Webster's New World
Secretarial Handbook

New Revised Edition

CONTRIBUTORS

Jeanette L. Bely, Ph.D., F.I.B.A., Professor of Education, Bernard M. Baruch College of The City University of New York

Ermalea Boning, M.A., Associate Professor, Head of the Department of Secretarial Administration and Office Management, San Bernardino Valley College

William W. Cook, J.D., Director of Development, Husson College, Bangor, Maine

Star Demetrion, M.B.A., Word Processing Coordinator, San Bernardino Valley College

Rose A. Doherty, M.A., Instructor, Business Communications Department, Katharine Gibbs School, Boston

Charlotte B. Holmquest, M.Ed., Business Teacher, Seabrook Intermediate School, Seabrook, Texas

Ruth Kimball Kent, M.A., Associate Editor, Dictionary Division, Simon and Schuster, Cleveland, Ohio

John I. McCollum, Ph.D., Professor, Department of English, University of Miami, Coral Gables, Florida

Emojean G. Novotny, B.S., Director, Secretarial Science Division, Dyke College, Cleveland, Ohio

Abba Spero, Ph.D., Associate Professor, Accounting, Cleveland State University

Betty L. Wooden, CPS, National Secretaries Association Representative, The National Secretaries Association (International), Kansas City, Missouri; Executive Secretary to Divisional Sales Manager, NABISCO, Inc., Irving, Texas

WEBSTER'S NEW WORLD
Secretarial Handbook

New Revised Edition

Simon and Schuster
New York

This new and revised edition of WEBSTER'S
NEW WORLD SECRETARIAL HAND-
BOOK includes some material previously
published in THE NEW WORLD SECRE-
TARIAL HANDBOOK copyright © 1968 by
Simon & Schuster and the revised edition
copyright © 1974 by Simon & Schuster.

Material from *Essentials of Grammar and
Style* by John I. McCollum copyright © 1966
is used by permission of the author.

Introduction

Webster's New World Secretarial Handbook has been prepared for the secretary who seeks efficiency and professionalism and for the person who strives to maintain the skills demanded of a career in office administration. While this book is directed toward the secretary and deals with the activities that confront a secretary in the business world, the typist, clerk, and stenographer will also find features here that are rewarding. This book may also be profitably consulted by the executive, for it contains a wealth of useful information that will contribute to the general efficiency of the office, especially in that phase of the work involving the secretary.

Today, the secretary's position is a challenge, demanding knowledge, a sense of responsibility, initiative, administrative ability, and office skills. As the executive's assistant, the secretary must display these qualities and exercise these skills, so as to lighten the employer's workload and keep the office functioning effectively. To make this task easier, the publisher has brought together the work of eleven authors, each with a specialized background, who have drawn on their experience and expertise to contribute to the understanding and knowledge necessary to your occupation.

Here you will find an abundance of factual information from wide-ranging sources, all related to your job and presented clearly to make your work easier. If the facts you want are not here, this book will tell you where to find them.

In addition to touching on all aspects of a secretary's occupation, the compilation of appendixes serves as a reference work in itself. Because it extends from dictionaries of abbreviations and business terms through a handbook of grammar and usage to a word book, which is a guide to the spelling and syllabification of the 33,000 most common words, the secretary will find that there will be little need to search for other reference material.

The handbook's usefulness will be enhanced if the index is consulted often.

The Editors

Contents

Chapter 1

The Secretary as a Professional

ROSE A. DOHERTY

THE BUSINESS WORLD is commonly divided into the white collar and the blue collar, the skilled and the nonskilled, and the professional and the nonprofessional. The secretary is a professional not only because of the knowledge and preparation that are necessary to secure the job but also because being a professional implies competence, pride in one's work, and a dedication to excellence. The secretary is a professional with each of these qualities.

The word secretary comes from the Latin *secretarius* meaning "confidential employee," and the secretary of today is still an employee who is privy to confidential information. However, the tools of the trade have changed since antiquity. The mass production of the typewriter and the development of systems of shorthand in the late nineteenth century gave women the opportunity to enter the work force in large numbers. The bulk of secretarial and clerical workers have been women since then.

Machine dictation and word-processing systems have further revolutionized the type of work that the secretary does. The changes that will take place in the future are impossible to predict, but the professional secretary will be able to learn and adapt to each new challenging development.

One change that can be commented upon now is the reentry of men as secretarial professionals into an area of employment where advancement is almost limitless. Gone are the days of the male executive and female secretary stereotypes. Men and women are working today as allies to promote the standards of the profession.

The National Secretaries Association (International) fosters an awareness of professional pride and the maintenance of high standards by promulgating the following definition:

A secretary shall be defined as an executive assistant who possesses a mastery of office skills, demonstrates the ability to assume responsibility without direct

1

supervision, exercises initiative and judgment, and makes decisions within the scope of assigned authority.

The importance of an organization like the NSA cannot be overemphasized. All professional people take pride in their affiliation with organizations which attest to the importance of their field. Lawyers have bar associations; doctors have the American Medical Association; teachers have national educational organizations. In each of these groups the purpose is to set standards for the profession and to honor those who meet the standards. The National Secretaries Association awards the title of Certified Professional Secretary to those who have passed a comprehensive two-day, six-part examination and who have fulfilled the experience requirements. The title of Certified Professional Secretary brings respect from peers and superiors and it may bring certain rewards.

The examination which the aspiring secretary must take calls upon knowledge which has been gained through education and work experience. Office procedures and administration, secretarial skills and decision making, accounting, economics and management, business law, and behavorial science in business are the areas covered by the test. For one who has not yet become a Certified Professional Secretary, membership in the NSA and participation in the local chapter's activities will bring a sense of the importance of a secretary's job to the functioning of society and will introduce the secretary to others who have similar professional goals in different organizations.

ENTERING AND SUCCEEDING

The relative ease with which a person can enter the secretarial profession is a plus in an era of rising educational costs. A high-school education and knowledge of typing and shorthand and perhaps machine transcription, filing, and office procedures will enable one to advance along a career path. The secretary entering the work force is faced with a multitude of possible job situations. Although the conditions under which a secretary works are fairly standard throughout the economy, a choice can certainly be made about location, the size of the company, and the company's services or products. Each and every area of the economy needs the expertise of a secretary, and the professional secretary has only to choose the most interesting field and the one in which career goals can be furthered. Weekly pay and fringe benefits are as important as ever, but today's secretary is also concerned with the possibilities for professional growth within a company.

Secretaries are now seen as professionals with career goals rather than people who have short-term job objectives. Most large organizations have a personnel or career-development department which is concerned with the occupational and professional growth of their employees. By providing training and educational opportunities for employees from date of hire until retirement, these organizations are able to enhance the effectiveness of their operations and to enrich the lives of their employees. The scope of this personnel development activity is immense, ranging from new employee orientation to retirement counseling.

On-the-job skill training is a matter of professional survival in a world where the methods of handling information are changing yearly, if not monthly. Refresher courses in shorthand, business writing, editing skills, the basics of English grammar, and so forth help to maintain employees' skills at the level desired by the company. Supervisor and management education and advanced technical and professional education are available to those who are interested in moving ahead in the organization.

The director of education at a nationwide insurance company states that one of the great benefits of a well-developed program is that people on the secretarial level can move into supervisory, administrative, and managerial positions if they have the desire and the ability to do so.

Developing the potential of secretarial personnel is the job of the career-development department which helps the individual examine the options for professional growth. The trained counselor helps the individual look at the present job as part of a career plan. Secretaries are encouraged to develop career paths and life plans just as executives do. The secretary's projected work life is just as long as the executive's; even with time out for child-rearing and other responsibilities, the secretary has many years in the work force. These years will be more pleasant if the individual takes steps to examine what kind of job will be the most satisfying now and in the future. It is also necessary for the secretary to decide what kind of job will give rewards that are personally satisfying. These career-development programs help the secretary to determine what is most important: money, security for the long run, exposure to high-pressure situations or famous personalities, or a low-key job which allows the individual to concentrate energies on activities or responsibilities outside the workplace. This kind of examination benefits the organization because it keeps personnel from changing companies when a change in work responsibility would be more satisfying, and career counseling allows the secretary to see today's work as part of an overall plan.

Many organizations give financial support and encouragement to outside educational opportunities. Frequently these outside courses must be job related or related to a degree which the company agrees would benefit the employee and employer. Sometimes, however, these courses are promoted for the personal enrichment of the employee. The development of valuable personal and professional skills, such as the ability to communicate effectively, or personal enrichment courses, such as "Introduction to Sculpture" and "Creative Writing," have been given on the premises of larger organizations. All of these personnel-development efforts increase the secretary's satisfaction with the job and the employer.

THE TOOLS OF THE PROFESSION

Typing, shorthand, filing, office procedures, and so forth are the skills for which the secretary was hired. However, the ability to use the language and a commitment to professionalism will earn respect and promotions.

LANGUAGE

The raw material on which the secretary uses the skills is the English language. A command of and a respect for the English language, both in writing and in speaking, are essential. A good dictionary, a thesaurus, and a grammar book must be close by for immediate checking of spelling, end-of-line division, usage, and sentence construction. Letters, whether the secretary composes them or transcribes them, represent the company, the employer, and the professional secretary. The recipient of a letter must never get the impression that any one of the three is less than first-rate. Most executives have a good speaking command of the language. This asset is often one of the reasons why the individual reaches a top management position. However, it is the secretary's responsibility to check details of grammar, spelling, and punctuation. An employer with an excellent command of English presents a double challenge to the secretary. Transcribed letters must be absolutely perfect, and letters composed for the executive must match in composition, tone, and clarity.

The secretary may occasionally be the final source for grammatical wisdom. The superior may have been hired for an area of technical expertise, not language ability. In this case the secretary will be responsible for editing all of the written communications from the office. The executive and the secretary in this situation must realize their mutual dependence and work to turn out superior written material. Correcting a dangling participle or making the verb and subject agree will demonstrate to the executive that the secretary is a professional with extremely valuable skills.

PROFESSIONAL READING

Trade journals are published for each area of the economy and for each profession. By reading these publications, the secretary demonstrates professional concern and also learns about new ideas and learns vocabulary which may soon find its way into transcription. The competent secretary does not have to read these magazines from cover to cover, but a system for skimming, using the table of contents as a guide, must be developed in order to stay abreast of developments.

Magazines pertaining to the profession of secretary and to efficient office management may not be available through the employer. These magazines will help the secretary to cope with difficult situations by discussions of the solutions of others and will alert the secretary to new products for the office. Reading current information that will make one a better professional is part of the commitment to professional excellence.

WORD PROCESSING

The new tool of word processing has revolutionized the way secretaries work. Word-processing systems and modifications are being developed so rapidly that by the time a book on the subject is published, it is dated. More and more offices will have this equipment in the future, and the secretary needs only the ability and the desire to grow and change with each new development or modification.

A word-processing system provides an automated typing center which improves office efficiency by increasing the speed and improving the quality of typed material. Today's businesses must deal with more written information than ever before, and they must duplicate and transmit that information quickly and accurately. The secretary who puts the material into the system is irreplaceable, but the word-processing system can perform at speeds that a typist would find impossible. Material for bulk mailing and form letters can be typed in a much shorter time by the machine. Having a boss decide to insert three paragraphs on page 60 of a 200-page report no longer means that the entire document must be retyped. The material to be inserted is typed into the machine, and the finished document is produced, often in seconds. At this writing, complete documents of hundreds of pages can be sent from one office to another in minutes, rather than days. By using satellite communication, the word-processing system can transmit a subsidiary company's entire monthly report to the home office half a continent away in 30 seconds.

New vocabulary and procedures must be learned, but training programs are offered by the vendor of the system or by the company. The competent secretary will learn not only how to respond to the instructions of the system but will also make every effort to understand how the machine works and how best to make use of the various options offered.

New systems of office management will result after the installation of word-processing equipment. Two types of secretaries will emerge because there will be two types of secretarial tasks. One will be the personal secretary who assists an executive in the day-to-day running of the office, handling mail, telephones, appointments, meetings, and so forth. The other type of secretary will work in the word-processing center typing correspondence which the executive has dictated into the telephone, editing documents on a screen in front of the keyboard, and performing typing tasks that the organization requires. One secretary will be in charge of monitoring the work flow through the word-processing center.

The future is unlimited for the secretary who takes advantage of all training opportunities and remains open and flexible to the changes that will certainly develop in the industry.

A PROFESSIONAL MANNER

The secretary is classified as a white-collar, rather than a blue-collar, worker because neither work clothes nor protective clothing are required in the office. However, the secretary should view clothing as a uniform which fits the image of the office and thus advances the secretary's career goals along with the purpose of the office. If there is no declared dress code, clues about formality should be taken from the other employees in the office. If the men always wear conservative business suits and the women are always dressed in conservatively tailored dresses or pantsuits, striking a blow for individuality in dress will do nothing for one's personal goals. If the office is very informal, the secretary who wishes to be noticed and moved ahead will wear clothing that is just a shade more formal, more professional—not the T-shirt with the funniest slogan. The goal is not to alienate other workers but to make oneself stand out as the secretary who takes work seriously. When the front office has an opening, the secretary who has demonstrated the most personal polish, in addition to superb skills, is the one who will be chosen.

We are a nation of coffee drinkers, gum chewers, and cigarette smokers. Unfortunately, each of these activities hampers our ability to work quickly on detailed matters. If one stops to sip or inhale, one cannot perform a task as quickly as would otherwise be possible. The competent secretary keeps smoking and coffee drinking away from the work area, and gum is strictly forbidden during working hours. This last proscription has nothing to do with grandmother's dire warnings about looking like a cow, although grandmother was correct. It is annoying, to say the least, to talk to someone on the telephone or in person who pauses to chew. This unbusinesslike attitude reflects on the company, and the secretary who chews gum while the employer dictates will probably not be put into an area of more responsibility. Certainly, this secretary will not be moved into an area in which contact with customers or clients is a possibility.

A proper office manner in dress and actions should be cultivated by the secretary, and this manner should be based on the fact that the executive and the secretary are expected to work as a team. The secretary should follow the lead of the executive in office style. Whether working for a single individual, a pair of executives, or a whole department, the secretary's duty is to help fulfill the executive job responsibilities. Therefore, assignments that appear in the job description (if there is one) are done conscientiously, and those chores which do not appear but which need to be done in order to free the executive from routine tasks will be done by the professional secretary without grumbling. Much has been written about people moving ahead in careers because of the mentor/protégé system whereby a seasoned hand in the business takes on the education of someone younger who has promise. Although the superior may be grooming someone for a place on the management level, the secretary can also be a protégé who moves upward in salary and responsibility with the boss or with the boss's blessing.

As part of the team, the professional secretary protects the employer, does not contribute information to office gossip, but does report any rumor that may be helpful to the superior, first qualifying the information as gossip. Also the professional does not spend company time on personal phone calls, in clock watching, or in being late.

THE COMPETENT SECRETARY

The secretary plans not only a career path but also plans short- and long-range work for the company. Short-range planning enables the secretary to do each day those things that must be done. For example, a routine is established whereby the secretary's and the employer's desks are ready for work at the beginning of each day. Standard procedures for handling mail, for advising the executive of telephone calls, and for handling dictation and transcription are set up, but this schedule does not lead to inflexibility. The competent secretary is capable of taking any kind of interruption in stride. When the emergency or interruption has been dealt with, the work routine is resumed at the point of interruption. Long-range planning makes it possible for the secretary to concentrate on low-priority projects at a slow time of the year and also makes it possible for the executive to call on secretarial aid at times when the work flow is heavy.

The secretary's time is a valuable and perishable commodity. All duties are performed as quickly as possible so that the unexpected may be dealt with. A sense of the relative urgency of activities is developed with experience, so that it is possible to distinguish the important from the trivial. A long-distance caller does not distract the secretary from the necessity to transcribe an urgent letter. The unexpected visitor is started on his or her way courteously and firmly, rather than being allowed to waste company time.

Business calls are evaluated for length, and they are not continued beyond the time that is absolutely essential for courtesy and the exchange of information. The secretary should structure the business call in the form of a business letter. It should be planned ahead and should have a beginning, middle, and end. If one is making a call, a clear statement of purpose should open, followed by details, questions, or whatever the call must accomplish. The call should be completed by thanking the person on the other end, stating the action you or your boss expect to be taken, or getting a firm commitment for future action or the time of a return call. Remember that this is a business call and avoid those verbal ticks like "you know" and slang that would be appropriate in a personal call.

By carefully following through on any tasks assigned, the secretary demonstrates a sense of responsibility every day. When the employer is out, the secretary displays professionalism by making sure that the office is covered at all times, especially when the workday begins in the morning. Every experienced secretary knows that this is when the problems start.

Take, for example, a situation in which the executive and the secretary are the only ones who know all aspects of a given situation. When the boss is away, something that vitally affects that matter happens. The competent secretary is present and immediately gets in touch with the employer so that the appropriate course of action can be decided and so that the secretary can set the wheels in motion.

The personal relationship between the executive and the secretary will vary according to the people involved and the formality of the company. The secretary should always remember that the relationship is a business arrangement and that the structure of any organization makes the executive more important than the secretary. Without the executive to set the overall objective and to plan for action to attain that objective, the secretary's job would not exist. Nevertheless, the indispensible contribution of the secretary to the execution of the executive's work should be a source of professional pride.

The executive may ask the secretary to explain a matter, but the secretary does not have the right to call upon the executive to justify decisions. However, when a good working relationship exists, office authority is not a source of discontent because both the secretary and the executive realize that they are there to make that office run at peak efficiency.

No job is without its dull routines as well as its stimulating aspect. No employer is without faults. There may be times when you consider your employer unreasonable. You may be asked to do chores that you consider demeaning or outside your province or job description. Decide how intrusive these jobs are, and discuss the matter with your employer. Perhaps the duties can be added to your job description, or see if you can arrange for the writing of a job description if there is none. Serving coffee and watering plants, for example, may not be your idea of the duties of a secretary. But if you like your job in most respects, if your employer is generally appreciative of your efforts and considerate of your personal needs you may be inclined to regard these services as part of the necessary work to keep your team in harness. Should you find it necessary to discuss your objection with your employer, do so reasonably and only after you have assured yourself that you are performing your legitimate duties fully and efficiently. Be sure too that the duties you object to in no way contribute to the overall objectives of your department or company or to your personal goals. Most important, bear in mind that you are working for your employer, not your employer for you.

Personal life must be separated from professional life in dealing with all office personnel. It is very possible to work well with people one does not like at all; likewise, it is possible to work professionally with people who are personal friends. Personal problems should not be brought into the office. However, worries about sickness at home, financial problems, and domestic difficulties do affect the quality of work, and the professional will do everything possible to keep the level of professional performance high. The fact that a doctor has personal troubles is not an acceptable excuse for a faulty diagnosis of a patient. One expects the doctor to perform well, and the executive has the right to expect the secretary to remain competent despite difficulties. People, however, are not machines and are not expected to behave as such. When overwhelming problems are present, the supervisor should be told before one's work is held up for censure.

Professional behavior as part of a team determines the relationships with the rest of the organization. In dealing with other members of the group, the secretary should make it clear that those others are viewed as the experts in their jobs. The professional secretary is courteous to everyone regardless of the individual's position on the company ladder. The order-processing clerk, the shipping clerk, the receptionist, the typist, and the file clerk will be much more helpful to the secretary/executive team if this attitude of professionalism is maintained.

The secretary must be very honest in all relationships within the company. Blame must be accepted if a mistake has been made. Everyone makes mistakes, and the good secretary will do everything possible to avoid them. The need to make use of other people's expertise must be recognized, and the secretary should help others in the office in an effort to foster a spirit of helpfulness to insure that good work is turned out. For example, even if a secretary's typing can be called excellent, proofreading of important documents should be done by two people. The secretary should therefore try to make arrangements to proofread material with a co-worker.

Alertness to the mistakes of others so that the mistakes may be corrected is characteristic of the competent secretary. Especially if work is done under pressure, people have a tendency not to check a figure, proofread a page, or make certain that a statement conforms to policy. The secretary must check and double-check to avoid errors that, more than simply being embarrassing, might affect important decisions adversely.

Differentiating between the executive's requests and the secretary's requests is very necessary. In the first instance, the secretary has a lot of authority; in the second instance, there is much less. If the executive needs the report by 4 P.M., the department responsible will recognize that the effort and expense are inconsequential compared to the importance of meeting the deadline. However, the secretary must not push co-workers unless the pressure is justified. Everyone has a schedule to which he or she must adhere. Remember to respect the importance and the schedules in other people's work. Never claim authority for yourself when you are passing on the executive's wishes. "Professor Brown would like all class schedules completed by Friday" will get a better response than "I would like all class schedules completed by Friday." Even with suggestions the same rule is followed. A suggested course is far more likely to be implemented if put forward as the boss's idea, particularly if it involves difficulty.

The secretary's filing system gets the same careful attention given to other duties. The employer must have an accurate record of what has happened in the past in order to take future action. For highly confidential matters or the employer's personal correspondence, a system consistent with filing rules but responsive to the needs of the office should be set up. If the company has a central files department, the secretary works closely with the assigned file clerk whose expertise should be recognized.

Filing is an historical recording of events that have occurred in a given aspect of company development. Filing requires intelligence, an intimate knowledge of the subject matter, and an organized method of recording. The secretary should work with the file clerk. All material should be carefully marked to indicate whether there has been any previous correspondence on the subject. If the previous reference could not be easily identified by the file clerk, a notation indicating the subject with which it should be filed is a courtesy that will save time, prevent confusion, and contribute to a helpful attitude in the office which will be to everyone's benefit. If a subject is especially important or unusually complicated, an exchange of ideas may enable the file clerk to set up the file intelligently. A sense of history on the part of the secretary and the file clerk will enable them to build up a file coherently, so that a person reading it will be able to determine the sequence of events and the actions taken. When the secretary recognizes the complexity of the file clerk's job, the employer will get the file or information sought, not an excuse.

THE EXECUTIVE SECRETARY

The executive secretary or the administrative assistant is more than just a secretary or an assistant to an executive. In some companies and organizations, the terms seem to be interchangeable; in other companies, one is placed above the other on the organizational ladder. Whether one uses the term executive secretary or administrative assistant, in terms of responsibility, knowledge of the company's business, judgment, and experience, this person is an executive. The executive secretary (the term we shall use in this discussion) may indeed employ a secretary or a whole staff. Making decisions which affect an important segment of the company's operations and, in some cases, taking charge of business while the executive is absent brings the executive secretary financial and personal rewards. But these benefits are earned. At this highest level of secretarial authority, the responsibilities are such that the greatest possible effort to check procedures and avoid errors is essential. Planning, discretion, knowledge, accuracy, efficiency, dependability are watchwords of the job. The executive secretary has top skills and keeps them serviceable. Technical skills may be used less, but they must remain in top condition so that should the executive have need of someone to transcribe an extremely confidential meeting and type the notes, the job will be done.

Confidence of the executive's staff is built slowly and carefully. These are the people who have the responsibility to carry out the objectives of the company or department. The executive secretary's duty is to screen demands on the executive's time, not to make the executive as unapproachable as Presidents of the United States have sometimes been made by their staffs.

Decisions must be made promptly; action must be taken swiftly. Anything that slows that action is detrimental to the overall operation of the company. When a member of the staff has to see the boss, it may be because that person faces some decision beyond the scope of his or her particular authority. It may seem a simple matter to give notice that the subordinate has to see the executive, but what if the secretary has six or seven calls from different staff members? Who sees the executive first, who next, and who not at all? It is up to the secretary to win the confidence of each member of the staff so that person will be absolutely honest as to the urgency of any particular request. Each has to know that if the employee says, "I must have five minutes before noon," he or she will have it if it is humanly possible, and that if the employee says, "Tomorrow will be fine," he or she will see the executive tomorrow without any further reminders to the secretary. In such circumstances, maximum use is made of everyone's time. The secretary can work out an orderly plan with the executive to conserve time. The subordinate can attend to other projects without wasting time calling back or attempting to waylay the executive in the hall. In this cooperative atmosphere, everyone realizes that the short-term advantage would not be worth the risk of losing the secretary's confidence.

The secretary must always be aware of being a representative of the executive, and while the staff is subordinate to the executive, the staff is not subordinate to the secretary. As the subordinates' confidence grows, they will ask advice or opinions on how the boss would like something done. The secretary has a responsibility to give accurate advice and to state only opinions which truly represent the executive's feelings. If the secretary's personal opinion is given, the subordinate may be misled as to the executive's actual sentiments on the matter.

The executive secretary cannot play favorites. The executive must view operations as a whole and must be able to depend upon the secretary to reflect this accurately in dealings with subordinates. It is important that each staff member be recognized as an integral part of the team and as making a contribution to the company. Each employee wants the good opinion of the boss, and perhaps even without consciously recognizing it, the secretary's reaction to an employee may be interpreted as a reflection of the boss's opinion. The secretary must remember that a personality trait which is unattractive to the secretary may be exactly the trait that makes the subordinate effective in a particular function. The subordinate who insists upon "dotting every i and crossing every t" may be far more effective in controlling costs than the easygoing, affable staff member who has difficulty in keeping even a personal expense account within proper bounds. The boss may have a higher opinion of the former than of the latter, and a secretary's favoring of the affable over the precise subordinate might be doing an injustice to both individuals and to the executive. By dampening the enthusiasm of one and giving a false sense of confidence to the other, the executive is misrepresented and the company's objectives may be impeded.

The job of executive secretary or administrative assistant is challenging and rewarding and a lot of hard work. Intelligence, interest, dedication, plus experience and training, are essential for success.

THE LEGAL SECRETARY

Accuracy and speed are the hallmarks of the legal secretary in the one-lawyer office or the large firm with a national reputation. Many legal forms must be prepared without erasures or other corrections on the paper, in conformance to exacting standards. Terminology is precise. As many legal procedures have to follow an initial action in exact sequence, timing and organization are essential.

Typing skills and the ability to learn legal terms quickly may be far more important to the beginning legal secretary than a course in which legal terms were taught. The director of a metropolitan employment agency which specializes in legal secretarial personnel says that a person with very good skills and one who is articulate can be placed easily. Verbal ability is important because in all except very large law offices, the legal secretary has client contact on the telephone and may also be responsible for greeting clients. The legal secretary must, of course, refrain from answering legal questions.

Word-processing systems have been added to large law offices to aid in the preparation of legal documents. The secretary who wishes to remain in the field should take advantage of every opportunity to train on these labor-saving devices.

The legal secretary's job is not easy because there is a lot of pressure, but it is one of the most lucrative in the secretarial field. Moreover, the fringe benefits are generally excellent, and the vacation periods are usually generous. Some law offices allow a secretary to advance to do some probate and paralegal work, but legal secretaries must recognize that advancement is generally open only to those with law degrees or legal training.

THE MEDICAL SECRETARY

Some medical secretaries have extensive contact with patients while others work in insurance companies, research foundations, medical textbook publishing houses, hospital administrations, city public health departments, and drug companies. Secretaries in most of these groups never see an ill person. Each job requires a good medical vocabulary and the need, in many cases, to take medical shorthand.

In a small office the secretary may have to know how to perform certain medical tasks, how to fill out insurance forms and the forms of different medical plans, how to take a patient's medical history, how to handle the doctor's billings and other clerical duties peculiar to a doctor's office. In addition, the secretary may need to deal with people who are ill, a task requiring patience, sympathy, and tact.

Regardless of the setting, a one-doctor office or a large facility which has no patient contact, the medical secretary must observe medical ethics. Cases should not be discussed except in the context of office business, and no comments or questions regarding a patient's condition or ailments should be made in the presence of other persons.

THE TECHNICAL SECRETARY

The growth of research, both governmental and private, and the explosion of knowledge have created the need for secretaries with the ability to deal with technical terms and symbols. Typing, editing, and proofreading are the necessary abilities, but these skills are exercised on extraordinary material. The ability to type accurately information that can be understood only by the researchers is essential, and the ability to proofread material which makes little or no sense to someone who is not technically trained in the field is indispensable.

The technical secretary must also recognize that the scientists and researchers have been hired for their technical competence, and frequently the secretary will have to edit material to make it grammatically correct. This task calls for much tact, patience, and humility in the face of material written in English but which is often incomprehensible to the layperson. However, for the secretary with the ability to deal with mathematical equations, Greek letters, and so forth, advancement to the level of technical aide and research assistant is possible. The technical secretary's job requires specialized skills, but the remuneration and benefits in these situations are usually quite good.

THE EDUCATIONAL SECRETARY

The opportunities for secretaries in educational institutions from preschool to graduate level are as varied as the institutions themselves. The secretary in the grade school may occasionally have to comfort a sick child who is waiting to go home or help a parent deal with the multiple forms that educational systems require. In higher education the secretary may be assigned to a specific academic or administrative area.

The duties of the secretary vary from school to school and often depend on its size. In a small school the secretary may have to handle student records, classroom assignments, transcripts of grades, and personnel records, and may even consult with parents and students concerning school policy and procedures. In larger institutions the secretary may be assigned just one of these duties or may be responsible for a specific department.

The minimum education required varies; in some institutions a high-school education is sufficient, whereas others, especially colleges and universities, may prefer secretaries to have some kind of college experience or even a degree. Secretaries and sometimes members of their families receive free tuition, use of athletic facilities and libraries, and discount tickets to sporting events. A college administrator's advice to the educational secretary is "Do not talk down to students." The secretary would be wise to include the student's parents in that warning. The students and their families may be subordinate to your boss, but not to you.

THE SECRETARY IN ADVERTISING, RADIO AND TELEVISION, JOURNALISM, AND THE ARTS

The skills required for these jobs are the same as for a job in any business, but the amount of contact with interesting personalities, public figures, and the public is increased. The secretary, when dealing with public personalities, must be able to maintain a professional manner. If your employer does not wish to talk to a local public figure or a network newsperson, you are going to have to be firm and diplomatic. Jobs in these fields require the ability to deal with people whose job it is to manipulate responses.

The professional secretary will decide just what kind of job will give the most satisfaction and the kind of atmosphere which will be pleasant. Will the high-pressure atmosphere of an advertising agency or television station make you nervous or will it challenge you? The fact that you are contributing to the success of a gallery or a museum may be the kind of reward that means the most to you. The excitement of putting any kind of publication "to bed" may be just what you want. Remember to take extras, such as house seats for a play, into consideration when you are considering a career.

THE SECRETARY IN GOVERNMENT

The federal government is the largest employer in the United States, and should not be overlooked by the professional secretary. The pay is good, the fringe benefits are excellent, and promotions are usually made from within based on availability and the demonstrated skill and industry of the applicant. In order to become eligible for a federal government job, the secretary must take a civil service examination and be put on a list of eligible applicants. Getting a government job can sometimes take months, but the delay may result in a job in pleasant surroundings with a secure future.

Other jobs are available in the public sector. State, county, municipal governments plus the many quasi-governmental agencies—all have need of skilled secretaries. The secretary who is interested in public service should contact the local civil service personnel office for particulars.

THE SECRETARY IN TRAVEL

Excitement and adventure are the fruits of secretarial work in the travel industry. Airlines, resorts, travel agencies, and so forth often offer free or reduced rates in transportation, hotel accommodations, and tours to their employees. A New York secretary can weekend in Miami; the secretary in San Francisco can spend a vacation in Hong Kong.

However, one does not get all this just for the asking. The job requires hard work. One must have a sincere liking for and a desire to help people. You are helping them to spend the money they have worked hard for all year. Also you must deal with harried offices who have to get an executive to Europe, and you will have to find an available flight. You must know geography well, be able to read different companies' timetables, plan itineraries, and make reservations through a computer or with a human being. In short, you must know how to do everything and anything that will contribute to the comfort and enjoyment of your company's customers. Above all you must be accurate. The pleasure of a vacation or a business opportunity can be lost by a single error.

Each year the volume of business and pleasure travel exceeds the previous year's. A person with the right combination or interest in people and ability to deal with details will find a bright future.

TEMPORARY EMPLOYMENT

Temporary employment services throughout the country fulfill a need for both the employer and the employee. Vacancies because of peak workload periods, vacation, illness, and resignations are filled by the temporary secretary.

Secretaries take on temporary employment for a number of reasons. Children or other responsibilities at home may keep a secretary from assuming a permanent job. Some secretaries use temporary service as a way to determine career paths because opportunities are available to explore different industries, organizations, and working conditions. Flexibility in time commitment is important to those who are pursuing an avocation or further education.

Agencies which engage temporary employees prefer secretaries who have had experience so that they will be able to go into an office and immediately assume the responsibilities of the job without oversight. Not only must the secretary fulfill the duties of the position, but also the secretary must be professional enough to fit into the organization in terms of dress and manner. The pay in temporary work is equivalent in many cases to that of permanent workers who have the same job skills and responsibilities. Fringe benefits are not generally available to temporary workers, but some agencies offer group hospitalization and major medical plans, paid luncheons, paid vacations, holiday pay, seniority bonuses, and credit unions to those who become temporary workers on a full-time permanent basis.

THE PART-TIME SECRETARY

Doctors, ministers, small businesses and to a growing extent large corporations often need part-time secretaries. The individual or the firm may need only a few hours of work a week and may be willing to have the work done at times convenient to the secretary. Some companies are now willing to divide a full-time job between two part-time secretaries. Part-time work enables the secretary to maintain skills while freeing the individual for home or other responsibilities.

THE FUTURE

The economy may heat up or the economy may cool down, but in either case, the need for skilled secretaries will continue to grow. The secretary of today and the future may be male or female; may be entering the field from high school, vocational school, or college; may be returning to work after many years of child-rearing; may be making a midlife career change. What all these secretaries have in common is their professionalism and their recognition of the importance of the work they do. The secretary of today and the future recognizes that a life's work deserves to be planned, and the professional secretary chooses a career path carefully with the help of a career-development program or the many self-help books that are available. The secretary of today and the future is a career conscious, professional man or woman who will assume an important place in business and society.

Chapter 2

The Secretary's Day
ROSE A. DOHERTY

JOB DESCRIPTIONS by their nature will make the task of organizing the workday a bit easier, but if your job does not have a formal description of duties, organization is the word to keep in mind. Not only must the secretary's desk be organized, but also the work that flows across the executive's desk must be ordered. Decisions about what is important must be made constantly since most secretaries will have more work to do in one day than can be reasonably accomplished. The principle to be used to help one decide what is most important is the principle which keeps the executive and the secretary working together as a team.

The interests of the superior must come first, and the good secretary will be sure to perform tasks that the executive wants completed quickly and thoroughly. Deadlines between the secretary and the executive in the office may be missed because of extraordinary circumstances, but if your boss misses a deadline with higher company executives because your work was not completed on time, do not expect to have an excuse accepted.

The schedule for the next day begins the afternoon before when the secretary goes through the tickler or follow-up folder to determine exactly what must be done the next day. The follow-up file should be set up in whatever way the secretary finds most convenient. If the office operates on a yearly schedule with certain meetings, promotions, and correspondence scheduled for the same time each year, the secretary may wish to have monthly files with notations about the amount of time it took to plan last year's fall sales meeting and the list of tasks to be performed in connection with that meeting. In an office that does not have this repetitive schedule, the secretary may use a desk calendar to keep track of letters to be answered, telephone calls that must be made, shipments expected, and so forth. The secretary should make a list of the items that must be taken care of the next day, and a list of appointments for the executive along with pertinent information and the materials which should be prepared. To conclude the day the typewriter should be covered and the desk cleared so that the maintenance staff will be able to work.

The office must be ready to function at whatever time it opens, and the secretary should be at work in the office, not returning from the washroom or talking in the next office. Certain jobs must be performed each day, and the secretary taking over an office would be wise to make a list of these in the order in which they should be done until the routine becomes second nature.

After opening the mail and putting the most important item on top, the trusted secretary may be required to call certain items to the executive's attention. This practice, however, should be begun only when permission has been given. The executive may ask that some of the journals and newspapers the office receives be skimmed and that pertinent articles, notices of new products, promotions, and so forth be marked for special notice.

Mail must be moved quickly from the secretary's desk to the appropriate correspondent; rerouting is done immediately. If some of the letters can be answered by the secretary, the executive may return them with notations about content. This letter-writing and typing task will then be completed as soon as possible.

The previous afternoon the secretary should have made a list of tasks for the following day by using the techniques of time management. Tasks fall into three categories: those that must be done immediately; those that may be done; those that may be put off. Just as the executive has a list of appointments, the secretary should have a list of tasks and some notation after the entry to indicate its relative importance. All necessary items can be given an A or 1; the tasks that should be done when there is time, a B or 2; and the tasks that can be left until a slack period, a C or 3. The mental exercise of deciding which items are the most important is the first step in getting the day's work finished. The trap of putting down jobs which are part of the daily routine or filling the list from the third category must be avoided. Putting down small jobs just for the satisfaction of crossing them out is a dangerous game to play. The executive will not want to hear that all of the filing is up-to-date and that the invitation for the annual office party has been sent to the printers if the report that was due in the president's office at 11 A.M. has not been typed.

The duties of a secretary are as varied as are jobs and employers. But in any situation it is safe to assume that the secretary is responsible for handling the mail, making calls and answering the telephone, taking and transcribing dictation, following up orders and work in progress, and organizing office work. More often than not, the secretary must keep track of the employer's appointments and maintain a filing system—all in addition to the specifics of the job.

How can one keep all of these duties in mind? The experienced secretary knows that it is impossible. Everything must be written down on the memo pad that is at hand at all times. Every request, every assignment, every message is noted. Nothing is left to memory or chance. The secretary's work procedure depends upon the nature of the job and the size of the company. Some offices have established routines; some employers will specify the methods they prefer; sometimes a departing secretary will train an incoming one. The basic tools of organization are a memo pad, a calendar, an appointment book, and a telephone-address book or file.

The memo pad will function as an added memory bank. Notations are made from each phone call, each request for an answer, each new assignment. By writing the information down, the secretary is freed from the need to keep small pieces of information in a mental notebook. Also, by writing all information down, the secretary is able to resume work at the point of interruption.

The appointment book is one of the most important records in the office. There are various methods of recording and following up appointments, but essential to each is the appointment book.

In some offices the book is kept on the executive's desk. The secretary must maintain an accurate duplicate appointment book so that both members of the office know how each day is to be spent. In other offices the executive assigns the appointment book to the secretary who makes all of the appointments. To examine the book, the executive will have to go to the secretary's desk and read it there or temporarily remove it.

Before making appointments, the secretary must be familiar with office procedure. Such matters as availability of executives, availability of conference rooms for meetings, daily arrival and departure times, and average schedules and length of conferences affect the making of appointments.

The appointment should be entered under the day and hour agreed upon by the person requesting the appointment and the secretary. The entry includes the names of the persons concerned, some notation of the topic to be discussed, and any other pertinent information. The secretary uses these notes to produce needed documents for the executive to read before the meeting. If the material is complex, the secretary may give it to the executive days ahead of time when the work flow is slow. On the day of the appointment the secretary follows through to be sure that there is no misunderstanding and to be sure that the appropriate materials and notes are on the executive's desk. If the appointment is canceled, arrangements for a new appointment should be made immediately.

The secretary who can find not only the names of those whom the employer must reach most frequently but also the names, addresses, and phone numbers for services, emergencies, and sources of information is a valuable asset to the office and is rewarded as such. Many secretaries in education and

Month January 25.
Day Monday
Year 1982

8:00 A.M.	P.M. 1:00
8:15	*Me - call printer* 1:15
8:30	1:30
8:45	1:45
9:00	*Mr. K - call to Seattle* 2:00
9:15 *Remind Mr. K - agenda*	2:15
9:30	*Exec. Comm. - Conf. Rm.* 2:30
9:45	2:45
10:00 *Ed Sparks to see*	3:00
10:15 *Mr. K. re type*	3:15
10:30	*Me - call travel agent* 3:30
10:45	*re Mr. K Paris trip* 3:45
11:00 *Staff meeting*	4:00
11:15 *(notify B)*	4:15
11:30	*Me - Jean L. Accounting* 4:30
11:45	4:45
12:00 *Mr. K - lunch with*	5:00
12:15 *Mr. Lyon - Amico's*	5:15
12:30 *reservations 12:15*	5:30
12:45	5:45
6:00	7:30
6:15	7:45
6:30 *Mr. + Mrs. K - dinner +*	8:00
6:45 *theater with*	8:15
7:00 *Mr. + Mrs. Owens -*	8:30
7:15 *Baltimore*	8:45

Appointment Book
with a typical day's appointments recorded

research organizations will keep a separate file of reference books or sources with notations about the contents and the call letters if they are in the public or the company library. The secretary would do well to become familiar with the area's Yellow Pages and with the various sources of information listed in the section on reference materials in this volume.

DAILY ORGANIZATION

Time is one of a business person's most precious commodities. The secretary who learns to organize work and plan time wisely will save minutes out of every hour, hours out of every week. This free time will be used by the professional to expand knowledge and expertise.

Here are a few time- and work-saving suggestions:

1. *Make efficient use of your desk.* Keep the surface clear of everything except your immediate work so you will not have to search through piles of other material when you want page 2. Form the habit of using filing folders for anything of a temporary nature—work in progress, incoming or outgoing communications, work being held for additional information— and keep these folders in the file drawer of your desk where they are instantly accessible but not in the way.

2. *Plan your time; never waste it.* When work is slow, plan ahead. Do what can be done to relieve the workload at peak periods. Try to learn more about your company's operations. Consider what you can do to make your part of it run more smoothly. Become familiar with reference materials; learn how to use the reference books your boss consults frequently. The next time you may be able to find that chart or graph that is needed badly. Bring the address book up-to-date. Get to know the filing system.

3. *Learn to schedule your time realistically.* It may take you an hour to type that stack of letters, provided that you are not interrupted; but you will be. The telephone will ring, your employer will call upon you to take care of something urgent, and people will stop at your desk to ask questions. That one hour may become two or three. If you learn to expect interruptions, you will not be flustered by them or lose time trying to pick up where you left off. Interruptions are part of your work and require a place in your schedule.

4. *Be part of the team.* When the workload is heavy, when your employers and other members of the staff are up against a deadline to get a job done, be willing to pitch in and help even if it is a little after closing time. Your ability to function as a professional will be remembered when you have a favor to ask and when you wish a promotion.

Chapter 3

Office Equipment and Supplies
RUTH KIMBALL KENT

A SECRETARY coming into a new office may quickly be aware of certain deficiencies in office supplies. On the other hand, the secretary who has been on the job for a considerable time may have to make a deliberate effort to keep track of new conveniences. The modern office can take advantage of a great many new products and newer styles of older aids that are skillfully designed to make the secretary's workday more pleasant and to help turn out work in the best possible form.

The secretary of a small office has full responsibility for taking care of office supplies and seeing to it that equipment is repaired or replaced as needed. The secretary in an office of a large company may have a supply officer or department to turn to. Still, this secretary should also have full knowledge of the varieties and kinds of supplies and new products available. This chapter discusses office equipment and supplies.

WORD-PROCESSING EQUIPMENT

Word processing is the automated production of records, documents, and correspondence as by the use of an electronic typewriter for preparation, editing, storage, and reproduction.

In a completely automated system, the material to be produced in the form of a printed document starts on its way as the originator talks into an electronic dictation unit. It is picked up for transcription by the word-processing secretary, who types it into a text-editing electronic typewriter. The copy appears on a computer terminal, variously called cathode-ray tube (CRT), video display terminal (VDT), computer work station, video terminal, or plasma-gas tube. The material is edited on the keyboard of the electronic typewriter. When all corrections and additions have been made, the letter, report, or other document is produced as a printout in its error-free form. The text remains stored in the computer or memory typewriter as long as there is need for it and can be retrieved in whole or in part at any time.

The benefits of word processing are many. Repetitive typing is no longer necessary. A long statistical report that needs to be revised only slightly each day, week, or month can now be stored in the computer. When the time for updating comes around, the secretary calls up the material on the CRT and makes only the few necessary changes. A legal contract or will that is changed only by names and amounts needs no longer to be typed by the secretary from first to last. Then again, typing the same letter to many different people calls for only one original typing and editing. After the main body of the letter has been typed into the memory of the typewriter, onto the tape of the automated typewriter, or into the computer, the letter needs only the insertion of variables such as name and address. Even the date can be temporarily programmed in if a great many of the same letters are to go out on a given day. In all of these tasks, word processing means that the material stored and then retrieved is error-free.

Word processing makes the correcting and revising of long reports or other documents a quick and simple task, for only the sections that need to be edited are worked over and retyped. If the executive finds at the last minute that a word, sentence, or paragraph is to be inserted in a "finished" letter, the insertion entails no more trouble than calling the copy up on the screen and keyboarding the changes.

AM JACQUARD SYSTEMS

Word Processor

Even though the letter is always thought of first in terms of typing in a business office, correspondence does not make up all of the paperwork of a secretary. A great deal of time is spent on forms. The form is made up of "constant data," that is, material that remains the same, with spaces left for "variable data," copy that will change. Word processing is invaluable for work with forms, an area in which some secretaries have traditionally spent many hours a week at the typewriter.

Statistical studies indicate that the most expensive paperwork put forth by a business office is reports. These documents supply data on company activities and give the information necessary for decisions to be made by the company for future action. Word-processing equipment makes it possible to turn out reports in considerably less time than old-fashioned methods and results in high quality, error-free finished work.

THE TEXT-EDITING TYPEWRITER

A text editor is an electronic word-processing typewriter that records copy, and can then be used to make corrections, deletions and additions, and to rearrange position of any element or segment of copy before the automatic printout of the finished text.

Among the various functions that are a feature of, or can be programmed into, the text editor are these:

automatic carriage return
automatic centering
proportional spacing
double- or triple-column printing
printing and positioning of subscripts and superscripts
margin settings and indentations
automatic respacing after material is inserted or deleted
automatic or semi-automatic hyphenation (some have the hyphen in the margin
    waiting for the operator to position it properly)
division into pages and automatic numbering of pages
automatic printing of running heads

The "automatic merge" capabilities make it possible, for example, to send a standardized form letter, or a new one made up of paragraphs searched and retrieved from three or four prerecorded documents, to the names and addresses on the company's mailing list—or to send the letter to a selection of names, as every fourth one on the list.

OFF-LINE TEXT EDITORS

Off-line text-editing equipment operates independent of a computer. The text-editing typewriter may be identified by the kind of medium used. The automated typewriter uses paper tape. The memory typewriter has a self-contained, built-in memory, often on semiconductor chips.

Other off-line text-editors record material that has been keyboarded by the secretary onto magnetic tape, cards, cassettes, or discs. After editing, the magnetic media is used to print the revised copy automatically. Some models of the "mag" typewriter can become a high-speed printer, printing up to 350 words per minute. The off-line text editor may or may not have a display screen.

Supplies for automated or mag typewriters. The secretary using an automated or "mag" typewriter must keep in stock not only the ribbons and correcting ribbons used by the particular kind of typewriter in the office, but also the storage media required. These storage units come in various forms. The kinds of *paper tape* used by an automatic typewriter, teletypewriter, or court reporter's machine, represent characters by combinations of holes that are punched across the strip. The *magnetic card* ("mag card") stores a page (about 50 lines) of text per card, while the *magnetic paper card* has a magnetic strip across it on which are stored 19 lines or less, as names and addresses, individual paragraphs, or other units of variable data to be merged with constant data on the printout.

Also available are cartridges or rolls of *magnetic tape* that will store up to 15 or 20 pages of typewritten matter. A *floppy disk* is a magnetic disc used in some word-processing typewriters. It is called "floppy" because it is flexible, unlike the stiff disc used in the computer memory. It can hold about 60 typed pages. The *flippy disk* stores material on both sides.

ON-LINE TEXT EDITORS

Any kind of computer-based or "on-line" word-processing equipment can use a communicating typewriter. This typewriter can receive and send material to its counterparts within the company or anywhere in the country or the world. It can also exchange material over telephone lines or other telecommunications media, or exchange copy with a computer. Communicating typewriters can send or receive at printout speeds of up to 120 characters per second.

On-line text editors that use telephone lines have a *modem*, a device that converts data to signals transmitted by telephone to the word-processing center, where a similar device reconverts it. The *acoustic coupler* holds the telephone handset through which the signals are transmitted.

Computer systems. On-line text editors can be involved with any of three computer systems:

The *minicomputer* is a desk-top unit that acts as an input-output (I/O) terminal with a direct cable or telephone line to the larger computer within the office.

The *shared-logic system* is an expansion of the minicomputer. The storage capacity is considerably larger. It has several terminals that share the memory and logic of a central word-processing computer. This means that many secretaries may work on the same document simultaneously and that each terminal can extract information from the central unit. This system can employ peripheral devices such as high-speed printers, phototypesetters, and page scanners.

The *time-sharing system* involves computers and peripheral devices operated by a bureau that services hundreds of users. Each user has one or more input terminals and is charged only for the time and particular devices put to use by its operators. The bureau delivers printouts to its users.

THE OCR SCANNER

The optical scanner, fully called the Optical Character Recognition (OCR) page reader, is a computer device that can "read" copy prepared in specified form compatible with the computer. The copy is stored on magnetic media and at the same time is reproduced immediately on the CRT or video terminal for correction and revision. The person working with the terminal usually has a carbon copy or rough draft to check against what appears on the screen and proceeds to prepare the material for printout by line printer, phototypesetter, or reproduction in whatever form is stipulated.

DICTATION EQUIPMENT AND METHODS

In some offices, the executive dictates to a secretary who takes shorthand, or, in an emergency, to a typist at a typewriter. Dictation may also be taken by machine shorthand, as legal testimony in a courtroom. Traditionally, the courtroom stenographer goes to the typewriter to spend many hours transcribing such testimony into typescript, but the shorthand machine is now compatible with some computers. Thus with the proper equipment, the computer can be programmed to transcribe machine shorthand.

In the modern business world, the executive is increasingly more apt to dictate into an electronic or portable battery-operated dictation unit or into a central recorder for which a microphone or telephone is used. In either of these cases, if the equipment is fitted with a phone-in adapter, up to thirty minutes of dictation can be recorded when the executive telephones from a remote location. Most of these recorders are now voice-activated, so that when the speaker pauses, the tape or other medium stops until the voice resumes.

All dictation machines allow the dictator to make simple corrections without going over the entire letter or report, and also allow the user to give special instructions to the transcriber.

Dictation Equipment Supplies. Cassettes are a commonly used dictation medium. The small metal or plastic cartridges contain magnetic tape that winds from one reel to a second. *Minicassettes* and *microcassettes* are smaller than the standard cassettes and fit into correspondingly smaller units. They were specifically developed to be used for dictation. There are *magnetic discs*, looking like small records but without grooves, and *magnetic belts* that fit over a pair of rollers in a dictation unit. These tapes, discs, and belts are all reusable but may be thought of as semipermanent. They may be stored for some time, but will eventually deteriorate.

Another type of dictation equipment is the *endless* (or *continuous*) *loop recorder*. It resembles the reel-to-reel tape recorder. The tape fits within a case called a tank. The tape is erased as the material on it is transcribed and is then ready for reuse.

To be used for permanent records, and therefore not erasable or reusable, are various media including some that use a plastic belt that is inscribed or "embossed" with visible grooves.

DICTATION AND THE WORD-PROCESSING CENTER

If the company has a word-processing center, the executive gains access to it in any of a number of ways for dictating. In one type of setup, the dictator uses the central equipment by dialing any telephone within the company. In another, the dictator's unit is connected to the system by a push-button phone. The central recorder can be accessed by use of any push-button telephone whether it is inside or outside the company. By a third kind of connection, the dictator has a private wire, and he or she uses a handset or microphone that is wired to the recorders in the company's word-processing center. These methods of dictation are called "on-line" systems because they are connected by wire or phone to the recorder. The portable dictating machine or one that is an independent unit within the dictator's own office is characterized as "off-line."

The advantages of machine dictation over in-person dictation are varied. It is faster for the executive to dictate into a machine than directly to the secretary—and it is faster for the secretary to transcribe from the spoken word than from notes, handwritten copy, or shorthand. A distinct advantage is that the secretary does not need to be present. At the time the executive is dictating, the secretary can be typing or doing other important office work.

When it comes time to transcribe the dictation, the transcription can be done by other office workers beside the secretary if this should be more convenient; the process is no longer limited to the one person who can decipher the boss's handwriting or the secretary's shorthand notes.

REPROGRAPHICS

The simplest way to reproduce office material is the carbon copy, but this is only applicable to three or four copies. The easiest method of reproducing material such as a form letter or report is through a word-processing center that has phototypesetting capabilities. The secretary feeds the copy into the CRT and has the copies quickly in hand.

Yet there are many instances when a limited number of copies are needed, or when the use of the word-processing center would not be cost effective. This is when the duplicating machine comes into its own. Directions on how to operate the various machines will not be attempted here, simply because all such machines are accompanied by operating instructions and manuals.

However, a review of types of duplicating machines could be valuable to the secretary in an office when the need for one becomes apparent.

Photocopying or xerography. The photocopier is perhaps the most commonly used office machine for reproduction of documents. Its speed and convenience is matched only by its cost, which is much higher than any other method in use today. It reproduces material at once, gives an exact copy, maintains the same quality of reproduction throughout the run, and demands no prior preparation. It may be used for book or catalog pages as well as for letters, office forms, and the like. The original is simply placed on the glass face of the machine, where it is exposed to light that will transfer the image to copy paper.

This expensive reproduction method costs from twice to fifteen times as much per page as other methods available. It is also subject to much misuse within the office. Careless operation results in many discards, office workers use it for nonbusiness or personal purposes, and unnecessary copies of office documents are made within the company. To prevent these abuses, many "copy control systems" have been worked out in various offices. Some office managers discover that the number of copies made in the office is suddenly reduced by a tenth to as much as half when a control system is put into effect.

Stencil duplicator or mimeograph. A stencil is a waxed sheet of somewhat fibrous paper. The stencil is prepared by writing or drawing with a stylus, by typing with the ribbon inoperative, or by a mechanical or electronic printer. The wax coating is perforated by the typebars, stylus, or other means and the ink flows through the openings to produce an exact reproduction on the highly absorbent paper. Ink is available in several colors.

Stencil corrections are relatively easy to make by applying a correction fluid over the error and retyping or drawing. The sheet is wrapped around a cylinder on the stencil machine, which may be operated manually by turning a handle, or by electricity.

Stencils or mimeos are used most often for runs of 25 to 2500 copies. Most stencil machines will handle anything from 3″ × 5″ cards to a sheet of 14″ × 18″ stock, and can print from 60 to 150 copies per minute.

The stencils must be stored very carefully if they are to be reused. They can be either kept flat between absorbent sheets or hung vertically from hangers.

Stencil copies are useful for announcements, price lists, diet lists or menus, weekly calendars, newsletters, company memos or bulletins, and programs.

The chief value of this process is simplicity and low cost. The last copy is as legible as the first, and there is good contrast between ink and paper.

Disadvantages: an operator must be carefully trained, and it takes time for an office worker to become proficient in the use of the stencil (mimeograph) machine. The storage of the used stencils is awkward and they take more space than storage of masters used to reproduce copies by other methods. A stencil must be prepared before copies can be made, and some secretaries find stencils difficult to type. To overcome this entirely, the electronic stencil maker or

HEYER INC.

Electronic Stencil Scanner

scanner "reads" ordinary typed material and makes a stencil by electronic means. With this advanced method of stencil duplication at hand, many companies use it for office forms and even letterheads.

Spirit duplicating. In this method of reproduction, spirit masters are prepared by typing or drawing on a glazed paper that is backed by a special hectographic carbon paper. The typebar or ballpoint pen transfers the wax layer from the carbon paper to the back of the master. After the carbon sheet is taken away, the master is inserted on the machine drum with the carbon side up. The wax layer contains a dye (in any of various colors) that is soluble in the alcohol-like solution in the moistening unit through which the paper passes. The moistened master sheet is then fed between the drum and impressions roller and duplication is achieved when the master is brought into contact with the copy sheet.

The spirit duplicator is very widely used, for it is the most economical process for duplicating up to 250 or 300 copies. It comes in manual or electric models. Duplication paper is available in white and colors, the most popular of which are blue, green, yellow, and pink.

Master units come in several colors and a single master may be made in two or more colors by inserting patches of the alternate carbon sheet in the areas where the different colors are to appear. The most commonly used color is purple, for this color dye will make the most copies before the dye on the master starts to fade. Spirit duplicating is a highly flexible reproduction method.

Disadvantages of the method are difficulty of learning the process of preparing (and correcting errors on) the master, difficulty in learning how to operate the machine efficiently, handling messy carbons, and poorer reproduction quality than other methods. There are many instances in which a high-quality copy is not necessary, and in these applications, the spirit duplicator is useful.

Offset printing. Initial cost for an office offset machine is high, but the resulting pieces of printing are nearly professional. Offset is designed for high-quality, long-run production.

Offset gets its name from the fact that it is indirect. The image from the printing surface is offset onto a blanket cylinder. As the paper passes between the blanket cylinder and impression cylinder, the inked impression is offset to the paper.

The principle used in offset (lithography) is that oil and water do not mix. The oil-based ink in the ink-water mixture is transferred only to the image area of the master, while the water is attracted to the nonimage area.

The master used for offset printing may be paper, metal, or plastic (electrostatic). The paper master will produce from 25 to 3,000 copies. The plastic master made on an electrostatic photocopier is used for a run of up to 5,000 copies, while the metal (aluminum) master can be used to produce up to 50,000 clear copies.

The secretary who runs an offset machine will need special training. Time necessary to set up operations and clean up afterward is greater than that needed for other office copying devices. But if high-quality reproduction of half-tone work is desired, the offset machine is available to the modern office.

ELECTRIC DEVICES

Electric equipment includes some items common in offices for many years, plus newer inventions that have been welcomed with pleasure. Some ensure greater accuracy, others bring relief from onerous chores.

The automatic electric copyholder is a boon for typists who handle either manuscript or tabular material. It is operated by a foot pedal or hand switch that allows a line guide to advance down copy as the typist progresses. If needed, the movement may be reversed, so that an up-or-down movement may alternate. A variable feature allows the guide to move from one side to the other. The copyholder fastens to the typewriter or stands independently and is generally made in four sizes to accommodate letter size, legal size, or two sizes of ledger paper. A simpler non-electric copyholder is also available. The line guide is simply moved by hand as the typist proceeds through the copy.

The electric paper shredder has provided needed security in a great many offices that handle sensitive material. It comes in a great many different models, and is usually selected according to the volume of paper that it must handle. The smaller paper shredders are desk-top, while large free-standing units can handle up to 140,000 sheets of paper an hour.

Various machines that help in the handling of paper are of great utility in the modern office. If the volume of mail is great, the electric letter opener is helpful. The electric collator is extensively used in offices where related material that runs to many pages is regularly produced. A manual paper cutter is fine in the smaller office, but an electric counterpart may be imperative in the larger concern. In an office that turns out a regular newsletter or ongoing reports, the electric paper folder, and the saddle stitcher or stapler get much use. If such reports or letters are regularly kept in ringed binders, an electric paper punch can be utilized.

Then there is, of course, the electric pencil sharpener, especially valuable in an office where much pencil work is done.

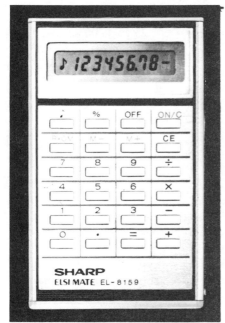

SHARP ELECTRONICS CORPORATION
Electronic Hand Calculator

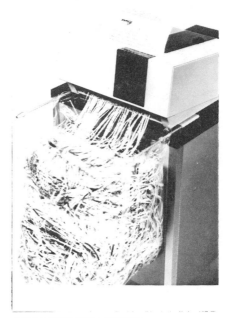

ELECTRIC WASTEBASKET CORPORATION
Paper Shredder

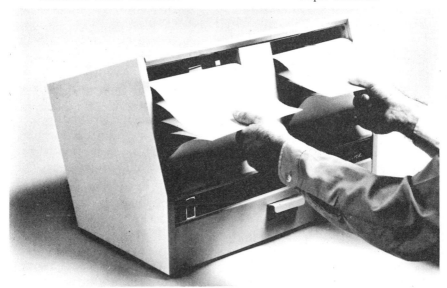

THE SWINGLINE COMPANY
Electric Collator

THE HAND CALCULATOR

While it is expected that a bookkeeper will be equipped with a calculator or adding machine, the modern secretary can also put to good use at least a hand calculator. It is only since the advent of these smaller devices that we have come to realize the extensive use of mathematics in day-to-day office dealings. The secretary's calculator should be sophisticated enough to cover the kind of figuring required by the particular business.

The smaller electronic calculators have a digital display section and have no printout tape; they show only the numbers pressed on the keyboard and then the result of the arithmetical calculation. In the early days of the hand calculator considerable difficulty arose because the only way to check whether every number entered had actually been recorded was to watch the digital record as the keys were being pressed; this made the calculating process lengthy and slow. This trouble has been sidestepped by the addition of a musical tone that beeps as each number is entered on the machine. This provides the operator with a signal so that errors are less frequent. Nevertheless, it is wise to do the calculation twice to be sure the results match. The desk calculator is usually electric, while the hand calculator is usually battery-operated.

If the calculator in use does have a printout tape, the secretary can review the figures on the tape, placing a check mark beside each as it is verified.

Hand Positions for Calculator Keys. Most calculators, with or without a printout tape, have a depression or more often a raised dot on the 5 key, which is located in the middle of the calculator keyboard. The 4, 5, and 6 keys across the board represent the "home position" for the index, middle, and ring fingers in the same way that the j, k, and l keys on the typewriter keyboard represent the home position for the fingers there.

Considerable speed can be attained by placing the fingers on this home position and practicing both the extension and downward movements of the fingers from this starting place, rather than employing a separate movement for each and every number entered on the keyboard. The positions are as follows:

index finger	7 extended = 4 home 1 retracted	middle finger	8 extended = 5 home 2 retracted	ring finger	9 extended = 6 home 3 retracted
thumb = 0					

The more advanced portable calculators are equipped with memories, have a number of programs that may be purchased with them or later, and have printout tape so that a hard copy of any given calculation is available.

The more advanced desk calculators are minicomputers, with storage capacity for either simple or highly sophisticated programs that are frequently used.

SUPPLIES

PAPER

A great many varieties of paper have been developed and perfected by the paper mills of today. The factors that the secretary must consider in choosing paper are (1) size, (2) type according to its intended use, (3) weight, (4) material from which it is made, and (5) finish and color.

SIZE. The standard paper size for ordinary office use is 8 1/2″ × 11″. The longer sheet used in the law office varies in different parts of the country. In some sections legal paper (also called "cap size" or "legal cap") is 8 1/2″ × 13″, while in others it is 8 1/2″ × 14″.

Some offices also keep on hand the 7 1/8″ × 10 3/8″ size sheet called "Monarch" for formal correspondence, and the 5 1/2″ × 8″ size called the "half-sheet."

TYPE. The type of paper selected is directly related to its intended use.

Typewriter paper. The best-known kind of typewriter paper is the so-called "bond paper." It was given this name because it was originally developed for the printing of bonds and other important documents. Typewriter papers have a dull, very smooth finish. The paper absorbs ink and is generally non-smearing. When selecting typewriter paper, the secretary will pay attention to its degree of whiteness, its weight, strength, and the kind of crispness ("crackle") usually associated with bond paper.

Second sheets. The most common use for second sheets is for carbon copies. This "onionskin" paper is available in the same qualities as is bond paper. The secretary may keep on hand two or three kinds of second sheets. The better quality, perhaps with a cockle finish, will be used for carbon copies to be sent to others, while the cheaper, lighter second sheet is used for the copy to be retained in the company files.

The kind of second sheet called "manifold" is dull on one side so that it won't slip in the typewriter, but is glazed on the other side so that it will be easy to file. The second sheets come in various colors so that the copies in the files can be easily color coded. Weight of second sheets is an important consideration. If the secretary needs to make several carbon copies of the same letter, the lightweight 9 lb. onionskin will make the clearest copies. It also occupies less room in the files.

Some second sheets have "COPY" printed in large red letters down one side, or diagonally or horizontally across the sheet. This feature may be desirable for instant identification.

Xerographic papers. This kind of paper has a smooth, hard finish and is carefully cut to exact dimensions, generally either the regular 8 1/2″ × 11″ letter size or the legal size used in a particular area. The exact cutting and the hard finish make sure that the paper feeds into the copying machine without jamming. The secretary may find it unwise to try to substitute another paper in the machine.

Xerographic paper must also be selected for the kind of machine in which it is used, depending on whether the copier uses a liquid toner process or a dry toner.

Duplicator paper. Duplicator papers are especially crafted to exert the least amount of wear on the duplicating master. They are to be used with spirit or gelatin (hektograph) machines. These papers are somewhat limp and soft and have a surface that is rougher than a xerographic paper but smoother than mimeograph paper.

Mimeograph paper. This bulky paper has a somewhat rough finish, a quality which allows the paper to absorb ink through the stencil rapidly so that the image is not offset to the following sheet; nor is the image blurred or feathered as it is reproduced. Opacity is another important factor; being completely opaque allows the sheet to be printed on both sides.

Scratch paper. Most offices want to keep on hand some kind of inexpensive paper for rough drafts or for handwritten drafts of letters, reports, or any kind of written composition. Many executives are happy with the so-called "legal pad," of the familiar lined, yellow sheets in legal size. If material is drafted in rough form on the typewriter, an inexpensive typewriter paper will serve. The secretary may also find it useful to keep a variety of notepads in the stock of supplies.

WEIGHT. The "basis weight" of paper refers to the weight in pounds of 500 sheets (a ream) of the paper cut to 17″ × 22″ size. (The terms "basic weight" or "substance" are sometimes used.) When cut to the standard size of 8 1/2″ × 11″, the basis weight shown on the box will be the weight of the ream from which the paper was cut. The most widely used office papers today range from a very lightweight 7 1/2 lb. (onionskin) to a very heavy weight 24 lb. The most commonly used office paper is 16 lb. The law office may make use of the heavy 20 lb. or even 24 lb. substance paper for important documents.

Paper is usually sold by the ream. It is also available in 80-sheet, 100-sheet, or 250-sheet packages, but these sizes are not economical for the business office.

MATERIAL. The best bond papers are the cotton fiber (or "rag content") papers. The 100% cotton fiber is called "parchment deed" and is used for documents, insurance policies, or the like, or for papers that are to constitute permanent records. Another heavy paper is called "vellum." This was originally lambskin, calfskin, or kidskin, but is now just an unusually strong paper. A 75% cotton fiber paper may be used for legal papers. It stands repeated folding well. The 50% and 25% cotton fiber papers have qualities of toughness and permanence to a lesser degree, but are excellent papers and much used. The 25% cotton fiber is the most common used for letterheads.

Some paper companies have the year of manufacture coded into the watermark of the 100% or 75% cotton fiber paper. This is an important feature for legal use.

Office papers are also made from wood-pulp chemical fibers or from combinations of chemical and cotton fibers. The most common of these is the chemical fiber sulphite which is less expensive than rag content, and is suitable for many office needs.

FINISH. The finish most suitable for the kinds of writing and typing done in the business office is the customary smooth finish. However, a favorite in good quality typing paper and onionskin is a finish known as "cockle." The surface of this finish has a puckery or ripply appearance that is distinctive and elegant.

Another finish is that of the so-called "erasable" papers. During the manufacturing process special coating is put on this paper that keeps the ink from penetrating it to any great extent. Thus the paper is very easy to erase, often with only a pencil eraser, while the ink is still wet. Once the ink has dried, the image is fairly permanent. This paper is often recommended for beginning typists, although they may become discouraged by smudging. Erasable paper is not to be used for documents that are to be kept on file indefinitely.

White is, of course, the common color for typing papers. However, there are degrees of whiteness, and the executive may prefer one type or brand of paper over another. Off-white papers are sometimes used for less formal correspondence.

CARBON PAPER

In spite of the advent of a great variety of copying methods for business letters and documents, carbon paper remains the most commonly used and ultimately the most convenient method of making copies. Only one person and one machine is involved. The secretary stays in one place. The copies are produced on lighter weight paper than is needed for other copying methods, so that a minimum amount of filing space is necessary for storage. And the method is, in any specific instance, the fastest copying method, for the original and its copy or copies are produced simultaneously.

Grades and types. There are a number of different grades of carbon paper, but just two basic types.

The standard typewriter wax carbon paper works as the typewriter key strikes the carbon through the first sheet and deposits a thin coat of carbon on the second sheet.

The solvent carbon paper or polyester carbon film is made variously of paper or of extremely thin sheets of polyester coated with a liquid ink formula. The "solvent carbon" soaks into the copy paper in the same way that typewriter ink does. This feature eliminates smudging and smearing. The solvent carbon paper or film carbon is durable, resists wrinkling, and may be reused 40 to 80 times, depending on the quality.

A maximum of eight or ten legible carbon copies is to be expected, or even less if the secretary is using a typewriter that is several years old. If more copies are needed a duplication process of one kind or another is preferable. Carbon copies should not be used when high quality of reproduction is important, or when the copy will be handled a great deal over a long period of time.

For many kinds of work, these conventional single sheets of standard carbon paper or film carbon are used. They come in weights designated as heavy, medium, and light. The lighter weight the carbon and the copy sheet, the more copies may be obtained.

Carbon sets. In many offices where the kind of work permits its use, the carbon set is a convenience much appreciated by the modern secretary. The sets of one piece of disposable carbon paper lightly fastened to one piece of tissue-thin copy paper may be purchased by the ream or in 100-sheet lots.

Carbon sets are also packaged in tablet form. The typist tears off the required number of copy sheets and carbons, puts the bond paper or letterhead on top of the pack and inserts the entire collection into the typewriter. Various printed office forms also come in carbon packs. For easy insertion in the typewriter, the secretary may put the pack into the flap of an envelope or a folded half-sheet, roll the unit behind the platen, and then remove the folded sheet and roll the paper back into proper beginning position for typing.

Carbon sets are more expensive than the conventional single-sheet carbon paper, but the savings in time may offset the increased cost.

Pencil or ballpoint carbon paper. This kind of carbon paper makes its copies by rubbing action of pen or pencil rather than the sharp impression of a typewriter key. It comes in black or blue. It is generally expected to make only one copy at a time, but can be reused. It has several uses; for example, an executive may consider it prudent to keep on file a copy of a hand-drawn sketch. Then again, some executives who prefer to write material by hand use this carbon for work that will need several revisions. They keep on hand a copy of rough drafts that have been turned over to an assistant for suggested changes.

Carbonless paper. Carbonless paper has a special coating on the back of the sheet and on the facing of the copy sheets. These coatings combine to produce an image when typed or marked upon. Printed office forms such as memorandums or reply-requested blanks are sometimes made up in carbonless paper sets. Up to six legible copies can be made by typewriter, while firm, sharp handwriting may produce up to three or four copies, depending on the thickness of the sheets.

Carbonless paper is expensive, but has the advantage of relative freedom from smudges. And of course there is no separate piece of carbon paper to handle or discard.

ENVELOPES

The quality of the paper used for envelopes should match exactly that used for the letterhead. Envelopes are designated by numbers according to size. The following list shows the names of the letterheads and the envelope numbers that can be used for the different sizes of letterhead sheets.

Letterhead	Envelope number	Envelope size
Standard	6 3/4	3 5/8″ × 6 1/2″
	9	3 7/8″ × 8 7/8″
	10	4 1/8″ × 9 1/2″
Half sheet	6 3/4	3 5/8″ × 6 1/2″
Monarch or Executive	7	4″ × 7 1/2″

ERASERS, CORRECTION TABS, CORRECTION FLUID

Erasers come in many types, and are of little use if not suited to the writing surface on which they are used. The general rule is to use a hard eraser on hard paper, and soft eraser for soft paper. The hard eraser used on soft paper will tear it; and the soft eraser used on hard paper will not do the work.

The *rubber eraser* is the soft, all-purpose eraser found at the end of a pencil.

The word "rubber" came from the fact that this substance was found to be valuable for rubbing away pencil marks when it was first discovered by the Western world. The rubber eraser comes in small rectangular or square blocks or in pencil-like sticks.

A *kneaded eraser*, as found in art shops, may prove to be handy in an office. It is not abrasive, can be shaped to any desired form, and works well on pencil, chalk, and charcoal. It is also useful for cleaning typewriter keys or the keys on an adding machine.

The pencil-shaped *typewriter eraser* is highly abrasive. It is invaluable for typed work, but must not be used on soft or thin paper. The brush is needed to whisk eraser dust away. The chief advantage of this eraser is that it may be sharpened to a point to erase a very small area. The *paper-wrapped eraser* is of similar substance and may be also sharpened to a point. The paper is peeled away to expose more erasing edge as needed. It has no brush. The chief disadvantage to each of these is the eraser dust that tends to fall downward into the typing mechanism. If it is possible to push the typewriter carriage over far enough so that the eraser dust falls outside of the typebar area, this should be done.

It is important to remember in the use of these erasers that they should be clean when they are applied to the paper, to avoid smudging. A piece of emery board taped to the side of the typewriter or kept elsewhere on the desk may be used to quickly clean an eraser.

The *fiberglass eraser* is a reasonably new development. It, too, is highly abrasive, and is effective on hard papers. It may be used on wood, plastic, or glass as well as paper. The fiberglass eraser should be handled with very light strokes, without the heavy touch used for the ordinary eraser. If ink smudges from the use of this eraser, use a common pencil eraser to clean the paper. *Do not touch the spun glass portion of this eraser*. A small particle of glass can lodge in the finger. If particles of glass are left on the paper, remove with a brush, and brush away from you.

An *electric eraser* is used most often in a drafting office, but the secretary may want to borrow it if a long line must be removed. Rotate gently. An electric eraser may have a hard or soft tip (they are interchangeable), so be sure the tip is suitable for the paper you want to erase.

In lieu of the eraser, the modern secretary may choose a *correction fluid* for the correction of typing errors. This fluid comes in a small bottle with an application brush attached to the cap. Originally only in white, the fluid is now available in colors to match various papers. There is a different fluid for use on carbon copies. Correction fluid tends to thicken rapidly, and the cap should never be left off of the bottle. Thinner can be purchased to make the fluid of usable consistency. At times, the secretary may find it prudent to erase an error before applying correction fluid.

Correction fluid is not desirable or permissible in every typing situation. It may crack and flake off of an erasable-finish or a cockle-finish paper. If the liquid is not carefully dabbed on any paper it may blend with the ink and result in a streaked, grayish patch. The ink may "bleed through" with age, and the correction fluid itself may rub off on documents that must stand a great deal of handling.

Then again, its use is totally unacceptable in legal typing or in copy that is to be fed into a scanner for reproduction on a cathode-ray tube (CRT) prior to being set in type. The scanner "sees through" the correction and comes to a halt.

Another useful typing correction method for the secretary is provided by *correction tabs*. These are small patches (usually 2 1/2" × 1 1/4") of coated papers or film to be inserted between the typed sheets and the typewriter ribbon.

The corrections made with these tabs may show up too plainly on some kinds of paper, but blend into others in a satisfactory manner. Then too, if the paper has slipped down slightly, the tops of the incorrectly typed characters may still show. Trial and error is the key. Correction tabs may be a convenience, but they cannot work magic.

Correction tabs are available in white or various colors. Be sure to purchase the kind needed for your particular typewriter ribbon. A different kind of tab must be used for polyethylene (carbon) ribbon than that used for the conventional nylon, silk, or cotton ribbon. Correction tabs come in cheaper or better quality; it is worthwhile to study the various kinds. A different tab is needed for carbon copies.

Also available for "correctable film" ribbons are special "lift-off" tabs that literally take the typed character off the paper. Corrections made by this method are rarely discernible.

To use correction tabs, backspace to the letter or letters that were typed incorrectly, place the correction tab over the error and on each carbon copy with coated side down. Retype using exactly the same type characters as the ones that are wrong. Remove correction tab or tabs, again backspace, and type in the correct characters.

KEYS

Among the miscellaneous equipment under the control of the secretary may be keys. In a small office, keys to special cabinets or closets should be plainly tagged with large pieces of cardboard and stored in a safe place. Such keys usually present no problem, because only a limited number of persons use them.

However, in a large business office, a suite of offices, or in a school office, for example, there may be keys for most of the rooms. It may be the secretary's duty to circulate and control all of these keys. A number of different key control systems have been devised. The way in which the system is set up depends upon the number of keys to be accounted for and whether they are for rooms or stores of material.

In one system, an index cross-referred three ways is kept separate from the location of the keys themselves. One index lists alphabetically the items that are kept locked up and their locations, and cross-refers to the number of the hook on which the key is kept. To go with this, a numerical index lists by hook number the locked items, and a second numerical index lists the serial number of the keys. Keys are tagged, but with the serial number, a key can be identified even when the tag is removed. A receipt is signed by each person as he or she takes a key.

Key cabinets come in a suitable variety. Such a cabinet may be recessed in the wall or mounted on the wall. For maximum security, the key cabinet can have a combination lock. Six- and eight-drawer key files are available for extremely complex systems. For a smaller number, a key index tray that fits into a regulation size file cabinet drawer is available.

STORAGE

Office supplies in storage should be arranged according to age, with the oldest stock in front for immediate use. Only one box of a single item should be opened at a time. Like items may be stacked one in front of the other on shelves. Unlike items should be kept separate to ensure that no stock is concealed from sight and forgotten. Shelves, boxes, and packages should be plainly marked to show contents and date of purchase. It is important to store supplies so that humidity and temperature are as close to ideal as possible.

INVENTORY

The secretary who has the obligation to look after office supplies will do well to keep a running record of what supplies are on hand, and the frequency with which each separate item needs to be reordered. A workable method is to place on the calendar or tickler file a reminder at the beginning of each month for the articles to be tended to in that time period. A yearly inventory is time-consuming. If an ongoing account can be maintained, it will generally serve the purpose better.

A card record should be kept for each item. This record should include name of supplier, name of salesperson, quantities usually purchased, sizes, colors, and other details. The cards may be filed alphabetically by supplier, item, or category. They may be used as inventory records, showing the quantities coming in, the quantities distributed, and the minimum quantity to be kept in stock. As the record approaches the minimum, the item should be added to an order list or immediately placed on order. The minimum order should be of a quantity large enough so that the stock is never exhausted and yet does not result in an overload of the item, for paper, typing ribbons, and certain other supplies deteriorate with age.

The following list of common office supplies is categorized. It recapitulates foregoing items discussed in detail and then goes on to include basic materials that the secretary will need to list on the inventory record.

PAPER AND FILING PRODUCTS

typing paper
carbon paper or carbon sets
scratch pads and paper
memo pads
dictation notebooks
telephone message pads
3″ × 5″ cards
4″ × 6″ cards
card files
business envelopes
manila envelopes
padded envelopes
mailing tape
address labels
postage stamps

manila or plastic file folders
  (color coded as needed)
hanging file folders
file folder tabs and labels
alphabetized dividers
file baskets, trays, and stacks
transparent tape
bookmarks
calendars
planning diaries
binders
looseleaf covers and fillers
telex paper
  (in rolls)
paper for calculating machines

TYPING SUPPLIES

typewriter ribbons
typewriter erasers
correction fluid (with thinner)
  (white and color as needed)
correction tabs (white and
  color as needed)
type cleaning brushes
exchangeable type elements
typewriter covers
typewriter "anchor" pads
copy-holders

DUPLICATING AND DICTATING SUPPLIES

stencil and/or memeograph masters
microfilm
microfiche film
microfiche index
cassette or reel tape
tape storage unit
tape demagnetizer
tape splicer

DESK SUPPLIES

staplers, staples, staple removers
pen and pencil holders
rulers
paper clips
rubber bands
magnifying glasses
scissors
pushpins
book holders

bookends
ashtrays
letter openers
tape dispensers
fineline, broad nib, or felt-tip pens
writing and marking pencils
erasers
rubber stamps, including date stamp
ink pads for rubber stamps

MISCELLANEOUS

postal scales
first aid kit
fire extinguisher
keys
batteries
globe
maps
easels
planning boards

DESK REFERENCE SOURCES

desk dictionary
secretarial handbook
current office supply catalog
style manual
almanac
chart for current postal rates
current telephone directory
telex directory, if needed
international area code booklet, if
    needed
office address and/or telephone
    directory (booklet, sheet, or rotary
    file)

Chapter 4

Dictation and Transcription
BETTY L. WOODEN

Taking and transcribing dictation are basic duties of the secretary. Dictation may be correspondence, reports, memos, telegrams, speeches, or in various other forms. A shorthand speed of 120 words per minute will be adequate in most instances; however, the secretary should be able to take notes at 150 words per minute for at least short periods of time. This will be determined by the dictating habits of the executive. The secretary is always ready to take dictation, whether in the executive's office, at the secretary's own desk, over the telephone, or directly onto the typewriter. In addition to shorthand notes the secretary may be expected to transcribe from discs, belts, or tapes used with dictating machines.

PREPARATION FOR DICTATION

Assuming the secretary has opened, sorted, and annotated the incoming mail, checked the appointment calendar and the tickler file, the correspondence files and materials needed by the executive can be anticipated and made available for the dictation period.

Some executives set aside the same time every day for dictation; others dictate as time is available. If the executive prefers that the office door be closed and phone calls held until the session is over, the secretary will arrange for another person to "cover" during that period. This will not be feasible in a "one executive, one secretary" office, in which case the executive will probably ask the secretary to answer the phone as usual, and then leave the door open so that either may see an incoming visitor.

Any work in progress or in the secretary's typewriter should be covered so that it cannot be seen or read by anyone who enters during the secretary's absence.

DICTATION TOOLS

1. A spiral-bound notebook, with a rubber band around the used portion. If dictation is taken from more than one executive, it might be well to have a separate notebook for each, to avoid confusion when transcribing. The first date of dictation should be entered on the front binder and the final date entered when the book has been filled. The dictator's initials can be shown on the cover also. The filled notebooks should be filed in the event there is a question later about a dictated item. The length of time such notebooks are kept will depend upon the policy of the employer.

2. A pen (ballpoint, felt-tip, or whatever is preferred by the secretary), one or two sharpened lead pencils, and a colored pencil, usually red. Notes written in ink are easier to read when transcribing than those written in pencil. The lead pencils are used if the pen runs dry; the colored pencil is for special notations.

3. A folder for correspondence and other reference materials.

4. A supply of paper clips, either along the binder of the notebook or clipped to the edge of the folder. These may be used for clipping memos of special instructions or small notes to the pages of the notebook.

5. A pocket-size calendar, taped to the binder of the notebook or to the front of the correspondence folder. The calendar will be used to check days and dates in the dictated material.

TAKING DICTATION

The current date should be entered in red pencil at the bottom of the first page to be used that day.

With the permission of the executive, the secretary's materials should be placed on a corner of the desk rather than in the lap. (Long periods of dictation can be difficult and very tiring if the secretary has to juggle papers, files, and other materials in the lap or retrieve them from the floor.) The executive's appointment calendar should be close at hand for checking dates and to avoid conflicts in scheduled meetings, travel arrangements, etc.

The executive should indicate the number of copies required for each dictated item. Following the dictation related correspondence should be given to the secretary and may be numbered to correspond with the number in the shorthand notebook. This correspondence will be placed in the folder and used by the secretary to check names, addresses, quoted dates, calculations, and other data, prior to transcribing.

Many secretaries use only the left hand column of the notebook, reserving the right hand side for corrections, insertions, special instructions, and so on. (Left-handed secretaries reverse this procedure.)

If the dictation becomes too rapid, the secretary should signal the dictator, reading back the last few words taken down. To avoid breaking the dictator's train of thought, the secretary should wait until the end of a sentence or paragraph before interrupting. (The new secretary may be reluctant to interrupt during dictation but the executive will usually realize a "breaking-in" period is to be expected and will make allowances.)

The secretary should feel free to ask that unusual names or terms be spelled out and then write them in longhand. This can be done at the end of the dictation.

If the dictation is interrupted by a phone call or a visitor, the secretary uses this time to read back over the shorthand notes, inserting punctuation, checking dates on the calendar, or filling in words that may have been missed. If the interruption is extended, the secretary should quietly gather up the materials and return to her or his desk to prepare for transcribing, returning to the executive's office when called.

SPECIAL DICTATION SIGNALS

The word "RUSH" may be written in red pencil to call attention to urgent letters. It is also a good idea to fold the lower left-hand edge diagonally and upward until the page protrudes one-half inch beyond the edge of the notebook as a signal to the secretary that this is a priority item.

A rough box should be drawn around special instructions and notations of attachments or enclosures to alert the secretary when transcribing.

A blank space should be left in the notes for material to be entered later, such as a date, a name, or other information to be provided by the executive (or the secretary) which might not have been available during the dictation period.

A caret or star may be used for small insertions and a circled capital A, B, and so on, for longer insertions.

A crosshatch is used to indicate the end of each dictated item.

A wavy line under the shorthand notes indicates underscoring; two lines indicate all capitals; three lines indicate both underscoring and typed in all capitals.

One or two diagonal lines should be drawn through the notes after they have been transcribed.

TRANSCRIPTION

Before transcribing anything, the secretary will establish priorities for the work to be done, sorting items quickly into stacks to be:

1. handled at once. (This may be a telegram, a phone call, or a letter to be typed, signed, and mailed immediately.)

2. transcribed before the day is over.
3. transmitted to others for handling.
4. handled by the secretary, but under no deadline.
5. placed in the tickler file for follow-up.
6. filed.
7. discarded.

Then the secretary will proceed according to the priorities set. The secretary should read through the notes, inserting needed punctuation, paragraphing (if not dictated), checking the calendar for conflicts in days and dates, correcting errors in grammar and facts, restructuring poor sentences, and so forth. It should be noted that most executives rely on their secretaries to make whatever changes are necessary. However, if the executive wants the material transcribed *exactly* as dictated, the secretary will do so.

A *new* dictionary and a current secretarial handbook should be on every secretary's desk to check spelling of unfamiliar words and place names, rules of punctuation, division of words at the end of a line, and so on.

With experience, the secretary can easily determine the length of a letter to be transcribed and the margins to be set on the typewriter. It will be necessary to take into consideration the size of the shorthand notes and the type style (pica, elite, and/or proportional spacing) of the typewriter. It may occasionally be necessary to type a rough draft when material not dictated is to be inserted, such as a list of names or a statistical tabulation.

Many companies have a standard format for correspondence and memos within the company, and a different style for letters to customers or clients. If this is not the case the secretary should use the style preferred by the executive or a generally accepted one in an up-to-date style manual.

If the transcription process is interrupted the secretary should put a small check mark in the shorthand notes to indicate the place to resume typing.

All materials should be proofread before removing from the typewriter. There must be no strikeovers and no detectable corrections.

Envelopes for letters should be typed as soon as the letter is transcribed. One method preferred by many executives is to place the letter and the enclosures, if any, under the flap of the envelope with the addressed side of the envelope on top. This same procedure may be used with those carbon copies that are to be sent to another party.

Because of the extended use of automated equipment the Postal Service has made available a leaflet entitled "Secretarial Addressing for Automation" (Notice 23-B) which may be obtained from customer-service representatives and postmasters. Some suggestions included are:

1. The address area should be in block form with all of the lines forming a uniform left margin. It should be at least one inch from the left edge of the

envelope and at least 5/8 inch up from the bottom of the envelope. No print should appear to the right or below it.

2. Mail addressed to occupants of multi-unit buildings should include the number of the apartment, room, suite, or other unit. The unit number should appear immediately after the street address on the same line—never above, below, or in front of the street address.

3. Street addresses or box numbers should be placed on the line immediately above the city, state, and ZIP Code. When indicating a box number at a particular station, the box number should precede the station name. Correct spelling of street names is essential since some machines match the names in the address to those like it on the machine's memory.

4. City, state, and ZIP Code should appear in that sequence on the bottom line of the address block. Automatic sorting equipment is instructed to look for this information in that position. Mail presorted by ZIP Codes bypasses many processing steps in the post office and can get to its destination quicker.

5. Type addresses in upper-case letters without punctuation. Example:

```
GENERAL XYZ CORP
ATTENTION SALES DEPT
1000 MAIN ST
PO BOX 23302 CENTRAL STATION
DALLAS TX  75223
```

It should be noted that this style of addressing envelopes is not mandatory and the secretary should consult with the executive before adopting it.

Special mailing instructions should be typed in all capital letters five or six spaces below the area where the postage will be placed. Or special labels may be used if available.

If a letter states or implies that materials are to be sent separately, the material should be prepared, placed in an envelope or mailing container, and a mailing label typed. If the mailing is to be taken care of by a different person or by another department the secretary should make a note to check and determine that the mailing was actually done.

The secretary should go back through the notebook to assure that no items or special instructions have been overlooked.

Notations should then be made on the secretary's calendar and follow-up items placed in the tickler file. The secretary will also post the executive's appointment calendar, if this was not done during the dictation period.

The completed correspondence should be put in a folder marked "FOR YOUR SIGNATURE" and placed on the executive's desk. Rush items should be taken in immediately; others may be accumulated and presented later in the day, allowing time for the letters to be signed and mailed on schedule.

Some executives prefer to personally sign each piece of mail; others authorize their secretaries to sign for them. The secretary's initials may be placed directly beneath the dictator's signature, unless otherwise instructed. If the executive prefers that the secretary's initials not appear on the original letter, it would be well to write them on the carbon copy, in the event that there should be a question later regarding the signature.

DICTATING MACHINES

Many executives use dictating machines to record some or all of their dictation. There are numerous kinds of machines available and the secretary should become familiar with them and learn to use them efficiently. Firms selling these machines are pleased to demonstrate them and the secretary should take advantage of this service.

The dictator speaks into a microphone, recording on a disc, belt, or tape. The dictator must speak distinctly, spell out any unusual words, and record the punctuation, capitalization, and paragraphs. For the transcriber's guidance, the number of required copies and other instructions should be dictated at the beginning.

Some machines are equipped with an indicator slip which enables the transcriber to determine length of letters, corrections, or special instructions. If the machine does not have an indicator slip, the transcriber must listen to an entire item first. It may also be necessary to take all or part of the dictation in shorthand or to make a rough draft on the typewriter.

The transcriber must learn to adjust the speed, volume, and tone controls, as well as the start, stop, and repeat mechanisms. The machine may be equipped with either a thumb or a foot control to start and stop the machine and a reverse control to replay the dictation when necessary.

The beginning transcriber usually starts the transcribing machine, listens to a few words or a phrase, stops the machine, and types the words or phrases, and then repeats the process—start, listen, stop, type. The goal of a good machine transcriber is to keep the typewriter moving with very few interruptions in the typing process.

Care should be taken that all items are transcribed before returning the disc, belt, or tape to the dictator's machine. Generally speaking, the discs can be used only one time; partially used discs should be marked to indicate what portion has been transcribed. Most of the belts or tapes can be used repeatedly, either by recording over the previous material or by erasing.

Transcribed material should be proofread and handled in the same manner as shorthand transcription.

DIRECT DICTATION AT THE TYPEWRITER

When taking dictation at the typewriter the secretary will ordinarily type a rough draft without bothering about placement or corrections. However, if the executive desires a final version without waiting for a retyping, the secretary should ask about the length of the material in order to determine placement and margins; corrections can be made after the executive has finished dictating.

TELEPHONE DICTATION

Executives who travel may frequently call and dictate letters, conference notes, instructions, and other messages to the secretary by telephone. The notes, especially names, dates, and figures, should be read back to the dictator before the conversation is terminated.

The secretary may be asked to monitor an important phone call to provide a record of what was discussed. A transcribed summary of what was said is usually sufficient and should be typed immediately while the conversation is still fresh in the secretary's mind.

ROUGH DRAFTS

The executive may request that the secretary type a rough draft of a letter, report, speech, or legal document. This should be done on inexpensive copy paper. A rough draft of a letter may be single spaced and corrections made in the margins. Speeches and reports should be double or triple spaced, leaving room for editorial changes. Rough drafts are retained until the final draft is approved.

On occasion the secretary may deem it advisable to type a rough draft of a letter without being asked, if experience dictates the probability of a rewrite. It could be diplomatically explained that the rough draft was for the secretary's own guidance in layout or because the shorthand notes were not clear. This will give the executive an opportunity to review the material before the final transcription and to make any changes desired.

Many offices are now equipped with "memory" or "display-screen" typewriters which enable secretaries to draft all items, making corrections or rearranging paragraphs, and then to "push a button" to produce a final copy with centered headings, justified margins, different types styles within the items, and so on. Special training is required to operate such machines.

These machines are excellent timesavers for secretaries who type manuscripts, technical materials, legal documents, or correspondence for executives who habitually make many changes in their dictation.

Chapter 5

Typewriter Techniques and Typing Problems

ERMALEA BONING, STAR DEMETRION

ONE OF THE SECRETS OF RAPID TYPING is to adopt a speed that allows you to keep the typewriter carriage moving constantly. Typing speed is obtained by quick key release. Only a light tap is needed when you let the typewriter mechanism carry the stroke for you. Use a quick, resilient touch and relax the finger the moment you feel contact with the key. A relaxed finger movement is probably the most important element in becoming a fast typist. One of the best ways to perfect your touch is to practice frequently used words and phrases over and over until you acquire a feel for typing them with a smooth, even rhythm. The more letter combinations you learn to type automatically, the greater your speed and control.

To acquire a very even touch, strike each key with the same force and timing.

Type with a steady pace. Never hurry or attempt to rush. The time it takes to correct errors will in the long run limit your typing speed and production rate. Concentrate word for word on what is being typed. Do not read ahead. When you read ahead, the fingers get confused.

Some words and combinations of letters are difficult to type. Good typists will slow down when typing these words or combinations because they know that they are difficult and want to type them accurately.

Many typing errors can be overcome by improving your posture and hand alignment. Adjust the typewriter so that the front edge of the frame is even with your typing desk. Let the chair comfortably support the center of your back so that your arms hang freely from the shoulders. Elbows should be in line with your hips or slightly ahead of the hip line. Wrists should be lower than your knuckles and the palms of your hands parallel to the keyboard slope. Fingers should be well curved. Fingernails should be short enough to allow the fingers to be well curved and not catch the edge of adjacent keys.

The ability to analyze and correct your own errors is an important and vital component in producing quality work and being a reliable and responsible typist. The accompanying list shows common errors and the possible reasons for them:

Error	*Analysis*
Misstroke	Typing too fast, reading copy too fast, difficulty with spelling.
Omission when typing double letters	Overemphasis on the first letter. (To prevent this, roll into the second letter by giving it greater emphasis.)
Omissions at the beginning and ending of words	Reading too far ahead in copy.
Inserting and rewriting letters	Watching letters as they are typed, faulty vision, poor light, reading too fast.
Transposition errors	Misreading, poor vision, bad light, typing too fast.
Adjacent key errors	Fingers not in correct position, improper position at typewriter, typewriter not at correct height, fingernails too long, not stroking the center of the key.
Failure to space	Poor concentration, hand movement in space bar stroke, swinging the thumb outward.

PROOFREADING

It is important to proofread each and every page before removing it from the typewriter. Performing this task is the sign of a responsible and efficient secretary. As a result your superior will have more faith and trust in your ability, and correspondence that leaves your office or firm is more likely to be error free.

Look for the following types of errors when proofreading:

1. *Formating.* Is the format correct? Is the material balanced on the page? Are all the components of the letter or document typed—date, inside address, salutation, closing, typed signature, title, reference initials, enclosure notation, etc? Has the material been arranged into proper paragraphs?
2. *Typographical errors.* Look for errors in spacing, mistyped words, repeated words, or missing letters or words.
3. *Errors in grammar.* Is there agreement between subjects and verbs? Are sentences complete? Are there run-on sentences?
4. *Errors in punctuation.* Have commas, semicolons, colons, question marks, apostrophes, and hyphens been used correctly?
5. *Errors in content or meaning.* Does the document make sense? Does it say what it was intended to say? Is something missing? Could it be misunderstood?
6. *Errors in names, numbers, addresses, amounts of money, or quantities.* Are names misspelled or the wrong names used? Are the correct addresses used? Are the numbers correct?

On important documents proofread twice—once for typing and punctuation errors, and once for content, format, and grammar errors. If possible, proofread with another person—one reading the newly typed document and one following the original.

HOW TO CORRECT ERRORS

Expert as you may be in handling the typewriter, there will be times when you may welcome hints on how to make erasing fast, clean, and inconspicuous.

There are a number of ways to correct errors on typewritten work—by eraser, correction paper, correction fluid, or with a self-correcting typewriter. However, there are advantages and disadvantages to each method.

Eraser. If you blot the error just before using your eraser, much of the surplus ink clinging to the top fibers is removed. The remaining portion of the error can be easily removed with a soft eraser. You have an erasing touch, just as you have a typing touch. If yours is a light touch, use a hard eraser; if you have a hard touch, use a softer eraser.

Manufacturers make a great effort to provide erasers suited to the different papers we use, as well as to the inks. Smooth-finished papers require a less abrasive eraser, the soft eraser. Linen-finished papers are not so easily damaged, and therefore erasing on these papers is easier. Impressions on onionskin paper are also easily removed; use a soft eraser with a light, lifting motion. On colored papers use the pencil-stick eraser with as light a motion as possible to avoid removing the color. Should you remove the color, cover it lightly with a pencil of the same color as the paper. Blend in the penciled area by brushing over it lightly with a soft eraser. The Multilith eraser makes a good, clean correction on green paper. Cockle-finished papers are not easily penetrated, and the soft eraser usually removes the ink impression readily. The pencil stick is best for cards and manila stock. To erase on this stock, you need to protect the glazed surface.

The paper-manufacturing process causes the fibers to run in a given direction; this effect is called the "grain" of the paper. The watermark, if there is one, usually indicates the grain. If the grain is horizontal (and it usually is on typewriting papers), the paper bends more easily around the platen. Erase with the grain of the paper, and you are less likely to rough up its fibers. If the fibers do become roughened in erasing, smooth them back by pressing the thumb or fingernail against the nap of the paper. Chalking the surface helps to cover the spot.

There are many ways to ensure clean erasures:
1. Keep the eraser clean by rubbing it on sandpaper or filing it with an emery board.
2. When erasing, protect the surrounding copy by using the shields provided by

equipment firms. These shields have small openings that match the space to be corrected. Frame the error with the shield and blot off the wet ink with either blotting paper, a soft eraser, or a plastic type cleaner. Kneaded rubber may also be used for blotting.

3. Remove only the necessary portion of the misstroke. If an "o" is struck for a "p," on most typewriters only the left side of the "o" needs to be erased, because the "p" fits over the "o." Other characters that fit easily over another are "h" over "n," "m" over "n," "s" over "e," "y" over "v," and "u" over "n."

4. Roll the paper far enough forward to make the error easily accessible and to secure good light on the error to be corrected. Engage the automatic line-position reset before rolling the copy up or down; re-engage it as it is returned to the line of writing. This ensures accurate realignment.

5. Avoid smearing the surrounding characters by using either the pencil type of eraser or an eraser with a sharp edge.

6. When erasing near the bottom edge of the paper, roll the sheet back to free it from the platen. If the typewriter has a copy guide, bring the bottom edge over this guide, erase, and then roll the page into typing position; otherwise, secure the sheets by rolling an extra piece of paper behind the pages in the typewriter. Now roll up, erase, return, and correct.

7. Use the margin release key and move the carriage or carrier to the extreme right or left.

8. Lift the paper bail.

9. Keep correction tools in the same location in order to eliminate wasted time and motion.

Correction paper. Correction paper is chalk-coated paper that comes in various types of dispensing containers. It is available in a variety of colors for use on colored paper. The disadvantage of correction paper is that it does not make permanent corrections. The corrections made with this device are often detectable as the chalk wears away. It is suggested that correction paper be used in conjunction with an eraser and only when the letter to be removed is similar in size and/or shape to the letter which will replace it. When an error is typed between words, it is suggested that an eraser or correction fluid be used.

To use correction paper properly:
1. Backspace or space forward to the error.
2. Place the correction paper between the paper and the card holder.
3. Strike the incorrect letter in order to coat it with the chalk from the correction paper.
4. Remove the correction paper. If the error is still visible, repeat the above process.
5. Now backspace and type the correct letter or letters.

Correction fluid. Correction fluid is chemical or water-based fluid that usually comes in small bottles with a small brush attached to the cap. The fluid is used to "paint" over the error. Correction fluid can be obtained in various colors to match the colors of paper available on the market. Correction fluid does dry out over a period of time. It may also become thick; when this occurs it makes poor corrections. A thinner can be purchased and should be used to thin out correction fluid periodically. In order to keep the fluid from being detected, skill in applying it is required.

To use correction fluid properly:
1. Roll the paper far enough forward to make the error easily accessible and to secure good light on the error to be corrected.
2. Shake the bottle of correction fluid to mix the contents well.
3. Allow only a small amount of fluid to remain on the brush.
4. Dab or dot the fluid on the error; do not stroke the error or errors because this will smear the ink and leave a dark spot where the error was located.
5. Always replace the cap tightly on the bottle immediately after use in order to prevent the fluid from drying up.
6. Allow the fluid on the paper to dry thoroughly. Otherwise fluid will attach to the card holder and/or the keys, a poor correction will result, and the keys and card holder will have to be cleaned.
7. After the fluid has dried, return to the location and type the correct letter or letters.

Self-correcting typewriters. Self-correcting typewriters contain adhesive correcting tape that lifts the error off the paper when a backspace/correction key is activated. The incorrect key is struck in order to lift the error off the page. The carriage or carrier remains in position after lifting the error off the page; backspacing to type the correct letter is therefore unnecessary. These corrections are permanent.

To make corrections using a self-correcting typewriter:
1. Strike the backspace/correction key.
2. Strike the mistyped letter.
3. Type the correct letter.

HOW TO ALIGN PAPER TO CORRECT ERRORS

If errors are discovered after work has been removed from the typewriter, the paper must be realigned properly in order to place the correction in the proper location. Use the paper release and align a straight letter (l, i, t) with one of the lines on the typewriter scale or card holder. Use the variable spacer or the left platen knob to align the typing so that it rests on the aligning scale. Your paper should then be located in the proper position to make the correction.

Some typists prefer to switch the ribbon-control lever to stencil position to test the location before the final typing of the correction. Other typists prefer to test their alignment position by striking over a period (also in stencil position) near the letter to be corrected. If the periods match, they then proceed to type the correct letters.

HOW TO CORRECT CARBONS

Before correcting carbons, erase the original first; it is your most important copy. Back the original with a plastic card or regular 3″ × 5″ card. One card serves for all copies. Put the card on top of the carbon paper, not behind it, and erase one copy at a time. Use a pencil eraser or soft eraser for carbon copies because carbon copies will erase very easily and quickly. Move the card back after each erasure. The card gives you a smooth surface to erase against and protects the copies and carbon sheets from damage.

If the correction on the carbon copy is lighter than the surrounding type, strike the key with the ribbon in stencil position. This leaves a darker impression on the carbon copy but keeps the original blank. You may want to match the retyped stroke to surrounding copy by inserting a small piece of carbon paper (carbon side facing carbon copy) between the type guide and the copy.

If the carbons have been removed from the typewriter before the correction is made, insert each carbon separately. To make the correction match the other typed characters, build a miniature carbon stack with the original, carbon paper, and copy paper. When you correct the first carbon copy, insert your miniature carbon stack between the type guide and your first carbon sheet so that you will stroke through the original. When correcting the second carbon copy, place your miniature carbon stack over the correction and strike through the original and one carbon.

When using correction tape with carbon copies, erase the carbon copies first, and then place a plastic card or 3″ × 5″ card behind the original when striking the incorrect letter to chalk it out. The same procedure would be used on a self-correcting typewriter.

HOW TO CROWD AND EXPAND CORRECTIONS

Did you leave out a letter? Did you type one or more extra letters in a word? If you leave off the last letter of a word and have already typed the next word, position the carriage so that the printing point is at the space immediately following the incomplete word, depress the backspacer halfway, and type the missing letter. On an electric typewriter without a half-space key, push the carriage back half a space with the right platen knob and hold it in this position as you type the missing letter. If the machine has a half-space key, position the carriage so that the printing point is at the last letter of the incomplete word, depress the half-space key, and type the missing letter. On a Selectric typewriter or a typewriter with an element, place your right hand along the right side of the carrier and press gently to the left. Hold the carrier in position while typing the correct letter.

If you are spreading three letters over a space formerly occupied by four, type in the initial letter and final letter first; then center the middle letter between them.

HOW TO TYPE OR CORRECT BOUND COPIES

Copies that are bound across the top of the sheets may be typed or corrected by front-feeding the bound pages as follows: Insert a blank sheet around the platen an inch or so above the typebar guide. Lift the paper bail to an upright position. Place the sheet to be typed or corrected behind the top of the already inserted paper in front of the platen. Turn the platen back to the typing location or the location of the error to be corrected.

slip bound sheet behind
already inserted paper

HOW TO USE THE TABULATOR KEY

The tab key is one of the most useful service features on your typewriter. Use it for indentions, for centering, for positioning the date line, the closing lines of your letters, and for addressing envelopes. If forms are typed repetitively, tabs are set for standard locations and positions on the forms. Many secretaries set and leave a tab stop at the center position of their typewriter for centering purposes.

On some electric typewriters you can use the tab key together with the carriage-return key to return the carriage to a desired point without returning it first to the left margin. Flick the carriage-return key and, as the carriage passes the tab stop setting, touch the tab key. Use this procedure in addressing envelopes, in positioning the carriage for the closing lines of the letter, and in columnar typing.

HOW TO TYPE SMALL CARDS

Make a pleat horizontally in the center of a sheet of bond paper. The depth of the pleat will determine how far down you can type on the card; that is, the depth of the pleat is equal to the margin to be left at the bottom of the card. Insert this sheet in the typewriter. Line up the folded edge of the pleat with the edge of the type guide. Place the bottom edge of the card in the pleat and roll back the platen to typing position. If you secure the pleat with transparent tape, it is easier to insert it in the machine. A pencil mark against the left edge of the first card can serve as a margin guide for all cards to be inserted in the typewriter.

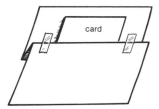

Side margins on the message side of post cards should be one-half inch. Leave two blank lines for top and bottom margins. Type the return address on the front of the card if there is not room to type it above the date on the message side. If the message is long, single-space between paragraphs and omit the salutation and closing.

If you have many post cards to type, chain-feed them from the front of the platen. After you have typed the first card, feed backward until the card has a 3/4-inch margin. Insert the next card so that the bottom is held in place by the first card. Each succeeding card will be held in position by the preceding card. The cards will pile up against the paper table as they are typed, and they will be in the same order in which they were inserted in the typewriter. This method is particularly useful when cards are stiff and smooth. You may also use this method for addressing envelopes in quantity.

CARBON PAPER AND ITS USE

Most organizations require at least one carbon copy of all documents for retention in their files. Onionskin paper, lightweight colored paper, or manifold paper is usually used for carbon copies.

Choose a carbon paper with as hard a finish and heavy a weight as you can use and still obtain good results. There are many variables that affect the quality of the carbon copy, such as make of typewriter and model, number of copies to be made, desired darkness of carbon copies, weight and finish of the copy paper, kind of type, kind of platen (soft or hard), weight of letterhead, and quality of carbon paper.

Some secretaries (or their employers) prefer black copies; others like a medium-black, and still others, a light-gray copy. Actually the grayer copies are more legible, and the writing is usually sharper. To obtain the effect that pleases you, select a finish that produces the desired degree of blackness. The intense finishes make an extremely black copy. Hard finish carbon paper should be used with pica type machines because they have larger characters and with electric typewriters because they strike with more force.

If you want more sharpness in your impression, back your carbon pack with a plastic backer, which may be obtained from your office-equipment supplier. Using the backer is like having a second platen.

Preassembled snap-out carbon packs are also available. These packs consist of alternate sheets of copy paper and carbon paper placed together with a perforated top. After the carbon copies are prepared, the carbon paper is removed and discarded.

Observe these considerations when using carbon paper:
1. Use the hardest finish and heaviest weight consistent with good results.
2. Use the rougher side of the sheet when using glazed second sheets, because carbon ink adheres best to rough surfaces.
3. If you want sharp, legible copies, select second sheets of the correct weight. The number of legible copies decreases as the weight of the second sheets is increased.
4. To obtain clearer copies when reusing carbon paper, turn the sheet around so that the top of the next page to be typed uses the section of the carbon paper that was used for the bottom of the preceding page.
5. Avoid excessive handling of carbon paper; keep hands clean to avoid smudges.
6. Use the paper release lever to prevent roller marks and/or wrinkles or creases.
7. Use carbon paper that is slightly longer than the paper because it is easier to remove the carbons from the pack when the document is completed.
8. Throw away carbon paper when it begins to show wear or begins to produce light or illegible copies.

To assemble a carbon pack:
1. Place a sheet of copy paper on the desk.
2. Place a sheet of carbon paper, glossy (carbon) side down, on top of the copy paper.
3. Repeat the above process until the desired number of copies has been assembled.
4. Place the letterhead or original sheet on top, letterhead facing you.

To insert a carbon pack into the typewriter:
1. Pick up the entire pack and turn it so that the back of the last copy sheet is facing you. Tap the bottom of the pack on the desk to straighten the pack.

2. If several carbon copies are to be produced, adjust the carbon copy indicator in order to lighten the pressure against the platen.
3. Be sure that the back of the pack is facing you and that the letterhead (facing away from you) is upside down.
4. Drop the pack into the typewriter. Use the paper release lever to get the pack into position. Some secretaries find it helpful to place the carbon pack into the folded edge of a half sheet of paper, which then guides the pack into the typewriter. The flap of an envelope may also be used for this purpose. After the pack has been inserted, the folded sheet (or envelope) is removed before typing begins.
5. When the carbon pack has been inserted, be sure that the letterhead is facing you and that the carbon or glossy side of the carbon paper is facing away from you.
6. To remove a carbon pack from the typewriter, always use the paper release.
7. To remove carbon paper from the carbon pack, hold the pack by one of the top corners and shake the pack gently. Remove the carbon paper from the bottom of the pack in one motion.

HOW TO CENTER PAPER

CENTERING HORIZONTALLY

For best paper feeding, center the paper in the typewriter and then move the paper-edge guide to the left edge of the paper. Determine the center point of your writing line by noting the figures on the writing scale against which the left and right edges of your paper rest, adding these figures, and dividing by 2. The result is the center of your page. Set a tab stop at the center point. From the center backspace once for every two spaces in the line to be centered. If there is an extra letter, disregard it.

CENTERING VERTICALLY

There is a short cut to vertical centering, too. It is based on the same principle as the one used in the backspace method of centering horizontally (backspacing once for every two spaces in the typed line). Start at the vertical center of your page. Standard size paper has 66 vertical lines; therefore, line 33 is the vertical center. Turn the platen forward to line 33. Now turn the platen back once for each two lines that you plan to type on the page. Begin typing at this point.

PIVOTING

Making lines end where you want them to end is called "pivoting." Set your carriage one space after the point where you wish to end the copy; backspace once for each letter and space in the line you are typing. If there are certain headings you frequently type, keep a list of them with the numbers on which you start them. With this reference list you can whiz through the heading of your typed reports.

TYPEWRITER CARRIAGE LENGTHS

Both manual and electric typewriters come with carriages that vary in length from 11 to 32 inches. If you are using a typewriter with a long carriage, center the paper by folding a sheet in half, lengthwise, opening it, and inserting it into the machine so that the fold lines up with the center point of the platen. Adjust the paper-edge guide so that it is flush with the left edge of the paper.

Some long carriages have a bar in the center of the margin rail, preventing you from moving the right margin stop beyond the center point of the carriage. This is why you should always type with the paper centered in the machine; besides, the paper will feed better because the little rollers under the platen will pull evenly on the sheet as it is inserted.

TYPE STYLES

Not only do typewriter carriages differ in length, but type styles vary also. Although elite and pica are probably still the most commonly used type styles, a number of other styles are available. Some have a broad face and others produce very sharply engraved characters. Some look like printing and one, Script Type, resembles handwriting. Interchangeable elements (with different type styles) may be purchased for use with typewriters that utilize an element instead of typebars.

HOW TO TYPE TABLES

The style of tables will vary according to the type of data to be used. However, the following *general information* is helpful in typing tables:

1. Move margin stops to the extreme far left and right. Clear all tab stops.
2. The *vertical placement* of tables is determined in the same way that was described under CENTERING VERTICALLY.
3. To determine the *horizontal placement* of tables:
   a. Use the longest item in each column as the size of that column.
   b. Determine the number of blank spaces to be placed between columns.
   c. To determine the left margin, from the center of the paper backspace once for every two spaces in the longest line of each column and for every two spaces between columns. Set the left margin.

    d. Space forward once for each letter and space in the first column and the space following the column. Set the first tab stop.

    e. Repeat the above procedures until all tab stops are set.

4. The main title is usually centered and typed in all caps.
5. If a secondary or subheading is used, it is typed a double space below the main heading, centered, and typed in lower case with major words capitalized.
6. Triple-space between the main heading (or subheading) and the body of the table.
7. Center column headings over columns. If a column heading is longer than the longest line in the column, the column heading should be used as the size of the column. The column is then indented and centered under the heading. Underline column headings. To determine the center of each column, find the center of the longest line in each column. Double-space to the body or first item in each column.
8. When typing a short table, double-space the body of the table. When typing a long table, single-space the body of the table.
9. When typing columns containing amounts of money, place the dollar sign only before the first figure in each column and before the totals.
10. Use leaders (a series of periods) to indicate omissions in a column.
11. Align figures on the right and words on the left.
12. Use abbreviations in tables, such as lb., ft., %.
13. To avoid confusion with figures in tables, indicate references or footnotes by the symbol * or the letters "a," "b," "c," etc.
14. Type credit lines at the left corner beneath the table.
15. Type tables of more than 30 lines on separate pages.

BALANCE OF PAYMENTS

(in thousands of dollars)

	Receipts	Payments	Net
Goods and Services	$ 164.20	$ 159.80	$ 4.40
Merchandise	114.69	123.92	-9.22
Services	49.51	35.89	13.63
Government	6.96	10.56	-3.60
Military	5.20	4.81	.39
Other	1.76	5.75	-3.99
Private	42.55	25.32	17.23
Grants	--	3.14	-3.14
Pensions, etc.	--	1.87	-1.87
Balance on current account			$ -.60

GENERAL SPACING REMINDERS

1. There are six lines of typing to one vertical inch.
2. There are 10 pica spaces to one horizontal inch.
3. There are 12 elite spaces to one horizontal inch.
4. There are 85 pica spaces and 102 elite spaces on an 8 1/2-inch line.
5. There are 66 vertical line spaces on an 8 1/2- × 11-inch page.
6. The center point on an 8 1/2- × 11-inch page: pica typewriter—42; elite typewriter—51.

TYPEWRITER UPKEEP AND MAINTENANCE

THE DAILY TWO-MINUTE CHECK

Spend two minutes at the end of each day wiping all exposed parts of your typewriter with a soft, dry cloth. Use a long-handled brush to get into the corners and brush toward you. Move the carriage or carrier all the way to the left or right and brush out any eraser dust that may be there. A soft paintbrush is good for this kind of dusting. Do not oil your typewriter; let the service representative do this for you.

CLEANING THE TYPE

Use a stiff, dry brush and brush out and away from the typewriter. If the "o's" and "e's" are filled up, tap them gently with your brush. Clean type at the end of the day's work. The ink is more easily removed then. If you are using nylon ribbons, leave a slight deposit of ink on the type bars or element. When you use a plastic type cleaner, do not press down on the keys too hard. With one finger lift a few keys at a time and apply the cleaner.

GENERAL CARE

A damp cloth will take off the excess carbon from the platen. If you clean the platen with alcohol, use it sparingly, because it has a tendency to harden the rubber. Disengage the paper release when you leave your typewriter for the night.

When erasing, move the carriage of the typewriter to keep the eraser dust from falling between the typebars.

If the keys jam, separate them carefully one at a time. Do not force them, or you may bend the typebars out of alignment.

Center the carriage and cover your typewriter when it is not in use. The cover protects the machine from dust and should be used whether the typewriter is on a desk or put away in a typewriter desk.

Record needed typewriter repairs as you notice them. Put your list on the underside of the typewriter cover. When the service representative comes, your list will be handy.

Chapter 6

The Business Letter: Format and Structural Parts

EMOJEAN NOVOTNY

THE LETTERS that issue from a business office are, in a very real sense, ambassadors of good will. The impression an individual letter creates may sometimes mean the difference between the gain or loss of a prospective customer, a client, or an influential friend for your company. This impression depends as much on the appearance of the letter as on the tone or contents of the letter.

This chapter will discuss the different letter styles that may be used to achieve a favorable impression.

LETTER STYLES

It has often been said that an ideal letter should resemble a picture in an appropriate frame, but this is not always practical today because of the many different letterhead styles; therefore, letters must be arranged and typed according to the style of the letterhead as well as the letter style which the company has chosen. Most organizations have a procedural manual for their employees giving the letter style and explaining how they want the various parts of the business letter typed.

The various letter styles being used in the business world are here listed and examples will be shown on the following pages.

Full block style (Letter 1). This style is the full or extreme block style with all lines beginning at the left margin.

Simplified style (Letter 2). This letter style is very similar to the full block letter style with the exception that the simplified style omits the salutation and complimentary closing. A subject line typed on the third line below the inside address in all capital letters replaces the salutation. The writer's identification and title is typed in all capital letters three lines below the body of the letter. This is a less formal letter style being used frequently today because of changes in the outlook of the business world. People are more informal and some executives feel their letters should also be less formal.

Modified or regular block style (Letter 3). The date line, complimentary closing, and typewritten signature lines begin at the center of the paper and all other lines begin flush with the left margin. If an attention line or subject line is used, it is also typed flush with the left margin. A five-space paragraph indention may be used in typing a very short letter.

Semiblock style (Letter 4). This style is very similar to the modified or regular block style letter. The paragraphs are indented five spaces, the inside address is blocked, and the date line, complimentary closing, and typewritten signature lines begin at the center of the paper.

Hanging indention style (Letter 5). This style starts each paragraph flush with the left margin. The rest of the lines in each paragraph are indented. The date line may be centered under the letterhead or it may be typed starting at the center of the sheet, as is the complimentary closing and the signature line.

Indented style (Letter 6). This style indents all lines five spaces, except for the main body of the letter. This letter style is almost obsolete, but may be encountered by the secretary in letters from foreign countries.

PUNCTUATION FOR BUSINESS LETTERS

The three punctuation styles for business letters are listed in their order of popularity:

Mixed or standard punctuation. Place a colon after the salutation and a comma after the complimentary closing.

Open punctuation. No punctuation is used after the salutation or the complimentary closing.

Closed punctuation. Each line (date, lines in the inside address, salutation, complimentary closing, firm name, dictator's signature) must be closed with a mark of punctuation. If there is only one line within the unit, then the line is closed with a period. If there is more than one line in a unit, use a comma at the end of each line and a period at the end of the closing line as shown in Letter 6. This punctuation style is seldom used, although some government offices still prefer it.

BASIC PARTS OF A BUSINESS LETTER

After the letter and punctuation styles have been determined, it is very important for the typist to place the basic parts of a business letter in proper format on company stationery.

These basic elements of the business letter will be discussed in order of appearance on business letterhead stationery.

Mead Johnson NUTRITIONAL DIVISION

Date   January 29, 19--

Inside address   MRI Media Research, Incorporated
                            25 Main Street
                            Ithaca, New York 14850

Salutation   Gentlemen

                            Enclosed find survey form MR43 that you have requested from us. We
                            have studied the results of your letter survey and are considering
                            using this style for business letters. Let us go over each element.

                            This letter is typed in the Full Block Style, sometimes called the
                            "extreme block style." All lines begin flush with the left margin.
Body   The salutation and complimentary closing are used.

                            The style is flexible. Some executives prefer to use the conven-
                            tional marks of punctuation. More often, the colon after the sal-
                            utation and the comma after the complimentary closing are omitted.

                            You will see that the company name is given before the signature
                            of the writer of the letter. It is typed in all capital letters.
                            The typed signature follows the space for the written signature.
                            Below or following the typed signature is the title of the writer.

Complimentary closing   Sincerely yours

Company   MEAD JOHNSON

Signature

Typed signature   John R. Starr
Title   Public Relations Director

Reference initials   JRS: mc
Enclosure line   Enc.

Carbon-copy notation   cc: Jean Winarchik

Letter 1
The Full Block Style of letter is much used in the business world today. It finds favor
because of speed and ease of typing. Many executives like its modern, straightforward
appearance. Yet others consider this style to look unbalanced because all elements
start at the left.

1375 east sixth street · cleveland, ohio 44114 · 216/696-9000

February 18, 19--

Ms. Joan Donest
14220 Trasket Avenue
Cleveland, New York 13042

SIMPLIFIED STYLE OF LETTER

This style of letter is typed in the full, or extreme, block form.
Each line begins flush with the left-hand margin. Note that there
is no salutation and no complimentary closing. This feature saves
the typist much time, not only in the typing, but sometimes in
trying to determine what title is proper for a salutation.

A subject line is always used, but the word "subject" is omitted.

Open punctuation is followed in this style of letter. No periods
are used after lines in the name and address block, nor after the
subject line.

Spacing is judged according to standard letter placement guides for
various sizes of type, except for these features:

A triple space is left above and below the subject line. The signature line is typed four spaces below the body, or perhaps five or
six lines if the executive has large handwriting. The signature
line is typed in all capital letters. If the name is followed by the
title of the signer, that too is in all capital letters.

JOSEPH H. FENG
ASSISTANT FILING SUPERVISOR

JHF:dh

Letter 2

The Simplified Style of letter is perhaps the least cluttered and the very easiest to type.
It is preferred by writers who dislike formality and want to get right to the point. Yet
even those who advocate the use of this style often vary it slightly by using a complimentary closing.

69

DIVISION OF UNIVERSITY RELATIONS
DEPARTMENT OF UNIVERSITY AND COMMUNITY RELATIONS   (216) 687-2296

                                        October 23, 19--

United Books International
909 Fifth Avenue   File No. 6931
New York, NY 10010

Gentlemen:

This is the Modified or Regular Block Style of letter, illustrated
with standard punctuation and file number. The date line, file
number line, complimentary closing, and typed signature all start
in the horizontal center of the sheet.

Sometimes instead of "File No.," the words "Re" or "In re" will be
used, generally followed by a colon. No punctuation is used after
the file number or after the subject mentioned in the "Re or "In
re" line.

Except for these elements, the lines of the letter start flush
with the left-hand margin.

Standard punctuation calls for the colon after the salutation and
comma after the complimentary closing.

                                    Very truly yours,

                                    (Mrs.) Maureen T. Reister
                                    Typing Supervisor
MTR/gp

cc: Ms. Lorraine Cooper
     Mr. Frederick Short

Letter 3
The Modified or Regular Block Style of letter is perhaps the best balanced in the page.
The body of the letter constitutes a complete block. Of the other elements, about half
start at the left while the other half start in the center. This placement creates a pleasing
unity of arrangement.

ARVIN/DIAMOND™

November 16, 19--

Ms. Teresa Nettles
Public Relations Department
Brokers Corporation
P. O. Box 420
New London, Iowa 52645

Dear Ms. Nettles:

Subject: Semiblock Style of Letter

      We have here an example of the Semiblock Style of letter
with standard punctuation and subject line. The address is a
block. The closing section also constitutes a block, with each
line starting at the center of the sheet, directly under the
beginning of the date line. The subject line may be centered
or flush left.

      This style of letter differs from the full block style in
that it features indention of the paragraphs. The practice of
indenting paragraphs is falling away as the years go on, but
some business executives and professionals still prefer the way
a letter appears with indented paragraphs.

      Standard punctuation is used; that is, a colon is typed
after the salutation and a comma after the complimentary closing.

                Sincerely yours,

                (Ms.) Imogene Jones
                Assistant to the Director

IJ:TY

DIAMOND ELECTRONICS P.O.BOX 200 LANCASTER, OHIO 43130 TEL: (614)756-9222
APPLIED TECHNOLOGY GROUP OF ARVIN INDUSTRIES INC.

Letter 4

The Semiblock Style of letter continues to be used by many companies. The paragraph indentions are thought to make the letter easy to read simply because the reader is accustomed to this in other printed matter. Then, too, the underlined subject is certain to catch the reader's attention at once.

THE PLAIN DEALER

OHIO'S LARGEST NEWSPAPER

1801 SUPERIOR AVE.

CLEVELAND, OHIO 44114

344-4124

OFFICE OF
DAVID L. HOPCRAFT
MANAGING EDITOR

December 18, 19--

Newsprint, Inc.
100 Public Square
Winters, California 95694

Dear Contributor:

This is the Hanging Indention Style of letter. It is also sometimes
called the "inverted paragraph style." It is used in advertising
letters, for it gives emphasis to the writer's message. The first
line of each paragraph starts at the left margin, and the remaining lines are uniformly indented.

MESSAGE IMPACT: The way in which the type is arranged calls immediate
attention to the various points the writer is trying to emphasize.

READING EASE: The eye follows the copy with surprising ease. The open
spacing and uniformity of arrangement account for this.

TYPING EASE: This letter can be typed speedily and with little effort.
If a great number of letters of the same kind are to be sent and
the executive objects to photocopies, the typist can zip through
this kind of letter in record time.

We are enclosing a copy of a guide for typists.

Yours truly,

(Ms.) Mary L. Fitzgibbons
Administrative Assistant

MLF:ms
Enclosure

Letter 5

The paragraphs of the Hanging Indention Style of letter are the reverse of the indented
paragraphs of the Semiblock Style shown in Letter 4 or the Indented Style of Letter 6.
This style is used for special purposes, and not for everyday business correspondence.

THE
VOLUME
LIBRARY Published by THE SOUTHWESTERN COMPANY

October 16, 19--

Capital Enterprises,
      100 Main Bridge Street,
            South Dennis, New Jersey 08245.

                    Attention: Miss Mary Lane.

Dear Miss Lane:

      This is the Indented Style of letter, with closed punctuation.
In this style the lines of the address and the closing section are
each indented five spaces from the line above. In order to avoid
having a long company name project into the right-hand margin, the
complimentary closing should be started five or more spaces to the
left of the horizontal center.

      Note that each line of typing above and below the body of the
letter ends with a punctuation mark. The last line of the inside
address and the last line of the closing section end with periods.
The lines preceding these end with commas.

      This style of letter is rarely used in the business offices
of America today.

                  Yours very truly,

                        THE SOUTHWESTERN COMPANY,

                              Robin L. Lewis,
                                Assistant Editor.
RLL:dd

Editorial Offices • 2080 West 117th Street, Cleveland, Ohio 44111   (216) 941-6930

Letter 6

The Indented Style of letter was the usual style taught in typing classes of an earlier era. The use of a punctuation mark at the end of each line has fallen into disfavor since. The indention of succeeding lines looks unnecessary, too, but some government offices continue to adhere to this style.

LETTERHEAD

Most business letters are typed on printed letterheads. The format of the letterhead will differ with each firm, but the contents of the letterhead are fairly standard. These elements consist of the company name, and usually the street address, the name of the city and state, and the ZIP Code. Other elements which may appear in the letterhead are the telephone number (with area code) of the firm, names and titles of the corporate officers, and an executive's name and position.

DATE LINE

The date line begins on the second or third line below the company letterhead or on line 14, whichever is lower or preferred. The date line consists of the month, the day, and the year.

The month is always spelled in full and never abbreviated. The date and the year are placed in figures, and the date is followed by a comma.

Preferred style	August 1, 1980
Military style	1 August 1980
INCORRECT STYLES	August 1st, 1980
	Aug. 1, 1980

If you use the full block style (Letter 1) or the simplified style (Letter 2), the date is typed flush against the left margin.

If you use the modified block style (Letter 3) or the semiblock style (Letter 4), the date begins at the center. For the indented letter style (Letter 6), the date is typed flush to the right margin.

When using any style except the full block or simplified style, some offices choose to center the date on the second or third line below the letterhead. This placement is illustrated in the hanging indention style (Letter 5).

INSIDE ADDRESS

The inside address may be typed anywhere from three to twelve lines below the date line, depending upon the length of letter (see placement chart on page 77).

The inside address should include the following elements: person's name, person's title, name of company or organization, street address, city name, state name, and ZIP Code. If a company or organization is being addressed, or a person at a company or organization, the inside address should be typed exactly as it appears in the addressee's letterhead.

If the name of a specific person is not known, then you may use a business title. In this way, the letter will be directed to the proper person.

Complete inside addresses are most important so that accurate files may be established. The inside address is typed directly at the left margin for all letter styles except the indented letter style (Letter 6).

If the address includes an apartment number or room number, these elements may be typed directly after the street address or on the line above the street address.

```
Mr. John Alexander, President        Mr. John Alexander
ABZ Company                          The ABZ Company
1234 East Sixth Street, Room 1410    Room 1410
New York, New York  10036            1234 East Sixth Street
                                     New York, New York  10036

Mr. John Alexander                   National Sales Manager
National Sales Manager               The ABZ Company
The ABZ Company                      Room 1410
1234 East Sixth Street               1234 East Sixth Street
New York, New York  10036            New York, New York  10036

National Sales Manager
The ABZ Company
Post Office Box 1614
New York, New York  10036
```

General guidelines to follow when typing the inside address:
1. Type names as they appear in the letterhead; always check the spelling of all proper names by referring to your files.
2. The number (#) symbol is not necessary when typing the house number, room number, or post office box number. House numbers with the exception of one are typed in figures.

One East Sixth Street

2 East Sixth Street

3. When street names are numbers write out names below ten and use figures for names above ten.
4. When figures are used in street addresses, it is not necessary to use endings such as st, d, nd, or rd after the numbered street name.

1234 East 12 Street

5. Do not abbreviate any part of the inside address unless it is shown in an abbreviated form on the firm's letterhead.
6. Type the city name, state name, and ZIP Code on the same line.
7. Type the city name in full followed by a comma, and then the two-letter state abbreviation or the state name in full.
8. The ZIP Code is typed two spaces after the name of the state, using no punctuation after the state name or its two-letter abbreviation.

SALUTATION

The salutation is typed two lines below the last line of the inside address. If an attention line is used, then the salutation is placed two lines following the attention line.

The salutation is omitted in the simplified letter style. In all other letter styles, the salutation is typed starting at the left margin and followed by a colon if mixed punctuation is used. There is no punctuation after the salutation if open style punctuation is used.

Capitalization of salutations. Capitalize the first word, the title, and any noun in the salutation:

```
Dear Mr. Jones

My dear Professor Clark

Dear Mrs. Morgan

Your Excellency
```

Abbreviations in salutations. Mr., Ms., Mrs., Messrs., and Dr. are abbreviated. Write out other titles such as Captain, Professor, Father, Reverend, etc.

Forms of salutations. For the forms of salutations to use in addressing church or government officials, judges, doctors, etc. see *Forms of Address* (Appendix 5).

When an organization is composed of men and women, the salutation used is still Gentlemen if the correspondence is addressed to a company. Although this style is frowned upon by some groups, it is still used simply because a more acceptable salutation has not yet evolved.

Guidelines for salutations when address is to a

1. Firm's name	Gentlemen
2. Firm's name and an attention line is used	Gentlemen
3. Married woman, a widow, or a divorced woman who uses the title Mrs.	Dear Mrs. Jones
4. Unmarried woman	Dear Miss Jones
	Dear Ms. Jones
5. Unknown whether woman is married or single	Dear Ms. Jones
6. Group (composed of men and women)	Ladies and gentlemen
7. Married couple	Dear Mr. and Mrs. Jones
8. Man and a woman	Dear Mr. Jones and Mrs. Black
	Dear Sir and Madam

LETTER PLACEMENT GUIDE

		Line	Spaces		Set Margins	
	Words in Body	Width	Pica	Elite	Pica	Elite
SHORT LETTERS	Under 100 words	4″	40	48	22-62	27-75
MEDIUM LETTERS	100 to 200 words	5″	50	60	17-67	21-81
LONG LETTERS	200 to 300 words	6″	60	72	12-72	15-87

The date is placed on line 14 on plain paper. When printed letterheads are used, the date is placed on the second or third line under the letterhead. However, if the letterhead is short (5 to 9 lines deep), bring date to line 14 for better placement.

	Words in Body	Lines from Date to Inside Address
SHORT LETTERS	0 - 50	12
	51 - 75	11
	76 - 100	10
MEDIUM LETTERS	101 - 125	9
	126 - 150	8
	151 - 175	7
	176 - 200	6
LONG LETTERS	201 - 225	5
	226 - 250	4
	251 - 300	3

At least a triple line space must be kept between date, or last line in return address, and the inside address.

Raise the inside address one line for each extra line of introductory or closing material:

1. Five-line inside address
2. Subject line
3. Attention line
4. Postscript
5. Enclosure line
6. Carbon copy line (one line for each name)

BODY OF THE LETTER

The part of the letter containing the message is known as the "body." It is typed a double space below the salutation or a double space below the subject line. The paragraphs should be blocked or indented depending upon the letter style that is used. The paragraphs are single-spaced except for the very short letter which is double-spaced.

Whether the lines are single-spaced or double-spaced, use only double spacing between paragraphs.

The body of the simplified letter style is typed on the third line below the subject line.

Tabulated matter in body of the letter. Tabulated matter in the body of a letter is indented at least five spaces from both the left- and right-hand margins.

Enumerated paragraphs. Enumerated paragraphs are also indented five spaces from both the right- and left-hand margins. These paragraphs begin with a number followed by a period. Two spaces after the period, begin typing the paragraph. Single-space each enumerated paragraph but double-space between the enumerated paragraphs. (If each enumerated paragraph contains only one line, you may single-space between paragraphs.)

    1.   ---
          ----

    2.   ---

COMPLIMENTARY CLOSING

The complimentary closing is typed two lines below the last line of the body of the letter.

Capitalize only the first word in the complimentary closing. Follow the complimentary closing by a comma, unless open punctuation is used. If open punctuation is used, no punctuation is needed.

Placement of complimentary closing. The placement of the complimentary closing depends upon which letter style is used. (See Letters 1-6.)

Degrees of formality. As with the salutation, there are also degrees of formality recognized in complimentary closings.

1. Formal tone: Yours truly, Yours very truly, Very truly yours.
2. More formal tone: Respectfully yours, Yours respectfully, Very respectfully yours, Yours very respectfully.
3. Less formal and more personal tone: Sincerely, Cordially, Sincerely yours, Cordially yours, Yours sincerely.

TYPEWRITTEN SIGNATURE AND TITLE

When a company name appears as part of the signature, it is typed in all capitals a double space below the complimentary closing. The typewritten signature is then typed on the fourth line below the company name or the complimentary closing. The penned signature is placed in the intervening space. If a letter is unusually short, place the typed signature on the sixth or eighth line below the company name or complimentary closing. If the writer's handwriting is unusually large, the signature may be typed from five to eight lines below the company name or complimentary closing.

The writer's title may appear on the same line with the typed signature or on the line below the typed signature, whichever gives a better balance to the page.

```
Yours very truly,          Yours very truly,



Clarence Brown, Manager    Clarence Brown
                           Manager
```

Simplified letter style. Beginning at the left margin, type the writer's name and title on the fifth line below the body of the letter in all capital letters, or the name on the fifth line and the title on the sixth line.

```
               Yours truly,

               ABZ CORPORATION

               C. M. Longfellow
               C. M. Longfellow
               Director of Research
```

Division or department. Frequently a division or department is used in the closing lines of a letter; it is typed below the typed signature and title.

```
               Very truly yours,

               R. M. Brown
               R. M. Brown, Supervisor
               Plastics Division
```

When a letter requires two signatures, you may use either one of the following forms:

Sincerely yours,

Jane R. Jones
(Ms.) Jane R. Jones
District Manager

Milton Trout
Milton Trout
General Manager

OR   Sincerely yours,

Jane R. Jones
(Ms.) Jane R. Jones
District Manager

Milton Trout
Milton Trout
General Manager

Signature for the employer. If, as a secretary, you are required to sign a letter for your employer, you may use either one of the following forms:

Sincerely yours,

Myrna Lane
Secretary to Ms. Jones

Sincerely yours,

Myrna Lane
Ms. Myrna Lane
Secretary to Ms. Jones

Signing someone else's name. When signing someone else's name, it is not necessary to write "per" or "by." Simply sign the individual's name and then use your initials.

If your employer has a facsimile signature, use it.

When the individual signing a letter for another person is not the person's secretary, use either one of these forms:

Sincerely yours,

Milton Trout
For Milton Trout
General Manager

Sincerely yours,

Milton Trout rk
Milton Trout
General Manager

Academic, military, and professional titles. These titles should appear in the typewritten signatures as given below.

Yours truly,   Yours truly,

Grace Johnson   *James Simpson*

(Ms.) Grace Johnson, C.P.S.   James Simpson, M.D.

Yours truly,   Yours truly,

Laura Willson,   *Leonard J. Richardson*

Laura Willson, Ph.D.   Leonard J. Richardson
Professor of Humanities   Colonel, USAF

The salutations in replies to each of these would be, respectively, Dear Ms. Johnson, Dear Dr. Simpson, Dear Professor Willson, and Dear Colonel Richardson.

When a man's first name could also be a woman's name, or if he uses initials, then he should use the courtesy title of Mr.

Sincerely,   Sincerely yours,

Dale Harrington   *D. K. Harrington*

(Mr.) Dale Harrington   (Mr.) D.K. Harrington

Courtesy titles for women. It is customary for a woman to include her courtesy title (Ms., Miss, Mrs.) in her signature. If she does not, she presents a problem to the person replying to her letter. Without a signature that lets respondents know what title the woman prefers, they have little choice than to use Ms., even though they risk offending some women who object to this title.

Sincerely yours,   Sincerely,

Francine Booth   *Francine Booth*

(Mrs.) Francine Booth   (Miss) Francine Booth

Yours truly,

Francine Booth

(Ms.) Francine Booth

If the writer is a single woman and wants to be recognized as being single, she should use Miss. If a woman is married and does not feel that her married status is relevant, she may use Ms. or Miss.

If a married woman prefers to be addressed by her husband's given name, then she should use the format:

Yours very truly,

Francine Booth

Mrs. Paul A. Booth

A divorced woman may use any courtesy title she wishes regardless of whether she has resumed her maiden name or retained her married surname.

REFERENCE INITIALS

All typed business letters should contain identifying initials. Usually there will be two sets of initials. The first set represents the author of the written document and the second set belongs to the typist. The reference initials are typed the second line below the typewritten signature and title. Some firms do not require the writer's identifying initials when there is a typewritten signature. Styles most commonly used are as follows:

ABC/jn   or typist's initials only jn

ABC:jn

jn   typist's initials only when typewritten
                          signature is given

Yours truly,

                          This style is used when there is a typewritten
                          title but no signature
President

Charles Brown:jn

Reference initials are typed flush left. The dictator's initials are upper case and the typist's initials are lower case. Occasionally an executive will type his or her own business letter. When this is done, the executive may repeat the personal initials (RK:rk) to indicate that a typist was not involved.

OCCASIONAL ELEMENTS IN BUSINESS LETTERS

ATTENTION LINE

The writer may wish to direct the letter to a particular person or department within the firm. When the inside address is directed to a firm name and the writer wishes a certain person or specific department to also be aware of the contents of the letter, an attention line should be used.

The attention line is typed two spaces below the last line of the inside address and flush with the left margin in any one of the styles presented below. Punctuation is not needed after the word ATTENTION unless the company prefers to use a colon.

ATTENTION Mr. John Little

Attention Mr. John Little

Attention Mr. John Little

Attention: Mr. John Little

SUBJECT LINE

When a subject line is used, it is typed a double space below the salutation. The subject line may be typed starting at the left margin, centered, or indented five spaces.

The subject line for these letter styles may be typed in all capital letters or in capital and small letters that are underscored.

SUBJECT: EMPLOYEE UPGRADING

Subject: Employee Upgrading

If the simplified letter style is used, the subject line should replace the salutation and be typed on the third line below the inside address against the left margin in all capital letters.

Re and In re. Some companies prefer to use the Latin expression, "Re" or "In re" rather than "Subject"; other companies may use both "Subject" and "In re," reserving the latter for use with numbers as for a policy, mortgage, etc. When both special lines are used, the Subject line is placed a double space below the salutation; and the "Re" or "In re" line is typed on the right-hand margin opposite the inside address.

ENCLOSURE NOTATION

Whenever an item is to be enclosed with a letter to be mailed, this should be indicated on the letter by typing an enclosure notation one or two lines below the reference initials. This tells the recipient that a check should be made to see that all items of enclosure have been received.

When more than one item is enclosed, any one of the following forms may be used:

```
Enclosures 2
Enclosures (2)
Enclosures--2
Enc. 2
```

Important enclosures are listed:

```
Enclosure--check

Enclosures:
   check
   contract

Enclosures:
   1.  check
   2.  contract
```

MAILING NOTATIONS

Any special mailing notation should be typed directly below the reference initials or below the enclosure notation if one is used.

```
jn
Enclosures
Certified

HRL:jn
Registered
cc:  Mr. H. R. Leonard
```

CARBON COPY NOTATIONS

When carbon copies of a letter are to be made and mailed to persons other than the addressee, a notation to this effect is typed two spaces below the identifying initials, flush with the left margin.

If there is an enclosure notation, the carbon copy notation is placed two lines (if space permits) below the enclosure notation and is also typed flush with the left margin.

The carbon copy notation (cc) may be typed in capital letters or in small letters. Any of the following styles is acceptable:

```
cc   Ms. Leonard
CC   H. R. Leonard
cc:  H. R. Leonard
CC:  H. R. Leonard
cc:  Mr. K. C. Fisher
CC:  Mrs. K. C. Fisher
```

Blind carbon copies. There are instances when it is necessary to send a carbon copy of a letter to one or more persons without the knowledge of the addressee. This is known as a blind carbon copy (bcc). To make this special notation, remove the original letter and any other copies on which the bcc should not appear. Then the typist will type the bcc notation on each of the remaining copies in the upper left corner. Make sure the firm's file copy shows all the bcc notations.

POSTSCRIPTS

Postscripts, as afterthoughts, are unnecessary in business-letter writing. The dictator who forgets to include a thought can simply dictate the missing paragraph and request the secretary to insert it at the appropriate place before transcribing the letter.

A postscript is often used in the business letter for the purpose of emphasis or sales effect and is typed a double space below the last notation in the letter.

The letters "ps" may be used in any one of the various forms shown or they may be omitted and the message typed two spaces below the last notation in the letter.

```
P.S.
P. S.
PS
PS:
```

CONFIDENTIAL

If the letter contains personal or confidential matter, the letter should be identified by typing *Personal* or *Confidential* two lines below the date line or halfway between the date line and the inside address. The special notation is placed flush with the left margin and may also be underlined.

MULTIPLE-PAGE LETTERS

When a letter consists of more than one page, the second page and successive pages are typed on plain paper of the same size and quality as the letterhead. Some organizations have simplified printed "continuation sheets" to be used for successive pages. A continuation sheet usually bears the name of the company and sometimes the company design, but not the full range of information given on the letterhead. Each successive page will require a heading.

The *Heading* will consist of the name of the addressee, page number of the letter, and the date; the heading will begin on line seven and may be typed in either of the following formats:

```
Mrs. J. R. Smith              2           August 1, 19--


Mrs. J. R. Smith
Page 2
August 1, 19--
```

The remainder of the message will begin on the third typing space below the heading and must consist of at least two typewritten lines. The last paragraph on the first page should also have at least two typewritten lines. *NEVER* carry over to a second page only the complimentary closing of a business letter.

The margins will conform to the same margins used on the first page.

ENVELOPES

There are several guidelines which should be observed when typing business envelopes because of the electronic equipment being installed in post offices today. Follow these rules in addressing the envelope:

1. The address should be typed exactly as it appears in the letter.
2. The address should be typed *single*-spaced, block style regardless of the number of lines.
3. The last line of the address should consist of the name of the city, the name of the state, and the ZIP Code. Leave two spaces between the state name and the ZIP Code.

    The name of the state may be spelled out in full or the two-letter state abbreviation may be used, but do not use a two-letter state abbreviation without a ZIP Code.

4. The address should begin on line 12 of a small envelope and line 14 of a large envelope. The address must be in correct position if mail is handled by a scanner; otherwise, it will be rejected.

5. Any special notation which you want to appear on the envelope (Confidential, Personal, Hold for Arrival, or Attention) is typed three spaces below the return address.

6. Special mailing procedures (Special Delivery, Registered, Certified) are typed in all capital letters three lines under the position for the stamp or the postal meter imprint, or on line 9.

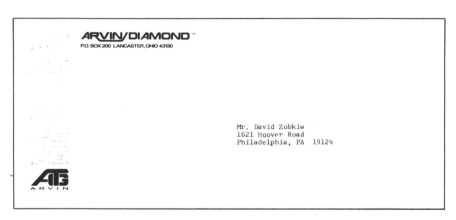

SPACING USED WITH PUNCTUATION MARKS

Period. Space twice after a period at the end of a sentence, after a term used as a subhead at the beginning of a line, or after a number as used in enumeration of items. Space once after the period following an abbreviation or following an initial.

Comma. Space once after a comma.

Question mark. Space twice after a question mark at the end of a sentence, once after a question mark within a sentence.

Exclamation point. Space twice after an exclamation point at the end of a sentence, once after an exclamation point within a sentence.

Semicolon. Space once after a semicolon.

Colon. Space twice after a colon. Exception: leave no space after the colon used in expressions of time (as 7:25).

Quotation marks. No space is left between the quotation marks and the material they enclose. When typing a list or quoting lines of poetry, leave the first quotation mark to the left of all the items or lines, so that the first words line up at the left. At the end of such material, the closing quotation marks come after the period (or closing word if no period is used) on the last line.

Double quotation marks. For a quotation within a quotation, single quotation marks are used. No space in typing is left between the single and double quotation marks.

Parentheses. If the material in parentheses falls within a sentence, leave one space before the opening parenthesis, two spaces when the material in parentheses follows a sentence, and no space after the opening parenthesis. The closing parenthesis requires no space before it, one space after it when the material in parentheses falls within a sentence, and two spaces when the material in parentheses constitutes a complete sentence and is followed by another sentence outside the parentheses.

Apostrophe. No space is left after an apostrophe within a word; one space is left after an apostrophe at the end of a word within a sentence.

Asterisk. The asterisk, used to refer a reader to a footnote, is typed immediately after a word or a punctuation mark with no space before it. In the footnote itself, one space is left after the asterisk.

Diagonal. No space precedes or follows the diagonal, sometimes called the slash mark or virgule.

Dash. No space is used before or after a dash made up of two hyphens (or the longer dash on a typewriter with this character on one of its keys). The dash should never be used at the beginning of a line.

For rules on the use of punctuation in writing, see Chapter 14, Part IV.

RULES FOR THE DIVISION OF WORDS

1. Avoid excessive word division.
2. Do not divide a word that contains only one syllable.
   Examples: brought, freight, friend
3. Divide only between syllables.
   Examples: ac knowl edg ment, har mo nize, tab u la tor
4. Do not divide a word unless it has at least six letters.
   Examples: ask ing, fil ter, man tel
5. Do not divide one or two letters from the remainder of a word.
   Examples: a gainst, a gend a
6. Do not divide a word immediately before a one-letter syllable.
   Examples: co ag u late, o bit u ar y, spec u late
   If the one-letter syllable is part of a common suffix, such as able or ible, carry the suffix over to the next line (reli-able, convert-ible, etc.)
7. If a consonant is doubled where syllables join, generally divide the word between the consonants.
   Examples: admis sion, confer ring, sug gestion
8. If a suffix has been added to a root word that ends in a doubled letter, ordinarily divide before the suffix.
   This rule could be considered an exception to the one preceding. A

word such as *telling* is made up of the root *tell* and the suffix *ing*. It would logically be divided after the second *l*. Here are several other words that would be governed by this rule:

Examples: cross ing, drill ing, fall ing, miss ing, ebb ing, stuff ing

9. Divide a hyphenated word only at the hyphen.

   Examples: self-explanatory, non-Communist

10. Do not end more than two consecutive lines with a hyphen. Also try to avoid dividing the first line of a paragraph.

11. Avoid the division of names.

    Proper nouns should be divided only when absolutely necessary. It is generally better to leave a line slightly short than to break a word such as Prendergast or Massachusetts. Divide proper noun groups so that they can be read with ease. The name Donald S. Crenshaw might be typed with Donald S. at the end of one line and Crenshaw at the start of the next.

12. DO NOT DIVIDE THE LAST WORD OF A PARAGRAPH OR THE LAST WORD ON A PAGE.

The following units cannot be divided:

June 12, 1979
8 percent
12 pounds
8:22 A.M.

See also Appendix 10, "33,000 Words Spelled and Syllabified."

Chapter 7

Business Letters Composed by the Secretary

EMOJEAN NOVOTNY

ONE ESSENTIAL SKILL that a secretary must possess is the ability to compose letters. It is not always easy to compose letters for someone else. Being asked to write letters for your employer indicates confidence in your ability. It gives you the opportunity to show your creativity. Accept the assignment as a challenge.

There are certain basic principles you must adhere to when you write a letter. It does not make any difference what type of letter you are composing. This chapter will present guidelines and discuss procedures for preparing several kinds of letters that a secretary may be asked to compose. Included are sample letters which will show how to use the principles and procedures for specific kinds of letters.

BASIC PRINCIPLES OF LETTER WRITING

THE FIRST AND MOST IMPORTANT PROCEDURE IS TO PLAN

1. Establish what kind of letter you are writing (purpose of letter). — FIRST PARAGRAPH
2. State items that need action. Answer questions. Give information. — MIDDLE PARAGRAPHS
3. Summarize briefly. End with a friendly greeting if this is appropriate. — CLOSING PARAGRAPH

ANSWERING A LETTER

1. Read the letter to be answered.
2. Jot down points of inquiry.

90

3. Place these items in priority.
4. Decide answers to questions.
5. Verify all data.

INITIATING A LETTER

1. Establish purpose of letter.
2. Collect necessary material.
3. Organize material.
4. Compose letter in style suitable for intended purpose.

Other guidelines in writing an effective business letter:
1. Reflect the employer's style of writing in presenting the message.
2. Write with clarity.
3. Write the message with conciseness.
4. Write the message in a personal tone.
5. Write with a positive approach.
6. Write with diplomacy.
7. Endeavor to create good will and interest.

Here are a few sample letters showing how the principles and guidelines which have been given are used in the development of a letter.

ACKNOWLEDGMENT LETTER

1. Answer immediately.
2. State what you are acknowledging.
3. Give information requested.
4. If appropriate, end with a "thank you" or expression of interest.

SAMPLE

```
     Your letter regarding the figures in our
current window display has been received. The dolls
that aroused your curiosity were made in Yugoslavia.
They are not antique, but were made and purchased
within the past year.

     Thank you for your kind words about this
display. Our decorators spent many hours planning
and setting up the scene and it is good to know
it is appreciated and enjoyed.

                    Sincerely yours,
```

ADJUSTMENT LETTER

1. Describe original action or purchase.
2. State complaint.
3. Request adjustment.

SAMPLE

On February 14 of this year, your company shipped a paper shredder to our office. It is the XX brand, Model 433. It was installed by your local agency, Richardson Electric Company.

Their service representative came at our request to try to adjust this piece of equipment twice in February and four times in March. It is inoperative most of the time, and at this time is again not working. It seems fairly clear by now that we have a defective machine. Richardson Electric Company says we must deal directly with you regarding this.

Please have a representative contact us for arrangements to replace this paper shredder with another.

Sincerely yours,

APPOINTMENT LETTER

1. Be specific as to time, place, and date of appointment.
2. Purpose of appointment.
3. Specify any special information, file, etc., necessary for the appointment.
4. Ask for confirmation.

SAMPLE

Mr. Thomas will be returning from his vacation next week and will be able to meet with you to discuss the audit report in the Board Room, Thursday, August 9, at 10 A.M.

Please bring File No. 306 with you to the meeting, as there are a few questions to be answered.

Please confirm this date by next Monday, August 6.

Sincerely yours,

APPRECIATION LETTER

1. State ceremony or occasion for which thanks is being expressed or enjoyment is being acknowledged.
2. State briefly subsidiary reasons, if any, for writing letter.
3. If appropriate, express wishes for future success.

SAMPLE

The speech that you gave at the In-house workshop last week was stimulating as well as informative. The people I spoke with after your presentation also responded favorably.

It has been ten years since we were in college, and it was good to see you again. It certainly brought back many memories for me.

I look forward to your presentation next weekend and know that it will be as successful as the last one.

Sincerely yours,

COVERING LETTER

1. Inform recipient of what is being sent, whether enclosed or sent separately.
2. Tell when item was (or will be) sent.
3. Tell by what class of mail or method of shipment.
4. Give further information (if appropriate).

SAMPLE

Your request to rent an 8 mm film, "Telephone Techniques," has been received. The film was sent this afternoon via Special Delivery.

We have other films on this subject and can furnish a list upon request.

Sincerely yours,

FOLLOW-UP OR REMINDER LETTER

1. Make reference to previous letter or request.
2. State what is needed and why.
3. Emphasize deadline.

SAMPLE

In the June Directors' Meeting, the chairmen were asked to submit their departmental budgets to the Vice-President within two weeks.

Three weeks have elapsed and your budget is needed so that we will be able to submit the overall budget report to the President. Our deadline is next week.

Office Services will be able to assist you in typing the report.

Sincerely yours,

NOTICE OF MEETING

1. Specify day, date, time, place, and purpose of meeting.
2. Specify if a special meeting.
3. Agenda of meeting.
4. Request for additional items to be placed on agenda.
5. Request reply.

SAMPLE

An Advisory Committee meeting will be held in the Board Room, Thursday, October 9, at twelve noon. This is a special meeting, called because of the upcoming change in price of our product.

An agenda for the meeting is enclosed. If you have any additional items to be placed on the agenda, please send them to Mr. Price by Monday, October 6.

Please notify me by Monday, October 6,
whether or not you will attend the meeting.

Sincerely yours,

Jean Jones
Secretary to Mr. Herbert Price

Enc.

LETTER OF REGRET OR REJECTION

1. State circumstances.
2. Give background information telling why decision was made.
3. End with expression of good will, showing appreciation or interest.

SAMPLE

Our President, Mrs. Beatrice R. Stokes, has
received your letter asking her to speak to the
Women's Club on "The Office of the Future,"
Saturday, August 4. Mrs. Stokes has asked me to
reply and I am glad to do so. However, I am sorry
to say that Mrs. Stokes will be on a business trip
at that time. Thus it will not be possible for her
to accept your kind invitation.

If your organization has a need for a speaker
at some other time, Mrs. Stokes hopes you will
remember her then.

Sincerely yours,

RESERVATION LETTER

1. State who wants the reservation and the number of people in the
   party.
2. State number of rooms, type of accommodations (one room, suite,
   two rooms, etc.).
3. Specify accommodations — twin beds, double bed, two double beds,
   single, tub, shower, etc.

4. Approximate rate.
5. Length of stay.
6. Arrival time and departure time. If arriving late, ask about guaranteed arrival and deposit requirements.
7. Mention business meetings/workshops party will be attending.
8. Request confirmation.

SAMPLE

        Please reserve a medium-priced living room
and bedroom suite (twin beds), with bath, for
Mr. and Mrs. Albert Clark, who will arrive late
Monday evening, April 6. They will leave Thursday
afternoon on April 9 on a 3 P.M. flight and will
require transportation to the airport.

        Please confirm that the room reservation
will be held for late arrival and advise me of
your deposit requirements.

        Mr. Clark, Vice-President of the ABZ
Corporation, will be attending the NSW workshop
which will be held in your hotel.

                            Sincerely yours,

DEFERRAL LETTER

1. Answer immediately.
2. State matter under discussion.
3. Explain why answer must be deferred.
4. Tell when answer may be expected.

SAMPLE

        Your letter to Ms. Jones asking her approval
of your new sales brochures has been received.
Ms. Jones is at present attending our annual
international conference in Denver. I am sure
she will give your letter her immediate attention
when she returns. You should hear from her within
the next three weeks.

                            Sincerely yours,

LETTER OF INQUIRY OR REQUEST

1. Give background to explain why letter is being written.
2. Ask question or make request.
3. Tell when information or material is needed.
4. Close with expression of appreciation or good will.

SAMPLE

> Our company is planning its annual sales meeting, to be held in Seattle. Over 200 salespersons will attend.
>
> We would appreciate having copies of your booklet "The Way to a Consumer's Heart" to pass out to those attending our conference.
>
> Could you please have them sent directly to the Seattle Hotel, addressed to me, by January 15? Your cooperation would be greatly appreciated.
>
> Sincerely,

ORDER LETTER

1. Tell where order is to be sent.
2. List items wanted, giving all pertinent numbers, description of the products, price, and any other necessary information such as color and size.
3. Tell how payment is to be made; that is, check may be enclosed, billing is to be sent to a specified address, the order is to be put on a regular account, etc.
4. Tell when order should be sent.

SAMPLE

Please send the following items to the above address:

Quantity	Catalog No.	Item	Unit Price	Total
200	N238	No. 2 Washington pencils (blue)	.15	$ 30.00
25	N357	plastic rulers	.84	21.60
				$ 51.60
		State sales tax		2.84
				$ 54.44

We understand that the state sales tax is applicable because we
are located in the same state as your company. Our check for
$54.44 is enclosed. We would appreciate having these items sent
at once.

                              Yours truly,

After you have planned and written the letter, ask yourself these questions:
1. Is my message clear?
2. Will the recipient interpret my message as I intended?
3. Have I presented facts clearly and correctly?
4. Have I kept the message concise?
5. Have I been diplomatic?
6. Have I used personal, positive, and natural tones throughout?
7. Have I created good will regardless of the situation?

INTEROFFICE MEMORANDA

The written communications passing between offices, departments, or
branches of an organization are usually transmitted in a form known as an
"interoffice memorandum." This form has the advantage of dispensing with
the salutation, the complimentary closing, and the signature of the dictator.

The four headings most frequently found on all interoffice memoranda are
To, *From*, *Subject*, and *Date*. Other headings, such as *File* or *Reference No.*,
may be added as needed. In firms where such memoranda are typed with
frequency and in large quantities, these headings, together with the firm name
and, perhaps, address, are printed. In typing interoffice memoranda, use
margins for a 6-inch line unless the headings are printed, in which case use
margins corresponding to these headings. Signed initials are frequently placed
on the memo to show that it has been read and approved. Sometimes the
initials of the dictator and the typist appear on the memorandum, just as in a
letter. Enclosures and attachments should be indicated.

Some organizations have memorandum forms prepared in carbon packs.
If these are not available the office copier may be put to use for multiple
copies. Several names may be typed after *To* or they may be listed at the
bottom of the memorandum. In this way, the recipients will know which
persons will be receiving the same message.

The secretary who writes an interoffice memorandum need not search for
an attention-getting opening sentence. This kind of communication has no
danger of being tossed in the wastebasket before it is read. However,
interoffice correspondence should include most of the essential characteristics

of a good letter. The tone should be considerate, courteous, and friendly. The message should be clear, concise, and complete.

Memoranda may be sent to confirm conversations, to report actions taken at meetings, and to apprise the entire staff of a directive from one of the administrators of the organization. Examples follow.

CLEVELAND PUBLIC LIBRARY
An Equal Opportunity Employer

A Second Century Of
BOOKS-INFORMATION-SERVICE

MEMORANDUM

August 15, 19--

TO: James Anderson
           Associate Editor

FROM: Elizabeth Stoneman *ɛs*
           Office Manager

SUBJECT: Memorandum Format

The purpose of the interoffice memorandum is to circulate correspondence within the institution rather than to outside organizations.

There are many different styles for typing interoffice memoranda, but this is the format that may be followed.

The typist may leave a minimum of three spaces and no more than six spaces before typing the body of the message. The same spacing format is also used when typing the reference initials.

Five spaces were used in this particular memorandum; therefore, five spaces have been left before typing the reference initials.

Signed initials are placed opposite the originator's name to show that it has been read and approved.

epm

Ervin J. Gaines, Director
325 SUPERIOR AVENUE CLEVELAND, OHIO 44114 216 623-2800

TO: J. Black, Comptroller   SUBJECT: Computer System

FROM: M. Sroka, Secretary to   DATE: October 29, 19--
      I. Cook, President

Ms. Cook has asked me to remind you that at the next
meeting of the Board of Directors to be held on November 5,
she would like you to present your ideas, which you and
Ms. Cook have been discussing, on the installation of the
new computer system. She would like you to emphasize the
timesaving, as well as the money-saving, aspects of this
system.

Please send to me as soon as possible any of your presentation
materials that will require duplicating, so that I can have
them ready for you in time for the meeting.

To: All Editorial Personnel   Date: May 14, 19--

From: N. Steigerwald, Secretary

Subject: Promotions

Please complete the information requested on the attached
questionnaire in good form for consideration in the fall.
You are to submit this information to J. Morgan, head of
the Departmental Committee, no later than October 1.

In completing the questionnaire, Mr. Morgan's directive
states that you should enter information concerning only
those accomplishments achieved since your last promotion.
Publications are of primary importance.

Attachment

Chapter 8

Special Typing Projects
ERMALEA BONING, STAR DEMETRION

REPORTS

The business report may include, along with the main body, all or some of the following: a title page, letter of transmittal, table of contents, list of tables, bibliography, appendix, and index. The secretary needs to know how to handle each of these elements and how to put them together. Secretaries wield an important influence in getting a report accepted. A report is much more likely to be looked upon with favor when it is well arranged and easy to read.

PAPER

In typing reports use a good quality of paper, usually 8 1/2″ × 11″, and use a black ribbon. Use white paper with rag content. The higher the rag content of paper, the longer its life. A watermark is imprinted on rag-content paper. It tells the brand of paper and the percentage of cotton fiber in it. The right side of the paper shows a readable watermark. Use either a 16- or a 20-pound paper.

Find out the number of carbon copies required. Carbon copies that are to be widely circulated should be on heavier paper, for readability is a factor in obtaining acceptance of a report.

Paper used for duplicates has a right and a wrong side. If you are duplicating the report, make certain that you place it on the right side of the paper for best results.

TYPE STYLE

Pica type is preferred for reports because its larger size makes it easier to read than elite type. As for design, the conventional roman type is still the most widely acceptable. It is the standard style on the modern typewriter. A variation such as the square-serif roman may be available. Then again, a sturdy, modern sans-serif design is clean, easy to read, and makes single-spaced or tightly packed data appear less crowded. Neither script nor italic type is suitable for reports.

FORMAT

You should be aware that the format, or arrangement and layout of material, in a report can vary—indentions, footnoting or citations, page numbering, spacing, etc. You may be required to follow the procedures for a certain format or have a preference for a certain style, but the format that you use should be consistent throughout the report.

TITLE PAGE

The title page will usually contain the name or title of the report, the name and title of the person or organization for whom it was written, the name and title of the person or group who wrote it, and the date it was submitted. The contents of a title page may include more information if necessary.

Type the main title in all capital letters approximately two inches from the top of the page. Type the date two inches from the bottom of the page. Space the other information equally between the top and bottom margins, typed in lower-case letters with the first letter of each main word capitalized. Center each line horizontally.

There are various formats for title pages. For an acceptable style, see the illustration on page 105.

LETTER OF TRANSMITTAL

A letter of transmittal is used to introduce the reader to the report. The content of the letter should tell the reader what the topic of the report is, why it was written, how it was compiled, who worked on it, and what major findings or conclusions resulted from the research.

The letter of transmittal appears directly after the title page, and it may be typed in any acceptable business letter format.

TABLE OF CONTENTS

The table of contents is one of the last things you prepare. It should be typed after all pages of the report are completed and numbered. The table of contents lists in order the numbers and titles of the sections or chapters in the report and the pages on which they begin. It should not be confused with the index, which is arranged alphabetically and includes more items.

Type the heading, TABLE OF CONTENTS, in all capital letters centered two inches from the top edge of the paper. Type "Page" a triple space below the heading, pivoted from the right margin. (See Chapter 5, page 61.)

Begin typing the contents a double space below "Page" at the left margin. Use the same margins that you use in typing the body of the report.

Use all capital letters in typing those entries of the contents page which refer to the major sections of the report. Those sections of lesser importance should be indented, typed in capital and lower-case letters, and placed in the same sequence as they appear in the report. Leaders should be used to guide the reader's eye across the page from a content's entry to the page number.

See page 106 for a sample of a TABLE OF CONTENTS.

LIST OF TABLES

When a report contains several tables, a list of tables should be included after the table of contents. It is typed in a format similar to the table of contents.

BODY OF THE REPORT

Use a report or manuscript typing guide for setting up reports. These may be purchased or you may design your own. See illustration on page 107.

Margins. Margins for reports and manuscripts are a minimum of one inch; however, many authors prefer one and one-fourth inches. When the report is to be bound on the left side, allow for the binding by making the left margin one and one-half inches wide. This makes the center point of the writing line three spaces to the right of the present center; if you are centering lines at 51, you will now center them at 54. You can accomplish the same result by merely moving the paper one-fourth inch to the left of the spot where you normally keep it.

The top margin on the first page should be at least two inches; on the other pages, it should be one inch. If the report is to be bound at the top, allow an additional half inch for this. Keep the bottom margins at least one inch deep; in some cases you may want to make them as much as one and one-half inches deep.

Spacing. Usually reports are double-spaced, and the first line of each paragraph is indented five spaces. The number of spaces paragraphs are indented may be eight or ten spaces, but paragraph indentions are always used.

When quotations are of three lines or more, indent the quoted material five spaces from the left and right margins or indent it the same number of spaces from these margins as you indent the paragraphs. Indent the first line of the quotation to show a paragraph indention. Copy the indented quotation in single spacing and omit the quotation marks. The indention tells the reader that the material is quoted.

If listings are included in your report, single-space them. Center the items on the page. If the length of items varies, select the longest one to be centered and line up the others with it. If your listings contain widely separated columns, use leaders to assist the eye in reading the material. Make these leaders by alternating periods with spaces. Note whether the periods fall on the odd or even spaces in the first line, and then match the location of the periods accordingly in succeeding lines.

Allow at least two lines of a paragraph to appear at the bottom and top of each page, adjusting the bottom margin, if necessary, to accommodate the ending and beginning lines. Avoid single lines that carry over to end a paragraph at the top of a new page. Avoid dividing the last word on a page.

PAGE NUMBERS

Number pages of the report with Arabic numbers. Number the pages in the preliminary section with small Roman numerals.

When the report is unbound or bound at the left, the page number of the first page (if numbered) is centered one-half inch (3 lines) from the bottom of the page. Other pages of the report are numbered in the upper right corner on line four, with the number ending flush with the right margin. Begin the first line of typing on line seven; this will leave a one-inch top margin for the body of the report.

Usually, if a manuscript is bound at the top, it is numbered at the bottom, centered on the third line from the bottom of the page.

In the preliminary section, count the title page as "i"; do not type the number. Number the remaining preliminary pages with small Roman numerals centered on the third line from the bottom of the page.

HEADINGS

The main heading is centered in all capital letters at the beginning of the report. No other heading should be typed in all capital letters. If the report has a subheading (secondary heading that explains or amplifies the main heading), separate it from the main heading with a double space, then triple space before beginning the body of the report. The subheading should be centered and the main word or words capitalized.

First-order subheadings (side headings) are preceded by a triple space and followed by a double space. Side headings should be typed at the left margin,

INTRODUCING WORD PROCESSING INTO THE SECRETARIAL CURRICULUM

AT SAN BERNARDINO VALLEY COLLEGE

Change Episode

for

The University of the Pacific Doctoral Program in School Management

By

Star Demetrion

May 16, 1979

Sample of the Title Page of a Report

TABLE OF CONTENTS

Sample of the Table of Contents of a Report

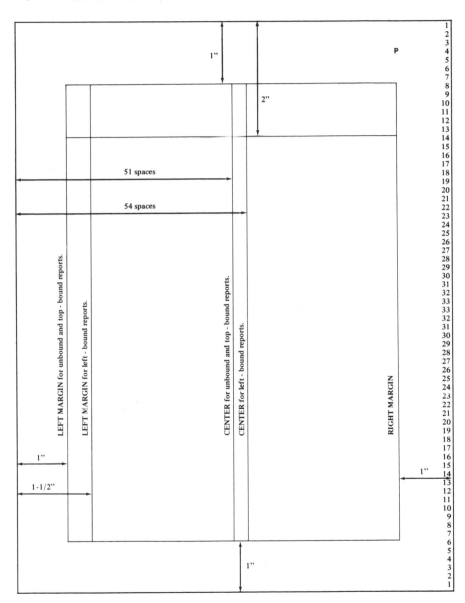

Sample of a Report Typing Guide

The report typing guide can be used for a report that is to be top-bound, left-bound, or unbound. All pages of the report must follow the same guide.

underlined, main words capitalized, and have no terminal period (or other terminal punctuation).

Second-order subheadings (paragraph headings) are preceded by a double space. They are indented to the paragraph point (usually only the first word is capitalized), underlined, and followed by a period. Begin typing the paragraph on the same line as the heading.

FOOTNOTES

Footnotes have a number of purposes: They may confirm or add meaning to the author's statements; they may refer to other parts of the report that have a bearing on the topic discussed; they may make acknowledgments; or they sometimes make additional explanations of the content or terms used.

Footnotes are identified in the text by raised figures called superscripts. The superscript is typed one-half space above the line of writing immediately after the word or statement to which the footnote applies. To type this superscript, engage the automatic line spacer and roll the paper down about one-half of the line. Type the figure and put the line spacer lever back in typing position. Touch the platen knob gently, and the paper will resume its former position. It is more convenient to use the automatic line-spacer lever (sometimes called "line finder" or "ratchet release lever") than to use the variable spacer on the platen knob, because the former will automatically bring the platen back to its original line of writing.

Footnotes may be numbered in one of two ways: consecutively throughout the article or chapter; or consecutively on each page, beginning with the number 1 for each new page. Be uniform in numbering the references. In rough-draft work and thesis work, it simplifies the typing if footnotes are numbered consecutively on each page. Then if there is an omission or correction, it can be accommodated without changing subsequent footnotes.

When you use footnotes, type the reference figure in the text following the passage to which the footnote refers. Type the footnote on the same page on which the reference figure following the passage appears. Type footnotes to end one inch from the bottom edge of the page. Use the page-end indicator on your typewriter or a guide sheet to determine where to begin the footnote in order to have this one-inch margin. Usually you are safe if you allow three or four lines for each footnote.

After you type the last line of the text before the footnote, single-space and type a horizontal underscore line one and one-half to two inches long, starting at the left margin and extending the line toward the center. Type the footnote a double space below this line. Precede the footnote with the corresponding reference number raised about one-half space above the line. Start the footnote at the paragraph indention. The second line of the footnote should begin at the left margin. Footnote entries should be single-spaced with a double space between each footnote.

For a footnote that refers to published material, give the same information that is given in a bibliographical reference plus the page number of the cited material.

Example of a footnote: book with two authors.

---

²Harold T. Smith and William H. Baker, The Administrative Manager (Chicago: Science Research Associates, 1978), p. 482.

Example of a footnote: magazine article.

---

⁴Willoughby Ann Walshe, "New Copiers Mean More Flexibility for WP/AS," Word Processing World, (July, 1979), pp. 18-24.

To avoid retyping the details of the identical footnote, use one of these three abbreviations for Latin phrases, whichever is appropriate—*Ibid.*, meaning "in the same place"; *loc. cit.*, meaning "in the place cited"; or *op. cit.*, meaning "in the work cited."

Use *Ibid.* when referring to the work cited in the immediately preceding footnote, without an intervening footnote. This abbreviation may be used several times in succession.

Example:

---

⁵Ibid. (Use when the reference is identical to the one in the preceding footnote.)
⁶Ibid., p. 35. (Use when the reference is identical to the one in the preceding footnote but on a different page.)

Use *loc. cit.* with nonconsecutive footnotes that refer to the same material, the same work, and the same page or pages. Use *op. cit.* with nonconsecutive footnotes that refer to the same work but different pages. Repeat the author's last name when using *loc. cit.* or *op. cit.*

Example:

---

⁸Walshe, loc. cit.
⁹Baker, op. cit., p. 77.

4

the College, considering the above circumstances, was most understandable.
It was and is a risky undertaking at this period of time when college
enrollment is declining.

Population Under Investigation

The population under investigation for this study is the administration
of the College, the Business and Economics Division, the Secretarial Administration Department, the students enrolled in the secretarial program, the
surrounding business community, and the certificated and classified staff of
San Bernardino Valley College.

Definition of Terms

Mag Card II Typewriter. Paula Cecil states in her word processing
textbook:

> In April 1973 IBM introduced the use of "memory" in word
> processing typewriters with its new Mag Card II. Previously,
> recording of typing had been made directly onto the magnetic
> tape. But on the Mag Card II the recording is made "in memory"
> from which it can be played back. If the operator wants to
> store the recording on a card, a button is depressed which
> records all information that was typed into memory.[4]

Memory Typewriter. In the same textbook Ms. Cecil describes the Memory
typewriter:

> In March 1974, another member of the IBM family was intro-
> duced: the Memory Typewriter. This unit has all the features
> of the Mag Card II except the use of cards, thereby eliminating
> long storage and merging applications. The Memory Typewriter
> has a 50-page memory storage and a 4000-character-per-page
> capacity for revising, which means a total memory capacity of
> 200,000 characters. This unit is sold mainly to small offices
> for production of regular correspondence, some stored letters
> or paragraphs, and short-turnaround revisions.[5]

---

[4]Paula B. Cecil, Word Processing in the Modern Office (Menlo Park,
California: Cummings Publishing Co., 1976), pp. 85-86.

[5]Ibid., p. 87.

Sample of a Page from the Body of a Report

BIBLIOGRAPHY

A bibliography includes the references used in the preparation of the report. Arrange it alphabetically by names of authors. When listing books, copy the information from the title page, rather than from the outside cover. When listing references from periodicals, take the title from the article itself.

Each reference lists the surname of the author, followed by given name or initials; the title of the work; the publisher; the place of publication; and the date of publication. When using references from periodicals, one may include such identifying information as volume and page numbers. Observe these rules:

Underscore the titles of books and magazines.

Enclose the titles of magazine articles in quotation marks.

Type the author's initials after the surname. If some references use a full name and others only initials, be consistent, particularly when the references come close together. Usually it is better to use the full name.

If the author has written some books alone and collaborated with other authors on some materials, list those books the author wrote alone first.

If the publication has more than three authors, list the publication under the name of the first mentioned author and then use the words "and others."

If the publication is out of print, indicate this in parentheses following the reference.

BIBLIOGRAPHY

Books

Cecil, Paula B., Word Processing in the Modern Office, Menlo Park, California: Cummings Publishing Co., 1976. 321 pp.

McCabe, Helen M., and Popham, Estelle L., Word Processing: A Systems Approach to the Office, New York: Harcourt Brace Jovanovich, 1977. 225 pp.

Waterhouse, Shirley A., Word Processing Fundamentals, San Francisco: Canfield Press, 1979. 252 pp.

Journals

Burdine, Gail, "Leading the Way in Education," Word Processing, (May/June, 1975).

Christensen, G. Jay, "Has Word Processing Been Oversold?" The Office, (September, 1977).

Collins, L. M., "Word Processing Business Education," Business Education Forum, (May, 1973).

Unpublished Reports

Demetrion, Star, "Word Processing Needs Assessment" (Change Episode, University of LaVerne, 1977), "Typewritten."

Volume numbers of periodicals are written with Arabic numerals.

To make the author's name stand out, type the first line of the entry at the left margin and indent all other lines.

If there are many sources of reference material, classify them according to books, periodicals, pamphlets, or other documents.

When two or more books by the same author are listed in succession, instead of retyping the author's name each time, simply use a solid line of five underscores followed by a comma.

Example:

Hegarty, Edward J., How to Run Better Meetings, New York: McGraw-Hill Book Company, 1957.

_____, How to Write a Speech, New York: McGraw-Hill Book Company, 1951.

See page 111 for sample of a bibliography.

APPENDIX

Material supportive to the report should be placed in a supplementary section called an appendix. It should follow the bibliography. Examples of items placed in the appendix are copies of questionnaires, maps, lists, tables, sample forms and letters, and detailed summaries of data.

The appendix may be preceded by an introductory page entitled APPENDIX, typed in all capital letters and centered both horizontally and vertically. This page may also include a list of the items included in the appendix. If this is used, both the title and the listing are centered vertically, or the title may be typed two inches from the top of the paper with the listing beginning a triple space below the title. When more than one item is appended, each item should be numbered or lettered and placed under a separate heading, such as Appendix A, Appendix B, etc.

INDEX

In long reports it may be necessary to prepare an index as well as a table of contents. Be extremely careful to see that the index is typed in alphabetical order. Put the entries first on $3'' \times 5''$ cards and then arrange them alphabetically. Then type the index from the cards.

NEWS RELEASES

News releases are typed double-spaced on $8\ 1/2'' \times 11''$ plain paper or on a special news-release form. Side margins should be generous, at least one and one-half inches or wider. Thus the editor has room for notations. Try to keep the release to one page.

The editor likes to see identifying information at the top of the sheet, including the date and the name, address, and telephone number of the person to whom requests may be made for more information.

The article itself starts with an indented date line consisting of the name of the city and the date. The city name is typed in all capital letters; the date is typed in capital and lower-case letters and is followed by a dash. The name of the state is given only if the city is not well known or if there is likely to be a doubt as to the proper identity of the city.

If the news release runs to more than one page, end each page with a complete paragraph and put the word MORE at the bottom, centered or at the right side of the page. Continuation pages are numbered and have a brief caption typed flush with the left margin near the top of the page. Copy is often divided so that it can be given to different typesetters. MORE tells the typesetters that there are more pages. End the news release with a concluding centered symbol such as ####, -0-, -end-, or (END).

The following is a sample of a news release heading.

```
N E W S   R E L E A S E        From Sandra Demous
                               Free Press
                               500 South Broadway
                               Los Angeles, California 90055
                               Telephone (213) 666-5555

                               Release July 30, 19--


                 CENTERED TITLE OF A NEWS RELEASE

        LOS ANGELES, July 30--Continue typing the news

release with double spacing in report form.
```

COPY FOR THE PRINTER

TYPING

When the copy is to be printed, keep the typewritten lines six inches long and use double spacing. Avoid dividing words at the ends of lines as much as possible. Type headings in the position they will occupy on the printed page and be consistent in style. Type on one side of the paper; make side margins at least one inch wide. Keep the pages equal in length. Do not staple pages together.

Proofread the material. It is a good idea to lay the material aside before giving it a final check. The second reading may reveal errors overlooked the first time. Two heads are better than one for proofreading. When working with an assistant, the typist should follow the original and the assistant the final copy. The secretary is really a stand-in reader. It is the secretary's job to find those errors so elementary that they escape the author's attention.

CORRECTING COPY

Use proofreading marks in making corrections. (See Appendix 7.) Short corrections can be made by crossing out the incorrect word and writing the correction over it. If the correction is lengthy, type it on a separate sheet of paper which should then be attached to the original. If a whole paragraph needs correction, you may find it convenient to type the correction on a separate sheet and staple or tape it over the original.

The best time to number the pages of the manuscript is after the whole job has been typed and all corrections have been made. Pages are numbered consecutively, and the page number usually appears in the upper right-hand corner of each page, indented one inch from the right edge, on line four from the top of the page.

ARTWORK

Identify all artwork either by number or by some other system of labeling, and keep a list. If you use numbers, make certain that the numbering agrees with the order in which the items will appear in the finished job. Avoid writing on photographs with either pen or pencil, because the marks may break the finish on the photograph and show in the reproduction. Type the identification line on a separate label and attach it to the back of the illustration.

LAYOUT

Your printer will advise you on the layout and will make up a dummy for you if it is part of your agreement. A dummy is a set of blank sheets, cut and folded to the size and shape of the finished job. In preparing the dummy, indicate the location of any artwork.

ESTIMATING LENGTH

Often it is necessary to tell the printer the approximate length of the material. Select three or four lines of the copy and count the number of words in these lines. From this count determine the average number of words per line. Now count the number of lines on the page and multiply this by the number of words in each line. Suppose in four lines you count 44 words. This means that you have an average of 11 words to each line. If there are 27 lines on your page, 27 times 11 gives you 297 words, or nearly 300 words to the page. A report, then, of ten full pages would be about 3,000 words.

GALLEY PROOFS

The printer will return the original manuscript to you with two or more copies, or proofs, set up in the type you selected. Compare the printer's copy, word for word, with the original. Again, it is always better if two people work together. Careful checking saves time and money, because the printer charges an extra fee for changes.

Reading these proofs, the galley proofs, is the next major step. This reading gives you the opportunity to not only detect and call attention to errors made by the printer but to make any last-minute alterations you may find desirable. However, if your revisions deviate much from the original, you pay a heavy penalty in time rates. Changes in the galley proof become very costly. Read material through for continuity in thought. Some of the things to watch for in checking are:

Spelling and punctuation errors
Inconsistencies in style, spelling, or paragraphing
Transposition of letters and lines
Errors in page numbers
Continuity from page to page (Does the last word on a page make sense with the top of the next page?)

If your employer frequently publishes manuscripts, keep a record of each manuscript on a $3'' \times 5''$ card. You will want to record such facts as the title, the date it was submitted to the printer, and how many pages it contained.

TECHNICAL SUBJECTS

The typing done for engineers, chemists, mathematicians, and other professionals is often referred to as "technical typing." The material often involves equation typing. In such work accuracy is extremely important, much more important than speed. Because you are typing symbols in patterns, spacing both horizontally and vertically becomes a consideration that may require some experimentation and technical knowledge.

Equations generally include raised and lowered symbols. Those symbols written above the regular line of writing are called superscripts; those written below, subscripts. It is essential, therefore, that technical reports be typed in double spacing to allow room for writing these subscripts and superscripts.

Typewriters can also have special keys with mathematical symbols and Greek letters. If you are operating a typewriter that utilizes an element, you may purchase a special element called the "universal symbol element." This element has the mathematical symbols and the letters of the Greek alphabet used frequently in equation typing.

For the larger symbols you will want a template. This is a small, plastic, rectangular guide that resembles the letter guides for stencil work, except that it provides outlines of symbols used in scientific reports. You trace the stencil symbol with a sharp-pointed pencil.

Always leave a space before and after the arithmetical operator symbol: $=$, $+$, $-$, $\div$, and $\times$. However, if the symbol is used adjectivally, as -3, there would be no space between the minus sign and the 3.

Multiplication is expressed by using the "$\times$" or a centered period ($4 \cdot 6$) or by parentheses enclosing an expression to be multiplied. Often the multiplication sign is omitted and the letters are typed together, as ab. Thus, in the equation $7ad(s - y) = mx$, there is no space between d and the opening parenthesis, but there is a space before and after the equal sign and the minus sign.

Type fractions as follows: If the equation is short, the fraction may be part of the running text and is typed in the shilling style, which looks like this: $4/5$. If you use mixed numbers, put a space between the whole number and the shilling fraction; for example, 43 $5/6$.

Equations are numbered consecutively throughout a report to make it easy to refer to any equation in the text. Each equation number is put in parentheses at the right margin. Set a tab stop for this location. Arrange the tab setting so that the closing parenthesis will be just inside of the right margin of your page. When making reference to these equation numbers, abbreviate equation to "Eq." Your reference will look like this: (Eq. 5).

Usually punctuation is not used with equations. If your author requests punctuation in equations, then observe these rules:

> Consider each equation as a clause of a complex sentence and follow it with either a comma or semicolon.
> If the equation concludes the sentence, a period follows it.
> If you have a series of equations, introduce them by a colon in the line preceding the equations.

Sometimes equations are too long for one line and must be placed on several lines. Break them before the equal sign when possible. Before any one of the operational signs ($+$, $-$, $\times$, $\div$) is another good place to divide an equation. You may also divide it between fractions or after brackets and parentheses. Do not put part of an equation on one page and the rest of it on the next page.

Some authors help their typists to read the symbols in an equation by writing all lower-case symbols and printing upper-case symbols. Why not suggest this to the author of the report? You will also find it helpful to draft all the equations in the report before typing. Let the author check your arrangement of the equations. If the author has no objection, then you are ready to do the finished report and can proceed with confidence that the material is arranged in the very best form.

LEGAL DOCUMENTS

Even though you may not be employed in a legal office, at times you may find it necessary to type a legal document or, at least, to fill in a printed legal form. Accuracy is essential, because a changed word or a correction may affect the validity of the paper. If you have any doubt about making a correction, consult your supervisor. When changes must be made in a document after it has been signed, all changes must be initialed by the signers. In some instances, erasures or corrections are not acceptable; the document with a correction would not be legally binding. For the above reasons, an electronic or correcting typewriter would be very useful.

Most legal documents are typed on "legal cap" paper. This paper is stronger than regular stationery and is usually slightly larger, measuring 8 1/2" × 13" or 8 1/2" × 14". It has a double-ruled line 1 1/4 inches from the left edge of the paper and a single-ruled line one-half inch from the right edge. Not all legal documents are put on these ruled sheets. Many wills, for example, are written on plain sheets of paper.

To avoid crowding the information in the document, type it double-spaced and use generous side margins (at least two spaces within the rulings). If your paper has no rulings, use a 1 1/2-inch left margin and a one-half-inch right margin. Start the first line of each page two inches from the top edge and end each page within an inch of the bottom. Indent all paragraphs ten spaces, and use only one side of the paper. Never end a page with the first line of a paragraph or begin a page with the last line of a paragraph. At least two lines of the document must appear on the page that is to have the signature.

Spell out sums of money and repeat them in figures enclosed within parentheses. Dates may either be spelled out or written in figures but not both ways.

The first page is usually not numbered, except on a will. Numbers of subsequent pages are centered between the margins, three blank lines from the bottom of the page. Type a hyphen before and another after the page number.

Use the underscore for signature lines. The signature lines for the principal signers start at the center of the page and extend toward the right margin. The signature lines for witnesses begin at the left margin and extend toward the center. Lines should be at least three spaces apart. Lightly pencil the respective initials at the beginnings of the signature lines to guide the signers. If you prefer, use the small "x" to mark the spot where the parties are to sign.

Type the introductory and closing phrases in all capitals. Put either a comma or a colon after the phrases, depending on how the phrase is used. Some of these phrases are:

> KNOW ALL MEN BY THESE PRESENTS, that . . .
> IN WITNESS WHEREOF, the parties . . .
> THIS AGREEMENT, made June . . .
> WHEREIN IT IS MUTUALLY AGREED AS FOLLOWS: 1. At that . . .

File copies can be made on onionskin paper. If carbon copies are to be signed, type the copies on the same quality of paper that you use for the original.

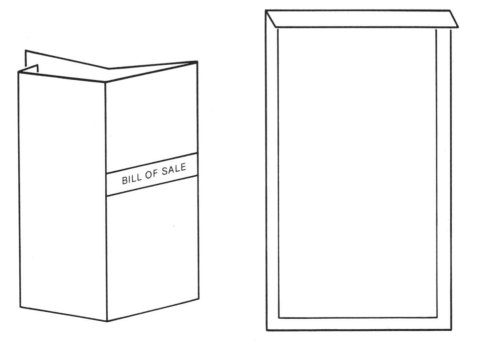

BILL OF SALE

Legal Binder
folded and endorsed (*left*), and flat with document in place

Most legal documents have cover sheets or binders, called "legal backs." These are endorsed with a brief description of the document. To prepare the binder, lay it on the desk and bring the bottom edge up to within one inch of the top; crease. Bring the creased end up to approximately one inch from the top and fold again. Open this fold and insert the binder in the typewriter. Do not type beyond the crease. After typing the endorsement, turn the top edge of the backing sheet down, crease it, and insert the document in the crease. Staple it in place. Fold the document to fit the creases in the binder.

TYPING NUMBERS

Typing numbers involves the observance of certain rules established by manuals of style. The following list will enable you to apply these rules quickly. The hyphen may be used to represent the word "to," as 1864-1872.

Use figures for	*Use words for*
Exact numbers above ten	Exact numbers, ten and below
35 club members	mail five boxes
Amounts of money	Round or approximate numbers
$29.95; $46; 9 cents	four hundred people
Percentages	Beginning of sentences
6 percent	Fourteen years
Dimensions, measurements, etc.	Names of centuries and decades
15 feet; size 9;	the sixteenth century
4 1/2 acres	the roaring twenties
Exact age	Approximate age
11 years, 4 months, 2 days	seventeen years old
Time with A.M. or P.M.	Time with "o'clock"
4 P.M.	four o'clock
Street names above ten	Street names ten and below
14 West 24 Street	Fifth Avenue
Word "number" followed by figure	Numbered sessions of Congress
No. 4	Seventy-eighth Congress
House or building numbers	Fractions standing alone
47 Genesee Street	send one-half of the order
Dates	Two numbers coming together
July 4, 1976	six 4-inch bolts
5th of May	210 six-pound crates
Plurals of numbers	Mixed numbers
16's	six and three-fourths
Large even amounts	Smaller amounts in round numbers
15 million dollars	fourteen hundred copies

Chapter 9

Filing and Finding
CHARLOTTE B. HOLMQUEST

THE SECRETARY MUST HAVE A WORKING KNOWLEDGE of the company's filing systems as they are used day by day. In a large company, the secretary's work in this line is augmented by that of the file clerk, who must have an extensive knowledge of all the filing systems.

The filing and finding of papers, documents, and letters is one of the most important activities in the office. Filing may be defined as the process of classifying and storing office papers. It is axiomatic that this classification and storage must be done efficiently so that any needed paper can be found quickly when needed. The files represent the past history and current activities of a company, and they may determine its future policies and decisions. The importance of correct and efficient filing cannot be overemphasized.

A large organization may have a sizable central file and a number of file clerks. A one- or two-person office may have only a small file. In either case, the files may be classified by two or more systems. Whatever size and complexity the filing system may be, the secretary should be thoroughly familiar with it.

FILING SYSTEMS

The basic filing systems in use in the modern office are: alphabetic, combination subject, numeric, and phonetic. Alphabetic filing encompasses filing papers by name, subject, or geographic location in alphabetic order. Combination subject systems utilize both numbers and words or numbers and letters arranged in alphabetic order. Such names as alpha-numeric, subject-numeric, and duplex-numeric appear in this category. Non-alphabetic filing exercises the use of numbers for filing purposes; and such terms as numeric, decimal, terminal digit, triple digit, and middle digit are in this category. The phonetic filing system involves using letters and sounds in code number form.

ALPHABETIC

Almost 90 percent of all the filing that is done in the office is alphabetic. The secretary usually files office correspondence and papers according to *name* or *subject*, in alphabetic order. Because a name file is arranged alphabetically, no cross-index file is necessary. It is very simple to expand a name file because the new name or subject is filed alphabetically without disturbing the name before or after it. The alphabetic system of filing is known as a "direct" method of filing. The direct method of filing means that a person can locate a file without first having to refer to a cross-index file.

GEOGRAPHIC

In the geographic system the papers are filed alphabetically according to the name of the state; then alphabetically according to the town or city within that state; then alphabetically according to the name of the correspondent within the town or city. Mail-order houses, public-utility companies, publishing houses, and organizations that serve a geographic district or have branch offices in different areas use this system of filing. It is helpful to have a cross index by names to show the location of a given firm. These name cards are filed alphabetically. The geographic system of filing is an indirect method.

SUBJECT

When a company deals with products, supplies, materials, advertising, and so forth, the subject system is used. It is an indirect system because a cross-index file is used to save time in filing and finding material and in locating correspondence by firm name when the subject is doubtful. The folders in the subject file are arranged alphabetically by the name of the product. The material within the folders is arranged by date, with the latest date in the front of the folder.

Often a combination of subject file and name file is used. If there is not enough material to set up a separate subject file, the subject captions are set up in a name file.

COMBINATION SUBJECT

Some companies which use the subject filing system have found it necessary to use major subject titles with separate sub-categories relating to that major topic so that locating specific information is quicker. A major subject outline containing the most important titles is set up in alphabetic order. Next, sub-category subject titles within each area are placed beneath the major subject titles. Then, numbers are used in combination with the subjects in the outline to make up the *combination subject filing system.*

Some of the combination subject filing systems used are:

Subject-Numeric. This system uses the major subject title with numbers assigned to the sub-categories underneath it. For example, the subject heading "Automobile Accessories" would be treated in this manner:

> AUTOMOBILE ACCESSORIES
> 1 Automobile Accessories: Tires
> 1-1 Standard Black
> 1-2 Whitewall

Duplex-Numeric. This system makes use of both numbers and letters of the alphabet. A digit is selected for the subject; this is followed by a dash and another digit for a division of the subject, plus a letter for further subdivision. For example, the subject heading "Automobile Accessories" might be given the number 8; the division "Automobile Accessories: Tires" would be numbered 8-1; a further subdivision "Automobile Accessories: Tires, Standard Black" would be numbered 8-1a; "Automobile Accessories: Tires, Whitewall" would be numbered 8-1b. The outline would look like this:

> 8   AUTOMOBILE ACCESSORIES
> 8-1 Automobile Accessories: Tires
> 8-1a   Standard Black
> 8-1b   Whitewall

Alpha-Numeric. This system uses letters of the alphabet for the major subject titles along with letters and numbers for subtopics.

> A   ADMINISTRATION
> A1   Long-Range Planning
> A1-1   Guidelines and Schedules
> A2   Competition
> A2-1   Survey Reports
> A3   Public Relations
>
> G   GOVERNMENT RELATIONS
> G1   Air Pollution Control
> G1-1   Vehicle Emissions
> G1-1-1   Health Hazards

When a company uses the combination subject filing system, it is extremely important that an up-to-date list be kept of all subjects and their code letters and numbers. This list should be circulated to all persons and departments needing access to the files. Likewise, a *relative index* should be made listing all possible subjects and where information might be located pertaining to that subject. This list, too, should be updated constantly and distributed to those using the files.

NUMERIC (NON-ALPHABETIC)

The numeric filing system is a non-alphabetic system because records are filed solely by numbers. The types of numeric filing systems are:

Straight Numeric. This system has records filed according to strict numeric sequence. Folder number 1 is given to the first client or account; folder number 2 is given to the second and so forth in strict numeric order.

Terminal Digit. In this system, numbers on a file are read from right to left. Usually, the last, or terminal, two digits are the drawer number, the next two digits are the folder number, and any other numbers indicate the sequence within the folders. For example, an insurance policy numbered 567,123 would be stored in drawer 23, folder 71, and the 56 would refer to its sequence in the folder.

Triple Digit. This system is similar to the terminal-digit system, except that the numbers are read in three digits instead of two. The terminal three digits of a number are called the "primary" numbers, and the remaining digits refer to the sequence of the papers in the folders bearing the primary numbers. For example, the insurance policy numbered 567,123 would be found in folder 123, and 567 would refer to its sequence in the folder.

Middle Digit. The third and fourth digits from the right are separated from the last two digits on the right. For example, in the insurance policy number 567,123, the policy would be filed in folder 71, and 23 would refer to its sequence in the folder.

When the numeric system is used, an *accession register* must be kept to make retrieving a particular file a quick process. The *accession register* is a book or card file which contains each file number beginning with the first number as well as the correspondent's name on that file. The correspondents' names should be alphabetized so that one can get the file quickly if a correspondent's file number has been forgotten.

DECIMAL

The decimal system of filing may be based on the Dewey decimal system. This is the system commonly used by public libraries, although many are switching to the Library of Congress Catalog card system. The decimal system is used only in highly specialized businesses.

PHONETIC

The phonetic filing system is a filing method based on the use of letters and sounds. Organizations which file records by individuals' surnames encounter the problem of filing names which sound alike but are spelled differently such as Smith, Smyth, Schmidt, Schmitt. To eliminate this problem, Remington Rand Office Systems Division of Sperry Rand Corporation developed the Soundex Phonetic Filing System. Soundex is a combination of spelling, or sounds, and numbers. Basic sounds are represented by six fundamental letters, the consonants B, C, D, L, M, and R, which make up the entire Soundex alphabet. Each of these consonants is given a separate code number: B is 1, C is 2, D is 3, L is 4, M is 5, and R is 6. The remaining consonants in the alphabet have the same relative sounds as the six basic Soundex consonants and are grouped with the *basic* consonant. All vowels and the letters W, H, and Y have no number and are not coded. To use this system, look at the *first* letter of the *surname* and sort by *that letter* first. Then code the *remaining* letters in the surname by looking at the following chart.

Code	Key Letters and Equivalents
1	B F P V
2	C G J K Q S X Z
3	D T
4	L
5	M N
6	R

To file the surname "Snyder," the first letter S is recorded. The next letter to be coded is N which is code 5. Y is disregarded, D is code 3, E is disregarded, and R is code 6. The surname "Snyder" is thus coded S536.

To file the surname "Day," code a D and three zeros to show that only vowels follow the first consonant D. When no consonants or not enough consonants follow the first letter in the surname, use one, two, or three zeros to give the name a three-digit code. The code for "Day" is D000. The surname "Shaw" is S000, Levy is L100, and Kelly is K400.

PHYSICAL SETUP OF FILES

The file drawer contains primary guides which divide the file into alphabetic sections or numeric sections. These primary guides are placed at the beginning of each section. The tabs may be on the left-hand side or in the middle of the file drawer. Secondary guides are used to subdivide the section or to call attention to important names or numbers. Individual folders, arranged alphabetically, chronologically, or in numeric sequence, are placed directly behind the guides. Individual folders are used for correspondents who communicate frequently with the firm. When there are from five to eight pieces of correspondence from the same source, an individual folder is set up. The full name of the correspondent is on the tab. Tabs are usually alternated in position so that one does not come directly behind another. When material is arranged in an individual folder, the latest date is always in the front of the folder.

When material is placed in a miscellaneous folder, it should be arranged alphabetically with the latest date in front for each person or subject. Miscellaneous folders follow the individual folders at the end of each major division. They are used for correspondence that does not warrant individual folders. The tab on the miscellaneous folder may be of a different size or be marked with a distinctive color so that it can be easily located.

In preparing index tabs and labels for guides and folders, type the letter of the alphabet or the name. The first typing space below the fold of the file-drawer label should be used, and typing should start two spaces from the left of the label. Use initial capitals and indent the second and each succeeding line two spaces so that the first word on the top line will stand out. Use abbreviations if the name or subject is long. Use the largest type possible when typing file-drawer labels, or print these labels.

PREPARATION OF MATERIAL FOR FILING

Check all papers to see whether they are to be filed and have been released for filing. Sort the correspondence into personal, business, contracts, and the like. Remove all staples, paper clips, or other paper holders. Underline the name in colored pencil to indicate where the letter is to be filed. Indicate the guide number in the upper right-hand corner. Use a colored pencil to circle important words to help to locate a particular paper when it is needed. Make any cross-reference sheets that are required. A cross-reference sheet is made out when a letter or a record may be filed in one of two places. File the letter or record under the most important name and cross-refer the second name or subject. For example, a letter may be received from Jordan Marsh Company. It would be filed under Jordan (first unit) Marsh (second unit) Company (third unit), and a cross reference made out for Marsh, Jordan Company. The cross-reference sheet would read:

```
Marsh, Jordan Company
SEE
Jordan Marsh Company
```

Below is a simple step-by-step checklist to use when getting ready to file material:

Step 1: *Inspection.* Read or scan the material. Put a check mark in the upper left-hand corner to signal that this material should be filed.

Step 2: *Indexing.* Determine which *name* or *subject* to use for filing the material. This is vital, as poor indexing means poor "finding," and a loss of time.

Step 3: *Coding.* Coding is the physical act of marking the name, subject, etc., under which the material is to be filed. Put the code in the upper right-hand corner. Make cross-reference sheets at this point.

Step 4: *Sorting.* Sort the material in a rough, superficial manner—all A's together, all B's together, etc., in alphabetic order. Put all 10's together, all 20's together, etc., for numeric filing. Then sort each stack according to "strict sorting," using the standard filing rules the firm uses.

Step 5: *Filing.* Place correspondence in the folders, top to the left of the folder. Put material in the miscellaneous folder alphabetically, with the latest date on top. Place material in individual folders chronologically, latest date on top.

When it is necessary to take material from the file, replace the record or correspondence with an "out" guide or card. On the "out" guide, record the date, the name of the record taken, who has it, and the date it is to be returned. The word "out" should be printed on the tab, and stock of a different color should be used so that the guide stands out. It is necessary to record the withdrawal of the material if it goes out of the office for a period of time, or if the employer is going to use it away from the office. Confidential records should be used in the office and returned to the files immediately.

CARD FILE

A card file (usually 3″ × 5″ cards) arranged alphabetically by name of person or subject is often imperative for finding needed manuscripts or correspondence. In many offices, two separate card files are maintained, one for subject and the second for the name of the writer of each piece of material. If there are a great many different sets of files in an office, each needs to be clearly identified to make the card file useful.

Each card should hold as much information as necessary for retrieval of needed material. It should contain subject, along with any pertinent sub-category, name of person and/or date (if pertinent), set of files in which the material is stored, and any notes that will aid the secretary or executive in learning exactly what will be found in the file being sought.

FILING EQUIPMENT

The standard office filing cabinet has four drawers that hold file folders enclosing material on the regulation 8 1/2″×11″ typing paper. A law office or company with many legal papers will need a wider cabinet to accommodate legal cap.

The standard drawer will carry a load of from 60 to 70 pounds. For efficient filing, the file drawers should not be overcrowded. The secretary should take note at what intervals the files start to become overcrowded, and take appropriate action.

The files should be arranged so that there is a minimum of walking required to and from the files. The file drawers may be labeled in either vertical (top to bottom), or horizontal (from left to right) order. Space may be saved if the file cabinets are backed up against a wall. If there are many cabinets, it may be more efficient to arrange them in a cluster in the center of a room. Floor space is expensive; therefore, some consideration should be given to arranging cabinets economically. Adequate aisle space between cabinets must be allowed. At least 28 inches must be allowed for a file drawer when it is opened into the aisle. There should be gaps in long rows of cabinets to save time in getting from one row to another. This is particularly important for the file supervisor who has to make spot checks of the file drawers and to assist the file clerks.

LATERAL OR OPEN-SHELF FILING

For certain kinds of filing, the open-shelf method is more appropriate than the use of file drawers. This "lateral" or shelf filing may result in the saving of as much as 40 percent of the office floor space needed for files. The aisles between the shelves can be considerably narrower than those needed between cabinets with drawers because the additional space for pulling out drawers is not needed. Also, files can be stacked higher than drawers—in many instances, to the ceiling.

Lateral filing is particularly useful for active files in which papers are inserted and withdrawn constantly, and which are not to be retained for a long period of time. Proponents of lateral filing claim much time is saved by having the files immediately at hand and in sight.

COLOR CODING

When file folders are kept on shelves, color coding may prove to be a worthwhile expedient. Color coding is usually employed to identify a filing series that has been categorized by the alphabetic system or any of the several numeric systems discussed earlier in this chapter. A specific color is assigned to each number or letter. One manufacturer of filing materials (Datafile) uses twelve colors twice, the second time with a white bar that sets it apart from the first. These 24, with white for Y and gray for Z, serve for the 26 letters of the alphabet.

This represents one of the great variety of color coding systems that have been worked out. The pattern used depends on the complexity of the material to be filed. Datafile, using its twelve colors, also has folders with two color bands for identification of the first two letters of a word or name. By identifying two letters the file is expanded from the 26 letters of the alphabet to about three or four hundred segments. The possible total is 26×26 or 676, but all combinations of letters do not occur at the beginning of words or names.

For some kinds of open-shelf filing, the plain manila folder and/or hanging file folders are used, with a much simpler color code. One company that keeps order files for exactly two years before discard uses a color coded dot on the folders holding the records for alternate years. Thus the file at any particular time consists of folders marked in one color for one of the years represented, unmarked folders for another, and a second colored dot for the third. If, for example, the date is March 1986, the folders for April through December of 1984 (January through March having been discarded) have dots of one color, the folders for 1985 are plain, and the folders for January to date in 1986 have dots of a second color. Folders for 1987 will be plain, and the system will repeat.

In summary, color coding may be effected on shelf filing by folders of a solid color, folders with color bands, by stick-on dots in an upper corner of a manila file folder, by tabs that protrude, or by tabs that slip on, clip on, or are pasted on the folders. The tabbed folders may be bought prepared or assembled by the secretary or file clerk.

Color coding of files within drawers can be equally effective. Durable plastic file folders are produced in a wide variety of colors, or a color tab may be affixed to manila folders or hanging dividers. One of the common ways to use these is to select a new color for each year within an alphabetic file.

Before making a decision about color coding, the secretary needs to study the various methods and patterns, and then determine which is the most efficient for the material filed in the office for which the system is intended.

INDEXING AND ALPHABETIZING

Indexing has to do with the arrangement of the names on the folder tab or on cards. The folders and cards are arranged alphabetically for simplicity of filing and finding. The following indexing rules are standard rules for filing. The Association of Records Managers and Administrators, Inc. (ARMA) uses these guidelines with minor exceptions which will be noted toward the end of this section.

Individual names. Names of individuals are indexed by the last name (the surname) first, then the first name, and then the middle initial or middle name, if any.

Name	*Indexing Order*
Alfred M. Amell	Amell, Alfred M.
Grace R. Gladd	Gladd, Grace R.
J. Thomas Williams	Williams, J. Thomas

Business Names. The names of business establishments, institutions, and organizations are indexed as they are written, unless they embody the name of an individual. An exception to this rule is the names of schools. When the individual's name is part of a firm name, index by considering the last name (surname) first, then the first name, and the middle initial or middle name, if any.

Name	*Indexing Order*
Atlantic Service Station	Atlantic Service Station
Earl A. Stone Book Publishers	Carson, James A. Company
General Department Store	General Department Store
James A. Carson Company	Morgan, J. M. Sign Company
J. M. Morgan Sign Company	Nathan Hale Junior High School
Nathan Hale Junior High School	Peter, Rose Beauty Shoppe
Rose and Peter Beauty Supplies	Rose and Peter Beauty Supplies
Rose Peter Beauty Shoppe	Rose's Beauty Salon
Rose's Beauty Salon	Stiles, Thomas Milford Florist Shop
Stone and Book Publishing Company	Stone Book Publishers
Stone Book Publishers	Stone and Book Publishing Company
Thomas Milford Stiles Florist Shop	Stone, Earl A. Book Publishers
Troy Sand and Gravel, Inc.	Troy Sand and Gravel, Inc.

Alphabetic Order. Names are alphabetized by comparing each letter in the names. If the first units are alike, compare the second units. If there is no second unit, the single name is filed first. The rule of "nothing before something" applies here. A surname followed by a first initial only goes before the same surname followed by a complete first name beginning with the same letter as the initial, again, "nothing before something."

Name	Indexing Order	
	Unit 1	Unit 2
Carson	Carson	
Carson Brothers	Carson	Brothers
J. Carson	Carson	J.
James Carson	Carson	James

Letters used as words. Consider any single letter as a word and not part of a cluster or part of an acronym.

Name	Indexing Order			
	Unit 1	Unit 2	Unit 3	Unit 4
N A P A Jobbers	N	A	P	A
N C R Accounting Company	N	C	R	Accounting
Pacific Car Company	Pacific	Car	Company	
R & B Auto Service	R	B	Auto	Service

Abbreviations. Abbreviations are indexed as though they are the words they are representing written out in full; hence, "Mme." is indexed as "Madame."

Name	Indexing Order		
	Unit 1	Unit 2	Unit 3
Mme. Sophie's Boutique	Madame	Sophie's	Boutique
Mr. Pete's Grocery	Mister	Pete's	Grocery
St. Alexis Hospital	Saint	Alexis	Hospital

Article "the." When "the" is part of the name, it is disregarded in filing. If it is the initial word, it is placed at the end of the name in parentheses.

If "the" occurs in the body of the name, it is placed in parentheses and disregarded.

Name	Indexing Order
The Cleveland Boat Company	Cleveland Boat Company (The)
Danny The Tailor	Danny (The) Tailor
Stanley of the Ritz	Stanley (of the) Ritz

(Such words as "and," "for," "on," "in," "by," and "of the" are disregarded in indexing and filing. However, they are placed in parentheses when writing names on folders and cards.)

Hyphenated names. Hyphenated firm names are treated as separate names, because they represent separate individuals; when listed among other proper names the second name is to be regarded as a given name for alphabetizing purposes.

Name	Indexing Order
Branch-Merrill Company	Branch Merrill Company
Richard T. Branch	Branch, Richard T.
Winifred I. Wilson	Wilson, Winifred I.
Wilson-Wyman, Inc.	Wilson Wyman, Inc.

Hyphenated individual names are treated as one name, because they represent one individual.

Name	Indexing Order
James A. Gladd-Monroe	GladdMonroe, James A.
Patricia Lloyd-Taylor	LloydTaylor, Patricia
Jane L. Marin-Jones	MarinJones, Jane L.

One- or two-word names. Names that may be spelled as one word or two words are usually considered as one word.

Name	Indexing Order		
	Unit 1	Unit 2	Unit 3
Raybrook Cleaners	Raybrook	Cleaners	
Ray Brook Paint Company	RayBrook	Paint	Company
South East Electric Shop	SouthEast	Electric	Shop
Southeast Supply Company	Southeast	Supply	Company
Good Will Cleaners	GoodWill	Cleaners	
Goodwill Industries	Goodwill	Industries	

Individual surnames with prefixes. Prefixes such as D', d', De, de, Del, Des, Di, Du, Fitz, l', La, Le, M', Mac, Mc, O', Van, Von, and so on, are indexed as written and treated as one word.

Name	Indexing Order		
	Unit 1	Unit 2	Unit 3
D'Aoust, James	D'Aoust	James	
Darling, John E.	Darling	John	E.
De Lancett, Morris	De Lancett	Morris	
DeLancey, Lincoln	DeLancey	Lincoln	
MacDonald, George H.	MacDonald	George	H.
McCasland, Raymond A.	McCasland	Raymond	A.
Van Cour, Elsie A.	Van Cour	Elsie	A.
Von Ottenfeld, Oscar M.	Von Ottenfeld	Oscar	M.

Words ending in "s." When a name ends in "s' " or " 's," the "s" is considered part of the name.

	Indexing Order		
Name	Unit 1	Unit 2	Unit 3
Bob's Sport Shop	Bob's	Sport	Shop
Boy Scout Camp	Boy	Scout	Camp
Boys' Clothing Store	Boys'	Clothing	Store
Williams' Dry Cleaning	Williams'	Dry	Cleaning
William's Service Station	William's	Service	Station
Wilson, John M.	Wilson	John	M.

Titles. A personal or professional title or degree is usually not considered in indexing and filing. When the name is written, the title is placed in parentheses at the end of the name.

Name	Indexed as
Dr. Richard P. Bellaire	Bellaire, Richard P. (Dr.)
Ms. Helen Hayles	Hayles, Helen (Ms.)
Grace M. Janson, D.D.	Janson, Grace M. (D.D.)

A religious or foreign title is considered as the first indexing unit when it is followed by a given name only.

Indexed and filed as

Brother Francis
Madame Eugenie
Prince Charles
Princess Grace
Sister Mary Megan

Married women's names. The name of a married woman is indexed according to the name by which she prefers to be known. Some women retain their maiden names after marriage and this preference should be respected. A married name could be her given first name, her maiden surname, and her husband's surname, or it could be her given first and middle names (or initial for the middle name), and her husband's surname. The title "Mrs." is disregarded in filing, but it is placed in parentheses after her name. If signatures on correspondence from her indicate that she prefers "Ms.," then that is the title placed in parentheses after her name. The name of the husband may be given in parentheses below the woman's legal name.

Name	*Indexing Order*
Mrs. John F. Matson (Mary Nelson)	Matson, Mary Nelson (Mrs.) (Mrs. John F. Matson)
Mrs. Lucien (Louise S.) Platt	Platt, Louise S. (Mrs.) (Mrs. Lucien Platt)
Mrs. Robert (Mary Lee) Young	Young, Mary Lee (Mrs.) (Mrs. Robert Young)

Names with numbers. When a name contains a number, it is considered as if the number was written as a single unit and is spelled as it is pronounced.

	Indexing Order		
Name	*Unit 1*	*Unit 2*	*Unit 3*
A 1 Garage	A	One	Garage
The 400 Club	Fourhundred	Club (The)	
7th Ave. Building	Seventh	Avenue	Building

Geographic names. An easy rule to follow in arranging geographic names is to treat them as they are written. Each element in a compound name of a geographic location is indexed as a separate unit.

	Indexing Order			
Name	*Unit 1*	*Unit 2*	*Unit 3*	*Unit 4*
Mount Holly, New Jersey	Mount	Holly	New	Jersey
New Bedford, Massachusetts	New	Bedford	Massachusetts	
New York Central R. R.	New	York	Central	Railroad
Newburgh, New York	Newburgh	New	York	

When the first element of a geographic name is not of English origin, that element is considered part of the first unit.

	Indexing Order	
Name	*Unit 1*	*Unit 2*
Des Moines, Iowa	DesMoines	Iowa
Las Vegas Hotel	LasVegas	Hotel
Los Angeles, California	LosAngeles	California
San Francisco, California	SanFrancisco	California

Government offices and departments. The name of a federal government office is indexed as follows:

1. United States Government (whether or not it is written as part of the name).
2. Principal word or words in the name of the department.
3. Principal word or words in the name of the bureau.
4. Principal word or words in the name of the division.

"Department of," "Bureau of," and "Division of" are disregarded but are usually placed in parentheses.

Name	*Indexing Order*
Bureau of the Census	United States Government
U.S. Department of Commerce	Commerce (Department of)
	Census (Bureau of the)
Office of Indian Affairs	United States Government
U.S. Department of the Interior	Interior (Department of)
	Indian Affairs (Office of)
U.S. Postal Service	United States Government
Bureau of Accounts	Postal Service
Division of Cost Ascertainment	Accounts (Bureau of)
	Cost Ascertainment (Division of)

Foreign government names. Names pertaining to foreign governments are indexed under names of countries and subdivided by title of the department, and then by bureau, division, commission, or board.

Name	*Indexing Order*
Republic of India	India (Republic of)
Department of Energy	Energy Department

Other political divisions. Names pertaining to other political divisions are indexed under the name of the political division followed by its classification such as *state*, *county*, or *city* and then subdivided by the title of the department, bureau, division, commission, or board.

Name	*Indexing Order*
Bureau of Statistics	Maine, State (of)
State of Maine	Statistics (Bureau of)
Harris County	Harris, County
Bureau of Personnel	Personnel (Bureau of)
Department of Safety	Anaheim, City (of)
City of Anaheim	Safety (Department of)

Banks. Banks are indexed under the names of the communities in which they are located, then by bank name. The state is the last indexing unit.

Name	*Indexing Order*
First National Bank Cleveland, Ohio	Cleveland: First National Bank, Ohio
Bank of New Jersey Newark	Newark: Bank of New Jersey, New Jersey
Wells Savings Bank Wells, Maine	Wells Savings Bank, Maine

If the name of the community is a part of the name of the bank, the name of the community is not repeated, but is considered the first unit as it occurs.

Churches, schools, and other organizations. The names of churches, schools, and other organizations are indexed as follows. Cross references may be used when necessary to file or find these names more efficiently.

Name	*Indexing Order*
American Legion	American Legion
University of California	California, University (of)
Lakewood Kiwanis Club	Kiwanis Club, Lakewood
First Lutheran Church	Lutheran Church, First
Martin Luther King High School	Martin Luther King High School
The Salvation Army	Salvation Army, The

Addresses. If two or more persons or firms have the same name but different addresses, alphabetize them according to city or town. In the event that the persons or firms also have the same city or town name, then alphabetize according to the state name. Should persons or firms having the same name be in the same community but have different addresses, alphabetize these names according to the name of the street. In the event that the same name has more than one address on the same street of that city or town, then index from the lowest to highest street number.

Example: 125 Main Street goes before 126 Main Street.

The Association of Records Managers and Administrators Indexing and Filing Rules. The Association of Records Managers and Administrators, Inc., in its book of indexing rules, *Rules for Alphabetical Filing*, has established three classifications for indexing: individual names, business establishment names, and government/political designations. ARMA recommends separating index units with the diagonal (/). ARMA rules are essentially the same as the ones given above with the following differences:

1. The hyphenated company name is treated as one unit.

   Example: Brown-Jacobs/Company/

2. Compound geographical names are treated as separate units.

   Example: Las/Vegas/Construction/Company/
   Del/Rio/Music/Store/

3. Company names which have compass points as part of the company name are indexed as separate units.

Name	*Indexing Order*
North East Alignment	North/East/Alignment/
Southeastern Transfer	South/eastern/Transfer/

4. The " 's" is included as part of the indexing unit; that is, the apostrophe, " ' ", is disregarded.

Name	*Indexing Order*
Leon's Barbecue	Leon's/Barbecue/
Leons' Music Store	Leons'/Music/Store/

5. Company names which are numbers and written in figure form such as *500 Club* are arranged in strict numeric sequence and are *not* spelled out. They are filed at the *front* of the entire alphabetic file.

Name	*Indexing Order*
1 Hour Cleaners	1/Hour/Cleaners/
7th Street Auto Shop	7(th)/Street/Auto/Shop/
8 Ball Eatery	8/Ball/Eatery/
400 Executive Clothiers	400/Executive/Clothiers/
500 Club	500/Club/

TRANSFERRING RECORDS

When records become inactive in the file, they should be transferred to storage files. Thus, the expensive filing equipment is used only for active material. The material that is removed from the active files and placed in the inactive, or transfer, files should be well arranged, so that no time is wasted in locating this material if it is needed. Many firms plan to transfer the material in the files annually. The entire file drawer is transferred to the inactive file. The secretary needs to make new guides and prepare new folders for the new file.

If the guides and folders are going to be kept in the office, the transferred material may be placed in inexpensive folders that have been labeled with the same captions as those in the active-file drawer.

All transfer files or boxes should be labeled to indicate their contents, dates, and so forth, so that they can easily be located when needed.

Many business papers, correspondence, and some records that will not be needed in the future may be destroyed to conserve space and save time in transferring files. Material should not be destroyed without consideration of the statute of limitations in the state and other laws which require business firms to retain certain types of records.

RECORDS RETENTION SCHEDULE

The secretary should keep a copy of the company's records retention schedule and update it when revisions occur. This schedule is a listing of all types of records a firm has and how long these items are to be kept in the office or in the records center. The schedule lists which records must be microfilmed and how long retained. Also, the schedule contains a timetable for disposing of records and a permanent records list.

The company's attorney and representatives of top management should set up the retention schedule following guidelines based on the many federal and state regulations which apply to the firm.

MICROGRAPHICS

Micrographics is the term used to designate reproduced information in miniature form on film. Storing information on microfilm has saved firms great amounts of money, space, and retrieval time. Records are photographed onto film in a microfilmer so that many small images in color or black and white will appear on a reel of 16-millimeter or 35-millimeter film. Records can be viewed in enlarged form on a reader. Roll film can be stored on rolls and put in cartons and cabinets. A plastic collar snapped over roll film becomes a magazine which self-threads to readers.

Other microfilm formats are:

Jackets contain chambers that hold short lengths of film. A 4" × 6" jacket holds 70 images of letter-size documents.

Microfiche (often called "fiche") contains rows of documents on sheet film about 4″ × 6″. Full-color or black-and-white images can appear on microfiche (98 full-color or more than 300 black-and-white images).

Aperture cards are tab-card-size cards which have chambers to hold one or more pieces of film and room on the card for identification.

Film folios are a combination of aperture cards and jackets; they are cards the size of microfiche with chambers to hold film of microfiche size. The card contains space for identification.

Computer Output Microfilm (COM). COM is a method of microfilming in which data that are stored in a computer can be recorded directly onto microfilm. This process eliminates recording the data on paper printouts before microfilming can take place. COM speeds getting information to persons needing it on film rather than on paper.

Chapter 10

Communications
JEANETTE L. BELY

I   The Office Mail

MAIL CONSTITUTES the most important method of communication between a firm or organization and its contacts in the business world. The way in which the mail is handled will affect every phase of the business. A secretary who can deal with the office mail efficiently is indeed a valuable asset to an employer.

INCOMING MAIL

A new secretary may find a well-established system of handling mail within an organization. Changes may need to be suggested tactfully. The size of the organization has a great bearing on the system that evolves. In a small office one person may sort and open all mail except that marked "Personal" or "Confidential." (Letters so marked are delivered unopened to the person to whom they are addressed.) A large organization usually has a mailing department, where both incoming and outgoing mail are handled according to a fixed system.

In an office where the secretary is assigned the responsibility for opening the mail for the employer, a routine procedure will permit rapid handling of each day's mail.

OPENING THE MAIL

To ensure that the contents will not be torn while the letter is being opened, tap the envelope firmly on the edge of the desk so that the contents will slip away from the top. Slit the upper edge of the envelope with a letter opener. If the contents of a letter are cut by the opener, use transparent tape to paste the parts together.

Checking the contents. After removing the contents of an envelope, check for a return address. If there is none, staple the envelope containing the return address to the contents. (Caution: If the contents include a punched card, use a paper clip for fastening rather than a staple.) The envelope should also be retained if the signature on the letter is not easily distinguishable.

Another check should be made to determine that all enclosures stipulated in the letter are accounted for. If not, a notation should be made immediately on the face of the letter, indicating what is missing.

Dating the mail. It is always wise to affix each day's date on incoming mail. The easiest procedure is to use a rubber stamp. Such a procedure is helpful if the letter has arrived too late to meet a deadline requested, has been in transit longer than it should have been, or is undated. In either of the latter two cases, it is well to staple the envelope to the letter in addition to dating the letter. This will give evidence of the date of mailing as well as the date of receipt.

Envelopes. Generally the envelope may be destroyed after it has been ascertained that everything has been removed and that there are no problems concerned with the names, addresses, or dates.

PREPARATION OF MAIL FOR EMPLOYER

In order to save the employer's time, the efficient secretary should take the time to prepare the mail. This involves two basic steps.

1. Read each letter, underlining important points which will aid you and your employer in answering the letter. Underline only those things which are of significance, such as publications, dates, and names of people.
2. Make annotations on each letter. This involves writing notes in the margins. Generally, annotations fall into three categories, namely, a note indicating:
    a. Action required by the letter—date of appointment for correspondent, reservations for a trip the employer may have to make as a result of the correspondence, etc.
        As the letters are being annotated, an efficient secretary will also make a list of files or pieces of correspondence and other information to be looked up before presenting the correspondence to the employer.
        Some employers wish to see the mail as soon as it has been opened. In that case the secretary may bring the mail in as soon as it has been annotated. While the mail is being read, the secretary may take the compiled list and seek the necessary files, reports, and other information for acting upon the urgent mail. To keep all papers pertaining to each piece of correspondence together, use file folders or small clips.
    b. Procedures to be followed. These may depend upon former correspondence

with the same person or related correspondence, which will have to be sought in the files.

c. The priority the letter should receive, symbolized by a code. In an agreement with the employer a given place on each letter should be established for this code. For example, a red number may be written in the upper left corner. Such a code might include:

Code 1. Mail and reports with high priority and requiring a decision should be answered the same day they are received. It is assumed that personal or confidential mail is delivered unopened to the addressee as soon as it arrives on the secretary's desk.

Code 2. Mail for which additional information must be procured and for which answering may have to be deferred for a day or two while data are being collected. *All mail should be answered withing 48 hours of receipt*, except under very unusual circumstances.

Code 3. Routine mail that the secretary may be able to handle. Many employers want to see all mail; it is wise to determine an employer's preference in this regard. After the relationship is well established, many secretaries have their employers' permission to reply to routine letters. In such instances it is usually good procedure to supply the employer with carbons of the letters sent and the original letter.

Code 4. Letters which require notations but no reply.

As the secretary reads and annotates the mail, it becomes a simple matter to encode and sort the mail as it is prepared for the employer. A fifth or even a sixth category may be added as needed. Usually important reports require a special category, while weekly, monthly, or semimonthly periodicals may require no encoding. Most employers prefer to examine the periodicals before they are made available to others in the office.

Arranging the mail. After the sorting process has been completed, the secretary may arrange the mail either in one pile with the high-priority mail on top or in any other arrangement which has been agreed upon. Whenever the mail is placed on the desk of the employer, some provision should be made to prevent others from reading the top letter. Some secretaries simply place the top letter face down.

Absence of the employer. When the employer is away from the office, letters requiring immediate replies may be handled in either of two ways. First, if a decision must be made immediately, it may be necessary to give the mail to the person in charge during the employer's absence. Second, if the employer will be in the office within a day or two and the decision can wait, the secretary should write the sender immediately and explain when a reply may be expected and the reason for the delay.

The efficient secretary to whom the employer has entrusted routine correspondence will maintain a file of materials handled during an absence of the employer. The folder should be readily at hand upon the employer's return.

OUTGOING MAIL

If the secretary is responsible for the preparation of outgoing mail, as it may well be in a firm too small to have a separate mailing and shipping department, time and expense can be saved by learning about the various postal and shipping services available and the general regulations and normal charges pertinent to these services. It is important to be alert to changes, for the charges tend to increase or change frequently.

An accurate scale for weighing postal matter is a worthwhile piece of office equipment. It saves time and eliminates guesswork.

SOURCES OF MAIL INFORMATION

To obtain correct information on postal procedures and rates, which are subject to change, consult the local postal authorities. From them, or from the Superintendent of Documents, Government Printing Office, Washington, DC 20402, may be obtained a number of useful pamphlets which are periodically brought up to date. These are some of them:

Mailers Guide
Packaging Pointers
Domestic Postage Rates, Fees, and Information
How To Prepare Second- and Third-Class Mailings
Mailing Permits
International Postage Rates and Fees

Some of the information in these pamphlets is taken from the *Postal Manual*, which contains complete data on postal regulations and procedures. Chapters 1 and 2 of this manual, which deal with domestic postal service and international mail, respectively, may be purchased separately.

A monthly publication called *Memo to Mailers* is available to business mailers without charge. It tells of rate and classification changes, along with other news of postal matters. Address:

MEMO TO MAILERS
P. O. Box 1600
La Plata, MD 20646

STAMPS, STAMPED ENVELOPES, AND POSTAL CARDS

Postage stamps may be purchased in several forms—single stamps, sheets, books, and coils—and denominations for both regular mail and overseas airmail. For the coil form, inexpensive dispensers are available at the post office. Stamped envelopes are also sold at the post office; these may be obtained in two standard sizes. Postal cards are available with the stamp printed on the address side; they come in single or double (reply) forms, with or without postage on the reply half.

Precanceled and meter stamps are two means of reducing the time and cost of mail handling. In order to use precanceled stamps (i.e., stamps canceled before mailing), a special permit must be obtained from the post office. For regulations applying to precanceled stamps, consult the *Postal Manual* or the local postal authorities.

Postage may be paid by printing meter stamps with a postage meter. Postage meters hasten the purchase, control, and attachment of postage and therefore facilitate mailing. Postage-meter machines may be leased from authorized manufacturers. Again, the *Postal Manual* or the local postal authorities should be consulted for regulations governing the leasing, use, and licensing of postal meters and also their manufacture and distribution.

ZIP CODES AND TWO-LETTER ABBREVIATIONS

The U.S. Postal Service uses a set of two-letter abbreviations, to be followed by the ZIP Code, for all of the states and possessions of the United States. Although traditional abbreviations, such as Calif. for California and Mich. for Michigan, are still used, the Postal Service suggests the use of these two-letter abbreviations with ZIP Codes.

AK	Alaska	IL	Illinois	ND	North	RI	Rhode Island
AL	Alabama	IN	Indiana		Dakota	SC	South
AR	Arkansas	KS	Kansas	NE	Nebraska		Carolina
AZ	Arizona	KY	Kentucky	NH	New	SD	South
CA	California	LA	Louisiana		Hampshire		Dakota
CO	Colorado	MA	Massachusetts	NJ	New Jersey	TN	Tennessee
CT	Connecticut	MD	Maryland	NM	New Mexico	TX	Texas
DC	District of	ME	Maine	NV	Nevada	UT	Utah
	Columbia	MI	Michigan	NY	New York	VA	Virginia
DE	Delaware	MN	Minnesota	OH	Ohio	VI	Virgin Islands
FL	Florida	MO	Missouri	OK	Oklahoma	VT	Vermont
GA	Georgia	MS	Mississippi	OR	Oregon	WA	Washington
HI	Hawaii	MT	Montana	PA	Pennsylvania	WI	Wisconsin
IA	Iowa	NC	North	PR	Puerto	WV	West Virginia
ID	Idaho		Carolina		Rico	WY	Wyoming

The U.S. Postal Service relies heavily on ZIP Codes in the processing of mail. While some letters (at this writing) are still delivered even if the ZIP Code is not used, they may be delayed by lack of the number code. On the other hand, the Postal Service will not accept quantity mailings of letters, circulars, brochures, catalogs, etc., unless the pieces to be mailed are ZIP Coded and sorted by the code.

ZIP stands for Zoning Improvement Plan. The ZIP Code itself is a designation by numbers that expedites mail deliveries by cutting down on the steps required to move a letter from sender to addressee. The digits identify state, city, and post office, enabling most efficient use of air, highway, and rail transportation of the letter or parcel.

The *National ZIP Code and Post Office Directory* is available from the Information Service, U.S. Postal Service, Washington, DC 20260, or at any post office or branch. Having the latest ZIP Code directory is important, for over a thousand ZIP Codes change each year. The *National ZIP Code and Post Office Directory* is printed by the Government Printing Office, and is exchangeable free of charge each year for the annually revised edition. ZIP Code manuals printed by private companies must be paid for anew each time an updated printing is desired.

Because of the many changes in ZIP Codes, even the latest printing of such a handbook may not provide the secretary with the one needed. In that case, local post offices generally have a separate department for this and a ZIP Code can easily be ascertained by telephone.

Your local telephone directory will usually show local ZIP Codes.

Canada uses a different coding system (called *National Postal Code*) to speed mail deliveries. The following two-letter abbreviations are recommended for use with this code.

AB	Alberta	NT	Northwest Territories
BC	British Columbia	ON	Ontario
LB	Labrador	PE	Prince Edward Island
MB	Manitoba	PQ	Quebec
NB	New Brunswick	SK	Saskatchewan
NF	Newfoundland	YT	Yukon Territory
NS	Nova Scotia		

Business offices that send a large amount of mail to Canada can write to the following address for Postal Code information:

Mail Collection & Delivery Branch
Postal Coding Division
Canada Post
Ottawa, Ontario K1A 0B1
Canada

CLASSES OF MAIL

There are six classes of domestic mail, and these will be discussed in detail. Postal regulations and rates change quite frequently. Those who are responsible for mailing packages and parcels, or large quantities of advertising material, or cards or letters of unusual size, will want to acquire a copy of the appropriate *Leonard's Guide* for your city, available by mail; write to 2121 Shermer Road, Northbrook, Illinois 60062.

Private, commercial "mail" services are now established providing an alternative to the U.S. Postal System which has had problems in effecting speedy delivery. Often such services operate only within a metropolitan area, but a few nationwide services also exist. All of these will be listed in the Yellow Pages, generally under "Delivery Services." There, too, will be found a listing of companies that will pick up mail and deliver it to the post office for speedier handling, or will make pickups of mail directed to a box number at a post office.

First class: all handwritten or typewritten material and all material sealed against postal inspection.

Priority mail: any mailable matter that requires the speediest transportation and expeditious handling, weighing more than 12 ounces.

Second class: newspapers and periodicals.

Third class: circulars, books, catalogs, and other printed matter, and merchandise not included in first or second class, weighing less than 16 ounces.

Fourth class: all mailable matter not included in first, second, or third class, weighing one pound or more, but no more than 40 pounds, and not exceeding 84 inches in combined length and girth (in some circumstances, 70 pounds and 100 inches).

Express mail: guaranteed fast, reliable, overnight delivery on a money-back basis, of mail and packages.

FIRST-CLASS MAIL

The rate for first-class mail is determined by weight (the ounce or fraction thereof), without regard to the distance the article is to travel.

Address. Instructions for typing envelopes are given in Chapter 6. To ensure prompt delivery, observe these precautions regarding the address:

Write the address clearly and legibly, if it cannot be typewritten.
Mail addressed for delivery through a city-delivery post office must include the street and street number, or post-office box number, or general delivery, or rural or star

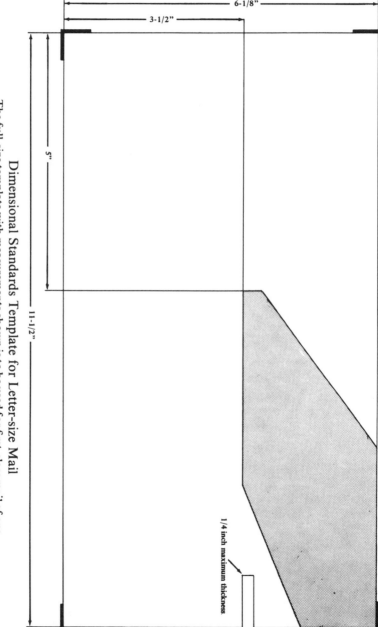

Dimensional Standards Template for Letter-size Mail

The full-size template with measurements shown is to be used for first-class mail of one ounce or less or third-class mail of two ounces or less. When the piece to be mailed is aligned with the lower left-hand corner the tip of the upper right-hand corner must touch the shaded area, to be mailed at regular postage.

6-1/8"

3-1/2"

5"

11-1/2"

1/4 inch maximum thickness

route designation. Mail for patrons on a rural route may be addressed to street names and numbers, provided that this type of address has been approved by the post office. The rural route number or the words "Rural Delivery" should be used in such addresses. Most patrons on rural routes have been assigned box numbers and this number should be included with the address.

All mail should bear the name and address of the sender, either in the upper left corner or on the back flap.

Include the ZIP Code on all mail.

Matter bearing more than one street address or the name of more than one city or town in the return address or in the recipient's address is not acceptable for mailing.

Some firms use both a post office box number and the street address. The U.S. Postal Service will deliver the item to the address immediately above the city-state-ZIP Code line. Therefore, if the company wants addressees to know its street address, yet prefers to have mail directed to its post office box, the box number will come next to last in its return address or letterhead. The secretary should be sure to address the envelope for return mail with the elements in the order shown. For the secretary's own company, such preferred order should be carefully specified when ordering letterheads, envelopes, or other company paper bearing an address.

	The BCX Company	The BCX Company
	200 Main Street	P.O. Box 456
Mail will be delivered ⟶	P.O. Box 456 ⟶	200 Main Street
	Small Town, NJ 06780	Small Town, NJ 06780

Envelope size. All envelopes differing widely from the standard sizes should be marked "FIRST CLASS." A rubber stamp is often used for this purpose, although it is not essential. First-class mail that weighs one ounce or less and exceeds 6 1/8 inches in height, 11 1/2 inches in length, 1/4 inch in thickness, and whose length is less than 1.3 times the height or more than 2.5 times the height is considered nonstandard mail. The secretary should call the post office to determine the rate for an outsized piece of mail, or should alert the company mail department that a nonstandard piece of mail is going out.

Certain minimum standards went into effect in 1979, and mail not meeting these standards will be refused. Mail must be at least .007 inch thick; that is, about the thickness of a postcard. Mail which is 1/4 inch thick or less must measure at least 3 1/2 inches in height, be at least 5 inches in length, and be rectangular in shape.

Postcards. Government-printed postal cards measure 3 1/2″ × 5 1/2″, while commercial postcards are 4″ × 6″ or slightly larger. In order to be mailed at the postcard rate, which is lower than the first-class letter rate, cards cannot be larger than 4 1/4″ × 6″. A larger card must bear the first-class letter postage. Cards less than 3 1/2″ × 5″ are not acceptable for mailing. Cards must be at least .007 inch thick but not over .0095 inch.

Double postal cards are two attached cards, one of which is to be detached by the receiver and returned through the mail as a reply. The reply portion does not have to bear postage when originally mailed. Double cards must have the address of the reply portion on the inside.

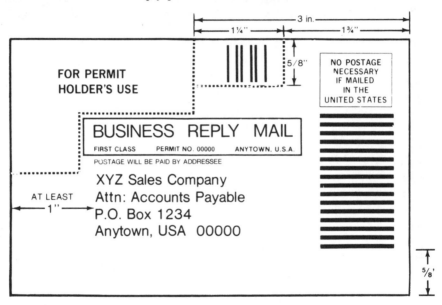

A standard format for the address side of a piece of business-reply mail

Business-reply mail. Specially printed business-reply cards, envelopes, cartons, and labels may be distributed so that they can be returned to the original mailer without prepayment of postage. A permit must be obtained from the local postmaster in order to distribute such mail. Postage is collected on each piece of business-reply mail at the time it is delivered to the original mailer. The rates are the regular postage rates, plus an additional fee. No special services may be included in these rates.

No limitation is made on the quantity of business-reply mail, but it cannot be sent to any foreign country except to U.S. military post offices overseas.

The forms of imprint and address for business-reply mail must conform to the requirements of the Postal Service. One of the standard formats is shown above.

PRIORITY MAIL

Mailable matter that weighs more than 12 ounces and is to be sent by the fastest means of transportation with the most expeditious handling may be sent by priority mail. Matter cannot exceed 70 pounds in weight nor 100 inches in length and girth combined.

Special envelopes or stickers should be used to clearly identify the package or envelope as priority mail. To ensure proper handling, the identification "PRIORITY MAIL" should be clearly marked in large letters on all sides.

SECOND-CLASS MAIL

The category of second-class mail includes newspapers and other periodical publications. The secretary may be concerned with the mailing of such matter if the company puts out a newsletter regularly. Special rates apply, according to the nature of the publication, the frequency of publication, and so on.

Publications issued by, and in the interest of, nonprofit organizations and associations, such as religious, educational, scientific, philanthropic, agricultural, labor, and fraternal groups, are categorized for mailing under a special-rate structure.

Because of the variation and specialization of postal regulations in this category, the secretary to whom the responsibility of handling this kind of mail is assigned should get specific information from the post office on the particulars applying to the publication with which the office is concerned. However, these few general observations on the wrapping or covering of second-class matter may be useful.

Preparation for mailing. Second-class mail must be prepared so that it can be easily examined. Even if envelopes, wrappers, or other covers are sealed, the use of second-class postage rates indicates that the sender consents to postal inspection of the contents.

Sealed or unsealed envelopes used as wrappers and sealed wrappers or covers must indicate, in the upper right corner, the "second-class" status, acknowledging the post office's right of examination; the upper left corner must have the name of the publication and the mailing address to which undeliverable copies or change-of-address notices are to be sent.

Special instructions must be followed for sorting the pieces before mailing. These are available through the local post office.

THIRD-CLASS MAIL

All pieces in the third-class category—circulars, books, catalogs, and other printed matter, and merchandise weighing less than 16 ounces—must be legibly marked "THIRD CLASS" whether they are sealed or not. They may be mailed and charged by the single piece or in bulk (see *Printed Matter* and *Bulk Mailing*, page 153). All the pieces in a bulk mailing must be identical in size, weight, and number of enclosures, although the printed textual matter need not be identical. Special rates are available for nonprofit organizations.

A single piece of third-class mail is considered nonstandard if it weighs two ounces or less and exceeds a height of 6 1/8 inches or a length of 11 1/2 inches or a thickness of 1/4 inch, and which is less than 1.3 times the height or more than 2.5 times the height. An additional charge will be made on such mail.

Preparation for mailing. Third-class mail must be prepared by the sender so that it can be easily examined. It need not be marked "May Be Opened for Postal Inspection," for this is implied in the sending of mail under this class.

Mailers must sort the mail and place each piece with the address side up and in the same position; the pieces should then be tied, lengthwise and crosswise, into packages, with twine strong enough to withstand handling in processing and shipping. The "Bulk Mail" labels should be large enough to cover the top piece of exposed mail and should be attached so that they will not slide out from under the twine. Mailers should follow special instructions from the post office. Wrapping, in general, should be handled as for parcel post (see below).

Writing permitted. Other than the address, the only writing permitted on the wrapper of third-class mail is in the form of instructions, such as "Printed Matter"; "Photograph—DO NOT BEND"; or "Do Not Open until Christmas."

Enclosures. With catalogs or booklets, one order form, a business-reply card or envelope, and one circular concerning the product being sent may be enclosed.

A letter may also be enclosed in the package if separate first-class postage is paid for the letter in addition to the third-class rate for the package and if the wrapper is marked "Letter Enclosed."

FOURTH-CLASS MAIL

Domestic parcel post makes up most of the fourth-class mail, but the classification also includes bound printed matter and the "special fourth-class rate" for books, 16-millimeter films (or films with less width), sound recordings, manuscripts, and a special library rate. Fourth-class mail includes merchandise, mailable live animals, and all other matter not included in first, second, or third class.

Parcel post service is provided for packages weighing one pound or more. In the conterminous United States, packages mailed from larger post offices are limited to 40 pounds and 84 inches in length and girth combined. However, parcels mailed from smaller offices and any office in Hawaii and Alaska are accepted up to 70 pounds and 100 inches. Rates are determined by weight (fractions of a pound are computed as a full pound) and by distance or zone. To find out which zone the place of destination is in, and also to learn of weight and size limitations on parcels, consult *Leonard's Guide* or the official zone chart furnished by your local post office. The zones are measured as follows:

* Local Zone (within delivery limits of local post office)
* Zone 1—Within the same sectional center area
* Zone 2—Up to 150 miles
* Zone 3—Up to 300 miles
* Zone 4—Up to 600 miles
* Zone 5—Up to 1,000 miles
* Zone 6—Up to 1,400 miles
* Zone 7—Up to 1,800 miles
* Zone 8—Beyond 1,800 miles

Special fourth-class rates apply to books, library materials, educational materials, and some advertising matter. Educational materials include 16-millimeter films and 16-millimeter film catalogs (except films and catalogs mailed to commercial theaters); printed music; printed objective-test materials; sound recordings and magnetic tapes; manuscripts of books, periodical articles, and music; printed educational reference charts processed for preservation; and loose-leaf pages, and their binders, consisting of medical information for distribution to doctors, hospitals, medical schools, and medical students. The outside of packages containing books or educational materials must be labeled "SPECIAL FOURTH-CLASS RATE: BOOK (or FILM, etc.)." To classify as a book to be mailed at the special fourth-class rate, a book must have 24 pages or more, at least 22 of which are printed, consisting wholly of reading matter.

Wrapping. Two or more packages may be mailed as a single parcel if they are about the same size or shape or if they are parts of one article. They must be securely wrapped or fastened together and must not, together, exceed the fourth-class weight and size limits.

Packages may be excluded from the mail unless they are wrapped in such a way as to ensure safe transport. A package sealed with masking tape or transparent adhesive tape is not acceptable for mailing.

Shipping containers. Containers in which the goods are to be shipped should be strong enough to retain the contents and protect them from the weight of other parcels with which they will be transported.

Cushioning contents. Corrugated cardboard may be used to protect contents. Cellulose materials, plastic bits, cotton, shredded paper, or tissue paper may be used for lighter items.

Outside wrapper. Nonfragile materials may be wrapped in heavy paper and sealed securely with tape. Thin paper bags are not acceptable.

Articles that are self-contained may be mailed without outside packaging or wrapping. However, the post office is not responsible if the surface or finish of the article becomes marred or damaged.

A cardboard carton in good condition may be wrapped and sealed with reinforced kraft paper tape or nylon filament tape. Avoid using twine if possible.

Mailing instructions. All parcel-post packages should be delivered to the post office and not deposited in mailboxes.

1. The return address of the sender must be shown on the face of each package. If the addresses of the sender and the addressee are close together, label the return address "from" and the addressee's "to." It is always wise to include inside each package the name and address of the sender as well as of the addressee.

Addresses should always be written with ink or an indelible marking pencil or typewritten on a label that is affixed to the package. Tied-on tags should be used only with packages too small to contain the complete address. Do not repeat the address on the back of the package.

2. Special inscriptions, such as "Merry Christmas," "Do Not Open until Christmas," or "Happy Birthday," may be written on the wrapper.

3. Packages containing fragile articles such as glassware, china, jewelry, and so forth, must be labeled "FRAGILE."

4. Products which may decay quickly, such as fresh meat or fresh produce, must be labeled "PERISHABLE."

5. The label "DO NOT BEND" may be used only when the contents are fully protected with fiberboard or corrugated cardboard.

Enclosures. Handwritten and typewritten materials to be included in parcel post are limited to the following:

1. Invoices and customers' orders may be enclosed with the merchandise stipulated thereon.

2. A letter may be enclosed, provided that the wrapper is marked "Letter Enclosed" or "First-class Enclosure" immediately below the place for postage. Separate first-class postage is charged for such an enclosure in addition to the fourth-class charge for the parcel.

Special handling. To ensure that a parcel-post package receives the fastest handling and transportation, the special-handling service may be used, for an additional fee. It does not include special-delivery service. Priority mail or express mail can be used for parcels going over long distances when faster delivery of the parcel is desired.

PRINTED MATTER

Books and catalogs of 24 or more bound pages (at least 22 of which are printed) and weighing less than 16 ounces apiece are considered third-class mail. Other material which may be mailed at the third-class rate includes circulars and other printed matter, such as proof sheets, corrected proof sheets with related manuscript copy, and bills or statements of account produced by any photographic or mechanical process.

All other matter wholly or partly in writing, except authorized additions to second-, third-, and fourth-class mail, should be sent as first-class mail.

BULK MAILING

Items that are to be mailed at the special bulk-mailing rate should be enclosed in mail sacks or other suitable containers and separated according to ZIP Code area. The containers must be taken to the post office.

If the third-class rate is to be used, postage is computed by rates per pound on the entire mailing at one time. An annual bulk-mailing fee must be paid at or before the first mailing of each calendar year. In addition, a postage permit is required. Under this permit, which may be obtained from the post office for a fee, mail must be prepaid.

If an imprint is used instead of precanceled stamps or meter stamps, the permit imprint may be made by printing press, hand stamp, lithograph, mimeograph, multigraph, addressograph, or similar device. It may not be typewritten or hand-drawn. The style must conform to the specifications set forth by the United States Postal Service. Each imprint must show the name of the post office and the permit number.

The fourth-class bulk rate may be used if at least 300 pieces of separately addressed pieces are involved and if they are identical in weight.

EXPRESS MAIL

This service is available for fast delivery of mail or parcels over long distances. It provides and guarantees overnight delivery on a money-back basis. Several options are available for both private and business customers who require urgent mail service. However, it is not available at all postal facilities. This is the most expensive service.

AIRMAIL

Airmail is no longer specified as such within the 50 states of the United States, as all first-class mail with a destination more than a certain number of miles is routinely transported by air. Airmail service is also available for some parcels and for overseas mail. The word "AIRMAIL" should appear on all sides of such a parcel. An adhesive label for this purpose is available without charge at the post office. The return address of the sender must be shown on the address side of each air parcel.

SPECIAL POSTAL SERVICES

Insurance. To assure the sender that payment may be obtained for loss of, rifling of, or damage to domestic mail, insurance is available. The fee, which is charged in addition to the regular postage, is based on assessed value. By paying an additional charge, the sender is assured that an insured package will be delivered only to the addressee.

Third-class and parcel-post mail may be insured up to $400. Insurance may be obtained for merchandise mailed at priority or first-class rates. The post office generally obtains a receipt of delivery from the addressee for all articles that are insured for more than $15. Insured mail may contain incidental first-class enclosures, so long as they are noted on the face of the package and paid for at the first-class rate. The mail must bear the complete names and addresses of sender and addressee. Articles not sufficiently well packed and wrapped to withstand normal handling are not acceptable for insurance.

Collect on delivery. A patron can mail an article which has not been paid for and have the price and the cost of the postage collected from the addressee when the article is delivered. Collect-on-delivery service may be used for merchandise sent by parcel post, first-class, or third-class mail; and the article may be sent as registered mail. Collection is made for the cost of the merchandise and postage, plus the C.O.D. fee; the merchandise cost is returned to the sender by postal money order. The fees include insurance against loss or damage of the merchandise and are limited to a maximum valuation of $400; fees vary according to the amount to be collected.

Registered mail. Additional protection for valuable pieces, irreplaceable articles, regardless of value, and all items valued above $400, may be obtained by using registered mail. This service gives the sender evidence of mailing and delivery and provides security; the mail is controlled throughout the postal system. The sender is required by law to tell the postal clerk or, if the sender is a company, to enter on the company mailing bill the full value of mail presented for registry. The following list offers a guide to the required declaration of values of various types of valuable mail:

Kind of mail	Value to be declared
Negotiable instruments Instruments payable to bearer and matured interest coupons	Market value
Nonnegotiable instruments All registered bonds, warehouse receipts, checks, drafts, deeds, wills, abstracts, and similar documents Certificates of stock, including those endorsed in blank	No value or replacement cost if postal insurance coverage is desired
Money	Full value
Jewelry, gems, precious metals	Market value or cost
Merchandise	Market value or cost

Only first-class and priority mail may be registered. C.O.D. parcels may be registered but they will be accepted only at the rate for first-class mail. The registry fees are in addition to postage and include insurance protection up to $25,000 for domestic mail only. In the registry of international mail, the indemnity varies according to the country of the addressee.

Special delivery. Immediate delivery at the address of the recipient during prescribed hours and within certain distance limits may be assured by payment of a special-delivery fee. Payment of this fee does not insure the safety of delivery or provide for payment of indemnity; therefore, money or other valuables sent special delivery should be registered also. Insured, certified, and C.O.D. mail may be sent special delivery.

Fees for special-delivery mail sent by regular first class are based on weight. For all other classes of mail, fixed special-delivery fees apply. Special-delivery fees must be paid in addition to regular postage.

Special handling. Special-handling service is available on third- and fourth-class mail only, including insured and C.O.D. mail. It provides preferential handling in transportation, but does not provide special delivery. Special-handling parcels are delivered as regular parcel post is delivered. The special-handling fee, which is based upon weight, must be paid on all parcels that require special care, such as baby chicks and packaged bees.

Certified mail. Certified-mail service provides a receipt for the person mailing the item and a record of the delivery of the item from the post office from which it is delivered. No record is kept at the post office at which it is mailed. Certified mail is handled in the ordinary mails and is not covered by insurance. If the matter mailed has no intrinsic value, but the sender wishes to be sure that it has been sent to the correct point of receipt, this service is worthwhile.

Any item on which first-class or priority postage has been paid will be accepted as certified mail. This matter may be sent special delivery if the required postage is also paid. An additional fee is involved if delivery is restricted (i.e., delivery only to the person named in the address) or if a return receipt is requested.

Certificates of mailing. At a fee somewhat lower than that for certified mail, certificates of mailing furnish evidence of mailing only. No receipt is obtained upon delivery of mail to the addressee. The fee does not insure the article against loss or damage.

Return receipt. For mail that is certified, insured for more than $15, registered, or sent C.O.D., the sender may wish to have evidence that the mail was received. When such proof of delivery is desired, a return receipt should be requested at the time of mailing. It identifies the article by number, the signer, and the date of delivery. Evidence of the exact address of delivery may also be requested. Restricted delivery service may be requested if the sender wants the mail to be delivered only to the addressee or to a particular individual authorized in writing to receive the mail of the addressee. Each of these services requires an additional fee as well as the regular postage.

Money orders. A practical and safe method of sending money through the mail is by postal money order. The fees vary according to the amount sent and also according to whether the order is domestic or international. Up to $400 may be sent by a single postal money order, but there is usually no limitation on the number of orders that can be purchased at one time. Lost or stolen money orders can be replaced and copies of payments can be obtained for two years after date of payment.

INTERNATIONAL MAIL

International mail is divided into two general categories; International Postal Union mail and parcel post. The Postal Union mail includes two classes of matter:

1. LC mail (letters and cards): letters, letter packages, Aerogrammes (air letters), post cards, and postal cards.

2. AO mail (other articles): printed matter, samples, commercial papers, matter for the blind, and small packets.

The special postal services which apply to Postal Union mail are registration with a standard limited indemnity, insurance (though not to all countries), and special delivery in most countries. Consult the post office for details, including what marking the mail should bear.

A person or company who wishes to prepay a reply letter from another country may do so by sending the correspondent one or more international reply coupons, which may be purchased at U.S. post offices.

To avoid delay and inconvenience, postage on all foreign mail should be prepaid according to weight.

Prohibited articles. Certain articles of a dangerous or objectionable nature are generally prohibited in the international mail: poisons, narcotics, intoxicating liquors, most live animals, explosive or flammable articles, obscene or libelous matter, and so on. In addition to these, each country generally prohibits or restricts the importation of various other articles. Such information may be obtained at the post office, provided the country named has made its restrictions known to the post office.

Preparation of Postal Union mail. The address on all articles must be legible and complete, showing the street name and house number, or post-office box number, the name of the post office, province (if known), and the country (on the last line). If the item is addressed in a foreign language, the name of the post office, province, and country must also be shown in English. The sender's name and address should be shown in the upper left corner of the address side.

All Postal Union articles except letters and letter packages are required to be left unsealed, even if registered.

Mailers must endorse the envelopes or wrappers of all Postal Union articles except letters and post cards to show the classification under which they are being mailed; for example, "Printed Matter," "Printed Matter—Books." The words "Letter (Lettre)" should be written on the address side of letters or letter packages which, because of their size or manner of preparation, may be mistaken for mail of another classification.

In addition, airmail articles should be plainly endorsed "Par Avion" or have such a label affixed; articles intended for special delivery should be marked boldly as "Express" or "Special Delivery."

International parcel post. Parcel-post packages that exceed certain size limitations are not accepted for mailing to foreign countries. Consult the post office about these and other restrictions.

Special services are subject to variation, but in certain cases registration and insurance are possible. Special handling, with the same provisions as for domestic mail, may be secured.

Packages for overseas mailing must be even more carefully packed and wrapped than those being sent within the United States. Containers should be strong enough to protect the contents from damage caused by pressures of other packages in the mail and by variations in climate and altitude.

Registered or insured parcels must be sealed. Consult the post office to determine restrictions of individual countries.

Customs declarations and other forms. A parcel-post sticker and at least one customs declaration are required for parcel-post packages (surface or air) mailed to another country. To some countries a dispatch note or more than one declaration form may be required. Detailed information may be obtained at the post office or by writing to: U.S. Customs Service, Treasury Department, Washington, DC 20229.

FORWARDING MAIL

First-class mail. First-class mail may be forwarded from one city or town to another without the payment of additional postage for one year, provided an official U.S. Postal Service change-of-address form is filed with the post office. It may also be reforwarded without the payment of additional postage.

Second-class mail. Second-class mail will be forwarded for three months. If the addressee has moved within the same city or town, the mail will be forwarded to the new address without payment of additional postage. If the addressee moves out of town, the mail will not be forwarded unless the addressee leaves instructions indicating that he or she will pay forwarding postage for second-class mail. If mail is sent to the old address more than three months after the person has moved, the mailer will receive a notice giving the addressee's new address. If the new address is not known, the sender will receive a statement indicating why the mail was not delivered. This notice costs the mailer a small fee.

Third-class mail. A locally addressed circular or pamphlet mailed to a person who has moved will be destroyed unless the mailer marks it "Return Requested." If the mailing piece is a package and apparently of some value, it will be forwarded, and the addressee will be charged the forwarding rate.

Mail marked "Return Requested" will be returned to the sender with a notation advising of the new address or an explanation of why it could not be delivered. This notice costs a small fee.

Fourth-class (parcel-post) mail. If the addressee has left a forwarding address, a package will be delivered and the addressee will be charged additional postage, depending upon the weight of the package and the distance forwarded. If there is no forwarding address, the package will be returned to sender, and a charge will be made for the return postage.

Forwarding foreign mail. Mail arriving in this country from a foreign country may be forwarded to any destination within the United States without additional postage.

Mail may not be forwarded to another foreign country without rewrapping, procuring a customs declaration, and affixing new postage.

U.S. mail to be forwarded to a destination outside the country should always have any additional postage affixed before leaving the United States, because some countries charge double postage for mail arriving with postage due.

OTHER INSTRUCTIONS ABOUT MAIL

Recall of mail. At times it is desirable to recall a piece of mail that has already been taken to a post office or dropped into a mailbox. In such instances the sender must go to the post office and complete a written application and present a similar envelope or wrapper to identify the piece of mail being recalled.

Change of address. Prior to moving, each individual or firm should procure from the post office and complete the official U.S. Postal Service change-of-address form. Change-of-address cards are available in quantity, so that all correspondents and publishers of periodicals regularly received may be notified of the new address and the date of its effect. If possible, it is wise to notify the publishers of periodicals six or eight weeks before the move takes place, so that magazines and newspapers are not sent to the old address.

Undeliverable mail. First-class mail that bears no return address cannot be returned to the sender in the event that it is undeliverable. Therefore, it is imperative that all mail have a return address typed or written on it.

Franked mail. The federal government uses "franked" mail, that is, mail sent free of postage. The franked envelope may be used only for surface mail; it may not be used for overseas airmail unless the airmail postage is affixed. There is a federal penalty for misuse of franked mail.

Unmailable items. The following items may not be sent through the U.S. mails. In fact, penalties are imposed on the mailers of these items.

Meat and meat-food products without certificate of inspection

Plants and plant products not accompanied by required certificate: certain plants are prohibited from shipment into certain states by quarantine order (Before attempting to mail plants, consult a postal authority)

Poisons, except those for scientific use and those sent to licensed dealers.

Intoxicating liquors

Narcotics and other controlled substances as defined by federal regulations

Explosive, flammable, corrosive, or toxic substances

Live animals, except tiny ones that need no care, as bees, earthworms, or day-old chicks

Poisonous reptiles and insects and all kinds of snakes

Foul-smelling articles

Dangerous mechanical devices or machines

Sharp-pointed or sharp-edged tools insufficiently protected

Firearms capable of being concealed on the person (with exceptions)

Radioactive material, unless special permission is granted and special packaging and labeling requirements are met

Matter tending to incite arson, murder, assassination, insurrection, or treason

Indecent matter, written or other

Defamatory, dunning, or threatening matter on post cards or on the outside of any piece of mail

Endless-chain enterprises, or fraudulent matter

Mail opened by mistake. At times mail is delivered to the wrong address and opened by mistake. When this happens, the person who opens it should simply reseal the envelope with tape and write "Opened by Mistake." The mail should then be dropped into a mailbox or handed to the mail carrier.

EXPRESS

Most things that can be transported can be sent by express, but nothing irreplaceable should be sent by this means. Valuable papers, such as bonds, can be sent by express, provided that they can be replaced. Certain items are barred from express shipments, such as those containing acids or corrosives, antiques, artworks, coins, explosives, gems or jewelry, or uncrated household goods. Consult the nearest express agency office for other specific limitations.

Preparation for shipment. The following information must be given to the express company before a shipment can be made:

Consignee's name and local address

Value of shipment

Number of pieces of shipment and type of container

Weight

    Description of articles shipped
    Shipper's name and address
    Information regarding payment

The address of the shipper and the consignee should both be written on the packing slip and also enclosed in the package.

DOMESTIC AIR EXPRESS

Air express is available for those cities having airports. The service is extended to the areas surrounding such cities, but an additional charge is made to "off-line" points outside the area served by the airport. The nearest express office should be queried as to the exact points to which delivery is made without additional charge.

Many airlines accept small packages and envelopes for airport-to-airport delivery; the item will be held for pickup at the luggage-return area or at the air express office.

PACKAGE EXPRESS BY BUS

Bus lines offer package express within the United States and Canada. Consult them for information on rates, requirements, and restrictions, and for up-to-date schedules.

Prohibited articles. The following articles are not accepted for shipment by bus:

    Acids or corrosive substances
    Alcoholic beverages and liquors
    Animals, live, including birds and reptiles
    Articles packed in wet ice or water
    Batteries, electric-storage, wet
    Dangerous articles, including ammunition, explosives, and flammable materials
    Fluorescent signs
    Gases in cylinders
    Jewelry, when the declared value is more than $50
    Materials having a disagreeable odor
    Money
    Neon signs or bent neon tubing
    Wild game, killed
    X-ray tubes.

II   Telegrams, Cables, and Radio Messages

A telegram or cable comes instantly to mind when speed is of vital importance in sending a written message at home or abroad.

However, sending a telegram or cable does not necessarily mean that the message will be delivered within minutes or hours. There are different classes of service, some of which are considerably faster than others. Often a phone call is not only much faster but also less expensive. Even an overseas call may cost only a little more than a brief cable, and if the message can be delivered verbally rather than in writing, the additional expense may be justified by speed and certainty of receipt.

A key question, then, is whether the message *must* be delivered in print on paper with a record of when sent (and in some cases when received). Many companies and organizations understandably insist that such information as prices and specifications be submitted in a form that can be kept by them as a record—if not in letter form, then by telegram, cable, or telex. In such cases, however, the person who sends the telegram *must specify* that it be actually delivered to the recipient; otherwise, the message will be simply telephoned by the local Western Union to the recipient. Delivery of the printed message will follow by local mail only if requested.

Another key question is whether one message to one person is involved, or whether the same message will go to many people—for example, to all the men and women on a large sales force, or to all the dealers who sell a particular product. Western Union has effective systems for wide distribution of a specific message, including a comparatively inexpensive overnight service. The overnight service can be used to assure quick delivery of important messages in all parts of the country.

If a response is desired, it is advisable to specify how that response should be sent. For example, a travel agency may be asked to send a cable requesting a hotel room, with a cabled response of confirmation. But if the agent sends the cable by reduced-rate night service, and if the hotel responds similarly by delayed service, the exchange of cables may take three days rather than a few hours.

Because the rates and rules of telegraph, cable, and radio change frequently, no attempt will be made to specify costs or to provide detailed instructions as to the number of words transmitted at various base rates. Where such details appear, they are to be taken as examples rather than as specifics. The local Western Union office will provide the latest printed material on request (along with blank forms). The companies that handle cable and radio services will be indicated in the appropriate sections of this chapter.

TELEGRAPH SERVICE

Time of day. The time of day at which a telegram is sent is of vital importance. When a New York business office closes, a Chicago (Central Time) office has one hour left in the business day; a Denver (Mountain Time) office, two more hours; and a San Francisco (Pacific Time) office, three more hours. At 4:45 P.M. in New York there is time left to complete a pending deal in Chicago, thereby perhaps saving the company dollars that a day's delay may cost. (See Appendix 8.)

CLASSES OF SERVICE

Full-rate telegram (speed service). There is no special indication needed for sending a full-rate telegram. If the sender does not specify otherwise the telegraph message will be sent as a full-rate telegram. The characteristics of this class of service are as follows:

15 words to start with
Additional words charged at low extra-word rate
Address and signature not charged
Immediate transmission and delivery
May be sent in plain language or code
Fastest type of a message service available for sending and telephone delivery
   24 hours a day, 7 days a week

Mailgram. This service can be used when a low-cost, high-impact message is desirable. These messages are sent over Western Union's microwave and satellite networks to the addressee's post office and delivered by letter carrier with the next day's mail. The characteristics are:

100 words to start with
Additional charge for extra words
Name, address, and signature included in word count
Delivery guarantees not made by Western Union
Messages received before 7 P.M. destination time are generally delivered the next
   postal service day
Messages received after 7 P.M. may not be delivered until the second postal service
   day

Night letter (NL). A night letter may be sent at any time up to 2 A.M. for delivery no later than 2 P.M. of the next business day. On weekends or holidays deliveries are made to business offices when open, and other disposition will be made if instructions from the addressee are on file or if the sender specifically requests it. Deliveries are made to residences on any day. The minimum rate is for 100 words. Additional words are counted individually.

SELECTING THE CLASS OF SERVICE

Full-rate telegrams usually provide the most efficient service. Night letters are less expensive and are used when the speed of delivery is not an important consideration. Night letters can be used effectively to send information on which action is not required until the following morning or messages going out late in the business day.

When speed of service is important, a choice must be made between a full-rate telegram, a Mailgram, or an overnight telegram. For messages of less than 15 words the full-rate telegram is most efficient. For messages of over 15 words, it is generally less expensive to select an overnight telegram or the Mailgram, which is by far the least expensive.

Code words as well as plain language may be sent in full-rate messages, Mailgrams, and night letters at the prevailing rates.

TELEPHONING A TELEGRAM

Messages are now most often telephoned to a Western Union office and charged either to the monthly telephone bill or to a credit-card account. The person answering at Western Union will take any message given. Simply give the following information:

> Calling telephone number (for billing purposes)
> Class of service
> Addressee's name and address
> Message
> Sender's name and address

When dictating a message over the telephone, spell each difficult word.

PREPARING THE TELEGRAPH MESSAGE

Even if the message will be transmitted by telephone, it would be helpful for the secretary to type the message on one of the telegraph blanks provided by Western Union. The file copies will then most closely resemble the recipient's message. On this blank, the following information should be recorded:

> In the box at the upper right, indicate the class of service to be used, such as an overnight telegram, so that this fact may be checked against the bill from Western Union.
> Always date the message. In business questions often arise as to when a message was sent and when it was received.

Type in double space, using capital letters so that you will see the message as it will appear on the telegram itself.

Type the full name and address of the recipient. Use as many words in the address as are necessary to indicate the exact location of the addressee. When sending a telegram to a person in a large office building, be sure to include either the name of the company or the room number of the office, or both.

The ZIP Code must be included on Mailgrams, as these messages are delivered by the U.S. Postal Service. The ZIP Code should also be included on full-rate telegrams or night letters for quick transmission to branch offices.

States should be designated by using the two-letter Postal Service abbreviations, without periods. (See page 143.)

A well-written telegraph message is concise. Because the charges are based upon the number of words sent, each word in the message should convey meaning, and no word necessary to the meaning should be omitted.

Use nouns and verbs freely to convey the message. Often prepositions, pronouns, adjectives, and adverbs may be omitted without affecting the meaning of the message.

Omit salutations and complimentary closings.

Do not divide words at the end of the line.

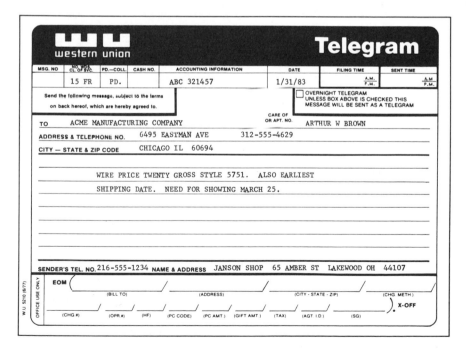

Western Union telegram form correctly filled out

TELEGRAPH COSTS

To calculate in advance the cost of telegraph messages, the secretary must have the rate sheets, which can be obtained from Western Union. Because rates are subject to change, it is important to check with the telegraph company to be sure that the rate sheets on file in the office are up to date.

The telegraph company charges nothing for the name and address of the addressee, unless more than one name is given (for example, "Henry Adams or Jeffrey Rose"). In this case, a charge is made for the alternate name.

The full name and address should be used, as:

```
Laura Allen  Room 304
Todd Leather Company
1616 West Berk Street
New York, NY  10003
```

"Mrs.," "Ms.," or "Miss" is generally used to signify that the recipient is a woman, although the use of a title is tending to decline in the business world. "Mr." is not used in telegrams unless no first name or intial is given. The titles "Dr.," "Rev.," "Major," "Hon.," and so forth may be used.

"Care of" may be sent without additional charge. "Hold for Arrival," followed by the time or a date, may be sent without additional charge.

```
Leon P. Adams, Hold for Arrival, 6 PM
        (or May 15)
Summit Hotel
New York, NY  10002
```

A telephone number may be sent free of charge when it accompanies the address of the addressee. The receiving telegraph office will then telephone the message and later mail a copy of the message to the addressee, if the request for this is made.

Report delivery. If a report of delivery of the message is desired, the words "Report Delivery" should be given after the addressee's name. The words "Report Delivery" are charged for. Immediately following delivery, a telegram is sent (and charged to) the sender, indicating the time and date of delivery.

Two addresses may be given, if necessary and a charge will be made for the alternate address. If report of delivery is to be requested, this may include (at an extra charge) the address to which the telegram was delivered as well as date and time. The inclusion of address must be requested in this case.

Personal delivery only. The notation "Personal delivery only" may be stipulated if the sender wishes to assure that delivery of the message will be made only to the addressee and to no one else.

"Will call" should be given immediately after the name in the address if someone is going to call at the telegraph office for a given message. The message will be held at the central telegraph station, but it can be quickly transmitted if it is called for at any branch office.

"Do not phone" may be given in the address at no extra charge.

Messenger delivery is available only to certain destinations, and the secretary will determine from Western Union whether the service can be requested in a particular instance. An additional charge is made for messenger delivery.

Multiple addressees. If copies of a message are to be sent to different persons, it is necessary to furnish only one copy of the message text and a list of the names and addresses. The message will be sent from the telegraph office to each of the addressees on the list.

Message to a passenger on a ship in port. Messages may be transmitted to ships at sea or to ships arriving in port and delivered to passengers. Give full details:

Name of passenger	Viola Acierno, passenger
Name of steamship line	Woodson Line
Name of ship and stateroom number (if known)	SS Calgary, Stateroom B202
Time of sailing and pier	4 PM sailing Pier 97
Departure port	New York, N.Y. 10004

WORD COUNT

Any word listed in a standard dictionary as one word will be counted as one word; this includes hyphenated words (as *self-defense*). That rule can be applied to all telegraphic messages. Nondictionary words or expressions are counted as one word for every five letters.

An abbreviation of five letters or less is counted as one word, provided it is written with no spacing: "COD" or "C.O.D." "AM" or "A.M."

Geographical names are counted according to the number of words as normally written. Examples:

New York City, 3 words	NYC, 1 word
St. Augustine, 2 words	
United States, 2 words	US, 1 word
North Carolina, 2 words	NC, 1 word

Proper names are counted by the number of words and initials they contain:

Van de Perle, 3 words
Vanderbilt, 1 word
P. Conners, 2 words

Each initial in a name is counted as a separate word:

A. F. Miller, 3 words
Sara B. Wolf, 3 words

A surname prefix, such as "Mac" in MacDougall, is not counted as a separate word when it is written without separation by a space. However, the "De" in De Berendinis is counted as a separate word because of the space.

Punctuation. Punctuation marks are free. Punctuation marks such as the period, comma, colon, semicolon, dash, hyphen, decimal point, parentheses, question mark, quotation marks, and apostrophe are neither counted nor charged for. On the other hand, an apostrophe used in a figure group to designate "feet" or a quotation mark used to designate "inches" is counted as a chargeable character (Example: $100'\ 7'' = 2$ words; $17'\ 9'' = 1$ word).

All words are counted; "stop," "comma," and "quote" are charged for as words when they are spelled out.

Figures and characters. Figures are counted as one word for a group of five figures or less:

67,383 = 1 word
1,343,682 = 2 words
1-12-65 = 1 word

Figures that are written out are counted as they are written:

thirty-six, 2 words
one hundred five, 3 words

Signs such as #, $, &, and the / (diagonal) for fractions are counted and charged for in figure groups, but the diagonal counts as a separate word in expressions such as "and/or."

#22 (3 characters), 1 word
$36.42 (5 characters), 1 word
2 1/2 (transmitted 2-1/2), 1 word
and/or, 3 words
12/2/68 (7characters), 2 words

The symbols ¢ and @ cannot be transmitted and should be written out. The percent sign %, is transmitted as 0/0 and counts as three characters.

Signatures. Only one individual's name is carried without extra charge, but a title, a department name, or the name of a firm added to an individual's name will be carried without charge. Examples:

> Ruth M. Henderson, Treasurer
> Ruth M. Henderson, Credit Department
> Ruth M. Henderson, Woodrow Lumber Company

When an individual's name is followed by a title and a firm name, the title is charged for. "Sales Manager" would be charged for in the following example:

> Ruth M. Henderson, Sales Manager
> Woodrow Lumber Company

MEANS OF TRANSMITTING MESSAGES

The secretary may have several choices as to how the domestic telegram may be filed with the telegraph company.

Desk-Fax. The Desk-Fax is a unit of facsimile equipment. The sender may either write or type the message and place it around the drum of the Desk-Fax. Inside the machine an electric eye then scans the telegraph message and automatically sends an exact reproduction of it directly to the Western Union office in the area.

Private-wire system. Regardless of size or complexity, the function of any private-wire system furnished and maintained by Western Union is to provide instantaneous, continuous communication between stations on the system.

The simplest private-wire system is a two-point channel with a teleprinter at each end that both sends and receives messages. These machines may be on two different floors of the same building or hundreds of miles apart, perhaps connecting the company with a branch office or a correspondent.

Large private-wire systems may be thought of as roughly resembling a huge wagon wheel in their physical layout. Around the rim of the wheel are the stations that send and receive messages. These stations are linked to each other by a switching center at the wheel's hub. In addition, if there is a large volume of communications between two points on the rim, these points can also be connected with each other by direct circuits as well as to the switching center at the hub. A major advantage of such a system is that it permits a message to be routed instantly from any station on the system to any or all of the other stations through the central switching station at the hub. Just as in the case of simple two-point circuits, the extensive private-wire systems are engineered to provide two-way record communication between any two stations on the system.

Because of such technological advancements as integrated data processing (IDP) and electronic computers, greater importance has devolved upon high-speed, reliable communications. Through private-wire systems it is possible to provide sufficient volumes of data at a centralized processing center to utilize the full potential benefits to be derived from a computer installation. Private-wire systems are engineered to handle either administrative messages or bits of data in machine language over the same system with equal facility.

SERVICES OFFERED

Telex service. Telex is a dial-direct subscriber-to-subscriber service for record and data communications made available by Western Union within the United States and, through connections with other carriers, to Canada, to Mexico, and to most overseas countries. A subscriber to this Western Union service is provided with a console-mounted teleprinter, supplemented with dial and automatic answer-back equipment. Connection with another subscriber in the United States, Canada, or Mexico is established within eight seconds by dialing the distant subscriber's station number. The automatic answer-back feature enables the subscriber to confirm the correctness of the connection established, thus permitting transmission even though the called subscriber's station is unattended. There is a fixed monthly service charge, plus a charge for the amount of actual time used during the connection of each telex call. There is no minimum period charged for on telex calls to stations in the United States, Canada, and Mexico. For subscribers desiring to prepare their communications in advance, and thereby keep their telex call usage time to a minimum, Western Union offers, at an additional charge, alternate equipment that enables the subscriber to prepare and transmit perforated tape.

Tel(T)ex service. An additional service available to Western Union telex subscribers permits the subscriber to send messages to nonsubscribers at major cities in the United States and Canada. The telex subscriber dials and transmits his message to the destination city telegraph office, where delivery is made to the addressee. A flat-rate delivery fee is made for each Tel(T)ex message, plus the usual charge for the time used in the telex transmission of the Tel(T)ex message.

Teletypewriter exchange service (TWX). Subscribed to by many companies for direct subscriber-to-subscriber transmission of telegraph messages, TWX service is made possible by the installation in the subscriber's office of a Teletype machine which can be connected by wire to Teletype machines of other TWX subscribers within the United States. A monthly rental is made for the equipment, and the subscriber is billed for each three-minute period of usage, with an additional charge made for each additional minute or fraction of a minute of usage. TWX service is also available to Canadian subscribers, the basic charge being for one minute.

Personal opinion message (POM) service. A special service offering reduced rates permits the sending of telegraph messages expressing the sender's views on current issues to the President of the United States, the Vice President, senators, and congressmen in Washington, or to the governor, lieutenant governor, and legislators at a state capital.

Speedata. At the point of origin, data on sales, payrolls, and inventory are sent on regular telegraph forms and converted to punched tape before being delivered to the recipient. The customer may select the speed of service desired and send data as a full-rate telegram or a night letter.

Wirefax. A public facsimile service between major cities provides direct transmission of letters, drawings, or any graphic materials.

Telegraphic money orders. Money may be sent quickly and safely as day money orders which are delivered within five hours during the open hours of the destination office or as overnight money orders which are delivered before 2 P.M. the following day. Money-order payments in foreign countries are usually made in the currency of the country of destination and are subject to prevailing exchange rates. In addition to the charges for a message to the destination city, a money-order fee applies, depending on the amount of money transmitted.

To send money by telegraph, complete a telegraphic money-order form, giving the name and address of the recipient, any message, and the sender's name and address; then deliver the money and the completed form to the telegraph office.

At the destination, the telegraph office will deliver a money-order draft or notify the recipient by telephone that the money may be called for at the telegraph office. Before a money-order draft can be cashed, the person is asked to present evidence of identity.

Special greetings. Suggested texts for greeting messages are available at the telegraph office, or the sender may compose an original message. Appropriate telegraph blanks are available for all major holidays and other occasions.

INTERNATIONAL COMMUNICATIONS

Technological improvements in communications have resulted in increased speed and capacity, as well as in reduction of costs for sending cablegrams. The use of sophisticated computers now permits automatic electronic handling of messages through high-frequency radio channels, submarine cable, or radio satellite.

In addition to international telegrams, also referred to as cablegrams, there are two other services: telex and leased-channel service.

Telex. Telex service (see page 170) is available for overseas written communications over Western Union telex or TWX. The service is offered by ITT World Communications, Inc., RCA Communications, Inc., and Western Union International, Inc. To communicate with firms having telex equipment in their offices overseas, the procedure is to call the Telex Center of any one of the three international carriers, identify yourself, and give the area code for the country being called, plus the telex number of the correspondent.

By means of Data Telex, it is now possible to send some 1,500 words per minute over special broad-band channels of the international carriers for the transmission of intelligence of any type. Special computers and data equipment must be installed at both ends of these circuits in the carrier's and the correspondents' offices in order to take advance of this high-speed service. The rates for Data Telex service, where it is available, carry a minimum charge for each connection. Special arrangements must be made with the international carriers, as this service is limited and must be scheduled in advance.

Leased-channel service. Through one of the major companies providing international communication service, leased-channel service provides instantaneous two-way radio communication 24 hours a day for firms whose volume of international messages warrants it. Service may be leased for a month or longer.

The company renting the service may transmit quickly and efficiently messages which would otherwise be handled by cable, airmail, or telephone.

Cablegrams. Cablegrams may be written in any language that can be expressed in roman letters or in secret language. A minimum charge is based on seven words, including the address and signature. Twenty-four-hour service is available for rapid transmission of messages. Each secret-language, nondictionary word is counted at the rate of five characters, or fraction of five characters, to the word.

SENDING INTERNATIONAL MESSAGES

ITT World Communications, Inc. issues periodically revised rate folders, which serve as a handy reference for sending international telegraph and telex messages to virtually all parts of the world. Free copies may be obtained from ITT World Communications, Inc., 67 Broad Street, New York, New York 10004.

Collect messages may not be used for foreign countries except for Canada and Mexico.

The basic regulations are:

Each word of the address, text, and signature is counted and charged for.

Each plain-language, standard dictionary word is counted at the rate of 15 characters, or fraction of 15 characters, to the word.

Figures, letters, signs, or combinations of them are counted as five characters per word.

If the name of a place is a compound word (e.g., Stratford on Avon), the name of destination point is joined and counted as one word, regardless of length.

In figure or letter groups, punctuation is counted as one character each.

Examples	No. of characters	Words charged
15,545	6	2
6,121	5	1
127,545	7	2

Punctuation used in conjunction with words is counted as one word each and transmitted only on special request of the sender. Exceptions are the two signs forming the parentheses ( ) and quotations marks (" " or ' '), which are counted as one word.

Examples	Words charged
( )	1
" "	1
' '	1

Those punctuation marks and signs acceptable for transmission upon the sender's recommendation are:

period (.)
comma (,)
colon (:)
division sign ($\div$)
question mark (?)
apostrophe or feet or minutes (')
inches or seconds (")
hyphen, dash, or subtraction sign (-)
diagonal (/)

Cable code address. A company which sends a volume of cable messages will find it economical to register a cable code address of its choice at any Western Union office. Such an address enables a company to economize on words in the signature of a message, thus reducing the cost.

Prepaid messages. A sender of a cablegram may wish to prepay the charges for a reply to the original message. When this is done, the indicator "RP" (reply paid) and figures showing the amount prepaid are inserted before the addressee's name.

Forwarding messages. Cablegrams may be forwarded to an addressee who has left the place to which the message was addressed. If the sender wishes to assure delivery in such cases, the indicator "FS" is placed before the addressee's name. A charge is made for the additional word.

Delivery after business hours. If the sender wishes to be assured that the message will be delivered by the foreign telegraph office after the close of the regular business day, the word "NUIT" should be indicated before the addressee's name. An additional charge is made for the one word. (For time differences in various parts of the world, see Appendix 8.)

Report of time delivery. When the sender wishes to receive a report as to the time of delivery of the cable, the indicator "PC" should be inserted before the addressee's name. The cost is for one word plus a six-word reply.

RADIO MARINE SERVICE

SHORE TO SHIP

Only full-rate telegraphic service is available from the United States to ships anywhere in the world.

Plain or secret language or a combination of both may be used. Plain-language words are counted at 15 characters to the word; secret-language words are counted at five characters to the word. Addresses and signatures are charged for.

Preparing messages. Write "INTL" above the name and address to stipulate "international message." The address must include the name of passenger, name of ship, ship's general location, and radio station.

Marine Radio stations are written as one word, as SANFRANCISCORADIO or KEYWESTRADIO.

```
INTL
William Alberts
SS United States
North Atlantic
Newyorkradio
```

Speeding messages. When speed is a primary factor, messages may be filed directly with the coast station serving the general vicinity of the ship. If the sender is not familiar with the coast station, the message may be telephoned or filed TWX (see page 170) by indication CHATHAMRADIO for ships in the Atlantic Ocean and SANFRANCISCORADIO for ships in the Pacific Ocean.

RECEIVING TELEGRAMS AND CABLEGRAMS

A message of such urgency that the sender selected telegraphic service should be delivered immediately to the addressee. In cases when the addressee is not in the office, the message may be read by the secretary or some other person given the responsibility of attending to urgent messages.

Code messages. If a code word is included in a message, the meaning of the word should be written above it before the message is passed along to the person for whom it was intended. Should a major part of the message be in code, the decoded message should be typed on a separate sheet and attached to the original message.

Copies. When a copy of a telegraphic message is desired, a facsimile may be made on any photographic duplicator.

III   The Telephone

TELEPHONE TECHNIQUES

The secretary is expected to be knowledgeable in the use of the telephone. It is also important to keep up with the constantly expanding and changing services available from the telephone company, as well as the many and varied pieces of equipment that can add to the efficient operation of the business office. The telephone is the most frequently used audio-communication

Remote Telephone Answering and Recording Device

Telex Teleprinter

176

medium in the business world. The dependence upon this instrument has grown so that currently over 800 million telephone calls are made daily.

The reputation and good will of the employer and the firm may depend upon the secretary's approach and skill in using the telephone. Although most people in our society begin to use the telephone in early childhood, perhaps the majority of them still need to be trained in proper telephone techniques. An impressive way to point out defects in techniques, and one that results in a rapid and desirable change, is to make a recording or tape of a telephone conversation. Such a recording emphasizes the faults in telephone techniques and vividly points out areas needing improvement. Many organizations, even though they are efficiently organized, lose customers, money, and good will simply because employees answering calls are incoherent, curt, or impolite.

The caller at the other end of the phone cannot see the person who is talking. This should be remembered at all times, for it means that the caller has no visual image on which to base impressions. The telephone caller's attention is focused entirely upon the audio impressions coming over the wires. If these sounds are jarring or unpleasant, a busy executive may quickly lose patience and discontinue association with the firm in question. On the other hand, a pleasant and understanding voice coming over an inanimate instrument can accomplish wonders. The power of the spoken word can and does exert a great impact upon the listener.

The telephone is not a nuisance instrument designed to interrupt the secretary in the midst of some important or complicated task. It is, rather, a vital business communication facility that assists the employee in carrying out duties and responsibilities owed to the employer.

In order to enhance one's telephone personality, it is necessary to inject variety and flexibility into the voice, so as to convey mood and attitude in telephone conversations. These qualities can be obtained through pitch, inflection, and emphasis. The development of these qualities is individual. A high-pitched voice may convey an impression of childishness and immaturity or of impatience and irritability. On the other hand, a voice that is well modulated carries the impression of culture and polish. "Pitch" in speaking, like "pitch" in music, refers to the key in which one speaks. Everyone has a range of tone within which a pleasant speaking voice is possible, and it can be consciously controlled. Each person must be conscious of his or her own range and practice utilizing it effectively. An individual is said to speak in a "modulated" voice when the pitch is in the lower half of the possible range. This tonal range carries best and is easiest to hear over the telephone.

Enunciation. In cultivating an interesting individual telephone personality, voice development alone is insufficient; it is essential also that the speaker enunciate clearly and distinctly. A garbled and indistinct speech pattern will annoy the listener who cannot understand what is being said. Do not be afraid to move the lips. One cannot form rounded vowel sounds or distinct consonants unless the lips accomplish their function. It is not necessary to exaggerate or to become stilted; clear enunciation should be made a part of the secretary's natural, daily speech pattern, because it is just as important in face-to-face conversations as in telephone conversations. Above all, be sure that your voice reflects your personality, that it transmits alertness and pleasantness, that is is natural, distinct, and expressive, and neither too loud nor too soft. Avoid repetitious, mechanical words and phrases, and try to enunciate in a manner that is neither too fast nor too slow.

ANSWER PROMPTLY

Answering a business telephone call is similar to welcoming a visitor. Therefore, it is essential that each call be greeted by a prompt, effective, and pleasing answer.

The telephone should be placed on the secretary's desk so that it is readily accessible. A pad and pencil or pen should be kept handy in order to jot down necessary information. These should not be used for doodling when speaking on the phone; this habit distracts the secretary from the business at hand and interferes with giving the caller undivided attention.

When the telephone rings, answer it promptly—at the first ring, if possible. Try not to put incoming calls immediately on "hold"; many callers find this practice infuriating. If it becomes increasingly necessary to do this, the employer should be alerted. It may be desirable to install another telephone line and to hire another person, if only for the busiest hours of the day, to help handle incoming calls.

If the secretary finds it necessary to leave the desk, arrangements should be made to have someone else answer the telephone and take the messages during that interval. The instrument should not be left unattended. An unanswered telephone becomes an instrument of failure—failure to the company because of the loss of customers and failure of the individuals responsible. It is well to inform the person who covers the telephone why the secretary will be away from the desk and for how long. Armed with this information, the one who answers the telephone can be more helpful to the caller.

This courtesy, of course, should be extended in both directions. Each secretary should reciprocally cover the calls of colleagues when it becomes necessary for them to be away from their desks so that telephones are never unattended for any period of time.

IDENTIFY WHO IS ANSWERING

For efficiency, the office should be identified immediately when the phone is answered. The secretary's name may also be given. It is correct to say, "Mr. Wright's office, Miss Dubrowski speaking," or the firm name may be used, as, "Smith and Grey; this is Mr. Lopez." The identification formula depends upon the size and structure of the organization. When the telephone is answered in this fashion, the caller is assured that the proper office has been reached. Avoid answering the business telephone by saying, "Hello." Using this form of greeting is much like saying, "Guess who this is," and is unbusinesslike. Business people have no time to play guessing games, and this form of address can become irritating particularly if it is necessary to call the office frequently.

In answering calls for others, identify yourself and the office of the person whose calls are being taken. For example, "Miss Jone's office, Mr. Liska speaking." Unless this is done, the caller will not know whether the right person has been reached at all. If the caller expects to hear the voice of Miss Jones's secretary, he or she may be taken aback when an unfamiliar voice comes over the wire. The fact that the correct office has been reached is made clear at once.

IDENTIFY WHO IS CALLING

The wise secretary develops a keen ear and learns to recognize the voices of important or frequent callers. However, a word of caution. Do not become too sure of an infallible ear, for voices may sound different over the telephone. If the voice is known beyond a doubt, use the caller's name when speaking. If the voice has been identified correctly, the caller will be pleased to be recognized and addressed by name. Then speak *to the person* at the other end of the wire, not *at the telephone*. If the secretary was incorrect in identifying the voice before divulging any information, little harm was done, since the caller will make the correction. Apologize tactfully and take up the business at hand. However, when the name of the caller is not revealed and/or the nature of the business is not identified, the secretary's skill at diplomacy comes into play. Many executives prefer their secretaries to screen incoming calls. This must be done with tact and discretion. In some cases the executive will speak with anyone who calls but would like to know beforehand who is calling and the nature of the business. It is the secretary's duty to obtain this information before transferring the call to the executive. Curtness and rudeness must be avoided in doing so. It is correct to say, for example, "May I tell Mr. Brown who is calling?" or "Mrs. Winslow is talking on another line. Would you care to wait, or may I have her call you? I believe her other call may take some time." or "Mr. Zobkiw is in conference. May I help you?" Be sincere and courteous in your explanation, but do not divulge information unnecessarily. Your goal is simply to find out tactfully who is calling if you can.

SCREENING CALLS

Although some executives answer the telephone themselves, many depend upon their secretaries to answer all incoming calls. The secretary must, therefore, be familiar with the executive's preferences. It is important to learn which calls the secretary is expected to handle, which are to be referred to the executive, and which should be transferred to someone else. Consequently, the secretary must classify telephone callers accurately and quickly. Every call is important. Enough information must be ascertained to classify the call. A caller cannot be allowed to get to the end of a long inquiry before being referred to the proper person. In order to forestall this, the secretary may make a discreet vocal sound that may cause the caller to pause slightly so that the secretary may say "Mr. Chan in the shipping department should be able to help you with this. Please let me transfer your call to him."

Generally the calls that can be handled by the secretary are as follows:

Requests for information. The secretary can handle this type of call if the information is not confidential, and if there is no doubt concerning the facts. Sometimes it may be necessary to check with the employer before imparting information. If any complications arise, it is always wiser to turn the call over to the executive.

Requests for appointments. The secretary is sometimes authorized to make appointments for the employer. However, both the executive's and the secretary's diary should be checked before any appointments are made in order to avoid conflicts. If the employer is out of the office, the appointment should be verified immediately upon return. Commitments could easily have been made about which the executive had either forgotten to inform the secretary or the opportunity had not yet arisen to have had them entered in the desk calendars.

Receiving information. Often the secretary can conserve the employer's time by taking down telephone information. If the message is taken in shorthand, this must be transcribed as soon as possible and placed on the employer's desk.

Transferring calls. If the call cannot be handled by the secretary or the employer, it should be transferred to the office that can give the caller the information sought. This should be done only with the caller's permission, however. If transferral is refused, obtain the information and call back. If the caller agrees to a transfer, make sure that the right office is reached before hanging up and give the person in that office sufficient information so that the caller will not need to repeat it.

In taking calls from persons who wish to speak to the executive directly, the secretary must know how to handle the following situations tactfully, discreetly, and diplomatically.

1. The employer is in and free. The executive is informed who is calling. On occasion, if the caller is well known to the employer and someone to whom the executive talks frequently, the secretary may signal the executive to pick up the telephone.

2. The employer is in but does not want to be disturbed. The caller is told that the executive is engaged at the moment and asks whether a message may be taken. If the caller insists on speaking to the executive personally, ask if a call back may be made as soon as the employer is free.

3. The employer is in another office in the building. The secretary should ascertain whether the executive will be available for telephone calls when away from the office. Generally only the most urgent calls should be transferred under such circumstances.

TAKING MESSAGES

It is good practice to keep a written record of all incoming calls, particularly when the executive is away from the office. In recording the call, the secretary should indicate the time the call was received; the name, business affiliation, and telephone number of the caller; and the message. The note may be signed with the secretary's initials. If the message is from an out-of-town caller, the area code or the telephone operator's number should also be recorded, so that the executive can return the call in a short time and without confusion. It is best when taking a message to read it back to the caller in order to avoid errors or misunderstandings. Messages should always be taken verbatim. Be patient and pleasant but persistent. If you do not understand, ask the caller to spell out both first and last names if necessary. If numbers are involved, repeat the sequence for verification. Taking a telephone message accurately often saves calling back to check information. Then again, if a message is completely garbled, it may be impossible to call back and a valuable contact could be forever lost.

When a call is taken, the "phone message" slip should be placed on the executive's desk immediately. The secretary will also anticipate the executive's needs by attaching to the slips any material (possibly annotated) that may be necessary for reference in order to conclude the transaction successfully— back correspondence, a bill, price lists, or whatever may assist the executive in handling the call intelligently.

To be able to handle the incoming calls more efficiently, the secretary should know where the executive will be when away from the office, whether urgent messages can be relayed, and the expected time of return to the office.

Also, in taking calls for other persons in the office, as suggested above, it is helpful if one can state when the person called will return or whether the call can be transferred somewhere else. It is best to offer whatever information possible; otherwise the caller may get the impression of being put off with an excuse. Be courteous, and use discretion in explaining an absence from the office. It is less offensive to say, "Miss Jones is away from her desk just now. May I have her call you, or would you prefer to leave a message?" than to say bluntly, "She's out," or "This is her coffee break," or "I don't know where she is." The secretary must always use tact in dealing with callers, whether it be for one's own executive or for another secretary whose calls are being taken.

TAKING ACTION

The secretary should promise the caller some definite action and see to it that the promise is kept. If the caller is told that the executive will call back, then this information must be conveyed to the employer so that the call can be made. A broken promise can result in a canceled order or a lost customer, and it may take many months to regain lost good will.

On some calls that the secretary can handle, more information may be needed than is within immediate reach. Therefore, if it becomes necessary to leave the telephone to look up the necessary information, inform the caller of this fact and of the length of time it may take to obtain the material. Offer the caller a choice of waiting or of being called back. The customer should never be left waiting for an unreasonable amount of time at the other end of the wire. If a promise is made to call back with the needed information, this promise must be honored.

If the caller is waiting to speak to the executive, the secretary should reassure the caller periodically that the call will be connected as soon as the employer is free. Otherwise the caller will be uncertain as to whether the call is still connected, and a minute's silent delay will seem like a half-hour's wait. When the secretary is ready to transfer the call, thank the customer for waiting.

COMPLETING THE INCOMING CALL

At the completion of the call, indicate readiness to terminate the conversation by summing up the details. Use the caller's name when saying a pleasant "Goodbye." It is courteous to wait for the caller to terminate the call first; the secretary who is too hasty in hanging up the receiver may cost the firm money. The impression may be given that the caller's business is of little importance to the organization because the call is cut short. Permitting the caller to say "Goodbye" first also allows time for last-minute orders or special instructions. The receiver should be replaced gently in its cradle, for the pleasantest "Goodbye" can be spoiled by the jarring sound of a receiver dropped into position. It is like slamming the door after a visitor. The abruptness may not be intentional, but the effect is the same. Do not hang up until your caller has done so first.

PERSONAL CALLS

Because of the secretary's status and the prestige of that position, an example should be set for the office personnel by refraining from making and accepting personal calls during business hours except those that stay strictly within the rules set by the employer. The policy of the company or executive should be determined by the secretary at the very beginning of employment.

TELEPHONE DICTATION

Frequently the secretary is called upon to take dictation over the telephone. For this reason a shorthand notebook and pen should be placed near the telephone and ready for use. The caller is always informed of the fact that the conversation will be taken by the secretary. The secretary picks up the receiver and indicates readiness to record the proceedings. In the case of telephone dictation, unlike dictation taken at the employer's desk, the dictator cannot tell whether the secretary is getting all the information. Therefore it is necessary for the secretary to repeat the material phrase by phrase as it is taken down in shorthand. This informs the dictator as to the rate of dictation, clarity of reception, and errors in grammar or facts. Corrections can then be made immediately instead of waiting until the end of the dictation, which may lead to confusion. If the dictation is too fast, it is best to indicate this immediately. It is a good practice to read back the notes at the termination of the dictation to ensure that the correct information was received and recorded and to correct any misinterpretations. The notes should be transcribed as soon as possible, and a copy should be sent to the telephone dictator. Of course, if the transcription equipment being used is one of those which can be utilized for recording telephoned dictation, the caller will be able to complete the dictation far more rapidly.

TELEPHONE REFERENCE MATERIALS

The efficient secretary must be cognizant of the available sources of information that will be of help in placing a call expeditiously, skillfully, and economically. A secretary should be familiar with the directories and booklets published by the telephone company, which contain reference information. Telephone directories contain three general sections—the introductory pages, the alphabetical listing of subscribers (which may be divided into subsections), and the classified section, familiarly known as "the Yellow Pages." In many areas of the country all three sections appear in one volume of the telephone directory. However, in metropolitan areas where the listings are voluminous, the classified section is a separate book.

The introductory section gives instructions on what numbers to call in various types of emergencies, where to place service calls, how to ask for directory assistance, how to make mobile and marine calls, and the different types of calls that can be made. It lists area codes for faster calling and sample rates for long-distance and person-to-person calls. It explains how to make collect calls; how to call overseas; how to call the telephone company's business office and the operators who handle customer information; where to pay bills and transact business in person; and what modern telephone services are available to the customer. A map illustrates area code zones.

The subscriber section lists in alphabetical sequence the names, addresses, and telephone numbers of all the telephone subscribers in a locality, borough, town, village, city, or county. Sometimes the kind of business or the occupation of a subscriber is also shown. In some large directories, business, professional, and organizational listings are given in a separate section from that for residences. Government offices may also be listed in still another section.

At the top outside corner of each page guide names, or "telltales," indicate the first and last listings on the page for quick location of the page on which a particular name appears. If a name might be spelled in several ways, a cross-reference spelling directs the user to additional listings. The divisions, departments, or branch offices of an organization with separate telephone listings are usually indented under the firm name. Alternate call listings can likewise be found in the telephone directory. These listings indicate telephone numbers to be called when no one answers the regular numbers. Governmental agencies and state, county, and municipal offices are shown with major headings for the principal listing and indented entries for subordinate departments and divisions.

The local alphabetical and classified directories are usually distributed to all subscribers. Out-of-town directories may be purchased by calling the telephone business office.

In some cities, street-address directories are available and may be rented from the telephone company. These directories list telephone numbers according to the alphabetical and numerical arrangements of streets in that city. They are of special value and usefulness to credit and collection agencies and for companies or organizations who desire to make up mailing lists.

DESK TELEPHONE FILES

For efficiency and expediency, a desk telephone file of numbers and area codes should be compiled. This list consists of (1) business numbers the employer calls frequently and, possibly, taxi, railroad-terminal, and airlines numbers; (2) emergency numbers for ambulance service, fire department, police department, and so on; (3) personal numbers of the employer's family; (4) extension numbers in other offices; and (5) frequently called long-distance numbers, with notations indicating the difference in time zones. Unlisted numbers should be added to this list, with an identifying mark indicating the nature of such a number. Unlisted numbers are never revealed without specific instructions from the executive to do so. They were given to the employer for personal use, and this fact should be respected.

It is a good idea when compiling a desk telephone list to make it as informative as possible. The secretary should identify individual names by noting title and company affiliation in addition to the address and telephone number and area code. In entering the name, address, and telephone number of an organization, also indicate the name and title or department of the person or persons with whom the secretary or the employer talk most frequently.

The placement of the desk telephone list depends upon its size. If quite short, it may be taped neatly to the top or the slide panel of the desk; if long, it may be kept in a book or on a rotary file attached to or near the telephone.

ASSEMBLING DATA FOR OUTGOING CALLS

In order to place outgoing calls quickly for the employer, the secretary should master all the telephone techniques that enable one to do this skillfully. Be absolutely certain of the telephone number before calling. It will save time, trouble, and irritation if the number is checked with the desk list, telephone directory, or correspondence file before calling.

Then assemble all the information that may be necessary to conduct the business transaction when the call is put through. It may be necessary to obtain materials from the files to refresh the executive's memory on previous business or other information that will be of help in making a successful call. All pertinent material should be placed on the executive's desk before the call is made.

It is also a good practice to be sure the executive will be free and available to take the call as soon as it goes through. No one likes to be called and then find that it is necessary to wait because the caller is talking on another line or is otherwise not ready to take the call immediately. Delay may not only lower the prestige of the company and the executive and cause annoyance but also prove costly to the firm making the call.

The question frequently arises as to which executive should answer first. Courtesy prescribes that the caller should be on the line, ready to talk, when the person called is put on the line by his or her own secretary, particularly if the person called outranks the caller. The secretary should put the executive on the line immediately, if possible. This can be done readily if the secretary identifies the employer when the call is answered. The secretary at the other end will then be able to transfer the call to the person called without delay or immediately inform the caller how to reach that individual.

TELEPHONE SERVICES

In addition to business calls within the local community or surrounding areas, it frequently becomes necessary to place calls to more distant points. The ability to handle long-distance calls capably will enhance the secretary's value to the employer.

TOLL CALLS

Long-distance calls are those made from one town or city to another town or city outside of a local calling area. A charge is made for such calls in addition to the charge for the regular telephone service. The amount of the charge depends upon the distance, the type of service requested, the time of day or night the call is made, and the time taken for the conversation.

There are two classes of long-distance calls—station-to-station and person-to-person.

Station-to-station calls. Any state in the United States can be reached by direct dialing today. The telephone directory carries a listing of cities and states and their area codes. In order to place a call to any of these localities, dial the area code and then the local telephone number of the individual to be reached. (In some areas, "1" must be dialed first.) If the city or town is not listed at the front of the telephone directory, refer to the area code directory, then call the directory assistance operator in that area and give the name and address of the party you want to reach. A station-to-station call is made to a particular telephone number, and the caller speaks to anyone who answers the telephone. Therefore, if someone answers the ring, the individual making the call is charged for it, and the charges start as soon as the call is answered. However, this type of call is less costly, is more frequently made, and is usually faster than the person-to-person call.

Person-to-person calls. To place a person-to-person call, the secretary dials zero, dials the three-digit area code, and then dials the telephone number; at this point the operator intercepts and the secretary gives the name of the individual being called. (Again, in some areas, "1" must be dialed first.) When the call is put through, the person called may not be present or available to take the call. Then a decision may have to be made as to whether someone else at that number can handle the transaction. A person-to-person call is made to a particular person only, and the caller is not charged for the call unless the person called is reached or the caller consents to speak to some other specifically identified individual. Charges start as soon as the caller consents to the call and begins speaking; therefore, the secretary should not start a conversation, but must make sure that the employer is ready to take the call immediately.

Direct distance dialing. Almost all calls in the United States and abroad may be put through by means of direct distance dialing. A list of the area codes one must use for direct dialing is found at the beginning of the telephone directory or in the expanded area code directory available from the telephone company. The direct dialing system works on a three-digit area code, which is dialed first, followed by the local telephone number. There are no two areas that have the same area code, nor are there two identical telephone numbers in an area. The numbers of adjacent geographical area codes are widely different numerically to help avoid confusion and error. It is a quick and accurate system. If a wrong number is reached, the secretary, before disconnecting, should ascertain the name of the city that was reached. Then dial the operator, or in some cases the credit bureau, and promptly report that an incorrect destination was reached, so that the telephone bill will not reflect a charge for the wrong number. Also, if the transmission was poor or the call was cut off, the operator or the credit bureau should be called in order that the appropriate adjustment may be made.

The phone directory also explains how to use direct dialing for credit-card and collect calls and for overseas calls.

Time differences. It is vital to check the differences in time when planning to place a long-distance call. One must be aware not only that this country is divided into time zones, but also that certain regions change to daylight-saving time during the summer months and that differences in time exist in all countries. For example, the United States (excluding Alaska and Hawaii) is divided into four standard-time zones: Eastern, Central, Mountain, and Pacific. Each zone is one hour earlier than the zone immediately to the east of it: when it is 12 noon Eastern Standard Time, it is 11 A.M. in the Central zone, 10 A.M. in the Mountain zone, and 9 A.M. Pacific time. Greenwich

Mean Time, which is the mean solar time of the meridian at Greenwich, England, is used as the basis for standard time throughout most of the world. For specific time information, consult the tables in Appendix 8.

APPOINTMENT CALLS

The telephone operator is asked to put through a person-to-person call at a specified hour. Contact will be established at the time indicated and the caller is then notified that the connection has been made. The charges for such calls are the same as those for an ordinary person-to-person call. This service is not available on international calls.

SEQUENCE CALLS

The sequence-calls service is of value when a number of calls are to be made to out-of-town points. Much time is saved by furnishing the operator with a list, oral or written, of the calls to be made at the specified times. The secretary should supply the names of the individuals to be called, the city and state where they are located, their telephone numbers, if known, and the hour at which the executive wishes to speak to each person on the list. However, it should be noted that this is an expensive procedure, as each call is charged at the "operator-assisted call" rate. If the secretary makes the calls by direct-dialing, money is saved.

CONFERENCE CALLS

Another instance of the various accommodations that the telephone company offers its subscribers is the conference service. It is of particular value to executives of organizations with branches and/ or plants located over a wide area who find it necessary to confer speedily with those at the different branches. The telephone company provides two methods for setting up a telephone conference.

1. An arrangement can be made with the conference operator to connect several people in various cities simultaneously for a conference or discussion. No special equipment is required for this hookup.

2. An arrangement can be made with the conference operator whereby a conference call can be placed to a large group of employees. This type of call requires setting up a loudspeaker at the called point in a different city, so that the executive can talk by phone to the entire group at one time.

When placing such a call, the secretary should signal the operator, ask for the conference operator, describe the setup desired, and furnish the names of the people to be called, their telephone numbers, if known, the city and state where each is located, and the time of the conference.

COLLECT CALLS

Calls can be charged to the phone of the person who is being called. The individual called may either accept the call and be charged for it or refuse the call and, of course, not be charged. Collect call rates are higher than direct-dialed station-to-station rates. A subscriber can also charge to his or her own phone long-distance calls placed from other phones. It behooves the efficient secretary to discuss with the employer when collect charges should be accepted. Determine from whom collect charges will be honored. If in doubt, ask the operator to wait while the matter is checked with the executive.

OVERSEAS CALLS

You can direct-dial many overseas points. Information on such calls can be obtained from the front pages of the directory, the International Dial brochures, or from the long-distance operator. For person-to-person overseas calls, the secretary must dial the long-distance operator and ask for an overseas operator. The name of the person to be called must be provided and the telephone number, if known. The charges for this service are higher than those for domestic calls. There are reduced rates for evenings, and for nights and weekends.

CALLS TO SHIPS, PLANES, TRAINS, AND AUTOMOBILES

Telephone calls to mobile conveyances by way of radio telephone are similarly made by the operator. Such service is not available without the installation of special equipment by the telephone company in the car, plane, or ship, of course. Calls can then be placed direct from the office telephone to the destination desired.

RETURNING LONG-DISTANCE CALLS

Frequently a long-distance call is received when the executive is not in the office to take it. In such a case, the long-distance operator will give the secretary the operator's number, the city calling, and the name and telephone number of the person calling. To return the call, dial the operator, ask by number for the operator who placed the call, and identify the city from which the call originated. When the connection is made with the proper operator, the secretary should tell the employer the name and telephone number of the person who placed the call. Collect calls are excluded from this service.

RECORD KEEPING

Many organizations require that a record be kept of all long-distance calls made, in order to verify the telephone bill, and have special printed forms for this purpose. The secretary may ask the telephone operator, when placing such calls, to provide the charges when the call is completed. However, the request for charges must be made in advance, not after the call is completed.

SPECIAL TELEPHONE EQUIPMENT AND SYSTEMS

A good secretary should be familiar with the various types of telephone equipment available, in order to facilitate the needs of the company and those of the executive. Tremendous strides have been made in the field of telephone research. Not only business but also the world in general benefits from the discoveries made by telephone technicians and telephone researchers.

Call Director. A push-button telephone which provides the capacity of several ordinary push-button phones in one compact, attractive unit is known as the Call Director. It can handle up to 29 lines and is available in 18- to 30-button models, which can be adjusted as needs change. The Call Director can be combined with the speakerphone feature (see below), which makes it possible to telephone with the hands free when needed. A plug-in headset model is also available; this frees the hands so that the secretary can take notes, consult records, and so forth.

The telephone company has also added the conference feature to the Call Director. This permits an executive to set up an intercom conference merely by dialing a code or pushing a button.

Speakerphone set. The speakerphone consists of a microphone and a loudspeaker and permits the user to carry on a telephone conversation clearly from anywhere in an office without lifting the receiver from its rest. The microphone picks up the user's voice, and the loudspeaker, with an adjustable volume control, broadcasts it to the party at the other end of the line. By sitting around the microphone, all members of a group can engage in a telephone conversation at one time. Everybody can talk and offer a viewpoint, and everybody can hear and understand fully what is being discussed.

Direct inward dialing. A setup is available whereby an outside caller can dial the central office designation, followed by the extension needed, and thereby put the call directly to the office desired instead of to the switchboard operator.

Dataphone. The Dataphone is a telephone-computer setup which, after activation by human hands, enables office machines to talk to one another and transmit data at tremendous speeds in various machine-usable forms.

Com Key. A telephone system for small offices that comes in four sizes as follows:

System			*Lines*	*Stations*
Com	Key	416	4	16
Com	Key	718	7	18
Com	Key	1434	14	34
Com	Key	2152	21	52

The Com Key system offers many standard and optional features and a choice of telephone sets in various colors.

Custom Calling services. These services are available on individual and auxiliary lines for both business and residence telephones. These features can be provided if a customer is served by the central office of ESS (Electronic Switching System). Custom Calling services will operate in connection with rotary or Touch-Tone service. There are four Custom Calling services.

Call waiting. This service is designed to let the called party know that someone is trying to call while the telephone is in use.

Call forwarding. This service transfers calls to another number when the called party is not at the office or at home.

Three-way calling. A third party may be cut into an existing conversation.

Speed calling. One or two digits can be dialed in order to reach local or long-distance numbers more quickly.

To obtain Custom Calling services, it is not necessary to install extra equipment nor to have an installer visit. These services are available with the regular telephone setup and may be attained by request at the central telephone office.

Dimension PBX. An electronic system that uses stored program control, a time division switching network, and switched loop consoles. It is modular in design and has a solid-state system; therefore it saves space, speeds operation, and simplifies installation and maintenance. There are two types of this system that are available to customers:

Dimension 400 has an approximate capacity of 400 lines and 90 trunks.

Dimension 2000 has an approximate capacity of 2000 lines and 350 trunks.

However, the capacity of lines and trunks for both Dimension 400 and 2000 may change depending upon the line and trunk combinations and how they are used. Information on Dimension PBX or any other type PBX telephone system or service may be obtained by calling the local telephone company.

Dataspeed 40 Service. A communication service that transmits the written word. It is available for private-line and expanded switched networks. The Dataspeed 40 Selective Calling System is designed for use with private-line applications in both half duplex and full duplex. ("Full duplex" pertains to a simultaneous two-way and independent transmission in both directions. "Half duplex" service permits communication alternately in either direction or in one direction only.) Data is always prepared on a typewriter prior to transmission. All transmissions are fast because the data proceeds at a maximum speed rather than the slower keyboard speed. The transmission accuracy is high, since the data is displayed on a monitor in its entirety before it is sent. This permits editing of data before transmission if necessary.

Horizon Communications System. A microprocessor controlled system that utilizes stored programs and multibutton electronic telephone (MET) sets. It has a capacity of 32 lines and 79 stations (excluding bridged, not MET, stations). A customer access unit (CAU) provides the ability to make feature changes or telephone set rearrangements. There are further standard and optional features that are too numerous to mention for both the stations and the system. Call the local telephone company for further detailed information.

Picturephone Meeting Service. With this service a videophone, which is a telephone combined with a television receiver and transmitter, enables users to see, as well as speak to, one another. The service is offered in color in a limited area and in black and white between several large cities. It brings people together for an important meeting so that everyone can participate. It makes it possible to conduct monthly or quarterly administrative reviews, to introduce new products to the sales force, to screen applicants for employment, to resolve production or distribution conflicts, to handle emergencies, etc. Visual aids such as slides, charts, artwork, or graphs may be used to illustrate or clarify facts discussed. Hard copies of information can be transmitted and videotapes can be sent or received.

Portable Conference Telephone Set. This permits individuals from an audience to speak directly to the speaker, to ask or answer questions, by means of a standard telephone receiver which may be carried anywhere; it connects to a standard telephone jack.

Touch-A-Matic. This automatic telephone dialer "remembers" up to 15 (or 31, depending on the type) numbers. It dials them at the touch of a button. Numbers may be added or changed at will.

Wide Area Telecommunications Service (WATS). This service allows subscribers to contract for station-to-station calls within a specified service area at a fixed monthly rate, in lieu of individual call billing. It includes a listing in the National Information Center Records (800-555-1212); by calling this number a subscriber can obtain the number of any other WATS-line subscriber.

Outward WATS provides outgoing direct-distance dialing of long-distance calls by means of a WATS line from the customer's premises to other telephones within a specified service area. Each WATS line has its own WATS number.

Inward WATS allows a subscriber to receive calls over a WATS line without charge to the originating party. The call is automatically charged to the called number without the announcement and acceptance necessary with a collect call.

Service areas number 1 through 7 indicate interstate service. Included within the range of WATS service is all of the United States including Alaska, Hawaii, Puerto Rico, and the U.S. Virgin Islands (St. Thomas, St. Croix, and St. John). The purchase of one service area, 2 through 7, includes the area or areas in the lower numbered service area or areas. Service area "0" is an intrastate service available only in some states. WATS service is available in either of two forms:

Full business day. The initial period allows 240 hours including up to 14,400 completed incoming station-to-station calls a month from any telephone within the specified service area.

Measured. The initial period allows 10 hours including up to 600 completed station-to-station calls a month from any telephone within the specified service area.

Card dialers. A plastic card is inserted in an automatic dialing telephone. The cards are coded with frequently called numbers. The number is dialed rapidly and accurately by the telephone mechanism. In a business that makes a great many calls to the same numbers, the amount of time saved by these cards can be considerable. The telephone that takes the cards may be used in a normal way.

Bellboy. This is a signaling device that may be kept in the pocket, purse, or briefcase. When the user is within a certain range of the office, the Bellboy will beep when the secretary dials its number. The user then goes to the nearest telephone and calls the office to receive the message.

TELEPHONE ANSWERING SERVICES

Many offices maintain contact with customers or others in the business world through an answering service that takes calls at night and on weekends and holidays. For a small office that closes entirely for vacations, an answering service is valuable.

The answering service may transfer the messages taken by calling at the beginning of the next business day. However, it is more common for the secretary to call in periodically and take the messages that have been received.

Trial and error may be necessary in finding a reliable answering service. If the service does not have enough lines or operators so that callers are put on "hold" for unreasonable lengths of time, much good will can be lost. Then again, it is important to have a service that can be trusted to take messages accurately. The secretary planning to engage an answering service will do well to consult other secretaries and take their recommendations. Once the system is in operation, the secretary should check response time regularly.

When it comes time to take the messages from an answering service, the secretary should have pen and paper on hand and be scrupulously accurate in transcribing any messages given, and especially so if the answering device does not have playback equipment. A set of priorities may be set up in advance with the employer as to which messages call for immediate action and which may be delayed for a shorter or greater length of time.

A sophisticated service available through the telephone company has an apparatus by which the subscriber can dial a two-digit code and have incoming calls transferred to an answering service. This does not "tie up" the line, as the subscriber may still make outgoing calls. When the subscriber wishes to disengage the service, a second two-digit code will restore the incoming calls to the client's own telephone line.

TELEPHONE ANSWERING DEVICES

A great variety of telephone answering devices, usually activating a cassette tape recorder, are available. The simplest of these give a recorded message, as for example a statement telling the caller when the person called will be available, telling hours when the business is open, or the like. An equally common type is the recorder in which the person called has prerecorded a message that invites the caller to leave a message. When a tone sounds, the caller can talk for varying lengths of time, depending upon the way in which the recorder is set to operate.

Messages recorded by such a device should be transcribed by the secretary as early as possible at the start of a business day. If it is not possible to understand clearly any portion of a message, a notation should be placed on the transcript to alert the employer that the secretary was not sure of the message given.

A remote control feature on such devices as the Phone-mate allows the user to call the device on any telephone from anyplace in the world and hear whatever messages have been recorded. One phone call plays all messages, and a special feature allows the user to replay any given message without waiting for the entire tape to rewind and replay.

Chapter 11

Special Secretarial Functions

JEANETTE L. BELY

MAKING TRAVEL ARRANGEMENTS

Many firms today have extended and expanded their interests and scope into the international picture. This broadening of the horizons makes it imperative for the executive to travel in order to maintain contacts with the firm's branches and customers, to attend meetings and conventions, to lecture, or just to relax. Commensurate with the need for increased travel, means of transportation have become more convenient and many-faceted. In order to ensure a smooth and enjoyable trip for the employer, the secretary should be familiar with the various means of transportation that are available. It is the secretary's responsibility to make sure that the executive gets to the destination on time, in comfort, well-fed and accommodated, and that the supplies and documents necessary for a successful trip are at the disposal of the traveler.

Before the secretary can make any arrangements for the trip, certain facts need to be compiled. The planner must know departure date and time, cities to be visited, length of time to be spent in each locality, the purpose of each visit, the time and day the traveler must arrive in each city to keep scheduled appointments, preferences as to means of travel, and whether travel accommodations will need to be made for one person only. Supplied with this information, the secretary can then take the next step in making travel arrangements—the compiling of an itinerary.

COMPILING AN ITINERARY

At first, as pieces and bits of information are gathered, it is a good practice to draw up a tentative itinerary or a work sheet on which notations of alternate flights, alternate train schedules, costs, and so forth can be presented for the executive's approval and selection. Such a work sheet might contain the following information: dates, destination, airport, railroad station, departure time, time of arrival, hotel accommodations, appointment (where and with whom), and reference materials.

The secretary should start the preliminary planning of the itinerary from the dates and times provided by the executive. Then a listing of whatever travel methods the employer prefers that are available at the times indicated should be added to the work sheet. If the means of transportation are left open, complete information on all airlines and railroads serving the city of destination, with arrival and departure times and the costs of each, should be obtained. Information about car rental agencies at the various destinations may be included. It is wise to indicate all possible choices available and permit the executive to make the decision as to which means of travel is preferred. The work sheet should be revised continually with the approval of the executive until the decisions are complete and the itinerary is ready for final typing.

In planning an itinerary, the secretary must bear in mind that the traveler is a human being and must eat regularly while traveling, must rest, must have enough time to get from a terminal to the place of an appointment, and so forth. Therefore, the following information should be included in the schedule:

> Eating locations (plane, train, hotel, restaurant, etc.)
> Allowance of time to go from the point of arrival to the appointment at the designated hour and without pressure
> Applicable time zone, noted in indicated time on the itinerary (EST, EDST, etc.)
> All confirmations for hotel accommodations, attached to the itinerary
> All confirmations for transportation, airline tickets, etc., attached to the itinerary

Multiple copies of the final draft should be prepared by the secretary: one for the office files, one or two for the executive, one for the traveler's family, and, if customary, copies for key people in the organization. The typed form of the itinerary would appear as follows:

```
        Charles Murray   Itinerary February 19, 19__

Tuesday, February 19 (New York to Raleigh)
10:00 a.m.  Leave West Side Airlines Terminal,
            New York, by limousine or van for
            Newark airport.

11:10 a.m.  Leave Newark airport on Eastern Airlines
            Flight #275 (lunch). (Ticket attached)

 1:19 p.m.  Arrive Raleigh.  Van to Hotel Hilton.
            (Reservation attached)
```

2:00 p.m.   Robert Lee, Office Manager at Raleigh
             branch, will pick you up at the Hilton.
             Conference scheduled at branch office.
             (File #1 in briefcase)

Wednesday, February 20 (Raleigh)
  9:00 a.m.   Robert Lee will pick you up at the
             hotel for inspection of Raleigh
             plant. (File #2 in briefcase contains
             facts and statistics on plant operation)

  8:00 p.m.   Company dinner at Hotel Hilton. (Speech
             in File #3 in briefcase)

Thursday, February 21 (Raleigh to Winston-Salem
  via Greensboro)
  9:30 a.m.   Robert Lee will pick you up at the hotel
             and drive you to the airport.

  9:56 a.m.   Leave Raleigh on Delta Airlines
             Flight #101. (Ticket attached)

 10:18 a.m.   Arrive Greensboro airport. Limousine
             or van to Winston-Salem Hotel in
             Winston-Salem. (Reservation attached)
             Lunch at hotel.

  3:00 p.m.   Appointment with John Spaaks, Office
             Manager at Winston-Salem branch; Karen
             Wilson, Personnel Director; Bob
             Meredith, Production Director; and Al
             Smith, Sales Director. Hotel Winston-
             Salem, Green Room. (File #4 in briefcase)

  7:00 p.m.   Dinner at Bill Lawson's home.
             (Telephone 722-1234)

Friday, February 22 (Winston-Salem)
  9:00 a.m.   Golf with Bill Lawson.

  1:00 p.m.   Conference with staff at Winston-Salem
             offices. (File #5 in briefcase)

  8:00 p.m.   Company dinner at Winston-Salem Hotel.
             (Speech in File #6 in briefcase)

<u>Saturday, February 23 (Winston-Salem to Greenville
    via Asheville)</u>

9:02 a.m.   Leave Winston-Salem on Southern Airlines
             Flight #501. (Ticket attached)

10:10 a.m.   Arrive Asheville. Limousine or van to
             Greenville Hotel in Greenville. (Reser-
             vation attached) Lunch at hotel.

2:00 p.m.   Conference with Greenville branch
             Office Manager Jim Turrell at Greenville
             Hotel, Mezzanine Lounge. (File #7 in
             briefcase)

7:00 p.m.   Company dinner at hotel. (Speech in File
             #8 in briefcase. Presentation of awards
             which will be brought by Turrell)

<u>Sunday, February 24 (Greenville)</u>
             Free day.

<u>Monday, February 25 (Greenville to Columbia)</u>

9:00 a.m.   Visit Greenville offices for inspection.
             Martin Blank, Office Manager, will pick
             you up at the hotel. Check out of hotel
             and bring luggage along, as you will go
             directly to airport after luncheon at
             restaurant adjoining Greenville office.

3:00 p.m.   Leave Greenville/Spartanburg airport on
             Southern Airlines commuter flight #38.
             (Ticket attached)

4:00 p.m.   Arrive Columbia. George Lewis, Office
             Manager, will meet you at airport.
             Magnolia Hotel. (Reservation attached)

<u>Tuesday, February 26 (Columbia)</u>

9:00 a.m.   Conference at Columbia offices. George
             Lewis will pick you up at the hotel.
             (File #9 in briefcase contains statistics
             and progress reports from this branch)

7:00 p.m.   Dinner meeting of Columbia staff at Hotel
             Magnolia. (Speech in File #10 in briefcase)

Wednesday, February 27 (Columbia to New York)
10:00 a.m.   George Lewis will pick you up to take you
              to the airport.

11:07 a.m.   Leave Columbia on Eastern Airlines Flight
              #666 (lunch). (Ticket attached)

 2:33 p.m.   Arrive Newark airport. Linda Grant will
              pick you up at airport and drive you to
              New York offices.

DATA AND SUPPLIES FOR TRIP

If the executive's trip is entirely for business or part business and part pleasure, the secretary's duties in making travel arrangements do not terminate with the completion of the itinerary. There is the further responsibility for the preparation of an appointments calendar of all the calls to be made while traveling. Such a schedule is made only for the executive and the secretary and it is not to be distributed to anyone else. It can be either combined with the itinerary or prepared as a separate schedule, depending upon the executive's preference. Regardless of which choice is made, the appointments schedule should include the following data: the name of city and state in which the call is to be made; the date and time of the appointment; the name and address of the firm to which the executive is going; the name of the individual with whom the appointment is made; the telephone number (if known); remarks or special reminders about each visit; and a reference to the file number of the data the traveler is taking along for each call.

The executive will not rely on memory alone for information pertaining to past associations with the individuals or firms. It will be helpful for the traveler if the secretary prepares a file for each firm to be visited. Such a memory refresher may help to make the call productive. A separate folder should be prepared for each call, and each folder should bear a reference number that is keyed to the schedule of appointments. In such folders the secretary should include carbons of past correspondence; letters or memos concerning the problem to be discussed; a list of the persons to see and their positions in the company; perhaps a list of the officers and executives of the organization; a list of the persons with whom the executive has had contact in the past, other than those with whom appointments are scheduled, and the circumstances of those contacts; and every other bit of information, regardless of how insignificant it may seem. These folders should be arranged in the order in which the executive will see the customers.

In addition to the files of correspondence and other data that the executive will take along, it is wise to provide the traveler with some stationery and supplies for communication with the office and with others while traveling.

For this purpose the secretary should draw up a checklist of those supplies to be taken, assemble all the materials, and pack them in the briefcase. Supplies that the executive might require include company stationery, plain paper, onionskin or copy paper, carbon paper, envelopes of various sizes, memo paper or pads, legal pad, address book, legal-size folders, letter-size folders, business cards, dictation equipment (portable recorder), cassette tapes or belts for recorder, mailing folders or boxes for dictation tapes or belts, office account checks, expense forms, other office forms, pens and pencils, erasers, clips, scissors, rubber bands, transparent tape, paste, calendar, pins, bottle opener, ruler, first-aid items, aspirin, timetable, and postage stamps. The materials that the executive selects from the checklist should be assembled by the secretary, checked by the executive, and made ready for packing at least the day before departure.

The expense record forms or expense book should be packed on top, so that expenses can be recorded as the executive goes along. This is a very important detail, because the expense record is needed for income-tax and accounting purposes. Generally the following information is needed if the executive is to be reimbursed in part or whole for the trip or to be able to deduct business-incurred travel expense from income tax: date of trip; description of how expense was incurred; types of expense (transportation, entertainment, breakfast, lunch, dinner, and so forth); amount reimbursed by company. In some instances receipts must be obtained for travel expenses. Therefore a secretary should be familiar with the company and income-tax requirements in this area and should attach a reminder to the expense forms or expense book for the traveling executive to obtain these receipts as the occasions arise.

ARRANGEMENTS FOR DOMESTIC TRIPS

Large organizations generally have traffic departments which make all the arrangements pertinent to a trip. If the company has a traffic department, the executive's secretary submits to this department the data that has been obtained from the executive about the trip and the department takes over. It works out the itinerary with the traveler's approval, makes all the reservations for transportation and accommodations, and obtains the confirmations. This information is sent to the executive's office well in advance of the departure date.

Where there is no traffic department in an organization, the secretary may either call on the services of a reliable travel agency or take care of the arrangements personally.

Using a travel agency. The easiest method for obtaining reservations for domestic and foreign travel is through the services of a reliable travel agency. Many executives rely on these services to plan their trips, and to make their reservations. This method saves the secretary considerable time. Furthermore, travel agencies can usually obtain better and faster services than an individual who lacks their contacts and their specialized experience and knowledge.

If the secretary or the executive does not know the name of a good travel agency, they could contact other firms whose executives travel, or get a list from The American Society of Travel Agents, Inc., at 501 Fifth Avenue, New York, NY 10017. However, not all of the good travel agents belong to this society. Others may be listed in the classified telephone directory.

The secretary must provide the travel agent with the executive's name, business and home telephone numbers, credit card number (if pertinent), detailed information on dates, times of arrival and departure desired for each city to be visited, and the type of transportation preferred. Although the agent will report periodically the progress made, it is the secretary's responsibility to keep in touch with the agent in order to see to it that tickets and reservations arrive at the office in plenty of time to check the dates, times, destinations, and so forth, before they are turned over to the traveler.

These agencies do not charge for making airline or hotel reservations, since they receive a commission from the hotel or airline with which the reservation is placed. There is sometimes a charge, however, for rail reservations unless they are part of a prearranged package tour. Refunds for any unused tickets are obtained by the agency and should be reflected as deductions from the charges made on bills. The agency should be instructed that all bills are to be sent to the attention of the executive or the secretary, so that they can be checked before being forwarded to the accounting department.

MAKING RESERVATIONS FOR TRANSPORTATION

Plane travel. The types of plane service available are first class and coach. Both types of accommodation are often available on the same plane. The differences between first class and coach are the size and comfort of the seats and the type of meals. First-class passengers enjoy wider seats and more leg room. They are served meals and complimentary alcoholic beverages. The coach section of the plane may be larger with smaller seats set closer together. The meals are less elaborate than in first class and alcoholic beverages must be purchased separately.

It has become the policy of many companies to request traveling personnel to use coach service on plane travel. The executive who prefers to travel first class must personally pay the difference between coach fare and first-class fare. The secretary should check company policy on this, then determine the executive's preference each time a trip is to be made. The executive may be willing to pay the difference if a very long flight is involved. If a first-class flight is to be made, the difference in cost must be entered in the correct place in the expense sheet.

Shuttle plane service may offer only a single class, especially when the flight is made in a smaller plane.

The secretary whose executive travels extensively should add an airline guidebook to the desk reference library for information on airlines servicing each city in the nation. The *Official Airlines Guide* may be obtained by writing to Official Airlines Guide, 2000 Clearwater Drive, Oak Brook, Illinois 60521. Each city in the United States and its possessions and each city in Canada that is serviced by an airline is listed in this book; the book indicates the airlines that service each city and gives information on car-rental and taxi service in each city.

Airline schedules may be kept on hand and the executive and the secretary may check the schedule before calling for reservations. The schedules need to be updated regularly, because flights may have been added, canceled, or have changes of time.

To make a plane reservation, the secretary should call the reservation desk of the airline chosen by the executive, give the executive's name, the name and address of the firm, the credit card number, the executive's home telephone number, the desired flight number, the city of departure and the city of destination, and the time that the flight is scheduled to leave. If the flight is already filled or a considerable change in time has been posted, the secretary should ask for alternative suggestions. If none of the suggestions is acceptable to the executive, ask to be placed on the standby list and then try to make reservations on some other airline. As soon as a reservation is available and a definite confirmation is received, the secretary should immediately cancel all the other pending alternative arrangements. This will ensure the good will of persons the secretary may want to deal with in the future.

In placing airline reservations, the secretary should get the name of the airline clerk who makes the original reservations. If flight plans are extremely involved, with layovers in different cities and changes of time zones, the secretary may avoid repeating the information if the same clerk is available when checking or changing plans.

Payment for airline tickets is generally made by credit card or standard billing. The secretary should be absolutely certain that there is time for an airline ticket to arrive in the mail prior to a flight. If there is some doubt, the executive should pick up the ticket at the airport before boarding the plane. If the ticket comes in advance, the various parts must be checked carefully against the information on the itinerary as to the correctness of flight numbers, the time of departure, the departure airport, and the city of destination. If any discrepancies are noted, the secretary must immediately notify the reservation clerk.

Train travel. The choice of available train accommodations may depend upon the length of the trip and the price of the accommodations. The least expensive way of traveling is by coach. For long trips the traveler may prefer a Pullman accommodation. The costs for such traveling space increase in sequential order of the means indicated below. For the most part, Pullman accommodations offered are:

> *Roomette:* a private room, usually for one person, with a bed folding into the wall, a sofa seat for daytime use, and toilet facilities in the same room.
> *Bedroom:* a private room with lower and upper berths, the lower berth serving as a sofa for daytime use, and toilet facilities in the same room.

The secretary should be aware that not all trains provide all the above accommodations. Railroad connections to many destinations are increasingly limited.

Automobile travel. Sometimes a trip may be more easily and conveniently made by car, or the executive may rent a car to reach the desired destination after disembarking from plane or train. In that case, and if the executive is a member of the American Automobile Association (AAA), help can be obtained from its travel department in planning the route that should be followed on the trip. The AAA will prepare a "Triptik," which is a detailed, up-to-the-minute strip map of the entire trip, listing recommended hotels and AAA service stations along the route. This association also assists members in obtaining hotel and resort accommodations.

If the executive is not a member of the AAA, the secretary's task is more complicated. Road maps and city maps may be obtained from the Tourist Bureaus in the various states and cities, but need to be sent for well in advance. Nowadays there is sometimes a fee involved and the secretary will have to write a second letter after the amount of this is made known.

Most drivers have a preferred method of mapping out the route for a trip. If the secretary is asked to determine the best driving route to a destination, the executive's preferred method of recording this should be determined. Some drivers mark out a route directly on the map with a transparent felt-tipped pen. Others write out an itinerary to be followed.

If a car is to be rented, arrangements should be made as far in advance as possible. Rates vary according to the size of car to be rented, so the executive's preference should be determined before the reservations are made. If the car is to be left at a different city or airport from the one where it is rented, the secretary will need to make sure that the car-rental agency has a branch at the second location.

Bus travel. With the improvements in equipment and services offered by bus lines, the economy-minded traveler may choose to use this means of travel for all or intervening portions of a trip. Bus lines have passenger service agents who will assist in planning either long or short trips. Timetables should be obtained and the route laid out well before reservations are placed for a bus trip.

REFUNDS FOR UNUSED TICKETS

On occasion the executive may need to change travel plans en route. In such a case the traveler is entitled to a refund on the unused portion of the ticket. The transportation line should be informed at once when the need for cancellation becomes apparent.

The secretary may send an unused flight ticket with a covering letter to the Refund Accounting Department of the airline involved. In the letter the secretary should mention the date of the flight that the executive was to have taken, the city of departure, the city of destination, the ticket number, the flight number, the credit card number, and the cost of the ticket. Refunds for train travel may be handled in a similar fashion.

MAKING MOTEL OR HOTEL RESERVATIONS

Reservations for motel or hotel accommodations should be made as soon as possible. Delay can cause the executive to arrive in a strange city without any place to stay. Therefore the secretary must be certain that reservations for all motel or hotel accommodations have been made and confirmed before the executive leaves on a trip.

If the motel or hotel at which the executive plans to stay is part of a chain, the easiest and quickest way for the secretary to make reservations is to call the chain's toll-free number for the central location through which all reservations for motels or hotels in the chain are handled.

In making reservations for overnight accommodations, the following sources contain information:

> *Hotel and Motel Red Book*, published annually by the American Hotel Association Directory Corporation, 888 Seventh Avenue, New York, New York 10019. This book lists the hotels and motels by city and state; indicates the number of rooms, rates, and plans under which they operate (American, with meals; European, without meals); lists recreational facilities; gives telephone and toll-free telephone or TWX numbers for each hotel; and indicates whether the hotel or motel belongs to a chain. A special section lists number and

types of meeting rooms of various seating capacities, along with facilities
available in these rooms for PA systems, lecterns, showing of films, etc.

*Leahy's Hotel Guide and Travel Atlas of the United States, Canada, Mexico, and
Puerto Rico*, published by the American Hotel Register Company, 2775
Shermer Road, Northbrook, Illinois 60062.

Chamber of Commerce or Tourist Information Bureau in city of destination.

Folders from the American Automobile Association which list motels, hotels, and
inns for automobile travelers.

In making reservations for overnight accommodations, the following
information must be supplied to the person taking reservations: the name and
address of the traveler, the type of accommodations desired, the date of
arrival, the approximate time of day of arrival, and the probable departure
date. The secretary should be sure to obtain the check-out time, since this
varies from one place to another, and to request a confirmation of the
reservation by mail. These confirmations should be attached to the traveler's
itinerary. Unless a request for accommodations has been confirmed, there is
no assurance that a room will be held for the traveler. Some motels and hotels
confirm reservations only if a deposit is made in advance.

Generally if a reservation is not picked up by 6 P.M., the room is not held.
Therefore, if the traveler will arrive later than 6 P.M., it would be wise to make
a deposit to ensure that the room will be held for the traveler. If such a deposit
is not made and the traveler is held up along the way, he or she should call the
motel or hotel if possible and ask that the reservation be held.

If the executive changes plans about itinerary or hotel after the reservation
is made, the secretary should contact the motel or hotel to cancel the
reservation.

ARRANGEMENTS FOR FOREIGN TRAVEL

Preparations for foreign travel should be made far in advance of the
departure date. There are many more details to be considered than in
domestic travel arrangements, and many phases of such an undertaking
involve much time. Before any arrangements for travel accommodations are
started, the traveler should know (1) the names of the persons to be seen in
what countries and for how long, (2) the U.S. government requirements
governing travel to foreign countries, (3) the requirements of the government
of the country or countries to be visited, (4) the conditions that are imposed on
business travelers and not on tourists, and (5) something about the countries
to be visited.

Using a travel agency. It is advisable that the arrangements for foreign
travel be made by a reliable travel agency, unless the organization has a traffic

department and foreign branches in the countries to be visited. Under any circumstances, the executive's secretary must know where to obtain information in preparation for the executive's trip abroad and the data that will be needed for such a trip. The travel agency chosen should be one that will work out a personal itinerary for the traveling executive, rather than an agency that specializes in package tours. A reliable agency will take care of all of the details pertaining to the trip and will perform the following services for its clientele:

Prepare a tentative itinerary, which the executive can approve or change.
Handle all the arrangements for traveling, for hotels, and perhaps for sightseeing for the entire trip.
Provide information as to exactly which documents will be needed (passport, visas, health and police certificates, etc.) and how to obtain them.
Obtain all the documents that they can (certain documents the executive must obtain personally).
Provide a small amount of currency in the denominations of the country or countries to be visited, in exchange for the equivalent in U.S. money.
Help to obtain a letter of credit or traveler's checks.
Arrange to have a rental car waiting for the executive at the destination point, if desired.
Handle both personal and baggage insurance, if desired.
If the executive is uncertain about accommodations and is unable to make arrangements before leaving, the agent will supply the name of a desirable hotel in the country of destination, as well as a letter of introduction to the manager of the hotel.

Preliminary preparations. For help in arranging a foreign business trip, the secretary could contact the Bureau of International Commerce in the Department of Commerce. This government department maintains a staff of specialists on individual countries and can contact foreign-trade experts who are stationed at each of the Department's field offices. This bureau will supply information on economic developments, regulations and trade statistics on any country, distribution methods, foreign costs and their effect on sales prices, types of distributors, and names of key commercial officers to contact both in the United States and in the countries to be visited. It will also set up the executive's overseas appointments and will notify all U.S. Foreign Service posts, such as the embassies, consulates, and consuls general, that the executive is coming to those countries and alert them as to the purpose of the visit. The bureau will request that these posts provide any assistance that is needed. Furthermore, the Washington Bureau of International Commerce maintains a trade complaint service, with which a traveler can communicate if any dispute with a foreign country should arise; this bureau safeguards and protects the industrial property rights to patents, trademarks, and copyrights abroad.

A very important secretarial duty in making preparations for the executive's trip abroad is to write letters to pave the way for a good reception in the countries to be visited. Write to the firms to be visited to make and confirm appointments, giving the time of arrival, the length of time the executive expects to stay, the address where reservations have been made, and any other pertinent information that will make it possible to aid the executive in the country of destination. The secretary should not overlook checking the holiday dates of the countries to be visited (see Appendix 6), so that an appointment will not be planned for a day when the offices will be closed. It should be borne in mind that many countries celebrate holidays that differ from those in the United States.

Visas. Some, but not all, countries require that visitors obtain permission to enter the country through a document referred to as a "visa." Therefore the secretary should call the consulates of the countries that the executive intends to visit and find out whether a visa is necessary. If it is, a passport must be presented by the traveler at the consulate and a visa form filled out. Since the length of time it takes to process a visa varies with the country to be visited, this must be done well in advance of the set departure date. The secretary should also find out from the consulate what the fee for the visa will be, since a charge for this document is generally made.

Customs regulations. In order to avoid difficulties upon the traveler's return to this country, the secretary should obtain information about the customs regulations for travelers abroad and present it to the executive. Such information can be procured from pamphlets issued by the U.S. Treasury Department, Bureau of Commerce, Washington, D.C. and from the travel agent who is arranging the trip.

The secretary should remind the executive that if a watch, a camera, or any other item of foreign manufacture that was purchased in the United States is being taken abroad, it will be necessary to carry proof of purchase such as a sales slip for each of the items. Such possessions should also be registered with the U.S. Customs officials before the executive leaves, in order to eliminate possible customs problems upon reentry.

During the trip, the executive will expect to be kept posted on events occurring at the home office. Therefore, it is important to determine which items are to be referred to other people in the organization, and which items are to be forwarded to the traveler. Some employers request that the secretary keep a log of daily events and send it on to them at specific times. If the secretary keeps abreast of the traveler's itinerary and uses airmail, the traveler can be kept informed about events in the home office. The secretary should keep a duplicate copy of all correspondence that is forwarded and number each packet sent, so that any loss can be detected.

If it is necessary to send a package to the executive in some foreign country, the secretary should first check with the post office about mailing regulations, restrictions, and requirements (see Chapter 10).

For urgent messages that need immediate attention, the secretary can rely on telephone, telegram, or cablegram services, which are described in Chapter 10.

THE TRAVELING SECRETARY

At times it is necessary for the executive to take along a secretary on a business trip. Although today the executive has several means to facilitate business needs, such as portable recorders, public stenographers, and the like, an employer may prefer to take the secretary on the trip because much of the work to be done would take a great deal of explaining to one unfamiliar with it.

A secretary who travels with an employer should be prepared for and try to foresee all contingencies that may arise during the trip. The secretary should study out which supplies should be taken along and which will be easily available at the destination.

If the executive will want material typed, arrangements for a typewriter must be made. A portable typewriter may be taken along if one is available. If not, the secretary may write ahead to the hotel or motel and arrange for the rental of a typewriter. Then again, it may be possible for the traveling secretary to type up reports or speeches as needed in a branch office of the company. If arrangements for this courtesy can be made in advance, the way may be paved for a harmonious sharing of space and office equipment during the trip.

SOCIAL AMENITIES

VISITING CARDS

Executives may use both business and personal cards. These cards should be uncluttered in the information they contain, yet informative and dignified. The secretary may be called upon to act as a consultant in choosing the format and type of card to order, or the entire job may be turned over to the secretary's good judgment. Therefore, the standard requirements for visiting cards should be known.

Personal calling cards are usually $3'' \times 1\ 1/2''$ in size, of heavy white card paper. The legend on such cards is generally engraved in black ink in roman letter style.

Business calling cards are slightly larger than personal cards. Customarily they are cut $3\ 1/2'' \times 2''$ in size, but for top executives they may be slightly larger. It is considered good form to use roman letters in black or gray ink on white pasteboard of good quality. The full name of the executive may be used, or now often only the initials. Titles such as "Mr.," "Mrs.," "Ms.," or "Dr." are rarely used, although the initials for a degree may occasionally follow the name. The identifications of junior or senior are abbreviated.

Placement of the name on the card varies. The name of the executive may be in the middle and that of the company in one of the corners, or vice versa. Address and phone number are commonly included.

A secretary encloses an executive's business card when a present goes to a business associate. However, if the individual becomes a personal friend— that is, one who is seen outside of business hours—the executive's personal visiting card should be used. The secretary should also enclose the executive's personal card in greetings and presents that are sent to personal friends and to relatives.

DONATIONS

An executive usually receives many requests for donations annually, and many individuals respond to these pleas. It is not the secretary's responsibility to screen such requests before submitting them to the employer. Every request for a donation must be submitted for the executive's attention and decision. However, it is the secretary's responsibility to keep a record, and (if possible) a receipt, for all donations made by the executive to educational, religious, and philanthropic organizations. These records are very important for income-tax purposes and for the donor's own information. When a request for a donation or contribution comes into the office, it will aid the executive if the secretary will note on each request the amount given to that organization in the preceding year and the total amount of contributions made during the current year. If a pledge was made that is payable in installments, the due dates of the payments should be entered on the secretary's calendar or in the card tickler and brought to the executive's attention as they occur. At the end of the year a list should be compiled of all the organizations to which the executive has contributed, with the amounts of the donations given to each organization clearly shown.

INVITATIONS

Invitations extended by the executive to two types of functions are of particular concern to the secretary. These functions are formal dinners that are given personally and official entertainments given by the executive in an official capacity.

Invitations for either of these functions are usually formal in style. This means that they should be written in the third person and may be engraved for the occasion, partly engraved, or handwritten.

Engraved invitations should be of traditional size, usually three units by four units, with the lettering in black. It is considered proper form and makes a very elegant-looking invitation to use a white or light-cream paper of a kid finish. No address, monogram, or initial should appear on an engraved invitation. If the family has a coat of arms, however, this may be embossed, but without color. The space for the name of the guest that is generally provided on invitations is omitted on official invitations from executives.

If a reply is expected, this is indicated on the bottom left-hand corner with the letters R.S.V.P. and directly underneath, the address to which the reply is to be sent if it differs from that where the entertainment will take place.

Etiquette prescribes that formal invitations should follow a standard format. The full name of the sender should appear on the invitation. The date and hour that the function is to take place should be specified, but the year is omitted. The time of day is written out in full. If the function begins at any time after the hour, the fraction should also be written out, for example, "half past seven o'clock."

Mr. Harold Jones
requests the pleasure of your company
at a reception
on Wednesday, the third of January
at half past six o'clock
The Executive Club
700 Locust Road

If the entertainment is given in someone's honor, a line would be inserted before the date on engraved invitations. On partially engraved invitations, the phrase "in honor of" or "to meet" may be handwritten at the top:

in honor of Ms. Linda Brown

or

to meet Ms. Linda Brown

"Honorable" and "Excellency" are used on invitations only when referring to the guest of honor:

To meet the Honorable Linda Brown

or

In honor of Her Excellency,
the Governor of Ohio

If the reception is being given at the executive's home with the executive's spouse acting as host or hostess, the invitation would read:

Mr. and Mrs. Harold Jones
at home
Wednesday, the third of January
from six to eight o'clock
36 Woodlawn Avenue

An executive who entertains frequently may wish to have a quantity of partially engraved invitations made up. When the time comes to put them to use, the name of the guest, the kind of gathering, and the time and date can be filled in by hand. A partially engraved invitation generally follows this form:

Mr. and Mrs. Harold Jones
request the pleasure of
(name written in)
company at
on
at   o'clock
35 Woodlawn Avenue

ANSWERS TO INVITATIONS

Etiquette requires that an invitation be answered promptly in the same form in which it was issued; that is, if the invitation was issued in the third person, it should be answered in the third person, and so forth. Formal answers are used in reply to formal invitations and are written by hand on personal writing paper.

Mr. and Mrs. John Smith
accept with pleasure
the kind invitation of
Mr. and Mrs. Harold Jones
for Wednesday, the third of March
from six until eight o'clock

Mr. Harold Jones
regrets that he is unable to accept
Mr. and Mrs. Alverez'
kind invitation for dinner
on Saturday, the second of August

The full name of the person answering the invitation should appear. If the invitation is proffered in more than one name, all the names mentioned should be shown in the reply. The date and the hour that the function is to take place should be specified in an acceptance, but only the date need be mentioned in a regret. The year of the date is omitted. When referring to the invitation in a reply, it is courteous to refer to it as a "very kind invitation."

Answers to invitations to social business functions, such as luncheons, dinners, or receptions, should also be written by hand but they should be on business letterhead paper. If it is necessary to explain the reason for declining such an invitation, a letter of explanation should follow the formal note of regret. Generally no reason need be given.

The secretary should keep a record of invitations received by the executive. The event should also be marked on the calendar or in the tickler file so that the employer can be reminded of the event in advance. Also, if the employer should take the invitation home, the secretary will have a record of the host, time, place, and date of the affair, so that the invitation can be answered correctly when the decision on attendance is made.

If the invitation originates with the executive, the secretary should type a list of the guests to whom the invitations were sent. As the acceptances and regrets come in, a notation should be made next to the name of each guest, and the letters should be attached to the list. It is helpful to make a daily summary of the total number of acceptances, regrets, and no replies to the invitations sent out. This summary should be placed on the executive's desk at the end of each day.

When dinner or luncheon invitations have specified a definite return date for reply and no reply has been received from some of the guests on the list, it is perfectly permissible for the secretary to telephone the invited guests three or four days before the event. This is done in order to determine the number of guests who will be present.

A good reference library for an office will contain at least one book on etiquette which should be consulted whenever there is a question of social form.

THEATER TICKETS

One of the extras that a secretary is sometimes called upon to attend to is that of obtaining theater tickets for the executive and guests. A little information about the shows and the critics' opinions will help the executive in making a choice. The executive may name several shows in order of preference. The usual procedure in buying tickets is to call the box office and charge tickets to the executive's credit-card account. Or the secretary may go in person to a Ticketron location if there is one nearby. Here, too, the tickets may be charged to any of several different credit-card accounts.

It is often difficult to obtain tickets by either of these methods for hit shows unless they are bought far in advance. However, advance notice is not always possible. The secretary may establish an account in the executive's name with a reliable theater-ticket agency in order to have a better chance of obtaining tickets on short notice.

When the tickets arrive at the office, the secretary should enclose them in an envelope on which have been typed the date and day of the week of the performance, the curtain time, the name and address of the theater, and the name of the show.

If the tickets must be sent through the mail for any reason, the secretary should enclose with them a letter of transmittal in which reference has been made to the name of the show, the name and address of the theater, the date of the performance, and the seat numbers. Thus, if the tickets are lost, and particularly if the executive has planned to attend several different shows, the carbon copy of the letter contains all the information necessary for follow-up. The letter also provides all the pertinent information to the individual receiving the tickets and acts as a reminder of the date.

GIFT AND CARD LISTS

Another of the responsibilities that sometimes devolve on the secretary is that of reminding the executive of an approaching occasion such as a birthday, anniversary, or graduation. The secretary may also be expected to tend to the sending of holiday remembrances. For this purpose a record of these events and lists of the persons to whom the executive sends cards and presents must be kept. Separate lists should be maintained for friends, relatives, and business acquaintances to whom holiday greetings are sent by the executive, those to whom cards are sent by the executive jointly with husband or wife, those who receive company cards, those to whom holiday gifts are given, and those who receive gifts at other times of the year.

These lists and records should be kept up to date, with names added or deleted and addresses checked periodically. It will aid the executive in the selection of gifts if the secretary keeps a cumulative record of the gifts previously given the individual, the cost of the gifts, and the occasion for such gifts. Since the secretary in many cases is asked to select and purchase the cards and gifts and address and mail them, these lists should be submitted to the employer well in advance of the occasion, so that sufficient time will be allowed for shopping, preparation, and mailing.

Holiday gifts or greeting cards should be thought of at least six or eight weeks in advance, particularly if the gift is to be sent abroad. If greeting cards are to have the executive's name imprinted, they need to be ordered early.

AT TIME OF DEATH

At the time of a death, a friend or acquaintance of the deceased usually expresses sympathy by sending a token remembrance to the bereaved family. The form of this expression of sympathy depends upon the religious affiliation, if any, of the deceased. Since no one wants to create a feeling of disrespect and disharmony on this most sensitive occasion, the secretary should know the correct procedure to follow in expressions of sympathy, so that the executive can be advised if the need should arise. These expressions may take any one or a combination of several of the following forms:

Flowers. It is customary to send flowers to the bereaved family, except one of the Jewish faith. From close friends or relatives, prepared dishes for meals that will save the family from food preparation is considered a proper and accepted expression of sympathy to the Jewish family in mourning.

Flowers may take the form of a floral piece, that is, a spray, wreath, or basket. Customs vary in different sections of the country. If the secretary telephones a florist long distance, it may be wise to ask for advice on what may be acceptable. It is also appropriate to send a floral piece to memorial services when the deceased is cremated or buried immediately. A card should always accompany the floral piece. If a visiting card is used for this purpose, the engraved name should be crossed out in ink and a few words of sympathy added. The floral piece is usually ordered by the secretary from the florist by telephone, and the florist supplies an appropriate card on which the name of the person sending the flowers is written, along with any message the sender desires. When ordering the floral piece, the secretary must be prepared to tell the florist the name of the deceased, where the flowers are to be sent, the time and date of the services, and the kind and size of floral piece desired.

Letters of sympathy. Letters expressing sympathy to the bereaved family may be sent to people of any faith and may be sent in addition to flowers or any of the other expressions noted here. Opinions differ on the proper form for a personal expression of sympathy. In some areas or sections of society, a sympathy letter or note is not considered proper unless it is written by hand, and a manufactured card as printed by a greeting-card company is totally unacceptable. In other sections, such a card is the most common way to express the message of sympathy. The secretary would be wise to inquire about the customs in the business and social community in which the executive is involved.

Mass cards. Mass cards indicate that arrangements have been made to have a Mass or Masses said in memory of the deceased and for the repose of the soul. It is appropriate to send such cards to a Roman Catholic family. They may be sent by either a Roman Catholic or a non-Catholic. The cards may be obtained from a priest. It is customary to make an offering when such cards are obtained. Although a Roman Catholic could ask a priest to say Mass for a non-Catholic, Mass cards are not usually sent to a non-Catholic family.

Charitable contributions. Some families specify that, instead of flowers, they would prefer friends and business associates to send contributions to charities or organizations in which the deceased was interested. If this is done, the organization that receives these donations in the name of the deceased usually notifies the bereaved family that such contributions were received. The donor may also write to the family to inform them that a donation is being sent to the charitable or educational institution in the name of the deceased.

Death of a member of the executive's family. The secretary may be asked to keep a record of those who send expressions of sympathy and what was sent when a member of the executive's family has died. A description of the floral piece that was received should be written on the back of each accompanying card. In addition, a separate alphabetic file of all Mass cards and letters should be kept. From these data, in order to facilitate sending acknowledgments, separate lists could be made if desired of those who sent flowers alone, of those who sent both Mass cards and flowers, of those who wrote and also sent flowers or Mass cards, and of those who sent contributions to institutions.

Two opinions exist as to the type of acknowledgment that is appropriate at this time. According to one, the cards acknowledging expressions of sympathy should be formal and engraved. According to the other, it is perfectly proper to have the acknowledgments typed. Acknowledgments may be written out in longhand if only a few need to be sent, but if the deceased was a prominent person and hundreds of remembrances were received, engraved cards should be sent only to those who are unknown to the bereaved, not to acquaintances. The type of remembrance sent—flowers, Mass cards, or contributions—should be mentioned in the acknowledgment.

The secretary should also keep a list of the names and addresses of those who performed outstanding services, such as doctors, nurses, a priest, minister, or rabbi, editorial writers, and the like, so that letters of appreciation can be sent to them for their kindness and understanding. Also, thank you letters should be sent to those who sent memorial contributions to organizations.

All the lists should be submitted to the executive, who will select those to whom letters will be dictated, those to whom acknowledgments will be written in longhand, and those for whom the secretary is to draft and type acknowledgments.

Death of the executive. The details that the secretary takes care of in the event of the executive's death depend upon the wishes of the family. The secretary could offer assistance in a number of ways:

Help to compile material for newspaper obituaries. This would include dates and history of the executive's career and the names of organizations to which the executive belonged and offices held in each. The secretary could write or help to write the obituary, or call the newspapers and give the information to the writer responsible for this. The funeral director supplies the funeral notice to the newspapers; the secretary could supply information for this.
Notify branch offices, foreign offices, or affiliates of the company of the death of the executive.
Notify the executive's lawyer and the secretaries of organizations to which the executive belonged.
Notify the insurance company or companies, the Social Security Administration, and any other institution or agency from which a monetary death benefit may derive.
Arrange for the personal effects of the executive to be removed from the office and taken home, or to be disposed of as the family requests.
Keep a file of clippings from the newspapers bearing items about the deceased.

Chapter 12

Managing Funds, Bookkeeping, and Record-keeping
ABBA SPERO

A SECRETARY will often be required to handle cash, either from the business operations or the employer's personal funds. This in turn may require the recording of these transactions. The figures recorded will be used in preparing income-tax returns and in determining the profitability of the firm's operations. It is important for the secretary to be able to handle various aspects of cash transactions and to be familiar with the basic procedures in record-keeping. The purpose of this chapter is to provide information that will enable the secretary to carry out these duties proficiently.

Specifically the chapter will deal with (1) managing all cash transactions, including receiving cash, writing checks, reconciling bank statements with records, and handling petty cash; (2) record-keeping as its affects the determination of profits; and (3) record-keeping for income-tax and payroll purposes.

MANAGING CASH TRANSACTIONS

Cash will come into the company from various sources, especially as fees collected for services or as the personal funds of the employer. Personal funds can be received for salaries, interest and dividends on investments, and rents from income-producing property. Usually this money will be in the form of checks; occasionally, cash itself is received.

It is important that all monies received be deposited into the appropriate bank account on the day they are received. This procedure is the best insurance against thefts and robberies. Checks should be examined to determine whether they are properly made out. Attention should be paid to the date; postdated checks cannot be deposited or cashed before the date written on the check. Checks that are irregularly made out should be set aside to be discussed with the employer. Whenever cash is received, the secretary should prepare a receipt in duplicate (blank forms are available at any stationery store), one copy to be given to the person making payment and the other to be retained as a record of the transaction.

If the secretary's duties include record-keeping, entries should be made in the proper records. Arrangements for night deposits should be made if funds cannot be deposited before the bank closes.

HANDLING THE BANK ACCOUNT

MAKING BANK DEPOSITS

When cash is to be deposited in a bank, a deposit slip is made out (see below). Although banks do accept deposit slips improperly prepared, the competent secretary is careful to do the job correctly. The company bank-deposit slips are usually imprinted with the company name and the bank account number. If these are not available then this information must be filled in on a blank slip. The account number is important since it is the number, rather than the name, that the bank uses for its records.

CHECKING DEPOSIT	00081-015-78)	NATIONAL CITY BANK

SUBJECT TO RULES AND REGULATIONS GOVERNING CHECKING ACCOUNTS — CLEVELAND, OHIO

DELUXE-N22494

DATE *Aug. 14, 19-* ACCOUNT NO. 0 4 7 5 2 6 1

CREDIT THE ACCOUNT OF *Dorothy Jones*

OFFICE WHERE ACCOUNT IS CARRIED

Broadway - 65th

Be Sure Each Item is Properly Endorsed.

CASH List Checks Singly	22	50
	150	00
	43	75
TOTAL	276	25

⑆041000124⑈

Currency is counted, and the total is entered on the slip. Coins, if in large quantities, should be rolled in wrappers provided by the bank. Each check included in the deposit is listed separately. Occasionally traveler's checks or money orders may be a part of the deposit. These are entered in the same manner as ordinary checks. After all checks have been listed, the amounts of all items on the slip are added and the total is placed in the space provided.

The bank will give a receipt for the deposit which should be retained until after the bank statement is received so as to ascertain that all deposits have been properly recorded.

ENDORSING CHECKS

Checks are written orders by which the depositor, known as the "drawer," directs the bank, referred to as the "drawee," to pay money to the "payee" or to a third party designated by the payee. Checks are sometimes made payable to "bearer," a practice generally frowned upon because they are negotiated by simple delivery and can be cashed by persons who wrongfully receive them. Checks need not be made payable to real persons. Business checks are frequently made out to "Petty Cash" or to "Payroll." A check is made payable to Payroll, for example, when money is needed in making up pay envelopes.

If a check is made out to a definite payee, this person must write on the back of the check directions for its disposition and sign his or her name. This is known as an "endorsement." Endorsements are placed on the back of the check on the left-hand side. The endorser should sign exactly as the name is written on the face of the check. If the name is misspelled or differs in any manner from the way it appears on the bank records, the payee should sign twice, first as it is written on the face and then correctly. There are three principal forms of endorsement: (1) in blank; (2) in full; and (3) restrictive (see below).

In a blank endorsement the endorser's signature is simply written across the back of the check. The effect of a blank endorsement is to make the check

Blank Endorsement
Payable to bearer
without further endorsement

Blank Endorsement
Name misspelled

Endorsement in Full
Payable as James Cavanaugh directs

FOR DEPOSIT ONLY IN
MECHANICS NATIONAL BANK
TO THE CREDIT OF
Grace Nelson

Restrictive Endorsement
Further negotiation prohibited

payable to the bearer. If it is lost or stolen, it can be cashed by the holder without further endorsement. Although they are commonly used, blank endorsements are not to be recommended. They should be made only at the time a check is being cashed or deposited at the bank.

In an endorsement in full the endorser transfers the check to a designated party by writing the words "Pay to the order of" followed by the name of the person to whom payment is to be made above the endorser's signature. A check so endorsed can be cashed or negotiated only after the person named in the endorsement has signed it. It is not good in the hands of a person who wrongfully possesses it.

In a restrictive endorsement the endorser limits further negotiation of the check by writing above his or her signature definite instruction on what may be done with it. Thus, a check might be made payable to one person only or it might be endorsed "For deposit only." Except when checks are being deposited in the bank, restrictive endorsements are almost never used. Business checks are usually endorsed for deposit with a rubber stamp; no written signature is needed.

DISHONORED CHECKS

A bank accepts checks for deposit subject to their final payment. If the drawer has directed the bank to refuse payment or if there are insufficient funds on deposit, the bank will return the check and charge it to the drawer's account. Such a check is known as a "dishonored check," or an "NSF (non-sufficient funds) check." Informal arrangements for payment or redeposit of a dishonored check are usually made with the drawer. However, if the drawer is a stranger, it would be advisable for the holder of a dishonored check to take legal steps and file a formal notice of protest. In this way, the holder is assured of protecting full rights against the drawer.

Dishonored checks that have been returned by the bank should be deducted from the bank balance on the depositor's cash records and then be redeposited or filed for safekeeping until the drawer has made settlement. Any fees that may have been paid for the protest or collection can rightfully be collected from the drawer.

BANK STATEMENT

At regular intervals, usually monthly, or sometimes upon request of the depositor, the bank renders a bank statement, showing what has taken place in the account since the last statement was prepared and the present balance according to the bank's records. The statement shows the balance carried forward from the previous statement, all deposits and all charges made to the account during the period, and the balance on the date the statement was rendered. Sent along with the statements are canceled checks, credit memos, and debit memos. Canceled checks are the depositor's checks that have been returned to the bank, charged against the account, and stamped "PAID." Credit memos are notices of amounts added to the account for such sums as interest allowed by the bank or proceeds of items left with the bank for collection—notes and bond coupons, for example. Debit memos are notices of deductions made from the account for service charges, interest on bank loans, checks accepted for deposit that were dishonored, and the like.

BANK RECONCILIATION

Seldom will the balance showing in the checkbook agree with the balance reported on the bank statement, even though no errors have been made in either place. Disagreement results from the following causes:

Deposits that were made near or after the date of the statement have not yet been posted on the bank records. They do, however, appear in the checkbook.

Credits that have been made to the account by the bank, as indicated on the credit memos, have not yet been entered in the checkbook.

Checks issued by the depositor and deducted in the checkbook are still outstanding; that is, they have not yet been presented to the bank for payment and therefore do not appear on the bank statement.

Charges that have been made against the account by the bank, as indicated on the debit memos, have not yet been entered in the checkbook.

Errors have been made either in the checkbook or on the bank's records, or in both places.

As soon as possible after receiving a statement, the depositor should locate the reasons for differences between the bank statement and the checkbook and find the correct balance in the account. This is done on a bank reconciliation statement, prepared by the following steps:

Compare deposits entered in the checkbook with those recorded on the bank statement. Check discrepancies against deposit slips to determine which record is correct. Make a note of deposits that do not appear on the bank statement and credits made by the bank that have not been added in the checkbook.

Arrange checks returned by bank in numerical order and compare them with their stubs, taking careful notice to see whether the amounts agree. Make a note of differences. Place a check mark, or other symbol, on stubs of the checks that have been returned. Prepare a list of the outstanding checks, noting the check numbers, the date, and the name of the payee. Do not include certified checks on this list, since they have already been charged against the account. Make a note of any bank charges that have not been entered in the checkbook.

Arrange the information that has been assembled on a bank reconciliation statement. The form and preparation of this statement are explained and illustrated below.

If the checkbook and bank statement are both correct, the balances can be brought into agreement and the reconciliation is complete. If the accounts cannot be reconciled after adjustments have been made for omissions, an error in addition or subtraction in the checkbook is indicated. The check stubs should be checked, with particular attention to the balances carried forward from one stub to another.

BANK RECONCILIATION STATEMENT

Bank reconciliation statements are prepared in three ways:

Adjustments are made to the balance reported by the bank to bring it into agreement with the checkbook balance.
Adjustments are made in the checkbook balance to bring it into agreement with the balance according to the bank statement.
Adjustments are made to both balances to get the correct balance.

Since neither of the first two methods provides the correct balance, the third method is the preferred procedure and is the one explained here. The sources of the data are the bank statement and the checkbook or a cash ledger account if one was prepared.

RECONCILIATION STATEMENT (July 31)

Balance on bank statement				$7,328
Add deposits made after date of statement				1,000
Deduct checks outstanding				$8,328

Check No.	Date	Payee	Amount	
633	7/22	Bean & Co.	$2,180	
634	7/28	Blue Cross	50	2,230

Corrected bank balance	6,098
Balance according to checkbook	6,100
Service charge not recorded	2
Corrected checkbook balance	$6,098

Comparison of the deposits that were made during the month with those recorded on the bank statement reveals that the bank has not entered a deposit of $1,000 made on July 31; this amount is added to the balance reported by the bank. Comparison of the canceled checks returned by the bank with the checks drawn during the period shows that the following checks are still outstanding:

Check No.	Date	Payee	Amount
633	7/22	Bean & Co.	$2,180
634	7/28	Blue Cross	50
			$2,230

The total of the outstanding checks is deducted from the balance reported on the bank statement. Adding the unrecorded deposits and deducting the outstanding checks take care of all omissions on the bank statement. The correct bank balance is determined to be $6,098.

The bank statement shows a service charge of $2.00 which has not been entered in the cash records; this amount is deducted from the checkbook balance. Now the corrected checkbook balance is also $6,098, and it has been proved that no errors have been made.

After the reconciliation has been completed, errors should be corrected and entries should be made in the depositor's cash records and checkbook for any omissions, such as the service charge discussed above, so that the records will reflect the correct balance. Adjustments in the checkbook can be made on the stub for the last check drawn. It is not necessary to correct all preceding balances. Any bank errors uncovered in the reconciliation should be reported to the bank immediately.

The bank reconciliation statement should be filed for future reference. It will prove useful when the next reconciliation is made. The canceled checks are receipts for payments that have been made. They should be kept on file as long as proof of payment might be necessary.

INVESTIGATING OUTSTANDING CHECKS

Ordinarily checks should clear through the bank and be returned to the depositor within a few weeks after issue. Checks that have been outstanding for unreasonably long periods of time should be investigated. Outstanding checks are not only annoying when bank accounts are being reconciled but they also pose a question as to what may have happened to them. Perhaps the checks have been lost or mislaid by the payee. Communication with the payee is in order.

If the payee claims to have not received a check, a new one will have to be issued in its place. This should be done, however, only after a stop-payment notice has been filed on the old check. How to stop payment on a check is described later in this chapter.

HANDLING CASH PAYMENTS

The secretary who takes care of the company bills accepts responsibility for paying the correct amount at the right time. To ensure proper payment, the secretary should (1) check to make sure that bills submitted to the employer are correct and (2) take measures to ensure that bills are at hand for payment when they are due.

Before drawing checks for the employer's signature, the secretary should thoroughly check the accuracy of the statements received. Compare the charges listed on the statement with the sales slips that are attached or other supporting evidence and make sure that proper credits have been allowed for returns and for payments that have been made on the account. The mathematical accuracy of all calculations on the statement should be verified.

Prompt payment of all bills is desirable; on some bills, payment on or before a given date is essential. Particular attention must be paid to insurance premiums, because policies lapse if premiums are not paid before a certain date, and to those bills that are subject to some form of additional charge if payment is not made within a stated period. Also bills that allow for cash discount if paid within a certain time should be earmarked for timely payment. For example, the expression "2/10; n/30" stands for a two percent discount off of the bill if paid within ten days; if not taken, the total is due within thirty days. In terms of annual notes this is the equivalent of almost a thirty-five percent interest charge if the discount is not taken. One method of ensuring payment at the right time is the use of a tickler file in which bills are filed by the dates on which they should be paid.

Occasionally payments must be made in a foreign currency (see Appendix 3). The easiest means of making remittances to foreign countries is a draft payable in the funds of the country to which it is to be sent; drafts can be purchased at any bank. Personal checks can be used in some instances; however, this poses the problem of exchange rates and presents the possibility of over- or underpayment. The exchange rates fluctuate.

WRITING CHECKS

Care should be exercised in writing checks. It is good policy to fill in the check stub first, to prevent the possibility of drawing a check without recording it. The date, the check number, the name of the payee, and the reason for the payment should all be listed on the stub. The reason for payment should contain enough information to permit later entry in the cash records. The check is filled in with the number, the date, the name of payee, the amount in both figures and words, and the signature. Checks should be written legibly. No blank spaces which might be used to alter the check should be left. The amount in figures is placed close to the dollar sign, and the amount in words is started close to the left-hand side. The amount in words should agree with the amount in figures. In case of disagreement, the bank may refuse to honor the check. If the check is honored, the amount written in words governs. If the amount of the check is less than one dollar, it is customary to cross out the word "Dollars" and write "Only . . . cents."

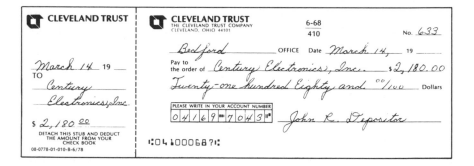

Titles such as "Dr." or "Rev." are not used; it is "Ben Kildare," not "Dr. Ben Kildare." "Mrs." is used only in connection with the husband's name; it is either "Mrs. Roy Roe" or "Ruth Roe." Checks issued to organizations should be made payable to the organization, not to some individual in the organization. Likewise, checks should be made payable to companies, rather than to their agents. Checks for insurance premiums, for example, would be drawn in favor of the insurance company, rather than the agent who handles the account.

It is not wise to sign blank checks. Should this be necessary when the employer will be absent from the office, the checkbook should be kept in a place where it will be safe from theft. Checks, like money, are a medium of exchange and should be guarded as carefully as money.

Erasures and alterations should never be made on checks. Banks are reluctant to accept checks if there is any suspicion that they have been tampered with. If mistakes are made in preparing a check, the word "VOID" should be written across the face of the check and on its stub. If the checks are prenumbered, spoiled checks should not be discarded; they should be kept with canceled checks so that there can be no question concerning the whereabouts of a missing check.

CERTIFIED CHECKS

Often checks for large amounts drawn by a person whose financial status is unknown to the payee must be certified by the bank before they are issued. To secure certification, the depositor takes a completed check to the bank. After the cashier has ascertained that the account has sufficient funds to cover it, the cashier stamps the check "CERTIFIED" and signs it. Immediately upon certification, the amount of the check is charged against the depositor's account. There can be no question of funds being available for payment when it is presented. So far as the bank is concerned, it has already been paid. Thus in a bank reconciliation a certified check is never outstanding, since it has been charged in advance.

Certified checks should never be destroyed. In the event that they are not sent to the payee, they should be redeposited in the bank.

STOPPING PAYMENT ON A CHECK

The drawer of a check has the power to stop payment on it at any time prior to its presentation to the bank for payment. This is accomplished by filing a stop-payment notice at the bank on a form that the bank will provide. Oral notice is insufficient. So that the bank can identify the check when it is presented, it will ask for such information as the number of the check, its date, the name of the payee, and the amount. Stop-payment notices should be filed immediately in case a check is lost.

As soon as the stop-payment notice is filed with the bank, the check stub should be marked "Payment stopped." The amount of the check should then be added to the current balance. This can be done on the check stub open at the time; it is not necessary to go back and correct all preceding balances.

PETTY-CASH FUND

Although it is good policy to make all payments by check, since a check provides a written record of the transaction and serves as a receipt, it is impractical to write checks for small amounts to cover items such as collect telegrams, postage due, carfare, supper money, and incidental purchases of office supplies. In some instances, too, cash is needed immediately. To meet these needs, it is customary to set up what is generally called a "petty-cash fund." Operation of the petty-cash fund is described in the following paragraphs.

Establishing the petty-cash fund. First, it is decided how much cash should be placed in the fund. This is determined by the expenditures that are anticipated. The amount should not be too high, yet it should not be so low that too frequent reimbursements are required. When the amount has been set, a check is drawn payable to Petty Cash. The check is cashed and the funds are placed in a locked cash box or drawer, generally referred to as the petty-cash drawer. Responsibility for the fund should be placed in one person, and this person alone should have access to it.

Payments from the petty-cash fund. All payments from the petty-cash fund should be supported by documentary evidence in the form of a petty-cash voucher, showing the date of payment, the name of the payee, the reason for payment, and the amount paid out (see below). The petty-cash voucher is initialed by the person making payment and signed by the person who has received the cash. Printed forms for this purpose can be purchased at any stationery store.

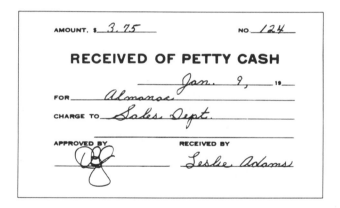

Petty-cash voucher

Paid vouchers are placed in the petty-cash drawer or in a special envelope kept for this purpose. In addition, some firms maintain a petty-cash record. This is simply a form on which paid vouchers can be summarized. Columns are provided for the voucher number, date, name of payee, explanation of payment, and a summary of the expenditures made. Seldom is there a real need for such a record; the petty-cash vouchers themselves usually provide an adequate record. However, in a company with a system of bookkeeping that accounts for every expenditure, regardless of how small, the inclusion of petty-cash payments in the accounting books as part of the daily record may be the best procedure.

Replenishing the petty-cash fund. Whenever the cash in the petty-cash fund gets low, the fund is replenished. A check is written payable to Petty Cash for the amount that has been spent from the fund. The check is cashed and the proceeds are placed in the petty-cash drawer. After replenishment, the cash in the fund should amount to the fund originally established. If replenishment of the fund is taking place too often consideration should be given to increasing the size of the fund.

BOOKKEEPING

There is a need to properly record the income and expense transactions of any business operation. There are two major purposes for this record-keeping. One objective is to determine the profitability of the business. By being able to calculate the profit or loss of the operation and then to be able to analyze in detail the individual items of income and expense, the company is in position to act with greater knowledge in its decisions. The second objective is to gather the necessary information required by the governmental tax agencies such as the Internal Revenue Service. These tax reports not only require a calculation of net income (income less total expense) but also detailed substantiation of individual amounts.

The preparation of these financial statements is usually the responsibility of the accountant. Much of the initial work, however, may be done by the bookkeeper. A secretary may be called upon to handle these bookkeeping duties. At this point, a brief description of these duties will be given. It should be understood that some of these tasks can be handled with little or no experience while others require complete training as an accountant.

   Recording business transactions originally in journals. Most companies use what is referred to as a "double entry" system which has a "debit" and "credit" entry for each item.

   Posting the journal to the ledger. There will be a general ledger and there may be subsidiary ledgers for specific accounts such as accounts receivable and accounts payable.

   Trial Balance of all accounts in the ledger to determine if the accounts are in balance in terms of debits and credits.

   Adjusting journal entries to bring all accounts up to date. For example, if there are any bills owed at the end of the year they are recorded even though they will not be paid until the next year.

   Preparation of the financial statements, primarily the Balance Sheet and the Income Statement. This usually involves the use of a worksheet.

The first two items and possibly the third are considered work normally done by the bookkeeper. The last two items are more often the job of the accountant. How a secretary fits into this process will, of course, depend upon the practice of the individual company.

TAX RECORDS

Aside from the bookkeeping described above, there is a need to keep adequate tax records. Every business must pay a tax on its profits. A corporation pays its own income tax while income from a partnership or an individually owned business is added to the personal tax return of the individual owner. In each case there must be proof of the amounts recorded in the tax returns for income and expense.

While the canceled check is often sufficient proof of the validity of a business expense, the company may be called upon to document specific items. A sales invoice, a bill, a receipt for cash payment, all of these can be useful in providing the necessary documentation. Providing a filing system which allows the accountant to find each of these papers is the basis for accomplishing this task. A filing system can be set up on the basis of (1) date—January bills, February bills, etc.; (2) type of expense—utilities, legal services, office supplies, etc., or (3) type of document—sales invoices, purchase orders, bills, etc. Combinations of these systems often are used. The main point in a good filing system is that it be based on a common sense approach that other people can follow. The secretary is in a central position to see to it that the filing is correctly handled.

There are specific expense items for which the IRS requires a detailed record. Where there are possibilities of abuse the government usually insists upon greater documentation. A taxpayer must clearly show that the expenses are for business reasons, not pleasure, and that they are neither lavish nor extravagant. An example of this type of expense and the additional record-keeping involved are travel and entertainment deduction (T & E). Adequate records would include:

The amount of the expenditure
The dates of departure and return for each trip and the number of days spent on
    business
The business purpose of the expenditure
The place of travel or entertainment
The business relationship to the taxpayer of the person(s) being entertained.

Documentary evidence in the form of credit-card stubs and receipts of paid bills is required for (1) all expenditures for lodging while traveling away from home, and (2) any expenditure over the amount specified by the Internal Revenue Service. Account books or diaries are quite helpful along with the

TRAVEL EXPENSE REPORT

Name	Harriet Blasko		Sales No.		Dept No. 510-076		Date 8/16	Approvals *RSM*

Business Purpose: Annual Convention of Purchasing Agents

Debit Acct.   Credit Acct.

Day	Date	Mil./Dr.	Location	Hotel	Meals	Ent'm't	Tel/Tel	Air	Transportation Gas/Oil	Other	Park/Tolls	Other	Amt.	TOTALS
Sun.														
Mon.														
Tue.														
Wed.														
Thu.	8/12		Kansas City	28.50	21.75	45.00	2.30	82.73	10.30			50.00		240.58
Fri.	8/13		"	--	19.80				10.50					30.30
Sat.														
			TOTALS											270.88

Miles @ 10¢

TOTAL 270.88
Less Airline Charges 82.73
Less Other Charges
TOTAL 188.15
Cash Advance
Due Me 188.15
Returned Herewith

ITEMIZED ENTERTAINMENT RECORD

Date	Location	Business Purpose	Persons Enter'd/Business Relationship	Amount
8/12	Jet Night Club	Inquiry on discounts for processing equipment	Elvin Hawes & Adele Vasquez, Acme Products	45.00

DETAIL OF OTHER EXPENDITURES

Date	Item	Total
8/12	cab: airport – hotel	10.30
8/13	" hotel – airport	10.50
8/12	Convention Registration fee	50.00

INSTRUCTIONS

1. Receipts for lodging, the customer copy of airline tickets, receipts for supplies and each item over $25 should be attached to the report.
2. Meal charges may be included in the report if the employee is away from home "overnight."
3. Include tips for meals and taxis in meal and transportation charges. Tipping for other services should be listed under "Other" expenses and itemized in the space provided.
4. Under "Other" expenditures include items such as luggage tips, supplies, postage, valet, and laundry.
5. Charges for transportation should be identified, such as bus, taxi, train, or rental car. Rental car receipts should be attached to the report.
6. If the space provided for entertainment is inadequate, use a separate memorandum for the overflow.
7. Expense reports are to be submitted weekly and should be sent to the office no later than the Friday following the week in which the expenditures occur.

Signed *Harriet B. Blasko*	Send Check To	Harriet Blasko, Purchasing Dept.

Report of travel expenses

attached receipts, paid bills, etc. on the back of the page that records the expenditures. Employers will expect their secretaries to handle this type of detailed record-keeping. Usually the employer will turn over the raw information to the secretary and then expect the secretary to put it together in a formal record.

AUTOMOBILE-EXPENSE RECORD

The Internal Revenue Service publishes a booklet entitled "Travel, Entertainment, and Expenses." The booklet is IRS Publication 463. Copies can be obtained by calling the local Internal Revenue office or by writing to the Superintendent of Documents, Government Printing Office, Washington, D.C. 20402. The IRS rules for record-keeping that are given in the publication are often used as a guide in the business office.

The taxpayer who uses a personal automobile in connection with business or employment is entitled to deduct automobile expenses (in whole if the auto is used exclusively for business, or in part if it is used for both business and pleasure) on the income-tax return. Expenses include not only all the operating costs but also a reasonable allowance for depreciation. To ensure receiving full benefit from allowable deductions, the taxpayer would be wise to keep careful account of expenses and mileage on an automobile-expense record. A simple form for this purpose, set up to accumulate expenses on an annual basis, is illustrated.

RECORD OF AUTOMOBILE UPKEEP FOR THE   Month of _January_   19*84*

DATE	MILEAGE	GASOLINE		OIL AND GREASE		STORAGE and PARKING		AUTO REPAIRS		CLEANING AND WASHING		ACCESS-ORIES		MISCEL-LANEOUS	
		No. Gals.	Amount												
1															
2	22,346	10	11	40											
3							2	00								
4											3	75				
5							2	75								
6					16	00			18	00					54	30
7		14	15	96												
29							3	15								
30		12	13	72												
31	24,180															
TOTAL	1,834				16	00	10	70	18	00	7	50			54	30

The secretary can keep the record by using information supplied by the employer or, better yet, by making entries from bills routinely filed. The calculation for depreciation can best be made by the accountant responsible for preparing the tax return.

If records are not kept on automobile expenses, an optional tax-deduction method is allowed by the IRS. A standard mileage rate for business use each year may be used by an individual instead of a record of the actual operating and fixed expenses and separate deduction for depreciation. Interest payments on loans and state and local taxes (other than the gasoline tax) attributable to the business use of the car are deductible in addition to the standard mileage rate.

EMPLOYER'S PERSONAL TAX RECORDS

There are a number of different nonbusiness expenses which are deductible on the individual's personal income tax return. As with business expenses, it is important that there exist adequate evidence of the payment of these expenses. The secretary may be called upon by the employer to keep an additional set of records for these personal expenses. The expense deductions include: (1) contributions to charities, colleges, etc., (2) medical and dental expenses, (3) interest on mortgages, loans, etc., and (4) taxes. The most important proof is the canceled check indicating payment. In most situations this is usually sufficient. However, occasionally more evidence is required. Thus a file of the bills would be helpful in substantiating a tax deduction. The employer should turn over personal bank statements with the canceled checks, or at least the ones to be recorded, along with the bills received. The degree that the employer wants the secretary involved in personal financial matters will obviously affect the amount of record-keeping that will be necessary.

PAYROLL

The secretary may be called in to handle the payroll of the company. This will involve (1) calculating the net amount to be paid out and (2) keeping payroll records required for computing the various kinds of payroll taxes and for the government reports. The following section describes these procedures in some detail.

The federal government requires that the employer withhold from each employee's salary a sufficient amount that will at year's end add up to the amount of income tax due. The employee when first hired must fill out Form W-4, the *Employee's Withholding Allowance Certificate* which indicates the number of exemptions claimed. The number of exemptions is then used in applying Circular E, *Employer's Tax Guide* of the Internal Revenue Service, which shows how much tax should be withheld for each salary level.

There also may be state and city income taxes which will require additional withholdings from the employee's payroll check. While the general procedures are basically the same, it is important that the secretary follow the specific requirements of each governmental agency.

Beside the various income taxes, the Federal Insurance Contributions Act

(FICA) requires employees to pay a percentage of their salary as their contribution to the social security program. (There is a matching contribution that is paid by the employer.) The rate is fixed at a certain percentage of the annual salary up to a given amount. After this figure is reached, no more FICA tax is to be paid. Circular E for each year will have tables prepared for the various salary levels.

The following example uses the figure 6.13% FICA tax to be withheld from the first $22,900 of annual salary:

> Employee A, married with 2 children may claim 4 exemptions.
> If A's weekly salary is $300, the payroll check would be calculated as follows:

Gross Pay		$300.00
Less: Federal Income Tax Withheld	$33.30	
FICA Tax Withheld (6.13% × $300)	18.39	
Total Withheld		−51.69
Net Pay—Amount of Check		$248.31

The illustration could have been more complex if state and city income taxes were included. Beside the taxes that are withheld the company sometimes withholds medical insurance, union dues, contributions to charity or retirement programs, and other agreed-upon items.

The monies withheld from the employee's pay check have to be remitted periodically to the respective agencies. Thus, for example, the federal income tax withheld, plus the FICA tax withheld, and the employer's matching FICA tax contribution must be sent to the Internal Revenue Service (or a bank authorized to act as the depositor). How often this is to be done depends upon the dollar amount:

> Less than $200 a month—Every three months
> More than $200 but less than $2000 a month—Every month
> More than $2000 a month—Every two weeks

At the end of each three-month period, a payroll tax return (IRS Form 941) is required to be filed with the IRS. This requirement normally is not the responsibility of the secretary. However, keeping the detailed payroll records may be one of the duties. This will require:

> A record of each pay period showing the dates, hours, and earnings of each employee; and
> A record of each employee's earnings showing
> Date of employment and discharge.
> Social security number.
> Rate or method of pay.
> Summary of wages and all deductions by quarter and calendar year.

There are additional reports required at the end of each year. These include the *Employer's Annual Federal Unemployment Tax Return* (Form 940) and a *Wage and Tax Statement* (Form W-2) for each employee. On the state and local governmental level, quarterly and annual income and unemployment tax returns may be required depending on state and local regulations.

It is important to point out that the ability to manage all of these tax and payroll reports is normally *not* the responsibility of the secretary. Usually the company has an accountant who handles these items. However, the accountant may delegate much of the work to the bookkeeper or the secretary and act only as a supervisor. Therefore, it is helpful to be familiar with payroll procedures and tax reports in case these areas become your responsibility.

Chapter 13

Business Law
WILLIAM W. COOK

BUSINESS LAW in a narrow sense involves the rules, regulations, and laws that pertain to business activities; and those activities are generally said to be the sale or exchange of goods or services for a profit. But business law in a broader sense and for a very practical reason involves the entire body of American law. A business, for example, may commit a crime or be responsible for the safety of its customers; its conduct may be regulated by the government or it may be bound by law to deal in good faith with an external organization such as a union. None of these situations directly involve profit.

When a business has legal problems, it seeks the services of a lawyer. But most legal problems can and should be prevented before they occur, and the secretary is often in a position to perform the important task of prevention. It is imperative, therefore, that the modern secretary have a basic understanding of the law. It is equally imperative that the secretary maintain an awareness of the dealings and activities of the employer as they may be affected by the law.

To be effective, a legal system must be flexible. It must adapt to changing social conditions and keep pace with technological advances. Thus, an ever increasing burden is placed on the secretary to be familiar not only with changes in the law but to cope with a proliferation of new laws. An example of change which might profoundly affect the secretary was the publication of new postal regulations that were necessary because of the installation by the Postal Service of sophisticated mail scanning and sorting machines. A secretary ordering stationery must now be aware of size and thickness restrictions.

BASIC CLASSIFICATIONS OF THE LAW

American law is classified by the "branches" into which it is divided. The first major distinction is that between criminal and civil laws. Essentially, a crime is an offense against society as a whole. The underlying purpose of criminal laws is to ensure that members of society have their constitutional rights of life, liberty, and the pursuit of happiness. To this end, criminal laws provide for the punishment of antisocial behavior. Traditionally, crimes have been punished by either a fine or imprisonment or both. Courts today are also increasingly ordering offenders to make restitution to their victims, that is to "pay back" or compensate the victim for the loss that has been sustained. A court may, for example, punish by imprisonment one who has embezzled funds from an employer. It may also order the offender to return the embezzled funds to the rightful owner.

Generally, to be a crime, the act must be committed intentionally, although negligence, if it is sufficiently wanton and willful, may be criminal. Crimes are also classified according to their seriousness.

Felonies are very serious crimes such as homicide, arson, larceny, and rape. Such crimes infringe upon the security of the person or the person's property. Felonies are punishable by imprisonment or even death. Homicide and rape obviously violate the security of the person whereas arson (the destruction by burning of another's property) and larceny (the taking away of another's property) violate the rightful owner's security in property.

All other crimes, less serious by their nature, are considered misdemeanors. Examples include traffic violations or disturbing the peace. The definition of an act as a felony or misdemeanor may differ from state to state.

Crimes may be committed by individuals and corporations. As will be subsequently discussed, the corporation is legally similar in many ways to a person. A corporation cannot, of course, do or be subject to things which are peculiar to persons. A corporation cannot, for example, commit perjury or be imprisoned. Corporate offenses can therefore be punished only by fines. A careful distinction should be made concerning a criminal offense by an individual within a corporation and an offense by the corporation itself. A corporate officer *could* commit perjury or be imprisoned for an offense committed in that officer's own right.

Other forms of doing business such as the proprietorship (one person doing business) or the partnership (two or more persons doing business jointly) cannot commit a criminal offense in the same way as a corporation.

Crimes fall under either federal or state jurisdiction. Jurisdiction is simply the power of a given type of court to hear and decide a case. A crime which crosses state lines is subject to federal jurisdiction. A federal statute, the Dyer Act for example, prohibits transporting a vehicle known to be stolen across state lines. Crimes committed on a federal property, such as a military reservation, also fall under federal jurisdiction.

THE CIVIL LAW

The civil law includes the remainder of the law after criminal law. The civil law has many branches, but the principal ones include the law of torts, contracts, real and personal property, estates and trusts, and domestic relations. Civil law exists to resolve conflicts between parties rather than between an offender and society. A civilly injured party is entitled to receive some type of compensation for the injury, and the party responsible for the injury cannot be fined or imprisoned for the act. "Injury" as used here refers not only to physical injury but to other types such as monetary injury.

THE LAW OF TORTS

The word "tort" means literally "twisted or crooked behavior." Generally, wrongs between two or more parties are considered to be either tortuous or contractual. The law of contracts will be discussed subsequently.

Torts fall into two main categories: intentional torts and negligence. Many intentional torts may be crimes as well. Assault and battery afford an example of this. If A commits battery upon B and damages B's teeth, it will do B little good if A is criminally fined or imprisoned. But B can sue A in tort and receive damages (money) to pay for repairing the damaged teeth or to compensate for suffering.

Several other intentional torts include fraud and deceit, libel and slander, the invasion of another's privacy, the maintenance of a nuisance, and antitrust violations, all of which may be committed by a business entity. Fraud and deceit, for example, involve the intentional misrepresentation of a material fact which leads another party to act upon it to his detriment and resulting damage. Such an offense could easily arise in a sales situation. But a salesperson's mere commendation of a product is not necessarily fraudulent or deceitful. A reference to a used car for sale as "a real cream puff" is a sales practice known as "puffing."

Businesses which are involved with mass communications, such as newspapers, magazines, and the broadcast media, are apt without utmost care to commit the tort of libel or slander. The damage suffered by a victim is essentially to the person's reputation as the result of a false statement or imputation. Thus, both libel (written statement) and slander (oral statement) are included in the broad term, defamation.

The tort of invasion of privacy stems from the right of the individual to be left alone and like other rights is not an absolute one. Because it is an individual right, it cannot be claimed by a corporation, institution, or business. Damages for intrusion into an individual's privacy might consist of humiliaton or shame, mental distress, or outrage by a person of ordinary sensibilities.

Nuisance consists of using one's property in such an unreasonable way as to hurt another. The doctrine is really a limitation on the use of property. Many businesses, as a part of a manufacturing process, could cause damage to adjacent property owners. The process could, for example, discharge noxious fumes which the business should take every precaution to prevent. Environmental pollution may be a public nuisance, and courts could order it abated or stopped. Nuisance can be a private one as well, and the victim may be entitled to damages for the hurt sustained. Public nuisance can be criminally prosecuted.

Antitrust violations involve the activities of an unlawful monopoly or combination which injure another. While state antitrust statutes provide for the recovery of actual damages by an injured party, the federal statute, the Sherman Act, provides for treble, or three times, the actual damages.

The employees of businesses should be alert to the possibility of their business committing an intentional tort, but a greater damage lies in the area of negligence. The law of negligence is very complex and is based upon the legal duty to use care. At the same time, the prevention of an action for negligence is largely a matter of common sense. It cannot, therefore, be overemphasized that all employees of a given business should be alert to the existence of negligent practices.

Traditionally, a subjective test has been used to determine liability for negligence. The courts will determine whether one party owing a duty of care to another party acted in a reasonable and prudent manner toward that other party. In essence, the law recognizes that accidents will happen despite reasonable precautions. On the other hand, the law will infer negligence when injury results from inherently dangerous activities such as blasting with an explosive. This doctrine is known as "strict liability."

Frequently, the victim of negligence will have contributed to the cause of injury. Under the doctrine of contributory negligence, the victim would be barred from recovering damages. Today, most states have enacted comparative negligence statutes which allow recovery of damages from the negligent party less the proportion of the victim's contribution of negligence to the accident. The doctrine of comparative negligence is most commonly invoked in motor vehicle negligence cases.

The secretary should be aware that the owner of property owes varying degrees of care to different classes of people who come upon the premises. Owners owe the highest degree of care to invitees on the property. Invitees are those who enter another's property and whose presence is of some interest or advantage to the owner. Customers in stores and shops and guests in hotels and restaurants would be considered invitees. To them the owner owes the care of keeping the premises reasonably safe.

THE LAW OF CONTRACTS

The underlying purpose of the law of contracts is to make agreements between two or more parties more certain. The vast majority of contracts are performed successfully to the satisfaction of the parties. It is only when a party breaches or fails to perform what has been agreed to that the law of contracts will be invoked. If at this time the contract is found to be valid, the courts will either order performance of it or award damages to be paid to the non-breaching party.

The determination of validity of a contract is based on many factors. The first step in making a valid contract is an offer by one party to another, and the terms of the offer must be reasonably certain. Next, the offer must be accepted as made since changing the terms of the offer would be a counteroffer which in turn would have to be accepted.

A second requirement for a valid contract is a true mutual assent of the parties which is often referred to as "a meeting of the minds." If one party procured the contract through fraud, duress, or undue influence on the other party, there can obviously be no mutual assent.

A valid contract must be supported by an exchange of consideration, that is, value. Consideration may consist of money or services and even a promise *not* to do something if the promise has value. In an old case, for example, a person's promise not to smoke until the age of twenty-one was held by the court to be adequate consideration for a promise to pay that person a sum of money.

Courts will not enforce a contract which is not for a legal purpose or contrary to the public welfare. If, for example, the performance of a contract is in violation of a law, it will be invalid. Formerly, many states had statutes which stipulated that contracts made on Sunday could not be enforced. These have largely been repealed. Frequently, contracts for the purchase and sale of a business will have a clause in which the seller agrees not to compete with the buyer for a period of time in a fixed geographical area. Such clauses are valid if they are not unreasonable. An agreement "not to compete in the State of New York for the next twenty years" would be considered unreasonable. An agreement "not to compete within a radius of three miles for the next six months" might be reasonable, however.

Although any person or corporation may enter into a contract, some persons are considered not to be competent to contract and a contract cannot be enforced against them. They include infants (persons under 18 years of age) and insane or intoxicated persons. Contracts made by these classes of people are said to be "voidable," in the sense that they may be considered void because such persons are under the disability of minority, insanity, or intoxication. When a disability is removed, such as by a party reaching eighteen years of age, the contract may be disaffirmed within a reasonable time or it is considered affirmed and enforceable.

Contracts need not be in writing to be valid. As a practical matter, however, it is advisable to have a written and signed contract because in the event of a breach and a court action, it will serve as proof of its own terms. The proof of oral contracts can be difficult.

Contracts which must be written are specified in the Statute of Frauds which was originally enacted in England in 1677. It has been enacted with some minor variations in all states. The most important types of contracts required to be in writing include contracts for the sale of real estate regardless of the amount of the purchase price, leases of real property usually for a period of a year or more, promises to answer for the debts or obligations of another, and contracts which are not to be performed within a year of the promise. Additionally, the Uniform Commercial Code requires that a contract for the sale of personal property for $500 or more be in writing unless part payment has been made, part of the goods have been delivered, or either the buyer or seller has signed a memorandum of agreement to the sale.

PERSONAL PROPERTY

The law relating to the *sale* of personal property is largely contained in Article 2 of the Uniform Commercial Code which will be discussed as a separate topic. Inherent in the ownership of property is the right to transfer or dispose of it. A sale is but one medium through which this may be done. The owner of property may transfer property by will (a bequest) or by making a gift of it. It is difficult to formulate a precise definition of personal property. Clearly the term includes objects other than real property which consists of land and the buildings on it. Personal property is frequently classified as corporeal and incorporeal. Corporeal refers to personal property which is tangible and includes goods which are also referred to as chattels. Another distinction of corporeal personal properties is that they are visible and movable.

Incorporeal personal property involves "rights" rather than tangible objects. Examples of such rights include patents, copyrights, and trademarks. A patent is a grant to the inventor to use, sell, or allow others to use the invention exclusively for a period of 17 years. A copyright, too, is a grant giving an author an exclusive right to possess, publish, or sell the production of his or her intellect. Formerly a copyright was a grant for 28 years with the right to renew it for another 28 years. Today, however, for copyrights granted during and after 1978, there is a single period consisting of the lifetime of the author plus 50 years. A trademark which is the property of a business is a sign, mark, name, or symbol which identifies it or its product. Trademarks may be registered for a period of 20 years and may be renewed at the end of each 20-year period.

The ownership of personal property should be distinguished from the possession of it. Frequently the owner of personal property will deliver it to another for some purpose, such as safekeeping or repair. When this happens, the possession by one other than the owner is known as a bailment. The one in possession (the bailee) has responsibilities for the property to the owner (the bailor). The bailee is responsible for using ordinary care as to the bailed property and returning or disposing of the property at the direction of the bailor. A bailment comes into being upon agreement of the parties and delivery of the property to the bailee.

A bailment does not exist when a party merely rents space for the safekeeping of personal property. A bank, for example, is not a bailee of goods kept in a safety-deposit box because it cannot enter the box without the owner's key. Similarly, a "park and lock" parking lot is not a bailee; but when a vehicle owner leaves the key to the vehicle with the parking lot operator, a bailment does exist. In the latter case the lot operator would be responsible if the owner's vehicle was damaged while stored.

Sometimes the law will infer a bailment which is known as a constructive bailment. A person who finds lost property is a constructive bailee who owes the owner the standard of ordinary care for it.

REAL PROPERTY

Much of the law relating to real estate is rooted in antiquity, although the modern consumer movement has modified or changed many of the traditional rights and responsibilities of owners.

Real estate consists of land, the buildings on it, and fixtures. Although it is not a particularly practical matter, land includes not only a surface area, but runs from the center of the earth to the reaches of space. More practically, the ownership of land includes subsurface mineral rights. Land also includes the things which naturally grow upon it such as trees and crops. When they are severed from the land they become personal property. Fixtures are personal property which are affixed to land or buildings in such a way as to be considered a part of the real property.

The ownership or right to possession of real estate falls into two categories: the freehold and leasehold estate. There are today only two types of freehold estates, and they essentially involve ownership. The most prevalent type of real-property ownership is called a fee simple and it is the most common type of home ownership. The owner of a fee simple has virtually full and usually unrestricted ownership including the right to transfer it by deed or will. A lesser type of ownership is the life estate where the holder owns the property during that person's life or that of another. As an example A, the owner of a fee simple estate, grants it to B for the life of B. During B's life he or she has full ownership; but upon the death of B, full ownership reverts back to A. B's interest could, of course, be sold to C, although the measuring life would still be that of B. Upon the death of B, C would lose the estate to A.

Leaseholds entitle a party to possess and use the real property of another and may be of definite or indefinite duration. Leaseholds are referred to as tenancies and may be for years, period to period, at will, or at the sufferance of the owner. A tenancy for years is one for a fixed period of time. The term is a misnomer because a tenancy for years may be for less than a year. The essential characteristic is a fixed period, be it six months or five years. The tenancy from period to period is the most common one. Such a tenancy may be from week to week, month to month, or year to year. It can be terminated by proper notice of either the landlord or tenant but could be of indefinite duration. A tenancy at will is simply one which may be terminated at any time and without notice at the will of either party. This type of tenancy usually does not involve the payment of rent. A tenancy at sufferance exists when a tenant for years "holds over" or remains in possession after the expiration of the lease. Such a tenancy is not really a tenancy because the tenant has absolutely no rights and remains in possession only through the consent of the landlord.

Businesses frequently select tenancies for years to ensure stability by maintaining the same location. Rental dwellings, however, are most commonly rented on a period to period basis. In recent years many states have enacted "consumer" statutes in favor of tenants. Landlords, for example, must maintain dwelling property in a habitable condition. Notice requirements have been strengthened to prevent arbitrary and sudden eviction.

ESTATES AND TRUSTS

Estate law provides for the transfer of property at the time of death. Such a transfer may be by will or be without a will. The maker of a will, a testator, provides his or her representative after death, the executor, with instructions for the distribution of property. In the absence of a will, distribution will be made as stipulated by law. It is certainly advisable for most people to make a will, not only so that their wishes may be effected but also because a will might be most advantageous to the relatives of the testator.

The basic requirement for a will is the intent, sometimes called the donative intent, of the maker. A will has no force until death and may be revoked or changed at any time by the testator. It creates no rights or benefits in others during the life of the maker. No special form is necessary for a will although the maker must know and understand the contents of it. Anyone who is "sound of mind" can make a will. Through the years there has been great controversy about what a sound mind really is. Because a will is a solemn document, the law requires with rare exceptions that it be written and signed by the testator. Signing must be attested to or witnessed in all states although the number of witnesses required varies.

Upon the death of the testator, a probate court in the appropriate jurisdiction appoints an executor, usually the person so-named in the will. The court is not bound in this respect, however, since the person named may be unavailable or unqualified at the time of probate. Following appointment, the executor distributes the personal property according to the will and under the supervision of the court. Finally, the executor must account to the court for the distribution.

When a person dies without a will, his or her property is distributed according to the various state statutes of descent and distribution. Such statutes provide for distribution to various classes of relationship. The most preferred class of persons are the lineal descendents who are in a direct line of the decedent such as children and grandchildren or parents and grandparents. A second relationship is that by affinity or marriage, and the third class consists of collateral relatives such as brothers and sisters and cousins. In default of the above classes, the decedent's estate goes to the "next of kin."

A person who dies without a will is said to be intestate. Distribution is made by an administrator rather than an executor, and the probate procedure is similar in many ways to that under a will.

A trust is a relationship between two or more parties where one party, a trustee, holds property for the enjoyment of the person creating the trust, the trustor or settlor, or a third party. The reasons for the creation of trusts are endless; but a trust once created must be for an active purpose. The decision to have a second party manage one's property would be a valid reason for establishing a trust.

Any legally competent person can create a trust and must manifest an intent to do so. The trust instrument must reasonably describe the property that is entrusted, and the duties of the trustee must be clear. If a trust is to be revocable, that is subject to cancellation by the trustor or another, it should be so stated in the instrument. Otherwise it will be irrevocable.

A trustor may also be the trustee but in such a case he or she cannot be a beneficiary or person who is to enjoy the benefits of the trust. Trusts must, of course, have a lawful purpose. As the term implies, the trustee has a fiduciary responsibility and must act in good faith.

SOURCES OF THE LAW

The secretary must have an understanding of general principles of law, but it is equally important to understand the source of laws, especially those which affect businesses. Through such understanding the secretary will be able to find specific laws as they are needed by the employer.

Unless the secretary works in a law office, few compilations of the law will be at hand. Many public libraries have excellent legal collections as do college and university libraries. Even more comprehensive collections are maintained in county seats, usually in or near the county courthouse. Many government regulations are available from the Superintendent of Documents in

Washington, D.C. and frequently the local office of the United States Senator or member of the House of Representatives will assist in obtaining such documents.

The highest legal authority is the Constitution of the United States and in the various states their respective constitutions. State constitutions are found in the collected statutes of each state. More specific laws are enacted by the federal and state legislatures. Federal laws are compiled in the *United States Code* (the working version is the *U.S. Code Annotated*), and state laws are compiled under a variety of names usually containing the word "statutes."

Many of the laws which affect businesses are promulgated by governmental agencies and are called regulations. Frequently, for example, Congress will enact legislation and leave the implementation of it to an appropriate agency. When this is done, the agency will publish "proposed rules" in *The Federal Register* for public comment. When they become final regulations, they are

A sample collection of books that a secretary might keep on hand, containing the rules, regulations, and laws that pertain to the employer's business.

again published in the *Register* and compiled in the *Code of Federal Regulations*. The latter publication may also be found in many libraries.

Local laws such as those of a town or city are called ordinances and are available at the town or city hall. Ordinances deal with purely local matters and can have considerable impact on a business. Zoning and opening and closing hours for stores are but two examples.

In recent years there has been a trend to enacting uniform laws, that is identically written laws among the states that accept them. The purpose of uniform laws is to to standardize the law, a practice which is particularly useful as to some business practices. As society becomes increasingly mobile, so do business transactions. The need for uniformity becomes apparent. One such uniform body of law is the Uniform Commercial Code which has been enacted in all states but Louisiana. The UCC will be discussed in detail.

A secretary should take responsibility for obtaining and maintaining a library of the most important rules, regulations, and laws that affect the business served. Many publications which should be readily available to the employer may be obtained at little or no cost.

THE UNIFORM COMMERCIAL CODE

The basic document governing the conduct of business is the Uniform Commercial Code (UCC). It covers the sale of goods; commercial paper; bank deposits and collections; letters of credit; bulk transfers; warehouse receipts, bills of lading, and other documents of title; investment securities; and secured transactions. The secretary should be thoroughly familiar with those articles of the UCC which affect the employer. A secretary in a bank should understand the articles on commercial paper and bank deposits and collections. A secretary in an establishment which sells goods should understand the articles on sale and secured transactions.

SALES

Article 2 of the UCC contains the basic law of sales. It is sometimes referred to as "the buyer's law" because it sets out remedies for the breach of sales contracts and defines various types of warranties for goods that are sold. But it also contains remedies for abuses suffered by the seller and delineates the responsibility for goods which are in the possession of a bailee such as a trucker or railroad.

When one considers the sheer number of sales transactions which occur each day and the fact that many of them are not cash transactions, it is apparent that both buyers and sellers need the protection of the law to clearly define their respective rights and responsibilities. The article on sales should, therefore, be considered in the light of the article on secured transactions. A secured transaction is simply one in which the seller maintains a right in that which is sold until the full purchase price has been paid.

Article 2 applies specifically to the sale of "goods" which are movable and identifiable. The term excludes money which is used to pay for the goods. Even more specifically, Article 2 governs contracts for the sale of goods and recognizes different types of buyers and sellers. A "merchant," for example, is one who has special occupational skills and knowledge of the particular type of goods sold. A merchant is charged with a higher standard of care in dealing than one who is not a merchant.

As noted, Article 2 basically governs *contracts* for the sale of goods. Most of the casual retail transactions which occur daily would thus be excluded. The Statute of Frauds in Article 2 further limits those transactions which must be covered by a written sales contract. Generally, a sales contract which provides for a price of $500 or more must be in writing. A special situation exists in Article 2 as to merchants. If a merchant receives a letter of confirmation of a transaction which is not written, he or she must, if desired, repudiate or reject the transaction within ten days just as though he or she had signed the writing. This provision cures a previous evil in which a party could repudiate a contract by simply ignoring a confirming letter. It is imperative that a buyer or seller who is in the "merchant" class closely monitor incoming mail. The secretary may therefore be instrumental in preventing an unwanted contract by default.

It should be emphasized that the requirement of the Statute of Frauds that certain contracts be in writing does not necessarily mean the existence of what most people consider a formal contract. The reason for the rule is evidentiary in the sense that as an agreement becomes more important, there is a greater need for written evidence of it. In the case of Article 2, $500 is the criterion which invokes the Statute.

A writing under the Statute must meet several requirements, however. It must be signed although this may be done by printing, stamping, typewriting, or even initials if it is the intent of the party to authenticate the writing. The terms of the writing should give assurance that there is or was a transaction and state the quantity of goods involved. The writing may be a single one or consist of several writings such as the exchange of letters, bills of sale, or even telegrams. Lesser documents such as cash register receipts usually do not satisfy the signature requirement.

There are situations in which a transaction is taken out of the Statute of Frauds even though the price is greater than $500. If, for example, the goods are delivered by the seller and accepted by the buyer, the contract will be enforceable without a writing. Delivery and acceptance of only a part of the goods will render a contract enforceable only as to that part.

Once a valid contract, written or oral, exists, each of the parties has certain rights and responsibilities. It may seem too obvious, but the essential two acts of performance are that the seller deliver the goods and that the buyer pay for them. Such a simplistic statement raises a variety of questons. Where, for example, is delivery to be made? How is payment to be made? While goods are in transit, who bears the risk of their destruction? What if the goods are not exactly of the quantity and quality ordered? Normally it is advisable to have specific provisions in the contract which answer these questions. But in practice such specific provisions are frequently omitted because customary practices in dealing are followed.

The UCC, Article 2, does provide some answers. Unless otherwise stated, the place of delivery is the seller's place of business or, if there is none, the seller's residence. Or if both parties know that the goods are at a location other than the seller's place of business, that location is the place of delivery. Such a situation might exist where the seller's goods are stored in another's warehouse.

Article 2 stipulates, unless otherwise stated, that the time for delivery is a *reasonable* time. In the event that a contract was breached on this basis, the court would decide what a reasonable time would have been. The type of goods would, of course, have a bearing upon the decision and even the hour of delivery must be reasonable. Without agreement to the contrary, a buyer is entitled to have all goods delivered at the same time.

If a contract states that the place of delivery of goods is that of the buyer, the seller must so deliver them and may do so through a carrier such as a trucking company or railroad. When the goods are turned over to the carrier, the carrier signs a bill of lading that lists goods, weight, etc. A bill of lading is a document by which the carrier acknowledges receipt of goods and agrees to transport them to the designated place of delivery. Generally, risk for the destruction of goods rests with the seller until time of delivery.

When the goods are delivered, the buyer has the right to inspect them to ensure that they comply with the contract. The time and place for inspection are described as reasonable ones by the UCC. And sometimes because of the complexity and nature of goods, the right of inspection extends to using the goods. Such is the case of a purchaser of an automobile since a visual inspection alone might not be sufficient to discover a defect.

If upon inspection the buyer determines that goods do not conform to the terms of the contract, they may be rejected or accepted. And the buyer may also elect to accept any commercial unit or units and reject the rest. If the buyer rejects all or part of the tendered goods, he or she must promptly notify the seller and hold them with reasonable care for a period of time sufficient for the seller to remove them. The buyer cannot, of course, use the goods after rejection.

Once the buyer has accepted goods, he or she must tender payment to the seller. Any method of payment is sufficient if it is in the ordinary course of business. The seller can demand payment in legal tender (money). When this is done, the buyer must be given a reasonable extension of time to procure it. Payment by check is conditional upon its being honored on due presentment.

The UCC sets out three kinds of warranties, the breach of which may create liability upon the seller. The most obvious warranty is an express one and need not be created by the words "warrant" or "guarantee." Any affirmation of fact or promise by the seller may create an express warranty and may be determined by whether or not it is a basis for the bargain between the seller and buyer. A seller's mere "puffing" of a product, that is an opinion or commendation of goods, does not create an express warranty. Since an express warranty is an affirmative statement, it cannot be excluded or modified as can implied warranties.

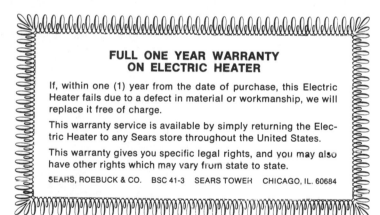

**FULL ONE YEAR WARRANTY
ON ELECTRIC HEATER**

If, within one (1) year from the date of purchase, this Electric Heater fails due to a defect in material or workmanship, we will replace it free of charge.

This warranty service is available by simply returning the Electric Heater to any Sears store throughout the United States.

This warranty gives you specific legal rights, and you may also have other rights which may vary from state to state.

SEARS, ROEBUCK & CO.   BSC 41-3   SEARS TOWER   CHICAGO, IL. 60684

Two types of implied warranties exist under the UCC. The first is the warranty of merchantability. For such a warranty to exist, the seller must be a merchant for a particular purpose as defined by the Code. Very generally, for the criteria are complex, goods are merchantable as they compare with the quality of other brands on the market and conform within variations permitted by the agreement. The reason for this warranty is that because of the merchant's special skill and knowledge, he or she is held to a higher standard for the quality of goods sold. And the UCC specifically includes the sale of food or drink for value in the warranty for merchantability.

A second implied warranty is that of fitness for a particular purpose. This warranty arises where the seller knows the purpose for which the goods are bought and that the buyer is relying on the seller's skill or judgment to furnish the appropriate goods.

Implied warranties may be modified or excluded. A warranty of fitness must be in writing and conspicuous. A warranty of merchantability must mention merchantability; and, if in writing, it too must be conspicuous. If a buyer examines or refuses to examine goods before entering a contract and such examination should have revealed a defect, there can be no implied warranty.

All warranties may extend to the family or those in the household of a buyer or even guests if they could reasonably expect to use or consume the product.

SECURED TRANSACTIONS

In recent years credit buying has become an American way of life. The practice is not new, however, although expansion of it has largely occurred in the consumer sector. Credit buying usually consists of a person's buying something and paying for it with a commitment against future income. The real estate mortgage is a form of credit buying and has its roots in antiquity.

The problem with a credit sale is that a seller parts with property to a buyer who may default on his or her promise to pay for the goods or who subsequently sells them to a third party. Article 9 of the UCC provides an orderly system which not only allows the seller's interest in goods sold on credit to be retained but gives notice of this interest to subsequent buyers. This system is similar in many ways to the mortgage system used in real estate.

Article 9 of the UCC essentially covers personal property and fixtures. Because personal property is movable and real estate is not, considerable differences also exist between Article 9 security interests and the real estate mortgage. What then is a security interest? It is simply an interest, which once established, secures the payment or performance of an obligation. Security interests are not limited only to a buyer-seller sales situation. A may lend B money to buy an automobile. When B has purchased the automobile, A may have a security interest in it to secure the loan to B. In this situation A would be called a lender, B would be called a debtor, and the automobile would be called collateral.

A security interest is said by the UCC to "attach" at a certain time. In essence it means to become effective. When three requirements have been met and coexist, a security interest is said to attach. There must first be agreement between the lender and debtor that it attach; the secured party must have given value; and the debtor must have rights in the collateral. In the example in the above paragraph, attachment would not occur at the time of the loan but at the time B had an interest in the collateral, that is, the automobile.

The medium for agreement is a document called a security agreement. It must reasonably identify the collateral and be signed by the debtor. Although the secured party does not have to sign the security agreement, such is the usual practice.

Once a security agreement has attached, the lender (or creditor) has enforceable rights in the collateral and is thus protected against the default of the debtor. The secured party is also *usually* protected against subsequent purchasers of the collateral and other creditors.

In the case of certain types of goods, the secured party must take one more step in order to have a fully protected interest. This procedure is known as "perfecting" the security interest and consists of filing a document called a financing statement with an appropriate agency. The place for filing varies from state to state, but typically it is with, say, the UCC Division in the Office of the Secretary of State. Here financing statements are filed and indexed under the name of the debtor.

The purpose behind the filing process is to give notice to another party considering extending credit to the debtor that there is a preexisting security interest in collateral. If, for example, A lends B $10,000 and takes a security interest in B's manufacturing equipment, A will file a financing statement to protect his or her interest. B might try to obtain another loan from C against the same collateral. If C checks with the place for filing, it will be apparent that there is another security interest in B's equipment and C will be well-advised not to extend a loan to B. If C does so anyway or fails to check for a previously filed security interest, C's interest will be subordinate to that of A.

Financing statements may be filed on very simple forms which are supplied by the Secretary of State. They must include the names and addresses of both the creditor and debtor and be signed by the latter. The description of collateral need not be as specific as in the security agreement because, as noted, the purpose is only to give notice to one considering a subsequent loan or extension of credit that a security interest already exists. Addresses are given so that a prospective creditor may further investigate the matter.

Security interests may be filed before attachment in which case perfection does not occur until attachment. If, for example, B borrows from A to buy equipment which will become the collateral in which A will have a security interest, A may file at the time of making the loan. The interest cannot attach until B purchases the equipment, and thus it is not perfected until that time.

A security interest is a perfected one if the creditor has the collateral in possession. The reason for this is that a prospective creditor is automatically put on notice of the security interest of a secured party.

Article 9 of the UCC generally classifies goods as consumer goods, equipment, farm products, and inventory. In the case of consumer goods, a security interest need not be perfected by filing, a rule largely based upon expediency. As a practical matter it would be nearly impossible to file the extremely large number of secured transactions in consumer goods. The burden of filing would be particularly heavy on retail merchants who typically sell their goods on installment contracts. Such a burden outweighs the interest of the possible creditor of the consumer. Consumer goods are defined by UCC as goods " . . . used or bought primarily for personal, family, or household purposes."

It has been noted that Article 9 covers secured transactions in fixtures as well as all other kinds of personal property. The place of filing a security interest in fixtures is usually the place of filing for the real property to which an item is affixed. This would usually be in a county office such as a Registry of Deeds. Filing may therefore be either local (in a county office) or central (in the Secretary of State's Office). The UCC does not, unfortunately, define fixtures. Thus a secured party must rely on individual state interpretations. If there is any doubt, the secured party should file *both* locally and centrally.

The system for secured transactions here described results in degrees of security for the creditor. Depending on the degree of security, the UCC establishes priorities among conflicting interests in the same collateral for

UNIFORM COMMERCIAL CODE — FINANCING STATEMENT — FORM UCC-2

INSTRUCTIONS
1. This form is designed to avoid double typing when filing with more than one office. Place this form over UCC-1.
2. PLEASE TYPE this form. Fold only along perforation for mailing.
3. Send all 3 copies with interleaved carbon paper to the filing officer. Enclose filing fee.
4. If the space provided for any item (s) on the form is inadequate the item(s) should be continued on additional sheets, preferably 5" x 8" or 8" x 10". Only one copy of such additional sheets need be presented to the filing officer with a set of three copies of the financing statement. Long schedules of collateral, indentures, etc., may be on any size paper that is convenient for the secured party.
5. If collateral is crops or goods which are or are to become fixtures, describe generally the real estate and give name of record owner.
6. When a copy of the security agreement is used as a financing statement, it is requested that it be accompanied by a completed but unsigned set of these forms, without extra fee.
7. At the time of original filing, filing officer will return third copy as an acknowledgment. At a later date, secured party may date and sign the termination legend and use third copy as a Termination Statement.

This FINANCING STATEMENT is presented to a filing officer for filing pursuant to the Uniform Commercial Code. | 3 Maturity date (if any):

1 Debtor(s) (Last Name First) and address(es) | 2 Secured Party(ies) and address(es) | For Filing Officer (Date, Time, Number, and Filing Office)

4 This financing statement covers the following types (or items) of property:

Check ☒ if covered: ☐ Proceeds of Collateral are also covered ☐ Products of Collateral are also covered No. of additional sheets presented:

Filed with:

This instrument prepared by

By: _____ Signature(s) of Debtor(s)   By: _____ Signature(s) of Secured Party(ies)

Filing Officer Copy — Alphabetical   STANDARD FORM - UNIFORM COMMERCIAL CODE - FORM UCC-2 Approved by The Secretary of State   The Ohio Legal Blank Co., Cleveland Publishers and Dealers Since 1883

Standard financing statement of the
Uniform Commercial Code

non-fixtures and fixtures respectively. Under these provisions a perfected security interest has priority over an unperfected interest. And the first party to perfect has priority over a party who perfects subsequently. If A advanced credit to B on January 1st and took a security interest in B's equipment but did not file a financing statement and on February 1st C executed the same transaction taking a security interest in the same equipment and did file a financing statement, C's interest would have priority over that of A. Even if A filed on March 1st, C's claim would be paramount. If B became insolvent on April 1st, C's rights in B's equipment would allow C to take it in satisfaction of the debt and A's rights would be defeated.

The secretary will often be the person in a business responsible for the documentation of a secured transaction. It should be apparent that the secretary must be alert to the need for timeliness and correct procedure in satisfying the requirements of Article 9. Procrastination in filing a financing statement, for example, might leave the business unprotected in the event of a buyer's or borrower's default. The secretary should live by the maxim that, "when in doubt, file!"

BULK SALES OR TRANSFERS

It is not, happily, a common occurrence; but a merchant could transfer the majority of his or her materials, supplies, or inventory to another with the purpose of defeating creditors' claims. Article 6 of the Uniform Commercial Code regulates just such transactions and serves to protect the creditors in a bulk transaction. A, for example, a merchant hounded by creditors, says to his friend B, "B, I'm tired of this business. I'll sell you my stock at a good price." B accepts and pays A in cash for his stock. A leaves the area. What recourse do the creditors of A have?

Article 6 of the UCC deals with the matter between the bulk transferee, B in the sample above, and the creditors of the transferor, A. First the transfer must be a "bulk" transfer. Article 6, Sec. 102 refers to a transfer not in the ordinary course of the transferor's business of " . . . a major part of the materials, supplies, merchandise, or other inventory." Article 6 does not proscribe bulk transfers; it merely dictates that certain procedures be followed, and the responsibility for so doing is largely on the transferee. In effect, an illegal or procedurally incorrect transfer is treated as no transfer at all with respect to the creditors.

The correct procedure is relatively simple. The transferee must require the transferor to supply him or her with a list of the transferor's property, that is, a schedule of the property transferred in bulk. The transferor is also required to furnish a list of his or her creditors. Next, the transferee must notify the creditors of the sale within ten days before either taking possession of the goods or paying for them. Finally, the transferee must maintain the list of creditors and schedule of property for six months and allow inspection or copying of them by the creditors.

Clearly, Article 6 is designed to prevent surprise or "midnight" sales which leave the creditor without protection. Since the very nature of a fraudulent bulk sale involves the absence of a transferor, the responsibility for compliance with Article 6 falls on the transferee. The creditors cannot be held responsible since they are not parties to the transaction nor do they ordinarily have knowledge of it.

Section 6-106 of the UCC requires that a bulk transferee apply the proceeds of the transferred goods to the creditors of the transferor as properly listed. Without correct procedure in the sale, creditors have a claim on the goods as though there had been no sale or transfer.

The law of bulk transactions logically follows that of secured transactions. It should again be noted that Article 6 does not invalidate a bulk transfer. It only provides protection to the creditors of the transferor and does not in any way affect the seller and buyer relationship in a bulk transfer.

RELATIONSHIPS BETWEEN BUSINESSES AND EMPLOYEES OR AGENTS

Aside from the rare if not improbable situation where one person goes into business and operates that business alone, various relationships exist between those who own or operate businesses and those who assist them. Historically such relationships have been those between the employer and employee and the principal and agent. The role of the independent contractor is also discussed here although the term in itself implies the absence of a relationship rather than the existence of one.

The role of a secretary in a business will usually involve performing a service for the employer. But it would not be uncommon for the secretary to serve as an agent as well. The employer and principal have definite responsibilities both for and toward their employees and agents. Similarly, their actions may create liability in employer or principal toward third persons.

EMPLOYMENT

In simplest terms an employment relationship exists when one person, an employee, performs services under the control of and for another, the employer. The relationship is consensual or by agreement of the parties. Otherwise employment would be slavery which is prohibited by the Constitution. The employee is entitled to compensation for services performed, a fact which is analagous to the requirement for consideration between parties to a contract. Employment is, in fact, a contractual relationship although the contract may be merely an implied one. It is interesting that the employment relationship was once known as the master-servant doctrine.

Although employers and employees are free to agree on most of the terms of employment, there are statutory requirements which must be met. The employer, for example, must compensate the employee at or above minimum wage levels and some classes of employees such as those under a certain age cannot be employed for some purposes. The employer may be bound by a union contract in which case he or she would have to conform not only to compensation provisions but many other types of provisions as well.

At one time employees worked simply for wages. Today, however, it is most common for the employee to receive additional compensation or benefits such as a retirement plan, health insurance, or even life insurance. In some cases the employer is required to contribute to a state insurance plan such as workers' compensation. And more and more employers are required by statute to provide safe and healthful working conditions for their employees.

One notable example of federal legislation to protect the rights of employees was the Employees Retirement Income Security Act, known as "ERISA," passed in 1974. Under it the pension rights earned by an employee cannot be arbitrarily denied by an employer. Once pension rights are earned, they are said to "vest" in the employee. The Act also requires detailed reporting to the Secretary of Labor by an employer or other person who administers a pension fund and stipulates that a person's pension rights are "portable" in that they may be taken from one employment to another. The Act was designed to prevent the practice of denying retirement benefits to an employee who terminates employment shortly before the usual age of retirement.

The employee is obligated to perform honest and faithful service to the employer. Unless they have a contractual provision to the contrary, an employee may serve two or more employers but not during the same hours. The employee must obey reasonable rules and regulations imposed by the employer and use due care and reasonable diligence in the performance of his or her work. When an employee is discharged before the end of a term of employment, the employer must provide compensation to the end of that term unless there is agreement to the contrary.

Modern statutes have considerably changed the liability of an employer for injury to the employees or injury to another *by* the employee. Workers' compensation statutes provide compensation to the employee or certain relatives regardless of fault on the part of either the employer or employee if an injury occurs as a part of employment. Today many occupational diseases are covered as well.

When an employee injures a third person, the employer is liable if the employee is at fault. The employer might, for example, direct the employee to perform an act which causes the injury. The employer is also responsible for injury caused by an employee if the causing act is within the scope of the employment. Such liability is known as the doctrine of *Respondeat Superior*, a legal term which means literally "let the master answer." Most employers seek to avoid the harshness of the doctrine by voluntarily carrying liability insurance.

One interesting exception to the rules of employer liability is the exemption of some governmental employers. Until waived by statute, the federal and state governments could not be sued for their employees' torts. The exception was based on the ancient concept that the sovereign (king or queen) could not be sued and the principle has been carried into modern times. Under the Federal Tort Claims Act, the exception is mostly waived, and most states have enacted similar legislation.

PRINCIPAL AND AGENT

The basic difference between an employee and an agent is degree of authority which is conferred upon the agent. An agent is one who on behalf of the principal may make contracts. An agent may also be an employee, such as in the case of delivery truck drivers who not only deliver goods but take orders for them.

Unfortunately, the term "agency" is loosely used to describe relationships which are not agencies at all. The real estate agent is usually a broker whose function is to find a buyer for property. If the broker has been authorized to enter a sales contract for the purchase of property on behalf of an absent buyer, however, he or she would be acting as an agent.

An agency relationship is both consensual and contractual and may be limited or unlimited. Usually an agency is created by the appointment of an agent by a principal. The appointment may be oral but in most states the appointment of an agent to acquire or dispose of land must be in writing. A written appointment is known as a power of attorney.

Agents may be classified as special, general, or universal. A special agent is one who has the power to make a specific transaction or do a specific act. A general agent is not so limited, however, and may transact all of the business at one place. One who manages a business, such as a store, for an owner would be a general agent. He or she could purchase and sell inventories and equipment. A universal agent has no limitations as to authority except those imposed by law. This type of agency is an appropriate one for a person who is geographically remote from the normal place of residence or doing business. A person going overseas in military service might grant a universal power of attorney to the spouse or a parent.

An agency may also be created by conduct because of the consensual nature of the relationship. If by his or her conduct one lets another act as an agent, the appearance of agency will exist. Then, in turn, if others can reasonably believe that one is an agent because the other's conduct so indicates, an agency will exist. Such a situation may seem unimportant; but because the existence of an agency raises questions about liabilities and duties in the principal, it may be important to a third person seeking to enforce a contract made by the apparent agent or seeking damages for his or her torts. It should be noted that a third person seeking legal redress from an apparent principal has the burden of proving that an agency relationship exists.

It has been noted that an agent may be an employee as well. As such he or she owes certain responsibilities to the employer. But because of the special nature of an agency, an agent has greater responsibilities to the principal. Because the agent is really standing in the place of the principal and making judgments for which the principal will in turn be responsible, the agent has a duty to keep the principal informed of all actions. The agent will often have the money or other property of the principal in possession. The agent must therefore periodically render an accounting to the principal and should never allow the principal's property to become comingled or mixed with that of the agent. Usually, a time for accounting is specified in the agency agreement or contract.

The agent must, of course, use reasonable care in transacting the principal's business and must avoid any conflict of interest. If an agency exists for the purpose of the agent to purchase a house for the principal, the agent cannot purchase it for himself or herself.

The principal also has duties toward the agent. Usually there is a contract provision for compensation although agencies frequently provide for a commission rather than salary. It is also common for an agent working on commission to receive an advance payment or "draw" against commissions to be received.

INDEPENDENT CONTRACTORS

The independent contractor differs from the agent and employee largely in the matter of control exerted over him or her. Thus when an owner (a term analagous to principal or employer) contracts with an independent contractor for the performance of a specified task, the owner has no control over how the work is to be done. Satisfaction of the contract is a matter of whether or not the task *is* performed. The contract may, of course, contain specifications such as the quality of materials used and a time for completion.

Because the owner does not control the independent contractor, he or she cannot be held responsible for the independent contractor's acts toward others. Nor is the owner liable for the independent contractor's employees.

THE FORMS OF DOING BUSINESS

Historically, there have been three basic forms of doing business: the proprietorship, the partnership, and the corporation. Each evolved into its present form today to meet the needs of the business community. In modern times new forms of doing business have come into existence. Some have developed in response to tax laws or other legislation. A discussion of the newer forms of doing business is deferred until after a discussion of the basic forms because they are more easily understood in the context of tradition.

A secretary will normally work for a business and the form of that business is essentially a matter of structure. The structure in turn delineates the authority of those in the organization. In order to perform effectively within an organization, a secretary must understand the concept of authority and how lines of authority are drawn.

THE PROPRIETORSHIP

The proprietorship is a relatively simple form of business. It is also called an individual or sole proprietorship to indicate but one person doing business. In a strictly legal sense a proprietor is one who has rights in something, that is, an owner. A proprietor in a business sense is then, one who owns and operates a business alone.

The term proprietorship gives no indication of size. A proprietor's business may be as small as a one-chair barber shop or employ thousands of people at many locations. What is common to all proprietorships is the centralization of control and authority in one person, the owner. A proprietor of a business is ultimately responsible for all decisions. For this he or she reaps the benefits of the business out of net profits.

There are distinct advantages and disadvantages in doing business as a proprietor. With the decision-making process in but one person, there is no need to go through the lengthy process of getting agreement such as is necessary in multi-owned businesses. A proprietor's rewards come in direct proportion to his or her diligence although proprietorships pose the greatest risk of failure among business forms. This is especially true of small businesses which frequently fail because of insufficient capitalization.

Probably the greatest disadvantage of the proprietorship is forming and acquiring capital for the conduct of the business. Where more than one person owns a business, each of the owners contributes or brings something of value into it. Thus by "pooling" assets, the multi-owned business is able to operate on a larger capital amount. While centralized decision-making may be an advantage in one sense, it may be a disadvantage in another sense. The collective skills of, say, a partnership may result in better decisions for the business. A proprietor can overcome the disadvantage of unilateral decision-making by hiring those with special skills to serve in advisory roles, but he or she must also understand that those hired do not have the same proprietary interest as the owner.

No special documentation is needed to form a proprietorship, and a proprietor's earnings out of profits are taxed to the individual. This is to be compared to corporate profits which are taxed first to the corporation and again as income to the shareholder. A double-taxation structure is therefore avoided by a proprietorship.

THE PARTNERSHIP

The partnership, like the corporation but unlike the proprietorship, reflects the notion that there is strength in numbers. A partnership provides for ownership of a business by two or more persons, and there is no limit on the number of partners which may participate.

A partnership is a voluntary, contractual association. Upon the formation of a partnership, each of the partners brings something of value to it such as money, other personal or real property, or even a skill. Based upon a negotiated agreement, partners usually enter a written partnership agreement which states the proportionate contribution of each partner. Partnership agreements do not necessarily have to be in writing, but they must satisfy the requirement of the Statute of Frauds which states that contracts which cannot be performed within one year must be in writing.

As a practical matter, it is sensible for partners to have a written partnership agreement. The agreement should clearly specify the rights, duties, and responsibilities of all concerned.

Each partner is, in addition to being a co-owner, a principal in the conduct of the business. As such each partner has the authority to do a variety of things on behalf of the business. The scope of a partner's authority includes making contracts which bind the partnership, selling goods (but not other assets) in the regular course of business, making purchases, obtaining loans, purchasing insurance, and hiring employees. In practice, partnerships assign the various areas of authority to individual partners.

A partnership might be formed in this way: Partner A has invented and patented a very superior mousetrap which he brings into the business as his contribution. In the written agreement it is stated that his contribution is worth $50,000, that he will be in charge of the manufacturing process for the traps and that he will share in the profits equally with the other partners. Partner B owns a building worth $50,000 which he will contribute and in which the mousetraps will be made. Partner B has an advertising background and it is agreed that he will be in charge of marketing. He, too, will receive a share of the profits. Partner C brings in $50,000 in cash which will be used as start-up and as operating capital. Partner C is assigned responsibility for the general administration of the business and will also receive a proportionate share of the profits.

This example serves to show how authority might be assigned and thus limited. Partner A might have authority to purchase raw materials and manufacturing equipment and to hire plant workers. Partner B might be given authority to sell the mousetraps on the market and hire salespeople to solicit orders. Partner C would logically have authority to obtain a loan for working capital, to purchase liability insurance, and to hire clerical workers. Such a division of labor is a sensible way to insure a smoothly functioning cooperative organization. An agreement among partners as to the scope of authority of each is binding between them.

Generally, partners have certain rights in the business. These may be and should be resolved in a written partnership agreement. Without such an agreement, all partners have equal rights. One such right is to manage the business. As noted, it is not very practical for all partners to manage all areas of the business. Also, without agreement to the contrary, all partners have a right to share equally in the profits of the business. Partners do not have a right to be compensated other than by a share of profits. If two partners manage the firm while a third partner is on vacation, they are not entitled to extra compensation for their extra work.

Partners have a right to inspect the books of a firm at any time. The books should be kept at the principal place of business for this purpose.

Partnerships may be dissolved or terminated in several ways. First, partnerships may be formed by agreement for a specific purpose or for a specific time. Upon the accomplishment of purpose or expiration of time, dissolution occurs. Even before that time *all* partners may agree to dissolution. Where no definite term is specified, a partnership may be dissolved by the express will of one partner only. If by agreement other partners can expel a partner, such expulsion for cause will result in dissolution. Other reasons for dissolution include the death or bankruptcy of any partner or the bankruptcy of the partnership itself.

Upon application of a partner, a court will decree a dissolution in several instances. These include the insanity or incapacity of a partner to perform his or her part of the partnership contract. A court will also decree dissolution where the conduct of a partner is prejudicial to carrying on the business or where a partner willfully breaches the partnership agreement. Finally, a court will dissolve a partnership which can only be continued at a loss or dissolve it for purely equitable reasons.

Once dissolution has occurred, someone must "wind up" or finally complete the business of the partnership. This may be done by the legal representative of the last remaining partner. Winding up consists generally of satisfying partnership liabilities and distribution of the partnership assets to qualifying parties.

There are several types of partnerships among which the most common is the general partnership. A newer type is the limited partnership which has some of the characteristics of a corporation. A limited partner may invest in a partnership but has no rights in the management of it. He or she shares the liabilities of the partnership only up to the amount invested. Most states have enacted the Uniform Limited Partnership Act which describes the relationships that may exist between limited and general partners.

A partnership which is for some other purpose than profit is known as an unincorporated association.

THE CORPORATION

Corporations exist under the authority of the states in which they are located and are subject to regulation in other states where they may do business. Many corporations do operate in all fifty states of the United States. The mere term "corporation" often brings to mind the corporate giants which may be owned by more than a million people. A corporation need not be large, however, and is often created for the one purpose of protecting its owners from a particular form of liability. In most states today a single person can incorporate. The former rule that three persons were needed to form a corporation was eased because of the prevalent practice of using two other persons merely for the purpose of incorporation.

The corporation is among some of the more interesting legal concepts created by the law. A corporation is a "person" in many respects and as such is entitled to certain constitutional protections such as the right to due process. As a person, the corporation can be immortal in the sense that it may perpetually exist.

The reasons for the corporate form of doing business are twofold. First, it permits a person to invest in a company and to share in the profits of it while having liability only to the degree of investment. If, for example, an individual purchases 10 shares of stock in a given company and the shares cost $100 each, he or she has a $1,000 investment. But the value of the shares may increase or decrease if they are traded on a market. If the market value rises to $120, the value of the total investment will be $1,200. If the company fails, the investor will be out of pocket $1,000.

This limitation on liability makes an investment far more attractive. In a proprietorship or partnership, the parties are responsible for all liabilities— even those above and beyond the amount invested.

The second reason for the corporate form follows from the first reason, the feature of limited liability. Because investors naturally want to keep risk at a minimum, they are more willing to invest in corporations. It is therefore easier for the corporation to acquire capital. For a corporation the pool of investors is virtually without limit. Proprietorships and partnerships do not have such an advantage.

Corporations are classified as public, private, and quasi-public. Public corporations exist for some governmental purpose such as a municipality. Private corporations are those which are privately owned and, as will be explained, may be for profit or nonprofit. Quasi-public corporations are those which serve a public need but which are privately owned. Public utilities are an example of quasi-public corporations. They usually are regulated by the government and have territorial protection from competition through a licensing process. Although it may be confusing, private corporations whose stock is publicly traded are known as public corporations in the business community.

Some corporations may qualify for designation as "close" corporations. A close corporation is typically owned by very few people, and in most states may not be owned by more than 20 people. The procedures to be followed by close corporations have been liberalized in many states.

The creation of corporations. The creation or formation of a corporation, like other business forms, begins with an idea. Someone feels that the idea has commercial value. When a person decides to form a business and it is to be in the corporate form, he or she is known as a promoter. Most corporations are formed to make a profit for the owners, but they may also be designated as "not-for-profit" which results in a tax-free status. A corporation may be created for any lawful purpose such as manufacturing a product, selling goods, or providing a service. Schools, hospitals, and religious organizations are examples of nonprofit corporations, and they may not be owned as such by individuals.

Once a decision has been made to incorporate and the type of corporation has been selected, the promoter begins preparations for eventual incorporation. The promoter has three basic tasks. First, he or she must promote the original idea which gave rise to the decision to form a new business. In effect, promotion of the idea is to get financial backing for the venture. The promoter works under a considerable handicap in that all of his or her efforts are tentative and depend upon eventual incorporation. The promoter cannot sell shares in the corporation until it exists. Instead, the promoter procures subscriptions or promises to buy shares when they are available.

The promoter's second task is to perform those acts which will enable the corporation to function once it has come into existence. Such acts might be to acquire a place of business, buy equipment, or hire employees. Again, the promoter is handicapped by the lack of existence of the corporation. If the promoter enters into contracts, he or she is personally bound by them unless the agreement states otherwise. While the promoter cannot bind the corporation, in practice the corporation once formed will agree to become a party in these contracts in order to relieve the promoter of personal liability. If for any reason the corporation is not formed as planned, the promoter remains liable on the contracts he or she has made.

The promoter's third and final task is to carry out the statutory procedure for incorporation. The first step is to prepare and submit a document commonly known as the Articles of Incorporation to, usually, the Secretary of State. The articles must include certain information such as the name of the corporation, its purpose, the amount of capital stock to be authorized together with the number of shares into which it is to be divided, the place of business, the duration of existence which many states permit to be perpetual, the names of officers and directors for the first year of operation, the names and addresses of the incorporators and the number of shares for which each has subscribed, and the name and address of an agent or clerk. The latter requirement exists to give one who is suing the corporation a contact for the service of process. There are variations in these requirements from state to state.

Once submitted, the Articles of Incorporation are examined by a government official, and, if approved, are returned to the new corporation. Articles may be amended at a later time if, for example, the purpose of the corporation changes. Approved Articles are in essence a contract between the state, the corporation, and the owners (shareholders). They become the document which confers authority upon the corporation.

Once created the corporation has powers and is required to follow certain procedures. Among the powers of a corporation are those to establish a corporate seal, make bylaws which supplement the Articles of Incorporation, issue stocks and bonds, borrow money, sell or acquire property, and even invest in other corporations.

Possibly one of the most important items of business at the first meeting of a corporation is to make bylaws for the conduct of the business. Bylaws are analagous to written partnership agreements. It is usually desirable to keep the Articles of Incorporation both brief and general and to provide specificity in bylaws. Articles should be effective for the life of the corporation and can be changed only upon application to the state. Bylaws can and should be changed when necessary, and this may be done within the corporation by the shareholders. Since the bylaws are a reflection of the will of the owners, they are binding on those who conduct the business of the corporation. Some states allow directors to amend bylaws. If a corporation wishes to retain this power for shareholders only, such must be done in the Articles of Incorporation.

Corporate organization. The lines of authority in a corporation run from the shareholders who are the owners, to the board of directors, to the officers. Directors are elected by the shareholders and in turn appoint the officers of the corporation. Usually the executive officers consist of a president, one or more vice-presidents, a secretary, and a treasurer. One person could be a shareholder, director, and officer; and some corporations require that directors be shareholders.

Shareholders may make policy indirectly through their power to elect directors. Frequently, too, a power is reserved to make broad policy changes such as the establishment of a pension plan. When a shareholder wishes to change policy, he or she does so by putting a resolution before the other shareholders for vote.

Frequently, because of geographical distribution or for other reasons, shareholders cannot attend meetings. In such an event, the shareholder is entitled to vote through another person, a practice known as "voting by proxy."

Although a few states forbid it, most states provide for a practice known as "cumulative voting." This process provides that each shareholder has a number of votes equal to the number of shares owned multiplied by the number of directors to be elected. Cumulative voting provides that a minority of shareholders can have representation on the board of directors.

Shareholders meet regularly, usually annually. No notice is required, although most corporations not only provide notice of regular meetings but provide forms for proxy votes as well. Special meetings do require notice and are usually called by the board of directors. In some cases special meetings are called by a fixed percentage of the shareholders. Quorum requirements for a valid meeting are based on either a specified percentage of shareholders present or on a specified percentage of voting stock represented. Once a quorum has been established, shareholders cannot obstruct the conduct of business by leaving and breaking a quorum.

The board of directors. The management of the corporation is the responsibility of the board of directors. Directors are considered to be fiduciaries or persons who are in a position of special trust by virtue of that position. They owe their allegiance to the corporation in general and specifically to the shareholders. As fiduciaries, directors should be careful to avoid any conflict of interest such as favoritism toward a relative or another business interest. A director should refrain from voting on a matter which might raise a conflict of interest. Similarly, a director should not use information acquired through the office for personal gain if such use is contrary to the interests of the corporation.

The bylaws of most corporations provide for regular board meetings, and directors usually cannot vote by proxy. The reason for requiring that a director be physically present is based on the idea that attendance is meeting a responsibility, whereas a shareholder's voting by proxy is the waiver of a right. As a rule, special meetings may be called by the chairperson, the president, or any two directors; bylaws frequently provide that an executive committee of the board can act on matters between meetings.

Corporate officers. As noted, officers are considered to be agents of the corporation which, in turn, is the principal. When in this role, officers' conduct is governed by the law of agency. The scope of authority of an officer includes those actions which are consistent with the general purposes of the corporation as delineated in the articles of incorporation and the bylaws.

Officers derive their authority from the board of directors which appoints them. Rarely, officers may be appointed by the shareholders. Logically directors should have the power of appointment because of their responsibility for management of the corporation and the fact that officers are the agents of management.

Termination of a corporation. Corporations may be terminated by either voluntary or involuntary actions. Unfortunately, the vast majority of corporate terminations are involuntary because of the failure of the business.

A corporation may be dissolved by written consent of shareholders, as by a vote on a resolution to dissolve. Such a resolution may be proposed by the board of directors or by shareholders possessing among them twenty percent of the outstanding shares of the corporation. After the voting procedure takes place, the corporation must file a "statement of intent to dissolve" with the Secretary of State and must notify all creditors of the filing. At this time the corporation ceases business and begins the winding-up process.

Insolvency in itself does not automatically terminate a corporation. But insolvency would probably lead to bankruptcy and that, in turn, would lead to a forced sale of the assets of the corporation. So as a practical matter, it could not continue to operate and exist without any assets.

Corporations may terminate because of a consolidation or merger of two or more corporations where it is legal under antitrust legislation. A consolidation occurs when two corporations join to form a third. If, for example, Company A and Company B consolidate to form Company C, A and B cease to exist and their combined assets are those of C. In a merger A would acquire B and continue as A while B would terminate. There is one other multi-corporate relationship, the conglomerate, which does not involve termination. A conglomerate exists when one corporation, a parent company, acquires another corporation which exists for a different purpose. If, for example, an oil company acquired a chain of motels, it would be a conglomerate. Usually corporations become conglomerates to diversify activities or to avoid the antitrust prohibition on consolidations and mergers.

Finally, corporations may be terminated for cause by the government authorizing it or by court decree. The latter method is used when a board of directors becomes so deadlocked that the company can't continue operations.

THE BUSINESS ORGANIZATION AND THE SECRETARY

A well-managed business, no matter what its form, will invariably have a procedure manual or similar document for the guidance of all personnel. A good manual will clearly describe the structure of the organization, and a good secretary will be thoroughly familiar with it.

The duties of a secretary involve far more than the mere task of typing letters. They involve as well the management of information which includes the creation, storage, retrieval, use, and transmittal of information. Within a business organization the smooth flow of information is vital to its success, and the secretary will be in a position to insure that the flow of information is smooth.

Furthermore, the secretary must understand the protocol within an organization. It is especially important to know which officers in the firm rank above and which rank below the executive for whom the secretary works. Once these matters are determined, the correct procedures in interoffice dealings and communications become clearer.

Through the centuries the law has changed to meet the needs of a changing society. Today technological changes alone have challenged those who make laws, and change is no more apparent than in the business world. The secretary must not only understand terminology which has come into existence in less than a generation, but a familiarity must be developed with the forces and interests, both scientific and societal, that affect the modern business community. The term "software" is of recent coinage, and its definition raises more questions than it answers. Assuming that software is a computer program, what are the implications of its theft? How is the creator (programmer) protected in his or her sole use of it? A program has intrinsic value but cannot be taken to a patent office as may be an invented "thing." And what is the value of a given program? A court can determine what a stolen horse is worth, but the problem is more difficult with software.

THE COMPUTER AND THE PROBLEM OF INFORMATION

Computers and similar devices such as calculators are relatively new. They are used in practically every business, and many businesses could not compete without them. The secretary must understand the concept which underlies

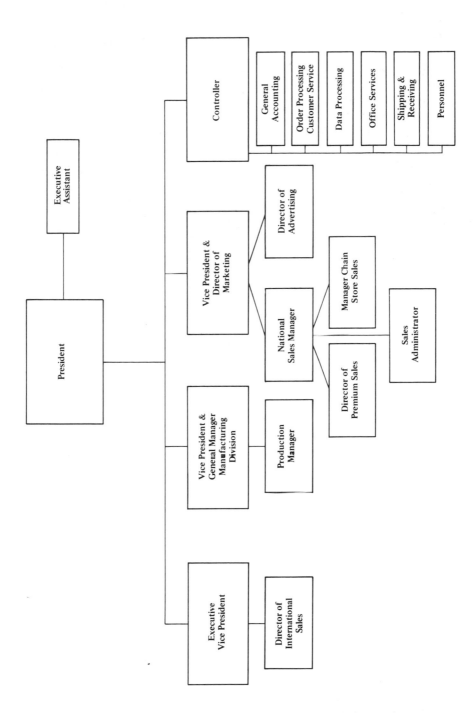

Organizational chart showing lines of authority in a typical business

computer systems in order to recognize the unauthorized or even illegal use of them. The misuse of a computer, whether intentional or unintentional, can result in considerable harm.

At the heart of the concept of computerization is data or information. Data is entered into the computer through the use of some form of coding device. Once entered, it is stored for future use. Depending on the way that the computer is programmed, the data may be retrieved as entered or in various other desired forms. A business may want, for example, to maintain a mailing list in a computer. As names and addresses of potential customers are acquired, they are entered into the computer. When the business wants to do a mailing of its catalog, it may retrieve the names and addresses printed on mailing labels and arrange them in ZIP Code order. If the business is to take advantage of bulk mailing rates, the Postal Service requires that all pieces be sorted and bundled according to ZIP Codes. The ability of the computer to so classify information which is unclassified when entered makes possible the compilation of mailing lists of a size that would have been impractical in the past.

The applications to which computers are put is practically infinite because of the ingenuity of those who design systems and programs. Computers are used for accounting of financial data, inventory and stock control, personnel records, medical records, banking transactions, marketing analyses, payroll preparation, and even library cataloging. Governments rely heavily on computers and use them to store tax records, vehicle registrations, even vital statistics.

The proliferation of computers and their applications has created some serious legal problems to which the secretary should be alert. First, much of the data stored in computers may be confidential by its very nature. Schools, colleges, and universities usually store student information in computers, but by law, the so-called Buckley Amendment, such information as student grades may not be divulged without the permission of the student. Another sensitive area involves consumer credit information, the incorrect disclosure of which could seriously damage an applicant for credit. At a time when confidential records were stored in locked file cabinets or safes, access could be more effectively controlled. Now, since a considerable number of people usually know the code enabling them to enter the computer for a given program, it is more difficult to control access.

A second but equally important problem inherent in computerization is inaccuracy. The problem is not, of course, a new one in record-keeping, but it is compounded by the sheer bulk of records that can be stored in a computer. It is axiomatic that no information is better than wrong information. A market analysis done by a computer may be totally invalid because of one erroneously entered set of data.

The job descriptions of many secretaries may require the ability to enter information into a computer. It is particularly important that a secretary be thoroughly accurate in performing this function because an error once entered is extremely difficult to find. This is because errors in a computer are not as visually apparent as they would be in, say, a ledger book.

Finally, both the information in a computer and the program by which information is manipulated have value to the owner. A mailing list may be worth thousands of dollars and may be sold or traded. A program, which is essentially an intellectual creation, may be vitally important to the competitive posture of a business. All employees of a business have an obligation to safeguard both data bases and programs owned by the employer. And employees should be aware that computer time is expensive. They should not, therefore, play "games" with the company computer.

BUSINESS AND THE ENVIRONMENT

Comparatively few businesses pollute the environment to any appreciable degree. Historically, there have been very few restrictions on businesses which damaged the environment although a Rivers and Harbors Act was passed as early as 1899. Also known as the "Refuse Act of 1899," it prohibited the deposit of refuse into navigable waters.

The largest part of environmental legislation was enacted in the 1960s and set not only air and water standards but provided for historic preservation, land use regulation and planning, noise control, the use of hazardous substances, and solid waste management. The result of this legislation was an extensive body of regulations which applied not only to the private sector, but to the government as well. As part of the regulatory process, those businesses and governments which were not in compliance were given deadlines for compliance. Federal legislation such as the National Environmental Policy Act of 1969 essentially regulated the acts of federal agencies which would affect the environment. The states at the same time enacted legislation which regulated the private sector. Today, a business contemplating an act which could adversely affect the environment has to obtain a permit. Permits are usually issued by a state agency such as a Board of Environmental Protection.

The secretary should be aware that businesses have to file a number of reports, if applicable, concerning the environment and may be subject to inspection by government officials charged with enforcing environmental regulations.

BANKRUPTCY

Bankruptcy is a method through which a person or business which is hopelessly in debt may be discharged from continuing liability. But its more important purpose is to protect creditors of the bankrupt by providing some relief however small. There is great potential for one contemplating bankruptcy to defraud the creditors by hiding or transferring assets. Invariably the bankrupt will have both assets and liabilities at the time that bankruptcy is declared. The law seeks to use as many assets as possible to satisfy in some proportion the valid claims of creditors.

The official determination of bankruptcy may be the result of voluntary action by the debtor or it may be forced involuntarily by a creditor. The timing of bankruptcy is largely a matter of judgment. A creditor may wish to avoid forcing a bankruptcy in the hope that the debtor will recover and pay his or her debts in full. But the creditor may abandon hope and force bankruptcy to salvage whatever is possible out of the assets of the debtor.

There are no special criteria for voluntary bankruptcy. The person or business wishing to enter bankruptcy simply files a petition in a federal bankruptcy court, an act which serves as an automatic determination of bankruptcy.

Generally involuntary bankruptcy proceedings may be brought against a person or business whose aggregate debts are $1,000 or more. If there are between one and eleven creditors, anyone may petition the court for involuntary bankruptcy. If there are twelve or more creditors, three of them must join in the petition; and each must have a provable claim in excess of $500. The commission of any one of six "Acts of Bankruptcy" may be justification for a creditor or creditors to bring a petition for involuntary bankruptcy. The act must have been committed within a period of four months before the petition is filed.

Only three of the six Acts of Bankruptcy involve insolvency. More to the point, the acts involve some action by the debtor which will make his or her assets unavailable to the creditor. A debtor contemplating or fearing bankruptcy or even a repossession, might hide or conceal property. Or the insolvent debtor might prefer one creditor over another and pay that creditor to the exclusion of another. The bankruptcy system is invoked, then, to provide *all* creditors who have a provable claim with a recourse against the debtor's assets according to their relative claim. The claim of a secured creditor would obviously be honored before that of an unsecured creditor.

Three kinds of officials handle the details of a bankruptcy case. Upon petition of creditors who fear the loss of the debtor's assets, the court will appoint a "receiver." A receiver is one who acts quickly to take custody of assets and to preserve them. Eventually, the court appoints a "trustee" who becomes, in effect, the owner of the bankrupt's assets. The trustee also holds the rights of the debtor's most favored creditor. This means that the trustee can set aside transfers of property made within four months of the petition for bankruptcy or up until the time of adjudication of bankruptcy if the transfer preferred one creditor over another with equal claims.

Some of the duties of the trustee are to hold meetings of the creditors, determine the extent of assets, and receive the claims of the creditors. Finally, he or she distributes the assets according to statutory priorities.

A "referee" in bankruptcy hears evidence in a bankruptcy case and reports his or her findings to the court. Referees are appointed to six-year terms and are, in effect, hearing examiners on behalf of the court.

Once the bankruptcy procedure has run its course, the bankrupt may be discharged (released from the obligations of the debts) by a decree terminating the bankruptcy. Several grounds exist which will bar a discharge, however. Most of these involve fraud or false representation by the debtor. But once discharged, the bankrupt is legally protected from the collection of his or her debts. The debts are not extinguished; creditors are merely enjoined by the court from enforcing them.

There are several "last chance" situations provided by bankruptcy laws which may prevent actual bankruptcy. One such provision allows a corporation with aggregate debts of $5,000 or more to file a voluntary petition for reorganization or three creditors of the corporation may petition for reorganization. With it the corporation may propose a plan for reorganization which the court will accept if it is fair, equitable, and feasible. Reorganization involves a reconstruction of a corporation's investment. If the reorganization is not successful, the only recourse remaining is bankruptcy.

The purpose of giving the corporation a last chance is so that it may avoid liquidation while providing at the same time for the eventual satisfaction of the creditors. A successful reorganization is far preferable to bankruptcy from the point of view of both debtor and creditor.

INSURANCE

Insurance is a method of spreading risk and is made necessary by the many laws which impose liability upon those who may or may not be responsible for the occurrence of certain events. Insurance is, then, a form of protection. This protection does not necessarily have to be for the owner of the insurance or policyholder but may be for the protection of others. Such, obviously, is the case with life insurance which may protect business associates, creditors, or the insured person's family.

A key concept to insurance is that the one purchasing insurance have an insurable interest in the property or person insured. Quite obviously one has an insurable interest in his or her life even though the beneficiary will be another. It is also possible to have an insurable interest in the life of another such as a key employee or partner. The interest extends to the pecuniary loss which would occur upon the death of the employee or partner. Creditors, too, have an insurable interest in their debtors. But if the creditor unreasonably overinsures the debtor, that is for an amount disproportionate to the debt, the policy may be found void.

The same rule requiring an insurable interest applies to property as well. A cannot insure B's farm against fire loss because recovery is based on actual pecuniary loss. If A and B both insured A's farm and it were destroyed 50 percent by fire, B could recover the actual loss; but A could recover nothing because A would not sustain a pecuniary loss. With life insurance, the insurable interest must exist at the time the policy is written. Conversely, with property the interest must exist at the time of loss.

An insurance policy is contractual, and as such is subject to the general rules for the formation of contracts. In most jurisdictions insurance contracts must be written although an oral affirmation of insurance between the time of application for insurance and the delivery of a written policy may be effective. By the better rule, the agent or broker should provide the applicant with a written memorandum called a binder.

Generally, the failure to pay premiums for insurance will cause the policy to lapse. Statutes provide for a period of grace, usually thirty days, during which the policy premiums may be paid without lapse. The policy remains in force for this period.

There are many types of insurance which protect against an infinite variety of losses. Common types include life insurance, motor vehicle insurance, fire insurance, health insurance, and liability insurance against a number of dangers. Automobile insurance may protect the owner not only for theft of his or her vehicle but an operator's liability for negligence.

Unfortunately, many people do not read their insurance policies when they purchase them. Rather, they rush to read them when a loss occurs and are often surprised to find that the insurance company has limited its liability in some way. The employer may wish the secretary to be familiar with the terms of company insurance policies. The secretary may assist in filing claims against the company's coverage. If an employer provides group health insurance coverage for employees, the secretary may be the one to file their claims.

COMMERCIAL PAPER

The law concerning commercial paper was once known as the law of negotiable instruments. The latter term was possibly more descriptive than the present one because the negotiability of commercial paper is one of its main characteristics. The law concerning commercial paper is largely contained in Article 3 of the Uniform Commercial Code.

Money is, as it always has been, the principal medium for the exchange of value. But because money has value as it stands, there is always the danger of losing it or having it stolen, and the finder or thief will have little trouble in using it. Commercial paper is in a sense "substitute money" but it acquires value only when signed or endorsed.

Name of Student: __ _____

Student No.: _____

PROMISSORY NOTE AND DISCLOSURES

$ _____   Date: _____, 19 ____

FOR VALUE RECEIVED, the undersigned (which includes all "undersigned" jointly and severally if more than one) promises to pay to the order of _____ , (which includes any holder hereof) at its offices: (i) the Amount Financed shown in item 1 below; (ii) interest on the balance of such Amount Financed from time to time remaining unpaid, at the rate per annum shown in item 3 below, from the date hereof, in accordance with the Payment Schedule shown in item 5 below. All payments shall be applied first to interest accrued to the date upon which payment is made, and the remainder in reduction of the Amount Financed. The undersigned and any guarantor agree that _____ may from time to time grant extensions or renewals for any period. Undersigned will pay reasonable attorney's fees not in excess of 15% of the unpaid balance after default and referral to an attorney. DEFAULT shall result from any of the following events: (a) failure to make a payment as required by this Note; (b) the significant impairment of the prospect of payment or performance, which includes, but is not limited to: death, insolvency, assignment for benefit of creditors, or the commencement of any proceeding under any bankruptcy or insolvency laws by or against undersigned. In the event of default, holder may, at its option, declare the entire unpaid balance of the Amount Financed and accrued interest thereon immediately due and payable without notice or demand, subject, however, to such rights, if any, as undersigned may have to cure a default for failure to make a required payment.

Terms and Disclosures

1. Amount Financed $ _____
2. **FINANCE CHARGE:** $ _____
3. **ANNUAL PERCENTAGE RATE**   _____ %
4. Total of Payments (1+2) $ _____
5. Payment Schedule: This Note is payable in _____ consecutive monthly installments of $ _____ each and one final monthly installment of $ _____ , commencing on _____, 19 ____ and on the same date of each month thereafter. If payments are not made when due, one or more additional payments may be necessary to pay in full.

NOTICE TO CONSUMER: 1. Do not sign this Note before you read it. 2. You are entitled to a copy of this Note. 3. You may prepay the unpaid balance at any time without penalty, except for minimum charges as permitted by law.

WITNESS:

_____

_____

                                             Address

Typical form of a promissory note (including terms) agreed to by a student and the financial officer of a college. This type of note is essentially an unconditional promise to pay the stipulated sum of money (often in designated installments) by some specified future date to the party named in the document. The note may be secured or unsecured.

Date of Issuance ...., 19 ....

Account No.

FIXED-RATE FIXED TERM CERTIFICATE ACCOUNT

HOME FEDERAL SAVINGS & LOAN ASSOCIATION OF LAKEWOOD
("ASSOCIATION")
LAKEWOOD, OHIO 44107

1. ACCOUNT SUMMARY SECTION
ACCOUNT
HOLDER

Opening Balance ....   Initial Maturity Date ....

Rate of Earnings .... % per annum   Extended Maturity Date ....

Frequency of Compounding   Renewal Term ....

Minimum Balance Requirement   Minimum Addition $ ....

        $ ....

EARNINGS DISTRIBUTION DATES

Beginning .... and ....
thereafter, with the last distribution on the final maturity date.

2. GENERAL SECTION This certifies that the Accountholder holds a savings account
with the Opening Balance and for the initial term expiring on the Initial Maturity
Date shown hereon in Home Federal Savings & Loan Association of Lakewood, Lakewood, Ohio.

The Accountholder may, from time to time, with the consent of the Association, make
additions to the balance in this account in any amount not less than the Minimum
Addition provided for in Section 1. In the event of any such addition, the term of this
account shall be extended so that the period from the date of such addition to the
Extended Maturity Date (which shall be recorded with the entry as to such addition)
shall not be less than the initial term (or Renewal Term, if the addition is made during
a Renewal Term).

3. EARNINGS SECTION This account shall receive earnings at the rate and with the
Frequency of Compounding as above set forth. Such earnings shall be payable on the
Earnings Distribution Dates above set forth, provided the balance in the account is
not reduced below the Minimum Balance Requirement. If such balance is reduced below
the Minimum Balance Requirement, the Rate of Earnings on the remaining balance
shall thereafter be reduced to the rate then paid on regular savings accounts. (See
also Section 5).

4. AUTOMATIC RENEWAL This account shall be automatically renewed at the close
of business on the Initial Maturity Date or the maturity date of any renewal or
extended term unless (1) withdrawn within the 10-day period referred to in Section 5
hereof or (2) at least 15 days prior to any such date, the Association gives written
notice to the Accountholder that this account will not be renewed at the Rate of
Earnings and/or the Renewal Term set forth above. In such event, the account will
either be extended for such additional term and at such rate of earnings as set forth
in said notice or the account will be converted to a regular savings account and receive
earnings at the rate then paid on regular savings accounts.

A form acknowledging that a certain person holds a certificate-of-deposit account in a
particular savings and loan association. Certificates of deposit of this kind are usually
time deposits; that is, they are payable on or after a stated future date at a stipulated
rate of interest. They are also payable on demand or subject to withdrawal, but in
either case the rate of interest is reduced. These certificates are transferable and negotiable instruments.

There are four types of commercial paper: promissory notes, drafts, checks, and certificates of deposit. A promissory note is basically a promise by one party to pay another party a certain sum of money either on demand or at a specific time. If the note is payable on demand, it is almost the same as money to the holder of it. If A signs a promissory note in favor of B on demand, B can use it to pay value to C because it can be immediately converted to cash. If a note is for payment on a certain future date, it serves to extend credit and is therefore not the same thing as money. Parties to a promissory note are the "maker," the one promising to pay, and the "payee," the one to whom the promise is made. Promissory notes must be in writing and signed by the maker. They may be secured by the borrower who provides some kind of collateral to the lender. When a mortgage on property is given to the lender, the note is known as a mortgage note; in the event of nonpayment, the lender can foreclose on the property for satisfaction.

A draft or bill of exchange involves three parties. One party orders a second party to pay a third party. For example, A, the drawer, orders B, the drawee, to pay a certain amount of cash to C, the payee. The system presupposes that B is in some way indebted to A. Drafts are the least common form of commercial paper.

Checks, of course, are very common and are a part of the fabric of modern business. A check is very simply a draft drawn on a bank. Here A, who has deposited money in the bank, orders it on demand to pay an amount to another, C. The bank would be similar to B in the example of a draft above.

Checks have a utilitarian value over money. When cashed by the payee, the check is canceled by the bank and returned to the maker. It thereby serves as a receipt or at least an indication that payment has been made. One of the characteristics of commercial paper is transferability. Thus, A may write a check in favor of C who, in turn, uses it to pay a debt to D. Transfer is done by C signing it over or "endorsing" it to D. When the check is finally returned to A, C's signature serves as evidence that C has received the face value of the check. It could also serve as evidence of the discharge of the debt of C to D.

A final type of commercial paper is the certificate of deposit. In recent years the certificate of deposit, or "CD" as they are popularly called, has gained in popularity. There are many forms of these certificates but what is common to them all, is redemption on demand. One popular form is the six-month CD. Usually a minimum amount of money is required, often $10,000. The purchaser is told that the money must be left in the bank for the full term of the certificate. If it is not left for the full period, a reduced interest rate will be applied. The latter situation is often referred to as a "penalty." But CD's of any kind must be redeemable on demand.

The law of commercial paper is essentially protective of the rights of the various parties to it. There are problems inherent in a system which allows people to "make" money even if it is only substitute money. The maker of a check, for example, may not have sufficient funds on deposit with the bank to cover it. Another problem, especially with checks, is the possibility of forgery or an intentionally written bad check. The secretary who may receive checks on behalf of the employer should insist on identification of the party writing a check. While many checks are overdrawn through a simple mistake by the drawer and may be eventually satisfied, it may require an unreasonable amount of time to collect on such a debt.

TAXATION

The laws of taxation affect virtually every business and person. It is impossible to discuss taxation with any specificity because of the many types of taxes that exist from state to state and in other localities. Taxes may be classified according to the governmental level which levies them, that is federal, state, and local.

Another classification scheme involves the type of event that is taxable. Typical taxable events include the receipt of income, the sale of an item, the transfer of property at death, the ownership of property, or even in some cases the gift of property by one to another.

Generally, income taxes are levied on natural persons and corporations. Although partnerships are required to file an information return, profits are taxable to the partners as individuals. Proprietorships are not taxed for income although the owner is taxed as he or she takes the profits from the business. Income taxes are levied by the federal government and by most states and many cities.

Most states and many cities have sales taxes. In effect the seller of goods serves as a collector of sales taxes and must forward them to the state or city treasurer. States also have special-purpose taxes such as that on gasoline which are used to maintain state highways. Such taxes and the so-called "sin taxes" on tobacco and liquor are not collected by the retail seller but are collected at the point of origin. They are subsequently passed along to the buyer.

The ownership of either real or personal property may give rise to taxation. Property taxes are levied as a percentage of an assessed valuation. The percentage or rate of property taxation may change as the needs of the taxing agency change. Traditionally, property taxes are collected on the local level and are used to pay for governmental services. The use of property may also be taxable; the tax on motor vehicles is such a tax.

Finally, estate and gift taxes are based on the transfer of property. Because of rate structures, it is often desirable to make gifts of property rather than have the estate taxed at a higher rate. Recent legislation has liberalized the amount of gifts which may be made without incurring a tax liability.

It should be noted that corporations and their shareholders are subject to a "double tax," a situation which has long been criticized. The corporation pays a tax on income and the shareholder pays income tax on dividends received from the same corporation.

Businesses are subject to a host of taxes which are commonly called by other names such as a "license." A license is official permission to perform some act for which the person or business receiving the permission invariably pays a fee.

THE BUSINESS, THE LAW, AND THE SECRETARY

The foregoing description of various branches of the law has emphasized the role of the secretary in preventing legal difficulties for the employer. A good general knowledge of business law will assist the secretary in this regard although good common sense and an awareness of legal implications in the activities of the business are equally important.

The following is a checklist of duties which the secretary should undertake although they are not a part of the job description.

1. The secretary should acquire and maintain a resource library of any rules, regulations, or laws which affect the business.

2. The secretary should have a docket-control system to insure the timely filing of reports or other documents required by law.

3. If the job involves handling money, the secretary should have an accounting system even if it only complements the business accounting system.

4. As an office administrator, the secretary should have a system for checking all legal documents, such as contracts, for accuracy.

5. Where applicable, the secretary should monitor computer printouts to insure that data is accurate.

The degree of secretarial involvement with each of the above tasks will vary according to the type of business served. Some businesses are heavily regulated while others are not. The secretary to a hospital administrator, for example, would have to maintain an extensive resource library. The secretary to the owner of a small retail business would have less involvement. But whatever the type of business, the secretary should develop a specialized knowledge of applicable law and be alert to the changes in it which inevitably occur.

Chapter 14

Grammar and Usage

JOHN I. McCOLLUM

CONTRARY TO THE VIEW held by a majority of people, grammar and rhetoric are not devices conjured by fiendish teachers to bedevil defenseless students. They are useful studies, the mastery of which is the mark of a sophisticated person. In general, it may be said that their value is both functional and esthetic. There is efficiency in a precisely worded statement, just as there may be pleasure in a well-turned phrase. The ability to use language is about all that distinguishes the human from some other animals. Possibly, the more highly developed one's ability to use language, the more distinct is one's transcendence of the lower animal forms.

Of the various theories relative to the development of language the social view seems most reasonable. The theory that languages have arisen, developed, and modified as a result of social necessity or convenience is the one from which most of the advice contained in the following pages springs. That is to say, the statements as to practice reflect usage widely adopted by informed writers and speakers. "Good" English is, in general, a somewhat debatable issue. What may at one time or in one place be good English may vary significantly from what is so considered at another time or in another place. The assumptions here are based on practices that may currently be considered acceptable by those who use the language clearly, efficiently, effectively, and artistically.

This section of the book contains basically useful advice for the development of an acceptable writing and speaking style. No attempt has been made to give a complete survey of the intricacies of grammar and rhetoric, and there is little or no theorizing. In many ways the material here is in the nature of a reminder of what should be brought to one's writing.

In matters of debate, and there are many, the practice is to adopt the more conservative position. To those who would argue that some of the best writers ignore, overlook, or transcend "mere rules," we offer the counterargument that in so doing such writers offer significant stylistic or artistic compensation and that they are generally capable of such compensation only after a long apprenticeship in which they acquired the tools with which to shape their greater achievement.

It may be argued, as well, that many decisions concerning propriety and style are essentially matters of taste. Indeed, such may be the case; one may, therefore, adopt a single rule: What is clearest, most precise, most useful, and most pleasing should prevail. One must learn to perceive and abhor vague, slovenly, impoverished, and inaccurate language.

The purpose of this section is to record useful statements of practice in the hope of leading secretaries easily and quickly through what is often considered a tangle of rule and rhetoric. What we generally call grammar is simply a description of the way words function and relate to one another in a sentence. This is to say that instead of prescribing a set of rules handed down by the gods of grammarians, rhetoricians, and linguists, we merely describe the way people have used their language in the past and thereby suggest possibilities for success through similar practice.

Effective communication is not easy, but we can reduce the difficulty somewhat by developing as great a familiarity with language as possible. The more we understand about how our sentences can be put together, how we can by punctuation marks pull together or separate a variety of ideas, how we can substitute one word for another to gain a more precise meaning or a more pleasing manner of expression, the easier and more successful our communication will be.

Part I

Parts of Speech

SENTENCES ARE COMPOSED by combining a series of words, each of which functions in a specific way within the particular context. That is to say, the word itself is called a *noun* or a *verb* or an *adjective* or an *adverb* because it functions as such in a sentence, not because it is arbitrarily a particular part of speech. In identifying parts of speech, always think of the *function* of the word (or word group) in a specific sentence. For example, the word *light* may function as a noun, a verb, an adverb, or an adjective.

> The *light* shines in the night. (Noun)
> *Light* the fire. (Verb)
> She struck him a *light* blow. (Adjective)

Obviously, it is necessary to identify a word (or word group) not as a particular part of speech but as a *functioning* part of the sentence. In this sense words may be divided according to four general functions:

1. To name or identify—a word or word group (noun, pronoun, gerund, infinitive, noun phrase, or noun clause—all substantives) that names a person, place, thing, condition, quality, or action.

2. To assert—a word or word group (verb) that indicates action, state of being, or occurrence.

3. To modify—a word, phrase, or clause (adjective, adverb, or participle) that describes, limits, restricts, or qualifies the meaning of another word or word group.

4. To connect—a word (preposition) that may join a substantive to another word in the sentence; a word (conjunction) that may join words, phrases, or clauses.

NOUNS

A noun is a word that names a person, place, thing, action, idea, quality, group, etc.

1. CLASSIFICATION

All nouns belong to one of two main classifications:

a. *Proper nouns* name specific persons, groups, organizations, places, things, ideas.

John Smith, Hamlet, Pittsburgh, White House

b. *Common nouns* name members of a group of persons, places, things, ideas, or conditions.

book, health, house, man, children, city, liberty

Common nouns are variously classified according to what they name: *collective, concrete, abstract, mass.*

2. AGREEMENT

a. For consistency, every verb must agree in number with its subject.

FAULTY: In each room *is* ten *typists.*
IMPROVED: In each room *are* ten *typists.*
FAULTY: The *quality* of a company's products often *determine* the reputation of the company.
IMPROVED: The *quality* of a company's products often *determines* the reputation of the company.

b. Nouns or pronouns placed between the subject and the verb do not affect the number of the subject.

The *sound* of the violins *seems* very faint.

c. The number of the subject is not changed by the use of parenthetical expressions that begin with such terms as *as well as, no less than, including, together with,* etc.

Dr. Smith, together with his wife and two sons, *is* to arrive on the evening flight.

d. Usually subjects joined by *and* take a plural verb.

A *dictionary* and a *typewriter are* two tools of a secretary.
Mother, Father, and *I were* at home when he called.

When the words joined by *and* refer to the same person or thing, the verb is singular:

Your family *physician* and *friend is* the man to see.

e. When *each* or *every* precedes a singular subject, the verb is singular. When *each* follows the subject and the subject is plural, the verb is plural.

Each member of the class *has* been urged to vote.
Every person *is* to vote if he possibly can.
They *each want* to go.

f. Singular subjects joined by *or, nor, either* . . . *or,* and *neither* . . . *nor* generally take a singular verb.

Neither a doctor *nor* a nurse *was* available.
Either the teacher *or* the principal *attends* the conference.

When one part of the subject is singular and one is plural, the verb usually agrees with the one closer to it.

Neither Bill nor his *parents are* at home.
He did not know where his pencil or his *books were.*
Either the eggs or the *milk has* to be used.
Either the milk or the *eggs have* to be used.

When the two parts of the subject are pronouns in different persons, usage is generally according to the following: If the sense is singular, the verb is singular and agrees with the closer pronoun.

Either you or *I am* able to attend the conference.

If the sense is plural, the verb is plural.

Neither you nor I *are* able to attend the conference.

g. Special care must be taken with sentences beginning with *there is* or *there are. There* is an expletive, not a substantive, and therefore cannot serve as a subject.

There *are* to be at least ten *floats* in the parade. (*Floats,* not the expletive *there,* is the subject.)
There *is* no *point* in questioning him further.

h. A collective noun (*class, committee, jury*) may be either singular or plural, depending upon the meaning of the noun in the particular context: If the items or people are considered as a group, the noun takes a singular verb; if they are considered as separate individuals in a group, the noun takes a plural verb. (Remember, too, that a collective noun can also be used in the plural form when more than one group is meant: *classes, committees, juries.* For some collective nouns the plural form is the same as the singular: *offspring.*)

The *jury was* in session for two days. (A group)
The *jury come* from several areas of the city. (Separate individuals)

A collective noun should not be used in both the singular and plural numbers within the same sentence.

FAULTY: Since the school *board hires* the teachers, *they may* also *dismiss* them. (*Board* is singular with *hires,* then inconsistently *plural* with *they.*)
IMPROVED: Since the school *board hires* the teachers, *it may* also *dismiss* them.

i. Some nouns that are plural in form but singular in meaning take singular verbs. *Esthetics, civics, economics, linguistics, mathematics, mumps, news,* and *semantics,* for example, are regularly singular. Verb agreement with words like *measles, physics,* and *politics* depends upon the specific use of the word.

Your *politics* are going to get you into trouble with the company. (Your political opinions are going to . . .)
Politics has always interested him. ([The subject of] politics has always interested him.)

A check with your dictionary will help you with similar words you are not sure of.

j. The title of a single published work or work of art takes a singular verb.

The *Canterbury Tales* was written by Chaucer.

k. A word used as a word, even when it is plural in form, takes a singular verb.

They is a pronoun.
Scissors comes before *scissortail* in the dictionary.

3. CASE
   Differentiations between the nominative and objective cases of nouns are not observed in the English language. A few special rules, however, are generally applied to nouns in the possessive case.
   a. The possessive case of nouns denoting inanimate objects is usually formed with an *of* phrase. (See also *Apostrophe* in Part IV, on punctuation.)

FAULTY: The room's ceiling
IMPROVED: The ceiling *of* the room

Exceptions to this practice are found in certain familiar expressions that are idiomatically correct.

a year's labor	his heart's content
a moment's notice	for heaven's sake
a stone's throw	a mile's end

b. A noun preceding a gerund is usually in the possessive case.

FAULTY: I don't understand William being gone so long.
IMPROVED: I don't understand William's being gone so long. (It is not *William* that is not understood; it is *being gone*, which is adjectivally identified by the word *William's*.)

Distinction should be made between gerunds and participles. (See *Verbals*, under *Verbs*, in this chapter.)

Everett doesn't like *Mary's working*. (Everett disapproves of the fact that Mary works. *Working* is a gerund here.)
Everett doesn't like *Mary working*. (Everett doesn't like Mary when she is at work. *Working* is a participle here.)

4. NOUNS USED AS ADJECTIVES
Although many nouns are used as adjectives effectively, especially when no suitable adjectives can be found, such forms should be avoided if they are awkward or ambiguous.

a. Nouns used acceptably as adjectives:

opera tickets   *automobile* race

b. Nouns used awkwardly or ambiguously as adjectives:

FAULTY: Many people now become seriously involved in a race argument. (Race is ambiguous; does the writer mean *racing* or *racial* issues?)
IMPROVED: Many people now become seriously involved in arguments about *racial issues*.
Many people now become seriously involved in arguments about *horse racing*.

PRONOUNS

A *pronoun* is a word that may be substituted for a noun. It performs all the functions of a noun but is not as specific. Because a pronoun is a substitute and depends on other words for its meaning, it must refer expressly or by clear implication to a noun or another pronoun previously mentioned (called the *antecedent*).

1. CLASSIFICATION

Pronouns are usually classified descriptively:

a. Personal pronouns designate the person speaking, the person spoken to, or the person or thing spoken of.

DECLENSION OF PERSONAL PRONOUNS

Person	Case	Singular	Plural
1st person	nominative	I	we
	objective	me	us
	possessive	my, mine	our, ours
2nd person	nominative	you	you
	objective	you	you
	possessive	your, yours	your, yours
3rd person	nominative	he, she, it	they
	objective	him, her, it	them
	possessive	his, her, hers, its	their, theirs

(Note that the possessive forms *ours, yours, hers, its,* and *theirs* are each written without the apostrophe.)

b. Demonstrative pronouns point out or identify specific objects (*this, that, these, those, such*). The choice of pronoun depends on the relative proximity of the speaker to the object.

this house, these houses (Near)
that house, those houses (Farther away)

c. Relative pronouns connect a subordinate clause to the main clause. *Who, whom, whose* (and the compounds *whoever, whomever, whosoever,* and *whomsoever*) refer to persons; *which* and *whichever* refer to things or objects and to living creatures (but not to persons except groups of people regarded impersonally or categories of persons regarded as such); *that* and *what* may refer to either persons or objects.

Homer, *who* is the first among the epic writers, has been called the father of heroic literature.
The writer of *whom* I speak is Sylvia Warner.
Is he the man *whose* hat is on my desk?
Whoever is first receives the award.
Grace will admit *whomever* she sees first.
This is the book of *which* I spoke.
The television set, *which* was repaired only last week, is broken again.
You may have *whichever* book you want.

He is a man *that* we all admire.
Is this the face *that* launched a thousand ships?
She is *what* I call a genius.
This is about *what* I would expect of him.

d. The pronouns *who, whose, which,* and *what* (and the compounds *whoever* and *whatever*) become *interrogative* when used to introduce a question.

Who shall cast the first stone?
Whose gloves are these?
Which is yours?
What do you want?
Whoever told you that lie?
Whatever does she mean?

e. *Indefinite pronouns* are ones whose antecedents are not explicit or precise persons, places, or things. Some of the most frequently used indefinite pronouns are listed below.

all	each one	neither	other
another	cither	nobody	some
any	everyone	none	somebody
anyone	everybody	no one	someone
anything	everything	nothing	something
both	few	one	such
each	much		

f. *Reflexive pronouns* direct or reflect the action back to the subject. In form they represent a compound of one of the personal pronouns and *self* or *selves.*

He taught *himself* to read.

g. *Intensive pronouns* appear in an appositive position and serve to emphasize or intensify a substantive. The forms are the same as the reflexive forms above.

The students *themselves* made the decision.

h. *Reciprocal pronouns* indicate an interchange or mutual action. *Each other* and *one another* are the only two such pronouns in English.

The two girls very seldom saw *each other.*
As they passed, all the soldiers nodded to *one another.*

2. CASE

The case of a pronoun is determined not by its antecedent but by the construction that it is a part of.

a. Personal pronouns have different forms for different cases. (See *Declension of Personal Pronouns*, above.)

(1) The subject of the verb is in the nominative case.

He and *I* are going.
Dave and *she* are going.

(2) The complements of all forms of the verb *to be* (except the infinitive) are in the nominative case.

This is *she* speaking.
The speaker was neither *he* nor *she*.
It is *they* whom you seek.
It is *we* who must remain to spread your message.

(3) The subject and the complement of the infinitive are in the objective case if the subject is also the object of a verb or preposition.

He invited *them* and *us* to go to the party.
We believed *him* to be wrong.
He asked *you* and *me* to be ready at noon.
The judges declared the winner to be *her*.

(4) The object of a preposition is in the objective case.

Let's keep this secret *between you* and *me*.
I bought birthday presents *for him* and *her*.
Come to lunch *with* Judy and *me*.
I typed the letters *for* Mr. Miller and *him*.

Note: In (1) through (4) above, when a pronoun follows *and*, it sometimes becomes a problem to choose the correct case (*I* or *me*, *he* or *him*, *she* or *her*, *we* or *us*, *they* or *them*). Very often the correct form can be determined if the sentence is tried out with the *pronoun in question used by itself*. Some of the sentences above would be tried out as follows:

Come to lunch *with* [Judy and] *me*.
I typed the letters *for* [Mr. Miller and] *him*.
He invited *them* [and us] to go to the party.
He invited [them and] *us* to go to the party.
He asked [you and] *me* to be ready at noon.

(5) The proper case for a pronoun used in an elliptical clause introduced by *than* or *as* can be determined by the meaning of the complete form of the clause.

He is more understanding than *I* [am understanding]. (*I* is the subject of the verb in the clause *I am understanding.*)

I can write as well as *he* [can write]. (*He* is the subject of the verb in the clause *he can write.*)

She speaks to Helen more often than [she speaks to] *me*. (*Me* is the object of the preposition *to.*)

She speaks to Helen more often than *I* [speak to Helen]. (*I* is the subject of the verb *speak* in the clause *I speak to* Helen.)

(6) With gerunds the possessive case is most often used, although the choice of case sometimes depends on the emphasis intended.

Your reading aloud disturbs me.

Have you ever thought about *his* leaving the company? (The *leaving* is emphasized here.)

Have you ever thought about *him* leaving the company? (The person named [*him*] is emphasized here.)

(See *Verbals*, under *Verbs.*)

(7) The possessive case of *it* has no apostrophe.

The bird built *its* nest in the tree.

b. The case of a relative pronoun is determined by the construction of the clause in which it appears. Difficulties frequently arise in the use of *who* and *whom*. In formal English *who* and *whoever* serve as subjects of a verb; *whom* and *whomever* serve as objects.

NOMINATIVE CASE	OBJECTIVE CASE	POSSESSIVE CASE
who	whom	whose
whoever	whomever	whosever
that	that	of that
which	which	of which, whose
what	what	of what

Jean, *who* lives next door, was married last week. (Subject of the verb *lives*)

Ann, *whom* I have known all my life, was there. (Object of the verb *have known*)

John, to *whom* we looked for help, was not at home. (Object of the preposition *to*)

He spoke to *whoever* answered the telephone. (Subject of the verb *answered* in a noun clause that serves as the object of the preposition *to*)

Whose is often used as the possessive of *which*, in place of *of which*, to avoid an awkward or formal-sounding construction.

I'd like to have a desk the drawers *of which* don't stick.

I'd like to have a desk *whose* drawers don't stick.

c. Some indefinite pronouns can be made possessive in form through the addition of an apostrophe and an *s.*

another's glove   anyone's house   everybody's responsibility

d. A pronoun used in apposition with a noun or another pronoun is in the same case as the noun or other pronoun.

We—James and *I*—will never betray your confidence. (*I*, in apposition with *we*, the subject, is in the nominative case.)
He asked three men—Bob, Joe, and *me*—to be ready. (*Me*, in apposition with *men*, the subject of the infinitive *to be*, is in the objective case.)
The men—Bob, Joe, and *I*—met him at the river. (*I*, in apposition with *men*, the subject, is in the nominative case.)

Note: The correct form may be determined easily by dropping the noun with which the pronoun is in apposition and allowing the pronoun to function alone; *e.g.*, *I* met him at the river.

3. REFERENCE

A pronoun should refer clearly to its antecedent if the meaning is to be precise. The following conventions concerning reference of pronouns should be noted.

a. The masculine pronoun (*he, him, his*) may be used to refer to an antecedent that is both masculine and feminine.

Each employee soon learns that *he* must accept responsibility for *his* actions. (Includes girls and women)

b. Each pronoun should refer clearly to a definite person, place, or thing in order to avoid the following difficulties:
  (1) Remote antecedent. The pronoun should be placed as close as possible to its antecedent.

FAULTY: He wore a flower in his lapel, *which* he had received from an admirer. (What had he received from an admirer, his lapel or a flower?)
IMPROVED: In his lapel he wore a flower, *which* he had received from an admirer.

  (2) Ambiguous reference. There should be no question as to the specific antecedent for each pronoun; if the antecedent involves the possibility of choice, it is ambiguous and thus the reference is faulty.

FAULTY: Last Tuesday James told Mr. Adams that *he* must find the money or face bankruptcy. (Who is to find the money or face bankruptcy?)

IMPROVED: Last Tuesday James told Mr. Adams to find the money or face bankruptcy.
> *or:*

IMPROVED: Last Tuesday James told Mr. Adams, "You must find the money or face bankruptcy."
> *or:*

IMPROVED: Last Tuesday James told Mr. Adams, "I must find the money or face bankruptcy."

(3) Broad or weak reference. A pronoun should refer to a definite word, not to an entire clause, idea, action, modifier, or understood or unexpressed word.

FAULTY: Bill was the star of the game, *which* led to his promotion to the first string.
IMPROVED: Bill's starring in the game led to his promotion to the first string.
FAULTY: Helen is studying the piano because her mother is a good *one.*
IMPROVED: Helen is studying the piano because her mother is a good pianist.
FAULTY: Helen is learning to play the piano. *It* is a subject I know nothing about.
IMPROVED: Helen is learning to play the piano. I know nothing about piano music.

(4) Indefinite reference with second- and third-person pronouns. Consistency of reference must be applied, or the passive voice may be used.

FAULTY: If you hope to pass, you must study; however, *anybody* can get help if *you* ask for it.
IMPROVED: If you hope to pass, you must study; however, *you* can get help if *you* ask for it.
> *or:*

IMPROVED: If one hopes to pass, he must study; however, *anyone* can get help if *he* asks for it.
FAULTY: *They* have no income-tax law in the state of Florida.
IMPROVED: Florida has no state income-tax law.

4. AGREEMENT

Although pronouns are effective instruments by which we can secure variety, emphasis, and economy, they may merely confuse if consistent grammatical patterns are not maintained.

a. The pronoun should agree with its antecedent in number, person, and gender.

If a new *secretary* wants to suceed, *he* or *she* must work hard. (Singular antecedent requires a singular pronoun.)

She is one of those people *who hate* early morning appointments. (*Who* refers to *people*; it is therefore plural and thus takes the plural form of the verb *hate*.)

b. The indefinite pronouns (*each, one, someone, somebody, any, anyone, everyone, everybody, none, nobody, either, neither*) are usually considered singular.

If *anyone* wishes to speak, *he* may do so now.
Neither of the men would answer when *he* was questioned.
Everyone present cast *his* vote.
Everybody must turn in *his* expense account by Thursday.

VERBS

A verb is a word that makes a statement about a subject. Its function is to convey a positive assertion, to make a statement of condition or probability, to give a command, to ask a question, or to make an exclamation.

1. CLASSIFICATION

a. A *transitive verb* is one that requires a direct object to complete its meaning (as the word *transitive* suggests, the action passes from one thing to another).

I *carried* the *book*.
Donne *wrote* intriguing *poetry*.
Alice *closed* the *book* with a sigh of relief.

b. An *intransitive verb* simply states something about the subject; there is no direct object to receive the action.

The sun *rose* at six o'clock.
The old dog *lay* sleeping in the sun.
James *sat* for two hours waiting for the train.

c. A *linking verb*, or *copula*, is an intransitive verb that makes no complete statement itself, but links the subject with a subjective complement (predicate noun or predicate adjective). *To be* is the most common linking verb; other principal ones are *taste, smell, become, feel, seem,* and *appear.*

The coffee *tastes* good.
I *am* the victor.
His account *seems* improbable.
She *felt* bad.

d. Many verbs serve an *auxiliary*, or *helping*, function; that is, they are used with another verb to form a verb phrase. They help indicate tense, mood, and voice. (See *Properties*, below.) Among the more common auxiliaries are *be, have, do, may, can, shall,* and *will.*

I <u>*am*</u> going.
She <u>*has*</u> been ill.
I <u>*do*</u> want to go.

2. PROPERTIES

Verbs regularly show the following qualities, or properties: *person, number, mood, voice,* and *tense.*

a. Verbs (except *to be*) change in form to denote *person* and *number* only in the third person singular of the present tense.

To stop	*Singular*	*Plural*
1st person:	I stop	we stop
2nd person:	you stop	you stop
3rd person:	he, she, it stops	they stop

To be	*Singular*	*Plural*
1st person:	I am	we are
2nd person:	you are	you are
3rd person:	he, she, it is	they are

b. Mood (or *mode*) is the property of a verb that denotes the state of mind in which the action is conceived:

(1) The *indicative* mood makes a statement or asks a question.

He *closed* the door.
Who *is* the hero of the play?

(2) The *imperative* mood expresses a command or makes a request.

Take time to compose a letter.
Listen well; respect wisdom.
Stop!
Please *come* as early as you can.

(3) The *subjunctive* mood expresses a condition contrary to fact, a doubt, a regret or a wish, a concession, or a supposition.

If I *were* you, I would study more regularly.
I wish I *were* in command here.
I move that the treasurer *be* instructed to pay our debts.
Suppose she *were* too late to be considered.
He acts as though he *were* the only person present.
If this *be* treason, make the most of it.

In English, the subjunctive mood has largely been displaced by the indicative. The subjunctive occurs most frequently in the third person singular of the present tense (*I desire that he go at once*, instead of the indicative form, *I desire that he goes at once*) and in the verb *to be*, as indicated below:

Present Indicative		Present Subjunctive	
I am	we are	if I be	if we be
you are	you are	if you be	if you be
he is	they are	if he be	if they be

c. *Voice* is the property of the verb that indicates whether the subject of a sentence or of a clause is *acting* or *being acted upon*. When the subject performs the action, the verb is said to be in the *active voice*. When the subject is acted upon, it is said to be in the *passive voice*; the subject is literally passive and is a receiver rather than an actor. The passive is formed by the use of some form of the verb *to be* as an auxiliary to the past participle of another verb.

The ball *struck* the player. (Active)
The player *was struck* by the ball. (Passive)
Mary *started* a rumor about two of her co-workers. (Active)
A rumor *was started* about two of Mary's co-workers. (Passive)

Although the passive voice is sometimes weak and should be avoided as a general rule, it has certain uses that are worth consideration by the careful writer.

(1) The passive voice may be used when the subject is not known or is not to be revealed.

A bomb *was found* in the railway station.
The invoice *was mailed* under separate cover.

(2) It may be used to emphasize the *action* in a sentence rather than the *actor*.

Good health *is sought* by everyone.
This lesson *will be learned* before we leave.

(3) It may be used to achieve variety in sentence structure.

Inexperienced writers often use the passive in an attempt to create an impression of authority and learning, but excessive use of the passive often results in vague and wordy constructions. When possible, use the active voice.

d. The word *tense* comes from the Latin word *tempus* (time) and refers to the forms of verbs denoting the time and the distinct nature of the action or existence (continuing or completed). In English six tenses are commonly used: present, past, future, present perfect, past perfect, and future perfect. (For more information on tenses, see *Principal Parts, Conjugation,* and *Sequence of Tenses,* below.)

3. PRINCIPAL PARTS

The *principal parts* of a verb are the *present stem* (*infinitive*) (*jump*), the *past tense* (*jumped*), and the *past participle* (*jumped*). The past tense and past participle of most verbs in English are formed by adding *–ed* to the present stem; these verbs are called "regular" verbs. The principal parts of many other verbs in English are formed in an "irregular" manner—some through a vowel change (*sing, sang, sung*), others in some other "irregular" manner (*catch, caught, caught*). The principal parts are important because the six tenses are built from the three principal parts. From the present stem are formed the present and future tenses; from the past participle are formed the present perfect, past perfect, and future perfect tenses.

Appendix 10 gives the principal parts of all irregularly formed verbs. You may also consult this list to learn when the final consonant is doubled to form the past tense, past participle, and present participle of a verb (*hop, hopped, hopping*) and to learn when a final *e* is dropped before the *–ed* is added to form the past tense and past participle or before the *–ing* is added to form the present participle (*hope, hoped, hoping*).

4. VERBALS

Because *participles, gerunds,* and *infinitives* are derived from verbs, they are called *verbals.* They are like verbs in that they have different tenses, may have subjects and objects, and may be modified by adverbs; but they cannot make a statement and therefore cannot be used in the place of verbs.

a. A *participle* may be used as an adjective.

A *working* man is generally busy. (Present participle used as an adjective to modify the noun *man*)
Polished silver always looks elegant. (Past participle used as an adjective to modify the noun *silver*)
Having completed his work, he retired for the night. (Perfect participle used as an adjective to modify the pronoun *he*)

b. A *gerund* ends in *–ing* and functions as a noun.

Your *working* is greatly appreciated. (Gerund used as the subject of the
  sentence)
He objected to my *speaking* without permission. (Gerund used as the object
  of the preposition *to*)

> A noun or pronoun preceding a gerund is usually in the possessive
> case.

Most companies disapprove of an *employee's* being late.

> However, a plural noun preceding a gerund is often not in the
> possessive case.

Most companies disapprove of *employees* being late.

> When the noun preceding the gerund denotes an inanimate object
> or an abstract idea, the noun is usually not in the possessive case.

They blamed the plane crash on the *engine* falling in midair.

c. An *infinitive* is usually preceded by *to* and functions as a noun, an
  adjective, or an adverb.

To *succeed* was my greatest ambition. (Infinitive used as a noun, subject of
  the verb *was*)
The person *to choose* is the one now in office. (Infinitive used as an adjective
  to modify the noun *person*)
We came *to help*. (Infinitive used as an adverb to modify the verb *came*)

5. CONJUGATION

Following is the conjugation of the verb *to see* in its various forms
(principal parts: *see, saw, seen*).

INDICATIVE MOOD

Present Tense

1st person
ACTIVE: I see   we see
PASSIVE: I am seen   we are seen

2nd person
ACTIVE: you see   you see
PASSIVE: you are seen   you are seen

3rd person
ACTIVE: he, she, it sees   they see
PASSIVE: he, she, it is seen   they are seen

Past Tense

1st person
ACTIVE: I saw   we saw
PASSIVE: I was seen   we were seen

2nd person
ACTIVE: you saw   you saw
PASSIVE: you were seen   you were seen

3rd person
ACTIVE: he saw   they saw
PASSIVE: he was seen   they were seen

Future Tense

1st person
ACTIVE: I shall see   we shall see
PASSIVE: I shall be seen   we shall be seen

2nd person
ACTIVE: you will see   you will see
PASSIVE: you will be seen   you will be seen

3rd person
ACTIVE: he will see   they will see
PASSIVE: he will be seen   they will be seen

Present Perfect Tense

1st person
ACTIVE: I have seen   we have seen
PASSIVE: I have been seen   we have been seen

2nd person
ACTIVE: you have seen   you have seen
PASSIVE: you have been seen   you have been seen

3rd person
ACTIVE: he has seen   they have seen
PASSIVE: he has been seen   they have been seen

Past Perfect Tense

1st person
ACTIVE: I had seen   we had seen
PASSIVE: I had been seen   we had been seen

2nd person
ACTIVE: you had seen   you had seen
PASSIVE: you had been seen   you had been seen

3rd person
ACTIVE: he had seen   they had seen
PASSIVE: he had been seen   they had been seen

Future Perfect Tense

1st person
ACTIVE: I shall have seen   we shall have seen
PASSIVE: I shall have been seen   we shall have been seen

2nd person
ACTIVE: you will have seen   you will have seen
PASSIVE: you will have been seen   you will have been seen

3rd person
ACTIVE: he will have seen   they will have seen
PASSIVE: he will have been seen   they will have been seen

SUBJUNCTIVE MOOD

Present Tense

Active Voice   *Passive Voice*
SINGULAR: if I, you see (if he sees)   if I, you, he be seen
PLURAL: if we, you, they see   if we, you, they be seen

Past Tense

SINGULAR: if I, you, he saw   if I, you, he were seen
PLURAL: if we, you, they saw   if we, you, they were seen

Present Perfect Tense

SINGULAR: if I, you have seen   if I, you have been seen
            (if he has seen)   (if he has been seen)
PLURAL: if we, you, they have seen   if we, you, they have been seen

Past Perfect Tense
(Same as the Indicative Mood)

IMPERATIVE MOOD

Present Tense
          see   be seen

INFINITIVES

Present Tense
          to see   to be seen

Present Perfect Tense
          to have seen   to have been seen

PARTICIPLES

Present Tense
          seeing   being seen

Past Tense
          seen   been seen

Present Perfect Tense
          having seen   having been seen

GERUNDS

Present Tense
seeing   being seen

Present Perfect Tense
having seen   having been seen

In addition to the six simple tenses in English, there are two other forms that are frequently recognized:
a. Progressive verb forms show action in progress.

I *am seeing*
I *was seeing.*
I *am being seen.*

   b. Emphatic verb forms employ *do* or *does* as an auxiliary. (These forms are used also for questions and negations.)

I *do see;* he *does see.*
Does he *see* it? *Did* he *see* it?
He *does* not *see* it; he *did* not *see* it.

6. SEQUENCE OF TENSES
   Tense reveals not only the time of the action (present, past, and future) but also the continuity of related action. Shifts in tense must conform to the logical order or sequence of action. In most instances a knowledge of the denotation of time in the six tenses and the application of common sense will aid in developing consistent practices.
   a. The tense of a verb in a subordinate element should *agree* logically with the thought suggested by the governing verb in the main clause. Note that statements regarded as universally or permanently true are expressed in the present.

   FAULTY: This book is *written* for an audience which *felt* that political favors *are* to be dispensed without particular regard for merit or justice.
   IMPROVED: This book *was written* for an audience which *feels* that political favors *are* to be dispensed without particular regard for merit or justice.

   b. A major difficulty arises from the use of verbals.
      (1) The *present infinitive* is used to express action of the same time as, or future to, that of the governing verb.

She wants *to read* each new book.
He wanted *to improve* his efficiency.

(2) The *perfect infinitive* is used to express action previous to that of the governing verb.

I *should* like *to have seen* his face when you told him.
I consider it a privilege *to have worked* with him in the recent political campaign.

(3) The *present participle* is used to express action simultaneous with that of the governing verb.

Looking up from her book, she was startled to see her supervisor enter the room.

(4) The *perfect participle* is used to express action prior to that of the governing verb.

Having found his place, he sat down hurriedly.

7. *SHALL* AND *WILL, SHOULD* AND *WOULD*

Although in informal usage the differences between *shall* and *will* and *should* and *would* are hardly discernible, careful writers still recognize the distinctions. In more conservative practice the use of *should* and *would* follows the same patterns as those established for *shall* and *will.*

a. In expressing expectation and in the simple future *shall* is used in the first person and *will* in the second and third persons.

I shall   we shall
you will   you will
he, she, it will   they will

I *shall* be in the office next Monday at 10 o'clock.
They said that they *would* be on time.
I *should* think that they *would* be more careful.

b. *Will* is used in the first person and *shall* in the second and third persons to express determination, command, or promise.

I *will* have my way in this matter.
I *would* do it if I could.
They *shall* not pass.

c. *Should* may be used in all persons to express obligation or condition.

I *should* follow your advice, but I'm too lazy.
If he *should* leave now, all work would stop.

    d. Would may be used in all persons to express determination, habitual action, or a wish.

Only on one condition *would* we be willing to consider such a proposal.
I *would* read for an hour or two each night before going to sleep.
If he *would* leave now, all work would stop.

ADJECTIVES AND ADVERBS

Modifiers are words or groups of words that describe or qualify other words. *To modify* means to describe, limit, or in any other way make the meaning more precise or exact. The two kinds of modifiers are *adjectives* and *adverbs*.

1. An *adjective* is a word that *modifies a noun or pronoun.*

blue bird	*the* chair
easy assignment	*his* grade
crushed flower	*several* people
a book	*seventh* day
an apple	*former* employer

Some adjectives form the comparative degree by adding *–er* and the superlative by adding *–est*; others form the comparative degree by the use of *more* (*less*) and *most* (*least*) for the superlative degrees. Still others have an irregular comparison.

Positive	*Comparative*	*Superlative*
cool	cooler	coolest
tired	more tired	most tired
bad	worse	worst
good	better	best

The comparative degree should be used to indicate the relationship between two persons or things.

I am the *taller* of the two children in our family.
This book is *better* than that one.
I am *more optimistic* than he.

The superlative degree should be used when three or more persons or things are compared.

This is the *warmest* day of the year.
I am the *tallest* of the three boys.
This is the *most pleasant* experience I can recall.

2. An *adverb* is a word that *modifies an adjective, a verb, or another adverb*. Frequently, adverbs can be distinguished from adjectives only by the context in which they appear.

Children like books. (No modifier)
Young children *usually* like *story* books. (*Young* and *story* are adjectives; *usually* is an adverb.)
Very young children *almost always* like *highly illustrated* books, books *that can be read quickly.* (*Young, illustrated,* and the clause *that can be read quickly* are *adjectives; very, almost, always, highly,* and *quickly* are adverbs.)

In the comparison of adverbs, some shorter adverbs form the comparative degree by adding *–er* (*fast, faster*) and the superlative by adding *–est* (*fastest*), but most adverbs form the comparative degree by using *more* (*less*) and the superlative by adding *most* (*least*). Others are irregularly formed.

Positive	Comparative	Superlative
badly	worse	worst
well	better	best
calmly	more calmly	most calmly

Adverbs have certain distinguishing characteristics:

a. They are frequently distinguished from corresponding adjectives by ending in *–ly*. Although many adverbs end in *–ly*, this ending is not a certain device for recognizing this part of speech; some adverbs do not and some adjectives (*early, cowardly*) do end in *–ly*. Several common words that do not end in *–ly* may be either adjectives or adverbs depending on their function in a given context: *fast, little, near, late, well.*

b. Some adverbs are distinguished from corresponding nouns by *–wise* or *–ways* used as a suffix: *sideways, lengthwise.*

c. Some adverbs are distinguished from the same word used as a preposition in that they have no noun as an object.

The sun came *up*. (Adverb)
Henry came *up* the hill. (Preposition)

d. Adverbs, like adjectives, may be preceded by words that intensify their meaning.

The *very hastily* written paper was much better than the author had expected.
He walked *right by* without speaking.

PREPOSITIONS

1. A *simple preposition* shows the relationship of a noun or a pronoun (the object of the preposition) to some other word: stayed *at* school, lived *in* the house, the neighborhood *across* the way. The following list contains the words most commonly used as prepositions:

about	beside	in	since
above	besides	inside	through
across	between	into	throughout
after	beyond	like	till
against	but	near	to
along	by	of	toward
amid	concerning	off	until
among	despite	on	under
around	down	onto	underneath
at	during	outside	up
before	except	over	upon
behind	excepting	per	with
below	for	regarding	within
beneath	from	save	without

A preposition is usually followed by its object, which may be a noun, a pronoun, a noun phrase, or a noun clause. Occasionally, however, the object may appear earlier in the sentence:

Which church are you going *to?*
The company I am employed *by* is a reliable one.

Although some writers object to the use of a preposition at the end of a sentence, others accept such usage unless the final preposition is weakening. The practice should always depend upon its effectiveness.

This is the sort of foolishness which we will not put up with.
We will not put up with this sort of foolishness.

2. A *compound preposition* serves the same purpose as a single one:

as for	for fear of	in view of
as to	for the sake of	on account of
aside from	in accordance with	owing to
because of	in addition to	pertaining to
by means of	in behalf of	regardless of
by way of	in case of	with reference to
contrary to	in favor of	with regard to
due to	in regard to	with respect to
exclusive of	in spite of	with the exception of

CONJUNCTIONS

Conjunctions are used to connect words or groups of words in sentences; they are identified generally according to their function as *coordinating* or *subordinating* elements. If the words or word groups are of equal value in the sentence, the conjunction is said to be *coordinating*; if the words or word groups are unequal, the conjunction is said to be *subordinating*.

1. *Coordinating conjunctions* link words, phrases, clauses, or sentences of equal rank—elements that are not grammatically dependent on one another.

   a. Pure, or *simple,* conjunctions join two or more words, phrases, clauses, or sentences of equal rank—that is, having similar importance in the grammatical unit. The simple conjunctions are *and, but, for, or,* and *nor* (some writers include *yet* or *so*).

   b. Correlative conjunctions are words used in pairs to emphasize the relationship between two ideas. The most commonly used correlatives are *either . . . or, both . . . and, neither . . . nor,* and *not only . . . but also.*

2. *Subordinating conjunctions* relate a noun clause or an adverb clause to its independent clause. (The adjective clause is usually related by a relative pronoun.) Some common subordinating conjunctions are *because, if, since, as, while, although, unless, before, so that.*

   Although English grammar is not difficult, many students never master it.
   Peter cannot hope to buy a car *unless* he begins to save money.

3. *Conjunctive adverbs* are words or phrases that ordinarily are used parenthetically but also are often used to relate two independent clauses or two words, phrases, or sentences; the more common are *however, thus, in fact, for example, still, then.*

   I worked for three hours on the bookkeeping; *then* I began to review the correspondence.
   English grammar is not difficult; *however,* many students never master it.

INTERJECTIONS

An *interjection* is an exclamatory or parenthetic word that has little relation to the remainder of the sentence. Frequently it is a sentence in itself:

Ouch!
Oh, why didn't you come earlier?
Alas, youth too soon is fled.

Commonly used interjections include the following:

ah	bravo	hurrah	so
aha	encore	hush	tut
ahoy	gosh	indeed	what
alas	hallo	lo	whoa
amen	hello	O	whoopee
ay	hey	off	why
bah	hist	oh	woe
behold	ho	ouch	
boo	huh	pshaw	

Interjections should be used sparingly in serious writing because they are for the most part colloquial and conversational. When overused, they give the effect of a strained, melodramatic, or immature style.

Part II

Clauses and Phrases

THE SENTENCE, which is in itself a group or cluster of words in a meaningful pattern, is often made up of a number of subordinate groups or clusters of words that form *clauses* and *phrases* and that function as individual parts of speech.

A *clause* is a closely related group of words containing a subject and a verb. There are two general types of clause:

1. An *independent* (principal or main) *clause* expresses a complete thought and may stand alone as a sentence. The underscored sections represent the independent clause.

Today's newspaper is on my desk.
The theater section, which begins on page 30, reviews the new play.

2. A *dependent* (subordinate) *clause* cannot stand alone as a sentence, although it contains a subject and a verb. Such a clause depends for its meaning upon the principal clause of the sentence in which it occurs; it functions as a noun or a modifier, and it is usually introduced by a subordinating conjunction, an adverb, or a relative pronoun. Dependent clauses are used as adverbs (adverbial clause), as adjectives (adjective clause), or as nouns (noun clause) and are identified according to their function.
   a. An *adverbial clause* modifies a verb, an adjective, or an adverb.

When the humidity is high, we suffer from the heat. (The adverbial clause modifies the verb *suffer*.)
We are sorry *that he is ill*. (The adverbial clause modifies the adjective *sorry*.)
He does his work more quickly *than I do*. (The adverbial clause modifies the adverbs *more quickly*.)

b. An *adjective clause* modifies a noun or a pronoun.

We saw a replica of the capsule *that John Glenn used in his orbital flight.*
(The adjective clause modifies the noun *capsule.*)
The employee *who applies himself* will succeed. (The adjective clause modifies the noun *employee.*)
The woman *who applies herself* will succeed. (The adjective clause modifies the noun *woman.*)
Give the book to anyone *who may want to use it.* (The adjective clause modifies the pronoun *anyone.*)

c. A *noun clause* serves as a subject, a complement, or an object.

What we need most is more money. (The noun clause is the subject of the verb *is.*)
That is *what he had in mind.* (The noun clause is a predicate nominative following the linking verb *is.*)
Macbeth stated *that he was governed only by his vaulting ambition.* (The noun clause is the direct object of the verb *stated.*)
Give *whoever needs one* a book. (The noun clause is the indirect object of the verb *give.*)
I will speak to *whoever answers the telephone.* (The noun clause is the object of the preposition *to.*)

3. A *phrase* is a group of related words having no subject and predicate. It is used as a noun or as a modifier (adjective or adverb) and is connected to the rest of the sentence by a preposition, a participle, a gerund, or an infinitive.

Her ambition was *to learn another language.* (The infinitive phrase is used as a noun, serving as a predicate nominative.)
Milton hoped *to write the great English epic.* (The infinitive phrase is used as a noun, serving as the direct object of the verb.)
To succeed was my greatest ambition. (The infinitive phrase is used as a noun, serving as the subject of the sentence.)
His energies were directed to *writing a notable epic.* (The gerund phrase is used as a noun, serving as the object of the preposition *to.*)
Fishing with his friends was his favorite pastime. (The gerund phrase is used as a noun, serving as the subject of the sentence.)
He considered *peddling old clothes* undignified. (The gerund phrase is used as a noun, serving as the object of the verb.)
The Greeks sailed *to Troy.* (The prepositional phrase is used as an adverb.)
We went *to visit our brother at camp.* (The infinitive phrase is used as an adverb.)
The cover *of the book* was blue. (The prepositional phrase is used as an adjective.)

Her ambition *to climb the mountain* was never fulfilled. (The infinitive phrase is used as an adjective.)

The mysterious stranger, *wearing a black coat*, disappeared into the night. (The participial phrase is used as an adjective.)

The *absolute phrase* is somewhat unlike other kinds of phrases in that it usually consists of a noun followed and modified by a participle or participial phrase. Because it cannot stand alone as a sentence, it is a phrase; but it modifies no single word in the sentence, although it is closely related in thought to the rest of the sentence or to some part of it. The phrase is *absolute* in that it has no grammatical relationship to the main clause.

The dishes having been done, she curled up in the chair for a nap.

The king having died, the prince assumed the throne.

An *appositive phrase* is a group of words naming again a substantive previously mentioned.

Washington, *our first president*, was an astute politician.

Chicago, *an inland city*, has grown in importance as an ocean port since the opening of the St. Lawrence Seaway.

Part III

Sentences

COMMUNICATION IN ENGLISH begins with the sentence. Depending on the circumstances, a sentence may be a fully developed statement, or it may contain implied elements. In many instances, our spoken language can be reduced to writing; however, the written statement does not have accompanying aids like gesture and vocal intonation, nor does it permit immediate questioning or requests for repetition when it is unclear. A good sentence, and thus effective communication, requires clarity, unity, and propriety. In order to achieve these qualities, writing generally follows a set of rules and conventions.

With the proper inflection a single word could be considered a sentence— or at least a sentence by implication.

> Oh? (Is that so?)
> Oh! (That hurts!)
> Come! (You come here!)
> [Who is that?] John. (That is John.)

As questions, exclamations, commands, and responses, such units may function satisfactorily as sentences. In general, however, it is convenient to define a sentence as *a group of words conveying a single complete thought.* If the group of words contains more than one statement, such statements should be so closely related that they convey a single impression.

1. The typical English sentence contains a *subject* and a *predicate.* As previously suggested, either the subject or the predicate may be expressed or implied. In order to work meaningfully with such matters, one must understand the structure of the sentence; one must recognize the function of words as they stand in a particular relationship with one another. The following comments are basic to that understanding.

    a. The *subject* (*S*) is the person, thing, or idea about which an assertion is made. The *predicate* (*P*) (in its most expanded form composed of a verb, its modifiers, and its object and modifiers) makes an assertion (of action, state of being, or condition) about the subject.

I read a book.

S   P

The old man spoke softly.

S   P

b. Both the subject and the predicate may be simple or compound.

John and Mary read and sing well.

S (compound)   P (compound)

John stated his opinion and sat down.

S (simple)   P (compound)

John and Mary are present.

S (compound)   P (simple)

John's briefcase and hat were found beside the wreck.

S (compound)   P (simple)

Note: A simple device by which the subject may be located is to ask *who* or *what* of the verb. Observe the sentences above:

Who read and sing well? *John and Mary* are thus identified as the subject.
Who stated his opinion and sat down? *John.*
Who are present? *John and Mary.*
What were found beside the wreck? *John's briefcase and hat.*

c. Although a sentence needs only a subject and a verb to fulfill the requirement of the definition, many sentences contain other elements to complete their meanings. Among these are two general classifications: *objects* and *complements.*

(1) The *direct object* (*DO*) is a word or group of words that receives the action of a transitive verb.

DO

Joan typed the *letter.*

DO

I have read *War and Peace.*

(2) The *indirect object* (*IO*) identifies the person or thing receiving the action suggested by the verb and direct object. The indirect object usually precedes the direct object; the preposition *to* or *for* is implied.

```
        IO    DO
```
He gave *her* a *box* of candy.
```
        IO              DO
```
She told *him* a bedtime *story*.
```
       IO      DO
```
Bring *me* the *report*. (Subject *you* understood)

> (3) The *object of a preposition* (*OP*) is the substantive that follows a preposition (*P*) and completes its meaning. The complete prepositional phrase functions either as an adjective or as an adverb.

```
                    P        OP
```
She wore a dress *with lace trim*.
```
                  P     OP
```
Your money is *in the bank*.
```
             P       OP
```
He spoke *to the manager*.
```
                      P          OP
```
The boat was built *by three old men*.

> (4) A *subjective complement* (*SC*) (also called a *predicate nominative* when a noun or pronoun, and a *predicate adjective* when an adjective) is a noun, pronoun, or adjective following a linking verb and completing the assertion made about the subject or modifying the subject. (For more about linking verbs, see *Verbs*, in *Part I*.)

```
              SC (or predicate nominative)
```
Tom is the *hero* of the play.
```
            SC (or predicate nominative)
```
This is *he* speaking.
```
                   SC (or predicate adjective)
```
This coffee smells *good*.

> (5) The *objective complement* (*OC*) is a noun, pronoun, or adjective following the direct object and completing the assertion made about the object.

```
                        OC
```
The president appointed him *chairman*.
```
                  OC
```
He washed his face *clean*.

2. Sentences are commonly classified according to their purpose: *declarative, imperative, interrogative,* and *exclamatory*.

I enjoy my work. (A declaration or a statement)
Learn to write well. (An imperative request or command)
Have you read the *Odyssey?* (An interrogation or question)
Look out! (An exclamation)

3. Sentences may also be classified according to their *structure*, that is, according to the kind and number of clauses of which they are composed.
   a. A *simple sentence* contains one independent clause.

I work in an office.

   b. A *compound sentence* contains two or more independent clauses.

She works in the city, but John works on the farm.
I like the theater; Bill, however, prefers the movies.

   c. A *complex sentence* contains one independent and at least one dependent clause.

Although she has traveled a great deal, she still finds charm in new places.

   d. A *compound sentence* contains two or more independent clauses, and one or more dependent clauses.

My black dress, which I wore to the party last week, is at the cleaner's, and my blue dress is not suitable for the occasion.

4. Usually, every sentence should be grammatically complete. Sometimes, however, a group of words stands alone as a sentence but is not grammatically complete and therefore not really a sentence in the strictest meaning. Such a group of words is called a *sentence fragment*.
   a. Although many skilled writers use fragments purposely to achieve particular effects, the inexperienced writer should be certain that he or she is able to write complete sentences when appropriate and that fragments are used knowingly and purposefully. The following sentences, while grammatically incomplete, are not considered real fragments, for the reader understands the writer's intent and the communication is complete.

QUESTIONS AND ANSWERS: Why are you going? Because I want to.
  Do you want to speak with me? No.
EXCLAMATIONS: Too bad!   So sorry!

The sentence fragments that should be avoided are those that have no specific meaning for the reader and do not communicate the intent of the author.

Increasingly large numbers of young people are seeking admission to colleges and universities, which are already overcrowded with students who have difficulty completing their work. Business and professions are demanding men and women with college degrees. *Because of a widespread idea that everyone should have a college education.*

> The fragment is not clearly related to the sentences preceding it. Are large numbers of young people seeking admission to colleges and universities because of the widespread idea that everyone should have a college education, or do businesses and professions demand men and women with college degrees for that reason? The ambiguity cannot be resolved without grammatically associating the fragment with one of the complete sentences.

    b. Many fragments occur because the writer is careless in making dependent elements a part of the sentence to which they belong; correction can usually be made by *modifying the punctuation.*

FAULTY: He asked me to forgive him. *Although I don't know why.*
IMPROVED: He asked me to forgive him, although I don't know why.
FAULTY: I was unable to gain admittance to the supply room. *The door having been locked five minutes before my arrival.*
IMPROVED: I was unable to gain admittance to the supply room, the door having been locked five minutes before my arrival.

    c. A sentence fragment is not to be confused with *elliptical construction* (also called *ellipsis*), an acceptable construction in which a word or more is omitted but whose meaning can be supplied from the rest of the sentence.

He is as tall as she [is tall].

5. Effective sentences must be more than grammatically correct; they must be unified, coherent, and skillfully arranged through the coordination and subordination of ideas and structure. Poor sentences frequently result from a failure to organize ideas in such a way as to indicate clearly their relationship and relative importance to one another.
    a. Coordination
    The basic principle of coordination is parallelism, a means of achieving unity, emphasis, and coherence. Ideas of equal importance and elements with similar functions in a sentence should be made structurally parallel; that is, coordinate elements in a compound structure are most effectively stated when given similar word patterns. In such compound constructions, nouns will be parallel with nouns, verbs with verbs, phrases with phrases, dependent clauses with dependent clauses, independent clauses with independent clauses.
    (1) Coordinating conjunctions (*and, but, for, or, nor*) are definite indicators of parallel structure; they should warn the writer to

be careful in constructing the sentence and alert the reader to look for ideas or elements of equal importance in the statement.

FAULTY: I like *to read, to listen* to good music, and *watching* television.
(The conjunction *and* joins improperly in this sentence two infinitive phrases —*to read, to listen*—and a gerund—*watching*.)
IMPROVED: I like *to read, to listen* to good music, and *to watch* television.
    or:
IMPROVED: I like *reading, listening* to good music, and *watching* television.
FAULTY: The duties of the president are *presiding* at meetings, *appointment* of committees, and *to call* special meetings.
IMPROVED: The duties of the president are *to preside* at meetings, *to appoint* committees, and *to call* special meetings.

(2) Comparisons should be stated in parallel structures.

FAULTY: A ditchdigger is a less rewarding occupation than teaching. (A ditchdigger is not an occupation; teaching is.)
IMPROVED: Ditchdigging is a less rewarding occupation than teaching.
FAULTY: He protested that his job was more rewarding than a common laborer.
IMPROVED: He protested that his job was more rewarding than a common laborer's [job].
    or:
IMPROVED: He protested that his job was more rewarding than that of a common laborer.

(3) A frequent error in parallelism occurs in the improper use of correlative conjunctions (conjunctions occurring in pairs): *either . . . or, neither . . . nor, not only . . . but also, both . . . and.* Elements compared or contrasted through the use of such conjunctions are best stated in parallel form: The second conjunction should be followed by a construction parallel to that following the first; if a prepositional phrase follows one conjunction, a prepositional phrase should follow the other conjunction.

FAULTY: She is not only a *tennis player* but *plays softball* as well.
IMPROVED: She is not only a *tennis player* but also a *softball player.*
FAULTY: He either was *a successful industrialist* or *an accomplished liar.*
IMPROVED: He was either *a successful industrialist* or *an accomplished liar.*
FAULTY: I talked both *to the student* and *his parents.*
IMPROVED: I talked to both *the student* and *his parents.*

b. Subordination

The mature writer recognizes that not all details and thoughts are of equal importance. He or she learns to give certain details a primary or secondary position in the sentence in order to communicate accurately to the reader; in other words, the writer learns to apply the principle of *subordination*. The relationships of the writer's ideas are thus revealed with greater exactness. The main clause will convey the major idea, and the modifiers (words, phrases, dependent clauses) will convey additional and clarifying information. Effective subordination is a means of achieving not only clarity but also variety and coherence.

(1) Short, choppy sentences (often a mark of immature writing) may be eliminated.

FAULTY: He is a man. He is fifty years old. He works hard. He wants to give his family a good home.

IMPROVED: He is a fifty-year-old man who works hard to give his family a good home.

(2) Rambling sentences composed of short clauses joined by *and's* and *but's* may be improved.

FAULTY: The alarm rings and she sits up in bed and she rubs her eyes.

IMPROVED: When the alarm rings, she sits up in bed and rubs her eyes.

(3) Important ideas may be expressed emphatically in main clauses, and less important ideas through subsidiary constructions (modifying words; prepositional, infinitive, participial, and gerund phrases; appositives; dependent clauses).

FAULTY: I came to the office and found that I was behind in my work.

IMPROVED: When I came to the office, I found that I was behind in my work.

(4) Faulty subordination frequently results when conjunctions fail to express clearly the relationship between ideas. (*Like* is not a subordinating conjunction and is not used to join two clauses; *as* is ordinarily used to show time, not causal, relationships.)

FAULTY: I don't know *as* I want to go.
IMPROVED: I don't believe I want to go.
       or:
IMPROVED: I don't want to go.
FAULTY: It looked *like* he would win the match.
IMPROVED: It looked *as if* he would win the match.
FAULTY: I liked the play *while* I didn't care for the movie.
IMPROVED: *Although* I liked the play, I didn't care for the movie.
FAULTY: I read in the paper *where* he had been elected.
IMPROVED: I read in the paper *that* he had been elected.

(5) *Because, where,* and *when* are subordinating elements and should not be used as the subject or the complement of a verb.

FAULTY: The reason he won is *because* he is fifty pounds heavier than his opponent.

IMPROVED: He won because he is fifty pounds heavier than his opponent.

FAULTY: Trusting him is *where* I made my mistake.

IMPROVED: My mistake was trusting him.

or:

IMPROVED: Trusting him was my mistake.

FAULTY: A quatrain is *when* you have a verse of four lines.

IMPROVED: A quatrain is a verse of four lines.

c. Consistent constructions

The careful writer avoids unnecessary or illogical shifts within the structure of an individual sentence or of closely related sentences. Although such a shift may not obscure the meaning, it may result in awkwardness, incongruity, and general loss of effectiveness and emphasis. In order to present ideas clearly and appropriately, the writer must be as consistent as possible in the use of voice, tense, mood, person, number, and style.

FAULTY: When Meg returned to her home, a new car was found waiting for her. (Illogical shift from active to passive)

IMPROVED: When Meg returned to her home, she found a new car waiting for her.

FAULTY: When he hears that his friend is here, he hurried home. (Inconsistency in sequence of tenses)

IMPROVED: When he heard that his friend was there, he hurried home.

FAULTY: Everyone should be careful of their grammar. (Inconsistency of number)

IMPROVED: Everyone should be careful of his grammar.

FAULTY: If a man is to succeed, you must work hard. (Illogical shift in person)

IMPROVED: If a man is to succeed, he must work hard.

FAULTY: First prepare your notes carefully; then the report may be written. (Unnecessary shift in voice)

IMPROVED: You should first prepare your notes carefully and then write your report.

FAULTY: She asked me would I help her with her expense account. (Inappropriate shift from indirect to direct discourse)

IMPROVED: She asked me to help her with her expense account.

FAULTY: Although the party has made significant contributions to the community, its weakness is that the big wheels grab all the glory. (Inappropriate shift from formal to colloquial diction)

IMPROVED: Although the party has made significant contributions to the community, its weakness is that the leaders do not recognize the contributions of others.

d. Modifiers

Modifiers, for clarity, must refer to specific words and should be placed as close as possible to the words they modify. A modifier is *misplaced* if it seems to modify a word that it logically should not or cannot; it is considered *dangling* if it has nothing to modify.

(1) Misplaced modifiers may be corrected by revising the sentence to place the modifier in such a position that its object of modification may be clearly discerned.

FAULTY: After driving blindly for hours, a local resident helped us find our way back to the main road.

IMPROVED: A local resident helped us find our way back to the main road after we had driven blindly for hours.

FAULTY: I only need a few more minutes.

IMPROVED: I need only a few more minutes.

(2) Dangling modifiers may be corrected by supplying the word that the phrase logically describes or by revising the dangling construction to make a complete clause.

FAULTY: Having taken our seats, the players began the game. (Dangling participial phrase)

IMPROVED: After we had taken our seats, the players began the game.

FAULTY: To appreciate good music, vigorous study must be undertaken. (Dangling infinitive phrase)

IMPROVED: To appreciate good music, one must study vigorously.

Part IV

Punctuation

FORMAL WRITING generally employs close punctuation because the sentences are often long and tend to contain more involved construction than informal writing. Punctuation serves two purposes: to make the structure of the sentence readily apparent and to establish minor relationships within the sentence. The marks of punctuation with conventional applications are listed in alphabetical order below.

1. APOSTROPHE

The apostrophe is used to indicate possession, contraction, and plurality of certain words and symbols.

a. To show possession in singular nouns and indefinite pronouns, add an apostrophe and *s.*

Tom's book   anybody's guess

b. To show possession in plural nouns ending in *s,* add only an apostrophe.

the students' grades   the soldiers' allegiance

c. To show possession in plural and collective nouns that end in a letter other than *s,* add an apostrophe and *s.*

the people's choice   the children's wishes

d. To show possession with names of inanimate objects, it is more common to use an "of" phrase, but the apostrophe with *s* is also used. Sound, meaning, rhythm in the sentence, and the emphasis desired determine the choice.

317

the brightness of the sun	the sun's brightness
the power of the state	the state's power
the lesson of today	today's lesson

e. To indicate measurement (of time, amount, degree, etc.) add an apostrophe (and with the singular an *s*).

| one day's work | a week's time |
| two weeks' notice | three dollars' worth |

f. To show joint possession, add an apostrophe and *s* only to the last element.

Tom and Robert's office (Both share one office.)

Note: Individual or alternative possession may be indicated by adding an apostrophe and *s* to each element.

Tom's and Robert's offices (Each has a separate office.)
Hitler's or Mussolini's dictatorship

g. To form the possessive of compounds, add an apostrophe and *s* to the last element of the unit only.

my brother-in-law's request   anyone else's belief

h. To indicate omission of letters in contractions, insert an apostrophe at the point of elision.

Can't, isn't, won't, haven't

Note: It's is a contraction of *it is; its* is the possessive pronoun.

i. To indicate the omission of the first figures from dates, insert an apostrophe at the point of elision.

Class of '09   Spirit of '76

j. To form the plural of a word used as a word, without regard to its meaning, add an apostrophe and *s*.

There are too many *but's* in this sentence.

k. To indicate the plural of symbols and letters, add an apostrophe and *s*.

10's, two 5's, H's, &'s

Note: The possessive forms of personal and relative pronouns do not require the apostrophe: *his, hers, its, ours, theirs, whose.* The possessive forms of indefinite pronouns do require an apostrophe: *one's* book, *anyone's* opinion, *somebody's* mistake.

2. BRACKETS

a. Brackets are commonly used to enclose comments, insertions, corrections, etc., made by a person other than the author of the quoted material.

"He [Abraham Lincoln] became known as a great humanitarian."

b. Brackets are used to enclose parenthetical material within parentheses to avoid the confusion of double parentheses.

The Voyages of the English Nation to America, before the Year 1600, from Hakluyt's Collection of Voyages (1598–1600 [III, 121–128]). Edited by Edmund Goldsmid.

3. COLON

a. The colon is a formal mark indicating introduction or anticipation. It is used ordinarily to precede a series or a statement that has already been introduced by a completed statement.

There is only one course of action: We must work more conscientiously.
The library has ordered the following books: *Don Quixote, The Pilgrim's Progress,* and *Alice in Wonderland.*
There are several schools and colleges in the university system: arts and sciences, business administration, education, music, and engineering.

b. The colon may be used to introduce an extended quotation.

In a long speech President Roosevelt said: "We have nothing to fear but . . ."

c. The colon is conventionally used after a formal salutation in a letter.

Dear Sir:
Dear Mr. Adams:

d. The colon is used to separate chapter and verse numbers in Biblical citations, and volume and page numbers in references containing Arabic numerals.

John 3:16   I Corinthians 13:1–12   *PMLA* 72:19–25

e. The colon is regularly used between numerals designating hours and minutes.

12:15 A.M.

4. COMMA

The comma is the most frequently used mark of punctuation; its misuse often produces confusion and misunderstanding.

   a. A comma is used to separate two independent clauses joined in a compound sentence by coordinating conjunctions (*and, but, for, or, nor*).

He spoke clearly, but his father did not hear him.

Note: In less formal writing the comma is frequently omitted between short clauses joined by *and;* it is rarely omitted before *or* or *but.*

   b. The comma is used to set off nonrestrictive modifiers. (A nonrestrictive modifier is one that is not essential to the meaning of the sentence but that supplies incidental information about a word already identified. A restrictive modifier restricts, limits, or defines; it cannot be left out without changing the meaning of the sentence.)

NONRESTRICTIVE MODIFIER: Grace's father, *who is a grocer*, ran for the city council. (The clause *who is a grocer* can be eliminated without robbing the sentence of meaning.)
   RESTRICTIVE MODIFIER: An employee *who is always late* may be fired. (The clause *who is always late* is necessary to the meaning of the sentence.)

   c. The comma is used to separate elements (words, phrases, clauses) in a series of three or more.

The vegetables included corn, beans, tomatoes, and asparagus.
Tell me what you wore, where you went, and what you did.

Note: Commas should not be used before the first or after the last element in the series unless needed for other reasons.

   d. The comma is used to set off terms of direct address.

Professor Jones, please be seated.

   e. The comma is used after a long introductory phrase or clause. Such "signal" words as *when, although, as, if, while, since, because* usually indicate that a comma will occur before the main clause.

After setting up our tent and getting the camp in order, we took a swim.
Although I am no scholar, I enjoy historical research.

   f. The comma is used both before and after a dependent clause that appears in the body of a sentence.

His car, although he bought it only last year, looked ready for the junk heap.

g. The comma is used to separate elements of a date, address, or other statistical details.

Monday, September 1, 1952, was an important day.
The address is 1172 Louis Plaza, Arlington, Kentucky.
The quotation occurs on page 16, line 6, of the manual.

h. The comma is used to set off direct quotations.

He said, "I am prepared."

i. The comma is used between coordinate adjectives (usually coordination can be tested by substituting *and* for the comma).

COORDINATE: He sat in a poorly made, old-fashioned chair.
NOT COORDINATE: He was a member of the large freshman class.

j. Commas should not be used to separate the subject from the verb or the verb from the complement.

FAULTY: Careful study, may produce good grades.
IMPROVED: Careful study may produce good grades.

k. One of the most common errors in punctuation is the *comma splice,* the separation of two independent clauses by only a comma. Fused or run-together sentences result when two or more independent clauses are included in a single sentence without punctuation to separate them. Independent clauses should be separated by a comma and a coordinating conjunction or by a semicolon.

FAULTY: It was raining, he could not walk to work.
IMPROVED: It was raining, and he could not walk to work.
        or:
IMPROVED: It was raining; he could not walk to work.

(1) Frequently a comma splice can be best corrected by effective subordination.

FAULTY: It was raining, he could not walk to work.
IMPROVED: Because it was raining, he could not walk to work. (The first clause is now a subordinate clause.)
        or:
IMPROVED: Because of the rain he could not walk to work. (The first clause is now a prepositional phrase.)
        or:
IMPROVED: The rain kept him from walking to work. (The two clauses are combined to form one simple sentence.)

(2) If the two independent clauses are not closely related in meaning, each may be made into a sentence.

FAULTY: Swimming is good exercise, I like to swim in the summer.
IMPROVED: Swimming is good exercise. I like to swim in the summer.

l. Conjunctive adverbs (such as *moreover, therefore, thus, hence, then, still*) should not be used to connect independent clauses unless a semicolon or a coordinating conjunction is also used.

FAULTY: The two boys meet each morning, then they spend the day together.
IMPROVED: The two boys meet each morning; then they spend the day together.
        or:
IMPROVED: The two boys meet each morning, and then they spend the day together.

m. When a conjunctive adverb of more than one syllable (*however, moreover, consequently, therefore,* etc.) is used to connect two independent clauses, a semicolon comes before the adverb and a comma after it. When a conjunctive adverb of only one syllable (*yet, then, still,* etc.) is used to connect two independent clauses, a semicolon comes before the adverb but a comma is not used after it.

The flood destroyed many houses; however, the church remained undamaged.
The flood destroyed many houses; yet the church remained undamaged.

n. The comma is used to set off conjunctive adverbs or short transitional phrases.

We do not, moreover, need your advice.

o. The comma is often used before the conjunction *for* to avoid faulty interpretation.

We hurried, for the plane was about to leave.

p. The comma is used after the complimentary closing of a letter.

Very truly yours,   Sincerely,

q. The comma is used after the salutation of a personal letter.

Dear Sandra,

5. DASH

Dashes are frequently overused by inexperienced writers; they are more emphatic than commas and less emphatic than parentheses.

a. The dash is used to emphasize or to indicate hesitation or a sharp break or change in thought.

I must tell you—now what was I going to tell you?
He ought to be satisfied—if he is ever to be satisfied.

b. The dash is used to set off parenthetical material when commas might be confusing or inadequately emphatic.

Three books—a dictionary, a grammar, and a novel—lay on the desk.

c. The dash is used before a statement or word that summarizes what has been said.

The mayor, the aldermen, the lesser officials, and the citizenry—all were gathered in front of the city hall.
Kindness, understanding, and honor—these are needed virtues.

6. ELLIPSIS

The ellipsis (. . .) is a mark used to indicate the omission of a part of quoted material or of words needed to complete a sentence. Three dots are used to indicate the omission; if the ellipsis occurs at the end of a sentence, a period is added.

The war, which had been in progress for ten years, was ended by mutual agreement.
The war . . . was ended by mutual agreement.
The war . . . was ended. . . .

7. EXCLAMATION POINT

The exclamation point is used to indicate an emphatic utterance.

For heaven's sake!   Ready, set, go!

8. HYPHEN

Whenever possible, avoid breaking words from one line to the next. When hyphenation is necessary, (a) the hyphen should be placed at the end of a line, never at the beginning; (b) only words of two or more syllables should be divided, with the division occurring only between syllables. The word list in Appendix 10 shows these syllable breaks.

a. The hyphen is used to divide at syllable breaks a word that must be carried over from one line to another. Words should be so divided that a single letter does not stand alone (*fault-y, a-bove*). Hyphenated words should be divided at the hyphen.

 b. The hyphen is used to join compound numbers from twenty-one through ninety-nine.
 c. The hyphen is used to join words that function as a single adjective before a substantive.

a broken-down nag
up-to-date methods

 d. The hyphen is used to join such prefixes as *self-, ex-, anti-* (when it is followed by a capital letter).

self-help   anti-American   ex-governor

 e. The hyphen is used in compounds containing forms like *-elect* and *-in-law*.

President-elect Wilson   sister-in-law

 f. The hyphen may be employed to eliminate confusion in the meaning of words to which prefixes are added.

re-creation (in contrast to *recreation*)
re-form (in contrast to *reform*)

 g. The hyphen is now frequently used to join a single capital letter to a noun.

H-bomb, I-beam, U-boat

 h. The hyphen is used to join a verb modifier except when the adverb ends in *-ly* or following such common adverbs as *very* and *most*.

a *fast-paced* horse
a *widely known* author

   Be careful to recognize that some words ending in *-ly* are adjectives (*cowardly, friendly*) and that there may be times when the adjective and another word should be joined with a hyphen to form a modifier of a noun.

a *friendly-acting* animal
a *cowardly-looking* bullfighter

 i. Although many modifiers are hyphenated when they come before the word which they modify, they are usually not hyphenated when they are in the predicate position.

He is a *well-known* scientist. The scientist is *well known*.

Sometimes, however, the meaning of the modifier is such that the hyphen should be retained even in the predicate position.

That man is *big-hearted.*
His appearance was *awe-inspiring.*

j. Usage is divided on hyphenating noun phrases used as modifiers (*income tax* laws, *income-tax* laws; *life insurance* policies, *life-insurance* policies). Usually a hyphen is not needed when the significance of the compound modifier is so well established that no ambiguity can result (*public health* program).

k. Sometimes two words mean one thing hyphenated and quite another without the hyphen. Contrast the difference in meaning between:

a light green coat   and   *a light-green coat*

Be careful not to use hyphens in constructions like *a long telephone conversation*, where each word modifies the noun separately.

a new company policy
a large cardboard box

The hyphen should be used in two-word modifiers like the following:

a *four-year* term
a *first-class* cabin

9. ITALICS

Italics are indicated in manuscript and typescript by underlining.

a. Italics are used to identify the titles of books, magazines, newspapers, and the names of ships and aircraft.

I have recently read Hemingway's novel *The Sun Also Rises.*
The *Queen Mary* was one of the world's finest ships.

b. Italics may be used to indicate emphasis.

I am *always* on time.

c. Italics are used to identify foreign words or phrases.

He is *persona non grata* in this country.
She lacks *joie de vivre.*

d. Italics (but frequently quotation marks) are used to identify words used as words (that is, without reference to their meanings).

The word *go* will be the signal.

10. PARENTHESES
Parentheses are used to set off explanatory or supplementary material (definitions, additional information, illustration) not essential to the meaning of the sentence, or to enclose numbers or letters in enumeration.

Many of our Presidents (Washington, Lincoln, Wilson, and Roosevelt, for example) rose above mere party politics.
(1), (a)

11. PERIOD
The period is used to indicate the end of a sentence and to mark abbreviations.

12. QUESTION MARK
a. The question mark is used to mark the end of a question.

Do you really care?

b. A question mark is used to show doubt, uncertainty, or approximation.

Sir Thomas Wyatt, the English poet, lived from 1503? to 1542.

c. Question marks are used in a series of questions.

Several questions remained to be answered: How many were going? How many cars would be needed? What time would we return?

d. The question mark is not needed at the end of a courteous request that is phrased as a question.

Will you please return the completed form as soon as possible.

e. A question mark is not used after an indirect question.

He asked whether he would be allowed to go.

f. When quotation marks and a question mark are used together, the question mark is placed *before* the closing quotation marks if the quoted material is a question and *after* the closing quotation marks if the whole sentence is a question. (If both are questions, only one question mark is used, *before* the closing quotation marks.)

He said, "Are you here?"
Did he say, "I am here"?
Did he say, "Are you here?"

(See also *Quotation Marks*, below.)

13. QUOTATION MARKS

Quotation marks serve to indicate spoken dialogue and to acknowledge specifically reproduced material.

a. Quotation marks are used to enclose direct quotations.

The supervisor said, "Come to my desk, young man."

Note: Single quotation marks (' ') are used to enclose a quotation within a quotation.

The student asked, "Who popularized the statement 'This is the best of all possible worlds'?"

b. Quotation marks should be used to enclose titles of short poems, stories, and articles that are usually printed as a part of a larger work.

She read "Ode on a Grecian Urn" from an anthology.

c. Quotation marks may be used to enclose a word used as a word (rather than for its meaning). (See also item *d* under *Italics*.)

The word "school" brings back pleasant memories.
Do not overuse the word "and" in formal writing.

Note: When other marks of punctuation are used with quotation marks, the following practices should be observed:

(1) A question mark or an exclamation point is placed inside the final quotation mark if it is a part of the quotation, outside if it is a part of the sentence that includes the quoted material.
(2) Periods and commas are always placed inside the closing quotation marks.
(3) Semicolons and colons are always placed outside the closing quotation marks.

14. SEMICOLON

a. A semicolon is used to separate two independent clauses not joined by a coordinating conjunction.

He annoyed me; I regretted having invited him.

b. A semicolon is used to separate two independent clauses which are joined by a coordinating conjunction when either or both of the clauses contain one or more commas.

The office manager, a woman I admired, was pleased with the results of the survey; but she was not happy to lose two of her best workers.

   c. A semicolon is used to separate two independent clauses joined by a conjunctive adverb.

We placed our order with your sales representative two weeks ago; however, we have not yet received delivery.

   d. A semicolon is used to separate two independent clauses when the second is introduced by such expressions as *namely, for example, that is, in fact.*

She is a poor example of what we expect; that is, she just doesn't meet our requirements for a person in such a position.

   e. The semicolon may be used to separate items in a series containing internal punctuation.

Our tour carried us to all parts of the country—from Seattle, Washington, to Miami, Florida; from El Paso, Texas, to Bangor, Maine.
Among our greatest Presidents we include George Washington, the father of our country; Abraham Lincoln, the great emancipator; and Theodore Roosevelt, the hero of San Juan.

Part V

Capitalization

THE USE OF THE CAPITAL LETTER generally is standardized, but some situations call for personal judgment based on the writer's taste and the level of writing in question. The following conventions are generally employed in formal writing.

1. Capitalize the first word of a sentence and of each line of poetry.

2. Capitalize the first word of a direct quotation. No capitalization is required at the resumption of a quotation interrupted by such expressions as *he said, he responded.*

He said, "This is your last opportunity to change your mind."
"This is your last chance," he said, "and I advise you to take it."

3. Capitalize proper nouns and adjectives derived from such nouns.
   a. Specific persons and places, their nicknames and titles.

Winston Churchill, Professor Smith, Major Adams, Grandma Moses, Boston, Bostonians

   b. Some words that were originally proper names but are no longer identified with those names are not capitalized. (Check the dictionary when in doubt.)

manila paper   india ink

   c. Titles used with a name, as on the envelope or inside address of a letter, are capitalized; but they are not capitalized when used alone.

John Jones, Director of Training
ABC Company
. . . the director of training of the ABC Company . . .

   d. Racial, religious, and political designations.

Indian, Negro, Baptist, Republican

e. Names of languages.

French, English, Latin, Aramaic

f. Days of the week, the months, and the holidays.

Monday, July, Christmas, Labor Day, Easter

g. Names of organizations and membership designations.

Phi Beta Kappa, Boy Scouts, Rotary Club, Rotarians, Socialists

h. References to a divine being.

Lord, Jehovah, Christ, Savior, Holy Ghost, God

i. Names of historical events and documents.

Renaissance, Monroe Doctrine, French Revolution, Magna Charta

j. Names of specific institutions, ships, airplanes, academic courses, geographical features, and regions.

First National Bank of Miami, *Queen Mary, Columbine,* History 101 (as distinguished from *my history class*), World War II (as distinguished from *a world war*), the South (as distinguished from *turn south on Main Street*)

k. Words denoting a definite geographical region or locality are proper names and therefore should be capitalized. However, compass points or words designating mere direction or position are not proper names and therefore should not be capitalized.

the Far East
Traveling south, we arrived . . .

4. Capitalize the first word and all important subsequent words (nouns, pronouns, adjectives, adverbs, verbs) in the titles of books, articles, musical compositions, motion pictures, and works of art.

The Sun Also Rises   A Place in the Sun

5. Capitalize names of family relationship when used with the person's name or in place of the name, but not otherwise.

I bought Mother a box of candy.
I bought my mother a box of candy.

6. Capitalize the pronoun *I* and the interjection *O* (but not *oh,* except at the beginning of a sentence).

7. Capitalize the word *the* in the title of a company or organization only when it is actually part of the name.

The Ohio Electric Company
the Girl Scouts of America

8. Once an organization or group has been referred to by name in full in a letter or other piece of writing, a shortened version of the name, using one of the words in the name, should be capitalized.

Acme Life Insurance Company .... the Company
Federal Communications Commission .... the Commission
Federal Bureau of Investigation .... the Bureau

(In expressions such as *our company policy, company* is not capitalized.)

9. Names of the seasons are ordinarily not capitalized.

10. Government organizations are capitalized when they are referred to by specific name.

House of Representatives   Peace Corps
Senate   Internal Revenue Service

11. Capitalize the material that follows a colon if it is in the form of a complete sentence. Do not capitalize it when it is not a sentence (unless the first word following the colon is capitalized for some other reason).

We had two alternatives: We could either go to the movies or stay home and watch television.
We had two alternatives: to go to the movies or to stay home and watch television.
We had two alternatives: Aileen's plan or Marilyn's plan.

Part VI

Spelling

SPELLING RULES represent generalizations that are applicable to large numbers of words; however, it should be noted that exceptions often occur. Proper understanding of prefixes, suffixes, syllabification, pronunciation, and definition will eliminate many spelling errors. Appendix 10 of this book is a guide to the correct spelling and syllabification of the 33,000 most frequently used words in English.

1. When the sound is long *e* (as in believe), *i* is placed before *e* except after *c*.

   achieve, chief, relief, yield, piece, receive, deceive, conceive, ceiling

   EXCEPTIONS: *neither, either, seize, weird, leisure*

   When the *ie* combination is pronounced as separate syllables, the rule does not apply.

   society, deity, science

   When the *ie* combination follows a *c* to produce the *sh* sound, *i* is placed before *e*.

   deficient, efficient, conscience, ancient

2. The final *e* is dropped before a suffix beginning with a vowel, retained before a suffix beginning with a consonant.

hope——hoping		pure——purely	
desire——desirable		use——useful	
allure——alluring		state——statement	

   EXCEPTIONS: *true, truly; acknowledge, acknowledgment* (but also *acknowlędgement*). With some words, both forms are used: *likable, likeable; lovable, loveable.*

332

After *c* or *g* the *e* is retained before a suffix beginning with *a, o,* or *u* to preserve the soft *c* or *g*.

peaceable, courageous, changeable, serviceable

3. Monosyllables and words accented on the last syllable ending in a single consonant preceded by a single vowel *double* the consonant before a suffix beginning with a vowel.

prefer——preferred   hop——hopped
occur——occurrence   forbid——forbidden
red——redder   control——controlled

When the accent shifts to another syllable with the addition of the suffix, the stress in the new word determines the application of the rule.

confer——conference   refer——reference   prefer——preference

4. Words ending in *y* usually change the *y* to *i* before all suffixes except *–ing*.

lonely— loneliness   try——tried   lady——ladies

The *y* is usually retained if preceded by a vowel.

valleys   plays

EXCEPTIONS: *lay——laid   pay——paid   say——said*

5. In the formation of plurals most nouns add *s* or *es*. Some ending in *s* or *z* double these letters.
   a. Nouns ending in *s, z, x, sh, ch* add *es*.

church——churches   box ——boxes
quiz——quizzes   loss——losses

   b. Nouns ending in *y* preceded by a consonant or by *u* sounded as *w* change the *y* to *i* and add *es*.

fly——flies   lily——lilies
sky——skies   soliloquy——soliloquies

   c. Compound nouns usually form the plural by adding *s* or *es* to the principal word.

attorneys-at-law   brothers-in-law
consuls-general   master sergeants
commanders in chief

   d. When the noun ends in *fe*, the *fe* is usually changed to *ve* and *s* is added.

knife——knives   wife——wives

   e. Nouns ending in *o* usually add *s* to form the plural.

radio——radios   cameo——cameos

EXCEPTIONS: echo——echoes   hero——heroes

6. When diacritical marks are a part of the foreign spelling, such marks are retained when the words are used in English sentences (fiancé, auto-da-fé, chargé d'affaires), but many words completely Anglicized no longer require diacritical marks.

cafe, canape, fete, habitue, naive, depot, denouement

7. Only one word ends in *sede* (supersede); three end in *ceed* (exceed, proceed, succeed); all other words with this final sound end in *cede* (precede, secede).

Part VII

Usage

THIS CHAPTER contains a list of words and phrases that are often used incorrectly or for some other reason cause a writer or speaker difficulty. In addition, the word list in Appendix 10 has many cross references to help you decide which is the appropriate word to use when confusion might arise (for example, *adapt, adept, adopt*).

A, AN: *a* is used before words beginning with consonants or with initial vowels that have consonant sounds (*a* book, *a* one-way street, *a* historian, *a* uniform); *an* is used before words beginning with vowels or with a silent *h* (*an* apple, *an* hour). Before an abbreviation that consists of letters sounded separately, use the article that agrees with the *pronunciation* of the first letter of the abbreviation (an S O S, an FM radio, a UN committee).

ACCEPT, EXCEPT: *accept* means *to receive something offered; except*, as a verb, means *to exclude*; as a preposition, *except* means *with the exclusion of.*

ACCIDENTLY: used incorrectly for *accidentally*; the *–ly* suffix should be added to the adjective and not to the noun.

ACQUIRE: often pretentious for *get.*

AFFECT, EFFECT: *affect* is a verb meaning, in one sense, *to pretend* or *to assume* and, in another sense, *to influence* or *to move*; *effect*, as a verb, means *to bring about*; as a noun, *effect* means *result* or *consequence.*

AGGRAVATE: in formal English, *to make worse or more severe*; in colloquial English, *to annoy* or *irritate.*

ALL RIGHT, ALRIGHT: *all right* means *satisfactory, correct,* or *yes*; *alright* is a misspelling.

ALOT: used incorrectly for *a lot.*

ALREADY, ALL READY: frequently confused: *Already* means *before* or *before this time*; *all ready* means *completely ready.*

ALTOGETHER, ALL TOGETHER: frequently confused: *Altogether* means *completely, on the whole*; *all together* means *in a group.*

A.M., P.M., a.m., p.m.: should not be used as synonyms for *morning* and *afternoon*; the abbreviations should be used only with the figures designating the time.

AND ETC.: redundant: *Etc.* is an abbreviation of the Latin *et* (and) *cetera* (others); *and etc.* would mean *and and so forth.*

AND WHICH: correct only when the clause that follows *and which* is coordinate with a previous clause introduced by *which.*

ANECDOTE, ANTIDOTE: an *anecdote* is a short, entertaining account of some event; an *antidote* is a remedy for poison.

ANGRY: *at* a thing and *with* a person.

ANYPLACE, EVERY PLACE, NO PLACE, SOMEPLACE: colloquialisms for *anywhere, everywhere, nowhere, somewhere.*

ANYWAY, ANYWAYS: colloquialisms for *in any case, in any event, anyhow.*

ANYWHERES: a misspelling of *anywhere.*

AS: sometimes used as a weak synonym for *since* or *because*; used incorrectly as a conjunction in place of *for, that,* or *whether* in sentences like these: I didn't buy the hat, *as* [use *for*] red is not my color. I don't know *as* [use *that* or *whether*] I can go. See also LIKE.

AT: redundant in such sentences as "Where are we at?"

AWFUL, AWFULLY: overworked intensives for *very.*

AWHILE: an adverb improperly used as the object of the preposition *for*; the acceptable form is *for a while.* Use *awhile* without the preposition *for*: He has been gone *awhile.*

BAD, BADLY: linking verbs *appear, be, seem, sound, taste, smell, feel, look, become* are followed by an adjective; hence *bad* is the proper form in such sentences as "This coffee tastes *bad.*" Remember, however, that a linking verb can also be used as a transitive verb, and the modifier may be an adverb, as in "He sounded the bell *loudly.*"

BADLY: colloquial for *very much, greatly.*

BECAUSE: a conjunction should not be used as a subject, object, or complement; thus, the construction beginning "The reason is because . . ." is incorrect.

BEFORE: redundant in such usage as "*Before, I used to* get sick if I saw blood."

BEING THAT, BEING AS HOW: misused for *as, since, because.*

BESIDE, BESIDES: only *beside* can be used as a preposition (That is *beside* the point), but both *beside* and *besides* can be used as an adverb (*Besides,* there is no place to go. *Beside,* there is no place to go).

BIANNUAL, BIENNIAL: *biannual* means twice (at any two times) every year (as distinguished from *semiannual,* which means once regularly every six months); *biennial* means once every two years.

CONTINUAL, CONTINUOUS: *continual* means happening again and again; *continuous* means going on without interruption.

CUTE: overused as a vague term of approval.

DEFINITELY: overused as an intensive modifier.

DEPRECIATE IN VALUE: redundant: *depreciate* means *lessen in value.*

DIFFERENT THAN: improperly used for *different from* except when the object is a clause: This room is *different from* that one. This room is *different than* I expected.

DUE TO: controversy among authorities exists about the use of *due to.* Some insist that *due to* should be used only as an adjective (The leak was *due to* a break in the line), never as a preposition (*Due to* a break in the line, there was a leak). *Owing to, because of,* or *as a result of* should be substituted for *due to* in the second example.

EACH AND EVERY: needless repetition; use one word or the other.

EDUCATIONAL: inaccurate and pretentious as a synonym for *instructive* or *informative*.

EFFECT: see AFFECT.

ENTHUSE: colloquially used as a verb; not acceptable in formal writing as a substitute for *be enthusiastic about.*

EQUALLY AS: redundant; use *equally* (Both men were *equally* guilty).

EXCEPT: improperly used for *unless.* See also ACCEPT.

EXCEPT FOR THE FACT THAT: wordy for *except that.*

FARTHER, FURTHER: now infrequently distinguished; in formal usage *farther* indicates distance and *further* indicates degree or extent.

FEWER, LESS: *fewer* refers to number; *less* refers to quantity or degree.

FIRST OFF: use instead *in the first place.*

FLAUNT, FLOUT: *flaunt* means to display defiantly or impudently (The little girl *flaunted* her new dress in front of her friends); *flout* means to show scorn or contempt for (The employee who continually reports late to work *flouts* discipline).

GOES ON TO SAY: wordy for *adds, continues.*

HARDLY: do not use a negative before *hardly* when you mean *with effort or difficulty* (I *can hardly* read his handwriting; not I *can't hardly . . .*).

HAVE: see OF.

IDEA: often vague for *belief, scheme, theory, conjecture, plan.*

INCREDIBLE, INCREDULOUS: *incredible*, said of a situation, means unbelievable (That he went swimming in the ocean in freezing weather is *incredible*); *incredulous*, said of a person, means unbelieving (I was *incredulous* that he would do such a thing).

INDULGE: often used improperly for *take part in.*

INFER, IMPLY: often confused: *Infer* means *to draw a conclusion from facts or premises*; *imply* means *to hint* or *suggest.*

IN MY ESTIMATION, IN MY OPINION: often unnecessary or pretentious for *I think, I believe.*

IN REGARDS TO: a confusion of the British idiom *as regards* with the American idiom *in regard to.*

INSIDE OF: colloquial for *within* when used in a time sense (I will see you *within* an hour).

IS WHEN, IS WHERE: frequently used erroneously in definitions; the verb *to be* requires a noun or an adjective as a complement.

IT BEING, THERE BEING: awkward for introducing a clause that should be introduced by *since* ("There being little time left, we hurried to the airport" should be changed to "Since there was little time left, . . .").

ITS, IT'S: *its* is the possessive form of the pronoun *it*; *it's* is a contraction of *it is.*

KIND OF: colloquial for *somewhat*.

LAY, LIE: often confused: *Lay* is a transitive verb meaning *to put* or *to place something* (*Lay* the book on the table); its principal parts are *lay, laid, laid*. *Lay* is also the past tense of the intransitive verb *lie*, meaning *to recline, to assume a position*, or *to remain in a position* (I will *lie* here until morning); the principal parts of the verb *lie* are *lie, lay, lain*.

LEARN: not to be confused with or used as a synonym for *teach*.

LEAVE, LET: *leave* should not be used as a synonym for *permit* or *let*; use *let me alone* to mean *do not bother me*.

LIABLE, LIKELY: *liable* means *subject to the possibility of*, but in a disagreeable way (He is *liable* to be caught if he continues stealing); *likely* means, simply, *subject to the possibility of* (If the Pirates continue to win games, they are *likely* to win the pennant this year).

LIKE: should not be used as a substitute for *as* or *as if*; *like* is a preposition and governs a noun or pronoun (He looks *like* me); *as* and *as if* introduce clauses (He looks *as if* he wants to speak to me).

–LOOKING: often a redundant suffix to an adjective.

LOT, LOT OF: vague, colloquial terms suggesting *many* or *much*.

MANNER: often unnecessarily used in phrases such as "in a clumsy manner"; a single adverb or a "with" phrase would suffice.

MARVELOUS: overused as a vague word of approval.

METHOD: a vague word for *manner, plan, scheme, way*.

MINUS: colloquial for *lacking* or *without*.

MR., MRS.: in American usage the abbreviations are followed by a period and are now rarely written out except ironically.

MYSELF: often improperly used as a substitute for *I* or *me*.

NEVER-THE-LESS: should be written as one solid word (*nevertheless*).

NOT TOO: colloquial for *not very*.

NOWHERES: incorrect for *nowhere*.

OBTAIN: often pretentious for *get*.

OF: *could of, may of, might of, must of, should of, would of* are often used incorrectly for *could have, may have, might have, must have, should have, would have*.

OFF OF, OFF FROM: a doubling of prepositions that should be reduced to *off* (She stepped *off* the escalator). However, verb-adverb combinations ending with *off* may be followed by *of* or *from* (The helicopter *took off from* the roof).

ONE AND THE SAME: needless repetition.

ONLY: should be placed in the sentence according to the meaning intended; contrast the following meanings: *Only* men work in these rooms. Men *only* work in these rooms. Men work in *only* these rooms.

OUTSIDE OF: *of* is usually superfluous; *outside of* should not be used as a substitute for *aside from, except, besides*.

PERSONS, PEOPLE: *persons* is used when the separateness of the individuals in a group is stressed (Five *persons* applied for the job); *people* is used when a large, indefinite, and anonymous mass is meant (Jackson was a man of the *people*).

PLAN ON: the idiom is *plan to*.

PLENTY: should not be used adverbially as a substitute for *very*, as in *plenty good* or *plenty tired*.

PLUS: colloquial for *in addition to, having something added*.

PRACTICAL, PRACTICABLE: *practical* stresses effectiveness as tested by actual experience; *practicable* stresses capability of being put into effect (Before the era of electronics, television did not seem *practicable*; today, however, it is only one of the *practical* applications of the science).

PRETTY: colloquial for *rather, somewhat, very*. (Faulty: He is a *pretty* good clerk. Improved: He is a *rather* good clerk. He is a *very* good clerk.)

PRINCIPAL, PRINCIPLE: often confused: *Principal* may be used as a modifier meaning *first in importance*, or as a noun naming a person or a thing of chief importance; *principle* is always a noun meaning *fundamental truth* or *motivating force*.

REASON WHY: *why* is redundant. See also BECAUSE.

SEEING THAT, SEEING AS HOW: an appropriate subordinating conjunction (*since, because*, etc.) should be substituted for these phrases.

SO: colloquial as a conjunction meaning *with the result that* between independent clauses. Colloquial as an intensive (He's *so* handsome); substitute *very*.

SOME TIME, SOMETIME, SOMETIMES: *some time* is used when a vague lapse of time is stressed (It has been *some time* since the objects were first sighted); *sometime*, used as an adverb, means at some unspecified time, usually in the future (He will come back *sometime*), and, used as an adjective, it means *having been formerly* (the *sometime* president of the company); *sometimes* means on various occasions, usually unspecified (*Sometimes* I wish I were still working there).

–STYLE, –TYPE: redundant suffixes to adjectives.

SURE: an adjective used colloquially as an adverb, as in "He was *sure* thorough."

THEIR, THERE, THEY'RE: frequently confused in spelling: *Their* is the possessive form of *they*; *there* is an adverb meaning *in that place*; *they're* is a contraction of *they are*.

TOO: overused as a substitute for *very*.

TRY AND: colloquial for *try to*.

WHILE: frequently overused as a substitute for *although, but*, and *whereas*.

WITHOUT: improperly used for *unless* ("I can't go *without* I get some money" should be changed to "I can't go *unless* I get some money").

YOU: often improperly used indefinitely, in the sense of *a person, anyone, someone, one*.

Chapter 15

Finding Facts and Figures

"THE FACTOR to be used in order to convert inches to millimeters? I think it's 25.4, but we'd better look it up."

"You are moving to Cedar Rapids, Iowa? Er . . . just how big a city is it?"

"The number of chemical elements? Well, over a hundred, certainly. The exact number escapes me."

Secretaries, business executives, students—all of us—are often faced with such questions. We "look up" the answers, and that is one form of research.

The subject for research might be the development of the computer, the hybridization of marigolds, the advertising rates for a metropolitan newspaper, the best hotel in Syracuse, New York, or the airline schedule between Nashville and London.

Resourcefulness often brings greater recognition for a researcher than does any other quality. Besides being an important part of general efficiency, it enables one to build up a reputation for knowing virtually everything.

Digging out information is first a matter of knowing *where* to dig. Following are sources of information with which all of us should be acquainted:

REFERENCE WORKS

Dictionaries. Your dictionary is indispensable as a quick reference for spelling, hyphenation, and syllabification of words and names. It is also valuable in finding definitions of words and phrases, synonyms, place names, biographical data, the usage of words, and the derivations of words from foreign languages.

The desk dictionary known as a "college edition" is the size and scope that has proved to be most useful in a business office. One of the best of these is *Webster's New World Dictionary of the American Language*, Second College Edition.

Some offices, families, and most libraries will also have an unabridged dictionary, larger in vocabulary coverage than the "college" editions. The principal dictionary of this scope is *Webster's Third New International Dictionary of the English Language* (Merriam-Webster).

Books of synonyms and antonyms. Synonyms and antonyms are groups of words with like or opposite meanings, respectively. "Sharp" and "keen" are synonyms, while "sharp" and "dull" are antonyms. Here again, your dictionary is a useful tool, but you may want a more concentrated resource. A *thesaurus* ("a treasury" or "storehouse") of synonyms and antonyms is then recommended; the best known is *Roget's International Thesaurus*, while another is *Webster's New World Thesaurus*, edited by Charlton Laird.

Books of quotations. Of the many volumes of quotations, the most useful are John Bartlett's *Familiar Quotations*, Burton Richardson's *The Home Book of Quotations*, H. L. Mencken's *New Dictionary of Quotations on Historical Principles*, and the *Oxford Dictionary of Quotations*.

Books on usage. The most concise advice on usage can be found in *Elements of Style* by William Strunk and E. B. White. The conservative view on usage is best represented by H. W. Fowler's *Dictionary of Modern English Usage*, while the liberal point of view is represented by Bergen and Cornelia Evans' *Dictionary of Contemporary American Usage*. Many writers use as their reference *The Careful Writer* by Theodore M. Bernstein, while others favor Wilson Follett's *Modern American Usage*.

Stylebooks and printing guides. An often-used guide for the preparation of manuscripts for printing is the *Manual of Style* published by the Chicago University Press, while others supplement it with or adhere strictly to the rules given by the United States Government Printing Office *Style Manual.* For newspaper and magazine style, one may use the *New York Times Manual of Style and Usage.* Other guides for writers, editors, and proofreaders are *Words Into Type* by Marjorie E. Skillin, *et al*, and Edmund Arnold's *Ink on Paper*.

Encyclopedias. A general encyclopedia is a good reference source because it summarizes what otherwise might take hours of reading to discover. Good encyclopedias also contain maps and lists of books on the subjects treated (bibliographies). Three of the standard multivolume works that are revised periodically are the *Encyclopaedia Britannica* (24 volumes), generally considered the finest reference set, *Collier's Encyclopedia* (24 volumes), and *Encyclopedia Americana* (30 volumes). A good one-volume work is the *Columbia Encyclopedia*.

Atlases and gazetteers. Even the best atlases, or books of maps and geographical data, find it hard to keep up with the rapidly changing boundaries and the formation of new countries in our world today. It is important for the secretary to check the publishing date of these works before purchase to be sure the information within is up to date. The best general reference atlases are the *Ambassador World Atlas* (Hammond), the

International Atlas (Rand McNally), and the *Times Atlas of the World* (Houghton Mifflin, compiled by the *London Times*).

Gazetteers, which are dictionaries or indexes of geographic names, include the *Columbia Lippincott Gazetteer of the World* and *Webster's New Geographical Dictionary* (Merriam-Webster). An extensive listing of geographical names is also contained in each of the atlases noted above.

Science encyclopedias. Most reference sources having to do with science are highly specialized, but *Van Nostrand's Scientific Encyclopedia* is a one-volume source of general scientific information. For more extensive research, the basic 15-volume *McGraw-Hill Encyclopedia of Science and Technology* is updated each year with a *Yearbook* supplement.

Yearbooks and almanacs. Although an almanac was originally and primarily a book of tables with astronomical information, data on tides, sunrise, etc., a number of commercial yearbooks and almanacs of a much broader scope are on the market. *The World Almanac and Book of Facts* and the *Information Please Almanac* are perhaps the best known. Both books are handy, inexpensive annual guides which give information and statistical data on scores of subjects of current interest, from sports to state histories.

The most comprehensive of the standard hardcover yearbooks is the *Facts on File* yearbook. *Facts on File* is a semimonthly periodical for which the subscriber receives at the beginning of each year a binder and updated maps along with the cumulative index of the preceding year. There are also the *International Yearbook and Statesman's Who's Who*, the *Statesman's Year-Book*, and the *Political Handbook and Atlas of the World*.

Directories. The volumes listing individuals and institutions in specialized fields are far too numerous to mention. The following titles—a few of the countless commercial, professional, biographical, and other types of directories—suggest the usefulness of these books:

Commercial directories (lists of companies)—
Thomas' Register of American Manufacturers
Kelley's Directory of Merchants, Manufacturers, and Shippers of the World
American Book Trade Directory
Directory of American Firms Operating in Foreign Countries
Poor's Register of Corporations, Directors and Executives
A Directory of Foreign Manufacturers in the United States
National Trade and Professional Associations of the United States and Canada and Labor Unions
International Business Bibliography
Professional directories (lists of lawyers, doctors, teachers, and members of other recognized professions) and biographical dictionaries—

American Medical Directory
Who's Who in Insurance
Leaders in Education
The World of Learning
American Men and Women of Science
Who's Who in Finance and Industry
Who's Who Among Black Americans
Who's Who in Computer Education and Research
Who's Who in America
Who's Who (British version)
Who's Who of American Women
International Who's Who
Who's Who in Canada
Who's Who in the World
Who's Who in Electronics
Who's Who in American Law
Dictionary of American Biography
Twentieth Century Authors, a Biographical Dictionary

City directories—These are intended to give the name, address, and occupation of each resident of the cities for which they are issued. Because Americans move frequently and businesses change names, a certain percentage of the information in each of these is out of date by the time it is published. In the cross index at the back of the book, entries are made by street and number so that by looking up a certain address, one can discover who lives there.

Telephone directories—In the larger cities, telephone directories of other large cities are usually on file at the central telephone offices and in libraries that have comprehensive reference departments. They are valuable not only for the telephone numbers listed, but for the street addresses as well. Telephone companies also publish directories in which entries are made under streets and numbers so that, given a certain address, they can tell whether there is a phone at that place. Although these directories are not available to the general public, they are rented to businesses.

If you had to secure a quantity of dry ice so that you could send a dozen brook trout in first-class condition to a friend or favored customer, the problem of finding a dealer in that unusual article might be difficult without the classified telephone directory. The "Yellow Pages" list the names, addresses, and telephone numbers of business houses, merchants, and professionals according to the specialties. Most big-city directories have indexes.

Other directories and lists—

Congressional Directory for the Use of the United States Congress (Gives comprehensive information regarding the legislative, judicial, and executive departments of the government, including biographical sketches of members of Congress and lists of members of diplomatic and consular services.)

Education Directory (Published by the U.S. Office of Education, it lists educational institutions, national and state educational officials and associations, county, town, and district superintendents, college presidents, etc.)

Patterson's American Education (One of several lists of schools, colleges, and other educational institutions in the U.S.)

Handbook of Private Schools

Yearbook of American and Canadian Churches

Yearbook of International Organizations

Directory of Special Libraries and Information Centers

Research Centers Directory

Ulrich's International Periodicals Directory

Ayer Directory of Publications (Geographical listing of newspapers and magazines, with address, name of editor, frequency of publication, advertising rates, and circulation figures.)

Indexes to various subjects. Recourse to the proper indexes will uncover many important newspaper and magazine articles that may answer questions arising in your work. Such indexes list thousands of subjects and the newspapers, periodicals, etc. where articles on those matters can be found. Individual subjects in various fields are indexed in the following reference books:

Cumulative Book Index (Lists all currently published books.)

United States Catalogue (Lists all books printed in the U.S., beginning in 1898; superseded by the *Cumulative Book Index.*)

Books in Print (Lists current books by title, author, and subject.)

Book Review Digest

The New York Times Index (Possibly the most comprehensive index of news, politics, scientific progress, international development, etc.)

Readers' Guide to Periodical Literature

Business Periodical Index

Index to Periodical Articles By and About Negroes

Index Medicus

Bibliography of Medical Reviews (Part of *Index Medicus*, but also published separately.)

Index to Legal Periodicals

Education Index

Applied Science and Technology Index

Social Sciences and Humanities Index
Biological and Agricultural Index

The question will arise as to how many of the reference books listed above should be purchased for home or business use. There can be no general answer. If you find that you must visit or phone the library frequently to get information from certain books, it might be wise to buy them. But a shelf of unused books serves the dubious purpose of decoration. It is more important for you to familiarize yourself with what is available and to know where to look.

If you are asked to get the name of a paper manufacturer in Calcutta, the digest of an article on fire hose that appeared in *The New York Times* sometime in August, 1908, or the rate for sending a telegram to Belgium, just remember that there are many research avenues open and many people and books to help you.

PUBLIC LIBRARIES

The public-library system of the United States has a high standard of helpfulness and courtesy. It is exceptional when a reference librarian is not alert to your requests for information. In any part of the country, the great majority of librarians are not only willing but eager to help.

At libraries you will find books on special subjects, both technical and general, including the reference books listed above. You will also find information on government activities, current events, current biographies, scientific advances, industrial and commercial developments, and many other subjects.

Most libraries have photocopying devices of one kind or another for reproducing printed material. It may be helpful to have a copy of a magazine article or of a page from a reference book to take back to the office. In some library departments permission to reproduce material or assistance from the librarian may be required.

The habit of going to the library for research will uncover many hitherto unsuspected sources of information. In using reference books, always check the date of publication; if a book was published in 1934, the data it contains may have no particular value today.

In making notes for your future use, be sure to cite the year in which the book, magazine, or newspaper was published. In the case of a book, the publisher and the city in which the book was published should be included.

U.S. GOVERNMENT

The United States Government is the largest publisher in the country. The Superintendent of Documents, United States Government Printing Office,

Washington, D.C. 20402, has catalogs of available government publications which cover a wide range of subjects. Some of the bulletins and pamphlets are free, but for some of them and for books a charge is made. Write the Superintendent of Documents to receive a monthly listing or to ask which government department or agency may have the specific information you are seeking. Otherwise, address the department or agency itself:

Department of Agriculture. For information regarding crops in general, statistics relating to agricultural production, the Forest Service, the combating of injurious insects and animal and plant pests and diseases, soil conservation, food and nutrition service, marketing, and farm prices.

Department of Commerce. For information on the national census, standards of weights and measures, government fisheries, lighthouses, and coast and geodotic surveys. Within the Department of Commerce, address specific inquiries to the Patent and Trademark Office and the National Weather Service.

Department of Defense. For information regarding the armed forces, the Joint Chiefs of Staff, training academies, and military installations of the United States.

Department of Education. For information on educational programs and opportunities for learning-disabled, mentally retarded, or handicapped students, the Head Start program and vocational rehabilitation, and on special classes for gifted students.

Department of Energy. For information about energy conservation, research, development, and technology; marketing of federal power; regulation of energy production; and nuclear weapons program.

Department of Health and Human Services. Within the department, address Public Health Services with inquiries about the Center for Disease Control, or for the Food and Drug Administration, the National Health Institutes, and the Alcohol, Drug Abuse, and Mental Health Administration. Address specific inquiries about social security to the Social Security Administration.

Department of Housing and Urban Development. For information on urban renewal and public and federal housing.

Department of the Interior. For information about government lands, national parks, national monuments, national forests, the geological survey, reclamation of wastelands, and control of mines. Within the Department of the Interior, address specific inquiries to the U.S. Fish and Wildlife Service and the Bureau of Indian Affairs.

Department of Justice. For information regarding the administration of the system of federal courts, the supervision of federal prisons, the violation of federal laws, and inquiries to the Immigration and Naturalization Service, the Antitrust Division, and the Federal Bureau of Investigation.

Department of Labor. For information on the welfare of wage earners' conditions in the United States, minimum wage and other wage-and-hour regulations, and statistics relating to labor and workers' compensation.

Department of State. To apply for passports for Americans traveling abroad. For information regarding ambassadors, ministers, consuls, and their staffs; the diplomatic relations of the United States with foreign countries; and activities of American citizens in foreign countries.

Department of Transportation. For information about transportation by air, road, and rail as well as programs involving urban mass transportation. For information about the St. Lawrence Seaway. Address the U.S. Coast Guard in the Transportation Department with inquiries about smuggling, law enforcement in coastal and other navigable waters of the United States, and assistance to vessels in distress.

Department of the Treasury. For information about minting and coinage, prosecution of counterfeiters, U.S. Savings Bonds, the U.S. Secret Service, and the Bureau of Alcohol, Tobacco and Firearms. Within the Department of the Treasury, address inquiries about income taxes to the Internal Revenue Service and about duties on imported products to the U.S. Customs Service.

Independent Government Agencies. In addition to the departments, there are nearly sixty independent agencies, commissions, boards, etc. of the federal government. They are listed with addresses in the *United States Government Manual.* Many of them have offices in major cities and some have offices in many smaller cities. Among these agencies are the United States Postal Service, the National Aeronautics and Space Administration, the Federal Trade Commission, the Environmental Protection Agency, the Equal Employment Opportunity Commission, the Civil Aeronautics Board, the Federal Reserve System, and the Veterans Administration.

PUBLIC ORGANIZATIONS AND FOUNDATIONS

The secretaries of organizations of a more or less public nature are usually willing to give information concerning that organization to the public. Directories of associations, such as *Foundations Directory*, *Encyclopedia of Associations* (3 volumes), and *Association Index: a Source-List of Directories and Other Publications Listing Associations*, list these organizations with addresses and, in many cases, the names of the secretaries. There are also directories of organizations by subject, such as the *Directory of Historical Societies and Agencies in the United States and Canada* and the *Directory of*

Religious Organizations in the United States. Some of the popular almanacs also list such associations.

PRIVATE INSTITUTIONS

Publicity departments. Large corporations, groups supporting causes, and public institutions such as universities, generally maintain departments of public information which handle inquiries regarding their products, services, policies, and plans. It is possible that the information they give out will seek to promote their own interests, but much valuable information may be secured from such sources. Inquiries or requests for photographs should be addressed to the director of public relations of the company or organization. Some businesses have a standard policy of enclosing a self-addressed, stamped envelope when requesting information from a charitable or other nonprofit organization.

Travel agencies. In most cities and towns, full information regarding transportation schedules and rates is on file with airline, bus, railroad, or ship offices or agencies. Travel agencies give efficient service free.

Departments of tourism. Each of the fifty states has a Department of Tourism, and many cities also have such a department, separate from or connected with the Chamber of Commerce. Brochures about historical sites, roadmaps, hotel and motel listings, and calendars of coming events are easily obtainable from these sources.

Newspaper offices. Newspapers maintain libraries or "morgues" which are sometimes open to the public, or at least to businesses in the community, for reference work. Here are filed thousands of news clippings under alphabetically arranged subject headings. Editors of special departments, such as society, finance, business, sports, etc., keep their own files and are often helpful. Furthermore, most photographic departments of newspapers make prints available for a fee. *The New York Times* has developed a computerized research system available to other newspapers, public libraries, business libraries, and so on.

Appendixes

ABBREVIATIONS*

A

A in *chemistry,* argon

A. academy; America; American; angstrom unit; answer; April; artillery

a. about; acre; acres; adjective; alto; ampere; anonymous; answer

AA Alcoholics Anonymous

A.A. Associate in Arts

AAA Agricultural Adjustment Administration

A.A.A. American Automobile Association

A.A.A.L. American Academy of Arts and Letters

A.A.A.S. American Academy of Arts and Sciences; American Association for the Advancement of Science

A.A.E. American Association of Engineers

A.A.U. Amateur Athletic Union

A.A.U.P. American Association of University Professors; Asssociation of American University Presses

A.A.U.W. American Association of University Women

ab. about

A.B. (*Artium Baccalaureus*) Bachelor of Arts

A.B., a.b. able-bodied (seaman)

A.B.A. American Bankers Association; American Bar Association

abb. abbess; abbot

abbr., abbrev. abbreviated; abbreviation

A.B.C., ABC American Broadcasting Company

abr. abridge; abridged; abridgment

abs. absent; absolute; abstract

Ac in *chemistry,* actinium

A/C, a/c in *bookkeeping,* account; account current

A.C. (*Ante Christum*) before Christ

A.C., a.c. in *electricity,* alternating current

acad. academic; academy

acc. acceptance; accompanied; account; accountant

acct. account

A.C.S. American Chemical Society; American College of Surgeons

A/cs pay. accounts payable

A/cs rec. accounts receivable

act. active

actg. acting

ad. adverb; advertisement

A.D. (*Anno Domini*) in the year of the Lord

A.D.A. American Dental Association; Americans for Democratic Action

ADC Aid to Dependent Children

A.D.C. aide-de-camp

ad inf. (*ad infinitum*) endlessly; forever; without limit

ad int. (*ad interim*) in the meantime

adj. adjective; adjourned

Adjt. Adjutant

ad-lib (*ad libitum*) to improvise; extemporize

Adm. Admiral; Admiralty

adm. administrator

adv. adverb; adverbial; advertisement

ad val. (*ad valorem*) according to value

advt. advertisement

AEC Atomic Energy Commission

A.E.F. American Expeditionary Force (or Forces)

AF Air Force

Af., Afr. Africa; African

A.F., a.f. audio frequency

A.F.A.M. Ancient Free and Accepted Masons

AFB Air Force Base

* For two-letter State abbreviations to be used with ZIP Codes see page 143.

351

AFL–CIO American Federation of Labor and Congress of Industrial Organizations

aft. afternoon

Ag (*argentum*) in *chemistry,* silver

A.G. Adjutant General; Attorney General

agcy. agency

agr., agric. agricultural; agriculture; agriculturist

agt. agent

A.I.C. American Institute of Chemists

AID Agency for International Development

A.I.E.E. American Institute of Electrical Engineers

A.I.G.A. American Institute of Graphic Arts

A.I.M.M.E. American Institute of Mining and Metallurgical Engineers

Al in *chemistry,* aluminum

A.L. American League; American Legion

Ala. Alabama

A.L.A. American Library Association

Alas. Alaska

Ald., Aldm. Alderman

alg. algebra

A.L.P. American Labor Party

alt. alternate; alternating; altitude; alto

Alta. Alberta

alum. alumnae; alumni

AM, A.M. amplitude modulation

Am in *chemistry,* americium

Am. America; American

A.M. (*Artium Magister*) Master of Arts

A.M., a.m. (*ante meridiem*) before noon

A.M.A. American Management Association; American Medical Association

Amb. Ambassador

A.M.E. African Methodist Episcopal

Amer. America; American

amp. amperage; ampere; amperes

amt. amount

an. anonymous; (*anno*) in the year

anal. analogous; analogy; analysis

anat. anatomical; anatomist; anatomy

ANC Army Nurse Corps

anc. ancient; anciently

ann. annual; annuity

anon. anonymous

ans. answer

ant. antiquity; antiquities; antonym

anthrop., anthropol. anthropological; anthropology

antiq., antiqu. antiquarian; antiquities; antiquity

AP Associated Press

Ap. Apostle

APO Army Post Office

Apoc. Apocalypse; Apocrypha; Apocryphal

app. appended; appendix; appointed; apprentice

appar. apparatus

approx. approximate; approximately

Apr. April

Apt., apt. apartment

Ar. Arabic; Aramaic

a.r. (*anno regni*) in the year of the reign

A.R.A. American Railway Association; Associate of the Royal Academy

Arab. Arabian; Arabic

ARC American Red Cross

Arch-Bish. Archbishop

arch. archaic; archipelago; architect; architectural; architecture

archaeol. archaeology

Arg. Argentina; Argentine

arith. arithmetic; arithmetical

Ariz. Arizona

Ark. Arkansas

Arm. Armenian

Armor. Armoric

arr. arranged; arrangements; arrival; arrives

art. article; artificial; artillery; artist

arty. artillery

A.R.U. American Railway Union

As in *chemistry,* arsenic

As. Asia; Asian; Asiatic

A.S. Academy of Science; Air Service; Anglo-Saxon

A.S.A. Acoustical Society of America; American Standards Association; American Statistical Association

ASC Army Service Corps

ASCAP American Society of Composers, Authors, and Publishers

A.S.P.C.A. American Society for Prevention of Cruelty to Animals

assn. association

assoc. associate; associated; association
asst. assistant
Assyr. Assyrian
astr., astron. astronomer; astronomical; astronomy
astrol. astrologer; astrological; astrology
At in *chemistry,* astatine
at. atmosphere; atomic
Atl. Atlantic
atm. atmosphere; atmospheric
at. no. atomic number
ATS Army Transport Service
att. attorney
atty. attorney
Atty. Gen. Attorney General
at. wt. atomic weight
Au (*aurum*) in *chemistry,* gold
aud. auditor
Aug. August
Aus. Austria; Austrian
Aust., Austl., Austral. Australia
auth. author; authoress; authorized
Auth. Ver., A.V. Authorized Version (of the Bible)
aux. auxiliary
a/v (*ad valorem*) according to value
av. average; avoirdupois
A.V.C. American Veterans Committee
avdp. avoirdupois
Ave., Av. Avenue
avg. average
avoir. avoirdupois
A.W.O.L., a.w.o.l. absent (or absence) without leave

B

B in *chemistry,* boron
B. in *medicine,* bacillus; Bible; British; Brotherhood
B., b. bachelor; battery; bay; bicuspid; bolivar; book; born; brother
Ba in *chemistry,* barium
B.A. (*Baccalaureus Artium*) Bachelor of Arts
bact. bacteriology
B.Ag., B.Agr. Bachelor of Agriculture
bal. balance; balancing
bank. banking
Bap., Bapt. Baptist
bap., bapt. baptized

bar. barometer; barrel; barrister
B.Ar., B.Arch. Bachelor of Architecture
B.A.S., B.A.Sc. Bachelor of Applied Science
bat., batt. battery
B.B.A. Bachelor of Business Administration
B.B.C. British Broadcasting Corporation
bbl. barrel; barrels
B.C. Bachelor of Chemistry; Bachelor of Commerce; before Christ; British Columbia
BCC, bcc blind carbon copy
B.C.E. Bachelor of Civil Engineering; before the Common Era
bch. bunch
B.Ch.E. Bachelor of Chemical Engineering
B.C.L. Bachelor of Civil Law
bd. board; bond; bound; bundle
B/D bank draft; bills discounted
B.D. Bachelor of Divinity; bills discounted
bd.ft. board feet; board foot
bdl. bundle
bds. boards; bundles
Be in *chemistry,* beryllium
B.E. Bachelor of Education; Bachelor of Engineering
B.E., B/E, b.e. bill of exchange
B.E.E. Bachelor of Electrical Engineering
bef. before
B.E.F. British Expeditionary Force
Bel., Belg. Belgian; Belgium
bet. between
bf, b.f. in *printing,* boldface
B/F in *bookkeeping,* brought forward
B.F. Bachelor of Forestry
B.F.A. Bachelor of Fine Arts
bg. bag
Bi in *chemistry,* bismuth
Bib. Bible; Biblical
Bibl., bibl. Biblical; bibliographical
bibliog. bibliography
bicarb. sodium bicarbonate; baking soda
biog. biographer; biographical; biography
biol. biological; biologist; biology
Bk in *chemistry,* berkelium
bk. bank; block; book

bkg. banking
bkpg. bookkeeping
bkpt. bankrupt
bkt. basket; bracket
B/L, b.l. bill of lading
bl. bale; bales; barrel; barrels; black
B.L. Bachelor of Laws; Bachelor of Letters
bldg. building
B.Lit., B.Litt. (*Baccalaureus Litterarum*) Bachelor of Letters; Bachelor of Literature
blk. black; block; bulk
B.LL. (*Baccalaureus Legum*) Bachelor of Laws
BLS Bureau of Labor Statistics
B.L.S. Bachelor of Library Science
Blvd. Boulevard
B.M. (*Baccalaureus Medicinae*) Bachelor of Medicine; (*Baccalaureus Musicae*) Bachelor of Music
B.M.A. British Medical Association
B.M.E. Bachelor of Mining Engineering
B.Mech.E. Bachelor of Mechanical Engineering
B.Mus. Bachelor of Music
B.N. bank note
B/O in *bookkeeping,* brought over
B.O. Board of Ordnance; body odor
b.o. back order; bad order; box office; branch office; broker's order; buyer's option
Bol. Bolivia; Bolivian
bor. borough
bot. botanical; botanist; botany; bottle
B.O.T. Board of Trade
bp. birthplace; bishop
b.p. below proof; boiling point
b.p., B/P bill of parcels; bills payable
b/p blueprint
B. pay. bills payable
B.P.E. Bachelor of Physical Education
B.Ph., B.Phil. Bachelor of Philosophy
B.Pharm. Bachelor of Pharmacy
bpl. birthplace
B.P.O.E. Benevolent and Protective Order of Elks
Br in *chemistry,* bromine
Br. Britain; British
br. branch; bronze; brother

b.r., B/R, B. Rec., b. rec. bills receivable
Braz. Brazil; Brazilian
B.R.C.S. British Red Cross Society
Brig. Gen. Brigadier General
Brit. Britain; Britannia; British
bro. brother
bros. brothers
B/s, b/s bags; bales
B.S. Bachelor of Science
b.s. balance sheet
b.s., B/S bill of sale
B.S.A. Boy Scouts of America
B.Sc. (*Baccalaureus Scientiae*) Bachelor of Science
B.S.Ed. Bachelor of Science in Education
bskt. basket
Bs/L bills of lading
B.T., B.Th. (*Baccalaureus Theologiae*) Bachelor of Theology
btry battery
B.T.U., Btu, B.t.u. British thermal unit (or units)
bu. bureau; bushel; bushels
bul., bull. bulletin
Bulg. Bulgaria; Bulgarian
Bur. Bureau
bus. business
B.W.I. British West Indies
BX base exchange
bx. box; boxes
Bz. benzene

C

C in *chemistry,* carbon
C, C. Celsius
C. Catholic; Church; Congress; Corps; Court
C., c. capacity; carat; carbon; carton; case; cent or cents; centimeter; century; chapter; circa; college; copyright; cubic; cup; cycle; hundredweight
Ca in *chemistry,* calcium
ca. cathode; centiare; circa
C/A capital account; credit account; current account
C.A. Central America; Coast Artillery; Court of Appeals
C.A., c.a. chartered accountant; chief ac-

countant; commercial agent; consular agent; controller of accounts

CAB Civil Aeronautics Board

C.A.F., c.a.f. cost and freight; cost, assurance, and freight

Cal. California; large calorie (or calories)

cal. calendar; caliber; small calorie (or calories)

Calif. California

Can. Canada; Canadian

Canad. Canadian

cap. capital; capitalize; captain

caps. capitals (capital letters)

Capt. Captain

car. carat; carats

Card. Cardinal

CARE Cooperative for American Relief Everywhere, Inc.

cat. catalog; catechism

Cath. Catholic; (*also* **cath.**) cathedral

cav. cavalier; cavalry

Cb in *chemistry,* columbium

C.B.S., CBS Columbia Broadcasting System

cc. chapters

cc., c.c. carbon copy; cubic centimeter; cubic centimeters

C.C., CC Community College

C.C., c.c. carbon copy; cashier's check; chief clerk; city council; county clerk; county commissioner; county council; county court

C.C.A. Chief Clerk of the Admiralty; Circuit Court of Appeals

CCC Commodity Credit Corporation

ccm. centimeters

C.C.R. Commission on Civil Rights

Cd in *chemistry,* cadmium

C/D, CD certificate of deposit

c.d. cash discount

Ce in *chemistry,* cerium

C.E. Chemical Engineer; Chief Engineer; Church of England; Civil Engineer

C.E.F. Canadian Expeditionary Force (or Forces)

cen. central; century

cent. centimeter; central; century

CEO chief executive officer

cert., certif. certificate

Cf in *chemistry,* californium

cf. (*confer*) compare

c/f in *bookkeeping,* carried forward

C.F., c.f. cost and freight

C.F.I., c.f.i. cost, freight, and insurance

cg. centigram; centigrams

C.G. Coast Guard

ch. chapter; chief; child; church

c.h. courthouse; customhouse

chap. chaplain; chapter

Ch.E., Chem. E. Chemical Engineer

chem. chemical; chemist; chemistry

chg. charge

chgd. charged

chgs. charges

Chin. China; Chinese

chm., chmn. chairman

Chr. Christ; Christian

Chron. Chronicles

chron., chronol. chronological; chronology

chs. chapters

CIA Central Intelligence Agency

C.I.C. Commander in Chief

C.I.F., c.i.f. cost, insurance, and freight

cit. citation; cited; citizen

civ. civil; civilian

ck. cask; check

Cl in *chemistry,* chlorine

cl. centiliter; centiliters; claim; class; clause; clearance; clerk; cloth

c.l. carload; carload lots; civil law

cld. called; cleared

clk. clerk; clock

Cm in *chemistry,* curium

cm. centimeter; centimeters

cml. commercial

C/N circular note; credit note

Co in *chemistry,* cobalt

C/O cash order

c/o, c.o. care of; carried over

Co., co. company; county

C.O. Commanding Officer; Conscientious Objector

C.O.D., c.o.d. cash on delivery; collect on delivery

C. of C. Chamber of Commerce

C. of S. Chief of Staff

Col. Colombia; Colombian; Colonel; Colorado; Colossians

col. collected; collector; college; colonial; colony; color; colored; column

coll. colleague; collect; collection; collector; college; colloquial

collab. collaboration; collaborator

collat. collateral; collaterally

colloq. colloquial; colloquialism; colloquially

Colo. Colorado

Com. Commander; Commission; Commissioner; Committee; Commodore; Communist

com. comedy; comma; commerce; commercial; common; commonly; communication

comb. combination

comdg. commanding

Comdr. Commander

Comdt. Commandant

comm. commander; commentary; commerce; commission; committee; communication

comp. companion; comparative; compare; compiled; compiler; composer; composition; compound

Comr. Commissioner

con. concerto; conclusion; consolidated; consul; continued

conc. concentrate; concentrated; concentration

Confed. Confederate

Cong. Congregational; Congregationalist; Congress; Congressional

conj. conjugation; conjunction; conjunctive

Conn. Connecticut

cons. consolidated; constitutional; construction; consulting

cons., Cons. constable; constitution

Cont. Continental

cont. containing; contents; continent; continue; continued; contra; contract

contd. continued

contemp. contemporary

contr. contract; contracted; contraction; contralto; contrary; contrasted; control; controller

contrib. contributor

co-op., coop. cooperative

cop. copper; copyrighted

Cor. Corinthians; Coroner

cor. corner; coroner; correct; corrected; correction; correspondence; correspondent; corresponding

Corp. Corporal

corp., corpn. corporation

corr. corrected; correction; correspondence; corresponding; corrugated; corruption

cos cosine

Cos., cos. companies; counties

C.O.S., c.o.s. cash on shipment

cosec cosecant

cot cotangent

cp. compare

C.P. Chief Patriarch; Common Pleas; Common Prayer; Communist Party

c.p. candlepower; chemically pure

C.P.A., c.p.a. Certified Public Accountant

CPI consumer price index

Cpl. Corporal

C.P.O. Chief Petty Officer

CPS Certified Professional Secretary

Cr in *chemistry,* chromium

cr. credit; creditor; creek; crown

C.R. Costa Rica

crim. criminal

crit. critical; criticism; criticized

cryst. crystalline; crystallography

Cs in *chemistry,* cesium

C.S. Christian Science; Christian Scientist

C.S., c.s. capital stock; civil service

CSC Civil Service Commission

csc cosecant

csk. cask

C.S.T. Central Standard Time

Ct. Connecticut; Court

ct. cent; certificate; county; court

ctf. certificate

ctg. cartage

ctn carton; cotangent

ctr. center

cts. cents

Cu (*cuprum*) in *chemistry,* copper

cu. cubic

cu. cm. cubic centimeter; cubic centimeters

cur. currency; current

CWA Civil Works Administration
C.W.O., c.w.o. cash with order
cwt. hundredweight
cyl. cylinder

D

D. December; Democrat; Democratic; Duchess; Duke; Dutch
d. date; daughter; day; days; dead; degree; delete; density; deputy; deserter; diameter; died; dime; director; dividend; dollar; dorsal; dose
da. daughter; day; days
D.A. District Attorney
Dan. Danish
D.A.R. Daughters of the American Revolution
D.A.V. Disabled American Veterans
db decibel
d.b. daybook
dba, d.b.a. doing business as
dbl. double
D.C. in *music*, (*da capo*) from the beginning; Dental Corps; District of Columbia; Doctor of Chiropractic
D.C., d.c. in *electricity*, direct current
D.C.L. Doctor of Civil Law
D.C.S. Doctor of Christian Science; Doctor of Commercial Science
dd., d/d delivered
D.D. (*Divinitatis Doctor*) Doctor of Divinity
D.D., D/D demand draft
D.D.S. Doctor of Dental Science; Doctor of Dental Surgery
DDT dichlorodiphenyltrichloroethane
D.E., D.Eng. Doctor of Engineering
deb. debenture
Dec. December
dec. deceased; decimeter; declaration; declension; declination; decrease
decl. declension
def. defendant; defense; deferred; defined; definite; definition
deg. degree; degrees
Del. Delaware
del. delegate; delete
Dem. Democrat; Democratic
Den. Denmark

dent. dental; dentist; dentistry
dep. department; departs; departure; deponent; deposed; deposit; deputy
dept. department; deponent; deputy
der., deriv. derivation; derivative; derived
Deut. Deuteronomy
D.F.C. Distinguished Flying Cross
di., dia. diameter
diag. diagonal; diagram
dial. dialect; dialectal; dialectic; dialectical
diam. diameter
dict. dictated (by); dictator; dictionary
dif., diff. difference
dig. digest
dil. dilute
dim. dimension; (*also* dimin.) diminuendo; diminutive
dir. director
dis. distance; distant; distribute
disc. discography; discount; discovered
dist. distance; distant; distinguish; distributor; district
div. divide; dividend; division; divisor; divorced
D.J., DJ disc jockey
D/L demand loan
D.Lit., D.Litt. (*Doctor Litterarum*) Doctor of Letters; Doctor of Literature
D.L.S. Doctor of Library Science
DM, Dm deutsche mark
D.Mus. Doctor of Music
DMZ demilitarized zone
D.N.B. Dictionary of National Biography
D/O, d.o. delivery order
do. ditto
D.O. District Office; Doctor of Osteopathy
DOA, D.O.A. dead on arrival
DOE Department of Energy
dol. dollar
dols. dollars
dom. domestic; dominion
Dom. Rep. Dominican Republic
DOT Department of Transportation
doz. dozen; dozens
D.P. displaced person
dpt. department; deponent

D.P.W. Department of Public Works
Dr. Doctor
dr. debit; debtor; dram; drams; drawer
d.r. dead reckoning; deposit receipt
D.S., D.Sc. Doctor of Science
D.S.C. Distinguished Service Cross
D.S.M. Distinguished Service Medal
D.S.O. Distinguished Service Order
D.S.T. Daylight Saving Time
d.t. delirium tremens; double time
D.Th., D. Theol. Doctor of Theology
Du. Dutch
dup. duplicate
D.V.M. Doctor of Veterinary Medicine
D.V.S. Doctor of Veterinary Surgery
DWI, D.W.I. driving while intoxicated
Dy in *chemistry,* dysprosium
dz. dozen; dozens

E

E in *chemistry,* einsteinium
E, E., e, e. east; eastern
E. Earl; Easter; English
E., e. earth; engineer; engineering
ea. each
E. A. in *psychology,* educational age
E. & O.E., e. & o.e. errors and omissions
  excepted
EC European Community
E.C. Engineering Corps; Established
  Church
eccl., eccles. ecclesiastical
Eccles. Eccl. Ecclesiastes
Ecclus. Ecclesiasticus
ecol. ecological; ecology
econ. economic; economics; economy
ed. edited; edition; editor; education
Ed.B. Bachelor of Education
Ed.D. Doctor of Education
Ed.M. Master of Education
EDP electronic data processing
educ. education; educational
E.E. Electrical Engineering
e.e. errors excepted
E.E.C. European Economic Community
Eg. Egypt; Egyptian
e.g. (*exempli gratia*) for example
EHF extremely high frequency
e.h.p. effective horsepower

elec., elect. electric; electrical; electricity
elem. element; elementary; elements
elev. elevation
Eliz. Elizabethan
E.M.F., e.m.f., EMF, emf electromotive
  force
Emp. Emperor; Empire; Empress
enc. enclosed; enclosure
ency., encyc., encycl. encyclopedia
Eng. England; English
eng. engine; engineer; engineering; en-
  graved; engraver; engraving
enl. enlarge; enlarged; enlisted
Ens. Ensign
EPA Environmental Protection Agency
Eph., Ephes. Ephesians
Epis. Episcopal; Episcopalian
eq. equal; equalizer; equation; equator;
  equivalent
equiv. equivalent
Er in *chemistry,* erbium
ERA Equal Rights Amendment
Esk. Eskimo
ESP, E.S.P. extrasensory perception
esp. especially
Esq., Esqr. Esquire
est. established; estimated
E.S.T. Eastern Standard Time
Esth. Esther
E.T.A. Estimated Time of Arrival
et al. (*et alibi*) and elsewhere; (*et alii*) and
  others
etc., &c et cetera
E.T.D. Estimated Time of Departure
Eth. Ethiopia; Ethiopian
et. seq. (*et sequens*) and the following
ETV educational television
Eu in *chemistry,* europium
Eur. Europe; European
Ex., Exod. Exodus
ex. examined; example; except; excepted;
  exchange; executive; export; express;
  extra; extract
exam. examination
Exc. Excellency
exc. excellent; except; excepted
exch. exchange
exec. executive; executor
exp. expenses; experiment; export; exported; express

ext. extension; exterior; external; extra
Ez., Ezr. Ezra
Ezek. Ezekiel

F

F in *chemistry,* fluorine
F. Fahrenheit; February; Fellow; France; French; Friday
F., f. farad; farthing; father; fathom; feet; feminine; fine; fluid; folio; folios; following; form; in *music,* forte; franc; francs
f.a. fire alarm; freight agent
FAA Federal Aviation Administration
F.A.A.S. Fellow of the American Academy of Arts and Sciences; Fellow of the American Association for the Advancement of Science
fac. facsimile
Fah., Fahr. Fahrenheit
F.A.M. Free and Accepted Masons
FAO Food and Agriculture Organization (UN)
f.a.s. free alongside ship
f.b. freight bill
FBI, F.B.I. Federal Bureau of Investigation; Federation of British Industries
f.c. in *printing,* follow copy
FCA Farm Credit Administration
FCC Federal Communications Commission
F.D. Fire Department
FDA Food and Drug Administration
FDIC Federal Deposit Insurance Corporation
Fe (*ferrum*) in *chemistry,* iron
Feb. February
Fed. Federal; Federation
fem. feminine
FEP Fair Employment Practices
feud. feudal; feudalism
ff. folios; following (pages); in *music,* fortissimo
F.F.A. Future Farmers of America
FFMC Federal Farm Mortgage Corporation
F.F.V. First Families of Virginia
FHA Federal Housing Administration

FHLBB Federal Home Loan Bank Board
FICA Federal Insurance Contributions Act
fict. fiction
fig. figurative; figuratively; figure; figures
Fin. Finland; Finnish
fin. finance; financial
Finn. Finnish
fl. floor; flourished; flower; fluid
Fla. Florida
fl. oz. fluid ounce; fluid ounces
FM frequency modulation
Fm in *chemistry,* fermium
fm. fathom; from
F.M. Field Marshal; Foreign Minister
F.O. Foreign Office
F.O.B., f.o.b. free on board
F.O.E. Fraternal Order of Eagles
fol. folio; following
for. foreign; forestry
F.O.R., f.o.r. free on rail
fp., F.P., f.p. foot-pound; foot-pounds
F.P., f.p. in *insurance,* fire policy, floating policy; fully paid
f.p., fp, fp. freezing point
FPC Federal Power Commission
FPO Fleet Post Office
Fr in *chemistry,* francium
Fr. Father; France; *Frau;* French; Friar; Friday
fr. fragment; franc; francs; frequent; from
FRB Federal Reserve Bank; Federal Reserve Board
freq. frequent; frequently
Fri. Friday
frt. freight
FSA Farm Security Administration; Federal Security Administration
FSCC Federal Surplus Commodities Corporation
FSLIC Federal Savings and Loan Insurance Corporation
FSR, F.S.R. Field Service Representative
Ft. Fort
ft. feet; foot
FTC Federal Trade Commission
fth., fthm. fathom

ft-lb foot-pound
fut. future
fwd. forward
F.Y.I. for your information

G

G. German; Germany; specific gravity
G., g. gauge; gold; grain; gram; grams;
   guilder; guilders; guinea; guineas; gulf
g. gender
Ga in *chemistry,* gallium
Ga. Gallic; Georgia
G.A. General Agent; General Assembly
G.A., G/A, g.a. in *insurance,* general
   average
gal. gallon; gallons
G.A.R. Grand Army of the Republic
gaz. gazette; gazetteer
G.B. Great Britain
g-cal. gram calorie; gram calories
G.C.D., g.c.d. greatest common divisor
G.C.F., g.c.f. greatest common factor
G.C.M., g.c.m. greatest common measure
Gd in *chemistry,* gadolinium
gds. goods
Ge in *chemistry,* germanium
Gen. General; Genesis; Geneva
gen. gender; genera; general; generally;
   generator; generic; genitive; genus
geneal. genealogy
genl. general
Gent., gent. gentleman; gentlemen
geog. geographer; geographical; geography
geol. geologic; geological; geologist; geol-
   ogy
geom. geometric; geometrical; geometri-
   cian; geometry
Ger. German; Germany
ger. gerund
g.gr. great gross
GHQ General Headquarters
gi. gill; gills
Gk. Greek
gl. glass; gloss
gloss. glossary
gm. gram; grams
G.M. general manager; Grand Master

Gmc. Germanic
G.M.T. Greenwich mean time
GNP gross national product
G.O., g.o. general office; general order
G.O.P. Grand Old Party (Republican
   Party)
Goth., goth. Gothic
Gov., gov. government; governor
Gov. Gen. Governor General
govt., Govt. government
G.P., g.p. general practitioner
G.P.O. General Post Office; (*also* **GPO**),
   Government Printing Office
Gr. Grecian; Greece; Greek
gr. grade; grain or grains; gram or grams;
   grammar; great; gross; group
grad. graduate; graduated
gram. grammar; grammarian; grammati-
   cal
Gr. Brit., Gr. Br. Great Britain
gro. gross
GSA, G.S.A. General Services Adminis-
   tration; Girl Scouts of America
GSC General Staff Corps
gt. gilt; great
Gt. Brit., Gt. Br. Great Britain
guar. guaranteed
Guat. Guatemala; Guatemalan

H

H in *physics,* henry; in *chemistry,* hydro-
   gen
H., h. harbor; hard; hardness; height;
   high; hour; hours; hundred; husband
ha. hectare; hectares
Hab. Habakkuk
Hag. Haggai
hal. halogen
Hb hemoglobin
H.B.M. His (or Her) Britannic Majesty
H.C. House of Commons
H.C.F., h.c.f. highest common factor
h.c.l., h.c. of l. high cost of living
hd. head
hdqrs. headquarters
HE, H.E. high explosive
He in *chemistry,* helium
H.E. His Eminence; His (or Her) Excel-
   lency

Heb. Hebrew; Hebrews
HEW (Department of) Health, Education, and Welfare
Hf in *chemistry,* hafnium
hf. half
H.F. high frequency
Hg (*hydrargyrum*) in *chemistry,* mercury
H.G. His (or Her) Grace; Home Guard
hgt. height
H.H. His (or Her) Highness; His Holiness
H.I.H. His (or Her) Imperial Highness
hist. historian; historical; history
H.L. House of Lords
H.M.S. His (or Her) Majesty's Service, Ship, or Steamer
Ho in *chemistry,* holmium
Hon., hon. honorable; honorary
Hond. Honduran; Honduras
hor. horizon; horizontal
Hos. Hosea
hosp. hospital
H.P., HP, h.p., hp high pressure; horsepower
H.Q., Hq. headquarters
hr. hour; hours
H.R. Home Rule; House of Representatives
H.R.H. His (or Her) Royal Highness
hrs. hours
H.S., h.s. high school
ht. heat; height; heights
hts. heights
HUD (Department of) Housing and Urban Development
hund. hundred; hundreds
Hung. Hungarian; Hungary
Hwy., hwy. highway
hyd. hydraulics; hydrostatics
hyp. hypotenuse; hypothesis; hypothetical
Hz, hz hertz

I

I in *chemistry,* iodine
I. Independent
I., i. island; islands; isle; isles
i. incisor; interest; intransitive
Ia. Iowa

I.A.M. International Association of Machinists
ib., ibid. (*ibidem*) in the same place
ICBM intercontinental ballistic missile
ICC Interstate Commerce Commission
Ice., Icel. Iceland; Icelandic
id. (*idem*) the same
ID, I.D. identification; Intelligence Department
Ida. Idaho
IDP integrated data processing
i.e. (*id est*) that is
I.G. Inspector General
ign. ignition; (*ignotus*) unknown
ILA International Longshoremen's Association
I.L.G.W.U., ILGWU International Ladies' Garment Workers Union
Ill. Illinois
ill., illus., illust. illustrated; illustration
ILO International Labor Organization
imp. imperative; imperfect; imperial; impersonal; import; imported; importer; imprimatur; imprint
imper., impv. imperative
imperf., impf. imperfect
In in *chemistry,* indium
in. inch or inches
inc. inclosure; included; including; inclusive; income; incorporated; increase
incl. inclosure; including; inclusive
incog. incognito
incorp., incor. incorporated
Ind. India; Indian; Indiana; Indies
ind. independent; index; indicative; industrial
indef. indefinite
indic. indicating; indicative; indicator
indiv. individual
Inf., inf. infantry
inf. infinitive; information; (*infra*) below
infin. infinitive
init. initial
ins. inches; insulated; insurance
insp. inspected; inspector
Inst. Institute; Institution
inst. instant (the present month); instrumental; installment
instr. instructor; instrument; instrumental

int. interest; interim; interior; interjection; internal; international; intransitive
inter. interrogation
interj. interjection
interrog. interrogation; interrogative
intl. international
intr. intransitive
in trans. (*in transitu*) on the way
Int. Rev. Internal Revenue
introd., intro. introduction; introductory
inv. invented; inventor; invoice
invt. inventory
I.O.F. Independent Order of Foresters
Ion. Ionic
I.O.O.F. Independent Order of Odd Fellows
IOU, I.O.U. I owe you
IPA International Phonetic Alphabet; International Phonetic Association
IQ, I.Q. intelligence quotient
Ir in *chemistry,* iridium
Ir. Ireland; Irish
I.R.A., IRA Irish Republican Army
Iran. Iranian
Ire. Ireland
IRS Internal Revenue Service
Is., Isa. Isaiah
is., isl. island; isle
i/t/a, I.T.A. Initial Teaching Alphabet
Ital., It. Italian; Italic; Italy
ital., it. italic; italics
i.v. intravenous; intravenously
I.W.W. Industrial Workers of the World

J

J in *physics,* joule
J. Judge; Justice
Ja. January
J/A, j/a joint account
J.A. Joint Agent; Judge Advocate
J.A.G. Judge Advocate General
Jam. Jamaica
Jan. January
Jap. Japan
Japan. Japanese
Jas. James
J.C. Jesus Christ

jct. junction
JD juvenile delinquency; juvenile delinquent
J.D. (*Jurum Doctor*) Doctor of Laws
Jer. Jeremiah
Jew. Jewish
j.g., jg junior grade
Josh. Joshua
jour. journal; journeyman
J.P. Justice of the Peace
Jpn. Japan; Japanese
Jr., jr. junior
Jud. Judges; Judith
Judg. Judges
Jul. July
jus. justice
J.W.V. Jewish War Veterans

K

K (*kalium*) in *chemistry,* potassium
K., k. in *electricity,* capacity; karat; kilo; kilogram; king; knight; kopeck or kopecks; krona; krone; kroner; kronor; in *nautical usage,* knot
Kan., Kans. Kansas
kc. kilocycle; kilocycles
K.C. King's Counsel; Knight (or Knights) of Columbus
K.D. in *commerce,* knocked down (not assembled)
Ken. Kentucky
kg. keg; kegs; kilogram; kilograms
kHz kilohertz
Ki. Kings (books of the Bible)
kilo. kilogram; kilometer
kilom. kilometer
K.K.K., KKK Ku Klux Klan
kl. kiloliter; kiloliters
km. kilometer or kilometers; kingdom
K.O., KO, k.o. in *boxing,* knockout
K. of C. Knight (or Knights) of Columbus
K. of P. Knight (or Knights) of Pythias
KP, K.P. kitchen police
Kr in *chemistry,* krypton
kr. krona; krone; kroner; kronor
kt. carat
K.T. Knight (or Knights) Templar
kw. kilowatt

kwh., K.W.H., kw-h, kw-hr kilowatt-
hour
Ky. Kentucky

L

L. Latin
L., l. lake; land; latitude; law; leaf; league;
left; length; (*libra*) pound; (*librae*)
pounds; line; link; lira; lire; liter; liters;
low
La in *chemistry,* lanthanum
La. Louisiana
L.A. Legislative Assembly; Los Angeles
Lab. Laborite; Labrador
lab. laboratory
Lam. Lamentations
lang. language
Lat. Latin
lat. latitude
lb. (*libra*) pound; (*librae*) pounds
L.B. (*Litterarum Baccalaureus*) Bachelor
of Letters
lbs. pounds
L/C, l/c letter of credit
l.c. in *printing,* lower case
L.C.D., l.c.d. lowest (or least) common
denominator
L.C.F., l.c.f. lowest (or least) common
factor
L.C.L., l.c.l. in *commerce,* less than carload lot
L.C.M., l.c.m. lowest (or least) common
multiple
L.D.S. Latter-day Saints
lect. lecture; lecturer
leg. legal; legislative; legislature
legis. legislation; legislature
Lev., Levit. Leviticus
lex. lexicon
L.F. low frequency
lg. large
lgth. length
lg. tn. long ton
L.H.D. (*Litterarum Humaniorum Doctor*) Doctor of the Humanities
Li in *chemistry,* lithium
Lib. Liberal; Liberia
lib. librarian; library
Lieut. Lieutenant

lin. lineal; linear
liq. liquid
lit. liter or liters; literal; literally; liter-
ary; literature
Litt.B. (*Litterarum Baccalaureus*) Bache-
lor of Letters; Bachelor of Literature
Litt.D. (*Litterarum Doctor*) Doctor of
Letters; Doctor of Literature
ll. lines
LL.B. (*Legum Baccalaureus*) Bachelor of
Laws
LL.D. (*Legum Doctor*) Doctor of Laws
loc. cit. (*loco citato*) in the place cited
log logarithm
log. logic
long. longitude
L.O.O.M. Loyal Order of Moose
LPN, L.P.N. Licensed Practical Nurse
Lr in *chemistry,* lawrencium
L.R. Lloyd's Register
L.S. (*locus sigilli*) place of the seal
Lt. Lieutenant
l.t. long ton
Lt. Col. Lieutenant Colonel
Lt. Comdr., Lt.-Comm. Lieutenant
Commander
Ltd., ltd. limited
Lt. Gen. Lieutenant General
Lt. Gov. Lieutenant Governor
Lu in *chemistry,* lutetium
Luth. Lutheran
Lux. Luxembourg
lv. leave; leaves

M

M. Manitoba; Master; Medieval; Monday; Monsieur
M., m. majesty; male; manual; married;
masculine; medicine; medium; meridian; (*meridies*) noon; meter; meters;
mile; miles; mill; mills; minim; minute;
minutes; month; moon; morning
M.A. (*Magister Artium*) Master of Arts
Mac., Macc. Maccabees
mach. machine; machinery; machinist
mag. magazine; magnetism; magnitude
Maj. Major
Maj. Gen. Major General
Mal. Malachi; Malay; Malaysia
Man., Manit. Manitoba

manuf., manufac. manufacture; manufacturer; manufacturing
Mar. March
mar. marine; maritime; married
marg. margin; marginal
masc. masculine
Mass. Massachusetts
math. mathematical; mathematician; mathematics
Matt. Matthew
max. maximum
M.B.A. Master of Business Administration
M.C. Master of Ceremonies; Medical Corps; Member of Congress
Md. Maryland
M.D. (*Medicinae Doctor*) Doctor of Medicine; Medical Department
Mdlle. Mademoiselle
Mdm. Madam
Mdme. Madame
M.D.S. Master of Dental Surgery
mdse. merchandise
Me. Maine
M.E. Mechanical Engineer; Methodist Episcopal; Middle English; Military Engineer; Mining Engineer
meas. measure
mech. mechanical; mechanics; mechanism
med. median; medical; medicine; medieval; medium
M.Ed. Master of Education
mem. member; memoir; memoranda; memorandum; memorial
Messrs. Messieurs
met. metaphor; metaphysics; metropolitan
metal. metallurgical; metallurgy
Meth. Methodist
Mex. Mexican; Mexico
M.F.A. Master of Fine Arts
mfd. manufactured
mfg. manufacturing
mfr. manufacture; manufacturer
Mg in *chemistry,* magnesium
mg. milligram; milligrams
Mgr. Manager; Monseigneur; Monsignor
M.H.R. Member of the House of Representatives

MHz, Mhz megahertz
mi. mile; miles; mill; mills; minor; minute
M.I. Military Intelligence; Mounted Infantry
Mic. Micah
Mich. Michigan
mid. middle; midshipman
mil. military; militia
min. mineralogy; minimum; mining; minister; minor; minute; minutes
Minn. Minnesota
misc. miscellaneous; miscellany
Miss. Mississippi
mkt. market
ml. mail; milliliter; milliliters
Mlle. Mademoiselle
Mlles. Mademoiselles
M.L.S. Master of Library Science
MM. Messieurs
mm. (*millia*) thousands; millimeter; millimeters
Mme. Madame
Mmes. Mesdames
Mn in *chemistry,* manganese
Mo in *chemistry,* molybdenum
Mo. Missouri; Monday
mo. month
M.O., MO (*modus operandi*) mode of operation; money order
mod. moderate; modern
Mon. Monastery; Monday; Monsignor
mon. monetary
Mong. Mongolia
Mont. Montana
Mor. Morocco
mos. months
MP, M.P. Military Police
M.P. Member of Parliament; Metropolitan Police; Mounted Police
M.P., m.p. melting point
mpg, m.p.g. miles per gallon
mph, m.p.h. miles per hour
Mr. Mister
Mrs. Mistress
MS multiple sclerosis
MS., ms. manuscript
Ms. courtesy title for any woman, married or unmarried
M.S., M.Sc. Master of Science
Msgr. Monsignor
M.Sgt., M/Sgt Master Sergeant

MSS, mss. manuscripts
M.S.T. Mountain Standard Time
MSW, M.S.W. Master of Social Work
Mt., mt. mount; mountain
mtg. meeting; mortgage
mtn. mountain
Mt. Rev. Most Reverend
mts. mountains
mun. municipal
mus. museum; music; musical; musician
Mv in *chemistry,* mendelevium
myth., mythol. mythological; mythology

N

N in *chemistry,* nitrogen
N, N., n, n. north; northern
N. National; Nationalist; Norse; November
N., n. nail; name; navy; neuter; new; nominative; noon; noun
n. nephew; net; note; number
Na (*natrium*) in *chemistry,* sodium
n/a in *banking,* no account
N.A. National Academy; Netherlands Antilles; North America
N.A.A.C.P., NAACP National Association for the Advancement of Colored People
Nah. Nahum
N.A.M., NAM National Association of Manufacturers
N.A.S. National Academy of Sciences
NASA National Aeronautics and Space Administration
nat. national; native; natural; naturalist
natl. national
NATO North Atlantic Treaty Organization
naut. nautical
Nb in *chemistry,* niobium
N.B. New Brunswick
N.B., n.b. (*nota bene*) note well
N.B.C., NBC National Broadcasting Company
NC, N.C. no charge
N.C. North Carolina
NCO noncommissioned officer
Nd in *chemistry,* neodymium
N.D., n.d. no date
N.D., N. Dak. North Dakota

Ne in *chemistry,* neon
N.E. Naval Engineer; New England
N.E.A. National Education Association
Neb., Nebr. Nebraska
N.E.D. New English Dictionary (the Oxford English Dictionary)
neg. negative
Neh. Nehemiah
Neth. Netherlands
neut. neuter
Nev. Nevada
New M. New Mexico
N.F., n/f in *banking,* no funds
N.F., Nfd., Nfld. Newfoundland
N.G. National Guard
N.G., n.g. no good
N.H. New Hampshire
Ni in *chemistry,* nickel
NIRA, N.I.R.A. National Industrial Recovery Administration
N.J. New Jersey
NLRB National Labor Relations Board
N.M., N. Mex. New Mexico
N.M.U., NMU National Maritime Union
No in *chemistry,* nobelium
No. north; northern
No., no. number
NOAA National Oceanic and Atmospheric Administration
nom. nominative
Nor. Norman; North; Norway; Norwegian
Norw. Norway; Norwegian
Nos., nos. numbers
Nov. November
Np in *chemistry,* neptunium
N.P., n.p. new paragraph; Notary Public
NRA National Recovery Administration
NRC, N.R.C. Nuclear Regulatory Commission
N.S. New Series; New Style; Nova Scotia
N/S, n/s, N.S.F. in *banking,* not sufficient funds
NSA National Secretaries Association; National Shipping Authority
NSC, N.S.C. National Security Council
NT., NT, N.T. New Testament
nt. wt. net weight
Num., Numb. Numbers (book of the Bible)
num. number; numeral; numerals

NW, N.W., n.w. northwest; northwestern
N.Y. New York
N.Y.C. New York Central; New York City
N.Z., N. Zeal. New Zealand

O

O in *physics,* ohm; in *chemistry,* oxygen
O. Ocean; October; Ohio; Ontario
O., o. old
o. off; only
OAS Organization of American States
OB, O.B. obstetrician; obstetrics
Ob., Obad. Obadiah
ob. (*obiit*) he (or she) died
obj. object; objection; objective
Obs., obs. observatory; obsolete
occas. occasion; occasional; occasionally
Oct. October
oct. octavo
O.D. Doctor of Optometry; Officer of the Day; overdraft; overdrawn
OE., O.E. Old English
O.E., o.e. omissions excepted
O.E.D., OED Oxford English Dictionary
OEO Office of Economic Opportunity
off. office; officer; official
O.K., OK, o.k. approval; approved
Okla. Oklahoma
OMB, O.M.B. Office of Management and Budget
Ont. Ontario
op. opera; operation; opposite; opus
O.P., o.p. out of print
op. cit. (*opere citato*) in the work cited
OPEC Organization of Petroleum Exporting Countries
opp. opposed; opposite
opt. optician; optics; optional
o.r. owner's risk
orch. orchestra
ord. ordained; order; ordinal; ordinance; ordinary; ordnance
Ore., Oreg. Oregon
org. organic; organization; organized
orig. origin; original; originally
Os in *chemistry,* osmium
O.S. Old Series; Old Style; ordinary seaman

o.s. out of stock
OSS Office of Strategic Services
OT, o.t. overtime
OT., OT, O.T. Old Testament
OTB offtrack betting
Ox., Oxf. Oxford
oz. ounce
ozs. ounces

P

P in *chemistry,* phosphorus; in *mechanics,* power, pressure
P., p. pastor; post; power; president; pressure; priest; prince
p. page; part; participle; past; penny; per; in *music,* piano; pint; pipe; population
Pa in *chemistry,* protactinium
Pa. Pennsylvania
P.A. Passenger Agent; public address (system); Purchasing Agent
Pac., Pacif. Pacific
Pan. Panama; Panamanian
par. paragraph; parallel; parenthesis
Parag. Paraguay; Paraguayan
paren. parenthesis
Parl. Parliament; Parliamentary
part. participial; participle; particular
pass. passenger; passim; passive
pat. patent; patented
patd. patented
path., pathol. pathological; pathology
Pat. Off. Patent Office
pat. pend. patent pending
Pb (*plumbum*) in *chemistry,* lead
PBS Public Broadcasting Service
PBX, P.B.X. Private Branch Exchange
P/C, p/c petty cash; prices current
pc. piece; price; prices
p.c. percent; postal card; post card
pct. percent
Pd in *chemistry,* palladium
pd. paid
P.D. Police Department; postal district; (*also* **p.d.**), per diem
P/E, P-E price-earnings ratio
P.E. probable error; Protestant Episcopal
Pen., pen. peninsula
Penn., Penna. Pennsylvania
Per., Pers. Persian

per. period; person
perf. perfect; perforated
pers. person; personal
pert. pertaining
Pet. Peter
pf. perfect; pfennig; pianoforte; preferred
Pfc. Private First Class
pfd. preferred
pfg. pfennig
Pg. Portugal; Portuguese
pg. page
Phar., Pharm. pharmaceutical; pharmacy
Ph.D. (*Philosophiae Doctor*) Doctor of Philosophy
Phil. Philippians; Philippine
phil. philosophy
phot., photog. photograph; photographer; photographic; photography
PHS, P.H.S. Public Health Service
phys. physical; physician; physics
phys. ed. physical education
pk. pack; park; peak; peck
pkg. package; packages
pl. place; plate; plural
plupf. pluperfect
Pm in *chemistry,* promethium
pm. premium
P.M. Paymaster; Postmaster; Prime Minister
P.M., p.m. (*post meridiem*) after noon
p.m. (*post-mortem*) after death
pmk. postmark
P/N, p.n. promissory note
Po in *chemistry,* polonium
P.O., p.o. petty officer; postal order; post office
poet. poetic; poetry
Pol. Poland; Polish
pol., polit. political; politics
pop. popular; popularly; population
Port. Portugal; Portuguese
pos. positive; possessive
poss. possession; possessive; possibly
pp. pages; past participle
P.P., p.p. parcel post; past participle; postpaid; prepaid
ppd. postpaid; prepaid
ppm, p.p.m., PPM parts per million

ppr., p. pr. present participle
P.P.S., p.p.s. (*post postscriptum*) an additional postscript
P.Q. previous question; Province of Quebec
Pr in *chemistry,* praseodymium
pr. pair; power; preferred (stock); present; price; pronoun
P.R. Puerto Rico; proportional representation; public relations
prec. preceding
pred. predicate
pref. preface; prefatory; preference; preferred; prefix
prelim. preliminary
prep. preparatory; preposition
Pres. Presbyterian; President
pres. present; presidency
Presb. Presbyterian
prim. primary; primitive
prin. principal; principally; principle
priv. private; privative
prob. probable; probably; problem
Prof. Professor
pron. pronoun; pronunciation
prop. properly; property; proprietor
Prot. Protestant
Prov. Provençal; Proverbs; Province
Prus. Prussia; Prussian
PS., P.S., p.s. postscript
Ps., Psa. Psalm; Psalms
ps. pieces; pseudonym
P.S. passenger steamer; Privy Seal; Public School
pseud. pseudonym
P.SS. postscripts
P.S.T. Pacific Standard Time
psych. psychological; psychology
Pt in *chemistry,* platinum
Pt. Point; Port
pt. part; payment; pint; point
p.t. past tense; pro tempore
P.T.A. Parent–Teacher Association
Pu in *chemistry,* plutonium
pub. public; publication; published; publisher; publishing
Pvt. Private
PWA, P.W.A. Public Works Administration
PX post exchange

Q

Q. Quebec; Queen; Question
q. quart; quarter; quarterly; quarto; quasi; queen; question; quintal; quire
q.e. (*quod est*) which is
Q.E.D. (*quod erat demonstrandum*) which was to be proved
Q.M. Quartermaster
qr. quarter; quire
qrs. quarters
qt. quantity; quart
qto. quarto
qts. quarts
qu. quart; quarter; quarterly; queen; question
quart. quarterly
Que. Quebec
ques. question
quot. quotation
q.v. (*quantum vis*) as much as you will; (*quod vide*) which see
qy. query

R

R in *chemistry,* radical
R. Radical; Republic; Republican
R., r. rabbi; radius; railroad; railway; (*Regina*) queen; (*Rex*) king; right; river; road; ruble; rupee
r. range; rare; received; residence; retired; rises; rod; rods; rubber
RA Regular Army
Ra in *chemistry,* radium
rad. radical; radius
RAdm. Rear Admiral
R.A.F., RAF Royal Air Force
R & D, R and D research and development
Rb in *chemistry,* rubidium
R.C. Red Cross; Roman Catholic
R.C.Ch. Roman Catholic Church
rcd. received
R.C.M.P. Royal Canadian Mounted Police
R.C.P. Royal College of Physicians
rcpt. receipt
R.C.S. Royal College of Surgeons
R/D, R.D. in *banking,* refer to drawer
Rd., rd. road; rod; round

R.D. Rural Delivery
Re in *chemistry,* rhenium
R.E. Reformed Episcopal
REA, R.E.A. Rural Electrification Administration
rec. receipt; received; recipe; record; recorded
recd., rec'd. received
Rec. Sec., rec. sec. recording secretary
ref. referee; reference; referred; reformed
Ref. Ch. Reformed Church
refl. reflection; reflex; reflexive
reg. regent; regiment; region; register; registered; registrar; regular; regulation
Rep. Representative; Republic; Republican
rep. repeat; report; reported; reporter
res. research; reserve; residence; resides; resistance; resolution
ret. retired; returned
Rev. Revelation; Reverend
rev. revenue; reverse; review; revise; revised; revision; revolution; revolving
RFC Reconstruction Finance Corporation
RFD, R.F.D. Rural Free Delivery
Rh in *chemistry,* rhodium
R.I. Rhode Island
R.I.P. (*requiescat in pace*) may he (or she) rest in peace
riv. river
rm. ream; room
rms. reams; rooms
Rn in *chemistry,* radon
R.N. Registered Nurse; Royal Navy
Rom. Roman; Romance; Romania; Romanian; Romans
Rom. Cath. Roman Catholic
ROTC Reserve Officers' Training Corps
RP reply paid
r.p.m. revolutions per minute
r.p.s. revolutions per second
rpt. report
R.R. railroad; Right Reverend
Rs. rupees
R.S. Recording Secretary; Reformed Spelling
RSV, R.S.V. Revised Standard Version (of the Bible)

R.S.V.P., **r.s.v.p.** (*répondez s'il vous plait*) please reply
rt. right
rte. route
Ru in *chemistry,* ruthenium
Russ. Russian
Rwy., **Ry.** Railway

S

S in *chemistry,* sulfur
S, S., s, s., south; southern
S. Sabbath; Saturday; Saxon; Senate; September; *Signor;* Socialist; Sunday
S., s. saint; school; society
s. second; seconds; section; see; series; shilling; shillings; sign; silver; singular; son; steamer; substantive
S.A. Salvation Army; South Africa; South America; South Australia
SAC Strategic Air Command
S. Afr. South Africa; South African
SALT Strategic Arms Limitation Talks
Sam., Saml., Sam'l. Samuel
Sans., Sansk. Sanskrit
Sask. Saskatchewan
SAT, S.A.T. Scholastic Aptitude Test
Sat. Saturday; Saturn
Sb (*stibium*) in *chemistry,* antimony
SBA Small Business Administration
Sc in *chemistry,* scandium
Sc, Scotch; Scots; Scottish
sc. scale; scene; screw; scruple
SC Signal Corps; Staff Corps
S.C. South Carolina; Supreme Court
s.c. in *printing,* small capitals
sch. school; schooner
sci. science; scientific
Scot. Scotch; Scotland; Scottish
S/D sight draft
S.D., S. Dak. South Dakota
Se in *chemistry,* selenium
SE, S.E., s.e. southeast; southeastern
SEC Securities and Exchange Commission
sec. secant; second or seconds; secondary; secretary; section or sections; sector; security
sect. section
secy., sec'y. secretary

Sem. Seminary
sem. semicolon
Sen., sen. Senate; Senator; senior
Sep., Sept. September; Septuagint
seq. (*sequentes*) the following
ser. series; sermon
serv. service
S.F. Sinking Fund
s.g. specific gravity
sgd. signed
Sgt., sgt. Sergeant
Shak. Shakespeare
shpt. shipment
shr. share; shares
Si, in *chemistry,* silicon
Sig., sig. signal; signature; *Signor; Signore; Signori*
sing. singular
S.J. Society of Jesus
Skr., Skrt., Skt. Sanskrit
Slav. Slavic; Slavonic
Sm in *chemistry,* samarium
Sn (*stannum*) in *chemistry,* tin
So. south; southern
Soc. Socialist; Society
sociol. sociological; sociology
sol. soluble; solution
SOP, S.O.P. standard (or standing) operating procedure
SOS international distress signal
Sp. Spain; Spaniard; Spanish
sp. special; species; specific; spelling
S.P., SP Shore Patrol; Submarine Patrol
Span. Spaniard; Spanish
S.P.C.A. Society for Prevention of Cruelty to Animals
S.P.C.C. Society for Prevention of Cruelty to Children
spec. special; specification
specif. specifically
sp. gr. specific gravity
spt. seaport
Sq., sq. square
Sr in *chemistry,* strontium
Sr. Senior; *Señor*
Sra. *Señora*
S.R.O. standing room only
Srta. *Señorita*
SS. Saints
S.S., SS, S/S steamship

S.S.A. Social Security Administration
St. Saint; Strait; Street
s.t. short ton
Sta. Santa; Station
std. standard
Ste. (*Sainte*) Saint
ster., stg. sterling
stge. storage
sub. substitute; substitutes; suburb; suburban
subj. subject; subjective; subjunctive
Sun. Sunday
sup. superior; superlative; supplement; supplementary; supply; (*supra*) above; supreme
Supt., supt. Superintendent
surg. surgeon; surgery; surgical
SW, S.W., s.w. southwest; southwestern
Sw., Swed. Sweden; Swedish
Switz. Switzerland
syn. synonym; synonymous; synonymy
Syr. Syria; Syriac; Syrian
syst. system

T

T. tablespoon; tablespoons; Testament; Thursday; Tuesday
T., t. tenor; territory; ton; tons; (*tomus*) volume
t. teaspoon; teaspoons; telephone; temperature; tense; time; town; township; transitive; troy
Ta in *chemistry,* tantalum
tab. table; tables; tablet; tablets
tan, tan. tangent
Tasm. Tasmania
TB, T.B., tb., t.b. tuberculosis
Tb in *chemistry,* terbium
tbs., tbsp. tablespoon; tablespoons
Tc in *chemistry,* technetium
Te in *chemistry,* tellurium
tech. technical; technically; technology
tel. telegram; telegraph; telephone
temp. temperature; temporary
Tenn. Tennessee
ter., terr. terrace; territory
Test. Testament
Teut. Teuton; Teutonic
Tex. Texas

Th in *chemistry,* thorium
Th. Thursday
theol. theologian; theological; theology
Thess. Thessalonians
Thur., Thurs. Thursday
Ti in *chemistry,* titanium
Tim. Timothy
tinct. tincture
Tit. Titus
tit. title
tkt. ticket
Tl in *chemistry,* thallium
Tm in *chemistry,* thulium
tn. ton; tons
tng. training
TNT, T.N.T. trinitrotoluene
topog. topographic; topography
tp. township
t.p. title page
tpk. turnpike
tr. trace; transitive; translated; translation; translator; transpose; treasurer
trans. transactions; transitive; translated; translation; translator; transportation; transpose
transl. translated; translation
treas. treasurer; treasury
trig., trigon. trigonometric; trigonometry
tsp. teaspoon; teaspoons
Tu., Tue., Tues. Tuesday
Turk. Turkey; Turkish
TV television
TVA Tennessee Valley Authority
twp. township

U

U in *chemistry,* uranium
U. Uncle; Union; United; University
U., u. unit; units; upper
U.A.W., UAW United Automobile, Aerospace, and Agricultural Implement Workers of America
u.c. in *printing,* upper case
UFO unidentified flying object
UHF, ultrahigh frequency
U.K. United Kingdom
Ukr. Ukraine; Ukrainian
UL Underwriters' Laboratories
ult. ultimate; ultimately; ultimo

UMT Universal Military Training
UMW, U.M.W. United Mine Workers of America
UN, U.N. United Nations
UNESCO United Nations Educational, Scientific, and Cultural Organization
UNICEF United Nations International Children's Emergency Fund
Unit. Unitarian
Univ. Universalist; University
univ. universal; universally
UPI United Press International
Uru. Uruguay; Uruguayan
U.S., US United States
U.S.A., USA United States of America; United States Army
USAF United States Air Force
USCG United States Coast Guard
USDA United States Department of Agriculture
USIA United States Information Agency
USIS United States Information Service
U.S.M. United States Mail; United States Mint
USMA United States Military Academy
USMC United States Marine Corps
USN United States Navy
USNG United States National Guard
USO, U.S.O. United Service Organizations
U.S.P., U.S. Pharm. United States Pharmacopoeia
U.S.S. United States Senate; United States Ship; United States Steamer; United States Steamship
U.S.S.R., USSR Union of Soviet Socialist Republics
Ut. Utah

V

V in *chemistry,* vanadium
V, v vector; velocity; volt; volts
v. verb; verse; version; versus; (*vide*) see; village; violin; voice; voltage; volume
VA Veterans Administration
Va. Virginia
var. variant; variation; variety; various
vb. verb; verbal

V.C. Vice-Chairman; Vice-Chancellor; Victoria Cross
V.D. venereal disease
Venez. Venezuela; Venezuelan
vet. veteran; veterinarian; veterinary
V.F.W., VFW Veterans of Foreign Wars
VHF very high frequency
V.I. Virgin Islands
v.i. intransitive verb; (*vide infra*) see below
V.I.P., VIP very important person
VISTA Volunteers in Service to America
viz. (*videlicet*) namely; that is
vocab. vocabulary
vol. volcano; volume; volunteer
vols. volumes
V.P. Vice-President
V. Rev. Very Reverend
vs. versus
V.S. Veterinary Surgeon
Vt. Vermont
v.t. transitive verb
Vulg. Vulgate
vv. verses; violins
v.v. vice versa

W

W (*wolfram*) in *chemistry,* tungsten; watt; watts
W, W., w, w. west; western
W. Wales; Wednesday; Welsh
W., w. warehouse; watt; watts; weight; width
W. week; weeks; wide; wife; with; won
WAC Women's Army Corps
Wash. Washington
W.B., W/B waybill
w.c. water closet; without charge
W.C.T.U. Woman's Christian Temperance Union
Wed. Wednesday
w.f., wf in *printing,* wrong font
WFTU, W.F.T.U. World Federation of Trade Unions
WHO World Health Organization (UN)
W.I. West Indian; West Indies
Wis., Wisc. Wisconsin
wk. week; work
wkly. weekly

w.l. wave length
WO Warrant Officer
wrnt. warrant
wt. weight
W.Va. West Virginia
Wyo., Wy. Wyoming

XYZ

Xe in *chemistry,* xenon
Y in *chemistry,* yttrium
y. yard; yards; year; years
Yb in *chemistry,* ytterbium
yd. yard; yards
Y.M.C.A. Young Men's Christian Association
Y.M.H.A. Young Men's Hebrew Association

yr. year; younger; your
yrs. years; yours
Yugo. Yugoslavia
Y.W.C.A. Young Women's Christian Association
Y.W.H.A. Young Women's Hebrew Association
Z. in *chemistry,* atomic number; in *astronomy,* zenith distance
Z., z. zero; zone
Zech. Zechariah
Zeph. Zephaniah
ZIP Zoning Improvement Plan
Zn in *chemistry,* zinc
zool. zoological; zoology
ZPG, Z.P.G. zero population growth
Zr in *chemistry,* zirconium

BUSINESS TERMS

A

abatement *n.* a deduction or rebate: the *order of abatement* establishes the order in which deficiencies in an estate are apportioned to the various types of bequest

abeyance *n.* a state of suspension: as, settlement of an estate is held in *abeyance* pending certain developments, such as proof of ownership

abstract of title a set of notes showing the history of transfers of ownership of real estate

acceleration clause provision in a mortgage or installment-purchase contract that states that if a payment is not made when due, the entire balance of the debt becomes due and payable at once

acceptance *n.* 1. endorsement of a bill of exchange by the person on whom it is drawn committing the signer of the endorsement to payment when due: the endorsement is written on the face of the bill, with the word "accepted" accompanying the signature: in event of the acceptor's failure to pay, the original maker of the bill is responsible; thus, the acceptance is a transaction between these two parties 2. an acknowledgement of receipt, as of goods, by a buyer 3. an acknowledgment of agreement, as to a contract, thus binding the purchaser

acceptor *n.* a person who signs a promise to pay a draft, or bill of exchange: also *accepter*

accommodation paper a bill of exchange or a note made or endorsed without consideration by one or more persons to enable the drawer to get credit or raise money on it

account *n.* 1. an itemized record of transactions, showing credits and debits 2. a business relation, especially one in which credit is used; charge account

account book a book in which business accounts are set down

account current a record of business dealings showing money owed

accounts payable amount of money a company owes to its creditors: a business liability

accounts receivable amount of money due to a company from its customers: a business asset

accrued dividends loosely, any unpaid dividends: strictly, dividends are not due until specifically declared

accrued expense charges incurred but not yet paid, as wages and other overhead for any period

accrued income income that has been earned but has not yet been received

accrued interest interest figured at a given time between the regular dates for payment: when a security is sold at a stated price "plus accrued interest," the buyer has to pay that price and the interest from the last interest date to the date of delivery: the buyer is recompensed by receiving interest for the full term

accumulative stock see **cumulative preferred stock**

acknowledgment *n.* a legal avowal, especially a notarized declaration of responsibility

active stock 1. an issue of stock currently figuring in market transactions 2. a stock for which there is a ready market

addendum *n.* something added or to be added

adjudicate *v.t.* 1. to submit (a contested matter) to judicial settlement 2. to settle (such a matter) by law

adjustment *n.* 1. settlement of an insurance claim 2. correction of errors in a charge account 3. refund for or replacement of goods lost or damaged in transit 4. lowering of price, as of soiled goods

admiralty court a court having jurisdiction in maritime matters

affiant *n.* one who makes an affidavit; deponent

affidavit *n.* a statement made under oath and in writing

agate line a unit of type measurement used in buying and selling space for advertising in newspapers: one fourteenth of an inch in a column, varying somewhat according to the width of the column

aggregate *n.* a total amount

agio *n.* 1. percentage paid as premium for exchange of one kind of currency for another, or in exchange of depreciated money for money of full value 2. agiotage

agiotage *n.* speculation on fluctuation of public securities

alien *v.t.* to transfer (land, etc.)

aliunde *adv. & adj.* in *law*, from some other source: as, evidence clarifying a document, but not deriving from the document itself, is evidence *aliunde*

allodium *n.* in *law*, land owned independently, without any rent, payment in service, etc.; a freehold estate

allonge *n.* a paper pasted on a note or bill of exchange to allow more endorsements than the bill has room for

amercement *n.* 1. punishment, especially by fine 2. the fine or penalty imposed

amortize *v.t.* 1. to put money aside at intervals, as in a sinking fund, for gradual payment of (a debt, etc.) 2. in *accounting*, to write off (expenditures) by prorating over a fixed period 3. in *law*, to transfer or sell (property) into a condition of mortmain

amount gross the total sum or aggregate

amount net total sum less proper deduction for expenses, discount, or charges

annual interest interest due yearly, rather than at more frequent intervals

annuity *n.* 1. a yearly payment of money 2. the right to receive such a payment 3. an investment yielding fixed payments during the holder's lifetime or for a stated number of years

A1 1. first class; best of its kind 2. in *shipping registry*, a first-class rating: *A* indicates first-class condition of the hull, *1* of the equipment

appraisal *n.* an estimate of the value of property or assets

appraise *v.t.* to examine and make an estimate of value

appreciation *n.* increase in value

arbitrage *n.* purchase of securities or goods in one market for immediate sale in another market where the price is higher: such trading tends to level out price differences

arbitration of exchange in *international business*, the process of arriving at a mutual understanding as to rates of exchange in the currencies of different countries

arrears *n.pl.* sums due but not paid: a delinquent customer is said to be *in arrears*, that is, behind in paying on an account

arson *n.* 1. the malicious burning of another's buildings or property 2. the burning of one's own property so as to collect insurance

article *n.* 1. the unit division of a document, as a constitution or a contract 2. a single piece of any kind of goods

assay office a department of the United States Mint, or a private firm, which tests metals and certifies them as to weight and purity

assessed valuation value placed upon property by an official assessor, as for determination of tax: it is commonly less than the true or market value

assessment *n.* 1. a charge against the owner of a property to cover his or her proportionate share of the cost of public improvements, as for street paving or the installation of sewer, water main, or sidewalks 2. a demand upon owners of securities, in proportion to the amount of their individual holdings, for the purpose of raising new capital for the corporation issuing the securities: most corporation securities are not subject to assessment, but bank stocks usually are: owners of assessable stocks are commonly held responsible for debts of the institution if it becomes insolvent

assets *n.* 1. everything owned by a business or that is owed to it: *fixed assets* include real estate and machinery; *current assets* include cash, investments, accounts receivable, inventory, and materials; *intangible assets* include goodwill and patents 2. in *accounting,* all the entries on a balance sheet showing such resources

assigned risks unreasonable risks that insurance companies do not want to insure, but for which insurance is required by law: such risks are assigned to insurers by turn

assignee *n.* the person to whom any asset, as a contract, right, or security, has been made over

assignment *n.* the making over to another of ownership or interest in any property or right: an assignment may be made to an individual person, a corporation, or one's creditors in general: if acceptable to the creditors in shares in proportion to the claims of each, it saves the cost of bankruptcy proceedings; but if it is not satisfactory to all the creditors, any of them may override the assignment by instituting bankruptcy action

assignment in blank an assignment, as of bonds or shares of stock, in which the name of the new owner does not appear

assume *v.t.* to take over, as bonds of one company by another, as in case of a merger or a transfer of control

assurance *n.* 1. [chiefly British] insurance. 2. an agreement to pay on a contingency sure to occur

attachment *n.* 1. seizure of property or person by legal writ 2. the writ authorizing such seizure

attorn *v.i.* to agree to continue as tenant under a new landlord

auditor *n.* one who checks claims and adjusts accounts

automation *n.* in *manufacturing,* a system or method in which all or many of the processes of production, movement, or inspection are performed or controlled by self-operating machinery, electronic devices, etc.

available assets unencumbered resources, especially those that can be converted into money through sale or can serve as security for a new obligation

average down to buy more shares of a security at a lower price than was paid for the first purchase, in order to reduce the average cost per share: thus if 100 shares were bought for $5,000, the average would be $50; another 100 shares at $30 would bring the investment to $8,000 for 200 shares, or $40 per share: compare **average up**

average of payments method of finding the time when payment may be made of several sums due at different dates, without loss to either party

average up to buy more goods or shares at a higher price, increasing the average payment per unit, in anticipation of a further advance in price and sale at a profit: compare **average down**

avulsion *n.* the sudden transference of a piece of land from one person's property to another's without change of ownership, as by a change in the course of a stream

B

bailment *n.* goods delivered in trust against an obligation and to be returned when that obligation is ended

bait-and-switch *adj.* of or using an illegal

or unethical sales technique in which a seller lures customers by advertising an often nonexistent item at a bargain price and then attempts to switch their attention to more expensive items

balance of trade the difference in value between all the merchandise imports and exports of a country: an excess of a country's exports over its imports is called a *favorable balance* and an excess of imports over exports is called an *unfavorable balance*

balance sheet a statement of assets and liabilities to show the standing of a business: it summarizes profits, losses, assets, liabilities, net worth, etc., and is usually figured at the close of a fiscal period

balloon payment final payment on a note that is much higher than the regular payments

bank acceptance a draft or bill of exchange drawn on a bank or other credit-loaning institution and accepted by it

bank annuities British government bonds; consols

bank balance the amount to a depositor's credit in a bank; the amount to which a bank or trust company is obligated to the depositor, and must hold subject to his or her order

bank bill 1. a bank note 2. a bill of exchange issued or accepted by a bank: also called *banker's bill*

bank discount interest deducted by a bank from a loan when the loan is made: it is equal to the normal interest from the date of the loan to the date of the final payment

bank draft an order by one bank for payment by another

bank holiday 1. a period when banks are closed by the government, as during a financial crisis 2. any weekday when banks are not open, as for a legal holiday

bank note a bank's promise to pay bearer on demand, at face value: these notes circulate as money

bank of deposit any bank, and in most of the states any trust company, which accepts deposits of money subject to order by check

bank of issue any bank empowered by law to issue notes for use as currency; in the United States, a Federal Reserve Bank

bank paper bank notes or commercial paper which can be handled by banks, as notes subject to discount

bank rate rate of discount fixed for a system of banks

bank statement 1. a bank's public report of its condition 2. a detailed report of financial condition given to a bank by an applicant for a loan 3. popularly, a bank's summary of activity in a depositor's account for a certain period

bank stock shares in a banking company; paid-up capital of a bank divided into shares

barratry *n.* 1. in *maritime law*, an act by a shipmaster hurtful to the owners of the vessel or its cargo 2. in common legal use, repeated deliberate attempts to cause resort to the courts

barrister *n.* [British] a lawyer who practices in the courts

bear *n.* a trader who gambles on prices going down; one who sells securities not yet owned, for future delivery at a certain price, counting on being able to buy the shares at a lower price before the delivery date

bear market a period of sustained downward tendency in prices on stock or commodity exchanges: see **cover; raid; short sale**

bench warrant order by a court that a certain person charged with a particular offense be brought before it

beneficiary *n.* a person named to receive the inheritance or income from a will, trust, insurance policy, etc.

billing terms conditions, as of time and rate of discount, on which an order is accepted

bill of entry a list of incoming and outgoing goods entered at the customs

bill of exceptions a written list of exceptions to a court's decisions

bill of lading 1. originally, a cargo list 2. a contract issued to a shipper by a transportation agency, listing the goods shipped, acknowledging their receipt, and promising delivery to the person named

bill of particulars specification of demands for which an action is brought

bill of sale a legally formal paper attesting that the ownership of something has been transferred by sale

bill of sight a form of customhouse entry allowing consignee to see goods before paying duty: it may be used to permit unloading of goods on which the importer lacks the information for a bill of entry

blank credit permission to draw money on account, no sum being specified

blank endorsement endorsement of a check or other commercial paper with signature only, making the endorsed amount payable to bearer, not to a named individual

blind trust an arrangement whereby a person, as a public official, in an effort to avoid conflicts of interest, places certain personal assets under the control of an independent trustee with the provision that the person is to have no knowledge of how those assets are managed

blue-sky law any law protecting the investing public against fraud or exploitation by promoters, some of whom are said to try to convert even the blue skies into capital

board n. 1. a group of directors, as of a company 2. the listing of current stocks and their prices, as at a stock exchange

bona fide in good faith; made or done in good faith; genuine; as, a *bona fide* offer

bond n. 1. in *commerce, a)* an agreement by an agency holding taxable goods that taxes on them will be paid before they are sold *b)* the condition of such goods *c)* an insurance contract by which a bonding agency guarantees payment of a specified sum to an employer, etc., in the event of a financial loss caused by the act of a specified employee or by some contingency over which the insured has no control 2. in *finance,* an interest-bearing certificate issued by a government or business, promising to pay the holder a specified sum on a specified date: it is a common means of raising capital 3. in *law, a)* a written obligation under seal to pay specified sums, or to do or not do specified things *b)* a person acting as surety for another's action; payer of bail *c)* an amount paid as surety or bail

bond creditor a creditor protected by bonds

bonded debt 1. amount of indebtedness, as of a corporation or government, represented by outstanding issues of bonds 2. a long-term indebtedness, as distinguished from current indebtedness represented by short-term obligations, such as notes

bonded goods goods held in bond, sense 1 *a):* their place of storage is known as a *bonded warehouse*

bondsman n. one who gives security for the payment of money, performance of an act, or integrity of another

book debts accounts on the books of record

books closed 1. designating a period when the books of a corporation are closed, to provide a period of adjustment during which the list of stockholders is checked to determine who is entitled to vote in a stockholders' meeting, after which the books are opened again to record transfers of shares 2. designating a period when the books are closed because an issue of shares has been fully subscribed and no more orders can be taken

book value 1. the worth of stock or any asset as shown in the financial records of the company that issues or owns it, as distinguished from par value or market value: it reflects the amount of capital invested per share of the stock 2. the value of a company's assets as carried on its books

bought-and-sold notes notes given by a broker to the buyer and seller, respectively

bounty *n.* a bonus or premium given to encourage trade

break bulk to open a package of goods in transit and remove a part

broker *n.* one who buys and sells for others on commission

brokerage *n.* 1. the business or office of a broker 2. a broker's fee

bull *n.* a trader who gambles on prices rising; one who buys securities counting on being able to sell them at a higher price

bull market a condition of sustained activity and rising prices in a stock market

buyers' market state of the market in which the buyer is at an advantage because supply is greater than demand: see **sellers' market**

buyer's option a buyer's privilege, when so stipulated in an agreement, to postpone completion of an order over a certain period but to demand delivery, should it be needed, on stated notice at any time within that period

C

calendar year 12 months beginning January 1 and ending December 31: distinguished from *fiscal year*

call *n.* 1. demand for payment 2. privilege of demanding fulfillment of an order at a given price within a stated period of time *v.t.* to redeem, as an issue of bonds, before maturity

callable *adj.* subject to call: said especially of bonds issued with reservation of the right to redeem on or after a specified date in advance of maturity

call loan a loan payable on demand of the lender: commonly made by banks or brokers: this lending provides a profit-

able use for available funds and protects the bank against a shortage of cash

call money money borrowed subject to the lender's demand for payment at any time within a stated limit

cancel *v.t.* to annul or erase: often done by stamp or punch

capital *n.* money available for investment; wealth (money or property) used to finance production or to produce more wealth

capital gain profit resulting from the sale of capital investment, as stocks, real estate, etc.

capital goods goods used productively, as raw materials, machinery, buildings, etc.; producers' goods: distinguished from *consumers' goods*

capitalize *v.t.* 1. to calculate the present value of (a periodical payment, annuity, income, etc.); convert (an income, etc.) into one payment or sum equivalent to the computed present value 2. to convert (floating debt) into stock or shares

carrier *n.* a person or firm that transports passengers or goods, or both, as a business: see **common carrier**

carrying charge a percentage paid by a customer making deferred payments, as in purchase of stock on margin or of goods on the installment plan

carte blanche a signed paper, as an order or other authorization, to be filled in as the holder may please

cash flow the pattern of receipts and expenditures of a company, government, etc., resulting in the availability or nonavailability of cash

cashier's check a check drawn by a bank against itself and carrying the signature of the cashier

cash sale sale of goods for immediate payment, or payment in full within a certain short period of time

certificate of deposit a paper given by a bank acknowledging receipt of money to be held for the customer in a time deposit that draws interest: it is subject to demand, but becomes mature on a specific date and is subject to penalty, usually a reduction of interest, if withdrawn before that date

certified check a check drawn on a depositor's bank account, and for which the bank guarantees payment

chattel mortgage a lien on personal property, taken to secure a loan or to enable seizure and sale of property bought on the installment plan should the buyer default

check *n.* a written order to a bank to pay the amount specified from money on deposit in one's account

chose *n.* a piece of personal property; chattel

chose in action a right, as to personal property which has not been taken into possession

clearinghouse *n.* an office maintained by a group of banks as a center for exchanging checks drawn against one another, balancing accounts, etc.

clearinghouse balance the amount which a bank owes to the clearinghouse at the end of a day or is to receive from it in settlement of its part in the day's debits and credits

close corporation a corporation whose stock is owned and controlled by only a few persons, as a family group

cognovit note in *civil law,* a promissory note with a clause acknowledging liability of a debt and authorizing any attorney, upon default, to take out and execute a judgment on the debt without a formal trial

coinsurance *n.* insurance on commercial property in which two or more insurers (*coinsurers*) carry the risk in proportion to the coverage of the full property value which each has insured: sometimes the insured stands as a coinsurer in assuming part of the risk

collateral *n.* property, such as securities, pledged by a borrower to protect a lender, or guarantee the discharge of an obligation

collateral note a note secured by collateral: it is given by a borrower to a lending bank, stating the terms of deposit of security on the loan, to protect the bank against the borrower's possible attempt to sell the pledged security

comaker *n.* a cosigner

commerce *n.* extended trade or traffic

commercial agency an organization which furnishes subscribers with information as to the financial standing and credit rating of individuals and corporations engaged in business: Dun and Bradstreet, Inc., of New York, is the foremost such agency in the United States

commercial bank a bank primarily concerned with checking accounts and short-term loans

commercial paper checks, promissory notes, bills of exchange, and other negotiable paper used in business

commission broker a broker who buys or sells on commission

commissioner of deeds in certain states, an attorney or notary authorized to take acknowledgment of deeds

commission house a brokerage firm that handles transactions, as purchase or sale of securities or goods, for others, on a percentage basis

commission merchant a merchant who buys or sells goods for others and is paid a commission by them

common carrier a person or company engaged in the business of transporting passengers or goods, or both: railroads, ships, ferries, bus lines, airlines, and trucking systems are common carriers: each state regulates their operation within its own boundaries, and the Federal Interstate Commerce Commission fixes rates and rules for operation across state lines

common law the unwritten law based on established custom: it is now largely regularized by legislative definition

common stock stock which does not carry the privileges granted to holders of preferred issues, and which shares in the profits of a business only after the claims of the preferred have been satisfied: income on preferred stock is usually a fixed percentage of par, or face, value; that on common stock is proportionate to earnings and may be very high or nothing at all: there is no rigidly fixed arrangement as between the two kinds of stock: the conditions of each issue are set forth on its certificates

composition *n.* 1. a payment by an insolvent debtor of a percentage of money due to a creditor as settlement in full 2. the sum offered and accepted in this way

compound interest interest on both principal and accumulated unpaid interest: distinguished from *simple interest*

consideration *n.* that which is given or promised by the parties to a contract: it may be money or another thing of value, or an action of some kind

consignee *n.* the person to whom a shipment of goods is addressed

consignment *n.* 1. an order of goods shipped 2. commitment of goods to an agent or distributor for sale: goods are said to be *on consignment* when they have been turned over to the agent with the understanding that the shipper will be paid only after the goods are sold

consignor *n.* one who ships goods, as to an agent or distributor; the maker of a consignment

consolidation *n.* the joining of two or more business houses under one management: technically distinguished from a *merger* in the details of financing and reorganizing

consols *n.pl.* funded government securities of Great Britain: abbreviation for *consolidated annuities* or *bonds*

consumers' goods goods, such as food, clothing, etc., for satisfying people's needs rather than for producing other goods or services: distinguished from *producers',* or *capital, goods*

contract *n.* an agreement between two or more people to do something: a contract follows an *offer* and *acceptance* and implies a legal means and purpose, as well as a sufficient *consideration*

convertible *adj.* of bonds, subject to surrender in exchange for stock, either by act of the issuing company or of the holder, or as required under certain stated conditions

corner *n.* control of the market for a security or commodity, as wheat, through acquisition of a major part of the supply

corporation *n.* a group of persons legally empowered to act as an individual in business

cosigner *n.* a person who signs a promissory note in addition to the maker, thus becoming responsible for the obligation if the maker should default: also called *comaker*

cost and freight a term of sale indicating that transportation charges will be paid by the seller

court of equity a court having equity jurisdiction: it is not limited by the common law: see **equity**, sense 1

cover *v.t.* 1. to provide payment for 2. to buy securities or commodities, after a short sale, in order to make good on a contract of future delivery: see **short sale**

craft union a labor union composed of workers belonging to a particular trade: see **industrial union**

credit *n.* 1. the power of a person or business to purchase goods or services on a promise to pay for them in the future 2. in *banking,* acknowledgment of money deposited in an account, or the amount of money on which a person or firm may draw at any time 3. in *accounting,* the entry on the right-hand side of a ledger in double-entry bookkeeping, recording a payment received

credit instrument a paper (aside from paper currency) acknowledging obligation to pay, as a check or draft, a note, a bond coupon, etc.

creditor *n.* one who extends credit or to whom money is owed

credit rating status of a person or firm as a credit risk, based on financial standing, past records of debt repayment, etc.

cumulative preferred stock a stock on which successive unpaid dividends accrue and have to be paid before any dividend can be paid on the common stock

current *adj.* passing freely; now in progress; of this day: as, *current* accounts

current assets resources that can be converted into cash quickly and easily

current expenses day-to-day costs of doing business

current liabilities obligations attendant upon the day-to-day conduct of business, such as wages

customs *n.pl.* 1. duties or taxes imposed by a government on imported and, occasionally, exported goods 2. the government agency in charge of collecting these duties

customs union a union of two or more nations that agree to eliminate customs restrictions among them and to follow a common tariff policy toward all other nations

cutback *n.* reduction or discontinuance, as of a contract, before the completion of what was originally called for

D

dating *n.* an extension of the period of credit by considering a transaction as made at a later date than that at which it actually was made: sometimes offered as an incentive to purchase, as during a slack season

dead weight freight for which charge is made by weight instead of bulk

debenture bond a bond not secured by a lien on property of the issuing corporation or backed by any security except the corporation's general assets and good faith

debit *n.* 1. in *banking*, a charge made

against a bank account 2. in *accounting*, the entry on the left-hand side of a ledger in double-entry bookkeeping, recording a debt

debt *n.* money owed by one to another

debtor *n.* a person or company that owes money to another

deed *n.* a paper in legal form conveying ownership of real estate

default *n.* failure of a debtor to pay money when due

deferred dividend a dividend, as on cumulative preferred stock, not paid when due but permitted to accrue

deficiency judgment a judgment in favor of a mortgagee for the remainder of a debt not completely cleared by foreclosure and sale of the mortgaged property

demand deposit a deposit in a bank, subject to withdrawal at any time: the usual form of checking account

deposit slip the printed form supplied by a bank on which the depositor makes an itemized statement of each deposit

depreciation *n.* 1. a decrease in the value of property through wear, deterioration, or obsolescence 2. the allowance made for this in accounting, bookkeeping, etc. 3. a decrease in the purchasing power of money

deviation *n.* a change from a set or prearranged plan: as, the *deviation* of a ship from her regular course to stop at other ports

discount *n.* 1. interest deducted in advance by one who buys, or lends money on, a bill of exchange, promissory note, etc. 2. a discounting, as of a bill, note, etc. 3. reduction from the regular price *v.t.* to pay or receive the present value of a bill or note, minus a deduction for interest

discount broker one who lends money on notes or bills

discount rate percentage at which commercial paper is discounted by the banks

dollar exchange bills of exchange drawn in other countries upon American banking houses and payable in United States money

domestic exchange issuance and acceptance of bills of exchange within the United States, chiefly in the form of bank drafts on Federal Reserve Banks

double-entry bookkeeping that system of bookkeeping in which every transaction is entered as both a debit and a credit

double-name paper a negotiable paper with an additional endorsement called for by the bank: also called *two-name paper*

double taxation taxation of one person or property by two governments, as state and federal, or by two states, as of a person who lives in one state on income derived from property in another state

draft *n.* a written order by which one person directs another to pay a certain sum to a third person, charging it to the maker of the draft: a check is a form of draft

draw *v.t.* to make a draft of or for; write (a check)

drawback *n.* an allowance or return of duties paid at the customhouse, made when a shipment is reexported

drawing account 1. an account showing money paid for expenses or as advances on salary, commissions, etc., as to a traveling agent or representative 2. the privilege of such an account

drop shipment an order for which the goods go to the retailer direct from the factory but the bill comes from the distributor or wholesale agent from whom the retailer would normally receive the goods

due bill a paper given to a customer who returns ordered or purchased goods, granting credit for the amount against a future purchase

E

earnest money money given as part payment and pledge, as in buying real estate

easement *n.* a right to certain uses of another's land, as of passage over it to a highway

easy *adj.* 1. lacking firmness in prices: said of a market 2. with funds plentiful and interest rates low: said of a money market: opposed to *tight*

effects *n.pl.* property; goods on hand; the possessions of a firm or an individual

ejectment *n.* the removal of a tenant from leased premises by legal means; a forcing out; eviction

endorse *v.t.* to place a signature on the back of a paper, as a check or note, in order to cash it or to assume responsibility for its payment: also *indorse*

endorsee *n.* one to whom a note or check is made over through endorsement by its holder: also *indorsee*

endorsement *n.* the act of writing on the back of a check, note, etc., or that which is written, as the signature of a payee, by which money or property is made over to someone: a *blank endorsement* or *endorsement in blank* is the usual form of endorsement, specifying no particular payee; a *restrictive endorsement* specifies the use to be made of the paper, as "Pay to X as agent," or "Deposit to the account of Y," with the maker's signature; a *special endorsement* designates the party to whom or to whose order payment is to be made: also *indorsement*

entrapment *n.* the arranging by a police officer, detective, etc., of circumstances that provide or encourage temptation to commit a felony or misdemeanor, as the encouragement of the offer of a bribe

entry *n.* 1. an item of record in an account 2. the officially recognized and recorded arrival of a ship or goods at a port

equity *n.* 1. a body of laws supplementary to statute law, designed to correct injustices due to legal technicality 2. a right or claim recognized in a court of equity 3. the value of property over and above the amount owed on it in liens, mortgages, etc.

equity of redemption the right of a mortgagor to redeem his or her forfeited estate by payment of capital and interest within a reasonable time: it is granted by a court of equity

escalator clause a clause in a contract providing for increases or decreases in wages, prices, etc., as in accordance with fluctuations in the cost of living

escrow *n.* a deed, bond, etc. held by a third party and not put into effect or delivered until certain conditions are fulfilled

estoppel *n.* the prevention of a person from asserting a fact or doing an act inconsistent with previous acts or declarations

examiner *n.* 1. a person named by state or federal authority to examine the records of a bank; bank examiner 2. a customhouse officer who compares goods with invoices

exchange *v.i.* 1. to make an exchange; barter; trade 2. in *finance,* to pass in exchange: as, the currency of this country *exchanges* at par *n.* 1. *pl.* the checks, drafts, etc., presented for exchange and settlement between banks in a clearinghouse 2. in *law,* a contract by which parties agree to exchange one thing for another *adj.* having to do with an exchange: as, an *exchange* broker

exchange broker a broker who deals in foreign bills of exchange and currencies

excise tax a government tax on goods made and sold within its domain, as the federal taxes on domestic liquors, automobiles, cigarettes, etc.: differentiated from *customs duties,* or *tariffs,* on imported goods

ex parte on, or in the interest of, one side only; one-sided

export duty a tax imposed on exports

exports *n.pl.* goods or merchandise exported; especially, all of the goods sent from one country to another or others

ex post facto acting backward; retrospec-

tive: an *ex post facto law* is one that can be applied to offenses charged as occurring before the law's enactment

express company a corporation engaged in the business of transporting goods and money from one place to another more quickly than can be done by sending as ordinary freight

extension *n.* 1. allowance of additional time for payment to a debtor 2. a carrying out of items of a bill or account, as by multiplying units by a unit rate

external loan an issue of bonds for buyers in other countries, often made payable in currency of the country in which the bonds are sold: distinguished from a *domestic* or *internal loan*

extinguish *v.t.* to bring to an end; settle; finish: as, to *extinguish* an obligation

F

facture *n.* 1. the act or method of making something 2. the thing made 3. an invoice or shipment of goods

fair copy an exact copy of a document after final corrections have been made on it

Federal Deposit Insurance Corporation a government corporation set up to protect bank depositors: all deposits are insured against loss, theft, etc., up to a limit of $100,000 for each account

Federal Reserve Bank any of the twelve district banks of the Federal Reserve System

Federal Reserve notes paper currency issued by the banks of the Federal Reserve System: most common form of legal tender

Federal Reserve System a centralized banking system in the United States under a Board of Governors which supervises twelve Federal Reserve Banks, each acting as the central bank for its district, and over 6,000 member banks: it was established in 1913 to develop a currency which would fluctuate with business demands and to regulate the member banks of each district

fee *n.* 1. originally, *a*) heritable land held from a feudal lord in return for service; fief; feudal benefice: also called *feud b*) the right to hold such land *c*) payment, service, or homage due to a superior 2. a payment asked or given for professional services, admissions, licenses, tuition, etc.; charge 3. in *law,* an inheritance in land

fee simple absolute ownership; ownership of property without limitations of heirs to whom it must descend: distinguished from *fee tail,* which limits the inheritance to a specified class of heirs

feud *n.* in the feudal system, land held from a lord in return for service given him: used in certain legal phrases: also *fee, fief*

feudist *n.* in *law,* a specialist in feudal law

fiduciary *n.* 1. a trustee of an estate or director of a corporation 2. a person engaged in a confidential financial capacity, as an agent

FIFO *n.* (*first in, first out*) a method of valuing inventories in which the items sold or used are priced at the cost of earliest acquisitions and those remaining are valued at the cost of most recent acquisitions: see also *LIFO*

first-mortgage bond a bond secured by a mortgage on part or all of a business property and having priority over other liens

fiscal year the 12-month period between settlements of financial accounts: in the United States, the government fiscal year legally ends June 30

fixed charges certain charges, as taxes, rent, interest, etc., which must be paid, usually at regular intervals, without being changed or shifted, and without reference to the amount of business done

flat *adj.* without interest charges, as a *flat* loan

floating *adj.* 1. not funded: said of a debt 2. not permanently invested, but held for speculation and frequently changing hands in the market: said of stock

3. not invested, but available for current expenses, as *floating* capital 4. fluctuating freely in relation to other currencies, as determined by supply and demand: said of a currency

forced sale sale of property, on legal order, to satisfy creditors' claims, as under a foreclosure action

foreclosure *n.* legal action for sale of mortgaged property to enable the mortgagee to recover loaned money in case of default by the mortgator: if the sale realizes more than the claim, the surplus goes to the holders of secondary liens; if there are none, it is paid to the mortgagor: foreclosure sales may also be held on pledged property other than real estate, and by a government, local, state, or federal, for unpaid taxes on lands and buildings

foreign bill a bill of exchange payable abroad: a bill payable in another state may also be classified under this heading

forestall *v.t.* to interfere with the trading in (a market) by buying up goods in advance, getting sellers to raise prices, etc.

forwarder *n.* a person or thing that forwards; specifically, a transmitting agent; person who receives goods and delivers them to the regular transportation agent for transmission to the proper destination

fractional currency currency of a denomination less than the standard monetary unit

franchise *n.* 1. right to operate a business in public service, granted by a government: as, a bus *franchise* 2. the right to market a product or provide a service, often exclusive in a specified area, as granted by the manufacturer or company

franchisee *n.* a person, business, etc. that has been granted a franchise

franchiser *n.* a company or manufacturer that grants franchises: also spelled *franchisor*

franking privilege right to send mail free of postage

free alongside ship (or **vessel**) delivered to the dock with freight charges paid by the shipper: said of goods to be hauled by ship

free and clear without encumbrance: said especially of title to real estate against which there is no mortgage or other legal lien

free list 1. a list of persons entitled to service without charge 2. a list of goods not subject to duty

free on board delivered (by the seller) aboard the train, ship, etc., at the point of shipment, after which the buyer pays all transportation charges: see also **cost and freight**

free port a port where goods may be unloaded, stored, and reshipped without payment of customs duties

front foot one foot of the edge of a plot of land facing on a road, street, or waterfront: used as a unit of valuation

frozen assets resources that cannot be quickly liquidated

funded debt indebtedness in the form of long-term obligations: debt is frequently funded by transforming a number of short-term issues into long-term, interest-bearing bonds

fungible *adj.* in *law,* designating goods, as grain, coffee, etc., any unit or part of which can replace another unit, as in discharging a debt; capable of being used in place of another *n.* a fungible thing

futures *n.pl.* securities or commodities bought and sold for delayed delivery: frequently done as speculation, selling of futures is a factor of business stability, enabling manufacturers to price their products with due regard to future cost of raw materials

G

general average in *marine insurance,* a proportionate contribution levied on ship and goods to cover necessary sacrifice of a part in order to save the remainder: all owners and shippers involved share in assuming this expense, even though the "necessary sacrifice" may have been goods belonging to only one of them

gold certificate 1. formerly, a United States Treasury note redeemable in gold 2. a United States Treasury note issued and used only within the Federal Reserve System

gold point the rate of foreign exchange which makes it cost no more to square accounts by shipping gold than to settle by buying or selling bills of exchange

gold reserve the gold held in the United States Treasury to back the gold certificates held by the Federal Reserve Banks and to meet foreign banking obligations

gold standard monetary standard based on gold, in which the basic currency unit is equal to a specified quantity of gold

goodwill *n.* favorable attitude of the buying public toward a business house, constituting an intangible asset in valuing the business: sometimes written *good will*

grand larceny in *law,* 1. theft in which the property stolen has a value equaling or exceeding a certain amount fixed by law: the amount varies from state to state but is usually between \$25 and \$60: distinguished from *petit* (or *petty*) *larceny* 2. in some states, the theft of property of any value directly from the person of the victim, but without the use of force

great gross 12 gross, i.e., 1,728 articles

gross *n.* 1. 12 dozen, i.e., 144 2. total amount: opposed to *net*

gross income total receipts, without deductions: distinguished from *net income*

gross national product the total value of a nation's annual output of goods and services

gross profit the amount by which receipts on sales exceed the cost of the goods, without deduction of costs of running the business

gross receipts total receipts from sale of goods, without expense deduction

gross ton a ton of 2,240 pounds: also called *long ton*

groundage *n.* a fee charged for permitting a ship to remain in port

H

harbor dues charges made for use of a habor; groundage

hedge *v.t.* to buy or sell in order to balance threatened loss in other transactions

hedge fund a partnership of investors who pool large sums for buying stocks they think will rise in price, at the same time selling shares they think will decline, so as to profit from both the rise and fall in prices

holder in due course one to whom a check, note, or other bill of exchange has come through earlier endorsements without protest or notice of defect

holding company a company organized to control subsidiary companies through possession of their stock issues

I

import duty a tax imposed on imports

increment *n.* increase: see **unearned increment**

indenture *n.* 1. a formal legal agreement, of which identical copies are held by each party: originally, the two copies had correspondingly notched edges for identification 2. an official, authenticated list, inventory, etc.

index numbers statistics in a table or record showing fluctuations of prices, volume of trade, or production, etc., from an assumed base

indulgence *n.* extension of time for payment, considered as a favor

industrial union a labor union composed of members of a particular industry, regardless of specialized occupation

inland bill a bill of exchange or draft drawn upon a person in one state or country and payable in the same state or country: also known as *domestic bill*

insurable interest a sufficient personal concern in the object of insurance to establish a reason for assuming responsibility for premium payment: for example, the *insurable interest* a company may have in the life of its chief executives

insurance broker one who negotiates insurance contracts

insurance trust an estate in the form of insurance policies, with a trustee to administer it in the beneficiary's interest

inter alios among other persons

interest *n.* money paid for the use of money, computed as a percentage per unit of time: see **compound interest**, **simple interest**

interest account in *bookkeeping*, a separate account of sums paid and received as interest

interfere *v.i.* in *patent law*, to claim priority for an invention, as when two or more applications for its patent are pending

interim certificate a paper acknowledging deposit of stock to be held, as by a designated trust company, during a period of reorganization of the issuing corporation, to be exchanged for new securities when the reorganization is completed

interplead *v.i.* in *law*, to go to trial with each other in order to settle a dispute in which a third party is concerned; initiate an interpleader

interpleader *n.* a legal proceeding by which a person sued by two others having the same claim may compel them to go to trial with each other to determine what settlement should be made

investment banking the business of buying all or part of new stock issues, for the purpose of resale in the expectation of making a profit: investment banking does not include conventional banking services

investment trust a firm that invests in securities the funds obtained from the sale of its own shares and distributes a return to its shareholders from the income on the securities: also called *investment company:* see **mutual fund**

invoice book (or **register**) a book for entering copies of invoices

IRA or **I.R.A.** (*Individual Retirement Account*) a personal retirement plan for a worker not covered by a group pension plan: a limited amount of annual earnings may be invested, as in a savings account or mutual fund, with the money invested and the earnings from it being tax-free until retirement

J

job analysis a study of a specific job, as in industry, with respect to operations and hazards involved, qualifications required of the worker, etc.

job description a brief description of the duties expected of a person filling a specific position

job printer a printer who does various kinds of printing, such as letterheads, circulars, posters, etc.

joint and several note a note with two or more signers: any or all signers can be held liable for performance of the pledge

joint tenancy ownership of property by two or more persons under which the holdings of any who die are held jointly by the survivors

judgment debtor a debtor against whom a creditor has obtained a court ruling

jump a claim to seize mining rights or land claimed by someone else

K

Keogh plan a retirement plan for self-employed persons and certain groups

of employees, similar to an IRA: see **IRA**

key punch a machine, operated from a keyboard, that records data by punching holes in cards that can then be fed into machines for sorting, accounting, etc.

kiting *n.* the practice of using bad checks or other worthless negotiable paper to raise money or maintain credit temporarily

knocked down in *commerce,* not assembled, as furniture, for convenience in shipping

L

law merchant all the rules and usages originating in the customs of merchants and now applied to dealings in trade and commerce, where not changed by statute

letter of advice a notification of completion of a commercial transaction; especially a letter in which the drawer of a bill of exchange notifies the drawee that the bill has been issued

letter of credit a letter from a bank asking that the holder of the letter be allowed to draw specified sums of money from other banks or agencies, to be charged to the account of the writer of the letter

liabilities *n.* 1. all the debts or legally enforceable obligations of a business: *current liabilities* are those due within one year and include accounts, dividends, wages, salaries, and accrued taxes payable; *long-term* or *fixed liabilities* are bank loans, debentures, mortgages, etc. 2. in *accounting,* the entries on a balance sheet showing money owed

liability *n.* 1. the responsibility of an owner, automobile or machine operator, employer, etc. for loss, damage, injury, etc. to another or others 2. the coverage for which an insurance company is liable as spelled out in a particular policy

lien *n.* a legal claim against property to protect a creditor, as one claiming pay for work done on the property

LIFO *n.* (*last in, first out*) a method of valuing inventories in which items sold or used are priced at the cost of the most recent acquisitions and those remaining are valued at the cost of earliest acquisitions: see also *FIFO*

limited *adj.* having liability of stockholders coincide with the actual amount of their investment: as, a *limited* company

limited partnership a partnership differing from a general partnership in that individual liability is limited to each partner's investment

linage, lineage *n.* amount of advertising space calculated in the number of lines of print: see **agate line**

line of credit the maximum amount of credit to which a customer is entitled

liquid assets assets that can be quickly and easily converted into cash

liquidation *n.* conversion, either voluntary or forced, of assets into cash, either to take profits or to close out a business

Lloyd's *n.* an association of insurance underwriters in London formed in the 18th century to subscribe marine insurance policies and to publish shipping news: it now handles many kinds of insurance

loan *n.* a sum of money lent for a specified period, usually at a specified rate of interest

loan society a group of people who pay various sums into a fund which is then used as a source of loans to them and, sometimes, to others

locum tenens [chiefly British] a person taking another's place for the time being; temporary substitute; lieutenant

long dozen 13 articles for the price of 12: it is sometimes given by way of effecting a discount: also called *baker's dozen*

longshoreman *n.* a laborer who loads and unloads ships at a waterfront

long-term bond a bond of slow maturity, running over a longer period than the average

long-term capital gain a capital gain (which see) taxed at less than the regular rate because the asset on whose sale it was realized had been held for a relatively long period

loss leader an article that a store sells cheaply or below cost in order to attract customers

M

managed currency currency that is regulated by various governmental agencies to alter the amount of money in circulation so as to control credit, price structure, etc.

margin *n.* 1. a customer's deposit of money or collateral used by a broker when buying or selling stocks or other commodities for the customer: on this credit the broker advances the rest of the price: margin requirements fluctuate under Federal Reserve regulations 2. equity remaining if a customer's account is closed at prevailing prices 3. difference between the face value of a loan and the market value of collateral put up to secure it

margin of profit the difference between what is paid and what is received in sales

market price the price that a commodity brings when sold in a given market; prevailing price

matched order an order to buy and to sell equal amounts of securities or goods: it is a trick to give the market an air of activity and cause advance in prices, and is illegal

measurement goods goods on which freight is charged by bulk rather than by weight

mechanic's lien a lien against property, as a building, filed by one who has been engaged in its construction or repair and has not been paid for work done or materials supplied: to safeguard against double liability, the owner may require the contractor to give a bond pledging payment to the contractor's own employees, thus confining the matter to the two principals, the owner and the contractor

mercantile paper same as **commercial paper**

merger *n.* a unification of business houses by concentration of their properties under the name of the corporation taking over the business of all

metallic currency coinage of silver, gold, copper, and other metals

middle management those persons in management at a level below that of upper executives

milline *n.* 1. a unit of measurement equal to a one-column agate line (of an advertisement) in one million copies of some publication 2. the cost per milline of an advertisement

money market the very active part of the stock exchange that deals in short-term funds, generally securities that mature in less than a year

money order an order for the payment of money, issued for a fee at one bank, post office, telegraph office, or express company office, and payable at another

moratorium *n.* a period of postponement, either permitted or ordered by government, as a *bank moratorium* in which banking operations are temporarily suspended as a check against panic

mortgage *n.* 1. the pledging of property to a creditor as security against a debt 2. the deed or contract recording this

mortgage bond a bond that is secured by a mortgage on property

mortmain *n.* 1. transfer of real estate to a school, church, or charitable institution 2. the ownership of such real estate

multinational *n.* a corporation with branches in a number of countries

municipal bond a bond issued by a municipality to raise money, as for

schools, improvements, and other needs of town or city government

mutual *adj.* involving common interest: in *life insurance,* a *mutual company* is one in which the holders of policies elect the officers of the company, share the profits of the business, and agree to indemnify one another against loss

mutual fund a type of investment company formed by the pooling together of funds contributed by a number of investors: the funds are usually invested in diversified securities and the profits from the investment are shared mutually by all concerned

mutual savings bank a savings bank in which the profits are distributed among the depositors: it has no capital

N

negotiable *adj.* capable of being transferred through endorsement or surrender to another: *negotiable paper* includes checks, drafts, bills of exchange, and bonds not registered but having coupons payable to bearer

negotiations *n.pl.* an agreeing upon a mercantile transaction; the making of a bargain

net *adj.* left over after certain deductions or allowances have been made, as for expenses, weight of containers or waste materials, nonessential considerations, etc. *n.* a net amount, profit, weight, price, result, etc. *v.t.* to get or bring in as a net; gain

net cash not subject to discount: said of goods

nonassessable *adj.* not subject to assessment: said of a stock whose holders cannot be required to participate in the raising of new capital for the issuing house

no protest note written on a check, draft, note, or other bill of exchange, to indicate to the one who cashes it that in case of nonpayment it is to be returned to the creditor and not protested

O

odd lot in the sale of securities and commodities, a lot of less than 100 shares of stock: see **round lot**

one-name paper commercial paper that is not endorsed and has no cosigner: also called *single-name paper*

open account an account with credit privileges

opening price the figure at which the first sale of the day is made on a stock exchange

open policy in *marine insurance,* a policy which covers specific shipments automatically and covers undefined risks either to a specific kind of goods or in a specific geographic location

overbuy *v.t. & v.i.* to buy more than is needed or justified by ability to pay

overdraft *n.* a check written for a higher amount than that credited to the drawer

overhead *n.* cost of conducting a business; costs which do not come under particular expenses but belong to the whole business, as rent, taxes, insurance, depreciation of plant, etc.

overissue *n.* an issue, as of bonds or stocks, that exceeds authorization, credit limit, etc.

oyer *n.* a copy of a bond or other instrument that is the subject of a suit, given to the opposite party instead of being read aloud, as formerly

P

paid-up shares securities for which the full price has been delivered; nonassessable shares

paid-up value in *insurance,* value of a policy on which payments have ceased, in advance of maturity

paper profits profits showing on outstanding deals but not yet realized or taken

par *n.* the face value of stocks, bonds, etc.: a commodity selling on the market *at par* is selling at face value

par of exchange the value of a unit of one country's currency expressed in terms of that of another country: see also **rate of exchange**

particular average in *marine insurance,* partial damage of a ship alone, or of cargo alone, arising from ordinary wear and tear or mishaps: loss caused by the damage must be borne by those sustaining it with no help from outside interests: see also **general average**

past-due account an account which has matured but has not been settled

patentee *n.* one who holds a patent giving sole right to manufacture and sell an invention

payable *adj.* 1. that can be paid: a paper designated *payable to bearer* need not be endorsed 2. due now or at a specified date

payload *n.* a cargo, or the part of a cargo, producing income

peg *v.t.* to maintain the price of, as a stock, by regulations or by buying and selling freely

penalty *n.* 1. interest forefeited if a security such as a certificate of deposit is redeemed before its date of maturity 2. forfeiture assessed to a contractor, etc. for nonfulfillment of a contract or obligation 3. specified charge if a note is paid up early in the event the note has a *prepayment penalty* clause

perpetual calendar a calendar that is mathematically so arranged that the correct day of the week can be determined for any given date over a wide range of years: see Appendix 8

petitioning creditor a creditor bringing bankruptcy proceedings against a debtor

petty cash a cash fund from which small incidental expenses are paid

petty (or petit) larceny theft involving a sum smaller than that which constitutes **grand larceny** (which see)

planned economy the organization of the economy of a country by which all phases of production are planned as an interdependent whole by some central authority, usually the government: in most modern countries, the phrase may be applied to some parts of the economy

point *n.* 1. a unit of value equal to $1 in quoting prices of stocks, or equal to $10 in quoting prices of bonds 2. one percent of the amount of a mortgage or other loan that is paid to the lender as a premium when the loan is obtained

pool *n.* 1. in the *stock exchange,* a combination of traders seeking market control 2. in *commodity trading,* a group posing as rivals but actually cooperating in an endeavor to control supply and prices

post *n.* a section of the floor of a trading room where trade in one stock is carried on

posting *n.* the transfer from a daybook or journal to the ledger

post-obit *n.* a bond given by a borrower, pledging to pay a debt upon the death of a specified person from whom an inheritance is expected

power of attorney a written statement legally authorizing one person to act for another

preferred creditor a creditor whose claims take legal precedence over others, such as a creditor who holds a first mortgage or one who is owed for personal services

preferred stock stock on which dividends must be paid before any are paid on the common stock, and whose holders have precedence when the assets of a dissolved corporation are distributed

premium *n.* 1. amount by which money or securities are valued above par 2. money paid in addition to interest in obtaining a loan 3. a fee paid by a borrower of securities to the lender, as in short selling 4. payment, usually in installments, for insurance

price current 1. the price named in a list of prices at a certain time, such as dealers circulate among their salespeople and customers 2. market price

price-earnings ratio the ratio of the current market price of a share of stock to

the corporation's annual earnings per share

price fixing artificial regulation of prices, as by a combination of sellers

price index a table of prices of commodities compiled as an indicator of the purchasing power of the dollar: see also **index numbers; price level**

price level average of prices of a number of commodities in relation to a price taken as base (an index number)

price maintenance control, by manufacturer, of price to be charged by retailers; fair-trade agreement or control

prime rate the most favorable rate of interest available on loans from banks

principal *n.* 1. the main body of an estate, as distinguished from income 2. a debt, investment, etc. on which interest is paid 3. the face value of a stock or bond 4. the person for whom a broker or lawyer acts as agent

procuration *n.* a power of attorney

producers' goods see **capital goods**

profit-and-loss account a ledger showing profits, losses, and expenses, with favorable or unfavorable balance: also called *income statement*

program *n.* 1. a logical sequence of operations to be performed by a computer in solving a problem or processing data 2. the coded instructions and data for such a sequence *v.t.* 1. to plan a computer program for (a task, problem, etc.) 2. to furnish (a computer) with a program

promissory note a written promise to pay a certain sum of money to a certain person or bearer on demand or on a specific date

prorate *v.t.* to divide in proportion to respective claims

protest *n.* 1. a formal declaration in writing made by a notary public in behalf of the holder of a bill or note, showing that it has not been honored by the drawer and protesting against all parties liable for any loss or damage by nonpayment 2. declaration by a shipmaster that damage to ship or cargo was due to no fault of ship, officers, or crew

proxy *n.* authority in writing which gives a person the right to vote for another or others, as at a stockholders' meeting

public-service corporation a corporation supplying some essential commodity or service to the public, as a bus company

put *n.* a contract calling upon the issuer to purchase a stock named in the agreement within a specified time at a fixed price, at the option of the purchaser

put and call see **straddle**

Q

qualified endorsement an endorsing signature, with the note "without recourse," or some other qualification which relieves the endorser of responsibility if the note is not paid or not accepted

quick assets current assets; goods or other resources which can readily be converted into cash

quit-claim deed a deed or other legal paper in which a person relinquishes to another a claim or title to some property or right without guaranteeing or warranting such title: distinguished from *warranty deed*

quota *n.* a proportional part

R

raid *n.* a concentrated endeavor by operators in the stock exchange to drive prices down

rate of exchange the ratio between currency of one country and that of another country: it fluctuates as conditions change

rating *n.* an evaluation of the credit or financial standing of a person or firm

rating book a commercial agency's book in which financial standings are given in a special code, with symbols for each rating

real property real estate; land, buildings, etc.

realtor *n.* a real-estate broker holding membership in the National Association of Real Estate Boards

receipt book a book in which receipts are filed

receiver *n.* a person appointed by a court to manage the property and affairs of a person or business house while bankruptcy proceedings or other legal processes affecting the property or business are under way

rediscount *v.t.* to give a second discount, as the action of a Federal Reserve Bank in discounting commercial paper for a member bank

rediscount rate the rate of interest charged for discounting a note or acceptance that has already been discounted once

redlining *n.* the systematic refusal by some lending institutions or insurance companies to issue mortgage loans or insurance on property in certain neighborhoods regarded by them as deteriorating

register *n.* 1. a ship's paper issued by the customhouse, stating description, name, tonnage, nationality, and ownership 2. a listing of the names of ships, together with pertinent information regarding each

registered bond a bond with principal and interest payable only to a listed owner or on his or her order

registrar *n.* an official of a company recording placement and transfers of stocks or bonds, and safeguarding against false transactions

reinsurance *n.* 1. renewed insurance 2. insurance taken out by an insurer with a second insurer to protect the primary insurer against excessive loss 3. the amount of such insurance

reloading *n.* the unscrupulous selling of additional shares of stock of doubtful value to individuals who have already purchased shares of the same stock

rental value the sum for which a property can be rented

repository *n.* a warehouse or storehouse

reserve ratio the amount of cash reserves kept in proportion to liabilities, as in bank statements

resources *n.pl.* assets

respondentia bond a bond for a loan secured on the cargo of a ship, as well as on the ship itself

retailer *n.* a dealer who sells single articles or small amounts to consumers: opposed to *wholesaler*

return *n.* 1. a statement of financial condition 2. the yield of an investment

reversion *n.* the right of succession or the future possession of property, as after the death of a person

risk *n.* 1. the hazard of a new undertaking: as, a good *risk;* a poor *risk* 2. degree of credit standing of an applicant for credit 3. chance of loss to an insurance company

rollover *n.* 1. the refinancing of a maturing note 2. the reinvesting of funds in such a way as to defer the payment of taxes

round lot in the sale of securities and commodities, a lot of shares in a normal trading unit, as 100 shares: see also **odd lot**

royalty *n.* a percentage fee paid the holder of a patent or copyright for the right to make or sell, etc. the article in question

running account an account settled from time to time, and held open: also *open account*

S

sag *n.* a letdown in stock-market prices

salvage *n.* compensation given those who rescue a ship or cargo from loss

saturation point state of a market when normal demands are met and sales depend upon demand at a decreased price

scrip *n.* 1. certificate for a fractional share of stock: such fractional shares may be paid in lieu of a cash dividend 2. a

certificate of indebtedness, issued as currency, as by a local government

secured creditor a creditor whose loan is protected by pledge of property or by unquestionable guarantee in the form of pledged securities

securities company a company depending for its supporting income on securities of other corporations which it holds for investment

security *n.* a document, as a stock certificate or bond, which establishes a right to some form of property: *usually used in pl.*

seigniorage *n.* a government's charge for minting coins from bullion: usually, the difference between face value and intrinsic value

self-insurance *n.* insurance of oneself or one's property by setting aside funds out of current income rather than paying an insurance company

self-liquidating *adj.* providing profit in a short time; converting itself into cash in the normal course of business

sellers' market state of the market in which the seller is at an advantage because demand exceeds supply: see **buyers' market**

seller's option a contract giving the seller of stock shares the privilege of delivering the shares to the buyer at an agreed price on one day's notice during a specified period

sell short 1. to sell securities not owned, but borrowed in expectation of a favorable change in the market 2. to sell a commodity, as wheat, for future delivery, in expectation of a drop in prices

sequestrator *n.* a person appointed to administer sequestrated, or confiscated, property

settlement *n.* full and final payment on a bill, debt, or other obligation

settlor *n.* in *law,* a person who makes a settlement of property

severable *adj.* in *law,* separable into distinct, independent obligations: said of a contract

shade *v.t.* to make a concession in the price of a commodity or security; reduce (a price) slightly

share *n.* 1. any of the parts into which the ownership of a piece of property is divided 2. any one of the equal parts into which the capital stock of a corporation is divided

shave *v.t.* to buy a note at a rate higher than the legal rate of interest or to give a discount exceeding the legal figure

shipping articles articles of agreement between a captain and seamen: also *ship's articles*

shipping clerk one who oversees the shipping of merchandise; one who prepares and keeps records of shipments

shipping order a form filled in with instructions for shipping

ship's papers all the documents that a merchant ship must carry to meet the requirements of port authorities, international law, etc.

short account 1. the account of one who sells securities or commodities short 2. the total short sales in a particular commodity or in the market as a whole

short exchange bills of exchange payable at sight or in a few days

short sale sale of securities or commodities not owned but borrowed, in expectation of buying at a lower price before the date of delivery as contracted

sight draft a draft that is due to be paid when presented

simple interest interest on principal alone, not on previously accumulated interest: distinguished from *compound interest*

single-entry bookkeeping that system of bookkeeping which requires only one entry for a single transaction: the single account consists of a record of cash and of debts owed to and by the concern in question

single-name paper commercial paper, unendorsed: also called *one-name paper*

sinking fund a fund made up of sums of

money set aside at intervals, usually invested at interest, to pay a debt, meet expenses, etc.

slow assets resources which require considerable time to be changed into cash, as real estate, buildings, etc.

slowdown *n.* a slowing down or being slowed down; specifically, a planned slowing down of industrial production on the part of labor or management

smart money 1. in *law*, money paid over and above usual damages, as an extra penalty for gross negligence, cruelty, etc.; exemplary damages 2. money invested cleverly

social insurance any government measure, as a pension plan, health and accident insurance, etc., providing people in low-income groups with assistance during economic and industrial hazards

specialty *n.* a written, sealed, and delivered contract.

speculation *n.* buying and selling of stocks, commodities, land, etc. for immediate profit rather than for investment

split commission a commission shared, as with a customer

stamp duty a law requiring stamps to be affixed to checks and proprietary articles before they may be lawfully sold or used

statement of account presentation of an account since the last payment

statute law a body of laws established by legislative enactment: written, as opposed to *unwritten* or *common law*

stock *n* 1. a debt owed to persons who have lent their money for interest, or the certificates representing this 2. the capital, or fund of invested money, used by a business firm in making its transactions 3. shares of corporate capital, or the certificates of ownership representing them: see **stock certificate**

stockbroker *n.* a person who acts as an agent in buying and selling stocks and bonds

stock certificate a paper evidencing

ownership of shares of stock: also *certificate of stock*

stock dividend a dividend paid in additional shares of the same stock instead of cash

stock in trade goods kept on hand, ready for sale

stocktaking *n.* inventory

stop-loss order an order to a broker to sell when the price falls to a certain figure, or, if selling short, to buy at a certain point: its purpose is to reduce or stop any loss

stop order an order to a broker to buy or sell a certain stock when a specified price is reached

stoppage in transit the right of the seller to stop goods on which delivery has not yet been completed, as when the purchaser has become insolvent

stop payment order by a bank's depositor to refuse payment on a check or draft that has been drawn on that depositor's account

straddle *n.* a combined put and call, giving the holder an option either to buy or sell a specified number of shares at a fixed price within a specified period: see **put; call**

straight bill of lading a bill of lading with no requirement beyond that of delivery to the consignee

subrogation *n.* substituting one creditor for another, along with transference of the rights and claims of the old creditor

sui juris in *law*, legally competent to manage one's own affairs, because of legal age and of sound mind

supercargo *n.* an officer on a merchant ship who is in charge of the cargo

surety *n.* a person who takes on the responsibility for another's debts, defaults of obligations, etc.: this is usually done by posting a *surety bond* to guarantee that a payment will be made, contract fulfilled, etc.

surveyor *n.* agent of an insurance company who examines and reports on applications or claims

suspense account a ledger account containing the amounts of items in doubt, to be credited or debited later to the right accounts

syndicate *n.* a group of individuals or corporations acting together for an agreed purpose, such as underwriting a new issue of securities

T

tally *n.* an account kept by checking off

tallyman *n.* [British] one who sells goods to be paid for in installments

tangible assets resources consisting of property that can be appraised for value, such as real estate or chattels

tare *n.* 1. an allowance for the weight of a container 2. the difference between gross and net weights of a shipment

tariff *n.* 1. a list or system of taxes placed by a government upon exports or, especially, imports 2. a tax of this kind, or its rate 3. any list or scale of prices, charges, etc. *v.t.* 1. to make a schedule of tariffs on; set a tariff on 2. to fix the price according to a tariff

taxpayer *n.* 1. a person who pays a tax; a person subject to taxation 2. a temporary building erected for the purpose of defraying taxes on the land

tenants in common persons holding the same property in common, i.e., with undivided possession and not as joint tenants: the shares held by the several tenants need not be equal

tie-in *adj.* designating a sale in which two or more articles are offered together, often at a reduced price, generally a scarce or desirable item with one of little value *n.* such a sale or item

tight *adj.* 1. difficult to get; scarce in relation to demand: said of commodities on a market 2. characterized by such scarcity, as, a *tight* market: opposed to *easy*

time bargain a firm contract between a buyer and seller for the future sale of stock at a specified price

time deposit a deposit not to be withdrawn until a certain period has elapsed or a specified number of days' notice of intention to withdraw has been given

time draft a draft payable at a future date specified on the draft

time money money borrowed or loaned for a specified period of time

title deed a document that establishes title to property

token payment a partial payment made as a token of intention to pay the remainder of a debt later

Torrenize *v.t.* to register (property) under a statute (called a *Torrens law*) that provides for the registration of the title to land with the government which issues a warranted title deed to said land

trade acceptance a bill of exchange in payment for goods, marked as accepted by the purchaser

trade association an association of merchants or business firms for the unified promotion of their common interests

trade discount percentage off from list price allowed a retailer

trade sale an auction by and for the trade, i.e., those in the same line of business

transfer agent a bank or other financial institution which acts as an agent for a corporation in the transfer of stock from one owner to another

transfer in blank the signing over of a stock certificate without endorsement in the customary place on the back of the certificate: said of a stock, bond, etc. left with a broker or dealer to be sold or transferred

transit duty a tax imposed on goods passing through a country

transportation *n.* conveying goods from one place to another

transshipment *n.* removing goods from one ship or conveyance to another

traveler's check one of a set of checks issued in various denominations by a bank, etc. for the use of a traveler: it is signed when issued and again in the presence of the person cashing it

treasury bill a short-term obligation of the U.S. Treasury, usually maturing in 91 days, bearing no interest and sold periodically on the open market on a discount basis

treasury bond a series of bonds issued by the U.S. Treasury, usually maturing over long periods

treasury certificate an intermediate-term obligation of the U.S. Treasury, usually maturing in one year, paying interest periodically on a coupon basis

treasury note an interest-bearing obligation of the U.S. Treasury with maturities between one and five years

treasury stock shares of issued stock reacquired by the issuing corporation and held by it

trover *n.* an action to recover damages for goods withheld or used by another illegally

trust account a savings account that is turned over to a designated beneficiary upon the death of the depositor

trust company a corporation, under the laws of a state, which administers estates and acts as guardian or trustee, also as fiscal agent

trust deed 1. a deed by which power is given to a group of creditors to foreclose mortgages upon default 2. a deed to property, serving as collateral for a bond issue, and held by a trustee

trustee *n.* 1. a person who holds title to, and administers, property of another 2. a member of a board (*board of trustees*) that manages the affairs of an organization or institution

U

ullage *n.* 1. the amount by which a container of liquid falls short of being full 2. the loss of liquid from a container through evaporation or leakage, or of grain, etc., through spilling or sifting

ultra vires beyond the legal power or authority of a court, corporation, etc.

underlying *adj.* in *finance*, prior, as a claim

underwriter *n.* 1. a person who guarantees against losses or who guarantees loans, stock or bond issues, etc. 2. an agent of an insurance company who determines the acceptability of risks, the premiums that should be charged, etc.

unearned increment increase in value of land or other property from causes other than those of management or direction

upset price the minimim price at which something will be sold at an auction

usance *n.* 1. the time allowed for the payment of a foreign bill of exchange, as established by custom and excluding any period of grace 2. income or other benefits derived from wealth or the use of wealth

usury *n.* excessive or unlawfully high interest on a loan

V

value-added tax a form of indirect sales tax paid on products and services at each stage of production or distribution, based on the value added at that stage and included in the cost to the ultimate consumer

value received a phrase used in notes and bills to express a monetary consideration, without specifying its nature

voidable *adj.* that can be made or adjudged void, or of no effect, as a contract

voucher *n.* 1. a receipt for a payment 2. a check that has been paid and returned to its maker by the bank 3. a document proving a transaction

W

wages *n.pl.* 1. money paid to an employee for work done 2. the share of the total product of industry that goes to labor, as distinguished from the share taken by capital

wage scale 1. a schedule of wages paid for the performance of related jobs or tasks in a given industry, plant, etc. 2. the schedule of wages paid by a given employer

warehouse receipt a receipt for goods deposited in a warehouse: sometimes it is made negotiable and used as collateral for a loan

warrant *n.* 1. a certificate granting the holder the right to buy certain securities at a specified price, usually for a limited time 2. [British] a receipt for goods stored in a warehouse *v.t.* in *law*, to guarantee the title of granted property to (the grantee)

warranty *n.* 1. a seller's assurance to the buyer that goods are as represented 2. a guarantee by the insured that the facts are as stated in regard to an insurance risk, or that specified conditions shall be fulfilled: it constitutes a part of the contract and must be fulfilled to keep the contract in force 3. a covenant by which the seller of real estate gives assurance of, and promises to defend, the security of the title: also called *covenant of warranty*

warranty deed a deed to real estate containing a covenant of warranty (see **warranty,** sense 3): distinguished from *quit-claim deed*

wash sales fake sales of shares of stock made to influence the market: see **matched order**

watered stock stock only partly covered by the capital of the issuing company

wholesaler *n.* one who buys in large quantities to sell to retailers

without recourse without liability on the part of an endorser of a promissory note to pay the amount of the note if the maker or any following endorser fails to do so

working capital capital needed for and used in actual operation of a business

workers' compensation the compensation to an employee for injury or occupational disease suffered in connection with his or her employment, paid under a government-supervised insurance system contributed to by employers

Y

yield *n*. 1. the amount yielded or produced, as on an investment 2. the ratio of the annual dividends or earnings per share of a stock to the market price

Z

zero-base *adj*. designating a technique for preparing a budget, in which each proposed item is evaluated on its merits without considering any previous budget: also **zero-based**

APPENDIX 3

CURRENCY UNITS OF FOREIGN COUNTRIES

(For evaluation in U.S. dollars, check with the foreign exchange department of a bank.)

Afghanistan: afghani
Albania: lek
Algeria: dinar
Andorra: franc; peseta
Angola: kwanza
Argentina: peso
Australia: dollar
Austria: schilling

Bahamas: dollar
Bahrain: dinar
Bangladesh: taka
Barbados: dollar
Belgium: franc
Benin: franc
Bhutan: ngultrum
Bolivia: peso boliviano
Botswana: pula
Brazil: cruzeiro
Bulgaria: lev
Burma: kyat
Burundi: franc

Cambodia (Kampuchea): riel
Cameroon: franc
Canada: dollar
Cape Verde: escudo
Central African Republic: franc
Chad: franc
Chile: peso
China: yuan
Colombia: peso
Comoros: franc
Congo: franc
Costa Rica: colon
Cuba: peso
Cyprus: pound
Czechoslovakia: koruna

Denmark: krone
Djibouti: franc

Dominica: dollar
Dominican Republic: peso

Ecuador: sucre
Egypt: pound
El Salvador: colon
Equatorial Guinea: ekuele
Ethiopia: birr

Fiji: dollar
Finland: markka
France: franc

Gabon: franc
Gambia: dalasi
Germany (East): mark
Germany (West): deutsche mark
Ghana: cedi
Greece: drachma
Guatemala: quetzal
Guinea: syli
Guinea-Bissau: peso
Guyana: dollar

Haiti: gourde
Honduras: lempira
Hungary: forint

Iceland: krona
India: rupee
Indonesia: rupiah
Iran: rial
Iraq: dinar
Ireland: pound
Israel: shekel
Italy: lira
Ivory Coast: franc

Jamaica: dollar
Japan: yen
Jordan: dinar

Kenya: shilling
Kiribati: dollar
Korea (North and South): won
Kuwait: dinar

Laos: kip
Lebanon: pound
Lesotho: rand
Liberia: dollar
Libya: dinar
Liechtenstein: franc
Luxembourg: franc

Madagascar: franc
Malawi: kwacha
Malaysia: ringgit
Maldives: rupee
Mali: franc
Malta: pound
Mauritania: ougiya
Mauritius: rupee
Mexico: peso
Monaco: franc
Mongolia: tugrik
Morocco: dirham
Mozambique: escudo

Nauru: dollar
Nepal: rupee
Netherlands: guilder
New Zealand: dollar
Nicaragua: cordoba
Niger: franc
Nigeria: naira
Norway: krone

Oman: rial

Pakistan: rupee
Panama: balboa
Papua New Guinea: kina
Paraguay: guarani
Peru: sol
Philippines: peso
Poland: zloty
Portugal: escudo

Qatar: riyal

Romania: leu
Rwanda: franc

San Marino: lira
Sao Tome and Principe: conto
Saudi Arabia: riyal
Senegal: franc
Seychelles: rupee
Sierra Leone: leone
Singapore: dollar
Solomon Islands: dollar
Somalia: shilling
South Africa: rand
Spain: peseta
Sri Lanka: rupee
St. Lucia: dollar
St. Vincent: dollar
Sudan: pound
Swaziland: lilangeni
Sweden: krona
Switzerland: franc
Syria: pound

Taiwan: dollar
Tanzania: shilling
Thailand: baht
Togo: franc
Tonga: paanga
Trinidad and Tobago: dollar
Tunisia: dinar
Tuvalu: dollar
Turkey: lira

Uganda: shilling
Union of Soviet Socialist Republics:
  ruble
United Arab Emirates: dirham
United Kingdom: pound
Upper Volta: franc
Uruguay: peso

Vatican City: lira
Venezuela: bolivar
Vietnam: dong

Western Samoa: tala

Yemen (People's Democratic Republic
  of): dinar
Yemen Arab Republic: riyal
Yugoslavia: dinar

Zaire: zaire
Zambia: kwacha
Zimbabwe: dollar

DISTANCES—AIR AND ROAD

AIR MILEAGE BETWEEN PRINCIPAL CITIES OF THE WORLD

	Berlin, Ger.	Bombay, Ind.	Buenos Aires, Arg.	Calcutta, Ind.	Capetown, S.Afr.	Gibraltar	Honolulu, U.S.A.	Istanbul, Turk.	London, Eng.	Los Angeles, U.S.A.	Manila, P.I.	Melbourne, Austl.	Mexico City, Mex.	Moscow, U.S.S.R.	New York, U.S.A.	Oslo, Nor.	Panama, Pan.	Paris, Fr.	Peking, Ch.	Port Said, Eg.	Quebec, Can.	Reykjavik, Ice.	Rio de Janeiro, Braz.	Rome, It.	Seattle, U.S.A.	Shanghai, Ch.	Singapore	Tokyo, Jap.	Valparaiso, Chile	Wellington, N.Z.
Berlin, Ger.	–	3910	7376	4376	5977	1453	7305	1078	574	5782	6128	9919	6037	996	3961	515	5849	542	4567	1747	3583	1479	6144	734	5041	5215	6166	5538	7795	11265
Bombay, Ind.	3910	–	9273	1041	5134	4814	8020	2991	4462	8701	3148	6097	9722	3131	7794	4130	9742	4359	2964	2659	7371	5191	8257	3843	7741	3133	2429	4188	10037	7677
Buenos Aires, Arg.	7376	9273	–	9963	4270	5963	7558	7920	6918	6005	11342	7238	4634	8375	5297	7613	3381	6877	11974	7234	5680	7099	1218	6929	6923	12197	9864	11400	761	6260
Calcutta, Ind.	4376	1041	9963	–	6024	5521	7037	3646	5219	8148	2239	5513	9493	3627	7493	4775	9074	4887	2011	3700	7362	5495	8518	4496	7224	2024	1804	3194	10993	7042
Capetown, S.Afr.	5977	5134	4270	6024	–	5076	11532	5219	6005	9969	7525	6843	8963	6294	7801	6646	6494	5841	8493	5130	7857	6862	3773	5249	10199	8059	6016	9774	5556	7019
Gibraltar	1453	4814	5963	5521	5076	–	7857	1874	1094	6005	7558	10501	5659	2179	3383	1595	4644	1016	5590	1950	3101	1818	4775	1034	5249	6353	7231	6735	6744	12060
Honolulu, U.S.A.	7305	8020	7558	7037	11532	7857	–	8104	7226	2557	5296	5513	3781	7033	4959	6843	5264	7438	5058	8767	5000	6200	8190	8022	2678	4934	6718	3850	6710	4708
Istanbul, Turk.	1078	2991	7920	3646	5219	1874	8104	–	1551	6843	5609	8829	7102	1088	5009	1518	6750	1400	4379	852	4644	2558	6395	854	6067	4959	5373	5556	8172	10663
London, Eng.	574	4462	6918	5219	6005	1094	7226	1551	–	5439	6667	10501	5550	1549	3458	714	5278	214	5054	2234	3101	1171	5772	887	4772	5710	6744	5938	7263	11682
Los Angeles, U.S.A.	5782	8701	6005	8148	9969	6005	2557	6843	5439	–	7269	7931	1542	6068	2451	5054	3101	5654	6251	7528	2579	4310	6750	6326	959	6477	8767	5470	5567	6714
Manila, P.I.	6128	3148	11342	2239	7525	7558	5296	5609	6667	7269	–	3941	8829	5130	8493	5813	9022	6673	1770	5619	8124	6651	11254	6457	6641	1152	1479	1863	11650	5162
Melbourne, Austl.	9919	6097	7238	5513	6843	10501	5513	8829	10501	7931	3941	–	8426	8963	10355	9926	8024	10504	5619	8493	10497	10544	8226	9929	8186	5005	3761	5089	6744	1595
Mexico City, Mex.	6037	9722	4634	9493	8963	5659	3781	7102	5550	1542	8829	8426	–	6663	2085	5666	1495	5706	7753	7706	2454	4622	4770	6353	2339	8039	10307	7035	4635	6899
Moscow, U.S.S.R.	996	3131	8375	3627	6294	2179	7033	1088	1549	6068	5130	8963	6663	–	4662	1016	6711	1541	3597	1710	4242	2050	7179	1474	5179	4235	5238	4650	8792	10279
New York, U.S.A.	3961	7794	5297	7493	7801	3383	4959	5009	3458	2451	8493	10355	2085	4662	–	3671	2231	3636	6844	5602	439	2600	4801	4273	2408	7371	9630	6757	5130	8946
Oslo, Nor.	515	4130	7613	4775	6646	1595	6843	1518	714	5054	5813	9926	5666	1016	3671	–	5706	832	3906	2211	3263	1083	6482	1243	4584	4591	5396	5020	7914	10974
Panama, Pan.	5849	9742	3381	9074	6494	4644	5264	6750	5278	3101	9022	8024	1495	6711	2231	5706	–	5382	8906	6823	2659	5691	3294	5703	3943	9324	11687	9043	2943	7433
Paris, Fr.	542	4359	6877	4887	5841	1016	7438	1400	214	5654	6673	10504	5706	1541	3636	832	5382	–	5106	1975	3235	1380	5699	682	5047	5752	6671	6033	7251	11791
Peking, Ch.	4567	2964	11974	2011	8493	5590	5058	4379	5054	6251	1770	5619	7753	3597	6844	3906	8906	5106	–	4706	6423	4584	10768	5047	5132	662	2774	1307	11774	6698
Port Said, Eg.	1747	2659	7234	3700	5130	1950	8767	852	2234	7528	5619	8493	7706	1710	5602	2211	6823	1975	4706	–	5250	3227	6244	1317	6417	5132	5088	5842	8088	10249
Quebec, Can.	3583	7371	5680	7362	7857	3101	5000	4644	3101	2579	8124	10497	2454	4242	439	3263	2659	3235	6423	5250	–	2189	5125	3943	2353	6981	9097	7160	6417	9228
Reykjavik, Ice.	1479	5191	7099	5495	6862	1818	6200	2558	1171	4310	6651	10544	4622	2050	2600	1083	5691	1380	4584	3227	2189	–	6118	2044	3614	5684	6891	5559	7225	10724
Rio de Janeiro, Braz.	6144	8257	1218	8518	3773	4775	8190	6395	5772	6750	11254	8226	4770	7179	4801	6482	3294	5699	10768	6244	5125	6118	–	5684	6891	11340	9774	11535	1855	7349
Rome, It.	734	3843	6929	4496	5249	1034	8022	854	887	6326	6457	9929	6353	1474	4273	1243	5703	682	5047	1317	3943	2044	5684	–	5684	5677	6232	6124	7235	11524
Seattle, U.S.A.	5041	7741	6923	7224	10199	5249	2678	6067	4772	959	6641	8186	2339	5179	2408	4584	3943	5047	5132	6417	2353	3614	6891	5684	–	5703	8001	4777	6891	7242
Shanghai, Ch.	5215	3133	12197	2024	8059	6353	4934	4959	5710	6477	1152	5005	8039	4235	7371	4591	9324	5752	662	5132	6981	5684	11340	5677	5703	–	2377	1094	10226	6054
Singapore	6166	2429	9864	1804	6016	7231	6718	5373	6744	8767	1479	3761	10307	5238	9630	5396	11687	6671	2774	5088	9097	6891	9774	6232	8001	2377	–	3304	10226	5292
Tokyo, Jap.	5538	4188	11400	3194	9774	6735	3850	5556	5938	5470	1863	5089	7035	4650	6757	5020	9043	6033	1307	5842	7160	5559	11535	6124	4777	1094	3304	–	10635	5785
Valparaiso, Chile	7795	10037	761	10993	5556	6744	6710	8172	7263	5567	11650	6744	4635	8792	5130	7914	2943	7251	11774	8088	6417	7225	1855	7235	6891	10226	10226	10635	–	5760
Wellington, N.Z.	11265	7677	6260	7042	7019	12060	4708	10663	11682	6714	5162	1595	6899	10279	8946	10974	7433	11791	6698	10249	9228	10724	7349	11524	7242	6054	5292	5785	5760	–

AIR MILEAGE BETWEEN PRINCIPAL CITIES OF THE UNITED STATES

	Atlanta, Ga.	Boston, Mass.	Buffalo, N.Y.	Charleston, S.C.	Cheyenne, Wyo.	Chicago, Ill.	Cleveland, Ohio	Dallas, Tex.	Denver, Colo.	Detroit, Mich.	Houston, Tex.	Indianapolis, Ind.	Jacksonville, Fla.	Kansas City, Mo.	Los Angeles, Cal.	Louisville, Ky.	Memphis, Tenn.	Miami, Fla.	Minneapolis, Minn.	New Orleans, La.	New York, N.Y.	Philadelphia, Pa.	Phoenix, Ariz.	Pittsburgh, Pa.	Portland, Ore.	St. Louis, Mo.	Salt Lake City, Utah	San Francisco, Cal.	Seattle, Wash.	Washington, D.C.
Atlanta, Ga.		937	697	267	1229	587	554	721	1212	596	701	426	285	676	1936	319	337	604	907	424	748	666	1592	521	2172	467	1583	2139	2182	543
Boston, Mass.	937		400	820	1735	851	551	1551	1769	613	1605	807	1017	1251	2596	826	1137	1255	1123	1359	188	271	2300	483	2540	1038	2099	2699	2493	393
Buffalo, N.Y.	697	400		699	1335	454	173	1198	1370	216	1286	435	879	861	2198	483	803	1181	803	1086	292	279	1906	178	2156	662	1699	2300	2117	292
Charleston, S.C.	267	820	699		1486	757	891	999	1227	663	1105	240	197	928	2203	316	500	594	1104	558	630	552	1857	528	2425	704	1845	2405	2428	453
Cheyenne, Wyo.	1229	1735	1335	1486		891	1199	663	96	1125	947	986	1605	493	950	882	1033	2049	726	1082	1604	1556	757	1453	1049	795	371	959	1006	1477
Chicago, Ill.	587	851	454	757	891		308	803	920	238	940	165	863	414	1745	269	482	1188	355	833	713	665	1453	410	1739	262	1260	1858	1737	597
Cleveland, Ohio	554	551	173	891	1199	308		1025	1227	95	1312	263	879	753	2049	308	630	1188	622	1091	405	360	1751	115	1991	492	1568	2166	2026	306
Dallas, Tex.	721	1551	1198	999	663	803	1025		663	999	225	763	879	451	1240	726	420	1111	862	443	1374	1299	887	1070	1633	547	999	1483	1744	1185
Denver, Colo.	1212	1769	1370	1227	96	920	1227	663		1156	879	879	1467	558	831	1038	879	1726	700	1082	1631	1579	586	1320	982	796	371	949	1021	1494
Detroit, Mich.	596	613	216	663	1125	238	95	999	1156		1105	240	865	643	1983	316	623	1152	543	939	482	443	1690	205	1955	455	1492	2091	1983	396
Houston, Tex.	701	1605	1286	1105	947	940	1312	225	879	1105		865	816	643	1374	803	484	968	1056	318	1420	1341	1009	1137	1825	679	1199	1645	1891	1220
Indianapolis, Ind.	426	807	435	240	986	165	263	763	879	240	865		585	453	1809	107	384	1024	511	712	646	585	1499	330	1420	231	1200	1949	1891	494
Jacksonville, Fla.	285	1017	879	197	1605	863	879	879	1467	865	816	585		699	2147	594	480	328	1329	481	831	752	1540	751	2439	838	1809	1954	2408	647
Kansas City, Mo.	676	1251	861	928	493	414	753	451	558	643	643	453	699		1356	480	369	1241	413	680	1198	1097	1041	781	1504	238	925	1506	1506	945
Los Angeles, Cal.	1936	2596	2198	2203	950	1745	2049	1240	831	1983	1374	1809	2147	1356		1829	1603	2339	1524	1673	2451	2394	357	2136	825	1589	579	347	959	2300
Louisville, Ky.	319	826	483	316	882	269	308	726	1038	316	803	107	594	480	1829		320	919	605	605	660	623	1508	344	2147	240	1356	1789	1943	476
Memphis, Tenn.	337	1137	803	500	1033	482	630	420	879	623	484	384	480	369	1603	320		872	699	358	957	881	1263	482	1867	240	1250	1802	1943	765
Miami, Fla.	604	1255	1181	594	2049	1188	1188	1111	1726	1152	968	1024	328	1241	2339	919	872		1511	669	1092	1019	1982	1010	2708	1061	2089	2594	2734	923
Minneapolis, Minn.	907	1123	803	1104	726	355	622	862	700	543	1056	511	1329	413	1524	605	699	1511		1051	1018	985	1280	743	1426	466	987	1584	1395	934
New Orleans, La.	424	1359	1086	558	1082	833	1091	443	1082	939	318	712	481	680	1673	605	358	669	1051		1171	1089	1316	919	2058	598	1434	1926	2101	966
New York, N.Y.	748	188	292	630	1604	713	405	1374	1631	482	1420	646	831	1198	2451	660	957	1092	1018	1171		83	2145	317	2445	875	1972	2571	2408	205
Philadelphia, Pa.	666	271	279	1131	1556	665	360	1299	1579	443	1341	585	752	1097	2394	623	881	1019	985	1089	83		2083	259	2445	811	1925	2523	2380	123
Phoenix, Ariz.	1592	2300	1906	1857	1038	1453	1751	887	586	1690	1009	1459	1540	1041	357	1508	1263	1982	1280	1316	2145	2083		1828	1009	1272	559	653	1114	1983
Pittsburgh, Pa.	521	483	178	528	1453	410	115	1070	1320	205	1137	330	751	781	2136	344	482	1010	743	919	317	259	1828		2145	559	1668	2089	2138	192
Portland, Ore.	2172	2540	2156	2425	1298	1739	1991	1633	982	1955	1825	1420	2439	1504	825	2147	1867	2708	1426	2058	2445	2445	1009	2136		1723	636	534	145	2354
St. Louis, Mo.	467	1038	662	704	795	262	492	547	796	455	679	231	838	238	1589	240	240	1061	466	598	875	811	1272	559	1723		1162	1744	1724	712
Salt Lake City, Utah	1583	2099	1699	1845	238	1260	1568	999	371	1492	1199	1200	1809	925	579	1356	1250	2089	987	1434	1972	1925	559	1668	636	1162		600	701	1848
San Francisco, Cal.	2139	2699	2300	2405	959	1858	2166	1483	949	2091	1645	1949	1954	1506	347	1789	1802	2594	1584	1926	2571	2523	653	2089	534	1744	600		678	2442
Seattle, Wash.	2182	2493	2117	2428	1006	1737	2026	1744	1021	1983	1891	1891	2408	1506	959	1943	1943	2734	1395	2101	2408	2380	1114	2138	145	1724	701	678		2329
Washington, D.C.	543	393	292	453	1477	597	306	1185	1494	396	1220	494	647	945	2300	476	765	923	934	966	205	123	1983	192	2354	712	1848	2442	2329	

ROAD MILEAGE BETWEEN PRINCIPAL CITIES OF NORTH AMERICA

City	Albuquerque	Atlanta	Birmingham	Boston	Chicago	Cleveland	Dallas	Denver	Detroit	Houston	Indianapolis	Kansas City	Los Angeles	Mexico City	Miami	Minneapolis	Montreal	Nashville	New Orleans	New York	Omaha	Philadelphia	Phoenix	Portland	St. Louis	Salt Lake City	San Francisco	Seattle	Toronto	Washington
Albuquerque, N. Mex.	—	1381	1251	2172	1281	1560	638	417	1525	834	1266	782	807	1414	1938	1190	2087	1218	1134	1979	858	1899	432	1371	1038	604	1115	1440	1847	1824
Atlanta, Ga.	1381	—	150	1037	674	672	795	1398	699	789	493	798	2182	1768	655	1068	1181	242	479	841	986	741	1793	2601	541	1878	2496	2618	925	608
Birmingham, Ala.	1251	150	—	1165	642	695	645	1286	724	639	475	697	2032	1618	751	1006	1270	196	342	969	898	898	1643	2505	465	1781	2366	2535	950	736
Boston, Mass.	2172	1037	1165	—	963	628	1748	1949	695	1804	917	1427	2979	2783	1504	1368	318	1088	1507	206	1412	296	2604	3046	1141	2343	2976	3095	554	429
Chicago, Ill.	1281	674	642	963	—	335	917	996	266	1067	181	499	2054	2045	1329	405	828	446	912	802	459	738	1713	2083	289	1390	2142	2013	492	671
Cleveland, Ohio	1560	672	695	628	335	—	1159	1321	170	1253	313	779	2367	2251	1264	740	561	513	1030	473	784	413	1992	2418	529	1715	2467	2348	287	346
Dallas, Tex.	638	795	645	1748	917	1159	—	781	1143	243	865	489	1387	1138	1300	936	1705	660	496	1552	644	1452	998	2009	630	1242	1753	2078	1369	1319
Denver, Colo.	417	1398	1286	1949	996	1321	781	—	1273	1019	1058	600	1059	1746	2037	921	2074	1207	1198	1771	537	1691	836	1238	857	504	1235	1307	1479	1616
Detroit, Mich.	1525	699	724	695	266	170	1143	1273	—	1265	273	743	2311	2243	1352	671	562	528	1045	637	716	573	1957	2349	513	1647	2279	2194	226	506
Houston, Tex.	834	789	639	1804	1067	1253	243	1019	1265	—	987	710	1538	1148	1190	1157	1827	769	356	1608	865	1537	1158	2037	779	1438	1912	2279	1479	1375
Indianapolis, Ind.	1266	493	475	917	181	313	865	1058	273	987	—	487	2073	1965	1190	600	841	287	796	713	587	633	1616	2519	243	1504	2209	2227	489	558
Kansas City, Mo.	782	798	697	1427	499	779	489	600	743	710	487	—	1589	1448	1589	447	1305	556	806	1198	201	1118	1208	1809	257	1086	1835	1858	1214	1043
Los Angeles, Cal.	807	2182	2032	2979	2054	2367	1387	1059	2311	1538	2073	1589	—	1917	2687	1889	2873	2025	1883	2786	1595	2706	389	959	1845	715	389	1131	2537	2651
Mexico City, Mex.	1414	1768	1618	2783	2045	2251	1138	1746	2243	1148	1965	1448	1917	—	2073	2169	2805	1917	1305	2786	1782	2587	1549	3256	2785	2291	2852	3273	2852	2354
Miami, Fla.	1938	655	751	1504	1329	1264	1300	2037	1352	1190	1190	1589	2687	2073	—	1723	1654	897	860	1308	1654	1198	2298	3256	1214	2256	3053	3273	1683	1075
Minneapolis, Minn.	1190	1068	1006	1368	405	740	936	921	671	1157	600	447	1889	2169	1723	—	1208	1163	1304	1207	357	1143	1616	1678	552	1143	1940	1678	1131	1076
Montreal, Que.	2087	1181	1270	318	828	561	1705	2074	562	1827	841	1305	2873	2805	1654	1208	—	1074	1591	378	1494	431	2519	2755	1075	2519	2961	2755	335	579
Nashville, Tenn.	1218	242	196	1088	446	513	660	1207	528	769	287	556	2025	1917	897	1163	1074	—	528	892	744	744	1654	2359	299	1636	2333	2376	754	659
New Orleans, La.	1134	479	342	1507	912	1030	496	1198	1045	356	796	806	1883	1305	860	1304	1591	528	—	1311	1007	1251	1490	2505	673	1738	2249	2574	1271	1078
New York, N.Y.	1979	841	969	206	802	473	1552	1771	637	1608	713	1198	2786	2786	1308	1207	378	892	1311	—	1251	100	2411	2885	948	2182	2934	2815	469	233
Omaha, Neb.	858	986	898	1412	459	784	644	537	716	865	587	201	1595	1782	1654	357	1494	744	1007	1251	—	1290	1290	1654	449	931	1683	1638	942	1116
Philadelphia, Pa.	1899	741	898	296	738	413	1452	1691	573	1537	633	1118	2706	2587	1198	1143	431	744	1251	100	1290	—	2331	2821	868	2114	2866	2751	453	133
Phoenix, Ariz.	432	1793	1643	2604	1713	1992	998	836	1957	1158	1616	1208	389	1549	2298	1616	2519	1654	1490	2411	1290	2331	—	1290	1470	648	763	1437	2566	2360
Portland, Ore.	1371	2601	2505	3046	2083	2418	2009	1238	2349	2037	2519	1809	959	3256	3256	1678	2755	2359	2505	2885	1654	2821	1290	—	2060	767	636	172	2625	2835
St. Louis, Mo	1038	541	465	1141	289	529	630	857	513	779	243	257	1845	2785	1214	552	1075	299	673	948	449	868	1470	2060	—	1337	2089	2137	767	793
Salt Lake City, Utah	604	1878	1781	2343	1390	1715	1242	504	1647	1438	1504	1086	715	2291	2256	1143	2519	1636	1738	2182	931	2114	648	767	1337	—	752	836	1873	2047
San Francisco, Cal.	1115	2496	2366	2976	2142	2467	1753	1235	2279	1912	2209	1835	389	2852	3053	1940	2961	2333	2249	2934	1683	2866	763	636	2089	752	—	808	2780	2799
Seattle, Wash.	1440	2618	2535	3095	2013	2348	2078	1307	2194	2279	2227	1858	1131	3273	3273	1678	2755	2376	2574	2815	1638	2751	1437	172	2137	836	808	—	2535	2684
Toronto, Ont.	1847	925	950	554	492	287	1369	1479	226	1479	489	1214	2537	2852	1683	1131	335	754	1271	469	942	453	2566	2625	767	1873	2780	2535	—	456
Washington, D.C.	1824	608	736	429	671	346	1319	1616	506	1375	558	1043	2651	2354	1075	1076	579	659	1078	233	1116	133	2360	2835	793	2047	2799	2684	456	—

© RAND McNALLY & COMPANY, RL 80-Y-28

APPENDIX 5

FORMS OF ADDRESS

PERSON BEING ADDRESSED	ENVELOPE ADDRESS	SALUTATION			IN SPEAKING
		FORMAL	LESS FORMAL OR PERSONAL		
Ambassador (United States)	The Honorable (full name), The Ambassador of the United States, Embassy of the United States of America (city and country)	Sir (or Madam):	My dear Mr. (or Madam) Ambassador:		Mr. Ambassador (or Madam Ambassador)
Ambassador (Foreign)	His (or Her) Excellency (full name), Ambassador of (country), Washington, D.C.	Excellency:	My dear Mr. (or Madam) Ambassador:		Excellency or Mr. Ambassador (or Madam Ambassador) or Sir (or Madam)
Archbishop (Roman Catholic)	The Most Reverend (full name), Archbishop of (city), (city and state, etc.)	Your Excellency: or Most Reverend Sir:	Most Reverend and dear Sir:		Your Excellency
Bishop (Methodist)	Bishop (full name), (city and state, etc.)	My dear Bishop (surname):	Dear Bishop (surname):		Bishop (surname)

Bishop (Protestant Episcopal)	The Right Reverend (full name), Bishop of (diocese), (city and state, etc.)	Right Reverend Sir:	My dear Bishop (surname):	Bishop (surname)
Bishop (Roman Catholic)	The Most Reverend (full name), (church), (city and state, etc.)	Most Reverend Sir:	My dear Bishop (surname):	Bishop (surname)
Brother (of a religious order)	Brother (religious name plus initials of his order), (address, city, and state)	My dear Brother:	Dear Brother (religious name):	Brother (religious name)
Cabinet Officer of the United States	The Honorable (full name), (title), Washington, D.C.	Sir (or Madam): or Dear Sir (or Dear Madam):	My dear Mr. (or Madam) Secretary: or Dear Mr. (or Mrs. or Ms. or Miss) (surname):	Mr. (or Madam) Secretary or Sir (or Madam)
Cardinal (Roman Catholic)	His Eminence (given name) Cardinal (surname), Archbishop of (city, etc.), (city and state, etc.)	Your Eminence:	Your Eminence:	Your Eminence
Common Form (Man)	Mr. (full name), (address, city, and state)	My dear Mr. (surname): or My dear Sir: in plural, Gentlemen:	Dear Mr. (surname): or Dear Sir:	Mr. (surname)
Common Form (Woman)	Mrs. (or Miss or Ms.) (full name), (address, city, and state)	My dear Mrs. (or Miss or Ms.) (surname): or My dear Madam: in plural, Ladies: or Mesdames:	Dear Mrs. (or Miss or Ms.) (surname): or Dear Madam:	Miss (or Mrs. or Ms.) (surname)

SALUTATION

PERSON BEING ADDRESSED	ENVELOPE ADDRESS	FORMAL	LESS FORMAL OR PERSONAL	IN SPEAKING
Consul (United States or other)	(full name), Esquire, American (or other) Consul, (city and country, or state)	Sir (*or* Madam): *or* My dear Sir (*or* My dear Madam):	Dear Mr. (*or* Mrs. *or* Ms. *or* Miss) (surname):	Mr. (*or* Mrs. *or* Ms. *or* Miss) (surname)
Doctor (of Philosophy, Medicine, Divinity, etc.)	(full name), Ph.D., M.D. D.D., etc., *or* Dr. (full name), (address, city, and state)	My dear Dr. (surname): *or* My dear Sir (*or* My dear Madam):	Dear Dr. (surname):	Dr. (surname)
Governor (of a state)	The Honorable (*or in some states* His *or* Her Excellency) (full name), Governor of (state), (capital city and state)	Sir (*or* Madam):	Dear Governor (surname):	Governor (surname) *or* Sir (*or* Madam)
Judge (see also Supreme Court)	The Honorable (full name), Justice (name of court), (city and state)	Sir (*or* Madam):	Dear Judge (surname):	Judge (surname)
Mayor	His (*or* Her) Honor, The Mayor, City Hall (city and state)	Sir (*or* Madam):	My dear Mr. (*or* Madam) Mayor; *or* My dear Mayor (surname):	Mr. (*or* Madam) Mayor
Military Enlisted Personnel (American)	(title of rank), (full name), (address)	Sir (*or* Madam): *or* Dear Sir (*or* Dear Madam):	Dear Private (*or* Airman, etc.) (surname)	Private (*or* Airman, etc.) (surname)

Military Officer (American)	(title of rank), (full name), (address)	Sir (*or* Madam): *or* Dear Sir (*or* Dear Madam):	Dear General (*or* Colonel, Major, Captain, etc.) (surname):	General (*or* Colonel, Major, Captain, etc.) (surname)
Minister (Protestant)	The Reverend (full name plus D.D. if applicable), (address, city, and state)	My dear Sir (*or* My dear Madam): *or* Sir (*or* Madam):	Dear Mr. (*or* Mrs. *or* Ms. *or* Miss *or* Dr.) (surname):	Mr. (*or* Mrs. *or* Ms. *or* Miss *or* Dr. *or, if a Lutheran*, Pastor) (surname)
Monsignor (Roman Catholic)	The Right Reverend Monsignor (surname), (church), (city and state)	Right Reverend and dear Monsignor (surname):	Reverend and dear Monsignor (surname):	Monsignor (surname)
Naval Enlisted Personnel (American)	(title of rank), (full name), (address)	Sir (*or* Madam): *or* Dear Sir (*or* Dear Madam):	Dear Seaman (*or* Quartermaster, etc.) (surname):	Seaman (*or* Quartermaster, etc.) (surname)
Naval Officer (American)	(title of rank), (full name), (address)	Sir (*or* Madam): *or* Dear Sir (*or* Dear Madam):	Dear Admiral (*or* Commodore, Captain, etc.) (surname):	Admiral (*or* Commodore, Captain, etc.) (surname)
Pope	His Holiness the Pope, Vatican City, Italy	Your Holiness:		Your Holiness (*or* Most Holy Father)
President (of the United States)	The President, The White House, Washington, D.C. 20500	Sir: *or* Mr. President:	My dear Mr. President: *or* Dear President (surname):	Mr. President *or* Sir
Priest (Roman Catholic)	The Reverend (full name plus initials of his order), (address, city, and state)	Reverend Father:	Dear Father (surname):	Father (surname) *or* Father

PERSON BEING ADDRESSED	ENVELOPE ADDRESS	SALUTATION		IN SPEAKING
		FORMAL	LESS FORMAL OR PERSONAL	
Professor	Prof. (*or* Dr. if Ph.D.) (full name), Department of (Mathematics, History, etc.), (name of university or college), (address, city, and state)	My dear Sir (*or* My dear Madam): *or* Dear Sir (*or* Dear Madam):	My dear Professor (surname): *or* Dear Dr. (surname):	Professor (*or* Dr. *or* Mr.) (surname). In certain universities (e.g., Harvard) all faculty members are orally addressed as Mr. (*or* Mrs. *or* Ms. *or* Miss) (surname)
Rabbi	Rabbi (full name plus D.D. if applicable), (address, city, and state)	Dear Sir:	Dear Rabbi (*or* Dr.) (surname):	Rabbi (*or* Dr.) (surname)
Representative (of a state legislature	The Honorable (full name), Member of Assembly (or other name of the legislature), (capital city and state)	Sir (*or* Madam):	My dear Mr. (*or* Mrs. *or* Ms. *or* Miss) (surname):	Mr. (*or* Mrs. *or* Ms. *or* Miss) (surname)
Representative (of the United States Congress)	The Honorable (full name), United States House of Representatives, Washington, D.C. 20515	Sir (*or* Madam):	My dear Mr. (*or* Mrs. *or* Ms. *or* Miss) (surname):	Mr. (*or* Mrs. *or* Ms. *or* Miss) (surname)
Senator (of a state legislature)	The Honorable (full name), The Senate of (state), (capital city and state)	Sir (*or* Madam):	Dear Senator (*or* My dear Senator) (surname):	Senator (surname) *or* Mr. (*or* Madam) Senator

Senator (of the United States)	The Honorable (full name), United States Senate, Washington, D.C. 20510	Sir (*or* Madam):	My dear Senator (surname):	Senator (surname) *or* Mr. (*or* Madam) Senator
Sister (of a religious order)	Sister (religious name plus initials of her order), (address, city, and state)	My dear Sister:	Dear Sister (religious name):	Sister (religious name)
Supreme Court (of a state) (Associate Justice)	The Honorable (full name), Associate Justice of the Supreme Court of (state), (address)	Sir (*or* Madam):	Dear Justice (surname):	Mr. (*or* Madam) Justice (surname) *or* Judge (surname)
Supreme Court (of a state) (Chief Justice)	The Honorable (full name), Chief Justice of the Supreme Court of (state), (address)	Sir (*or* Madam):	Dear Mr. (*or* Madam) Chief Justice:	Mr. (*or* Madam) Chief Justice *or* Chief Justice (surname) *or* Judge (surname)
Supreme Court (of the United States) (Associate Justice)	Mr. Justice (surname), The Supreme Court, Washington, D.C. 20543	Sir:	My dear Mr. Justice (surname):	Mr. Justice *or* Mr. Justice (surname) *or* Sir
Supreme Court (of the United States) (Chief Justice)	The Chief Justice, The Supreme Court, Washington, D.C. 20543	Sir:	My dear Mr. Chief Justice:	Mr. Chief Justice *or* Sir
United Nations Delegate (other than U.S.)	His (*or* Her) Excellency, (country) Representative to the United Nations, United Nations, New York 10017	Sir (*or* Madam): *or* Your Excellency:	My dear Mr. (*or* Madam) Ambassador: *or* My dear Mr. (*or* Ms. or Miss or Mrs.) (surname):	Your Excellency

PERSON BEING ADDRESSED	ENVELOPE ADDRESS	SALUTATION		IN SPEAKING
		FORMAL	LESS FORMAL OR PERSONAL	
United Nations Delegate (United States)	The Honorable (full name), United States Permanent Representative to the United Nations, United Nations, New York 10017	Sir (*or* Madam):	My dear Mr. (*or* Madam) Ambassador: *or* My dear Mr. (*or* Ms. *or* Miss *or* Mrs.) (surname):	Mr. Ambassador (*or* Madam Ambassador)
Vice President (of the United States)	The Vice President, United States Senate, Washington, D.C. 20510	Sir:	My dear Mr. Vice President:	Mr. Vice President *or* Sir
Warrant Officer	Warrant Officer (*or* Chief Warrant Officer) (full name), (address)	Sir (*or* Madam): *or* Dear Sir (*or* Dear Madam):	Dear Mr. (*or* Mrs. *or* Ms. *or* Miss) (surname):	Mr. (*or* Mrs. *or* Ms. *or* Miss) (surname)

APPENDIX 6

HOLIDAYS

CHIEF LEGAL OR PUBLIC HOLIDAYS IN THE UNITED STATES

Each state has jurisdiction over holidays that will be observed in that state. They are designated either by the state legislature or by executive proclamation and, therefore, may be changed with each new state executive or legislature. There are no national holidays in the United States. The President and Congress designate holidays only for the District of Columbia and for Federal employees throughout the nation. In most states, holidays that fall on Sunday are observed on the following day.

New Year's Day (January 1)—All the states.

Martin Luther King Birthday (January 15)—Connecticut, Illinois, Louisiana, Maryland, Massachusetts, Michigan, New Jersey, & Ohio. Many groups and institutions in other states also observe this day.

Robert E. Lee's Birthday (Third Monday in January)—Mississippi & (as *Lee-Jackson Day*) Virginia: (January 19)—Arkansas, Georgia, Louisiana, North Carolina, & South Carolina.

Inauguration Day (January 20)—District of Columbia (observed every fourth year).

Mardi gras or *Shrove Tuesday* (Last day before Lent; February or early March)—Alabama & Louisiana.

Lincoln's Birthday (February 12)—Alaska, Arizona, California, Colorado, Connecticut, Delaware, Illinois, Indiana, Iowa, Kansas, Maryland, Michigan, Missouri, Montana, Nebraska, New Jersey, New Mexico, New York, Oregon, Pennsylvania, Rhode Island, Tennessee, Utah, Vermont, Washington, West Virginia.

Washington's Birthday (Third Monday in February)—All the states except Florida. In several states the holiday is called *President's Day* or *Washington-Lincoln Day*.

Good Friday (Friday before Easter Sunday)—All the states. It is a legal holiday in Connecticut, Delaware, Hawaii, Indiana, Kentucky, Louisiana, Maryland, New Jersey, North Dakota, & Tennessee. It is a partial holiday in New Mexico & Wisconsin.

Memorial Day (Last Monday in May)—All the states except Alabama, Mississippi, & South Carolina: (May 30)—Delaware, Florida, Kentucky, Maryland, New Hampshire, New Mexico, South Dakota, & Vermont.

Independence Day (July 4)—All the states.

Labor Day (First Monday in September)—All the states.

Columbus Day (Second Monday in October)—All the states except Alaska, Arkansas, Hawaii, Io-

411

wa, Mississippi, Nevada, North Dakota, Oregon, South Carolina, South Dakota, & Washington: (October 12)—Maryland.

General Election Day (First Tuesday after First Monday in November)—Colorado, Delaware, Hawaii, Illinois, Indiana, Kentucky, Louisiana, Michigan, Missouri, Montana, New Hampshire, New Jersey, New York, North Carolina, Pennsylvania, Rhode Island, South Carolina, Tennessee, Virginia, Wisconsin, & Wyoming. It is observed only when presidential or general elections are held. (Days on which primary elections are held are observed as holidays or partial holidays in some states.)

Veterans Day or *Armistice Day* (November 11)—All the states.

Thanksgiving Day (Fourth Thursday in November)—All the states. The day after Thanksgiving Day is observed as a full or partial holiday in several states.

Christmas Day (December 25)—All the states.

HOLIDAYS IN OTHER COUNTRIES

The following list is of the legal holidays observed in various countries. Business firms and banks are closed on these days. Travelers and others doing business in foreign countries should check with the individual consulates, cultural attachés, or United Nations delegations of the countries with which they are concerned to be sure of the calendar of legal holidays in any particular year. Furthermore, individual provinces and cities may celebrate holidays not included in the national calendar.

Canada—New Year's Day, Jan. 1; Good Friday; Easter Monday (general holiday but some businesses open); Victoria Day and Queen's Day, May 24; Dominion Day, July 1; Civic Holiday in Manitoba, Ontario, and Northwest Territories, usually first Monday in Aug.; Labour Day, first Monday in Sept.; Thanksgiving Day, second Monday in Oct.; Remembrance Day, Nov. 11; Christmas, Dec. 25; Boxing Day, Dec. 26. Each province also has its own holidays.

Denmark—New Year's Day, Jan. 1; Twelfth Night, Jan. 5; Shrove Tuesday; Good Friday; Easter Monday; Queen's Birthday, April 16; General Prayer Day, fourth Friday after Easter; Ascension Day; Constitution Day, June 5 (half holiday); Midsummer Day, June 24; American Independence Day, July 4; Christmas Eve, Dec. 24 (half holiday); Christmas, Dec. 25; New Year's Eve, Dec. 31 (half holiday).

England—New Year's Day, Jan. 1; Easter Monday; Whitmonday; Spring Bank Holiday, last Monday in May; Summer Bank Holiday, last Monday in August; Christmas, Dec. 25; Boxing Day, first weekday after Christmas.

France—New Year's Day, Jan. 1; Easter Monday; Labor Day, May 1; Ascension Day; Bastille

Day, July 14; Assumption, Aug. 15; All Saints' Day, Nov. 1; Armistice Day, Nov. 11; Christmas, Dec. 25. August is a general month of vacations in France, during which very little business is transacted.

Germany, West—New Year's Day, Jan. 1; Good Friday; Easter Monday; Labor Day, May 1; Ascension Day; Whitmonday; Corpus Christi (in Catholic regions); German Unity Day, June 17; Repentance Day, Nov. 21 (except in Bavaria); Christmas, Dec. 25 and 26.

Italy—New Year's Day, Jan. 1; Epiphany, Jan. 6; St. Joseph's Day, Mar. 19; Holy Thursday; Good Friday; Easter Monday (Little Easter); Liberation Day, April 25; Labor Day, May 1; Republic Day (or Constitution Day), June 2; St. Peter and St. Paul Day, June 29; Assumption, Aug. 15; All Saints' Day, Nov. 1; Victory Day (or Unity Day), Nov. 4; Immaculate Conception, Dec. 8; Christmas Eve, Dec. 24 (half holiday); Christmas, Dec. 25; St. Stephen's Day, Dec. 26; New Year's Eve, Dec. 31 (half holiday). August is a general month of vacations in Italy, during which very little business is transacted.

Japan—New Year's Day, Jan. 1; Adults' Day Jan. 15; National Foundation Day, Feb. 11; Vernal Equinox Day, Mar. 20 or 21; Emperor's Birthday, Apr. 29; Constitution and Memorial Day, May 3; Children's Day, May 5; Day of Respect for the Aged, Sept. 15; Autumnal Equinox, Sept. 23 or 24; Sports Day, Oct. 10; Culture Day, Nov. 3; Labor-Thanksgiving Day, Nov. 23. Any holiday that falls on Sunday is celebrated the following day.

Mexico—New Year's Day, Jan. 1; Constitution Day, Feb. 5; Benito Juarez's Birthday, Mar. 21; Good Friday; Easter Monday; Labor Day, May 1; Battle of Puebla Day, May 5; Independence Day, Sept. 16; Columbus Day, Oct. 12; Revolution Day, Nov. 20; Fiesta of Our Lady of Guadalupe, Dec. 12; Christmas, Dec. 25.

Netherlands—New Year's Day, Jan. 1; Queen's Birthday; Good Friday; Easter Monday; Liberation Day, May 5 (in years ending in 0 or 5); Ascension Day; Whitmonday; Christmas, Dec. 25 and 26.

Norway—New Year's Day, Jan. 1; Holy Thursday; Good Friday; Easter Monday; Public Holiday, May 1; Ascension Day; Constitution Day (or Independence Day), May 17; Whitmonday; Christmas, Dec. 25; Boxing Day, Dec. 26.

Sweden—New Year's Day, Jan. 1; Epiphany, Jan. 6; Good Friday; Easter Monday; Labor Day, May 1; Ascension Day; Whitmonday; Midsummer Day, June 24; All Saints' Day, Nov. 1; Christmas, Dec. 25 and 26.

Switzerland—New Year's Day, Jan. 1; Good Friday; Easter Monday; Labor Day, May 1; Ascension Day; Whitmonday; Confederation Day, Aug. 1; Christmas Eve, Dec. 24; Christmas, Dec. 25; St. Stephen's Day, Dec. 26.

MAJOR JEWISH HOLIDAYS, 1980–1988
Holidays begin at sundown of the preceding day. For observances extending two days or more only the first day of the celebration is noted here.

1980—Rosh Hashana, Sept. 11; Yom Kippur, Sept. 20; Sukkot, Sept. 25; Simhat Torah, Oct. 3, Hanuka, Dec. 3

1981—Rosh Hashana, Sept. 29; Yom Kippur, Oct. 8; Sukkot, Oct. 13; Simhat Torah, Oct. 21; Hanuka, Dec. 21; Purim, March 20; Passover, Apr. 19; Shavuot, June 8

1982—Rosh Hashana, Sept. 18; Yom Kippur, Sept. 27; Sukkot, Oct. 2; Simhat Torah, Oct. 10; Hanuka, Dec. 11; Purim, Mar. 9; Passover, Apr. 8; Shavuot, May 28

1983—Rosh Hashana, Sept. 8; Yom Kippur, Sept. 17; Sukkot, Sept. 22; Simhat Torah, Sept. 30; Hanuka, Dec. 1; Purim, Feb. 27; Passover, Mar. 29; Shavuot, May 18

1984—Rosh Hashana, Sept. 27; Yom Kippur, Oct. 6; Sukkot, Oct. 11; Simhat Torah, Oct. 20; Hanuka, Dec. 19; Purim, Mar. 18; Passover, Apr. 17; Shavuot, June 6

1985—Rosh Hashana, Sept. 16; Yom Kippur, Sept. 25; Sukkot, Sept. 30; Simhat Torah, Oct. 8; Hanuka, Dec. 8; Purim, Mar. 7; Passover, Apr. 6; Shavuot, May 26

1986—Rosh Hashana, Oct. 4; Yom Kippur, Oct. 13; Sukkot, Oct. 18; Simhat Torah, Oct. 26; Hanuka, Dec. 27; Purim, Mar. 25; Passover, Apr. 24; Shavuot, June 13

1987—Rosh Hashana, Sept. 24; Yom Kippur, Oct. 3; Sukkot, Oct. 8; Simhat Torah, Oct. 16; Hanuka, Dec. 16; Purim, Mar. 15; Passover, Apr. 14; Shavuot, June 3

1988—Rosh Hashana, Sept. 12; Yom Kippur, Sept. 21; Sukkot, Sept. 26; Simhat Torah, Oct. 4; Hanuka, Dec. 4; Purim, Mar. 3; Passover, Apr. 2; Shavuot, May 22

APPENDIX 7
SIGNS AND SYMBOLS

ASTRONOMY

1. SUN, MOON, PLANETS, ETC.

☉ (1) the sun (2) Sunday
☾, ☽(1) the moon (2) Monday
● new moon
☽, ☽ first quarter
○ full moon
☾, ☾ last quarter
✶, ✱ fixed star
☿ (1) Mercury (2) Wednesday
♀ Venus (2) Friday
⊕, ♁, ⊗ Earth
♂ (1) Mars (2) Tuesday
♃ (1) Jupiter (2) Thursday
♄ (1) Saturn (2) Saturday
♅ Uranus
♆ Neptune
♇ Pluto
☄ comet
①, ②, ③, etc. asteroids in the order of their discovery
α, β, γ, etc. stars (of a constellation) in the order of their brightness; the Greek letter is followed by the Latin genitive of the name of the constellation

2. SIGNS OF THE ZODIAC

Spring Signs
1. ♈ Aries (the Ram)
2. ♉ Taurus (the Bull)
3. ♊ Gemini (the Twins)

Summer Signs
4. ♋, ⊗ Cancer (the Crab)
5. ♌ Leo (the Lion)
6. ♍ Virgo (the Virgin)

Autumn Signs
7. ♎ Libra (the Balance)
8. ♏ Scorpio (the Scorpion)
9. ♐ Sagittarius (the Archer)

Winter Signs
10. ♑, ♑ Capricorn (the Goat)
11. ♒ Aquarius (the Water Bearer)
12. ♓ Pisces (the Fish)

3. ASPECTS AND NODES

☌ conjunction: with reference to bodies having the same longitude, or right ascension
✶ sextile: being 60° apart in longitude, or right ascension
□ quadrature: being 90° apart in longitude, or right ascension
△ trine: being 120° apart in longitude, or right ascension
☍ opposition: being 180° apart in longitude, or right ascension
☊ ascending node
☋ descending node

4. SIGNS AND ABBREVIATIONS USED IN ASTRONOMICAL NOTATION

α mean distance
α, R.A. right ascension
β celestial latitude

4. SIGNS AND ABBREVIATIONS USED IN ASTRONOMICAL NOTATION

D   diameter
α   mean distance
δ   declination
△   distance
e   eccentricity of orbit
G   universal gravitational constant
h, ʰ   hours: as, 5h or 5ʰ
i   inclination to the ecliptic
L, l   mean longitude in orbit
λ   longitude
M   mass
m, ᵐ   minutes of time: as, 5m or 5ᵐ
μ, η mean daily motion
+   north
Ω   longitude of ascending node
π, ω   longitude of perihelion
q   perihelion distance
R   radius or radius vector
—   south
S̄   mean position of satellite
s, ˢ   seconds of time: as, 16s or 16ˢ
T   periodic time
φ   geographical latitude
°   degrees of arc
′   minutes of arc
″   seconds of arc

BIOLOGY

○,⊙,⊕   annual plant
⊙,⊛   biennial plant
♃   perennial herb
△   evergreen plant
⊙   monocarpic plant, that bears fruit but once

♂, ♂   (1) male organism or cell   (2) staminate plant or flower
♀   (1) female organism or cell   (2) pistillate plant or flower
☿   perfect, or hermaphroditic, plant or flower
○   individual, especially female, organism
□   individual, especially male, organism
☿ ♀   unisexual; having male and female flowers separate
☿ — ♀   monoecious; having male and female flowers on the same plant
☿ ∶ ♀   dioecious; having male and female flowers on different plants
♀ ☿ ♀   polygamous; having hermaphroditic and unisexual flowers on the same or different plants
∞   indefinite number, as of stamens when there are more than twenty
0   lacking or absent, as a part
)   turning or winding to the left
(turning or winding to the right
×   crossed with: used of a hybrid
P   parental (generation)
F   filial (generation); offspring
$F_1, F_2, etc.$ offspring of the first, second, third, etc. filial generation
+   possessing a (specified) characteristic
—   lacking a (specified) characteristic
⁎   northern hemisphere
⁎   southern hemisphere
⁑   Old World
⁎   New World
°, ″, ‴   feet, inches, lines
°, ″, ‴   feet, inches, lines (in European usage)

COMMERCE AND FINANCE

$ dollar or dollars: as, $100
¢   cent or cents: as, 13¢
£   pound or pounds sterling: as, £100
/   shilling or shillings: as, 2/6, two shillings and sixpence
@   (1) at: as, 200 @ $1 each   (2) to: as, shoes per pr. $30 @ $50
℔   per

% (1) per cent: as, 5% (2) order of
‰ per thousand
a/c account
B/L bill of lading
B/S bill of sale
c/d, C/D carried down (in bookkeeping)
c/f, C/F carried forward (in bookkeeping)
c/o (1) care of (2) carried over (in bookkeeping)
d/a days after acceptance
d/s days after sight
L/C letter of credit
O/S out of stock
w/ with
w/o without
(1) number (before a figure): as, #5 can (2) pounds (after a figure): as, 25#

COMPUTER SYSTEMS FLOWCHART

terminal: beginning, end, or interruption of a flowchart

input/output: any input/output function, as processing information (input) or printout of processed information (output)

process: any processing function that results in a change in form or location of information

preparation: instructions to modify a program

decision: choice of alternatives at this point

predefined process: a process that is specified elsewhere, as in a subroutine

connector: entry from or to another part of the flowchart

offline storage: on perforated or magnetic tape, cards, or paper

online storage: in a storage unit, as a disc, magnetic tape, etc.

flow direction: direction of data flow: arrows not required if flow is top to bottom or left to right

communication link: transmission of data from one location to another by telephone or other telecommunications medium

annotation: addition of explanatory notes: dotted line extends to flowchart symbol

manual input: data input by an online device, usually a keyboard

manual operation: manual offline operation

punched card

punched tape

document

magnetic tape

transmittal tape

display

MATHEMATICS

1. NUMERATION

Capital letters were sometimes used for the Greek numerals, and lower-case letters are often used for the Roman. In the Roman notation, the value of a character to the right of a larger numeral is added to that of the numeral: as, VI = V + I = 6. I, X, and sometimes C, are also placed to the left of larger numerals and when so situated their value is subtracted from that of such numerals: as, IV, that is, V − I = 4. After the sign IƆ for D, when the character Ɔ was repeated, each repetition had the effect of multiplying IƆ by ten: as, IƆƆ, 5,000; IƆƆƆ, 50,000; and the like. In writing numbers twice as great as these, Ɔ was placed as many times before the stroke I as the Ɔ was written after it. Sometimes a line was drawn over a numeral to indicate thousands: as, C̄ = 100,000

Arabic	Greek	Roman
0	· · ·	· · ·
1	α	I
2	β	II
3	γ	III
4	δ	IV or III
5	ε	V
6	s	VI
7	ζ	VII
8	η	VIII or IIX
9	θ	IX or VIIII
10	ι	X
11	ια	XI

Arabic	Greek	Roman
12	ιβ	XII
13	ιγ	XIII or XIIV
14	ιδ	XIV or XIIII
15	ιε	XV
16	ιϛ	XVI
17	ιζ	XVII
18	ιη	XVIII or XIIX
19	ιθ	XIX or XVIIII
20	κ	XX
30	λ	XXX
40	μ	XL or XXXX
50	ν	L
60	ξ	LX
70	ο	LXX
80	π	LXXX or XXC
90	ϟ	XC or LXXXX
100	ρ	C
200	σ	CC
300	τ	CCC
400	υ	CD or CCCC
500	φ	D or IↃ
600	χ	DC or IↃC
700	ψ	DCC or IↃCC
800	ω	DCCC or IↃCCC
900	· · ·	CM, DCCCC, or ICCCCC
1,000	· · ·	M or CIↃ
2,000	· · ·	MM or CIↃCIↃ

2. CALCULATION

+ (1) plus, the sign of addition: used also to indicate that figures are only approximately exact, some figures being omitted at the end: as, 2.1557 + (2) positive

— (1) minus, the sign of subtraction: used also to indicate that figures have been left off from the end of a number, and that the last figure has been increased by one: as, $2.9378 = 2.94-$ (2) negative

±, ∓ plus or minus: indicating that either of the signs + or – may properly be used; also used to introduce the probable error after a figure obtained by experimentation, etc.

× multiplied by: $5 \times 4 = 20$: multiplication is also indicated by a centered dot $(5 \cdot 4 = 20)$ or by placing the factors in immediate juxtaposition $(2ab = 2 \times a \times b)$

÷ divided by: division is also indicated by the sign: $(x \div y = x : y)$, by a straight line between the dividend and the divisor $(\frac{a}{b})$, or by an oblique line (x/y)

= is equal to; equals

≠ is not equal to

> is greater than: as, $x > y$; that is, x is greater than y

< is less than: as, $x < y$; that is, x is less than y

≮, ≧ is not less than; is equal to or greater than

≯, ≦ is not greater than; is equal to or less than

≎ is equivalent to: applied to magnitudes or quantities that are equal in area or volume, but are not of the same form

≡ is identical with

≅ is congruent to

~ the difference between: used to designate the difference between two quantities without indicating which is the greater: as, $x \sim z =$ the difference between x and z

∝ varies as; is directly proportional to: as, $x \propto y$; that is, x varies as y

∺ geometric proportion: as, $\overset{\cdot\cdot}{\cdot\cdot} x : y : : a : b$; that is, the geometric proportion, x is to y as a is to b

: is to; the ratio of

: : as; equals: used between ratios

∞ indefinitely great; the symbol for infinity

!, ∟ the factorial of, or the continued product of numbers from one upward: as, $5! = 5 \times 4 \times 3 \times 2 \times 1$

∴ therefore

∵ since; because

... and so on

∠ angle: as, $\angle XYZ$

Σ sum: algebraic sum: when used to indicate the summation of finite differences, it has a sense similar to that of the symbol ∫ the continued product of all terms such as (those indicated)

Π pi, the number 3.14159265+: the ratio of the circumference of a circle to its diameter, of a semicircle to its radius, and of the area of a circle to the square of its radius

e, ε the number 2.7182818+: the base of the Napierian system of logarithms; also, the eccentricity of a conic section

M the modulus of a system of logarithms, especially of the common system of logarithms, where it is equal to 0.434294819+

° degrees; as, 90°
' (1) minutes of arc (2) feet
" (1) seconds of arc (2) inches
h hours
m minutes of time
s seconds of time

MEDICINE AND PHARMACY

ĀĀ, Ā, āā [Gr. *ana*] of each
a.c. [L. *ante cibum*] before meals
ad [L.] up to; so as to make: as, *ad*3ij; so as to make two drams
add. [L. *adde*] let there be added; add
ad lib. [L. *ad libitum*] at pleasure; as needed or desired
aq. [L. *aqua*] water
b. (i.) d. [L. *bis (in) die*] twice daily
c̄. [L. *cum*] with
coch. [L. *cochleare*] a spoonful
D. [L. *dosis*] a dose
dil. [L. *dilue*] dilute or dissolve
ess. [L. *essentia*] essence
ft. mist. [L. *fiat mistura*] let a mixture be made
ft. pulv. [L. *fiat pulvis*] let a powder be made
gr. [L. *granum*] a grain
gtt. [L. *guttae*] drops
guttatim [L.] drop by drop
H. [L. *hora*] hour

⌐ right angle
⊥ the perpendicular; is perpendicular to: as, EF ⊥ MN = EF is perpendicular to MN
∥ parallel; is parallel to: as, EF ∥ DG
○ circle; circumference; 360°
⌒ arc of a circle
△ triangle
□ square
▭ rectangle
▱ parallelogram
√, ∛ radical sign; root, indicating, when used without a figure placed above it, the square root: as,$\sqrt{9} = 3$. When any other than the square root is meant, a figure (called the *index*) expressing the degree of the required root, is placed above the sign: as,$\sqrt[3]{27} = 3$
1,2,3, *etc.* exponents, placed above and to the right of a quantity to indicate that it is raised to the first, second, third, etc. power: as, a^2, $(a + b)^3$
', ", ''', *etc.* prime, double (or second) prime, triple (or third) prime, etc., used to distinguish between different values of the same variable; as, x', x'', x''', etc.

These signs indicate that the quantities connected or enclosed by them are to be taken together, as a single quantity

─ vinculum: as, $\overline{x + y}$
( ) parentheses: as, $2(x + y)$
[ ] brackets: as, $a[2(x + y)]$
{ } braces: as, $b + \{2 - a[2(x + y)]\}$
f, F function; function of: as, $f(a)$, a function of a
d differential of: as, da
δ variation of: as, δa
△ finite difference, or increment
D differential coefficient, or derivative
∫ integral; integral of, indicating that the expression following it is to be integrated: as, $\int f(x)dx$ indicates the indefinite integral of $f(x)$ with respect to x
$\int_a^b$ definite integral, indicating the limits of integration: as, $\int_a^b f(x)dx$ indicates the integral of $f(x)$ with respect to x, between the limits a and b

419

MEDICINE AND PHARMACY (con.)

haust. [L. *haustus*] a draft
hor. decub. [L. *hora decubitus*] at bedtime
in d. [L. *in dies*] daily
lot. [L. *lotio*] a lotion
M. [L. *misce*] mix
mac. [L. *macera*] macerate
O., o. [L. *octarius*] a pint
p.c. [L. *post cibum*] after meals
pil. [L. *pilula(e)*] pill(s)
p.r.n. [L. *pro re nata*] as circumstances may require
pulv. [L. *pulvis*] powder
q. (i.) d. [L. *quater (in) die*] four times daily
q.l. [L. *quantum libet*] as much as you please
q.s. [L. *quantum sufficit*] as much as will suffice
q.v. [L. *quantum vis*] as much as you like
℞ [L. *recipe*] take: used at the beginning of a prescription
S., Sig. [L. *signa*] write: used in prescriptions to indicate the directions to be placed on the label of the medicine
t. (i.) d. [L. *ter (in) die*] three times daily
tab. [L. *tabella*] tablet

℥ ounce; ℥i = one ounce; ℥ij = two ounces; ℥ss = half an ounce; ℥iss = one ounce and a half, etc.; ƒℨ = a fluid ounce

ℨ dram; ℨi = one dram; ℨij = two drams; ℨss = half a dram; ℨiss = one dram and a half, etc.; ƒℨ = a fluid dram

Э scruple; Эi = one scruple; Эij = two scruples; Эss = half a scruple; Эiss = one scruple and a half, etc.

♏, ℳ minim

WEATHER

◎ calm
○ clear
● cloudy
◐ partly cloudy
||| fog
∞ haze
⌇ tropical storm
⦂ rain
△ sleet
✳ snow
⍛ thunderstorm

MISCELLANEOUS

&, ℰ (the ampersand) and: as A. B. Smith & Co.
&c. [L. *et cetera*], and others; and so forth
© copyright; copyrighted
® registered trademark
☾ crescent: symbol of Islam
† cross: symbol of Christianity
† Celtic cross: symbol of Protestant Episcopal Church
‡ Russian cross: symbol of Russian Orthodox Church
† Greek cross: symbol of Greek Orthodox Church
℟ response: in religious services, used to mark the part to be uttered by the congregation in answer to the officiant
* in Roman Catholic service books, a mark used to divide each verse of a psalm into two parts, indicating where the response begins
℣,V,v versicle: in religious services, used to mark the part to be uttered by the officiant
☧ (1) a sign of the cross used by the pope, by archbishops, and by bishops, before their names (2) in religious services, used to mark the places where the sign of the cross is to be made
✡ star of David: symbol of Judaism
🕎 menorah: symbol of Judaism
† died: used in genealogies, etc.
× (1) by: used in dimensions, as paper 8 × 11 inches (2) a mark representing a signature, as on a legal document, made by someone unable to write; the name is added by someone else; e.g.

```
                his
       John ×  Doe
               mark
```

☢ radioactive

PROOFREADER'S MARKS

⊙ Insert period
⌃ Insert comma
⊙ or ⁏ Insert colon
⁏ Insert semicolon
! Insert exclamation point
↗ Insert apostrophe or single
   quotation mark
∜ | ∜ Insert quotation marks
(/) Insert parentheses
[/] Insert brackets
‗ Insert hyphen
⅟ Insert en dash
⅟ Insert em dash
?/ Insert question mark
⊙ Query to author
< Insert marginal addition
∝ Delete
⊙/⊙ Delete and close up
⌒ Close up
Insert space
∨ or ⊛ Less space
∨⌃ or ⊛ # Equalize spacing
¶ Paragraph
No ¶ Run in same paragraph

[or] Move to left or to right
⌐ or ⌐ Raise or lower
= Straighten type horizontally
‖ Align type vertically
↝ Transpose
stet Let crossed-out words stand
ctr Center
lc Set in lower-case letters
caps Set in capital letters
sc Set in small capitals
rom Set in roman type
ital Set in italic type
bf Set in boldface type
⊗ Replace imperfect letter
⊃ Reverse upside-down letter
wf Push down space that prints
   Wrong font (wrong size or
   style of type)
sp Spell out word or figure
ldin Insert lead, or space,
   between lines
dld Delete lead, or space,
   between lines

421

APPENDIX 8

TIME

TIME ZONES AND AREA CODES IN THE UNITED STATES

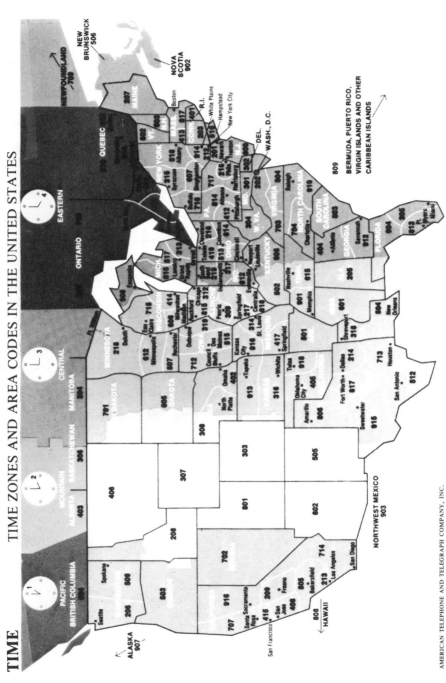

AMERICAN TELEPHONE AND TELEGRAPH COMPANY, INC.

Most of Alaska and all of Hawaii are on Alaska, or Hawaiian, Time; that would be 11 o'clock on the map. Westernmost Alaska and the Aleutian Islands have Bering Time (10 o'clock on the map).

STANDARD TIMES AT 12 NOON, EASTERN STANDARD TIME

(Selected Areas of the World)

AREA	TIME	AREA	TIME
Argentina	2 P.M.	Korea	2 A.M.*
Austria	6 P.M.	Mexico (Mexico City)	11 A.M.
Australia (Sydney)	3 A.M.*	Morocco	5 P.M.
Bangladesh	11 P.M.	Netherlands	6 P.M.
Belgium	6 P.M.	Neth. Antilles (Aruba,	
Brazil	2 P.M.	Bonaire, Curaçao)	1 P.M.
Burma	11:30 P.M.	New Zealand	
Canada (Toronto)	12 noon	(Auckland)	5 A.M.*
Canada (Vancouver)	9 A.M.	Newfoundland	1:30 P.M.
Chile	1 P.M.	Nigeria	6 P.M.
China (Shanghai)	1 A.M.*	Norway	6 P.M.
Colombia	12 noon	Pakistan	10 P.M.
Costa Rica	11 A.M.	Peru	12 noon
Cuba	12 noon	Philippines	1 A.M.*
Czechoslovakia	6 P.M.	Poland	6 P.M.
Denmark	6 P.M.	Portugal	6 P.M.
Dominican Republic	1 P.M.	Romania	7 P.M.
Egypt	7 P.M.	Senegal	5 P.M.
Ethiopia	8 P.M.	Singapore	12:30 A.M.*
Finland	7 P.M.	South Africa	7 P.M.
France	6 P.M.	Spain	6 P.M.
Germany	6 P.M.	Sweden	6 P.M.
Gibraltar	6 P.M.	Switzerland	6 P.M.
Greece	7 P.M.	Thailand	12 midnight
Haiti	12 noon	Tunisia	6 P.M.
Hong Kong	1 A.M.*	Turkey	7 P.M.
Hungary	6 P.M.	United Kingdom	5 P.M.
India	10:30 P.M.	Uruguay	2 P.M.
Indonesia (Java)	12 midnight	U.S.A. (Chicago)	11 A.M.
Iran	8:30 P.M.	U.S.A. (Salt Lake City)	10 A.M.
Iraq	8 P.M.	U.S.A. (San Francisco)	9 A.M.
Ireland	5 P.M.	U.S.S.R. (Moscow,	
Israel	7 P.M.	Leningrad)	8 P.M.
Italy	6 P.M.	U.S.S.R. (Vladivostok)	3 A.M.*
Ivory Coast	5 P.M.	Venezuela	1 P.M.
Jamaica	12 noon	Vietnam	12 midnight
Japan	2 A.M.*	Zaire (Kinshasa)	6 P.M.

* Morning of the following day

CALENDAR TIME

The early Roman calendar was based on the lunar month of 29 1/2 days and had 354 days. But the solar year (the time it takes the earth to circle the sun) is about 365 1/4 days. The Romans added an extra month from time to time to bring the calendar into agreement with the seasons.

A more consistent calendar was instituted by Julius Caesar in 46 B.C. Its year was 365 days with an extra day added in February every fourth year (leap year). The Julian calendar set the length of a month at 30 or 31 days, except for February.

By 1582, the calendar was again out of phase with the seasons. In October of that year, Pope Gregory XIII dropped ten days from the calendar to correct the error that had accumulated. To keep the error from recurring, the Gregorian calendar has leap year every fourth year except those centesimal years which can be divided by 400. Many countries adopted the new calendar at once, but Great Britain and its American colonies waited until 1752. Sometimes two dates are specified for an early event. "Old Style" means the Julian calendar and "New Style" means the Gregorian calendar.

A year is divided into 12 months, 52 weeks, or 365 days (except a leap year, which has 366 days):

January	31 days	July	31 days	
February	28 days	August	31 days	
	(leap year 29)			
March	31 days	September	30 days	1 week has 7 days
April	30 days	October	31 days	1 day has 24 hours
May	31 days	November	30 days	1 hour has 60 minutes
June	30 days	December	31 days	1 minute has 60 seconds

To compute actual days between two dates, find the number of days between months in the chart below and to that add the difference between the days (after February in a leap year, add one day).

FROM ANY DATE IN	TO THE SAME DATE IN											
	Jan.	Feb.	Mar.	Apr.	May	June	July	Aug.	Sept.	Oct.	Nov.	Dec.
January	365	31	59	90	120	151	181	212	243	273	304	334
February	334	365	28	59	89	120	150	181	212	242	273	303
March	306	337	365	31	61	92	122	153	184	214	245	275
April	275	306	334	365	30	61	91	122	153	183	214	244
May	245	276	304	335	365	31	61	92	123	153	184	214
June	214	245	273	304	334	365	30	61	92	122	153	183
July	184	215	243	274	304	335	365	31	62	92	123	153
August	153	184	212	243	273	304	334	365	31	61	92	122
September	122	153	181	212	242	273	303	334	365	30	61	91
October	92	123	151	182	212	243	273	304	335	365	31	61
November	61	92	120	151	181	212	242	273	304	334	365	30
December	31	62	90	121	151	182	212	243	274	304	335	365

PERPETUAL CALENDAR (A.D. 1–2400)

To find calendar for any year, first find Dominical letter for the year in the upper section of table. Two letters are given for leap year; the first for January and February, the second for other months. In the lower section of table, find column in which the Dominical letter for the year is in the same line with the month for which the calendar is desired; this column gives the days of the week that are to be used with the month.

For example, in the table of Dominical letters we find that the letter for 1960, a leap year, is CB; in the line with July, the letter B occurs in the third column; hence July 4, 1960, is Monday.

DOMINICAL LETTERS

				Julian Calendar							Gregorian Calendar				
				0	100	200	300	400	500	600	1500‡	1600	1700	1800	1900
	Century			700	800	900	1000	1100	1200	1300		2000	2100	2200	2300
				1400	1500+										
Year															
0				DC	ED	FE	GF	AG	BA	CB		BA	C	E	G
1	29	57	85	B	C	D	E	F	G	A	F	G	B	D	F
2	30	58	86	A	B	C	D	E	F	G	E	F	A	C	E
3	31	59	87	G	A	B	C	D	E	F	D	E	G	B	D
4	32	60	88	FE	GF	AG	BA	CB	DC	ED	CB	DC	FE	AG	CB
5	33	61	89	D	E	F	G	A	B	C	A	B	D	F	A
6	34	62	90	C	D	E	F	G	A	B	G	A	C	E	G
7	35	63	91	B	C	D	E	F	G	A	F	G	B	D	F
8	36	64	92	AG	BA	CB	DC	ED	FE	GF	ED	FE	AG	CB	ED
9	37	65	93	F	G	A	B	C	D	E	C	D	F	A	C
10	38	66	94	E	F	G	A	B	C	D	B	C	E	G	B
11	39	67	95	D	E	F	G	A	B	C	A	B	D	F	A
12	40	68	96	CB	DC	ED	FE	GF	AG	BA	GF	AG	CB	ED	GF
13	41	69	97	A	B	C	D	E	F	G	E	F	A	C	E
14	42	70	98	G	A	B	C	D	E	F	D	E	G	B	D
15	43	71	99	F	G	A	B	C	D	E	C	D	F	A	C
16	44	72		ED	FE	GF	AG	BA	CB	DC	—	CB	ED	GF	BA
17	45	73		C	D	E	F	G	A	B	—	A	C	E	G
18	46	74		B	C	D	E	F	G	A	—	G	B	D	F
19	47	75		A	B	C	D	E	F	G	—	F	A	C	E
20	48	76		GF	AG	BA	CB	DC	ED	FE	—	ED	GF	BA	DC
21	49	77		E	F	G	A	B	C	D	—	C	E	G	B
22	50	78		D	E	F	G	A	B	C	—	B	D	F	A
23	51	79		C	D	E	F	G	A	B	—	A	C	E	G
24	52	80		BA	CB	DC	ED	FE	GF	AG	—	GF	BA	DC	FE
25	53	81		G	A	B	C	D	E	F	—	E	G	B	D
26	54	82		F	G	A	B	C	D	E	C	D	F	A	C
27	55	83		E	F	G	A	B	C	D	B	C	E	G	B
28	56	84		DC	ED	FE	GF	AG	BA	CB	AG	BA	DC	FE	AG

Month	Dominical letter						
Jan., Oct.	A	B	C	D	E	F	G
Feb., Mar., Nov.	D	E	F	G	A	B	C
Apr., July	G	A	B	C	D	E	F
May	B	C	D	E	F	G	A
June	E	F	G	A	B	C	D
Aug.	C	D	E	F	G	A	B
Sept., Dec.	F	G	A	B	C	D	E

Day											
1	8	15	22	29	Sun.	Sat.	Fri.	Thrus.	Wed.	Tues.	Mon.
2	9	16	23	30	Mon.	Sun.	Sat.	Fri.	Thurs.	Wed.	Tues.
3	10	17	24	31	Tues.	Mon.	Sun.	Sat.	Fri.	Thurs.	Wed.
4	11	18	25		Wed.	Tues.	Mon.	Sun.	Sat.	Fri.	Thurs.
5	12	19	26		Thurs.	Wed.	Tues.	Mon.	Sun.	Sat.	Fri.
6	13	20	27		Fri.	Thurs.	Wed.	Tues.	Mon.	Sun.	Sat.
7	14	21	28		Sat.	Fri.	Thurs.	Wed.	Tues.	Mon.	Sun.

+ On and before 1582, Oct. 4 only. ‡ On and after 1582, Oct. 15 only.

This calendar was prepared by G. M. Clemence, U. S. Naval Observatory, and is reprinted from the Smithsonian Physical Tables, Ninth Edition, by permission of the Smithsonian Institution.

APPENDIX 9

WEIGHTS AND MEASURES

Linear Measure

1 inch	=	2.54	centimeters
12 inches = 1 foot	=	0.3048	meter
3 feet = 1 yard	=	0.9144	meter
5 1/2 yards or 16 1/2 feet = 1 rod	=	5.029	meters
40 rods = 1 furlong	=	201.17	meters

8 furlongs or 1,760 yards
or 5,280 feet = 1 (statute) mile = 1,609.3   meters
3 miles = 1 (land) league =   4.83   kilometers

Square Measure

1 square inch   =   6.452   square centimeters
144 square inches = 1 square foot = 929   square centimeters
9 square feet = 1 square yard =   0.8361 square meter
30 1/4 square yards = 1 square rod   =   25.29   square meters
160 square rods or
4,840 square yards or
43,560 square feet = 1 acre   =   0.4047 hectare
640 acres = 1 square mile = 259   hectares or 2.59
square kilometers

Cubic Measure

1 cubic inch   = 16.387   cubic centimeters
1,728 cubic inches = 1 cubic foot =   0.0283 cubic meter
27 cubic feet   = 1 cubic yard =   0.7646 cubic meter
(in units for cordwood, etc.)
16 cubic feet   = 1 cord foot   =   0.453   cubic meter
8 cord feet   = 1 cord   =   3.625   cubic meters

Nautical Measure

6 feet = 1 fathom   = 1.829 meters
100 fathoms = 1 cable's length (ordinary)
(In the U.S. Navy 120 fathoms or 720
feet = 1 cable's length; in the British
Navy, 608 feet = 1 cable's length.)
10 cables' lengths = 1 nautical mile (6,076.11549 feet,
by international agreement)   = 1.852 kilometers
1 nautical mile = 1.1508 statute miles (the length of a
minute of longitude at the equator)
3 nautical miles = 1 marine league (3.45 statute miles) = 5.56 kilometers
60 nautical miles = 1 degree of a great circle of the earth

Dry Measure

1 pint	=	33.60 cubic inches =	0.5505 liter
2 pints	= 1 quart =	67.20 cubic inches =	1.1012 liters
8 quarts	= 1 peck =	537.61 cubic inches =	8.8098 liters
4 pecks	= 1 bushel =	2,150.42 cubic inches =	35.2383 liters

1 British dry quart = 1.032 U.S. dry quarts.

According to United States government standards, the following are the weights avoirdupois for single bushels of the specified grains: for wheat, 60 pounds; for barley, 48 pounds; for oats, 32 pounds; for rye, 56 pounds; for corn, 56 pounds. Some states have specifications varying from these.

Liquid Measure

1 gill	= 4 fluid ounces =	7.219 cubic inches =	0.1183 liter
	(see next table)		
4 gills	= 1 pint	= 28.875 cubic inches =	0.4732 liter
2 pints	= 1 quart	= 57.75 cubic inches =	0.9464 liter
4 quarts	= 1 gallon	= 231 cubic inches =	3.7854 liters

The British imperial gallon (4 imperial quarts) = 277.42 cubic inches = 4.546 liters. The barrel in Great Britain equals 36 imperial gallons, in the United States, usually 31 1/2 gallons.

Apothecaries' Fluid Measure

1 minim		= 0.0038 cubic inch	= 0.0616 milliliter
60 minims	= 1 fluid dram =	0.2256 cubic inch	= 3.6966 milliliters
8 fluid drams	= 1 fluid ounce =	1.8047 cubic inches	= 0.0296 liter
16 fluid ounces	= 1 pint	= 28.875 cubic inches	= 0.4732 liter

See table immediately preceding for quart and gallon equivalents.
The British pint = 20 fluid ounces.

Circular (or Angular) Measure

60 seconds (")	= 1 minute (')
60 minutes	= 1 degree (°)
90 degrees	= 1 quadrant or 1 right angle
4 quadrants or 360 degrees	= 1 circle

Avoirdupois Weight

(The grain, equal to 0.0648 gram, is the same in all three tables of weight)

1 dram or 27.34 grains		= 1.772 grams
16 drams or 437.5 grains	= 1 ounce	= 28.3495 grams
16 ounces or 7,000 grains	= 1 pound	= 453.59 grams
100 pounds	= 1 hundredweight	= 45.36 kilograms
2,000 pounds	= 1 ton	= 907.18 kilograms

In Great Britain, 14 pounds (6.35 kilograms) = 1 stone, 112 pounds (50.80 kilograms) = 1 hundredweight, and 2,240 pounds (1,016.05 kilograms) = 1 long ton.

Troy Weight

(The grain, equal to 0.0648 gram, is the same in all three tables of weight)

3.086 grains	= 1 carat	= 200	milligrams
24 grains	= 1 pennyweight	= 1.5552	grams
20 pennyweights or 480 grains	= 1 ounce	= 31.1035	grams
12 ounces or 5,760 grains	= 1 pound	= 373.24	grams

Apothecaries' Weight

(The grain, equal to 0.0648 gram, is the same in all three tables of weight)

20 grains	= 1 scruple	= 1.296	grams
3 scruples	= 1 dram	= 3.888	grams
8 drams or 480 grains	= 1 ounce	= 31.1035	grams
12 ounces or 5,760 grains	= 1 pound	= 373.24	grams

THE METRIC SYSTEM
Linear Measure

10 millimeters	= 1 centimeter	= 0.3937	inch
10 centimeters	= 1 decimeter	= 3.937	inches
10 decimeters	= 1 meter	= 39.37	inches or 3.28 feet
10 meters	= 1 decameter	= 393.7	inches
10 decameters	= 1 hectometer	= 328.08	feet
10 hectometers	= 1 kilometer	= 0.621	mile
10 kilometers	= 1 myriameter	= 6.21	miles

Square Measure

100 square millimeters	= 1 square centimeter	= 0.15499	square inch
100 square centimeters	= 1 square decimeter	= 15.499	square inches
100 square decimeters	= 1 square meter	= 1,549.9	square inches or 1.196 square yards
100 square meters	= 1 square decameter	= 119.6	square yards
100 square decameters	= 1 square hectometer	= 2.471	acres
100 square hectometers	= 1 square kilometer	= 0.386	square mile

Land Measure

1 square meter	= 1 centiare	= 1,549.9	square inches
100 centiares	= 1 are	= 119.6	square yards
100 ares	= 1 hectare	= 2.471	acres
100 hectares	= 1 square kilometer	= 0.386	square mile

Volume Measure

1,000 cubic millimeters	= 1 cubic centimeter	= .06102	cubic inch
1,000 cubic centimeters	= 1 cubic decimeter	= 61.02	cubic inches
1,000 cubic decimeters	= 1 cubic meter	= 35.314	cubic feet

(the unit is called a *stere* in measuring firewood)

Capacity Measure

10 milliliters	= 1 centiliter =	.338	fluid ounce
10 centiliters	= 1 deciliter =	3.38	fluid ounces
10 deciliters	= 1 liter =	1.0567	liquid quarts or 0.9081 dry quart
10 liters	= 1 decaliter =	2.64	gallons or 0.284 bushel
10 decaliters	= 1 hectoliter =	26.418	gallons or 2.838 bushels
10 hectoliters	= 1 kiloliter =	264.18	gallons or 35.315 cubic feet

Weights

10 milligrams	= 1 centigram =	0.1543	grain
10 centigrams	= 1 decigram =	1.5432	grains
10 decigrams	= 1 gram =	15.432	grains
10 grams	= 1 decagram =	0.3527	ounce
10 decagrams	= 1 hectogram =	3.5274	ounces
10 hectograms	= 1 kilogram =	2.2046	pounds
10 kilograms	= 1 myriagram =	22.046	pounds
10 myriagrams	= 1 quintal =	220.46	pounds
10 quintals	= 1 metric ton =	2,204.6	pounds

APPENDIX 10

33,000 WORDS SPELLED AND SYLLABIFIED

Each of the words listed alphabetically in the following list will be referred to here as an *entry* or an *entry word*.

1. CONTENT

This list is a quick, accurate, up-to-date guide to the correct spelling and syllabification of more than 33,000 words, based on the widely used *Webster's New World Dictionary of the American Language, Second College Edition.* A special feature is the *Word Finder Table*, which will help you locate a word even though all you know about the word is how to pronounce it.

Many of the entries will settle questions as to whether a certain term is written as one word or with a hyphen or as two words. Answers to specific questions such as the following can be found easily: Do I want the word *anecdote* or *antidote*? When is *hanged* preferred as the past tense and past participle of *hang*? Is the word I want spelled *moot* or *mute*? When is *ringed* used correctly as a verb?

An almost infinite number of words can be formed through the addition of certain prefixes or suffixes to base words. Many of these derived words have been entered. Those that present any question of spelling have been included. For example:

a·gree'a·ble	di·ag'o·nal	di·dac'tic	gar'lic
a·gree'a·bly	di·ag'o·nal·ly	di·dac'ti·cal·ly	gar'lick·y

Obsolete, rare, and archaic forms have been omitted. Many technical terms, especially those in general use, and many colloquial words in common use have been included.

In all, this list has been designed to be as complete and timesaving an aid to spelling and syllabification as possible.

2. WORD DIVISION

All the entry words have been divided into syllables. Each syllable break is indicated by a centered dot, an accent mark, or, in certain cases, a hyphen. Wherever a hyphen *is* used in an entry word, that hyphen is part of the spelling of the word.

A word can be divided from one line to the next between any of its syllables except in the following cases:

a. Never separate from the rest of the word a first or last syllable of only one letter or, if you can avoid it, two letters.

b. Never divide a hyphenated word at any point other than the hyphen.

3. ACCENT MARKS

Accent marks are included to help you find words more quickly. In some cases the accent mark will distinguish one word from another word spelled almost the same way.

lo'cal / lo·cale'   kar'at / ka·ra'te

Two kinds of accent marks are used. The accent mark in heavy type shows that the syllable preceding it receives the main stress, or accent. The lighter one, wherever used, indicates that the preceding syllable receives less stress than the main one but somewhat more than an unmarked syllable.

ag'gra·vate' / dem'on·stra'tion / su'per·vise'

4. PARTS OF SPEECH

Part-of-speech labels (*n.* = noun, *v.* = verb, *adj.* = adjective, *adv.* = adverb) are included here only in special cases. Sometimes this label will give you information about current usage. In all cases the main purpose is to help you be sure you have the word you are looking for. Two of these special cases are explained here.

a. Sometimes a word is accented and syllabified in one way as one part of speech and differently as another. These changes in accent and syllabification are indicated, and the word is identified with the appropriate part-of-speech label; for example: re·cord' *v.* / rec'ord *n.*

b. Sometimes two words are related in meaning and close in spelling and pronunciation. A part-of-speech label is all that is needed to identify each word:

ad·vice' *n.*   proph'e·cy *n.*
ad·vise' *v.*   ·cies
·vised' ·vis'ing   proph'e·sy' *v.*
                       ·sied' ·sy'ing

5. INFLECTED FORMS

Inflected forms include the plurals of nouns, the parts of the verb, and the comparative and superlative forms of the adjective and adverb. All irregularly formed inflected forms have been entered as part of the entry for the base word. To save space, these forms have been shortened in most cases to show only those syllables that are different from the base word. For example:

please   li'a·bil'i·ty   pic'nic
  pleased pleas'ing   ·ties   ·nicked ·nick·ing
fly   eas'y   date
  flies   ·i·er ·i·est   dat'ed dat'ing
  flew flown fly'ing

For verbs, when two forms are given, the first is the past tense and past participle and the second is the present participle. When three forms are given, the first is the past tense, the second is the past participle, and the third is the present participle. Noun, adjective, and adverb forms are easy to identify.

Again to save space, inflected forms of some compound words and derived words have been omitted. These forms can easily be found with the entry for the base word. For example:

   po·lice'man   pre·pack'age   un'der·score'

Occasionally certain inflected forms are used for certain meanings. These are identified. For example:

   staff   ring
    staffs *or* staves   rang rung ring'ing
    (*stick; music*)   (*sound* . . .)
   staffs   ring
    (*people*)   ringed ring'ing
                                (*circle* . . .)

This system of enterng inflected forms as part of the entry for the base word accomplishes at least three things: (1) It helps you distinguish between words that might be confused if entered separately, as in:

   hop   hope
    hopped hop'ping   hoped hop'ing

(2) It saves the time and trouble of searching for a word you might think is spelled one way but is, in fact, spelled differently, as in:

        swim
         swam swum swim'ming

(3) It establishes, without further identification under a separate entry, the specific inflected form that you are looking for (see *fly* above).

One last point: when an entry contains verb forms, this does not necessarily mean that the word is used only as a verb. On the contrary, many of the entries represent the spelling for more than one part of speech. If, for example, a word used as an adjective is already entered as a verb form, and the spelling and syllabification are exactly the same, this word is not entered again separately. You may accept the verb form as the correct spelling for the adjective (see *please* above). If, too, a noun has the same spelling as a verb, no special notation is given (see *picnic* above). Where confusion might exist, some kind of identification is given.

6. USE OF IDENTIFYING DEFINITIONS

It is no doubt clear that this list is not meant to replace the dictionary. It is also clear that in attempting to learn the correct spelling for a specific word, you may run into the difficulty of confusing another word with it. Many instances of such confusion are present in the English language. To help you find the exact word you are seeking, this list contains many cross-references.

Each cross-reference supplies you with a very short *identifying definition* and refers you to another word that may be the one you want.

Confusion may result for any of several reasons. Two of the most common are: (1) similar (but not exactly the same) pronunciation:

mou'ton′
(*fur*; see mutton)

mut'ton
(*food*; see mouton)

(2) exactly the same pronunciation but, usually, a different spelling (such words are called *homonyms*):

la'ma
(*monk*; see llama)
lla'ma
(*animal*; see lama)

leak
(*escape*; see leek)
leek
(*vegetable*; see leak)

Often the words involved are very close alphabetically. In such cases only the identifying terms are given, as in:

less'en
(*make less*)
less'er
(*smaller*)

les'son
(*instruction*)
les'sor
(*one who leases*)

An important thing to note here is that these *identifying definitions* are meant only as an aid to your locating or identifying the word you want. They are not meant to replace or by any means cover the entire dictionary definition.

7. MORE THAN ONE ACCEPTED SPELLING

Many words in the English language have more than one accepted spelling in use today. Because of space limitations, only the variant spellings of the more common words have been included. To help you identify them as variants of the same word, they have, in most cases, been entered together, as part of the same entry. Usually, the first spelling given is the one more frequently used. Sometimes, if they are far apart alphabetically, they are entered as separate entries. Whichever variant spelling you decide on, it is advisable to be consistent and use that same spelling throughout any one piece of writing.

8. PREFIXES

Many derived words have been entered. Since all such words cannot possibly be included, the information given below about certain prefixes will be helpful.

The prefix . . . is usually added to the base word . . .

self ....with a hyphen.
out ....without a hyphen.
over ....without a hyphen.

The prefix . . . is usually added to the base word . . .

---

anti ......
pre ...... } without a hyphen *except* when the prefix is followed by a
pro ......   capital letter.
semi .....
un ....

non ....without a hyphen *except* when the prefix is followed by a capi-
                   tal letter or a word that has a hyphen in it.

re ....without a hyphen *except* to distinguish between a word in
                   which the prefix means *again* or *anew* and a
                   word having a special meaning (*re-lay* and
                   relay).

WORD FINDER TABLE

HAVE YOU EVER tried to look up a word in order to find its spelling when you don't have any idea how to find it—simply because you can't spell it? This *Word Finder Table*, which gives the most common spellings for sounds, will help you end this vicious circle.

Think of the word in terms of its pronounced syllables. *Be sure you are pronouncing the word correctly.*

If the sound is like the	try also the spelling . . .	as in the words . . .
a in fat	ai, au	pl*ai*d, dr*au*ght
a in lane	ai, ao, au, ay, ea, ei, eigh, et, ey	r*ai*n, g*ao*l, g*au*ge, r*ay*, br*ea*k, r*ei*n, w*eigh*, sach*et*, th*ey*
a in care	ai, ay, e, ea, ei	*ai*r, pr*ay*er, th*e*re w*ea*r, th*ei*r
a in father	au, e, ea	g*au*nt, s*e*rgeant, h*ea*rth
a in ago	e, i, o, u, *and combinations, as* ou	*a*gent, san*i*ty, c*o*mply, foc*u*s, vici*ou*s
b in big	bb	ru*bb*er
ch in chin	tch, ti, tu	ca*tch*, ques*ti*on, na*tu*re
d in do	dd, ed	pu*dd*le, call*ed*
e in get	a, ae, ai, ay, ea, ei, eo, ie, u	*a*ny, *ae*sthete, s*ai*d, s*ay*s, br*ea*d, h*ei*fer, l*eo*pard, fr*ie*nd, b*u*ry
e in equal	ae, ay, ea, ee, ei, eo, ey, i, ie, oe	alumn*ae*, qu*ay*, l*ea*n, fr*ee*, dec*ei*t, p*eo*ple, k*ey*, mach*i*ne, ch*ie*f, ph*oe*be
e in here	ea, ee, ei, ie	*ea*r, ch*ee*r, w*ei*rd, b*ie*r
er in over	ar, ir, or, our, re, ur, ure, yr	li*ar*, elix*ir*, auth*or*, glam*our*, ac*re*, aug*ur*, meas*ure*, zeph*yr*
f in fine	ff, gh, lf, ph	cli*ff*, lau*gh*, ca*lf*, *ph*rase
g in go	gg, gh, gu, gue	e*gg*, *gh*oul, *gu*ard, prolo*gue*
h in hat	wh	*wh*o

If the sound is like the	try also the spelling . . .	as in the words . . .
i in it	a, e, ee, ia, ie, o, u, ui, y	usage, English, been, carriage, sieve, women, busy, built, hymn
i in kite	ai, ay, ei, ey, ie, igh, uy, y, ye	aisle, aye, sleight, eye, tie, nigh, buy, fly, rye
j in jam	d, dg, di, dj, g, gg	graduate, judge, soldier, adjective, magic, exaggerate
k in keep	c, cc, ch, ck, cqu, cu, lk, q, qu, que	can, account, chorus, tack, lacquer, biscuit, walk, quick, liquor, baroque
l in let	ll, sl	call, isle
m in me	chm, gm, lm, mb, mm, mn	drachm, paradigm, calm, limb, drummer, hymn
n in no	gn, kn, mn, nn, pn	gnu, kneel, mnemonic, dinner, pneumatic
ng in ring	n, ngue	pink, tongue
o in go	au, eau, eo, ew, oa, oe, oh, oo, ou, ough, ow	mauve, beau, yeoman, sew, boat, toe, oh, brooch, soul, dough, row
o in long	a, ah, au, aw, oa, ou	all, Utah, fraud, thaw, broad, ought
oo in tool	eu, ew, o, oe, ou, ough, u, ue, ui	maneuver, drew, move, shoe, group, through, rule, blue, fruit
oo in look	o, ou, u	wolf, would, pull
oi in oil	oy	toy
ou in out	ough, ow	bough, crowd
p in put	pp	clipper
r in red	rh, rr, wr	rhyme, berry, wrong
s in sew	c, ce, ps, sc, sch, ss	cent, rice, psychology, scene, schism, miss
sh in ship	ce, ch, ci, s, sch, sci, se, si, ss, ssi, ti	ocean, machine, facial, sure, schwa, conscience, nauseous, tension, issue, fission, nation
t in top	ed, ght, pt, th, tt	walked, bought, ptomaine, thyme, better
u in cuff	o, oe, oo, ou	son, does, flood, double
u in use	eau, eu, eue, ew, ieu, iew, ue, ui, you, yu	beauty, feud, queue, few, adieu, view, cue, suit, youth, yule
ur in fur	ear, er, eur, ir, or, our, yr	learn, germ, hauteur, bird, word, scourge, myrtle
v in vat	f, lv, ph	of, salve, Stephen
w in will	o, u, wh	choir, quaint, wheat
y in you	i, j	onion, hallelujah
z in zero	s, sc, ss, x, zz	busy, discern, scissors, xylophone, buzzer
z in azure	ge, s, si, zi	garage, leisure, fusion, glazier

Sometimes, certain letter combinations (rather than single sounds) cause problems when you are trying to find a word. Here are some common ones:

If you've tried . . .	then try . . .	If you've tried . . .	then try . . .	If you've tried . . .	then try . . .
pre	per, pro, pri, pra, pru	cks, gz us	x ous	fiz ture	phys teur
per	pre, pir, pur, par, por	tion	sion, cion, cean, cian	tious air	seous are
is	us, ace, ice	le	tle, el, al	ance	ence
ere	eir, ear, ier	kw	qu	ant	ent
wi	whi	cer	cre	able	ible
we	whe	ei	ie	sin	syn, cin, cyn
zi	xy	si	psy, ci		

A

aard'vark'
aard'wolf'
·wolves'
ab'a·cus'
·cus·es *or* ·ci'
ab'a·lo'ne
a·ban'don
a·base'
·based' ·bas'ing
a·bash'
a·bat'a·ble
a·bate'
·bat'ed ·bat'ing
ab'a·tis
ab'at·toir'
ab'ax'i·al
ab'ba·cy
·cies
ab'bé
ab'bess
ab'bey
ab'bot
ab·bre'vi·ate'
·at'ed ·at'ing
ab·bre'vi·a'tion
ab·bre'vi·a'tor
ab'di·cate'
·cat'ed ·cat'ing
ab'di·ca'tion
ab'di·ca'tor
ab'do·men
ab·dom'i·nal
ab·duct'
ab·duc'tion
ab·duc'tor
ab·er'rant
ab'er·ra'tion
a·bet'
·bet'ted ·bet'ting
a·bey'ance
ab·hor'
·horred' ·hor'ring
ab·hor'rence
ab·hor'rent
a·bide'
·bode' *or* ·bid'ed
·bid'ing
a·bil'i·ty
·ties
ab'ject
ab·jec'tion
ab'ju·ra'tion
ab·jure'
·jured' ·jur'ing
ab'la·tive
a·blaze'
a'ble
·bler ·blest
a'ble-bod'ied
ab·lu'tion
ab'ne·gate'
·gat'ed ·gat'ing
ab'ne·ga'tion

ab·nor'mal
ab'nor·mal'i·ty
·ties
ab·nor'mi·ty
·ties
a·board'
a·bode'
a·bol'ish
ab'o·li'tion
A'-bomb
a·bom'i·na·ble
a·bom'i·nate'
·nat'ed ·nat'ing
a·bom'i·na'tion
a·bom'i·na'tor
ab'o·rig'i·nal
ab'o·rig'i·ne
·nes
a·bort'
a·bor'ti·cide
a·bor'ti·fa'cient
a·bor'tion
a·bor'tive
a·bound'
a·bout'-face'
-faced' -fac'ing
a·bove'bóard'
ab'ra·ca·dab'ra
ab·rade'
·rad'ed ·rad'ing
ab·ra'sion
ab·ra'sive
ab're·act'
ab're·ac'tion
a·breast'
a·bridge'
·bridged'
·bridg'ing
a·bridg'ment
or ·bridge'ment
a·broad'
ab'ro·gate'
·gat'ed ·gat'ing
ab'ro·ga'tion
ab'ro·ga'tor
a·brupt'
ab'scess
ab'scessed
ab·scis'sa
·sas *or* ·sae
ab·scond'
ab'sence
ab'sent *adj.*
ab·sent' *v.*
ab'sen·tee'ism
ab'sent-mind'ed
ab'sinthe *or* ·sinth
ab'so·lute'
ab'so·lu'tion
ab'so·lut'ism
ab·solve'
·solved' ·solv'ing
ab·solv'ent
ab·sorb'
·sorbed' ·sorb'ing
ab·sorb'a·ble
ab·sorb'en·cy
ab·sorb'ent

ab·sorp'tion
ab·stain'
ab·ste'mi·ous
ab·sten'tion
ab'sti·nence
ab'sti·nent
ab·stract'
ab·strac'tion
ab·struse'
ab·surd'
ab·surd'i·ty
·ties
a·bun'dance
a·bun'dant
a·buse'
·bused' ·bus'ing
a·bus'er
a·bu'sive
a·but'
·but'ted ·but'ting
a·but'ment
a·but'ter
a·bys'mal
a·bys'mal·ly
a·byss'
a·ca'cia
ac'a·de'mi·a
ac'a·dem'ic
ac'a·dem'i·cal
ac'a·dem'i·cal·ly
a·cad'e·mi'cian
ac'a·dem'i·cism
a·cad'e·my
·mies
ac'a·jou'
a·can'thus
·thus·es *or* ·thi
a' cap·pel'la
A'ca·pul'co
ac·cede'
·ced'ed ·ced'ing
(*agree;* see
exceed)
ac·cel'er·an'do
ac·cel'er·ant
ac·cel'er·ate'
·at'ed ·at'ing
ac·cel'er·a'tion
ac·cel'er·a'tor
ac·cel'er·om'e·ter
ac'cent
ac·cen'tu·al
ac·cen'tu·al·ly
ac·cen'tu·ate'
·at'ed ·at'ing
ac·cen'tu·a'tion
ac·cept'
(*receive;* see
except)
ac·cept'a·bil'i·ty
ac·cept'a·ble
ac·cept'a·bly
ac·cept'ance
ac'cep·ta'tion
ac·cept'ed
(*approved;* see
excepted)
ac·cep'tor

ac'cess
(*approach;* see
excess)
ac·ces'si·bil'i·ty
ac·ces'si·ble
ac·ces'sion
ac·ces'so·ry
or ·sa·ry
·ries
ac'ci·dent
ac'ci·den'tal
ac'ci·den'tal·ly
ac·claim'
ac'cla·ma'tion
ac'cli·mate'
·mat'ed ·mat'ing
ac·cli'ma·tize'
·tized' ·tiz'ing
ac·cliv'i·ty
ac·cli'vous
ac'co·lade'
ac·com'mo·date'
·dat'ed ·dat'ing
ac·com'mo·da'·
tion
ac·com'pa·ni·
ment
ac·com'pa·nist
ac·com'pa·ny
·nied ·ny·ing
ac·com'plice
ac·com'plish
ac·com'plished
ac·cord'
ac·cord'ance
ac·cord'ant·ly
ac·cord'ing
ac·cor'di·on
ac·cost'
ac·count'
ac·count'a·bil'·
i·ty
ac·count'a·ble
ac·count'a·bly
ac·count'ant
ac·count'ing
ac·cou'ter
ac·cou'ter·ments
ac·cred'it
ac·cred'it·a'tion
ac·cre'tion
ac·cru'al
ac·crue'
·crued' ·cru'ing
ac·cul'tu·rate'
·rat'ed ·rat'ing
ac·cul'tu·ra'tion
ac·cu'mu·la·ble
ac·cu'mu·late'
·lat'ed ·lat'ing
ac·cu'mu·la'tion
ac·cu'mu·la'tive
ac·cu'mu·la'tor
ac'cu·ra·cy
ac'cu·rate
ac'cu·rate·ly
ac·curs'ed *or*
ac·curst'

ac·cus'al
ac'cu·sa'tion
ac·cu'sa·tive
ac·cu'sa·to'ry
ac·cuse'
·cused' ·cus'ing
ac·cus'tom
ac·cus'tomed
a·cer'bi·ty
·ties
ace'e·tate'
ace'e·tone'
a·cet'y·lene'
ache
ached ach'ing
a·chiev'a·ble
a·chieve'
·chieved'
·chiev'ing
a·chieve'ment
ach'ro·mat'ic
a·chro'ma·tism
a·chro'ma·tize'
·tized' ·tiz'ing
A'chro·my'cin
ach'y
ach'i·er ach'i·est
ac'id-fast'
ac'id-form'ing
a·cid'ic
a·cid'i·fi'er
a·cid'i·fy'
·fied' ·fy'ing
a·cid'i·ty
ac'i·do'sis
a·cid'u·late'
·lat'ed ·lat'ing
a·cid'u·lous
ac·knowl'edge
·edged ·edg·ing
ac·knowl'edge·
a·ble
ac·knowl'edg·
ment *or*
·edge·ment
ac'me
ac'ne
ac'o·lyte'
ac'o·nite'
a'corn
a·cous'tic *or*
·ti·cal
a·cous'ti·cal·ly
ac·quaint'
ac·quaint'ance
ac·qui·esce'
·esced' ·esc'ing
ac'qui·es'cence
ac'qui·es'cent
ac·quir'a·ble
ac·quire'
·quired' ·quir'ing
ac·quire'ment
ac·qui·si'tion
ac·quis'i·tive
ac·quit'
·quit'ted
·quit'ting

ac·quit'tal
a'cre
a'cre·age
ac'rid
a·crid'i·ty
ac'ri·mo'ni·ous
ac'ri·mo'ny
ac'ro·bat'
ac'ro·bat'ic
ac'ro·bat'i·cal·ly
ac'ro·nym
ac'ro·pho'bi·a
a·crop'o·lis
a·cross'
a·cros'tic
a·cryl'ic
act'a·ble
act'a·bil'i·ty
act'ing
ac·tin'i·um
ac·ti·nom'e·ter
ac'ti·no·my'cin
ac'tion
ac'ti·vate'
·vat'ed ·vat'ing
ac'ti·va'tion
ac'ti·va'tor
ac'tive
ac'tiv·ism
ac'tiv·ist
ac·tiv'i·ty
·ties
ac'tiv·ize'
·ized ·iz'ing
ac'tor
ac'tress
ac'tu·al
ac'tu·al'i·ty
·ties
ac'tu·al·ize'
·ized' ·iz'ing
ac'tu·al·ly
ac'tu·ar'i·al
ac'tu·ar'y
·ies
ac'tu·ate'
·at'ed ·at'ing
ac'tu·a'tion
ac'tu·a'tor
a·cu'i·ty
·ties
a·cu'men
ac'u·punc'ture
a·cute'
a·cute'ly
ad'age
a·da'gio
·gios
ad'a·mant
a·dapt'
(*fit;* see adept,
adopt)
a·dapt'a·bil'i·ty
a·dapt'a·ble
ad'ap·ta'tion *or*
a·dap'tion
a·dapt'er *or*
a·dap'tor

a·dap'tive
add'a·ble or ·i·ble
ad·den'dum
·da
ad'der
(snake)
add'er
(one who adds)
ad'dict
ad·dic'tion
ad·dic'tive
ad·di'tion
(an adding; see edition)
ad·di'tion·al
ad·di'tion·al·ly
ad'di·tive
ad'dle
·dled ·dling
ad'dle·brained'
ad·dress'
ad'dress·ee'
ad·duce'
·duced' ·duc'ing
ad·duc'i·ble
ad·duc'tion
ade·e·noi'dal
ad'e·noids'
ad·ept'
(skilled; see adapt, adopt)
ad'e·qua·cy
ad'e·quate
ad'e·quate·ly
ad·here'
·hered' ·her'ing
ad·her'ence
ad·her'ent
ad·he'sion
ad·he'sive
ad·hoc'
ad·hom'i·nem'
a·dieu'
ad·in·fi·ni'tum
ad·in'ter·im
ad'i·pose'
ad·ja'cen·cy
ad·ja'cent
ad'jec·tive
ad·join'
(be next to)
ad·journ'
(suspend)
ad·judge'
·judged'
·judg'ing
ad·ju'di·cate'
·cat'ed ·cat'ing
ad·ju'di·ca'tion
ad·ju'di·ca'tor
ad'junct
ad·ju·ra'tion
ad·jure'
·jured' ·jur'ing
ad·just'
ad·just'a·ble
ad·just'er or

·jus'tor
ad·just'ment
ad'ju·tant
ad'-lib'
-libbed' -lib'bing
ad'man'
·men'
ad·min'is·ter
ad·min'is·tra·ble
ad·min'is·trate'
·trat'ed ·trat'ing
ad·min'is·tra'tion
ad·min'is·tra'tive
ad·min'is·tra'tor
ad'mi·ra·ble
ad'mi·ra·bly
ad'mi·ral
ad'mi·ral·ty
·ties
ad'mi·ra'tion
ad·mire'
·mired' ·mir'ing
ad·mir'er
ad·mis·si·bil'i·ty
ad·mis'si·ble
ad·mis'si·bly
ad·mis'sion
ad·mit'
·mit'ted ·mit'ting
ad·mit'tance
ad·mit'ted·ly
ad·mix'
ad·mix'ture
ad·mon'ish
ad·mo·ni'tion
ad·mon'i·to'ry
ad'nau'se·am
a·do'
a·do'be
ad·o·les'cence
ad·o·les'cent
a·dopt'
(choose; see adapt, adept)
a·dop'tion
a·dop'tive
a·dor'a·ble
ad·o·ra'tion
a·dore'
·dored' ·dor'ing
a·dorn'
a·dorn'ment
ad·re'nal
ad·ren'al·in
a·drift'
a·droit'
ad·sorb'
ad·sor'bent
ad·sorp'tion
ad'u·late'
·lat'ed ·lat'ing
ad'u·la'tion
a·dul'ter·ant
a·dul'ter·ate'
·at'ed ·at'ing
a·dul'ter·a'tion
a·dul'ter·er
a·dul'ter·ess n.

a·dul'ter·ous adj.
a·dul'ter·y
a·dult'hood
ad·um'brate
·brat·ed ·brat·ing
ad'va·lo'rem
ad·vance'
·vanced'
·vanc'ing
ad·vance'ment
ad·van'tage
ad'van·ta'geous
ad'ven·ti'tious
ad·ven'ture
·tured ·tur·ing
ad·ven'tur·er
ad·ven'ture·some
ad·ven'tur·ous
ad'verb
ad·ver'bi·al
ad'ver·sar'y
·ies
ad·verse'
(opposed; see averse)
ad·verse'ly
ad·ver'si·ty
·ties
ad·vert'
ad·vert'ent
ad'ver·tise' or
·tize'
·tised' or ·tized'
·tis'ing or
·tiz'ing
ad'ver·tise'ment
or ·tize'ment
ad·vice' n.
ad·vis'a·bil'i·ty
ad·vis'a·ble
ad·vis'a·bly
ad·vise' v.
·vised' ·vis'ing
ad·vis'ed·ly
ad·vise'ment
ad·vis'er or
·vi'sor
ad·vi'so·ry
ad'vo·ca·cy
ad'vo·cate'
·cat'ed ·cat'ing
Ae·ge'an
ae'gis
ae'on
aer'ate'
·at'ed ·at'ing
aer·a'tion
aer'a·tor
aer'i·al
aer'i·al·ist
aer'ie or ·y
aer'o·bal·lis'tics
aer'o·bat'ics
aer'obe
aer'o·dy·nam'i·cal·ly
aer'o·dy·nam'ics
aer'o·me·chan'·ics

aer'o·med'i·cine
aer'o·nau'ti·cal
aer'o·nau'tics
aero'o·neu·ro'sis
aer'o·sol'
aer'o·space
aer'o·stat'ics
Ae'sop
aes'thete'
aes·thet'ic
aes·thet'i·cal·ly
aes·thet'i·cism
af'fa·bil'i·ty
af'fa·ble
af'fa·bly
af·fair'
af·fect'
(to influence; see effect)
af'fec·ta'tion
af·fect'ed
af·fec'tion
af·fec'tion·ate
af·fec'tive
(of feelings; see effective)
af·fi'ance
·anced ·anc·ing
af'fi·da'vit
af·fil'i·ate'
·at'ed ·at'ing
af·fil'i·a'tion
af·fin'i·ty
af·firm'
af·fir·ma'tion
af·firm'a·tive
af·firm'a·tive·ly
af·fix'
·fixed' or ·fixt'
·fix'ing
af·flict'
af·flic'tion
af'flu·ence
af'flu·ent
(rich; see effluent)
af·ford'
af·fray'
af·front'
af'ghan
a·fi'cio·na'do
a·field'
a·fire'
a·flame'
a·float'
a·fore'men'tioned
a·fore'said'
a·fore'thought'
a·fore'time'
a·foul'
a·fraid'
A'-frame'
a·fresh'
Af'ri·can
af'ter
af'ter·birth'
af'ter·burn'er
af'ter·damp'

af'ter·ef·fect'
af'ter·glow'
af'ter·im'age
af'ter·life'
af'ter·math'
af'ter·noon'
af'ter·shock'
af'ter·taste'
af'ter·thought'
af'ter·ward
a·gain'
a·gainst'
a·gape'
ag'ate
ag'ate·ware'
age
aged, ag'ing or age'ing
age'less
age'long'
a'gen·cy
·cies
a·gen'da
a'gent
age'-old'
ag·glom'er·ate'
·at'ed ·at'ing
ag·glom'er·a'tion
ag·glu'ti·nant
ag·glu'ti·nate'
·nat'ed ·nat'ing
ag·glu'ti·na'tion
ag·gran'dize'
·dized' ·diz'ing
ag·gran'dize·ment
ag'gra·vate'
·vat'ed ·vat'ing
ag'gra·va'tion
ag'gre·gate'
·gat'ed ·at'ing
ag'gre·ga'tion
ag·gres'sion
ag·gres'sive
ag·gres'sor
ag·grieve'
·grieved'
·griev'ing
a·ghast'
ag'ile
ag'ile·ly
a·gil'i·ty
ag'i·tate'
·tat'ed ·tat'ing
ag'i·ta'tion
ag'i·ta'tor
ag'it·prop'
a·gleam'
ag'let
a·glow'
ag·nos'tic
ag·nos'ti·cal·ly
ag·nos'ti·cism
a·gog'
ag'o·nize'
·nized' ·niz'ing
ag'o·ny
·nies

ag·o·ra·pho'bi·a
a·grar'i·an
a·gree'
greed' ·gree'ing
a·gree'a·bil'i·ty
a·gree'a·ble
a·gree'a·bly
ag'ri·busi'ness
ag'ri·cul'tur·al
ag'ri·cul'ture
ag'ri·cul'tur·ist
or ·tur·al·ist
a·gron'o·my
a·ground'
a'gue
a'gu·ish
a·head'
aid
(help)
aide
(assistant)
aide'-de-camp' or
aid'-de-camp'
aides'- or aids'-
ail
(be ill; see ale)
ai'le·ron'
ail'ing
ail'ment
aim'less
air
(gases; see heir)
air base
air'borne'
air brake
air'bra'sive
air'brush'
air coach
air'-con·di'tion
air'-con·di'tioned
air conditioner
air conditioning
air'-cool'
air'-cooled'
air'craft'
air'drome'
air'drop'
·dropped'
·drop'ping
air'-dry'
-dried' -dry'ing
air express
air'field'
air'foil'
air force
air'frame'
air gun
air hole
air'i·ly
air'i·ness
air'ing
air lane
air'lift'
air'line'
air'lin'er
air lock
air'mail'

air'man
·men
air'-mind'ed
air'mo'bile
air'plane'
air'port'
air pressure
air'proof'
air pump
air raid
air'scape'
air'ship'
air'sick'
air'space'
air'speed'
air'-sprayed'
air'stream'
air'strip'
air'tight'
air'waves'
air'wor'thy
air'y
air'i·er air'i·est
aisle
(passage; see isle)
a·kim'bo
Al'a·bam'a
al'a·bas'ter
a' la carte'
a·lac'ri·ty
à' la king'
a' la mode'
or à' la mode'
a·larm'ing
a·larm'ist
A·las'ka
al'ba·core'
al'ba·tross'
al·be'it
al'bi·nism
al·bi'no
·nos
al'bum
al·bu'men
(egg white)
al·bu'min
(class of proteins)
Al'bu·quer'que
al'che·mist
al'che·my
al'co·hol'
al'co·hol'ic
al'co·hol·i·cal·ly
al'co·hol'ism
al'cove
al'der·man
·men
ale
(a drink; see ail)
a'le·a·to'ry
ale'house'
a·lert'ly
A·leu'tian
ale'wife'
·wives'
al·fal'fa
al·fres'co
al'gae

al'gae·cide'
al'ge·bra
al'ge·bra'ic
al'ge·bra'i·cal·ly
al'i·as
al'i·bi'
·bis
·bied' ·bi'ing
al'ien
al'ien·ate'
·at'ed ·at'ing
al'ien·a'tion
a·light'
·light'ed or ·lit'
·light'ing
a·lign' or a·line'
·ligned' or ·lined'
·lign'ing or
·lin'ing
a·lign'ment
or a·line'ment
a·like'
al'i·men'ta·ry
(nourishing; see
elementary)
al'i·mo'ny
al'i·quant
al'i·quot
a·live'
al'ka·li'
·lies' or ·lis'
al'ka·line
al'ka·lize'
·lized' ·liz'ing
al'ka·loid'
al'kyd
all'-A·mer'i·can
all'-a·round'
al·lay'
·layed' ·lay'ing
all'-clear'
al'le·ga'tion
al·lege'
·leged' ·leg'ing
al·leg'ed·ly
Al'le·ghe'ny
al·le'giance
al·le·gor'i·cal
al'le·go·rize'
·rized' ·riz'ing
al'le·go'ry
·ries
al·le·gret'to
al·le'gro
al·le·lu'ia
al'ler·gen
al·ler·gen'ic
al·ler'gic
al'ler·gist
al'ler·gy
·gies
al·le'vi·ate'
·at'ed ·at'ing
al·le'vi·a'tion
al'ley
·leys
(narrow lane;
see ally)

al'ley·way'
al·li'ance
al·lied'
al'li·ga'tor
all'-im·por'tant
all'-in·clu'sive
al·lit'er·ate'
·at'ed ·at'ing
al·lit'er·a'tion
al'lo·cate'
·cat'ed ·cat'ing
al'lo·ca'tion
al·lot'
·lot'ted ·lot'ting
al·lot'ment
al·lot'tee'
all'-out'
all'o'ver
al·low'
al·low'a·ble
al·low'ance
al·lowed'
(permitted; see
aloud)
al'loy
all'-pur'pose
all right
all'spice'
all'-star'
all'-time'
al·lude'
·lud'ed ·lud'ing
(refer to; see
elude)
al·lure'
·lured' ·lur'ing
al·lu'sion
(mention; see
elusion, illusion)
al·lu'sive
(mentioning; see
elusive, illusive)
al·lu'vi·al
al·lu'vi·um
·vi·ums or ·vi·a
al·ly' v. al'ly n.
·lied' ·ly'ing
·lies
(join; partner;
see alley)
al'ma ma'ter
al'ma·nac'
al·might'y
al'mond
al'mon·er
al'most
alms
a·loft'
a·lo'ha
a·long'shore'
a·long'side'
a·loof'
a·loud'
(loudly; see
allowed)
al'pac·a
al'pen·stock'
al'pha·bet'

al'pha·bet'i·cal
al'pha·bet'i·cal·ly
al'pha·bet·ize'
·ized' ·iz'ing
al·read'y
al'so·ran'
al'tar
(table for
worship)
al'ter
(to change)
al'ter·cate'
·cat'ed ·cat'ing
al'ter·ca'tion
al'ter·nate'
·nat'ed ·nat'ing
al'ter·na'tion
al·ter'na·tive
al'ter·na'tor
al·though'
al·tim'e·ter
al'ti·tude'
al'to
·tos
al·to·geth'er
al'tru·ism
al'tru·is'tic
a·lu'mi·num
a·lum'na n.fem.
·nae
a·lum'nus
n.masc.
·ni
al'ways
a·mal'ga·mate'
·mat'ed ·mat'ing
a·mal'ga·ma'tion
a·man'u·en'sis
·ses
am'a·ryl'lis
am'a·teur'
am'a·to'ry
a·maze'
·mazed'
·maz'ing
a·maze'ment
Am'a·zon'
am·bas'sa·dor
am·bas'sa·do'ri·al
am'ber
am'ber·gris'
am'bi·ance
am'bi·dex·ter'i·ty
am'bi·dex'trous
am'bi·ent
am'bi·gu'i·ty
am·big'u·ous
am·bi'tion
am·bi'tious
am·biv'a·lence
am'ble
·bled ·bling
am·bro'sia
am'bu·lance
am'bu·late'
·lat'ed ·lat'ing
am'bu·la·to'ry

am'bus·cade'
·cad'ed ·cad'ing
am'bush
a·me'ba
·bas or ·bae
a·mel'io·rate'
·rat'ed ·rat'ing
a·mel'io·ra'tion
a·mel'io·ra'tive
a·me'na·bil'i·ty
a·me'na·ble
a·mend'
(revise; see
emend)
a·mend'ment
a·men'i·ty
·ties
A·mer'i·can
A·mer'i·ca'na
A·mer'i·can·ism
A·mer'i·can·i·
za'tion
A·mer'i·can·ize'
·ized' ·iz'ing
Am'er·ind'
am'e·thyst
a'mi·a·bil'i·ty
a'mi·a·ble
a'mi·a·bly
am'i·ca·bil'i·ty
am'i·ca·ble
am'i·ca·bly
a·mid'
a·mid'ships
a·midst'
a·mi'no
Am'ish
a·miss'
am'i·ty
·ties
am'me'ter
am·mo'nia
am'mu·ni'tion
am·ne'sia
am·ne'si·ac' or
am·ne'sic
am'nes·ty
·ties, ·tied ·ty·ing
a·moe'ba
·bas or ·bae
a·mok'
a·mong'
a·mongst'
a·mon'til·la'do
a·mor'al
a'mor·al'i·ty
am'o·rous
a·mor'phous
am'or·ti·za'tion
am'or·tize'
·tized' ·tiz'ing
a·mount'
a·mour'
am'per·age
am'pere
am'per·sand'
am·phet'a·mine'
am·phib'i·an

am·phib'i·ous
am'phi·the'a·ter
am'pho·ra
·rae or ·ras
am'ple
am'pli·fi·ca'tion
am'pli·fi'er
am'pli·fy'
·fied' ·fy'ing
am'pli·tude'
am'ply
am'pul
am·pul'la
·las or ·lae
am'pu·tate'
·tat'ed ·tat'ing
am'pu·ta'tion
am'pu·tee'
a·muck'
a·mu'let
a·muse'
·mused'
·mus'ing
a·muse'ment
a·nach'ro·nism
a·nach'ro·nis'tic
an'a·con'da
a·nae'mi·a
a·nae'mic
an·aes·the'sia
an·aes·thet'ic
an·aes'the·tize'
·tized' ·tiz'ing
an'a·gram'
a'nal
an'al·ge'si·a
an'al·ge'sic
an'a·log' computer
a·nal'o·gize'
·gized' ·giz'ing
a·nal'o·gous
a·nal'o·gy
·gies
a·nal'y·sis
·ses'
an'a·lyst
(one who
analyzes; see
annalist)
an'a·lyt'i·cal
or an'a·lyt'ic
an'a·lyt'i·cal·ly
an'a·lyze'
·lyzed' ·lyz'ing
an'a·pest'
an·ar'chic
or an·ar'chi·cal
an'ar·chism
an'ar·chist
an'ar·chis'tic
an'ar·chy
·chies
an'as·tig·mat'ic
a·nas'tro·phe
a·nath'e·ma
·mas
a·nath'e·ma·tize'
·tized' ·tiz'ing

an'a·tom'i·cal
or an'a·tom'ic
an·a·tom'i·cal·ly
a·nat'o·mist
a·nat'o·mize'
·mized' ·miz'ing
a·nat'o·my
·mies
an'ces'tor
an·ces'tral
an'ces'tress
an'ces'try
·tries
an'chor
an'chor·age
an'cho·rite'
an'cho'vy
·vies
an'cient
an'cil·lar'y
an·dan'te
and'i'ron
and/or
an'dro·gen
an'ec·dot'al
an'ec·dote'
(story; see
antidote)
a·ne'mi·a
a·ne'mic
a·nem'o·graph'
an'e·mom'e·ter
a·nem'o·ne'
an'er·oid'
an'es·the'sia
an'es·the'si·
ol'o·gy
an'es·thet'ic
an·es'the·tist
an·es'the·tize'
·tized' ·tiz'ing
an'gel
(spirit; see angle)
an'gel·fish'
an·gel'ic
or an·gel'i·cal
an·gel'i·cal·ly
An'ge·lus
an'ger
an·gi'na
an'gle
·gled ·gling
(corner; scheme;
see angel)
an'gler
an'gle·worm'
An'gli·can
An'gli·cism
An'gli·cize'
·cized' ·ciz'ing
an'gling
An'glo-A·mer'i·
can
An'glo·ma'ni·a
An'glo·phile'
An'glo-Sax'on
An·go'ra
an'gos·tu'ra

an'gri·ly
an'gry
·gri·er ·gri·est
an'guish
an'gu·lar
an·gu·lar'i·ty
·ties
an·gu·la'tion
an·hy'drous
an'ile
a·nil'i·ty
an'i·mad·ver'
sion
an'i·mal
an'i·mal'cule
an'i·mal·ism
an'i·mal·is'tic
an'i·mal·ize'
·ized' ·iz'ing
an'i·mate'
·mat'ed ·mat'ing
an'i·ma'tor
or ·mat'er
an'i·ma'tion
an'i·mism
an'i·mos'i·ty
·ties
an'i·mus
an'i'on
an'ise
an'i·seed'
an'i·sette'
ankh
an'kle
an'kle·bone'
an'klet
an'nal·ist
(a writer of
annals; see
analyst)
an'nals
An·nap'o·lis
an·neal'
an'ne·lid
an·nex' v.
an'nex n.
an·nex·a'tion
an·ni'hi·late'
·lat'ed ·lat'ing
an·ni'hi·la'tion
an·ni'hi·la'tor
an'ni·ver'sa·ry
·ries
an'no·tate'
·tat'ed ·tat'ing
an'no·ta'tion
an·nounce'
·nounced'
·nounc'ing
an·nounce'ment
an·nounc'er
an·noy'
an·noy'ance
an'nu·al
an'nu·al·ly
an·nu'i·tant
an·nu'i·ty
·ties

an·nul'
·nulled'
·nul'ling
an'nu·lar
an·nul'ment
an'nu·lus
·li' or ·lus·es
an·nun'ci·ate'
·at'ed ·at'ing
(announce; see
enunciate)
an·nun'ci·a'tor
an'ode
an'o·dize'
·dized' ·diz'ing
an'o·dyne'
a·noint'
a·nom'a·lous
a·nom'a·ly
·lies
an'o·mie
a·non'y·mi·ty
a·non'y·mous
a·noph'e·les'
an·oth'er
an'swer
ant·ac'id
an·tag'o·nism
an·tag'o·nis'tic
an·tag'o·nize'
·nized' ·niz'ing
ant·al'ka·li'
·lies' or ·lis'
ant·arc'tic
Ant·arc'ti·ca
an'te
·ted or ·teed
·te·ing
an'te- prefix
(before; see
anti-)
ant'eat'er
an'te·bel'lum
an'te·cede'
·ced'ed ·ced'ing
an'te·ced'ence
an'te·ced'ent
an'te·cham'ber
an'te·date'
an'te·di·lu'vi·an
an'te·lope'
an'te me·ri'di·em
an·ten'na
·nae or ·nas
an'te·pe'nult
an·te'ri·or
an'te·room'
an'them
an'ther
an·thol'o·gist
an·thol'o·gy
·gies
an'thra·cite'
an'thrax
·thra·ces'
an'thro·poid'
an'thro·pol'o·gist
an'thro·pol'o·gy

an'thro·po·mor'·
phic
an'ti- prefix
(against; see
ante-)
an'ti·air'craft
an'ti·bac·te'ri·al
an'ti·bi·ot'ic
an'ti·bod'y
·ies
an'tic
·ticked ·tick·ing
an·tic'i·pant
an·tic'i·pate'
·pat'ed ·pat'ing
an·tic'i·pa'tion
an·tic'i·pa·to'ry
an'ti·cli·mac'tic
an'ti·cli'max
an'ti·de·pres'sant
an'ti·dote'
(remedy; see
anecdote)
an'ti·freeze'
an'ti·gen
an'ti·he'ro
an'ti·his'ta·mine'
an'ti·knock'
an'ti·la'bor
An·til'les
an'ti·ma·cas'sar
an'ti·mat'ter
an'ti·mo'ny
an'ti·nov'el
an'ti·par'ti·cle
an'ti·pas'to
an'ti·pa·thet'ic
an·tip'a·thy
·thies
an'ti·per'son·nel'
an'ti·phon
an·tiph'o·nal
an'ti·po'dal
an'ti·pode'
an'ti·po·des'
an'ti·quar'i·an
an'ti·quar'y
·ies
an'ti·quate'
·quat'ed
·quat'ing
an·tique'
·tiqued'
·tiqu'ing
an·tiq'ui·ty
·ties
an'ti·Sem'ite
an'ti·Se·mit'ic
an'ti·Sem'i·tism
an'ti·sep'sis
an'ti·sep'tic
an'ti·so'cial
an·tith'e·sis
·ses'
an'ti·thet'i·cal
an'ti·thet'i·
cal·ly
an'ti·tox'in

an'ti·trust'
ant'ler
an'to·nym'
an'trum
·trums or ·tra
a'nus
·nus·es or ·ni
an'vil
anx·i'e·ty
·ties
anx'ious
an'y·bod'y
an'y·how'
an'y·one'
an'y·thing'
an'y·way'
an'y·where'
A'-OK' or
A'-O·kay'
a·or'ta
·tas or ·tae
a·pace'
a·part'heid
a·part'ment
ap'a·thet'ic
ap'a·thet'i·
cal·ly
ap'a·thy
·thies
ap'pe·ri·tif'
ap'er·ture
a'pex
a'pex·es or
ap'i·ces
a·pha'si·a
aph'o·rism
aph'ro·dis'i·ac'
a'pi·ar'y
·ies
a·piece'
a·plomb'
a·poc'a·lypse'
a·poc'a·lyp'tic
a·poc'ry·phal
ap'o·gee'
a·pol'o·get'ic
a·pol'o·get'i·
cal·ly
ap'o·lo'gi·a
a·pol'o·gize'
·gized' ·giz'ing
ap'o·logue'
a·pol'o·gy
·gies
ap'o·plec'tic
ap'o·plex'y
a·pos'ta·sy
a·pos'tate
a' pos·te'ri·o'ri
a·pos'tle
ap'os·tol'ic
a·pos'tro·phe
ap'os·troph'ic
a·pos'tro·phize'
·phized'
·phiz'ing
a·poth'e·car'y
·ies

ap'o·thegm'
(short saying)
ap'o·them'
(math. term)
a·poth'e·o'sis
·ses
Ap'pa·la'chi·an
ap·pall' or pall'
·palled' ·pall'ing
ap'pa·loo'sa
ap'pa·ra'tus
·tus or ·tus·es
ap·par'el
·eled or ·elled
·el·ing or ·el·ling
ap·par'ent
ap'pa·ri'tion
ap·peal'
ap·pear'ance
ap·peas'a·ble
ap·pease'
·peased'
·peas'ing
ap·pease'ment
ap·peas'er
ap·pel'lant
ap·pel'late
ap'pel·la'tion
ap·pend'
ap·pend'age
ap·pend'ant or
·ent
ap·pen·dec'to·my
·mies
ap·pen·di·ci'tis
ap·pen'dix
·dix·es or
·di·ces'
ap'per·cep'tion
ap·per·tain'
ap'pe·tite'
ap'pe·tiz'er
ap'pe·tiz'ing
ap·plaud'
ap·plause'
ap'ple·jack'
ap'ple·sauce'
ap·pli'ance
ap'pli·ca·bil'i·ty
ap'pli·ca·ble
ap'pli·cant
ap'pli·ca'tion
ap'pli·ca'tor
ap·plied'
ap'pli·qué'
·quéd' ·qué'ing
ap·ply'
·plied' ·ply'ing
ap·pog'gia·tu'ra
ap·point'
ap·point·ee'
ap·poin'tive
ap·point'ment
ap·por'tion
ap'po·site
ap'po·si'tion
ap·prais'a·ble
ap·prais'al

ap·praise'
·praised'
·prais'ing
(estimate; see
apprise)
ap·prais'er
ap·pre'ci·a·ble
ap·pre'ci·ate'
·at'ed ·at'ing
ap·pre'ci·a'tion
ap·pre'ci·a'tive
ap'pre·hend'
ap'pre·hen'sion
ap'pre·hen'sive
ap·pren'tice
·ticed ·tic·ing
ap·prise' or
·prize'
·prised' or
·prized'
·pris'ing or
·priz'ing
(inform; see
appraise)
ap·proach'
ap·proach'·
a·ble
ap'pro·ba'tion
ap·pro'pri·ate'
·at'ed ·at'ing
ap·pro'pri·ate·ly
ap·pro'pri·a'tion
ap·prov'a·ble
ap·prov'al
ap·prove'
·proved'
·prov'ing
ap·prox'i·mate'
·mat'ed ·mat'ing
ap·prox'i·mate·ly
ap·prox'i·ma'·
tion
ap·pur'te·nance
a'pri·cot'
A'pril
a·pri·o'ri
ap'ro·pos'
apt'i·tude'
apt'ly
aq'ua·cade'
aq'ua·lung'
aq'ua·ma·rine'
aq'ua·naut'
aq'ua·plane'
a·quar'i·um
·i·ums or ·i·a
a·quat'ic
aq'ua·tint'
aq'ue·duct'
a'que·ous
aq'ui·line'
ar'a·besque'
A·ra'bi·an
Ar'a·bic
ar'a·ble
a·rach'nid
ar'bi·ter
ar'bi·tra·ble

ar·bit'ra·ment
ar'bi·trar'i·ly
ar'bi·trar'i·ness
ar'bi·trar'y
ar'bi·trate'
·trat'ed ·trat'ing
ar'bi·tra'tion
ar'bi·tra'tor
ar'bor
ar·bo're·al
ar'bo·re'tum
·tums or ·ta
ar'bor·vi'tae
arc
arced or arcked
arc'ing or arck'ing
(curve; see ark)
ar'cade'
ar'chae·o·log'i·cal
ar'chae·ol'o·gy
ar·cha'ic
arch·an'gel
arch'bish'op
arch'dea'con
arch'di'o·cese
arch'duch'y
·ies
arch'duke'
arched
arch'en'e·my
·mies
ar'che·o·log'i·cal
ar'che·ol'o·gy
arch'er·y
ar'che·type'
arch'fiend'
ar'chi·pel'a·go'
·goes' or ·gos'
ar'chi·tect'
ar'chi·tec·ton'ics
ar'chi·tec'tur·al
ar'chi·tec'tur·
al·ly
ar'chi·tec'ture
ar'chi·trave'
ar'chives
arch'priest'
arch'way'
arc'tic
ar'dent
ar'dor
ar'du·ous
ar'e·a·way'
a·re'na
aren't
Ar'gen·ti'na
ar'gon
ar'got
ar'gu·a·ble
ar'gu·a·bly
ar'gue
·gued ·gu·ing
ar'gu·ment
ar'gu·men·
ta'tion
ar'gu·men'ta·
tive
a'ri·a

a·rid'i·ty
ar'id·ness
a·rise'
·rose' ·ris'en
·ris'ing
ar'is·toc'ra·cy
·cies
a·ris'to·crat'
a·ris'to·crat'ic
a·ris'to·crat'i·
cal·ly
Ar'is·to·te'li·an
Ar'is·tot'le
a·rith'me·tic' n.
ar·ith·met'ic adj.
ar'ith·met'i·cal
ar·ith·me·ti'cian
Ar'i·zo'na
ark
(enclosure;
see arc)
Ar'kan·sas'
ar·ma'da
ar'ma·dil'lo
·los
ar'ma·ment
ar'ma·ture
arm'chair'
armed
arm'ful
·fuls
arm'hole'
ar'mi·stice
arm'let
ar'mor
ar'mored
ar'mor-plat'ed
ar'mor·y
·ies
arm'pit'
arm'rest'
ar'my
·mies
ar'ni·ca
a·ro'ma
ar'o·mat'ic
ar'o·mat'i·cal·ly
a·round'
a·rous'al
a·rouse'
·roused'
·rous'ing
ar·peg'gio
·gios
ar·raign'
ar·range'
·ranged'
·rang'ing
ar·range'ment
ar·rang'er
ar'rant
ar·ray'
ar·ray'al
ar·rear'age
ar·rears'
ar·rest'

ar·riv'al
ar·rive'
·rived' ·riv'ing
ar'ro·gance
ar'ro·gant
ar'ro·gate'
·gat'ed ·gat'ing
ar'ro·ga'tion
ar'row·head'
ar'row·root'
ar·roy'o
·os
ar'se·nal
ar'se·nic
ar'son
ar'son·ist
ar'te·fact'
ar·te'ri·al
ar·te'ri·o·scle·
ro'sis
ar·te'ri·o·scle·
rot'ic
ar'ter·y
·ies
ar·te'sian
art'ful
art'ful·ly
ar·thrit'ic
ar·thri'tis
Ar·thu'ri·an
ar'ti·choke'
ar'ti·cle
ar·tic'u·late'
·lat'ed ·lat'ing
ar·tic'u·late·ly
ar·tic'u·la'tion
ar'ti·fact'
ar'ti·fice
ar·tif'i·cer
ar·ti·fi'cial
ar·ti·fi'cial·ly
ar·ti·fi'ci·al'i·ty
·ties
ar·til'ler·y
ar'ti·san
art'ist
ar·tiste'
ar·tis'tic
ar·tis'ti·cal·ly
art'ist·ry
art'less
art'mo·bile'
art'sy-craft'sy
art'y
·i·er ·i·est
Ar'y·an
as·bes'tos
as·cend'
as·cend'a·ble
as·cend'an·cy
as·cend'ant
as·cen'sion
as·cent'
(a rising; see
assent)
as'cer·tain'
as·cet'ic

as·cet'i·cal·ly
as·cet'i·cism
a·scor'bic
as'cot
as·crib'a·ble
as·cribe'
·cribed'
·crib'ing
as·crip'tion
a·sep'tic
a·sep'ti·cal·ly
a·sex'u·al
a·shamed'
ash'can'
ash'en
ash'es
a·shore'
ash'y
·i·er ·i·est
A'sia
A'si·at'ic
as'i·nine'
as'i·nin'i·ty
·ties
a·skance'
a·skew'
a·sleep'
a·so'cial
as·par'a·gus
as'pect
as'pen
as·per'i·ty
as·perse'
·persed' ·pers'ing
as·per'sion
as'phalt
as·phyx'i·a
as·phyx'i·ant
as·phyx'i·ate'
·at'ed ·at'ing
as·phyx'i·a'tion
as·phyx'i·a'tor
as'pic
as'pir·ant
as'pi·rate'
·rat'ed ·rat'ing
as'pi·ra'tion
as'pi·ra'tor
as·pire'
·pired' ·pir'ing
as'pi·rin
as·sail'
as·sail'ant
as·sas'sin
as·sas'si·nate'
·nat'ed ·nat'ing
as·sas'si·na'tion
as·sault'
as·say'
(analyze; see
essay)
as·sem'blage
as·sem'ble
·bled ·bling
as·sem'bly
·blies
as·sem'bly·man
·men

as·sent'
(consent; see ascent)
as·sert'
as·ser'tion
as·ser'tive
as·sess'
as·ses'sor
as'set
as·sev'er·ate'
·at'ed ·at'ing
as·sev'er·a'tion
as·si·du'i·ty
as·sid'u·ous
as·sign'
as·sign'a·ble
as·sig·na'tion
as·sign'ee'
as·sign'ment
as·sim'i·la·ble
as·sim'i·late'
·lat'ed ·lat'ing
as·sim'i·la'tion
as·sim'i·la'tive
as·sim'i·la'tor
as·sist'
as·sist'ance
as·sist'ant
as·size'
as·so'ci·ate'
·at'ed ·at'ing
as·so'ci·a'tion
as·so'ci·a'tive
as'so·nance
as'so·nant
as·sort'
as·sort'ed
as·sort'ment
as·suage'
·suaged'
·suag'ing
as·sua'sive
as·sum'a·ble
as·sume'
·sumed'
·sum'ing
as·sump'tion
as·sur'ance
as·sure'
·sured' ·sur'ing
as·sur'ed·ly
As·syr'i·a
as'ter·isk'
as'ter·oid'
asth'ma
asth·mat'ic
asth·mat'i·cal·ly
as·tig·mat'ic
as·tig·mat'i·cal·ly
a·stig'ma·tism
as·ton'ish
a·stound'
a·strad'dle
as'tra·khan
or ·chan
as'tral
a·stride'
as·trin'gen·cy
as·trin'gent

as'tro·dome'
as'tro·labe'
as·trol'o·ger
as'tro·log'i·cal
as·trol'o·gy
as'tro·naut'
as'tro·nau'ti·cal
as'tro·nau'tics
as·tron'o·mer
as'tro·nom'i·cal
  or ·nom'ic
as'tro·nom'i·cal·ly
as·tron'o·my
as'tro·phys'i·cal
as'tro·phys'i·cist
as'tro·phys'ics
as·tute'
a·sun'der
a·sy'lum
a'sym·met'ri·cal
  or ·met'ric
a·sym'me·try
as'ymp·tote'
at'a·vism
at'a·vis'tic
at'el·ier'
a'the·ism
a'the·ist
a'the·is'tic
ath·lete'
ath·let'ic
ath·let'i·cal·ly
at-home'
a·thwart'
a·tin'gle
At·lan'tic
at'las
at'mos·phere'
at'mos·pher'ic
at'mos·pher'i·
  cal·ly
at'oll
at'om
a·tom'ic
a·tom'ics
at'om·ize'
  ·ized' ·iz'ing
at'om·iz'er
a·ton'al
a'to·nal'i·ty
a·tone'
  ·toned' ·ton'ing
a·tone'ment
a'tri·um
  ·tri·a or ·tri·ums
a·tro'cious
a·troc'i·ty
  ·ties
at'ro·phy
  ·phied ·phy·ing
at·tach'
at·ta·ché'
at·tach'ment
at·tack'
at·tain'
at·tain'a·ble
at·tain'der
at·tain'ment

at·taint'
at'tar
at·tempt'
at·tend'
at·tend'ance
at·tend'ant
at·ten'tion
at·ten'tive
at·ten'u·ate'
  ·at'ed ·at'ing
at·ten'u·a'tion
at·ten'u·a'tor
at·test'
at'tes·ta'tion
at'tic
at·tire'
  ·tired' ·tir'ing
at'ti·tude'
at'ti·tu'di·nal
at·tor'ney
  ·neys
at·tract'
at·trac'tion
at·trac'tive
at·trib'ut·a·ble
at'tri·bute' n.
at·trib'ute v.
  ·ut·ed ·ut·ing
at·tri·bu'tion
at·trib'u·tive
at·tri'tion
at·tune'
  ·tuned' ·tun'ing
a·typ'i·cal
a·typ'i·cal·ly
au'burn
auc'tion
auc'tion·eer'
au·da'cious
au·dac'i·ty
  ·ties
au'di·bil'i·ty
au'di·ble
au'di·bly
au'di·ence
au'di·o
au'di·ol'o·gy
au'di·o·vis'u·al
au'di·phone'
au'dit
au·di'tion
au'di·tor
au·di·to'ri·um
au'di·to'ry
au'ger
  (tool; see augur)
aught
  (anything; see
  ought)
aug·ment'
aug'men·ta'tion
aug·ment'a·tive
au·gra'tin
au'gur
  (soothsayer;
  see auger)
Au'gust
au jus'

au na·tu·rel'
au'ra
  ·ras or ·rae
au'ral
  (of the ear; see
  oral)
au're·ole'
Au're·o·my'cin
au'·re·voir'
au'ri·cle
  (earlike part;
  see oracle)
au·ric'u·lar
au·ro'ra bo're·
  a'lis
aus'cul·ta'tion
aus'pi·ces'
aus·pi'cious
aus·tere'
aus·tere'ly
aus·ter'i·ty
  ·ties
Aus·tral'ia
au·then'tic
au·then'ti·cal·ly
au·then'ti·cate'
  ·cat'ed ·cat'ing
au·then'ti·ca'tion
au'then·tic'i·ty
au'thor
au·thor'i·tar'i·an
au·thor'i·ta'tive
au·thor'i·ty
  ·ties
au'thor·i·za'tion
au'thor·ize'
  ·ized' ·iz'ing
au'to
  ·tos
  ·toed ·to·ing
au'to·bi'o·
  graph'ic or
  graph'i·cal
au'to·bi·og'ra·
  phy
  ·phies
au·toc'ra·cy
  ·cies
au'to·crat'
au'to·crat'ic
au'to·crat'i·
  cal·ly
au'to·graph'
au'to·mat'
au'to·mate'
  ·mat'ed ·mat'ing
au'to·mat'ic
au'to·mat'i·cal·ly
au'to·ma'tion
au·tom'a·tism
au·tom'a·ton'
  ·tons' or ·ta
au'to·mo·bile'
au'to·mo'tive
au'to·nom'ic
au·ton'o·mous
au·ton'o·my
  ·mies

au'top'sy
  ·sies
au'to·sug·ges'·
  tion
au'tumn
au·tum'nal
aux·il'ia·ry
  ·ries
a·vail'a·bil'i·ty
a·vail'a·ble
a·vail'a·bly
av'a·lanche'
  ·lanched'
  ·lanch'ing
a·vant'-garde'
a·vant'-gard'ism
a·vant'-gard'ist
av'a·rice
av'a·ri'cious
a·venge'
  ·venged'
  ·veng'ing
a·veng'er
av'e·nue'
a·ver'
  ·verred'
  ·ver'ring
av'er·age
  ·aged ·ag·ing
a·verse'
  (unwilling; see
  adverse)
a·ver'sion
a·vert'
a'vi·ar'y
  ·ies
a'vi·a'tion
a'vi·a'tor
a'vi·a'trix
av'id·ly
av'o·ca'do
  ·dos
av'o·ca'tion
a·void'a·ble
a·void'a·bly
a·void'ance
av'oir·du·pois'
a·vow'al
a·vowed'
a·vun'cu·lar
a·wait'
a·wake'
  ·woke' or
  ·waked',
  ·waked',
  ·wak'ing
a·wak'en
a·wak'en·ing
a·ward'
a·ware'
a·weigh'
awe'some
awe'-struck'
aw'ful
aw'ful·ly
aw'ful·ness
a·while'
awk'ward

awn'ing
a·wry'
ax or axe
ax'es
  axed ax'ing
ax'i·om
ax'i·o·mat'ic
ax'i·o·mat'i·
  cal·ly
ax'is
  ax'es
ax'le
Ax'min·ster
a·zal'ea
az'i·muth
Az'tec
az'ure

B

bab'bitt
bab'ble
  ·bled ·bling
ba·boon'
ba·bush'ka
ba'by
  ·bies
  ·bied ·by·ing
ba'by-sit'
  -sat' -sit'ting
baby sitter
bac'ca·lau're·ate
bac'ca·rat'
bac'cha·nal
bac'cha·na'li·an
bac'chant
  ·chants or
  bac·chan'tes
bac·chan'te
bach'e·lor
ba·cil'lus
  ·li
back'ache'
back'bite'
  ·bit', ·bit'ten or
  ·bit', ·bit'ing
back'bend'
back'board'
back'bone'
back'break'ing
back'court'
back'date'
  ·dat'ed ·dat'ing
back'door'
back'drop'
back'field'
back'fire' ·fir'ing
back'gam'mon
back'ground'
back'hand'
back'lash'
back'list'
back'log'
  ·logged'
  ·log'ging

back'rest'
back'side'
back'slide'
  ·slid', ·slid' or
  ·slid'den, ·slid'ing
back'space'
  ·spaced'
  ·spac'ing
back'spin'
back'stage'
back'stairs'
back'stop'
back'stretch'
back'stroke'
  ·stroked'
  ·strok'ing
back'track'
back'up' or
back'-up'
back'ward
back'wash'
back'wa'ter
back'woods'man
  ·men
ba'con
bac·te'ri·a
  (sing. bac·te'ri·um)
bac·te'ri·cide'
bac·te'ri·o·log'i·
  cal·ly
bac·te'ri·ol'o·gist
bac·te'ri·ol'o·gy
bad
  worse worst
badge
  badged badg'ing
badg'er
bad'i·nage'
  ·naged' ·nag'ing
bad'lands'
bad'min·ton
bad'-tem'pered
baf'fle
  ·fled ·fling
bag
  bagged bag'ging
bag'a·telle'
ba'gel
bag'ful'
  ·fuls'
bag'gage
bag'gy
  ·gi·er ·gi·est
bag'pipe'
ba·guette' or
  ·guet'
Ba·hai'
Ba·ha'mas
bail
  (money; see
  bale)
bai'liff
bai'li·wick
bails'man
  ·men
bait'ed
  (lured; see
  bated)

bake
  baked bak'ing
bak'er
bak'er·y
  ·ies
bal'a·lai'ka
bal'ance
  ·anced ·anc·ing
bal'ance·a·ble
bal·brig'gan
bal'co·ny
  ·nies
bal'der·dash'
bald'faced'
bald'head'ed
bald'ness
bale
  baled bal'ing
  (bundle; see
  bail)
bale'ful
balk'y
  ·i·er ·i·est
ball
  (round object;
  see bawl)
bal'lad
bal'lad·eer'
bal'last
ball bearing
bal'le·ri'na
bal'let
bal·lis'tic
bal·loon'ist
bal'lot
ball'park'
ball'play'er
ball'room'
balm'y
  ·i·er ·i·est
ba·lo'ney
bal'sa
bal'sam
Bal'tic
Bal'ti·more'
bal'us·ter
bal'us·trade'
bam·bi'no
  ·nos or ·ni
bam·boo'
bam·boo'zle
  ·zled ·zling
ban
  banned ban'ning
ba'nal
ba·nal'i·ty
  ·ties
ba·nan'a
band'age
  ·aged ·ag·ing
band'-aid' or
  band'aid'
ban·dan'na
band'box'
ban·deau'
  ·deaux'
ban'de·role'
ban'dit

band'mas'ter
ban'do·leer'
  or ·lier'
band saw
bands'man
  ·men
band'stand'
band'wag'on
ban'dy
  ·died ·dy·ing
ban'dy·leg'ged
bane'ful
ban'gle
bang'-up'
ban'ish
ban'is·ter
  or ban'nis·ter
ban'jo
  ·jos or ·joes
ban'jo·ist
bank'book'
bank note
bank'roll'
bank'rupt
bank'rupt·cy
  ·cies
ban'ner
banns or bans
  (marriage notice)
ban'quet
ban'tam
ban'tam·weight'
ban'ter
ban'zai'
bap'tism
bap·tis'mal
bap'tis·ter·y
  or ·tis·try
  ·ies or ·tries
bap'tize
  ·tized ·tiz·ing
bar
  barred bar'ring
bar·bar'i·an
bar·bar'ic
bar'ba·rism
bar·bar'i·ty
  ·ties
bar'ba·rous
bar'be·cue'
  ·cued ·cu'ing
barbed wire
bar'bel
bar'bell'
  (bar with weights)
bar'ber
bar'ber·shop'
bar'bi·tal'
bar·bi'tu·rate
bar'bule
bare
  bared bar'ing
  (uncover; see
  bear)
bare'back'
bare'faced'
bare'fac'ed·ly

bare'foot'
bare'foot'ed
bare'hand'ed
bare'head'ed
bare'leg'ged
bare'ly
bar'gain
barge
  barged barg'ing
bar'i·tone'
bar'keep'er
bark'en·tine'
bark'er
bar'ley·corn'
bar'maid'
bar'man
  ·men
bar mitz'vah or
  bar miz'vah
bar'na·cle
bar'na·cled
barn'storm'
barn'yard'
bar'o·graph'
ba·rom'e·ter
bar'o·met'ric
bar'on
  (nobleman; see
  barren)
bar'on·ess
bar'on·et
ba·ro'ni·al
ba·roque'
ba·rouche'
bar'racks
bar'ra·cu'da
bar·rage'
  ·raged' ·rag'ing
barred
bar'rel
  ·reled or ·relled
  ·rel·ing or
  ·rel·ling
bar'ren
  (empty; see
  baron)
bar·ette'
  (hair clasp;
  see beret)
bar'ri·cade'
  ·cad'ed ·cad'ing
bar'ri·er
bar'ris·ter
bar'room'
bar'row
bar'tend'er
bar'ter
Bart'lett pear
bas'al
bas'al·ly
ba·salt'
bas'cule
base
  bas'es
based bas'ing
  (foundation; vile;
  see bass)

base'ball'
base'board'
base'born'
base'burn'er
base hit
base'less
base line
base'ly
base'man
  ·men
base'ment
base'ness
bas'es
  (pl. of base)
ba'ses
  (pl. of basis)
bash'ful
bash'ful·ly
bash'ful·ness
bas'ic
bas'i·cal·ly
bas'il
ba·sil'i·ca
ba'sin
ba'sis
  ·ses
bas'ket
bas'ket·ball'
bas'ket·work'
bas'-re·lief'
bass
  (singer; see base)
bass
  (fish)
bass clef
bass drum
bas'set
bass horn
bas'si·net'
bas·soon'
bass viol
bass'wood'
bas'tard
baste
  bast'ed bast'ing
bas·tille'
bas'tion
bat
  bat'ted bat'ting
batch
bate
  bat'ed bat'ing
ba·teau'
  ·teaux'
bat'ed
  (held in; see
  baited)
bathe
  bathed bath'ing
bath'er
bath'house'
bath'i·nette'
ba'thos
bath'robe'
bath'room'
bath'tub'
bath'y·sphere'
ba·tik'

ba·tiste'
bat mitz'vah or
  bat miz'vah
ba·ton'
bat·tal'ion
bat'ten
bat'ter
bat'ter·y
  ·ies
bat'ting
bat'tle
  ·tled ·tling
bat'tle-ax' or -axe'
bat'tle·dore'
bat'tle·field'
bat'tle·ground'
bat'tle·ment
battle royal
battles royal
bat'tle-scarred'
bat'tle·ship'
bau'ble
baux'ite
bawd'y
  ·i·er ·i·est
bawl
  (shout; see ball)
bay'o·net'
  ·net'ed or ·net'ted
  ·net'ing or ·net'ting
bay'ou
ba·zaar'
  (market; see
  bizarre)
ba·zoo'ka
be
  was or were,
  been be'ing
beach
  (shore; see
  beech)
beach'comb'er
beach'head'
bea'con
bead'ing
bead'work
bead'y
  ·i·er ·i·est
bea'gle
beak'er
bean'bag'
bean'stalk'
bear
  (animal; see
  bare)
bear
  bore, borne or
  born,
  bear'ing
  (carry; see bare)
bear'a·ble
bear'a·bly
beard'ed
bear'ish
bear'skin'
beast'li·ness
beast'ly
  ·li·er ·li·est

beat
  beat beat'en
  beat'ing
be'a·tif'ic
be·at'i·fi·ca'tion
be·at'i·fy'
  ·fied' ·fy'ing
be·at'i·tude'
beat'nik
beau
  beaus or beaux
  (sweetheart; see
  bow)
beau'te·ous
beau·ti'cian
beau'ti·fi·ca'tion
beau'ti·fi'er
beau'ti·ful
beau'ti·ful·ly
beau'ti·fy'
  ·fied' ·fy'ing
beau'ty
  ·ties
bea'ver
bea'ver·board'
be·calm'
be·cause'
beck'on
be·come'
  ·came' ·come'
  ·com'ing
bed
  bed'ded
  bed'ding
bed'bug'
bed'cham'ber
bed'clothes'
bed'cov'er
be·dev'il
  ·iled or ·illed
  ·il·ing or ·il·ling
bed'fast'
bed'fel'low
bed'lam
Bed'ou·in
bed'pan'
bed'post'
be·drag'gle
  ·gled ·gling
bed'rid'den
bed'rock'
bed'roll'
bed'room'
bed'side'
bed'sore'
bed'spread'
bed'spring'
bed'stead'
bed'time'
beech
  (tree; see beach)
beech'nut'
beef
  beeves or beefs
beef'eat'er
beef'steak'
beef'y
  ·i·er ·i·est

bee'hive'
bee'keep'er
bee'line'
beer
 (drink; see bier)
beer'i·ness
beer'y
 ·i·er ·i·est
bees'wax'
Bee'tho·ven
bee'tle
bee'tle-browed'
be·fall'
 ·fell' ·fall'en
 ·fall'ing
be·fit'
 ·fit'ted ·fit'ting
be·fog'
 ·fogged'
 ·fog'ging
be·fore'hand'
be·friend'
be·fud'dle
 ·dled ·dling
beg
 begged beg'ging
be·get'
 ·got', ·got'ten or
 ·got', ·get'ting
beg'gar
be·gin'
 ·gan' ·gun'
 ·gin'ning
 (start; see beguine)
be·gin'ner
be·gird'
 ·girt' or ·gird'ed,
 ·girt', ·gird'ing
be·gone'
be·gon'ia
be·grime'
 ·grimed'
 ·grim'ing
be·grudge'
 ·grudged'
 ·grudg'ing
be·guile'
 ·guiled' ·guil'ing
be·guine'
 (dance; see begin)
be·half'
be·have'
 ·haved' ·hav'ing
be·hav'ior
be·head'
be·he'moth
be·hest'
be·hind'hand'
be·hold'
 ·held' ·hold'ing
be·hold'en
be·hoove'
 ·hooved'
 ·hoov'ing
beige
be·jew'el
 ·eled or ·elled
 ·el·ing or ·el·ling

be·la'bor
be·lat'ed
be·lay'
 ·layed' ·lay'ing
belch
be·lea'guer
bel'fry
 ·fries
be·lie'
 ·lied' ·ly'ing
be·lief'
be·liev'a·bil'i·ty
be·liev'a·ble
be·liev'a·bly
be·lieve'
 ·lieved' ·liev'ing
be·liev'er
be·lit'tle
 ·tled ·tling
be·lit'tler
bel'la·don'na
bell'boy'
 (errand boy)
bell buoy
 (signal bell)
belle
 (pretty girl)
belles-let'tres
bell'-bot'tom
bel'li·cose'
bel'li·cos'i·ty
bel·lig'er·ence
bel·lig'er·en·cy
bel·lig'er·ent
bell'-like'
bell'man
 ·men
bel'low
bell'weth'er
bel'ly
 ·lies
 ·lied ·ly·ing
bel'ly·band'
be·long'
be·lov'ed
be·low'
belt'ing
be·mire'
 ·mired' ·mir'ing
be·moan'
bend
 bent bend'ing
be·neath'
ben'e·dict'
Ben'e·dic'tine
ben'e·dic'tion
ben'e·fac'tion
ben'e·fac'tor
ben'e·fac'tress
ben'e·fice
be·nef'i·cence
be·nef'i·cent
ben'e·fi'cial
ben'e·fi'ci·ar'y
 ·ar'ies
ben'e·fit
 ·fit·ed ·fit·ing
be·nev'o·lence

be·nev'o·lent
ben'ga·line'
be·night'ed
be·nign'
be·nig'nan·cy
be·nig'nant
be·nig'ni·ty
ben'i·son
be·numb'
ben'zene
 (in chemistry)
ben'zine
 (cleaning fluid)
be·queath'
 ·queathed'
 ·queath'ing
be·queath'al
be·quest'
be·rate'
 ·rat'ed ·rat'ing
be·reave'
 ·reaved' or ·reft'
 ·reav'ing
be·reave'ment
be·ret'
 (flat cap; see barrette)
ber'i·ber'i
Berke'ley
Ber·mu'da
ber'ry
 ·ries
 ·ried ·ry·ing
 (fruit; see bury)
ber·serk'
berth
 (bed; see birth)
ber'yl
be·ryl'li·um
be·seech'
 ·sought' or
 ·seeched'
 ·seech'ing
be·set'
 ·set' ·set'ting
be·side'
be·sides'
be·siege'
 ·sieged' ·sieg'ing
be·smirch'
be·sot'
 ·sot'ted ·sot'ting
Bes'se·mer
bes'tial
bes'ti·al'i·ty
 ·ties
be·stow'
best seller
bet
 bet or bet'ted
 bet'ting
be'ta·tron'
be·tray'al
be·troth'
be·troth'al
be·trothed'
bet'ter
 (compar. of good)

bet'tor or ·ter
 (one who bets)
between'
be·twixt'
bev'a·tron'
bev'el
 ·eled or ·elled
 ·el·ing or ·el·ling
bev'er·age
bev'y
 ·ies
be·wail'
be·ware'
 ·wared' ·war'ing
be·wil'dered
be·witch'
be·yond'
bez'el
bi·an'nu·al
bi·an'nu·al·ly
bi'as
 ·ased or ·assed
 ·as·ing or ·as·sing
Bi'ble
Bib'li·cal
Bib'li·cal·ly
bib'li·og'ra·phy
 ·phies
bib'li·o·phile'
bib'u·lous
bi·cam'er·al
bi·car'bon·ate
bi·cen·te'nar·y
 ·ies
bi'cen·ten'ni·al
bi'ceps
 ·ceps or ·ceps·es
bick'er
bi·cus'pid
bi'cy·cle
 ·cled ·cling
bi'cy·clist
bid
 bade or bid,
 bid'den or bid,
 bid'ding
bid'da·ble
bi·det'
bi·en'ni·al
bi·en'ni·al·ly
bier
 (coffin stand; see beer)
bi'fo'cals
bi'fur·cate'
 ·cat'ed ·cat'ing
big
 big'ger big'gest
big'a·mist
big'a·mous
big'a·my
 ·mies
big'gish
big'heart'ed
big'horn'
big·no'ni·a
big'ot
big'ot·ed

big'ot·ry
 ·ries
bi'jou
 ·joux
bi·ki'ni
bi·la'bi·al
bi·lat'er·al
bilge
bi·lin'gual
bil'ious
bill'board'
bill'let
bil'let-doux'
 bil'lets-doux'
bill'fold'
bill'head'
bil'liards
bill'ing
bil'lings·gate'
bil'lion
bil'lion·aire'
bill of fare
 bill of lad'ing
bill of sale
bil'low
bil'low·i·ness
bil'low·y
 ·i·er ·i·est
bil'ly
 ·lies
bi·man'u·al
bi·man'u·al·ly
bi'me·tal'lic
bi·met'al·lism
bi·month'ly
bin
 binned bin'ning
bi'na·ry
bind
 bound bind'ing
bind'er
bind'er·y
 ·ies
binge
bin'go
bin'na·cle
bin·oc'u·lars
bi·no'mi·al
bi·no'mi·al·ly
bi'o·as'tro·nau'tics
bi'o·chem'ist
bi'o·chem'is·try
bi'o·cide'
bi'o·e·col'o·gy
bi'o·graph'i·cal
bi'o·graph'i·cal·ly
bi·og'ra·phy
 ·phies
bi'o·log'i·cal
bi'o·log'i·cal·ly
bi·ol'o·gy
bi·on'ics
bi'o·phys'ics
bi'op'sy
 ·sies
bi'o·sat'el·lite'

bi·par'ti·san
bi·par'tite
bi'pro·pel'lant
bi·quar'ter·ly
bi·ra'cial
bird'bath'
bird'call'
bird'ie
bird'lime'
bird'man'
 ·men'
bird'seed'
bird's'-eye'
bi·ret'ta
birth
 (being born; see berth)
birth'day'
birth'mark'
birth'place'
birth'rate'
birth'right'
birth'stone'
bis'cuit
bi·sect'
bi·sec'tion
bi·sec'tor
bi·sex'u·al
bi·sex'u·al·ly
bish'op
bish'op·ric
bis'muth
bi'son
bisque
bis'tro
bitch
bite
 bit, bit'ten or
 bit, bit'ing
bit'ter
bit'tern
bit'ter·sweet'
bi·tu'men
bi·tu'mi·nous
bi·va'lent
bi'valve'
biv'ou·ac'
 ·acked' ·ack'ing
bi·week'ly
 ·lies
bi·year'ly
bi·zarre'
 (odd; see bazaar)
bi·zarre'ly
black'-a-moor'
black'-and-blue'
black'ball'
black'ber'ry
 ·ries
black'bird'
black'board'
black'en
black'face'
black'guard
black'head'
black'heart'ed
black'jack'
black'list'

black'mail'
black'out'
black'smith'
black'top'
· topped'
· top'ping
blad'der
blam'a · ble or
blame'a · ble
blame
blamed blam'ing
blame'wor'thy
blanc · mange'
blan'dish
blan'ket
blare
blared blar'ing
blar'ney
bla · sé'
blas · pheme'
· phemed'
· phem'ing
blas'phe · mous
blas'phe · my
· mies
blast'off' or
blast'-off'
bla'tan · cy
· cies
bla'tant
blaze
blazed blaz'ing
blaz'er
bla'zon
bleach'ers
bleak'ly
blear'i · ness
blear'y
· i · er · i · est
blear'y-eyed'
bleed
bled bleed'ing
blem'ish
blend
blend'ed or blent
blend'ing
blend'er
bless
blessed or blest
bless'ing
bless'ed · ness
blight
blind'fold'
blintz
bliss'ful
bliss'ful · ly
blis'ter
blithe
blithe'some
blitz'krieg'
bliz'zard
bloat'ed
bloc
(group)
block
(solid piece)
block · ade'
· ad'ed · ad'ing

block'bust'ing
block'head'
block'house'
blond or blonde
blood bank
blood count
blood'cur'dling
blood'hound'
blood'i · ness
blood'i · ly
blood'less
blood'let'ting
blood'mo · bile'
blood pressure
blood'shed'
blood'shot'
blood'stained'
blood'stream'
blood test
blood'thirst'y
blood vessel
blood'y
· i · er · i · est
· ied · y · ing
Bloody Mary
blos'som
blot
blot'ted blot'ting
blotch'y
· i · er · i · est
blot'ter
blouse
bloused
blous'ing
blous'on
blow
blew blown
blow'ing
blow'gun'
blow'hole'
blow'out'
blow'pipe'
blow'torch'
blow'up'
blow'y
· i · er · i · est
blowz'y
· i · er · i · est
blub'ber
blu'cher
bludg'eon
blue
blued, blu'ing or
blue'ing
blue'ber'ry
· ries
blue'bird'
blue'-blood'ed
blue book
blue'-chip'
blue'-col'lar
blue'fish'
blue'grass'
blue jay
blue law
blue'-pen'cil
· ciled or · cilled
· cil · ing or · cil · ling

blue'print'
blue'stock'ing
bluff'er
blu'ing or
blue'ing
blu'ish or
blue'ish
blun'der
blun'der · buss'
blunt'ly
blur
blurred blur'ring
blur'ri · ness
blur'ry
· ri · er · ri · est
blus'ter
blus'ter · y
bo'a
boar
(hog; see bore)
board'er
board foot
board feet
board'ing · house'
boarding school
board'walk'
boast'ful
boast'ful · ly
boat'house'
boat'ing
boat'load'
boat'man
· men
boat'swain
bob'bin
bob'ble
· bled · bling
bob'o · link'
bob'sled'
· sled'ded
· sled'ding
bob'white'
bode
bod'ed bod'ing
bod'ice
bod'ied
bod'i · ly
bod'kin
bod'y
· ies
bod'y · guard'
bo'gey
· geys
· geyed · gey · ing
(golf term)
bog'gy
· gi · er · gi · est
(like a bog)
bo'gus
bo'gy
· gies
(spirit)
boil'ing
bois'ter · ous
bold'face'
bold'faced'
bo · le'ro
· ros

boll
(pod; see bowl)
boll weevil
boll'worm'
bo · lo'gna
bol'ster
bom · bard'
bom'bar · dier'
bom'bast
bom · bas'tic
bom · bas'ti · cal · ly
bomb'proof'
bomb'shell'
bomb'sight'
bo'na fi'de
bo · nan'za
bon'bon'
bond'age
bonds'man
· men
bone'-dry'
bon'fire'
bon'go
· gos
bon'i · ness
bon' mot'
bons' mots'
bon'net
bon'ny
· ni · er · ni · est
bon · sai'
bo'nus
bon' vi · vant'
bons' vi · vants'
bon' voy · age'
bon'y
· i · er · i · est
boo'by
· bies
boo'hoo'
· hoos'
· hooed' · hoo'ing
book'bind'er
book'case'
book club
book'end'
book'ish
book'keep'er
book'keep'ing
book'let
book'mak'er
book'mark'
book'mo · bile'
book'plate'
book'rack'
book'sell'er
book'shelf'
· shelves'
book'stack'
book'stall'
book'stand'
book'store'
book'worm'
boom'er · ang'
boom'let
boon'docks'
boon'dog'gle
· gled · gling

boor'ish
boost'er
boot'black'
boot'ee
(baby's shoe; see
booty)
boot'leg'
· legged'
· leg'ging
boot'leg'ger
boot'strap'
boo'ty
· ties
(spoils; see
bootee)
bo'rax
bor'der
bor'der · line'
bore
(dull person;
see boar)
bore
bored bor'ing
bore'dom
born
(brought into
life)
borne
(participle of
bear)
bor'ough
(town; see burro,
burrow)
bor'row
borsch or borsht
bos'om
boss'i · ness
boss'y
· i · er · i · est
bo · tan'i · cal
bot'a · nist
bot'a · ny
botch
both'er · some
bot'tle
· tled · tling
bot'tle · neck'
bot'tle · nose'
bot'tom
bot'u · lism
bou · clé' or
bou · cle'
bou'doir
bouf · fant'
bough
(tree branch;
see bow)
bought
bouil'la · baisse'
bouil'lon
(broth; see
bullion)
boul'der
boul'e · vard'
bounce
bounced
bounc'ing
bounc'er

bound'a · ry
· ries
bound'en
bound'less
boun'te · ous
boun'ti · ful
boun'ti · ful · ly
boun'ty
· ties
bou · quet'
bour'bon
bour · geois'
bour'geoi · sie'
bourse
bou · tique'
bou'ton · niere'
bo'vine
bow
(curve; see beau)
bow
(of a ship; see
bough)
bowd'ler · ize'
· ized' · iz'ing
bow'el
bow'er
Bow'er · y
bow'ie knife
bow'knot'
bowl
(dish; see boll)
bow'leg'ged
bow'line
bowl'ing
bow'sprit'
bow'string'
bow tie
box'car'
box'er
box office
box'wood'
boy
(child; see buoy)
boy'cott
boy'friend'
boy'hood'
boy'ish
boy'sen · ber'ry
· ries
brace
braced brac'ing
brace'let
brack'et
brack'ish
brad'awl'
brag
bragged
brag'ging
brag'ga · do'ci · o'
brag'gart
Brah'ma
Brah'man · ism
braid
Braille
brain'child'
brain'i · ness
brain'pow'er
brain'storm'

brain'wash'
brain wave
brain'y
  ·i·er ·i·est
braise
  braised brais'ing
  (cook; see braze)
brake
  braked brak'ing
  (stop; see break)
brake'man
  ·men
bram'ble
branch'ing
bran'dish
brand'-new'
bran'dy
  ·dies
  ·died ·dy·ing
bras'sard
brass'ie n.
bras·siere'
brass'i·ness
brass'ware'
brass'-wind' adj.
brass winds
brass'y adj.
  ·i·er ·i·est
braun'schwei'ger
bra·va'do
brave
  braved brav'ing
brave'ly
brav'er·y
bra'vo
  ·vos
brawl
brawn'y
  ·i·er ·i·est
braze
  brazed braz'ing
  (solder; see
  braise)
bra'zen
bra'zen·ness
bra'zen·faced'
bra'zier
Bra·zil'
bra·zil'wood'
breach
  (a gap; see
  breech)
bread'bas'ket
bread'board'
bread'box'
breadth
  (width; see
  breath)
breadth'ways'
bread'win'ner
break
  broke bro'ken
  break'ing
  (smash; see
  brake)
break'a·ble
break'age
break'down'

break'fast
break'front'
break'neck'
break'out'
break'through'
break'up'
break'wa'ter
breast'bone'
breast'-feed'
  -fed' -feed'ing
breast stroke
breast'work'
breath
  (air; see breadth)
breath'a·lyz'er
breathe
breathed
breath'ing
breath'er
breath'less
breath'tak'ing
breech
  (rear; see
  breach)
breech'cloth'
breech'es
breech'-load'ing
breed
  bred breed'ing
breez'i·ly
breez'i·ness
breeze'way'
breez'y
  ·i·er ·i·est
breth'ren
bre'vi·ar'y
  ·ies
brev'i·ty
brew'er·y
  ·ies
brib'a·ble
bribe
  bribed brib'ing
brib'er·y
  ·ies
bric'-a-brac'
brick'bat'
brick'lay'ing
brick'work'
brick'yard'
brid'al
  (wedding; see
  bridle)
bride'groom'
brides'maid'
bridge
bridged
bridg'ing
bridge'a·ble
bridge'head'
bridge'work'
bri'dle
  (harness; see
  bridal)
brief'case'
bri'er or bri'ar
bri·gade'
brig'a·dier'

brig'and
brig'an·tine'
bright'en
bril'liance
bril'liant
bril'lian·tine'
brim
  brimmed
  brim'ming
brim'ful'
brim'stone'
brin'dled
brine
  brined brin'ing
bring
  brought
  bring'ing
brin'i·ness
brink'man·ship'
brin'y
  ·i·er ·i·est
bri·oche'
bri·quette'
  or ·quet'
bris'ket
brisk'ly
bris'tle
  ·tled ·tling
bris'tli·ness
bris'tly
  ·tli·er ·tli·est
Bris'tol board
Brit'ain
  (place)
Brit'i·cism
Brit'on
  (person)
brit'tle
brit'tle·ly or
  brit'tly
broach
  (open; see
  brooch)
broad'ax' or ·axe'
broad'cast'
  ·cast' or ·cast'ed
  ·cast'ing
broad'cloth'
broad'leaf'
broad'-leaved'
broad'loom'
broad'-mind'ed
broad'side'
broad'sword'
bro·cade'
  ·cad'ed ·cad'ing
broc'co·li
bro·chette'
bro·chure'
bro'gan
brogue
broil'er
bro'ken-down'
bro'ken·heart'ed
bro'ker
bro'ker·age
bro'mide
bro·mid'ic

bro'mine
bro'mo selt'zer
bron'chi·al
bron·chi'tis
bron'chus
  ·chi
bron'co
  ·cos
bron'to·sau'rus
bronze
bronzed
bronz'ing
brooch
  (pin; see broach)
brood'i·ness
broom'stick'
broth'el
broth'er-in-law'
  broth'ers-in-law'
brougham
brought
brou'ha·ha'
brow'beat'
  ·beat' ·beat'en
  ·beat'ing
brown'ie
brown'out'
brown'stone'
browse
browsed
brows'ing
bruise
  bruised bruis'ing
bruis'er
bru·net' or
  bru·nette'
brush'wood'
brush'work'
brusque
brusque'ly
brusque'ness
Brus'sels sprouts
bru'tal
bru·tal'i·ty
  ·ties
bru'tal·ize'
  ·ized' ·iz'ing
brut'ish
bub'ble
  ·bled ·bling
bub'bler
bub'ble-top'
bub'bly
bu·bon'ic
buc'ca·neer'
buck'board'
buck'et·ful'
  ·fuls'
bucket seat
buck'le
  ·led ·ling
buck'-pass'er
buck'ram
buck'saw'
buck'shot'
buck'skin'
buck'tooth'
  ·teeth'

buck'toothed'
buck'wheat'
bu·col'ic
bud
  bud'ded bud'ding
Bud'dha
Bud'dhism
budge
  budged budg'ing
budg'et
budg'et·ar'y
buf'fa·lo'
  ·loes' or ·los'
buff'er
buff'et
buf·foon'er·y
bug'bear'
bug'gy
  ·gies
  ·gi·er ·gi·est
bu'gle
  ·gled ·gling
build
  built build'ing
build'up' or
  build'-up'
built'-in'
built'-up'
bul'bar
bul'bous
bulge
  bulged bulg'ing
bulg'i·ness
bulk'i·ness
bulk'y
  ·i·er ·i·est
bull'dog'
bull'doze'
  ·dozed' ·doz'ing
bull'doz'er
bul'let
bul'le·tin
bul'let-proof'
bull'fight'er
bull'frog'
bull'head'ed
bull'horn'
bul'lion
  (gold; see
  bouillon)
bull'ish
bull'ock
bull'pen'
bull's'-eye'
bull'whip'
bul'ly
  ·lies
  ·lied ·ly·ing
bul'rush'
bul'wark
bum'ble·bee'
bum'bling
bump'er
bump'kin
bump'tious
bump'y
  ·i·er ·i·est
bun'combe

bun'dle
  ·dled ·dling
bun'ga·low'
bung'hole'
bun'gle
  ·gled ·gling
bun'ion
bunk'er
bun'ting
Bun'sen burner
buoy
  (marker; see boy)
buoy'an·cy
buoy'ant
bur'ble
  ·bled ·bling
bur'den·some
bu'reau
  ·reaus or ·reaux
bu·reau'cra·cy
  ·cies
bu'reau·crat'
bu'reau·crat'ic
bu'reau·crat'i·
  cal·ly
bu·rette' or ·ret'
bur'geon
bur'glar
bur'gla·rize'
  ·rized' ·riz'ing
bur'gla·ry
  ·ries
Bur'gun·dy
bur'i·al
bur'lap
bur·lesque'
  ·lesqued'
  ·lesqu'ing
bur'ley
  (tobacco)
bur'li·ness
bur'ly
  ·li·er ·li·est
  (muscular)
burn
  burned or burnt
  burn'ing
burn'a·ble
bur'nish
bur·noose'
burn'out'
bur'ro
  ·ros
  (donkey; see
  burrow, borough)
bur'row
  (hole; see burro,
  borough)
bur'sa
  ·sae or ·sas
bur'sar
bur·si'tis
burst
  burst burst'ing
bur'y
  ·ied ·y·ing
  (cover; see
  berry)

bus
  bus'es or bus'ses
  bused or bussed
  bus'ing or bus'sing
  (motor coach; see
  buss)
bus'boy'
bus'by
  ·bies
bush'el·bas'ket
bush'ing
bush'man
  ·men
bush'rang'er
bush'whack'er
bush'y
  ·i·er ·i·est
bus'i·ly
busi'ness
busi'ness·like'
busi'ness·man'
  ·men'
busi'ness·wom'an
  ·wom'en
bus'kin
bus'man
  ·men
buss
  (kiss; see bus)
bus'tle
  ·tled ·tling
bus'y
  ·i·er ·i·est
  ·ied ·y·ing
bus'y·bod'y
  ·ies
bus'y·ness
butch'er·y
but'ler
butte
but'ter·fat'
but'ter·fin'gers
but'ter·fly'
  ·flies'
but'ter·milk'
but'ter·nut'
but'ter·scotch'
but'ter·y
but'tocks
but'ton-down'
but'ton·hole'
  ·holed' ·hol'ing
but'tress
bux'om
buy
  bought buy'ing
buz'zard
buz'zer
by'gone'
by'law'
by'line'
by'pass'
by'path'
by'play'
by'prod'uct or
  by'-prod'uct
by'road'
by'stand'er

by'way'
by'word'

C

ca·bal'
  ·balled' ·bal'ling
cab'a·lism
ca·bal·le'ro
  ·ros
ca·ba'na
cab'a·ret'
cab'bage
cab'driv'er
cab'in
cab'i·net
cab'i·net·mak'er
cab'i·net·work'
ca'ble
  ·bled ·bling
ca'ble·gram'
ca·boose'
cab'ri·o·let'
cab'stand'
ca·ca'o
cac'ci·a·to're
cache
  cached cach'ing
ca·chet'
cach'in·nate'
  ·nat'ed ·nat'ing
cach'in·na'tion
cack'le
  ·led ·ling
ca·cog'ra·phy
ca·coph'o·nous
ca·coph'o·ny
cac'tus
  ·tus·es or ·ti
ca·dav'er
ca·dav'er·ous
cad'die or ·dy
  ·dies
  ·died dy·ing
  (in golf)
cad'dish
cad'dy
  ·dies
  (tea box)
ca'dence
ca·den'za
ca·det'
cad'mi·um
ca'dre
ca·du'ce·us
  ·ce·i
Cae·sar'e·an
cae·su'ra
  ·ras or ·rae
ca·fé' or ca·fe'
caf'e·te'ri·a
caf'fe·ine or ·in
cage
  caged cag'ing
ca'gey or ca'gy
  ·gi·er ·gi·est

ca'gi·ly
ca'gi·ness
cais'son
cai'tiff
ca·jole'
  ·joled' ·jol'ing
ca·jole'ment
ca·jol'er·y
cake
  caked cak'ing
cal'a·bash'
ca·lam'i·tous
ca·lam'i·ty
  ·ties
cal·car'e·ous
cal'ci·fi·ca'tion
cal'ci·fy'
  ·fied' ·fy'ing
cal'ci·mine'
  ·mined' ·min'ing
cal'ci·um
cal'cu·la·ble
cal'cu·late'
  ·lat'ed ·lat'ing
cal'cu·la'tion
cal'cu·la'tor
cal'cu·lus
  ·li or ·lus·es
cal'dron
cal'en·dar
  (table of dates)
cal'en·der
  (roller; see
  colander)
cal'ends
ca·les'cent
calf
  calves
calf'skin'
cal'i·ber or ·bre
cal'i·brate'
  ·brat'ed ·brat'ing
cal'i·bra'tion
cal'i·co'
  ·coes' or ·cos'
Cal·i·for'ni·a
cal'i·pers
ca'liph
cal'is·then'ics
calk
call'board'
cal·lig'ra·phy
cal'lous adj.
cal'low
call'-up'
cal'lus n.
  ·lus·es
calm'ly
ca·lor'ic
cal'o·rie or ·ry
  ·ries
cal'o·rim'e·ter
cal'u·met'
ca·lum'ni·ate'
  ·at'ed ·at'ing
ca·lum'ni·ous
cal'um·ny
  ·nies

Cal'va·ry
  (Biblical place;
  see cavalry)
calve
  calved calv'ing
Cal'vin·ism
ca·lyp'so
ca'lyx
  ca'lyx·es or
  ca'ly·ces'
ca·ma·ra'de·rie
cam'ber
cam'bric
Cam'bridge
cam'el
ca·mel'li·a
Cam'em·bert'
cam'e·o'
  ·os'
cam'er·a
cam'er·a·man'
  ·men'
cam'er·a-shy'
cam'i·sole'
cam'o·mile'
cam'ou·flage'
  ·flaged' ·flag'ing
cam·paign'
cam'pa·ni'le
  ·les or ·li
camp'er
camp'fire'
camp'ground'
cam'phor
cam'phor·ate'
  ·at'ed ·at'ing
camp'o·ree'
camp'site'
camp'stool'
cam'pus
cam'shaft'
can
  canned can'ning
Ca'naan
Can'a·da
Ca·na'di·an
ca·naille'
ca·nal'
ca·nal'boat'
ca·nal'ize'
  ·ized ·iz'ing
ca'na·pé'
  (food; see
  canopy)
ca·nard'
ca·nar'y
  ·ies
ca·nas'ta
can'can'
can'cel
  ·celed or ·celled
  ·cel·ing or
  ·cel·ling
can'cel·la'tion
can'cer
can'cer·ous
can·de·la'bra
  ·bras

can·de·la'brum
  ·bra or ·brums
can·des'cence
can·des'cent
can'did
  (frank; see
  candied)
can'di·da·cy
  ·cies
can'di·date'
can'died
  (sugared; see
  candid)
can'dle·light'
candle power
can'dle·stick'
can'dle·wick'
can'dor
can'dy
  ·dies
  ·died ·dy·ing
can'dy-striped'
cane
  caned can'ing
ca'nine
can'is·ter
can'ker
can'na·bis
can'ner·y
  ·ies
can'ni·bal
can'ni·bal·ize'
  ·ized' ·iz'ing
can'ni·ly
can'ni·ness
can'non
  (gun; see canon,
  canyon)
can'non·ade'
  ·ad'ed ·ad'ing
can'not
can'ny
  ·ni·er ·ni·est
ca·noe'
  ·noed' ·noe'ing
can'on
  (law; see cannon,
  canyon)
ca·non'i·cal
can'on·ize'
  ·ized' ·iz'ing
can'o·py
  ·pies
  (hood; see
  canapé)
can·ta'bi·le'
can'ta·loupe'
  or ·loup'
can·tan'ker·ous
can·ta'ta
can·teen'
can'ter
  (gallop; see
  cantor)
can'ti·cle
can'ti·le'ver
can'to
  ·tos

can'ton
can·ton'ment
can'tor
  (singer; see
  canter)
can'vas
  (cloth)
can'vass
  (to solicit)
can'yon or ca'ñon
  (valley; see
  cannon, canon)
caou·tchouc'
cap
  capped cap'ping
ca·pa·bil'i·ty
  ·ties
ca'pa·ble
ca'pa·bly
ca·pa'cious
ca·pac'i·tance
ca·pac'i·tor
ca·pac'i·ty
  ·ties
ca'per
cap'ful'
  ·fuls'
cap'il·lar'y
  ·ies
cap'i·tal
  (city; chief; see
  capitol)
cap'i·tal·ism
cap'i·tal·is'tic
cap'i·tal·is'ti·
  cal·ly
cap'i·tal·i·za'tion
cap'i·tal·ize'
  ·ized' ·iz'ing
cap'i·tal·ly
cap'i·ta'tion
cap'i·tol
  (building; see
  capital)
ca·pit'u·late'
  ·lat'ed ·lat'ing
ca·pit'u·la'tion
ca'pon
ca·price'
ca·pri'cious
cap'ri·ole'
  ·oled' ·ol'ing
cap'size
  ·sized ·siz·ing
cap'stan
cap'stone'
cap'su·lar
cap'sule
  ·suled ·sul·ing
cap'sul·ize'
  ·ized' ·iz'ing
cap'tain
cap'tain·cy
  ·cies
cap'tion
cap'tious
cap'ti·vate'
  ·vat'ed ·vat'ing

cap'tive
cap·tiv'i·ty
·ties
cap'tor
cap'ture
·tured ·tur·ing
car'a·cul
ca·rafe'
car'a·mel
car'a·mel·ize'
·ized' ·iz'ing
car'a·pace'
car'at
(weight; see
caret, carrot)
car'a·van'
car'a·van'sa·ry
·ries
car'a·way'
car'bide
car'bine
car·bo·hy'drate
car·bol'ic
car'bon
car·bo·na'ceous
car'bon·ate'
·at'ed ·at'ing
car'bon·a'tion
car'bon-date'
-dat'ed -dat'ing
car'bon·if'er·ous
car'bon·ize'
·ized' ·iz'ing
car'bo·run'dum
car'bun·cle
car'bu·re'tion
car'bu·re'tor
car'cass
car·cin'o·gen
car·ci·no'ma
car'da·mom
card'board'
card'-car'ry·ing
car'di·ac'
car'di·gan
car'di·nal
car'di·o·gram'
car'di·o·graph'
card'sharp'
care
cared car'ing
ca·reen'
ca·reer'
care'free'
care'ful
care'ful·ly
care'less
ca·ress'
ca·res'sive·ly
car'et
(insert mark; see
carat, carrot)
care'tak'er
care'worn'
car'fare'
car'go
·goes or ·gos
car'hop'

Car'ib·be'an
car'i·bou'
car'i·ca·ture
·tured ·tur·ing
car'i·ca·tur·ist
car'ies
(decay; see
carries)
car'il·lon'
car'load'
car'man
·men
car'mine
car'nage
car'nal
car'nal·ly
car·na'tion
car·nel'ian
car'ni·val
car'ni·vore'
car·niv'o·rous
car'ol
·oled or ·olled
·ol·ing or ·ol·ling
car'ol·er or ·ol·ler
Car'o·li'nas
Car'o·lin'i·an
car'om
car'o·tene' or ·tin
ca·rot'id
ca·rous'al
ca·rouse'
·roused'
·rous'ing
car'ou·sel'
car'pen·ter
car'pen·try
car'pet
car'pet·bag'ger
car'pet·ing
carp'ing
car'port'
car'riage
car'ri·er
car'ries
(form of carry;
see caries)
car'ri·on
car'rot
(vegetable; see
carat, caret)
car'rou·sel'
car'ry
·ried ·ry·ing
car'ry·all'
car'ry·out'
car'ry-o'ver
car'sick'
cart'age
carte' blanche'
cartes' blanches'
car·tel'
car'ti·lage
car'ti·lag'i·nous
car'to·gram'
car·tog'ra·phy
car'ton
car·toon'

car·toon'ist
car'tridge
carve
carved carv'ing
car'wash'
car'y·at'id
·ids or ·i·des'
ca·sa'ba
or cas·sa'ba
cas'bah
cas·cade'
·cad'ed ·cad'ing
cas·car'a
case
cased cas'ing
case'book'
case'hard'ened
ca'se·in
case'load'
case'mate'
case'ment
case'work'er
cash'-and-car'ry
cash'book'
cash'ew
cash·ier'
cash'mere
cas'ing
ca·si'no
·nos
(gambling room)
cas'ket
cas·sa'va
cas'se·role'
cas·sette'
cas·si'no
(card game)
cas'sock
cas'so·war'y
·war'ies
cast
cast cast'ing
cas'ta·nets'
cast'a·way'
caste
(social class)
cas'tel·lat'ed
cast'er
cas'ti·gate'
·gat'ed ·gat'ing
cast'-i'ron
cas'tle
cast'off'
cas'tor
cas'trate
·trat·ed ·trat-ing
cas·tra'tion
cas'u·al
cas'u·al·ly
cas'u·al·ty
·ties
cas'u·ist
cas'u·is'tic
cas'u·ist·ry
cat'a·clysm
cat'a·comb'
cat'a·falque'
cat'a·lep'sy

cat'a·lep'tic
cat'a·lo'
·loes' or ·los'
cat'a·log' or
·logue'
·loged' or
·logued'
·log'ing or
·logu'ing
cat'a·log'er or
·logu'er
ca·tal'y·sis
·ses'
cat'a·lyst
cat'a·ma·ran'
cat'a·pult'
cat'a·ract'
ca·tarrh'
ca·tarrh'al
ca·tas'tro·phe
cat'a·stroph'ic
cat'a·stroph'i·
cal·ly
cat'a·to'ni·a
cat'call'
catch
caught catch'ing
catch'all'
catch'er
catch'ing
catch'pen'ny
·nies
catch'up
catch'word'
catch'y
·i·er ·i·est
cat'e·chism
cat'e·chize'
·chized' ·chiz'ing
cat'e·chu'men
cat'e·gor'i·cal
cat'e·go·rize'
·rized' ·riz'ing
cat'e·go'ry
·ries
ca'ter
cat'er-cor'nered
ca'ter·er
cat'er·pil'lar
cat'er·waul'
cat'gut'
ca·thar'sis
ca·thar'tic
ca·the'dral
cath'e·ter
cath'e·ter·ize'
·ized' ·iz'ing
cath'ode
cath'o·lic
Ca·thol'i·cism
cath'o·lic'i·ty
ca·thol'i·cize'
·cized' ·ciz'ing
cat'li'on
cat'nap'
·napped'
·nap'ping
cat'nip

cat'-o'-nine'-tails'
cat's'-eye'
Cats'kill'
cat's'-paw'
cat'sup
cat'tail'
cat'ti·ly
cat'ti·ness
cat'tle
cat'tle·man
·men
cat'ty
·ti·er ·ti·est
cat'ty-cor'nered
cat'walk'
Cau·ca'sian
Cau'ca·soid'
cau'cus
cau'dal
cau'date
cau'li·flow'er
caulk
caus'a·ble
caus'al
caus'al·ly
cau·sal'i·ty
·ties
cau·sa'tion
caus'a·tive
cause
caused caus'ing
cau'se·rie'
cause'way'
caus'tic
cau'ter·i·za'tion
cau'ter·ize'
·ized' ·iz'ing
cau'ter·y
·ies
cau'tion
cau'tion·ar'y
cau'tious
cav'al·cade'
cav·a·lier'
cav'al·ry
·ries
(troops; see
Calvary)
cav'al·ry·man
·men
cave
caved cav'ing
ca've·at' emp'tor
cave'-in'
cav'ern
cav'ern·ous
cav'i·ar'
cav'il
·iled or ·illed
·il·ing or ·il·ling
cav'i·ty
·ties
ca·vort'
cay·enne'
cease
ceased ceas'ing
cease'-fire'

cease'less
ce'dar
cede
ced'ed ced'ing
ce·dil'la
ceil'ing
ceil·om'e·ter
cel'e·brant
cel'e·brate'
·brat'ed ·brat'ing
cel'e·bra'tion
cel'e·bra'tor
ce·leb'ri·ty
·ties
ce·ler'i·ty
cel'e·ry
ce·les'ta
ce·les'tial
cel'i·ba·cy
cel'i·bate
cel'lar
cel'lar·et'
cel'lar·way'
cel'list
or 'cel'list
cell'-like'
cel'lo
or 'cel'lo
·los or ·li
cel'lo·phane'
cel'lu·lar
cel'lu·loid'
cel'lu·lose'
Cel'o·tex'
Cel'si·us
ce·ment'
cem'e·ter'y
·ies
cen'o·bite'
Ce·no·zo'ic
cen'ser
(incense box)
cen'sor
(prohibiter)
cen'sored
cen·so'ri·al
cen·so'ri·ous
cen'sor·ship'
cen'sur·a·ble
cen'sure
·sured ·sur·ing
(blame)
cen'sus
cen'taur
cen·ta'vo
cen'te·nar'i·an
cen'te·nar'y
cen·ten'ni·al
cen·ten'ni·al·ly
cen'ter
cen'ter·board'
cen'tered
cen'ter·piece'
cen·tes'i·mal
cen·tes'i·mal·ly
cen'ti·grade'
cen'ti·gram'
cen'ti·li'ter

cen'time
cen'ti·me'ter
cen'ti·pede'
cen'tral
cen'tral·i·za'tion
cen'tral·ize'
·ized' ·iz'ing
cen·trif'u·gal
cen'tri·fuge'
cen·trip'e·tal
cen'trist
cen'tu·ple
cen·tu'ri·on
cen'tu·ry
·ries
ce·phal'ic
ce·ram'ic
ce·ram'ist or
ce·ram'i·cist
ce're·al
(grain; see serial)
cer'e·bel'lum
·lums or ·la
cer'e·bral
cer·e'bral·ly
cer'e·brate'
·brat'ed ·brat'ing
cer'e·bro·spi'nal
cer'e·brum
·brums or ·bra
cer'e·ment
cer'e·mo'ni·al
cer'e·mo'ni·al·ly
cer'e·mo'ni·ous
cer'e·mo'ny
·nies
ce·rise'
cer'tain
cer'tain·ly
cer'tain·ty
·ties
cer'ti·fi'a·ble
cer'ti·fi'a·bly
cer·tif'i·cate
cer'ti·fi·ca'tion
cer'ti·fy'
·fied' ·fy'ing
cer'ti·o·ra'ri
cer'ti·tude'
ce·ru'le·an
ce·ru'men
cer'vi·cal
cer'vix
·vi·ces' or ·vix·es
ces·sa'tion
ces'sion
(a giving up; see
session)
cess'pool'
chafe
chafed chaf'ing
(rub)
chaff
(husks of grain)
chaf'finch
cha·grin'
·grined'
·grin'ing

chain'man
·men
chain'-re·act'
chain'-smoke'
chair'lift'
chair'man
·men
chair'wom·an
·wom·en
chaise longue
chaise or chaises
longues
chaise lounge
chaise lounges
chal·ced'o·ny
cha·let'
chal'ice
chalk'board'
chalk'i·ness
chalk'y
·i·er ·i·est
chal'lenge
·lenged ·leng·ing
chal'leng·er
chal'lis
cham'ber
cham'ber·lain
cham'ber·maid'
cham'bray
cha·me'le·on
cham'fer
cham'ois
·ois
·oised ·ois·ing
cham'o·mile'
cham·pagne'
(wine)
cham·paign'
(open field)
cham'pi·on
chance
chanced
chanc'ing
chan'cel
chan'cel·ler·y
·ies
chan'cel·lor
chance'-med'ley
chan'cer·y
·ies
chan'cre
chan'croid
chanc'y
·i·er ·i·est
chan·de·lier'
chan·delle'
chan'dler·y
·ies
Cha·nel'
change
changed
chang'ing
change'a·bil'i·ty
change'a·ble
change'a·bly
change'ful
change'ful·ly
change'less

change'ling
change'o'ver
change'-up'
chan'nel
·neled or ·nelled
·nel·ing or
·nel·ling
chan'nel·ize'
·ized' ·iz'ing
chan·teuse'
chan'tey or ·ty
·teys or ·ties
Cha'nu·kah
cha'os
cha·ot'ic
cha·ot'i·cal·ly
chap
chapped
chap'ping
chap'ar·ral'
cha·peau'
·peaus' or
·peaux'
chap'el
chap'er·on'
or ·one'
·oned' ·on'ing
chap'fall'en
chap'lain
chap'let
chap'ter
char
charred
char'ring
char'ac·ter
char'ac·ter·is'tic
char'ac·ter·is'ti·
cal·ly
char'ac·ter·i·
za'tion
char'ac·ter·ize'
·ized' ·iz'ing
cha·rade'
char'coal'
chare
chared char'ing
charge
charged
charg'ing
charge'a·ble
charge plate or
charge'-a-plate'
charg'er
char'i·ly
char'i·ness
char'i·ot
char'i·ot·eer'
cha·ris'ma
char'is·mat'ic
char'i·ta·ble
char'i·ty
·ties
cha·riv'a·ri'
char'la·tan
charm'ing
char'nel
char'ry
·ri·er ·ri·est

char'ter
char·treuse'
char'wom·an
char'y
·i·er ·i·est
chase
chased chas'ing
chasm
chas·sé'
·séd' ·sé'ing
chas'sis
·sis
chaste'ly
chas'ten
chas·tise'
·tised' ·tis'ing
chas·tise'ment
chas'ti·ty
chas'u·ble
chat
chat'ted
chat'ting
châ·teau'
·teaux' or ·teaus'
chat'e·laine'
cha·toy'ant
chat'tel
chat'ty
·ti·er ·ti·est
Chau'cer
chauf'fer
(stove)
chauf'feur
(driver)
chau·tau'qua
chau'vin·ism
chau'vin·ist
chau'vin·is'tic
chau'vin·is'ti·
cal·ly
cheap
(low in cost;
see cheep)
cheap'en
cheat'er
check'book'
check'er·board'
check'ered
check'list' or
check list
check'mate'
·mat'ed ·mat'ing
check'off'
check'out' or
check'-out'
check'point'
check'rein'
check'room'
check'up'
Ched'dar
cheek'bone'
cheek'i·ly
cheek'i·ness
cheek'y
·i·er ·i·est
cheep
(sound; see cheap)

cheer'ful·ly
cheer'i·ly
cheer'i·ness
cheer'lead'er
cheer'less
cheer'y
·i·er ·i·est
cheese'burg'er
cheese'cake'
cheese'cloth'
chees'i·ness
chees'y
·i·er ·i·est
chee'tah
chem'i·cal
che·mise'
chem'ist
chem'is·try
·tries
chem'ur·gy
che·nille'
cher'ish
Cher'o·kee'
che·root'
cher'ry
·ries
cher'ub
·ubs or ·u·bim
che·ru'bic
che·ru'bi·cal·ly
cher'vil
chess'board'
chess'man'
ches'ter·field'
chest'nut
chev'i·ot
chev'ron
chew'y
·i·er ·i·est
Chi·an'ti
chi·a'ro·scu'ro
·ros
chic
chic'quer
chic'quest
chi·can'er·y
chi'chi or chi'-chi
chick'en-heart'ed
chicken pox
chic'le
chic'o·ry
chide
chid'ed or chid,
chid'ed or chid
or chid'den,
chid'ing
chief'ly
chief'tain
chif·fon'
chif·fo·nier'
chig'ger
chi'gnon
chig'oe
·oes
Chi·hua'hua
chil'blain'
child
chil'dren

child'bear'ing
child'bed'
child'birth'
child'hood'
child'ish
child'like'
chil'i
·ies
chill'i·ness
chill'y
·i·er ·i·est
chime
chimed chim'ing
chi·me'ra
chi·mer'i·cal
chim'ney
·neys
chim'pan·zee'
chin
chinned
chin'ning
chi'na·ware'
chin·chil'la
Chi·nese'
chi'no
chin'qua·pin
chintz
chip
chipped
chip'ping
chip'munk'
chi·rog'ra·phy
chi·rop'o·dist
chi·rop'o·dy
chi'ro·prac'tic
chi'ro·prac'tor
chir'rup
chis'el
·eled or ·elled
·el·ing or ·el·ling
chis'el·er or
chis'el·ler
chi'-square'
chit'chat'
chit'ter·lings
chiv'al·rous
chiv'al·ry
chlor'dane
chlo'ric
chlo'ride
chlo'ri·nate'
·nat'ed ·nat'ing
chlo'ri·na'tion
chlo'rine
chlo'ro·form'
chlo'ro·phyll'
or ·phyl'
chlo'rous
chlor·tet'ra·cy'·
cline
chock'a·block'
chock'-full'
choc'o·late
choice
choic'er choic'est
choir
(singers; see
quire)

choke
choked chok'ing
chok'er
chol'er·a
chol'er·ic
cho·les'ter·ol'
choose
chose cho'sen
choos'ing
chop
chopped
chop'ping
chop'house'
chop'pi·ness
chop'py
·pi·er ·pi·est
chop'sticks'
chop su'ey
cho'ral
(of a chorus)
cho·rale' or ·ral'
(hymn tune)
chord
(music; see cord)
chore
cho·re'a
chor'e·og'ra·pher
chor'e·o·graph'ic
chor'e·o·graph'-
i·cal·ly
chor'e·og'ra·phy
chor'is·ter
chor'tle
·tled ·tling
cho'rus
cho'sen
chow'der
chow mein
chrism
chris'ten
Chris'ten·dom
Chris'tian
Chris'ti·an'i·ty
Chris'tian·ize'
·ized' ·iz'ing
chris'tie or ·ty
Christ'like'
Christ'mas
Christ'mas·tide'
chro·mat'ic
chro'ma·tin
chrome
chro'mic
chro'mi·um
chro'mo·some'
chron'ic
chron'i·cle
·cled ·cling
chron'o·log'i·cal
chro·nol'o·gy
chro·nom'e·ter
chro·nom'e·try
chrys'a·lis
chrys·an'the·
mum
chrys'o·lite'
chrys'o·prase'
chub'bi·ness

chub'by
·bi·er ·bi·est
chuck'-full'
chuck'hole'
chuck'le
·led ·ling
chug
chugged chug'ging
chuk'ka boot
chuk'ker or ·kar
chum'mi·ness
chum'my
·mi·er ·mi·est
chunk'i·ness
chunk'y
·i·er ·i·est
church'go'er
church'man
church'wom'an
church'yard'
churl'ish
churn
chute
chut'ney
chyle
chyme
ci·bo'ri·um
·ri·a
ci·ca'da
·das or ·dae
cic'a·trix
ci·cat'ri·ces
cic'e·ly
Cic'er·o'
ci'der
ci·gar'
cig'a·rette'
or ·ret'
cig'a·ril'lo
·los
cil'i·a
(sing. cil'i·um)
cil'i·ar'y
cin·cho'na
Cin'cin·nat'i
cinc'ture
·tured ·tur·ing
cin'der
cin'e·ma
cin'e·mat'o·
graph'
cin'e·rar'i·um
·rar'i·a
cin'er·a'tor
cin'na·bar'
cin'na·mon
cinque'foil'
ci'pher
cir'ca
cir'cle
·cled ·cling
cir'clet
cir'cuit
cir·cu'i·tous
cir'cuit·ry
cir'cu·lar
cir'cu·lar·i·
za'tion

cir'cu·lar·ize'
·ized' ·iz'ing
cir'cu·late'
·lat'ed ·lat'ing
cir'cu·la'tion
cir'cu·la·to'ry
cir'cum·cise'
·cised' ·cis'ing
cir'cum·ci'sion
cir·cum'fer·ence
cir'cum·flex'
cir'cum·lo·
cu'tion
cir'cum·nav'i·
gate'
·gat'ed ·gat'ing
cir'cum·po'lar
cir'cum·scribe'
·scribed' ·scrib'ing
cir'cum·
scrip'tion
cir'cum·spect'
cir'cum·spec'tion
cir'cum·stance'
cir'cum·stan'tial
cir'cum·stan'ti·
ate'
·at'ed ·at'ing
cir'cum·vent'
cir'cum·ven'tion
cir'cus
cir·rho'sis
cir'ro·cu'mu·lus
cir'ro·stra'tus
cir'rus
·ri
cis·al'pine
cis·at·lan'tic
cis'tern
cit'a·del
ci·ta'tion
cite
cit'ed cit'ing
(mention; see
sight)
cit'i·fied'
cit'i·zen
cit'i·zen·ry
cit'i·zen·ship'
cit'rate
cit'ric
cit'ron
cit'ron·el'la
cit'rous adj.
cit'rus n.
cit'y
·ies
cit'y·scape'
cit'y-state'
civ'et
civ'ic
civ'il
ci·vil'ian
ci·vil'i·ty
·ties
civ'i·li·za'tion
civ'i·lize'
·lized' ·liz'ing

civ'il·ly
civ'vies
claim'ant
clair·voy'ance
clair·voy'ant
clam
clammed
clam'ming
clam'bake'
clam'ber
clam'mi·ness
clam'my
·mi·er ·mi·est
clam'or
clam'or·ous
clan·des'tine
clan·des'tine·ly
clan'gor
clan'gor·ous
clan'nish
clans'man
clap
clapped
clap'ping
clap'board
clap'per
clap'trap'
claque
clar'et
clar'i·fi·ca'tion
clar'i·fi'er
clar'i·fy'
·fied ·fy'ing
clar'i·net'
clar'i·net'ist or
clar'i·net'tist
clar'i·on
clar'i·ty
clas'sic
clas'si·cal
clas'si·cal·ly
clas'si·cism
clas'si·fi'a·ble
clas'si·fi·ca'tion
clas'si·fi'er
clas'si·fy'
·fied' ·fy'ing
class'mate'
class'room'
clat'ter
clause
claus'tro·
pho'bi·a
clav'i·chord'
clav'i·cle
cla·vier'
clay'ey
clay'i·er
clay'i·est
clean'a·ble
clean'-cut'
clean'er
clean'hand'ed
clean'li·ly
clean'li·ness
clean'ly
·li·er ·li·est

clean'ness
cleanse
cleansed
cleans'ing
cleans'er
clean'shav'en
clean'up'
clear'ance
clear'-cut'
clear'eyed'
clear'head'ed
clear'ing·house'
clear'sight'ed
cleats
cleav'age
cleave
cleaved or cleft
or clove, cleaved
or cleft or
clo'ven,
cleav'ing
(to split)
cleave
cleaved cleav'ing
(to cling)
cleav'er
clem'en·cy
clem'ent
clere'sto'ry
·ries
cler'gy
·gies
cler'gy·man
·men
cler'ic
cler'i·cal
cler'i·cal·ly
cler'i·cal·ism
clev'er
clew
cli·ché'
click
cli'ent
cli'en·tele'
cliff'-dwell'ing
cliff'hang'er or
cliff'-hang'er
cli·mac'ter·ic
cli·mac'tic
(of a climax)
cli·mac'ti·cal·ly
cli'mate
cli·mat'ic
(of climate)
cli·mat'i·cal·ly
cli'ma·tol'o·gy
cli'max
climb'er
clinch'er
cling
clung cling'ing
clin'ic
clin'i·cal
cli·ni'cian
clink'er
cli·nom'e·ter
clip
clipped clip'ping

clip'board'
clip'per
clique
cli'to·ris
clo·a'ca
·cae
cloak'room'
clob'ber
cloche
clock'wise'
clock'work'
clod'dish
clod'hop'per
clog
clogged
clog'ging
cloi'son·né'
clois'ter
close
closed clos'ing
close
clos'er clos'est
closed'-end'
close'fist'ed
close'fit'ting
close'grained'
close'-hauled'
close'ly
close'mouthed'
clos'et
close'-up'
clo'sure
clot
clot'ted clot'ting
cloth n.
clothe v.
clothed or clad
cloth'ing
clothes'line'
clothes'pin'
clothes'press'
cloth'ier
cloth'ing
clo'ture
cloud'burst'
cloud'i·ness
cloud'y
·i·er ·i·est
clo'ver·leaf'
·leafs'
cloy'ing·ly
clown'ish
club
clubbed
club'bing
club'foot'
club'house'
clue
clued clu'ing
clum'si·ly
clum'si·ness
clum'sy
·si·er ·si·est
clus'ter
clut'ter
coach'man
co·ad'ju·tor
co·ag'u·la·ble

co·ag'u·lant
co·ag'u·late'
·lat'ed ·lat'ing
co·ag·u·la'tion
co·ag'u·la'tor
co'a·lesce'
·lesced' ·lesc'ing
co'a·les'cence
co'a·les'cent
co'a·li'tion
coarse
(common; see
course)
coarse'grained'
coars'en
coarse'ness
coast'al
coast'er
coast guard
coast'land'
coast'line'
coat'ing
coat'tail'
co·au'thor
co·ax'i·al
coax'ing·ly
co'balt
cob'ble
·bled ·bling
cob'bler
cob'ble·stone'
co'bel·lig'er·ent
co'bra
cob'web'
co·caine'
or ·cain'
coc'cus
coc'ci
coc'cyx
coc·cy'ges
cock'a·lo'rum
cock'boat'
cock'crow'
cock'er·el
cock'eyed'
cock'i·ly
cock'i·ness
cock'ney
·neys
cock'pit'
cock'roach'
cocks'comb'
cock'sure'
cock'tail'
co'coa
co'co·nut'
or co'coa·nut'
co·coon'
cod'dle
·dled ·dling
code
cod'ed cod'ing
co'de·fend'ant
co'de·ine'
co'dex
·di·ces'
cod'fish'
codg'er

cod'i·cil
cod'i·fi·ca'tion
cod'i·fy'
·fied' ·fy'ing
co'ed·u·ca'tion
co·ef·fi'cient
co·erce'
·erced' ·erc'ing
co·er'cion
co·er'cive
co·e'val
co·ex·ist'ence
cof'fee·house'
cof'fee·pot'
cof'fer
cof'fer·dam'
cof'fin
co'gen·cy
co'gent
cog'i·tate'
·tat'ed ·tat'ing
cog'i·ta'tion
cog'nac
cog'nate
cog·ni'tion
cog'ni·tive
cog'ni·zance
cog'ni·zant
cog·no'men
·no'mens or
·nom'i·na
cog'wheel'
co·hab'it
co·hab'i·ta'tion
co'heir'
co·here'
·hered' ·her'ing
co·her'ence
co·her'ent
co·he'sion
co·he'sive·ness
co'hort
coif·fure'
coign
(position; see
coin, quoin)
coin
(metal money;
see coign, quoin)
coin'age
co'in·cide'
·cid'ed ·cid'ing
co·in'ci·dence
co·in'ci·dent
co·in'ci·den'tal
co·in'ci·den'tal·ly
co·i'tion
co'i·tus
col'an·der
(draining pan;
see calender)
cold'blood'ed
cold'heart'ed
co'le·op'ter·ous
cole'slaw'
col'ic
col'ick·y
col'i·se'um

co·li'tis
col·lab'o·rate'
·rat'ed ·rat'ing
col·lab'o·ra'tion
col·lab'o·ra'tor
col·lage'
col·lapse'
·lapsed' ·laps'ing
col·laps'i·bil'i·ty
col·laps'i·ble
col'lar
col'lar·bone'
col·late'
·lat'ed ·lat'ing
col·lat'er·al
col·lat'er·al·ly
col·la'tion
col·la'tor
col'league
col·lect'a·ble
or ·i·ble
col·lec'tion
col·lec'tive·ly
col·lec'tiv·ism
col·lec'tiv·is'tic
col·lec'tiv·i·ty
col·lec'tiv·ize'
·ized' ·iz'ing
col·lec'tor
col'leen
col'lege
col·le'gi·al'i·ty
col·le'gi·an
col·le'giate
col·lide'
·lid'ed ·lid'ing
col'lie
col'li·gate'
·gat'ed ·gat'ing
col'li·mate'
·mat'ed ·mat'ing
co·lin'e·ar
col·li'sion
col'lo·ca'tion
col·lo'di·on
col'loid
col·loi'dal
col·lo'qui·al
col·lo'qui·al·ism
·qui·a
col'lo·quy
·quies
col'lo·type'
col·lude'
·lud'ed ·lud'ing
col·lu'sion
col·lu'sive
co·lo'cate'
·cat'ed ·cat'ing
co'-lo·ca'tion
co·logne'
co'lon
colo'nel
(officer; see
kernel)
co·lo'ni·al
col'o·nist

col'o·ni·za'tion
col'o·nize'
·nized' ·niz'ing
col'on·nade'
col'o·ny
·nies
col'o·phon'
col'or
Col'o·rad'o
col'o·rant
col'or·a'tion
col'o·ra·tu'ra
col'or·bear'er
col'or·blind'
col'or·cast'
·cast' or cast'ed
·cast'ing
col'ored
col'or·fast'
col'or·ful
col'or·less
co·los'sal
Col'os·se'um
co·los'sus
·los'si or
·los'sus·es
colt'ish
Co·lum'bi·a
col'umn
co·lum'nar
col'um·nist
co'ma
(stupor; see
comma)
com'a·tose'
com·bat'
·bat'ed or
·bat'ted
·bat'ing or
·bat'ting
com'bat·ant
com·bat'ive
comb'er
com·bin'a·ble
com·bi·na'tion
com·bine'
·bined' ·bin'ing
comb'ings
com·bus'ti·
bil'i·ty
com·bus'ti·ble
com·bus'ti·bly
com·bus'tion
com·bus'tor
come
came come
com'ing
come'back'
co·me'di·an
co·me'dic
co·me'di·enne'
come'down'
com'e·dy
·dies
come'li·ness
come'ly
·li·er ·li·est
co·mes'ti·ble

com'et
come'up'pance
com'fit
com'fort
com'fort·a·ble
com'fort·a·bly
com'fort·er
com'ic
com'i·cal
com'i·cal·ly
com'i·ty
·ties
com'ma
(punctuation
mark; see coma)
com·mand'
com'man·dant'
com'man·deer'
com·mand'er
com·mand'ment
com·man'do
·dos or ·does
com·mem'o·rate'
·rat'ed ·rat'ing
com·mem'o·
ra'tion
com·mem'o·
ra'tive
com·mence'
·menced'
·menc'ing
com·mence'·
ment
com·mend'
com·mend'a·ble
com·mend'a·bly
com'men·da'tion
com·mend'a·
to'ry
com·men'su·
ra·ble
com·men'su·
ra·bly
com·men'su·rate
com'ment
com'men·tar'y
·ies
com'men·tate'
·tat'ed ·tat'ing
com'men·ta'tor
com'merce
com·mer'cial
com·mer'cial·ism
com·mer'cial·i·
za'tion
com·mer'cial·ize'
·ized' ·iz'ing
com·min'gle
·gled ·gling
com·mis'er·ate'
·at'ed ·at'ing
com·mis'er·
a'tion
com'mis·sar'
com'mis·sar'i·at
com'mis·sar'y
·ies
com·mis'sion

com·mis'sion·er
com·mit'
·mit'ted ·mit'ting
com·mit'ment
com·mit'ta·ble
com·mit'tal
com·mit'tee
com·mit'tee·man
com·mode'
com·mo'di·ous
com·mod'i·ty
·ties
com'mo·dore'
com'mon·al·ty
·ties
com'mon·er
com'mon·ness
com'mon·place'
com'mon·weal'
com'mon·wealth'
com·mo'tion
com'mu·nal
com·mu'nal·ly
com·mu'nal·ism
com·mune' v.
·muned'
·mun'ing
com'mune n.
com·mu'ni·ca·ble
com·mu'ni·cant
com·mu'ni·cate'
·cat'ed ·cat'ing
com·mu'ni·
ca'tion
com·mu'ni·
ca'tive
com·mu'ni·ca'tor
com·mun'ion
com·mu'ni·qué'
com·mu'nism
com'mu·nist
com'mu·nis'tic
com·mu·nis'ti·
cal·ly
com·mu'ni·ty
·ties
com'mu·nize'
·nized' ·niz'ing
com·mut'a·ble
com'mu·tate'
·tat'ed ·tat'ing
com'mu·ta'tion
com·mu'ta·tive
com'mu·ta'tor
com·mute'
·mut'ed
·mut'ing
com·mut'er
com·pact'
com·pan'ion
com·pan'ion·
a·ble
com·pa'ny
·nies
com'pa·ra·ble
com'pa·ra·bly
com·par'a·tive
com·par'a·tive·ly

com·pare'	com·plic'i·ty	con·cede'	con·cur'rence	con·fes'sed·ly	con·gres'sion·al
·pared' ·par'ing	com·pli'er	·ced'ed ·ced'ing	con·cur'rent	con·fes'sion	con'gress·man
com·par'i·son	com'pli·ment	con·ceit'	con·cus'sion	con·fes'sion·al	con'gru·ence
com·part'ment	(praise; see	con·ceit'ed	con·demn'	con·fes'sor	con'gru·ent
com·part'men'·	complement)	con·ceiv'a·	con·dem'na·ble	con·fet'ti	con·gru'i·ty
tal·ize'	com'pli·men'·	bil'i·ty	con'dem·na'tion	con'fi·dant' n.	con'gru·ous
·ized' -iz'ing	ta·ry	con·ceiv'a·ble	con·dem'na·to'ry	con·fide'	con'ic
com'pass	com'pli·men·	con·ceiv'a·bly	con·demn'er	·fid'ed ·fid'ing	con'i·cal
com·pas'sion	tar'i·ly	con·ceive'	con·den'sa·ble	con'fi·dence	con'i·cal·ly
com·pas'sion·ate	com·ply'	·ceived' ·ceiv'ing	or ·si·ble	con'fi·dent adj.	co'ni·fer
com·pat'i·bil'i·ty	·plied' ·ply'ing	con'cen·trate'	con'den·sa'tion	con'fi·den'tial	co·nif'er·ous
com·pat'i·ble	com·po'nent	·trat'ed ·trat'ing	con·den'sa·ble	con'fi·den'tial·ly	con·jec'tur·al
com·pat'i·bly	com·port'ment	con'cen·tra'tion	con·dense'	con·fig'u·ra'tion	con·jec'ture
com·pa'tri·ot	com·pose'	con·cen'tric	·densed'	con·fin'a·ble or	·tured ·tur·ing
com'peer	·posed' ·pos'ing	con·cen'tri·cal·ly	·dens'ing	con·fine'a·ble	con·join'
com·pel'	com·pos'er	con'cept	con·dens'er	con·fine'	con·joint'ly
·pelled' ·pel'ling	com·pos'ite	con·cep'tion	con'de·scend'	·fined' ·fin'ing	con'ju·gal
com·pen'di·ous	com'po·si'tion	con·cep'tu·al	con'de·scend'ing	con·fine'ment	con'ju·gal·ly
com·pen'di·um	com·pos'i·tor	con·cep'tu·al·ize'	con'de·scen'sion	con·firm'	con'ju·gate'
·ums or ·a	com'pos men'tis	·ized' ·iz'ing	con·dign'	con'fir·mand'	·gat'ed ·gat'ing
com·pen'sa·ble	com'post	con·cep'tu·al·i·	con'di·ment	con'fir·ma'tion	con'ju·ga'tion
com'pen·sate'	com·po'sure	za'tion	con·di'tion	con·firm'a·to'ry	con·junc'tion
·sat'ed ·sat'ing	com'pote	con·cep'tu·al·ly	con·di'tion·al	con·firmed'	con·junc'tive
com'pen·sa'tion	com·pound' v.	con·cern'	con·di'tion·al·ly	con'fis·cate'	con·junc·ti·vi'tis
com'pen·sa'tive	com'pound n.	con·cerned'	con·do'la·to'ry	·cat'ed ·cat'ing	con·junc'ture
com·pen'sa·tor	com'pre·hend'	con·cern'ing	con·dole'	con'fis·ca'tion	con'jure
com·pen'sa·to'ry	com'pre·hen'si·	con'cert	·doled' ·dol'ing	con'fla·gra'tion	·jured ·jur·ing
com·pete'	ble	con·cert'ed	con·do'lence	con·flict'	con'jur·er or ·or
·pet'ed ·pet'ing	com'pre·hen'sion	con·cer·ti'na	con'dom	con·flic'tion	con·nect'
com'pe·tence	com'pre·hen'sive	con'cert·mas'ter	con·do·min'i·um	con'flu·ence	Con·nect'i·cut
com'pe·ten·cy	com·press'	con·cer'to	·i·ums or ·i·a	con·form'	con·nec'tion
com'pe·tent	com·pressed'	·tos or ·ti	con·do·na'tion	con·form'a·ble	con·nec'tive
com·pe·ti'tion	com·pres'si·ble	con·ces'sion	con·done'	con·form'a·bly	con·nec'tor
com·pet'i·tive	com·pres'sion	con·ces'sion·aire'	·doned' ·don'ing	con·form'ance	or ·nect'er
com·pet'i·tor	com·pres'sor	conch	con'dor	con'for·ma'tion	conn'ing tower
com·pi·la'tion	com·prise'	conchs or	con·duce'	con·form'ist	con·niv'ance
com·pile'	·prised' ·pris'ing	conch'es	·duced' ·duc'ing	con·form'i·ty	con·nive'
·piled' ·pil'ing	com'pro·mise'	con·chol'o·gy	con·du'cive	con·found'ed	·nived' ·niv'ing
com·pil'er	·mised' ·mis'ing	con'ci·erge'	con'duct'	con·front'	con'nois·seur'
com·pla'cence	comp·tom'e·ter	con·cil'i·ar	con·duct'ance	con'fron·ta'tion	con·no·ta'tion
com·pla'cen·cy	comp·trol'ler	con·cil'i·ate'	con·duct'i·ble	Con·fu'cius	con·no·ta'tive
com·pla'cent	com·pul'sion	·at'ed ·at'ing	con·duc'tion	con·fuse'	con·note'
(smug; see	com·pul'sive	con·cil'i·a·to'ry	con'duc·tiv'i·ty	·fused' ·fus'ing	·not'ed ·not'ing
complaisant)	com·pul'so·ri·ly	con·cise'	con·duc'tor	con·fu'sion	con·nu'bi·al
com·plain'	com·pul'so·ri·ness	con·cise'ly	con'duit	con·fu·ta'tion	con'quer
com·plain'ant	com·pul'so·ry	con·cise'ness	co'ney	con·fute'	con'quer·or
com·plaint'	com·punc'tion	con'clave	·neys or ·nies	·fut'ed ·fut'ing	con'quest
com·plai'sance	com·punc'tious	con·clude'	con·fab'u·late'	con·geal'	con·quis'ta·dor
com·plai'sant	com·put'a·bil'i·ty	·clud'ed	·lat'ed ·lat'ing	con·gen'ial	·dors or ·dores
(obliging; see	com·put'a·ble	·clud'ing	con·fec'tion	con·gen'ial·ly	con'science
complacent)	com'pu·ta'tion	con·clu'sion	con·fec'tion·ar'y	con·ge'ni·al'i·ty	con'sci·en'tious
com'ple·ment	com·pute'	con·clu'sive	adj.	con·gen'i·tal	con'scious
(completing part;	·put'ed ·put'ing	con·coct'	con·fec'tion·er	con·gen'i·tal·ly	con'script'
see compliment)	com·put'er	con·coc'tion	con·fec'tion·er'y	con·gest'	con·se'crate'
com'ple·	com·put'er·ize'	con·com'i·tance	n.	con·ges'tion	·crat'ed ·crat'ing
men'ta·ry	·ized' ·iz'ing	con·com'i·tant	·ies	con·glom'er·ate'	con'se·cra'tion
com·plete'	com·put'er·i·	con'cord	con·fed'er·a·cy	·at'ed ·at'ing	con·sec'u·tive
·plet'ed ·plet'ing	za'tion	con·cord'ance	·cies	con·glom'er·a'tion	con·sen'sus
com·ple'tion	com'rade	con·cor'dat	con·fed'er·ate'	con·grat'u·late'	con·sent'
com·plex'	con·cat·e·na'tion	con'course	·at'ed ·at'ing	·lat'ed ·lat'ing	con'se·quence
com·plex'ion	con·cave'	con·crete'	con·fed·er·a'tion	con·grat'u·	con'se·quen'tial
com·plex'i·ty	con·cav'i·ty	con·cre'tion	con·fer'	la'tion	con'se·quent'ly
·ties	·ties	con'cu·bine'	·ferred' ·fer'ring	con·grat'u·	con·ser'van·cy
com·pli'ance	con·ca'vo-con·	con·cu'pis·cence	con'fer·ee'	la·to'ry	con·ser·va'tion
com·pli'ant	cave'	con·cu'pis·cent	con'fer·ence	con'gre·gant	con·ser'va·tism
com'pli·cate'	con·ca'vo-con·	con·cur'	con·fer·en'tial	con'gre·gate'	con·ser'va·tive
·cat'ed ·cat'ing	vex'	·curred'	con·fer'ment	·gat'ed ·gat'ing	con·ser'va·to'ry
com'pli·ca'tion	con·ceal'	·cur'ring	con·fer'ral	con'gre·ga'tion	·ries
			con·fess'		

con·serve'
·served'
·serv'ing
con·sid'er
con·sid'er·a·ble
con·sid'er·a·bly
con·sid'er·ate
con·sid'er·a'tion
con·sid'ered
con·sign'
con·sign'a·ble
con·sign·ee'
con·sign'ment
con·sign'or
or ·er
con·sist'
con·sis'ten·cy
·cies
con·sis'tent
con·sis'to·ry
·ries
con·sol'a·ble
con'so·la'tion
con·sol'a·to'ry
con·sole'
·soled' ·sol'ing
con'sole
con·sol'i·date'
·dat'ed ·dat'ing
con·sol'i·da'tion
con·sol'i·da'tor
con'som·mé'
con'so·nance
con'so·nant
con'so·nan'tal
con'sort
con·sor'ti·um
·ti·a
con·spec'tus
con·spic'u·ous
con·spir'a·cy
·cies
con·spir'a·tor
con·spire'
·spired' ·spir'ing
con'sta·ble
con·stab'u·lar'y
·ies
con'stan·cy
con'stant
con'stel·la'tion
con'ster·na'tion
con'sti·pate'
·pat'ed ·pat'ing
con'sti·pa'tion
con·stit'u·en·cy
·cies
con·stit'u·ent
con'sti·tute'
·tut'ed ·tut'ing
con'sti·tu'tion
con'sti·tu'tion·al
con'sti·tu'tion·al'i·ty
con'sti·tu'tion·al·ly
con·strain'
con·straint'

con·strict'
con·stric'tion
con·stric'tor
con·stru'a·ble
con·struct'
con·struc'tion
con·struc'tive
con·struc'tor or
con·struct'er
con·strue'
·strued' ·stru'ing
con'sul
con'sul·ar
con'sul·ate
con·sult'
con·sult'ant
con'sul·ta'tion
con·sul'ta·tive
con·sum'a·ble
con·sume'
·sumed'
·sum'ing
con·sum'er
con'sum·mate'
·mat'ed ·mat'ing
con·sum'mate·ly
con'sum·ma'tion
con'sum·ma'tor
con·sump'tion
con·sump'tive
con'tact
con·ta'gion
con·ta'gious
con·tain'er
con·tain'er·ize'
·ized' ·iz'ing
con·tain'ment
con·tam'i·nant
con·tam'i·nate'
·nat'ed ·nat'ing
con·tam'i·na'tion
con·tam'i·na'tor
con·temn'
con·tem'plate'
·plat'ed
·plat'ing
con'tem·pla'tion
con'tem·pla'tive
con'tem·pla'tor
con·tem'po·ra'ne·ous
con·tem'po·rar'y
con·tempt'
con·tempt'i·bil'i·ty
con·tempt'i·ble
con·tempt'i·bly
con·temp'tu·ous
con·tend'
con·tent'
con'tent
con·tent'ed·ly
con·ten'tion
con·ten'tious
con·tent'ment
con·test'
con·test'a·ble
con·test'ant

con'text
con·tex'tu·al
con·ti·gu'i·ty
con·tig'u·ous
con'ti·nence
con'ti·nent
con'ti·nen'tal
con·tin'gen·cy
·cies
con·tin'gent
con·tin'u·a·ble
con·tin'u·al
con·tin'u·ance
con·tin'u·a'tion
con·tin'ue
·ued ·u·ing
con·ti·nu'i·ty
·ties
con·tin'u·ous
con·tin'u·um
·u·a or ·u·ums
con·tort'
con·tor'tion
con'tour
con'tra·band'
con'tra·bass'
con'tra·cep'tion
con'tra·cep'tive
con'tract
con·tract'i·bil'i·ty
con·tract'i·ble
con·trac'tile
con·trac'tion
con'trac·tor
con·trac'tu·al
con·trac'tu·al·ly
con'tra·dict'
con'tra·dic'tion
con'tra·dic'to·ry
con'tra·dis·tinc'tion
con'trail'
con·tral'to
·tos or ·ti
con'tra·pun'tal
con'trar·i·ly
con'trar·i·ness
con'trar·i·wise'
con'trar·y
con·trast'
con'tra·vene'
·vened' ·ven'ing
con'tra·ven'tion
con·trib'ute
·ut·ed ·ut·ing
con'tri·bu'tion
con·trib'u·tor
con·trib'u·to'ry
con·trite'
con·tri'tion
con·triv'a·ble
con·triv'ance
con·trive'
·trived' ·triv'ing
con·trol'
·trolled'
·trol'ling
con·trol'la·bil'i·ty

con·trol'la·ble
con·trol'ler
con'tro·ver'sial
con'tro·ver'sy
·sies
con'tro·vert'
con'tro·vert'i·ble
con·tu·ma'cious
con·tu·ma·cy
con·tu·me'li·ous
con'tu·me·ly
con·tuse'
·tused' ·tus'ing
con·tu'sion
co·nun'drum
con'ur·ba'tion
con'va·lesce'
·lesced' ·lesc'ing
con'va·les'cence
con'va·les'cent
con·vec'tion
con·vec'tive
con·vec'tor
con·vene'
·vened' ·ven'ing
con·ven'ience
con·ven'ient
con'vent
con·ven'ti·cle
con·ven'tion
con·ven'tion·al
con·ven'tion·al'i·ty
·ties
con·ven'tion·al·ize'
·ized' ·iz'ing
con·ven'tion·eer'
con·verge'
·verged'
·verg'ing
con·ver'gence
con·vers'a·ble
con'ver·sa'tion
con'ver·sa'tion·al
con·verse'
·versed' ·vers'ing
con'verse
con·ver'sion
con·vert'
con·vert'er
or ·ver'tor
con·vert'i·ble
con·vex'
con·vex'i·ty
con·vex'o-con·cave'
con·vex'o-con·vex'
con·vey'
con·vey'ance
con·vey'or or ·er
con·vict'
con·vic'tion
con·vince'
·vinced'
·vinc'ing

con·vin'ci·ble
con·viv'i·al
con·viv'i·al'i·ty
con'vo·ca'tion
con·voke'
·voked' ·vok'ing
con'vo·lut'ed
con'vo·lu'tion
con'voy
con·vulse'
·vulsed'
·vuls'ing
con·vul'sion
con·vul'sive
cook'book'
cook'out'
cook'ie or ·y
·ies
cool'ant
cool'head'ed
coo'lie
(Oriental laborer;
see coolly,
coulee)
cool'ly
(in a cool manner;
see coolie,
coulee)
co'-op'
co·op'er·ate'
or co-op'·
·at'ed ·at'ing
co·op'er·a'tion
or co-op'·
co·op'er·a·tive
or co-op'·
co-opt'
co·or'di·nate'
or co-or'·
·nat'ed ·nat'ing
co·or'di·na'tor
or co-or'·
co·part'ner
cope
coped cop'ing
cop'i·er
co'pi·lot
co'pi·ous
cop'-out'
cop'per
cop'per·plate'
co'pra
cop'u·late'
·lat'ed ·lat'ing
cop'u·la'tion
cop'y
·ies
·ied ·y·ing
cop'y·cat'
cop'y·hold'er
cop'y·read'er
cop'y·right'
cop'y·writ'er
co·quet'
·quet'ted
·quet'ting
co'quet·ry
co·quette'

co·quet'tish
co·quille'
cor'al
cor'bel
cord
(string; see
chord)
cord'age
cor'date
cor'dial
cor·di·al'i·ty
·ties
cor'dil·le'ra
cord'ite
cor'don
cor'do·van
cor'du·roy'
cord'wood'
core
cored cor'ing
co're·spond'ent
(in law; see
correspondent)
Cor'fam
co'ri·an'der
Co·rin'thi·an
cork'screw'
cor'mo·rant
corn borer
corn bread
corn'cob'
cor'ne·a
cor'nered
cor'ner·stone'
cor'ner·wise'
cor·net'
cor·net'ist
or ·net'tist
corn'field'
corn'flow'er
corn'husk'ing
cor'nice
corn'meal'
corn'stalk'
corn'starch'
cor'nu·co'pi·a
corn'y
·i·er ·i·est
co·rol'la
co·rol'lar'y
·ies
co·ro'na
·nas or ·nae
cor'o·nar'y
cor'o·na'tion
cor'o·ner
cor'o·net'
cor'po·ral
cor'po·rate
cor'po·ra'tion
cor'po·ra·tive
cor·po're·al
corps
corps
(group of people)
corpse
(dead body)
corps'man

cor'pu·lence
cor'pu·lent
cor'pus
  cor'po·ra
cor'pus·cle
cor·ral'
  ·ralled' ·ral'ling
cor·rect'
cor·rect'a·ble
cor·rec'tion
cor·rec'tive
cor·rec'tor
cor're·late'
  ·lat'ed ·lat'ing
cor're·la'tion
cor·rel'a·tive
cor're·spond'
cor're·
  spond'ence
cor're·
  spond'ent
  (*writer;* see
  corespondent)
cor'ri·dor
cor'ri·gi·ble
cor'ri·gi·bly
cor·rob'o·rate'
  ·rat'ed ·rat'ing
cor·rob'o·ra'tion
cor·rob'o·ra'tive
cor·rob'o·ra'tor
cor·rode'
  ·rod'ed ·rod'ing
cor·rod'i·ble
cor·ro'sion
cor·ro'sive
cor'ru·gate'
  ·gat'ed ·gat'ing
cor·ru·ga'tion
cor·rupt'
cor·rupt'i·bil'i·ty
cor·rupt'i·ble
cor·rupt'i·bly
cor·rup'tion
cor·rup'tive
cor·sage'
cor'sair
corse'let
cor'set
cor'se·tiere'
cor·tege' *or* ·tège'
cor'tex
  ·ti·ces'
cor'ti·cal
cor'ti·cal·ly
cor'ti·sone'
co·run'dum
cor'us·cate'
  ·cat'ed ·cat'ing
cor·vette'
co·se'cant
co'sign'
co'sign'er
co·sig'na·to'ry
  ·ries
co'sine'
cos·met'ic
cos'me·ti'cian

cos·me·tol'o·gy
cos'mic
cos'mi·cal·ly
coun'ter·man'
cos·mog'o·ny
cos·mog'ra·phy
cos'mo·line'
cos·mol'o·gy
cos'mo·naut'
cos·mop'o·lis
cos'mo·pol'i·tan
cos·mop'o·lite'
cos'mos
cos'mo·tron'
co'spon'sor
cost
  cost cost'ing
cost'li·ness
cost'ly
  ·li·er ·li·est
cost'-plus'
cos'tume
  ·tumed ·tum·ing
cos·tum'er
co·tan'gent
co'te·rie
co·til'lion
cot'tage
cot'ton
cou'gar
cough
cou'lee
  (*gulch;* see
  coolie, coolly)
cou·lomb'
coun'cil
  (*legislature;* see
  counsel)
coun'cil·man
coun'ci·lor
  or ·cil·lor
  (*council member;*
  see counselor)
coun'sel
  ·seled *or* ·selled
  ·sel·ing *or*
  ·sel·ling
  (*advice; advise;*
  see council)
coun'se·lor
  or ·sel·lor
  (*adviser;* see
  councilor)
count'down'
coun'te·nance
count'er
  (*one that counts*)
coun'ter
  (*opposite*)
coun'ter·act'
coun'ter·ac'tion
coun'ter·at·tack'
coun'ter·bal·
  ance
coun'ter·claim'
coun'ter·clock'·
  wise
coun'ter·feit
coun'ter·foil'

coun'ter·ir'ri·
  tant
coun'ter·man'
coun'ter·mand'
coun'ter·march'
coun'ter·meas'·
  ure
coun'ter·move'
coun'ter·of·fen'·
  sive
coun'ter·pane'
coun'ter·part'
coun'ter·plot'
coun'ter·point'
coun'ter·poise'
coun'ter·sign'
coun'ter·sink'
  ·sunk' ·sink'ing
coun'ter·spy'
coun'ter·weight'
count'less
count'less
coun'tri·fied'
coun'try
  ·tries
coun'try·man
coun'try·side'
coun'ty
  ·ties
coup de grâce'
coup d'é·tat'
coupe
cou'ple
  ·pled ·pling
cou'pler
cou'plet
cou'pon
cour'age
cou·ra'geous
cou'ri·er
course
  coursed
cours'ing
  (*way; run;* see
  coarse)
cour'te·ous
cour'te·san
cour'te·sy
  ·sies
  (*polite act;*
  see curtsy)
court'house'
cour'ti·er
court'li·ness
court'ly
  ·li·er ·li·est
court'-mar'tial
courts'-mar'tial
  ·tialed *or*
  ·tialled
  ·tial·ing *or*
  ·tial·ling
court'room'
court'yard'
cous'in
cou·ture'
cou·tu·rier'
cou·tu·rière'

cov'e·nant
Cov'en·try
cov'er·age
cov'er·alls'
cov'ered
cov'er·ing
cov'er·let
cov'ert
cov'er-up'
cov'et·ous
cov'ey
cow'ard
cow'ard·ice
cow'ard·li·ness
cow'ard·ly
cow'boy'
cow'catch'er
cow'er
cow'herd'
cow'hide'
  ·hid'ed ·hid'ing
cowled
cow'lick
cowl'ing
co'-work'er
cow'pox'
cow'rie *or* ·ry
  ·ries
cow'shed'
cox'comb'
cox'swain
coy'ly
coy·o'te
co'zi·ly
co'zi·ness
co'zy
  ·zies
  ·zi·er ·zi·est
crab
  crabbed crab'bing
crab'bed
crab'bi·ness
crab'by
  ·bi·er ·bi·est
crack'brained'
crack'down'
cracked
crack'er
crack'ing
crack'le
  ·led ·ling
crack'lings
crack'up'
cra'dle
  ·dled ·dling
cra'dle·song'
craft'i·ly
craft'i·ness
crafts'man
craft'y
  ·i·er ·i·est
crag'gi·ness
crag'gy
  ·gi·er ·gi·est
cram
  crammed
cram'ming
cramped

cram'pon
cran'ber'ry
  ·ries
crane
  craned cran'ing
cra'ni·al
cra·ni·ol'o·gy
cra'ni·um
  ·ni·ums *or* ·ni·a
crank'case'
crank'i·ness
crank'shaft'
crank'y
  ·i·er ·i·est
cran'ny
  ·nies
crap'u·lence
crash'-land'
crass'ly
crass'ness
cra'ter
cra·vat'
crave
  craved crav'ing
cra'ven
crawl'er
cray'fish'
cray'on
craze
  crazed craz'ing
cra'zi·ly
cra'zi·ness
cra'zy
  ·zi·er ·zi·est
creak
  (*squeak;* see
  creek)
creak'i·ness
creak'y
  ·i·er ·i·est
cream'er·y
  ·ies
cream'i·ness
cream'y
  ·i·er ·i·est
crease
  creased
creas'ing
cre·ate'
  ·at'ed ·at'ing
cre·a'tion
cre·a'tive
cre'a·tiv'i·ty
cre·a'tor
crea'ture
cre'dence
cre·den'tial
cre·den'za
cred'i·bil'i·ty
cred'i·ble
cred'i·bly
cred'it·a·bil'i·ty
cred'it·a·ble
cred'it·a·bly
cred'i·tor
cre'do
  ·dos
cre·du'li·ty

cred'u·lous
creek
  (*stream;* see
  creak)
creep
  crept creep'ing
creep'i·ness
creep'y
  ·i·er ·i·est
cre'mate
  ·mat·ed ·mat·ing
cre·ma'tion
cre'ma·to'ry
  ·ries
cre'o·sote'
crepe *or* crêpe
cre·scen'do
  ·dos
cres'cent
crest'fall'en
cre'tin
cre'tonne
cre·vasse'
crev'ice
crew'el·work'
crib'bage
crick'et
cri'er
crim'i·nal
crim'i·nol'o·gy
crim'son
cringe
  cringed
cring'ing
crin'kle
  ·kled ·kling
crin'o·line
crip'ple
  ·pled ·pling
crip'pler
cri'sis
  ·ses
crisp'er
crisp'i·ness
crisp'y
  ·i·er ·i·est
criss'cross'
cri·ter'i·on
  ·i·a *or* ·i·ons
crit'ic
crit'i·cal
crit'i·cal·ly
crit'i·cism
crit'i·cize'
  ·cized' ·ciz'ing
cri·tique'
croak
cro·chet'
  ·cheted'
  ·chet'ing
crock'er·y
croc'o·dile'
cro'cus
crois·sant'
crom'lech
cro'ny
  ·nies
crook'ed·ness

croon'er
crop
 cropped
 crop'ping
crop'-dust'ing
cro·quet'
 ·queted'
 ·quet'ing
 (game)
cro·quette'
 (food)
cro'sier
cross'bar'
cross'beam'
cross'bow'
cross'breed'
 ·bred' ·breed'ing
cross'-check'
cross'-coun'try
cross'cur'rent
cross'cut'
cross'-ex·am'i·
 na'tion
cross·ex·am'ine
cross'-eyed'
cross'-fer'ti·lize'
cross'-grained'
cross'hatch'
cross'-in'dex
cross'ing
cross'-leg'ged
cross'o'ver
cross'piece'
cross'-pur'pose
cross'-re·fer'
cross'-ref'er·ence
cross'road'
cross'ruff'
cross section
cross'-stitch'
cross'tie'
cross'-town'
cross'walk'
cross'wise'
cross'word'
crotch'et·i·ness
crotch'et·y
crou'pi·er'
crou'ton
crow'bar'
crowd'ed
crow's'-foot'
 -feet'
crow's'-nest'
cru'cial
cru'cial·ly
cru'ci·ble
cru'ci·fix'
cru'ci·fix'ion
cru'ci·form'
cru'ci·fy'
 ·fied' ·fy'ing
crude'ly
cru'di·ty
 ·ties
cru'el·ly
cru'el·ty
 ·ties

cru'et
cruise
 cruised cruis'ing
cruis'er
crul'ler
crum'ble
 ·bled ·bling
crum'bly
 ·bli·er ·bli·est
crum'by
 ·bi·er ·bi·est
crum'pet
crum'ple
 ·pled ·pling
crunch'i·ness
crunch'y
 ·i·er ·i·est
crup'per
cru·sade'
crush'a·ble
crus·ta'cean
crust'ed
crust'i·ness
crust'y
 ·i·er ·i·est
crux
 crux'es or cru'ces
cry
 cries
 cried cry'ing
cry'o·gen'ics
crypt
cryp'tic
cryp'ti·cal·ly
cryp'to·gram'
cryp'to·gram'mic
cryp'to·graph'ic
cryp'to·graph'i·
 cal·ly
cryp·tog'ra·phy
crys'tal
crys'tal·line
crys'tal·liz'a·ble
crys'tal·li·za'tion
crys'tal·lize'
 ·lized' ·liz'ing
crys'tal·log'ra·phy
cub'by·hole'
cube
 cubed cub'ing
cu'bic
cu'bi·cal
 (cube-shaped)
cu'bi·cal·ly
cu'bi·cle
 (compartment)
cu'bit
cuck'old
cuck'oo'
cu'cum·ber
cud'dle
 ·dled ·dling
cud'dly
 ·dli·er ·dli·est
cudg'el
 ·eled or ·elled
 ·el·ing or
 ·el·ling

cue
 cued cu'ing
 or cue'ing
 (signal; see
 queue)
cui·rass'
cui·sine'
cul'-de-sac'
cu'li·nar'y
cull
cul'mi·nate'
 ·nat'ed ·nat'ing
cul'mi·na'tion
cu·lottes'
cul'pa·bil'i·ty
cul'pa·ble
cul'pa·bly
cul'prit
cult'ist
cul'ti·va·ble
cul'ti·vate'
 ·vat'ed ·vat'ing
cul'ti·va'tion
cul'ti·va'tor
cul'tur·al
cul'ture
 ·tured ·tur·ing
cul'vert
cum'ber·some
cum'mer·bund'
cu'mu·late'
 ·lat'ed ·lat'ing
cu'mu·la'tive
cu'mu·lous adj.
cu'mu·lus n.
 ·li
cu·ne'i·form'
cun'ning·ly
cup'board
cup'ful'
 ·fuls'
cu·pid'i·ty
cu'po·la
cur'a·ble
cu'ra·çao'
cu'rate
cur'a·tive
cu·ra'tor
curb'stone'
cur'dle
 ·dled ·dling
cure
 cured cur'ing
cure'-all'
cur'few
cu'rie
cu'ri·o'
 ·os'
cu'ri·os'i·ty
 ·ties
cu'ri·ous
curl'i·cue'
curl'i·ness
curl'y
 ·i·er ·i·est
cur·mudg'eon
cur'rant
 (fruit)

cur'ren·cy
 ·cies
cur'rent
 (a flowing)
cur·ric'u·lar
cur·ric'u·lum
 ·u·la or ·u·lums
cur'ry
 ·ried ·ry·ing
cur'ry·comb'
curse
 cursed or curst
 curs'ing
cur'sive
cur'so·ri·ly
cur'so·ri·ness
cur'so·ry
cur·tail'
cur'tain
curt'ness
curt'sy
 ·sies
 ·sied ·sy·ing
 (knee bend;
 see courtesy)
cur'va·ture
curve
 curved curv'ing
cur'vi·lin'e·ar
curv'y
 ·i·er ·i·est
cush'ion
cus'pid
cus'pi·dor'
cus'tard
cus·to'di·al
cus·to'di·an
cus'to·dy
cus'tom
cus'tom·ar'i·ly
cus'tom·ar'y
cus'tom-built'
cus'tom·er
cus'tom·house'
cus'tom-made'
cut
 cut cut'ting
cu·ta'ne·ous
cut'a·way'
cut'back'
cut'i·cle
cut'lass or ·las
cut'ler·y
cut'let
cut'off'
cut'out'
cut'-rate'
cut'ter
cut'throat'
cy'a·nide'
cy'ber·cul'ture
cy'ber·na'tion
cy'ber·net'ics
cy'cla·mate'
cy'cle
 cy'cled cy'cling
cy'clic
cy'cli·cal

cy'clist
cy'cli·zine'
cy'clom'e·ter
cy'clone
cy'clo·pe'di·a
cy'clo·ra'ma
cy'clo·tron'
cyg'net
cyl'in·der
cy·lin'dri·cal
cym'bal
 (brass plate;
 see symbol)
cyn'ic
cyn'i·cal
cyn'i·cal·ly
cyn'i·cism
cy'no·sure'
cy'press
cyst'ic
cyst'oid
cy·tol'o·gy
cy'to·plasm
czar
Czech'o·slo·
 va'ki·a

D

dab'ble
 ·bled ·bling
dachs'hund
Da'cron
dac'tyl
dad'dy
 ·dies
da'do
 ·does
daf'fo·dil'
dag'ger
da·guerre'o·type'
dahl'ia
dai'ly
 ·lies
dain'ti·ly
dain'ti·ness
dain'ty
 ·ti·er ·ti·est
dai·qui·ri
dair'y
 ·ies
dair'y·maid'
dair'y·man'
da'is
dai'sy
 ·sies
dal'li·ance
dal'ly
 ·lied ·ly·ing
Dal·ma'tian
dam
 dammed
 dam'ming
 (barrier; see
 damn)

dam'age
 ·aged ·ag·ing
dam'age·a·ble
dam'a·scene'
dam'ask
damn
 damned
 damn'ing
 (condemn; see
 dam)
dam'na·ble
dam'na·bly
dam·na'tion
dam'na·to'ry
damp'-dry'
 -dried' -dry'ing
damp'en
damp'er
dam'sel
dance
 danced danc'ing
danc'er
dan'de·li'on
dan'dle
 ·dled ·dling
dan'druff
dan'ger
dan'ger·ous
dan'gle
 ·gled ·gling
Dan'ish
dan·seuse'
dap'ple
 ·pled ·pling
dare
 dared dar'ing
dare'dev'il
Dar·jee'ling
dark'en
dark'room'
dar'ling
Dar·win'i·an
dash'board'
das'tard·li·ness
das'tard·ly
da'ta
 (sing. da'tum)
date
 dat'ed dat'ing
daugh'ter
daugh'ter-in-law'
 daugh'ters-
 in-law'
daunt'less
dav'en·port'
dav'it
daw'dle
 ·dled ·dling
day'bed'
day'book'
day'break'
day'dream'
day letter
day'light'
day'long'
day room
day'time'
day'-to-day'

day'work'
daze
  dazed daz'ing
daz'zle
  ·zled ·zling
D'-day'
dea'con
dea'con·ess
de·ac'ti·vate'
dead'en
dead'-end'
dead'head'
dead'line'
dead'li·ness
dead'lock'
dead'ly
  ·li·er ·li·est
dead'wood'
deaf'en·ing·ly
deaf'-mute'
deal
  dealt deal'ing
deal'er·ship'
dean'er·y
  ·ies
dear'ly
dearth
death'bed'
death'blow'
death'less
death'ly
death'trap'
death'watch'
de·ba'cle
de·bar'
  ·barred' ·bar'ring
de·bark'
de'bar·ka'tion
de·base'
  ·based' ·bas'ing
de·bat'a·ble
de·bate'
  ·bat'ed ·bat'ing
de·bauch'
deb·au'chee'
de·bauch'er·y
  ·ies
de·ben'ture
de·bil'i·tate'
  ·tat'ed ·tat'ing
de·bil'i·ta'tion
de·bil'i·ty
  ·ties
deb'it
deb'o·nair'
  or ·naire'
deb'o·nair'ly
de·brief'
de·bris'
debt'or
de·bunk'
de·but'
deb'u·tante'
dec'ade
dec'a·dence
dec'a·dent
dec'a·gon'
dec'a·gram'

dec'a·he'dron
  ·drons or ·dra
de·cal'ci·fy'
  ·fied' ·fy'ing
de·cal'co·ma'ni·a
dec'a·li'ter
Dec'a·logue'
  or ·log'
dec'a·me'ter
de·camp'
de·cant'
de·cant'er
de·cap'i·tate'
  ·tat'ed ·tat'ing
de·cap'i·ta'tion
de·cath'lon
de·cay'
de·cease'
  ·ceased'
  ·ceas'ing
de·ce'dent
de·ceit'ful
de·ceiv'a·ble
de·ceive'
  ·ceived'
  ·ceiv'ing
de·cel'er·ate'
  ·at'ed ·at'ing
de·cel'er·a'tion
de·cel'er·a'tor
de·cel'er·on'
De·cem'ber
de'cen·cy
  ·cies
de·cen'ni·al
de'cent
  (proper; see
  descent, dissent)
de·cen'tral·i·
  za'tion
de·cen'tral·ize'
  ·ized' ·iz'ing
de·cep'tion
de·cep'tive·ly
dec'i·bel
de·cide'
  ·cid'ed ·cid'ing
de·cid'ed·ly
de·cid'u·ous
dec'i·mal
dec'i·mal·ize'
  ·ized' ·iz'ing
dec'i·mal·ly
dec'i·mate'
  ·mat'ed ·mat'ing
de·ci'pher
de·ci'sion
de·ci'sive
deck'le
de·claim'
dec'la·ma'tion
de·clam'a·to'ry
de·clar'a·ble
dec'la·ra'tion
de·clar'a·tive
de·clare'
  ·clared'
  ·clar'ing

de·clas'si·fy'
  ·fied' ·fy'ing
de·clen'sion
dec'li·na'tion
de·cline'
  ·clined' ·clin'ing
de·cliv'i·ty
  ·ties
de·code'
de·cod'er
de'com·pos'a·ble
de'com·pose'
de'com·po·si'tion
de'com·pres'sion
de'con·gest'ant
de'con·tam'i·nate'
de'con·trol'
  ·trolled'
  ·trol'ling
dé·cor' or de·cor'
dec'or·ate'
  ·at'ed ·at'ing
dec'o·ra'tion
dec'o·ra·tive
dec'o·ra'tor
dec'o·rous
de·co'rum
de'cou·page'
de·coy'
de·crease'
  ·creased'
  ·creas'ing
de·cree'
  ·creed' ·cree'ing
de·crep'it
de·crep'i·tude'
de'cre·scen'do
de·cres'cent
de·cri'al
de·cry'
  ·cried' ·cry'ing
de·crypt'
de·cum'bent
ded'i·cate'
  ·cat'ed ·cat'ing
ded'i·ca'tion
ded'i·ca·to'ry
de·duce'
  ·duced' ·duc'ing
de·duc'i·ble
de·duct'
de·duct'i·ble
de·duc'tion
de·duc'tive
de·em'pha·sis
de·em'pha·size'
deep'-chest'ed
deep'-dyed'
deep'freeze'
  ·froze' or
  ·freezed'
  ·fro'zen or
  ·freezed'
  ·freez'ing
deep'-fry'
  -fried' -fry'ing

deep'-laid'
deep'-root'ed
deep'-seat'ed
deep'-set'
deer'skin'
de·es'ca·late'
de·es'ca·la'tion
de·face'
de·fac'to
de·fal'cate
  ·cat·ed ·cat·ing
def'a·ma'tion
de·fam'a·to'ry
de·fame'
  ·famed'
  ·fam'ing
de·fault'
de·fea'sance
de·feat'
de·feat'ist
def'e·cate'
  ·cat'ed ·cat'ing
def'e·ca'tion
de·fect'
de·fec'tion
de·fec'tive
de·fec'tor
de·fend'
de·fend'ant
de·fense'
de·fen'si·ble
de·fen'sive
de·fer'
  ·ferred' ·fer'ring
def'er·ence
def'er·en'tial
de·fer'ment
de·fi'ance
de·fi'ant
de·fi'cien·cy
  ·cies
de·fi'cient
def'i·cit
de·fi'er
de·file'
  ·filed' ·fil'ing
de·fin'a·ble
de·fine'
  ·fined' ·fin'ing
def'i·nite
def'i·ni'tion
de·fin'i·tive
de·flate'
  ·flat'ed ·flat'ing
de·fla'tion
de·fla'tion·ar'y
de·fla'tor
de·flect'
de·flec'tion
de·flec'tor
de·flow'er
de·fo'li·ate'
  ·at'ed ·at'ing
de'for·ma'tion
de·formed'
de·form'i·ty
  ·ties
de·fraud'

de·fray'
de·fray'al
de·frost'
de·funct'
de·fuse'
de·fy'
  ·fied' ·fy'ing
dé'ga·gé'
de·gen'er·a·cy
de·gen'er·ate'
  ·at'ed ·at'ing
de·gen'er·a'tion
de·gen'er·a·tive
de·grad'a·ble
deg'ra·da'tion
de·grade'
  ·grad'ed
  ·grad'ing
de·gree'
de'hu·mid'i·fy'
  ·drat·ed ·drat·ing
de'hy·dra'tion
de·hy'dra·tor
de·ic'er
de'i·fi·ca'tion
de'i·fy'
  ·fied' ·fy'ing
deign
de'ism
de'i·ty
  ·ties
de·ject'ed
de·jec'tion
Del'a·ware'
de·lay'
de·lec'ta·ble
del'e·gate'
  ·gat'ed ·gat'ing
del'e·ga'tion
de·lete'
  ·let'ed ·let'ing
del'e·te'ri·ous
de·le'tion
delft'ware'
de·lib'er·ate
de·lib'er·ate·ly
de·lib'er·a'tion
del'i·ca·cy
  ·cies
del'i·cate
del'i·cate·ly
del'i·ca·tes'sen
de·li'cious
de·light'ful
de·light'ful·ly
de·lin'e·ate'
  ·at'ed ·at'ing
de·lin'e·a'tion
de·lin'e·a'tor
de·lin'quen·cy
de·lin'quent
de·lir'i·ous
de·lir'i·um
de·liv'er·a·ble
de·liv'er·ance
de·liv'er·y
  ·ies

de·lude'
  ·lud'ed ·lud'ing
del'uge
  ·uged ·ug·ing
de·lu'sion
de·lu'sive
de·luxe'
delve
  delved delv'ing
de·mag'net·ize'
dem'a·gog'ic
dem'a·gog'i·cal·ly
dem'a·gogue'
  or ·gog'
dem'a·gog'y
de·mand'ing
de·mar'cate
  ·cat·ed ·cat·ing
de·mar·ca'tion
de·mean'or
de·men'tia
de·mer'it
de·mesne'
dem'i·john'
de·mil'i·ta·rize'
de·mise'
dem'i·tasse'
de·mo'bi·lize'
de·moc'ra·cy
  ·cies
dem'o·crat'ic
dem'o·crat'i·cal·ly
de·moc'ra·ti·
  za'tion
de·moc'ra·tize'
  ·tized' ·tiz'ing
de·mog'ra·phy
de·mol'ish
dem'o·li'tion
de'mon
de·mon'e·tize'
  ·tized' ·tiz'ing
de·mo'ni·ac'
de·mon'ic
de·mon'i·cal·ly
de·mon'stra·ble
dem'on·strate'
  ·strat'ed
  ·strat'ing
dem'on·stra'tion
de·mon'stra·tive
dem'on·stra'tor
de·mor'al·ize'
de·mote'
  ·mot'ed ·mot'ing
de·mo'tion
de·mount'
de·mul'cent
de·mur'
  ·murred'
  ·mur'ring
  (to object)
de·mure'
  (coy)
de·mur'rage
de·mur'rer
de·na'tion·al·ize'
de·nat'u·ral·ize'

de·na'ture
·tured ·tur·ing
de·ni'a·ble
de·ni'al
de·nier'
de·ni'er
den'im
den'i·zen
de·nom'i·nate'
·nat'ed ·nat'ing
de·nom'i·na'tion
de·nom'i·na'tor
de'no·ta'tion
de·note'
·not'ed ·not'ing
de·noue'ment
de·nounce'
·nounced'
·nounc'ing
dense
dens'er dens'est
dense'ly
den'si·ty
·ties
den'tal
den'tal·ly
den'ti·frice'
den'tin
den'tist
den'tist·ry
den'ture
de·nude'
·nud'ed ·nud'ing
de·nun'ci·a'tion
de·ny'
·nied' ·ny'ing
de·o'dor·ant
de·o'dor·ize'
·ized' ·iz'ing
de·o'dor·iz'er
de·part'ed
de·part'ment
de·part'men'tal
de·part'men'tal·ize'
·ized' ·iz'ing
de·par'ture
de·pend'a·bil'i·ty
de·pend'a·ble
de·pend'a·bly
de·pend'ence
de·pend'en·cy
·cies
de·pend'ent
de·per'son·al·ize'
de·pict'
de·pic'tion
de·pil'a·to'ry
·ries
de·plane'
de·plete'
·plet'ed ·plet'ing
de·ple'tion
de·plor'a·ble
de·plore'
·plored'
·plor'ing
de·ploy'

de·pon'ent
de·pop'u·late'
de·port'a·ble
de'por·ta'tion
de·port'ment
de·pose'
de·pos'it
de·pos'i·tar'y
dep'o·si'tion
de·pos'i·tor
de·pos'i·to'ry
·ries
de'pot
dep'ra·va'tion
(a corrupting; see deprivation)
de·prave'
·praved'
·prav'ing
de·prav'i·ty
·ties
dep're·cate'
·cat'ed ·cat'ing
dep're·ca'tion
dep're·ca·to'ry
de·pre'ci·a·ble
de·pre'ci·ate'
·at'ed ·at'ing
de·pre'ci·a'tion
dep're·da'tion
de·pres'sant
de·pressed'
de·press'ing
de·pres'sion
de·pres'sive·ly
dep'ri·va'tion
(a taking away; see depravation)
de·prive'
·prived' ·priv'ing
depth
dep'u·ta'tion
dep'u·tize'
·tized' ·tiz'ing
dep'u·ty
·ties
de·rail'
de·range'
·ranged'
·rang'ing
der'e·lict'
der'e·lic'tion
de·ride'
·rid'ed ·rid'ing
de ri·gueur'
de·ri'sion
de·ri'sive
der'i·va'tion
de·riv'a·tive
de·rive'
·rived' ·riv'ing
der'ma·tol'o·gist
der'o·ga'tion
de·rog'a·to'ri·ly
de·rog'a·to'ry
der'rick

der'ri·ère'
der'ring·do'
der'rin·ger
de·sal'i·na'tion
de·salt'
des'cant
de·scend'
de·scend'ant
de·scend'i·ble
de·scent'
(going down; see
decent, dissent)
de·scrib'a·ble
de·scribe'
·scribed'
·scrib'ing
de·scrip'tion
de·scrip'tive
de·scry'
·scried'
·scry'ing
des'e·crate'
·crat'ed ·crat'ing
des'e·cra'tion
de·seg're·gate'
·gat'ed ·gat'ing
de·seg're·ga'tion
de·sen'si·tize'
de·sen'si·tiz'er
de·sert'
(abandon; see
dessert)
des'ert
(dry area)
de·ser'tion
de·serts'
(reward, etc.)
de·serve'
·served'
·serv'ing
de·serv'ed·ly
des'ic·cant
des'ic·cate'
·cat'ed ·cat'ing
des'ic·ca'tion
de·sign'
des'ig·nate'
·nat'ed ·nat'ing
des'ig·na'tion
des'ig·na'tor
de·signed'
de·sign'er
de·sir'a·bil'i·ty
de·sir'a·ble
de·sir'a·bly
de·sire'
·sired' ·sir'ing
de·sir'ous
de·sist'
des'o·late'
·lat'ed ·lat'ing
des'o·la'tion
de·spair'
des'per·a'do
·does or ·dos
des'per·ate
(hopeless; see
disparate)

des'per·a'tion
des'pi·ca·ble
de·spise'
·spised'
·spis'ing
de·spite'
de·spoil'
de·spo'li·a'tion
de·spond'en·cy
de·spond'ent
des'pot
des·pot'ic
des·pot'i·cal·ly
des'pot·ism
des·sert'
(food; see desert)
des'ti·na'tion
des'tine
·tined ·tin·ing
des'tin·y
·ies
des'ti·tute'
des'ti·tu'tion
de·stroy'er
de·struct'
de·struct'i·bil'i·ty
de·struct'i·ble
de·struc'tion
de·struc'tive
de·struc'tor
des'ue·tude'
des'ul·to'ry
de·tach'
de·tach'a·ble
de·tach'ment
de·tail'
de·tain'
de·tect'
de·tect'a·ble
or ·i·ble
de·tec'tion
de·tec'tive
de·tec'tor
dé·tente'
de·ten'tion
de·ter'
·terred'
·ter'ring
de·ter'gent
de·te'ri·o·rate'
·rat'ed ·rat'ing
de·te'ri·o·ra'tion
de·ter'ment
de·ter'mi·na·ble
de·ter'mi·na·bly
de·ter'mi·nant
de·ter'mi·nate
de·ter'mi·na'tion
de·ter'mine
·mined ·min·ing
de·ter'min·ism
de·ter'rence
de·ter'rent
de·test'
de·test'a·ble
de·test'a·bly
de·tes·ta'tion

de·throne'
·throned'
·thron'ing
det'o·nate'
·nat'ed ·nat'ing
det'o·na'tion
det'o·na'tor
de'tour
de·tract'
de·trac'tor
det'ri·ment
det'ri·men'tal
de·tri'tus
deuce
de·val'u·a'tion
de·val'ue
dev'as·tate'
·tat'ed ·tat'ing
dev'as·ta'tion
de·vel'op·ment
de·vel'op·men'tal
de'vi·ant
de'vi·ate'
·at'ed ·at'ing
de'vi·a'tion
de·vice'
dev'il·ish
dev'il·ment
dev'il·try
·tries
de'vi·ous
de·vis'a·ble
(that can be devised;
see divisible)
de·vise'
·vised' ·vis'ing
de·vi'tal·ize'
de·void'
de·volve'
·volved'
·volv'ing
de·vote'
·vot'ed ·vot'ing
dev'o·tee'
de·vo'tion
de·vour'
de·vout'
dew'drop'
dew'lap'
dew'y
·i·er ·i·est
dex·ter'i·ty
dex'ter·ous
or dex'trous
dex'trose
di'a·be'tes
di'a·bet'ic
di'a·bol'ic
di'a·bol'i·cal
di'a·bol'i·cal·ly
di'a·crit'i·cal
di'a·dem'
di'ag·nos'a·ble
di'ag·nose'
·nosed' ·nos'ing
di'ag·no'sis
·no'ses
di'ag·nos'tic

di'ag·nos'ti·cal·ly
di'ag·nos·ti'cian
di·ag'o·nal
di·ag'o·nal·ly
di'a·gram'
·gramed' or
·grammed'
·gram'ing or
·gram'ming
di'a·gram·mat'ic
di'al
·aled or ·alled
·al·ing or ·al·ling
di'a·lect'
di'a·lec'tal
di'a·lec'tic
di'a·lec·ti'cian
di·al'o·gist
di'a·logue' or
·log'
di·am'e·ter
di'a·met'ri·cal
di'a·met'ri·cal·ly
di'a·mond
di'a·pa'son
di'a·per
di·aph'a·nous
di'a·phragm'
di'a·rist
di'ar·rhe'a
or ·rhoe'a
di'a·ry ·ries
di'a·stase'
di'a·ther'my
di'a·ton'ic
di'a·tribe'
dib'ble
·bled ·bling
dice
diced dic'ing
(sing. die or dice)
di·chot'o·mize'
·mized' ·miz'ing
di·chot'o·my
dick'er
dick'ey
·eys
Dic'ta·phone'
dic'tate
·tat·ed ·tat·ing
dic·ta'tion
dic·ta'tor
dic·ta·to'ri·al
dic'tion·ar'y
·ies
Dic'to·graph'
dic'tum
·tums or ·ta
di·dac'tic
di·dac'ti·cal·ly
die
dice
(cube)
die
dies
died die'ing
(mold; stamp)

die
　died dy'ing
　(*stop living;*
　see dye)
die'-hard' *or*
　die'hard'
diel'drin
di'e·lec'tric
di·er'e·sis
　·ses'
die'sel
die'sink·er
di'e·sis
　·ses'
di'e·tar'y
di'e·tet'ic
di'e·tet'i·cal·ly
di'e·ti'tian
　or ·cian
dif'fer·ence
dif'fer·ent
dif'fer·en'tial
dif'fer·en'ti·ate'
　·at'ed ·at'ing
dif'fer·en'ti·a'tion
dif'fi·cult
dif'fi·cul'ty
　·ties
dif'fi·dence
dif'fi·dent
dif·fract'
dif·frac'tion
dif·fuse'
　·fused' ·fus'ing
dif·fus'i·ble
dif·fu'sion
dif·fu'sive
dig
　dug dig'ging
dig'a·my
di'gest
di·gest'i·ble
di·ges'tive
dig'ger
dig'it
dig'it·al
dig'i·tal'is
dig'i·ti·grade'
dig'ni·fy
　·fied' ·fy'ing
dig'ni·tar'y
　·ies
dig'ni·ty
　·ties
di·gress'
di·gres'sion
di·lan'tin
di·lap'i·date'
　·dat'ed ·dat'ing
di·lat'a·ble
di·late'
　·lat'ed ·lat'ing
di·la'tion
dil'a·to'ry
di·lem'ma
dil'et·tante'
　·tantes' *or* ·tan'ti
dil'et·tant'ish

dil'i·gence
dil'i·gent
dil'ly·dal'ly
　·lied ·ly·ing
dil'u·ent
di·lute'
　·lut'ed ·lut'ing
di·lu'tion
di·lu'vi·al
dim
　dim'mer
　dim'mest
　dimmed
　dim'ming
di·men'sion
di·min'ish
di·min'u·en'do
dim'i·nu'tion
di·min'u·tive
dim'i·ty
dim'out'
dim'ple
　·pled ·pling
din
　dinned din'ning
dine
　dined din'ing
din'er
　(*person eating;*
　see dinner)
din·ette'
din'ghy
　·ghies
　(*boat*)
din'gi·ness
din'gy
　·gi·er ·gi·est
　(*not bright*)
din'ner
　(*meal;* see diner)
din'ner·ware'
di'no·saur'
di·oc'e·san
di'o·cese
di'o·ra'ma
di·ox'ide
dip
　dipped dip'ping
diph·the'ri·a
diph'thong
di·plo'ma
di·plo'ma·cy
　·cies
dip'lo·mat'
　(*government*
　representative)
dip'lo·mate'
　(*doctor*)
dip'lo·mat'i·cal·ly
dip'so·ma'ni·a
di·rect'
di·rec'tion
di·rec'tive
di·rec'tor
di·rec'tor·ate
di·rec'to'ri·al
di·rec'to·ry
　·ries

dire'ful
dirge
dir'i·gi·ble
dirn'dl
dirt'i·ness
dirt'y
　·i·er ·i·est
dis'a·bil'i·ty
　·ties
dis·a'ble
　·bled ·bling
dis·a·buse'
　·bused' ·bus'ing
dis'ad·van'tage
dis·ad·van·ta'·
　geous
dis'af·fect'ed
dis'a·gree'
dis'a·gree'a·ble
dis'a·gree'a·bly
dis'a·gree'ment
dis'al·low'
dis'ap·pear'ance
dis'ap·point'ment
dis'ap·pro·ba'tion
dis'ap·prov'al
dis'ap·prove'
dis·ar'ma·ment
dis·arm'ing
dis'ar·range'
dis'ar·ray'
dis'as·sem'ble
dis'as·so'ci·ate'
dis·as'ter
dis·as'trous
dis'a·vow'
dis'a·vow'al
dis·band'
dis·bar'
dis·be·lief'
dis'be·lieve'
dis'be·liev'er
dis·burse'
　·bursed'
　·burs'ing
dis·burse'ment
disc
dis·card'
dis·cern'
dis·cern'i·ble
dis·cern'ing
dis·cern'ment
dis·charge'
dis·ci'ple
dis'ci·plin·a·ble
dis'ci·pli·nar'i·an
dis'ci·pli·nar'y
dis'ci·pline
　·plined ·plin·ing
disc jockey
dis·claim'
dis·claim'er
dis·close'
dis·clo'sure
dis·cog'ra·phy
dis'coid
dis·col'or
dis·col'or·a'tion

dis·com'fit
dis·com'fi·ture
dis·com'fort
dis·com·pose'
dis'com·po'sure
dis·con·cert'
dis·con·nect'
dis·con'so·late
dis·con·tent'
dis·con·tin'u·ance
dis·con·tin'ue
dis·con'ti·nu'i·ty
dis·con·tin'u·ous
dis'co·phile'
dis'cord
dis·cord'ant
dis'co·thèque
dis'count
dis·cour'age
　·aged ·ag·ing
dis·cour'age·ment
dis'course
dis·cour'te·ous
dis·cour'te·sy
dis·cov'er
dis·cov'er·er
dis·cov'er·y
　·ies
dis·cred'it
dis·crect'
　(*prudent;* see
　discrete)
dis·crep'an·cy
　·cies
dis·crete'
　(*separate;* see
　discreet)
dis·cre'tion
dis·cre'tion·ar'y
dis·crim'i·nate'
　·nat'ed ·nat'ing
dis·crim'i·na'tion
dis·crim'i·na·
　to'ry
dis·cur'sive
dis'cus
　·cus·es *or* dis'ci
dis·cuss'
dis·cus'sion
dis·dain'ful
dis·ease'
　·eased' ·eas'ing
dis'em·bark'
dis'em·bod'y
dis'em·bow'el
　·eled *or* ·elled
　·el·ing *or*
　·el·ling
dis'en·chant'
dis'en·cum'ber
dis'en·gage'
dis'en·tan'gle
dis'es·tab'lish
dis·fa'vor
dis·fig'ure
dis·fig'ure·ment
dis·fran'chise
　·chised ·chis·ing

dis·gorge'
dis·grace'
　·graced'
　·grac'ing
dis·grace'ful
dis·grun'tle
　·tled ·tling
dis·guise'
　·guised'
　·guis'ing
dis·gust'
dis'ha·bille'
dis·har'mo·ny
dish'cloth'
dis·heart'en
di·shev'el
　·eled *or* ·elled
　·el·ing *or*
　·el·ling
dis·hon'est
dis·hon'es·ty
dis·hon'or
dis·hon'or·a·ble
dish'pan'
dish towel
dish'wash'er
dish'wa'ter
dis'il·lu'sioned
dis·in·cli·na'tion
dis·in·cline'
dis·in·fect'
dis·in·fect'ant
dis·in·gen'u·ous
dis·in·her'it
dis·in'te·grate'
　·grat'ed
　·grat'ing
dis·in'te·gra'tion
dis·in·ter'
dis·in'ter·est·ed
dis·join'
dis·joint'
dis·junc'tion
disk
dis·like'
dis'lo·cate'
dis'lo·ca'tion
dis·lodge'
dis·loy'al
dis·loy'al·ty
dis'mal
dis'mal·ly
dis·man'tle
dis·may'
dis·mem'ber
dis·miss'
dis·miss'al
dis·mount'
dis'o·be'di·ence
dis'o·be'di·ent
dis'o·bey'
dis·or'der
dis·or'der·ly
dis·or'gan·i·za'·
　tion
dis·or'gan·ize'
dis·o'ri·ent'
dis·own'

dis·par'age
　·aged ·ag·ing
dis'pa·rate
　(*not alike;* see
　desperate)
dis·par'i·ty
dis·pas'sion·ate
dis·patch'
dis·patch'er
dis·pel'
　·pelled' ·pel'ling
dis·pen'sa·bil'i·ty
dis·pen'sa·ble
dis·pen'sa·ry
　·ries
dis'pen·sa'tion
dis·pense'
　·pensed'
　·pens'ing
dis·pen'ser
dis·per'sal
dis·perse'
　·persed' ·pers'ing
dis·pers'i·ble
dis·per'sion
dis·pir'it·ed
dis·place'
dis·place'ment
dis·play'
dis·please'
dis·pleas'ure
dis·port'
dis·pos'a·ble
dis·pos'al
dis·pose'
　·posed' ·pos'ing
dis'po·si'tion
dis'pos·sess'
dis·proof'
dis'pro·por'tion
dis'pro·por'tion·
　ate
dis·prove'
dis·pu'ta·ble
dis·pu'tant
dis·pu·ta'tion
dis·pu·ta'tious
dis·pute'
　·put'ed ·put'ing
dis·qual'i·fi·ca'·
　tion
dis·qual'i·fy'
dis·qui'et
dis·qui'e·tude
dis·qui·si'tion
dis·re·gard'
dis·re·pair'
dis·rep'u·ta·ble
dis·rep'u·ta·bly
dis·re·pute'
dis're·spect'ful
dis·robe'
dis·rupt'
dis·rup'tion
dis·rup'tive
dis·sat'is·fac'tion
dis·sat'is·fy'
　·fied' ·fy'ing

dis·sect'
dis·sec'tion
dis·sec'tor
dis·sem'blance
dis·sem'ble
 ·bled ·bling
dis·sem'i·nate'
 ·nat'ed ·nat'ing
dis·sem'i·na'tion
dis·sen'sion
dis·sent'
 (*disagree;* see
 decent, descent)
dis·sen'tient
dis·sen'tious
dis'ser·ta'tion
dis·serv'ice
dis·sev'er
dis'si·dence
dis'si·dent
dis·sim'i·lar
dis·sim'i·lar'i·ty
dis·sim'i·la'tion
dis·sim'u·late'
dis'si·pate'
 ·pat'ed ·pat'ing
dis'si·pa'tion
dis·so'ci·ate'
 ·at'ed ·at'ing
dis·so'ci·a'tion
dis·sol'u·ble
dis'so·lute'
dis'so·lu'tion
dis·solv'a·ble
dis·solve'
 ·solved'
 ·solv'ing
dis·sol'vent
dis'so·nance
dis'so·nant
dis·suade'
 ·suad'ed
 ·suad'ing
dis·sua'sion
dis·sym'me·try
dis'taff
dis'tance
dis'tant
dis·taste'ful
dis·tem'per
dis·tend'
dis·ten'si·ble
dis·ten'tion *or*
 dis·ten'sion
dis'tich
dis·till' *or* ·til'
 ·tilled' ·till'ing
dis'til·late
dis'til·la'tion
dis·till'er
dis·till'er·y
 ·ies
dis·tinct'
dis·tinc'tion
dis·tinc'tive
dis·tin·gué'
dis·tin'guish
dis·tin'guish·a·ble

dis·tin'guish·a·bly
dis·tort'
dis·tor'tion
dis·tract'
dis·tract'i·ble
dis·trac'tion
dis·trait'
dis·traught'
dis·tress'
dis·trib'ut·a·ble
dis·trib'ute
 ·ut·ed ·ut·ing
dis'tri·bu'tion
dis·trib'u·tive
dis·trib'u·tor
dis'trict
dis·trust'ful
dis·turb'
dis·turb'ance
dis·un'ion
dis·u·nite'
dis·un'i·ty
dis·use'
ditch
dith'er
dit'to
 ·tos
 ·toed ·to·ing
dit'ty
 ·ties
di·u·ret'ic
di·ur'nal
di'va
di·van'
dive
 dived *or* dove
 dived div'ing
di·verge'
 ·verged'
 ·verg'ing
di·ver'gence
di·ver'gent
di'vers
 (*sundry*)
di·verse'
 (*different*)
di·ver'si·fi·ca'·
 tion
di·ver'si·form'
di·ver'si·fy'
 ·fied' ·fy'ing
di·ver'sion
di·ver'sion·ar'y
di·ver'si·ty
di·vert'
di·ver'tisse·ment
di·vest'
di·vest'i·ture
di·vid'a·ble
di·vide'
 ·vid'ed ·vid'ing
div'i·dend'
div'i·na'tion
di·vine'
 ·vined' ·vin'ing
di·vin'i·ty
 ·ties
di·vis'i·bil'i·ty

di·vis'i·ble
 (*that can be divided;*
 see devisable)
di·vi'sion
di·vi'sor
di·vorce'
 ·vorced' ·vorc'ing
di·vor·cé' *masc.*
di·vor'cée' *or*
 ·cee' *fem.*
div'ot
di·vulge'
 ·vulged'
 ·vulg'ing
di·vul'gence
diz'zi·ly
diz'zi·ness
diz'zy
 ·zi·er ·zi·est
 ·zied ·zy·ing
do'a·ble
dob'bin
do'cent
doc'ile
doc'ile·ly
do·cil'i·ty
dock'age
dock'et
dock'yard'
doc'tor
doc'tor·al
doc'tor·ate
doc'tri·naire'
doc'tri·nal
doc'trine
doc'u·ment
doc'u·men'tal
doc'u·men'ta·ry
 ·ries
doc'u·men·ta'tion
dod'der·ing
dodge
 dodged
 dodg'ing
dodg'y
 ·i·er ·i·est
do'er
does
doe'skin'
does'n't
dog'catch'er
dog'ear'
dog'ged·ly
dog'ger·el
dog'gy *or* ·gie
 ·gies
 (*dog*)
do'gie *or* ·gy
 ·gies
 (*calf*)
dog'ma
 ·mas *or* ·ma·ta
dog·mat'ic
dog·mat'i·cal·ly
dog'ma·tism
dog'ma·tize'
 ·tized' ·tiz'ing
dog'nap'

do'-good'er
dog'trot'
dog'watch'
dog'wood'
doi'ly
 ·lies
do'-it-your·self'
doll'ce
doll'drums
dole
 doled doll'ing
dole'ful
dol'lar
dol'lop
dol'man
 ·mans
 (*robe*)
dol'men
 (*tomb*)
do'lor·ous
dol'phin
dolt'ish
do·main'
do·mes'tic
do·mes'ti·cate'
 ·cat'ed ·cat'ing
do'mes·tic'i·ty
 ·ties
dom'i·cile'
dom'i·nance
dom'i·nant
dom'i·nate'
 ·nat'ed ·nat'ing
dom'i·na'tion
dom'i·neer'ing
dom'i·cal
do·min'ion
dom'i·no'
 ·noes' *or* ·nos'
don
 donned don'ning
do'nate
 ·nat·ed ·nat·ing
do·na'tion
do·nee'
Don' Ju'an
don'key
 ·keys
don'ny·brook'
do'nor
do'-noth'ing
Don' Qui·xo'te
don't
doo'dle
 ·dled ·dling
doo'hick'ey
dooms'day'
door'bell'
do'-or-die'
door'jamb'
door'keep'er
door'knob'
door'man'
door'mat'
door'nail'
door'plate'
door'sill'
door'step'

door'stop'
door'-to-door'
door'way'
dope
 doped dop'ing
dor'man·cy
dor'mant
dor'mer
dor'mi·to'ry
 ·ries
dor'mouse'
 ·mice'
dor'sal
do'ry
 ·ries
dos'-à-dos'
dos'age
dos'si·er'
dot
 dot'ted dot'ting
dot'age
dot'ard
dote
 dot'ed dot'ing
dou'ble
 ·bled ·bling
dou'ble-bar'reled
dou'ble-breast'ed
dou'ble-check'
dou'ble-cross'
dou'ble-date'
dou'ble-deal'ing
dou'ble-deck'er
dou'ble-edged'
dou'ble-
 en·ten'dre
dou'ble-faced'
dou'ble-head'er
dou'ble-joint'ed
dou'ble-knit'
dou'ble-park'
dou'ble-quick'
dou'ble-space'
dou'blet
dou'ble-tongued'
dou'bly
doubt
doubt'ful
doubt'ful·ly
doubt'less
douche
 douched
 douch'ing
dough
dough'i·ness
dough'nut'
dough'y
 ·i·er ·i·est
doup'pi·o'ni *or*
 dou'pi·o'ni
douse
 doused dous'ing
dove'cote'
dove'tail'
dow'a·ger
dow'di·ness
dow'dy
 ·di·er ·di·est

dow'el
dow'er
down'beat'
down'cast'
down'fall'
down'grade'
down'heart'ed
down'hill'
down'i·ness
down'pour'
down'range'
down'right'
down'spout'
down'stage'
down'stairs'
down'state'
down'stream'
down'swing'
down'time'
down'-to-earth'
down'town'
down'trod'den
down'turn'
down'ward
down'wash'
down'wind'
down'y
 ·i·er ·i·est
dow'ry
 ·ries
dox·ol'o·gy
doze
 dozed doz'ing
doz'en
drab
drab'ber
drab'best
draft·ee'
draft'i·ness
drafts'man
draft'y
 ·i·er ·i·est
drag
 dragged
 drag'ging
drag'gle
 ·gled ·gling
drag'gy
 ·gi·er ·gi·est
drag'net'
drag'o·man
 ·mans *or* ·men
drag'on
drag'on·fly'
 ·flies'
dra·goon'
drain'age
drain'pipe'
dra'ma
dra·mat'ic
dra·mat'i·cal·ly
dram'a·tist
dram'a·ti·za'tion
dram'a·tize'
 ·tized' ·tiz'ing
dram'a·tur'gy
drape
 draped drap'ing

dra'per·y
·ies
dras'tic
dras'ti·cal·ly
draughts'man
·men
draw
drew drawn
draw'ing
draw'back'
draw'bridge'
draw·ee'
draw'er
draw'knife'
knives'
drawl
drawn'work'
draw'string'
dray'age
dray'man
dread'ful
dread'ful·ly
dread'nought'
dream'i·ly
dream'i·ness
dream'y
·i·er ·i·est
drear'i·ly
drear'i·ness
drear'y
·i·er ·i·est
dredge
dredged
dredg'ing
drenched
dress
dressed or drest
dress'ing
dress'er
dress'i·ly
dress'i·ness
dress'ing-down'
dress'mak·er
dress'y
·i·er ·i·est
drib'ble
·bled ·bling
drib'let
dri'er or dry'er
drift'wood'
drill'mas·ter
drill press
drink
drank drunk
drink'ing
drink'a·ble
drip
dripped or dript
drip'ping
drip'-dry'
drive
drove driv'en
driv'ing
drive'-in'
driv'el
·eled or ·elled
·el·ing or
·el·ling

driv'er
drive'way'
driz'zle
·zled ·zling
driz'zly
droll'er·y
·ies
droll'ly
drom'e·dar'y
·ies
drone
droned dron'ing
droop'i·ly
droop'i·ness
droop'y
·i·er ·i·est
drop
dropped
drop'ping
drop'cloth'
drop'-forge'
-forged'
-forg'ing
drop'let
drop'out'
drop'per
dross
drought
or drouth
dro'ver
drown
drowse
drowsed
drows'ing
drow'si·ly
drow'si·ness
drow'sy
·si·er ·si·est
drub
drubbed
drub'bing
drudge
drudged
drudg'ing
drudg'er·y
drug
drugged
drug'ging
drug'gist
drug'store'
drum
drummed
drum'ming
drum'beat'
drum'head'
drum'mer
drum'stick'
drunk'ard
drunk'en·ness
drunk·o'me·ter
drupe'let
dry
dri'er dri'est
dried dry'ing
dry'as·dust'
dry'-clean'
dry cleaner
dry cleaning

dry'er
dry'-eyed'
dry ice
dry'ly or dri'ly
dry'ness
du'al
(of two; see duel)
du'al·ism
du'al·is'tic
du'al·ly
du'al-pur'pose
dub
dubbed dub'bing
du·bi'e·ty
du'bi·ous
du'cal
duc'at
duch'ess
duch'y
·ies
duck'ling
duck'pins'
duc'tile
duct'less
dudg'eon
due bill
du'el
·eled or ·elled
·el·ing or
·el·ling
(fight; see dual)
du·et'
duf'fel or ·fle
dug'out'
dul'cet
dul'ci·mer
dull'ard
dull'ness
dul'ly
(in a dull manner)
du'ly
(as due)
dumb'bell'
dumb'found' or
dum'found'
dumb'ly
dumb'wait·er
dum'dum'
dum'my
·mies
dump'i·ness
dump'ling
dump'y
·i·er ·i·est
dun
dunned
dun'ning
dun'der·head'
dun'ga·ree'
dun'geon
dung'hill'
dun'nage
du'o
du'os or du'i
du'o·dec'i·mal
du'o·de'nal
du'o·logue'
du·op'o·ly

du'o·tone'
du'o·type'
dupe
duped dup'ing
du'ple
du'plex
du'pli·cate'
·cat'ed ·cat'ing
du'pli·ca'tion
du'pli·ca'tor
du·plic'i·ty
·ties
du'ra·bil'i·ty
du'ra·ble
du'ra·bly
dur'ance
du·ra'tion
du·ress'
dur'ing
du'rum
dusk'i·ness
dusk'y
·i·er ·i·est
dust'i·ness
dust'pan'
dust'y
·i·er ·i·est
du'te·ous
du'ti·a·ble
du'ti·ful
du'ti·ful·ly
du'ty
·ties
du'ty-free'
dwarf
dwarfs or
dwarves
dwell
dwelt or dwelled
dwell'ing
dwin'dle
·dled ·dling
dy'ad
dyb'buk
dye
dyed dye'ing
(color; see die)
dyed'-in-the-wool'
dy'er
dye'stuff'
dy·nam'ic
dy·nam'i·cal·ly
dy'na·mism
dy'na·mite'
·mit'ed ·mit'ing
dy'na·mo'
·mos'
dy'na·mom'e·ter
dy'na·mo'tor
dy'nas·ty
·ties
dyne
dy·nel'
dys'en·ter'y
dys·func'tion
dys·pep'si·a
dys·pep'tic
dys'tro·phy

E

ea'ger
ea'gle
ea'gle-eyed'
ear'ache'
ear'drum'
ear'ly
·li·er ·li·est
ear'mark'
ear'muffs'
ear'nest
carn'ings
ear'phone'
ear'plug'
ear'ring'
ear'shot'
earth'en·ware'
earth'i·ness
earth'ly
earth'quake'
earth'shak·ing
earth'ward
earth'y
·i·er ·i·est
ear'wax'
ease
eased eas'ing
ea'sel
ease'ment
eas'i·ly
eas'i·ness
east'er·ly
east'ern
east'ward
eas'y
·i·er ·i·est
eas'y·go'ing
eat
ate eat'en
eat'ing
eat'a·ble
eaves'drop'
ebb tide
eb'on·y
e·bul'lient
e·bul·li'tion
ec·cen'tric
ec·cen'tri·cal·ly
ec'cen·tric'i·ty
·ties
ec·cle'si·as'ti·cal
ech'e·lon'
ech'o
·oes
e·cho'ic
é·clair'
é·clat'
ec·lec'tic
ec·lec'ti·cism
e·clipse'
·clipsed'
·clips'ing
e·clip'tic
ec'o·log'i·cal

ec'o·log'i·cal·ly
e·col'o·gist
e·col'o·gy
e'co·nom'ic
e'co·nom'i·cal
e'co·nom'i·cal·ly
e·con'o·mist
e·con'o·mize'
·mized' ·miz'ing
e·con'o·my
·mies
e'co·sys'tem
e'co·tone'
ec'ru
ec'sta·sy
·sies
ec·stat'ic
ec·stat'i·cal·ly
ec'u·men'i·cal
ec'ze·ma
ed'dy
·dies
e'del·weiss'
e·de'ma
·mas or ·ma·ta
edge
edged edg'ing
edge'ways'
edge'wise'
edg'i·ly
edg'i·ness
edg'y
·i·er ·i·est
ed'i·bil'i·ty
ed'i·ble
e'dict
ed·i·fi·ca'tion
ed'i·fice
ed'i·fy'
·fied' ·fy'ing
e·di'tion
(form of book;
see addition)
ed'i·tor
ed·i·to'ri·al
ed·i·to'ri·al·ize'
·ized' ·iz'ing
ed·i·to'ri·al·ly
ed'u·ca·bil'i·ty
ed'u·ca·ble
ed'u·cate'
·cat'ed ·cat'ing
ed·u·ca'tion
ed'u·ca'tive
ed'u·ca'tor
e·duce'
·duced' ·duc'ing
e·duc'i·ble
ee'rie or ·ry
·ri·er ·ri·est
ee'ri·ly
ee'ri·ness
ef·face'
·faced' ·fac'ing
ef·face'a·ble
ef·fect'
(result; see
affect)

ef·fec'tive
  (*having effect;*
  see affective)
ef·fec'tu·al
ef·fec'tu·ate'
  ·at'ed ·at'ing
ef·fem'i·na·cy
ef·fem'i·nate
ef'fer·ent
ef'fer·vesce'
  ·vesced'
  ·vesc'ing
ef'fer·ves'cence
ef'fer·ves'cent
ef·fete'
ef'fi·ca'cious
ef'fi·ca·cy
ef·fi'cien·cy
ef·fi'cient
ef'fi·gy
  ·gies
ef'flo·resce'
  ·resced'
  ·resc'ing
ef'flo·res'cence
ef'flu·ence
ef'flu·ent
  (*flowing;* see
  affluent)
ef·flu'vi·um
  ·vi·a *or* ·vi·ums
ef'fort
ef·fron'ter·y
  ·ies
ef·ful'gence
ef·fu'sion
ef·fu'sive
e·gal'i·tar'i·an
egg'nog'
egg'shell'
e'go
e'go·cen'tric
e'go·cen'tri·cal·ly
e'go·ism
e'go·ist
e'go·ma'ni·a
e'go·tism
e'go·tist
e'go·tis'tic
e'go·tis'ti·cal·ly
e·gre'gious
e'gress
e'gret
ei'der·down'
ei·det'ic
eight'een'
eighth
eight'i·eth
eight'y
  ·ies
ei'ther
ei'ther-or'
e·jac'u·late'
  ·lat'ed ·lat'ing
e·jac'u·la'tion
e·jac'u·la'tor
e·ject'
e·jec'tion

e·jec'tor
eke
  eked ek'ing
e·kis'tics
e·kis'ti·cal
e·lab'o·rate'
  ·rat'ed ·rat'ing
e·lab'o·rate·ly
e·lab'o·ra'tion
e·lapse'
  ·lapsed'
  ·laps'ing
e·las'tic
e·las'tic'i·ty
e·las'ti·cize'
  ·cized' ·ciz'ing
e·late'
  ·lat'ed ·lat'ing
e·la'tion
el'bow·room'
eld'er·ly
eld'est
e·lec'tion
e·lec'tion·eer'
e·lec'tive
e·lec'tor
e·lec'tor·al
e·lec'tor·ate
e·lec'tric
e·lec'tri·cal
e·lec'tri·cal·ly
e·lec·tri'cian
e·lec·tric'i·ty
e·lec'tri·fi·ca'tion
e·lec'tri·fy'
  ·fied' ·f ·g
e·lec'tro·cute'
  ·cut'ed ·cut'ing
e·lec'tro·cu'tion
e·lec'trode
e·lec'trol'y·sis
e·lec'tro·lyte'
e·lec'tro·lyt'ic
e·lec'tro·lyze'
  ·lyzed' ·lyz'ing
e·lec'tro·mag'net
e·lec'trom'e·ter
e·lec'tro·mo'tive
e·lec'tron
e·lec'tron'ic
e·lec·tron'i·cal·ly
e·lec'tro·plate'
e·lec'tro·scope'
e·lec'tro·stat'ics
e·lec'tro·ther'a·py
e·lec'tro·type'
e·lec'tro·typ'y
el'ee·mos'y·nar'y
el'e·gance
el'e·gant
el'e·gi'ac
el'e·gize'
  ·gized' ·giz'ing
el'e·gy
  ·gies
el'e·ment
el'e·men'tal
el'e·men'ta·ri·ness

el'e·men'ta·ry
  (*basic;* see
  alimentary)
el'e·phant
el'e·phan·ti'a·sis
el'e·phan'tine
El'eu·sin'i·an
el'e·vate'
  ·vat'ed ·vat'ing
el'e·va'tion
el'e·va'tor
e·lev'enth
elf
  elves
elf'in
e·lic'it
  (*draw forth;*
  see illicit)
e·lide'
  ·lid'ed ·lid'ing
el'i·gi·bil'i·ty
el'i·gi·ble
el'i·gi·bly
e·lim'i·nate'
  ·nat'ed ·nat'ing
e·lim'i·na'tion
e·li'sion
e·lite' *or* é·lite'
e·lix'ir
E·liz'a·be'than
el·lipse'
el·lip'sis
  ·ses
el·lip'ti·cal
el·lip'ti·cal·ly
el'o·cu'tion
e·lon'gate
  ·gat·ed ·gat·ing
e·lon'ga'tion
e·lope'
  ·loped' ·lop'ing
e·lope'ment
el'o·quence
el'o·quent
else'where'
e·lu'ci·date'
  ·dat'ed ·dat'ing
e·lu'ci·da'tion
e·lude'
  ·lud'ed ·lud'ing
  (*escape;* see
  allude)
e·lu'sion
  (*an escape;* see
  allusion, illusion)
e·lu'sive
  (*hard to grasp;*
  see allusive,
  illusive)
e·ma'ci·ate'
  ·at'ed ·at'ing
e·ma'ci·a'tion
em'a·nate'
  ·nat'ed ·nat'ing
em'a·na'tion
e·man'ci·pate'
  ·pat'ed ·pat'ing
e·man'ci·pa'tion

e·man'ci·pa'tor
e·mas'cu·late'
  ·lat'ed ·lat'ing
e·mas'cu·la'tion
e·mas'cu·la'tor
em·balm'
em·bank'ment
em·bar'go
  ·goes
  ·goed ·go·ing
em·bark'
em'bar·ka'tion
em·bar'rass
em·bar'rass·ment
em'bas·sy
  ·sies
em·bat'tle
  ·tled ·tling
em·bed'
em·bel'lish
em'ber
em·bez'zle
  ·zled ·zling
em·bez'zler
em·bla'zon
em'blem
em'blem·at'ic
em·bod'i·ment
em·bod'y
em·bold'en
em'bo·lism
em'bo·lus
  ·li
em·boss'
em'bou·chure'
em·brace'
  ·braced'
  ·brac'ing
em·brace'a·ble
em·bra'sure
em·broi'der
em·broi'der·y
  ·ies
em·broil'
em'bry·o'
  ·os'
em'bry·ol'o·gy
em'bry·on'ic
em'cee'
  ·ceed' ·cee'ing
e·mend'
  (*to correct;*
  see amend)
e'men·da'tion
em'er·ald
e·merge'
  ·merged'
  ·merg'ing
  (*appear;* see
  immerge)
e·mer'gence
e·mer'gen·cy
  ·cies
e·mer'i·tus
em'er·y
e·met'ic
em'i·grant

em'i·grate'
  ·grat'ed
  ·grat'ing
em'i·gra'tion
em'i·nence
em'i·nent
  (*prominent;* see
  imminent)
em'is·sar'y
  ·ies
e·mis'sion
e·mit'
  ·mit'ted
  ·mit'ting
e·mol'li·ent
e·mol'u·ment
e·mo'tion·al
e·mo'tion·al·ize'
  ·ized' ·iz'ing
em·path'ic
em'pa·thize'
  ·thized' ·thiz'ing
em'pa·thy
em'pen·nage'
em'per·or
em'pha·sis
  ·ses'
em'pha·size'
  ·sized' ·siz'ing
em·phat'ic
em'phy·se'ma
em'pire
em·pir'i·cal
em·pir'i·cism
em·place'ment
em·ploy'
em·ploy'a·ble
em·ploy'ee
em·ploy'er
em·ploy'ment
em·po'ri·um
  ·ri·ums *or* ·ri·a
em·pow'er
em'press
emp'ti·ly
emp'ti·ness
emp'ty
  ·ti·er ·ti·est
  ·ties
  ·tied ·ty·ing
emp'ty-hand'ed
emp'ty-head'ed
em·u'late'
  ·lat'ed ·lat'ing
em·u·la'tion
em'u·lous
e·mul'si·fi·ca'tion
e·mul'si·fi'er
e·mul'si·fy'
  ·fied' ·fy'ing
e·mul'sion
en·a'ble
  ·bled ·bling
en·act'ment
en·am'el
  ·eled *or* ·elled
  ·el·ing *or*
  ·el·ling

en·am'el·ware'
en·am'ored
en·camp'ment
en·case'
  ·cased' ·cas'ing
en·caus'tic
en·ceph'a·li'tis
en·chant'ment
en'chi·la'da
en·cir'cle
en'clave
en·close'
  ·closed'
  ·clos'ing
en·clo'sure
en·code'
en·co'mi·ast'
en·co'mi·um
  ·ums *or* ·a
en·com'pass
en'core
en·coun'ter
en·cour'age
  ·aged ·ag·ing
en·cour'age·ment
en·croach'
en·cum'ber
en·cum'brance
en·cyc'li·cal
en·cy'clo·pe'di·a
  or ·pae'di·a
en·dan'ger
en·dear'
en·dear'ment
en·deav'or
en·dem'ic
end'ing
en'dive
end'less
end'most'
en'do·crine'
en·dog'a·my
en'do·me'tri·um
en·dorse'
  ·dorsed'
  ·dors'ing
en·dor'see'
en·dorse'ment
en·dors'er
en·dow'
en·dow'ment
end'pa'per
en·dur'a·ble
en·dur'a·bly
en·dur'ance
en·dure'
  ·dured' ·dur'ing
end'ways'
en'e·ma
en'e·my
  ·mies
en'er·get'ic
en'er·get'i·cal·ly
en'er·gize'
  ·gized' ·giz'ing
en'er·giz'er
en'er·gy
  ·gies

en'er·vate'
· vat'ed vat'ing
en·fee'ble
· bled · bling
en'fi·lade'
· lad'ed · lad'ing
en·fold'
en·force'
· forced'
· forc'ing
en·force'a·ble
en·fran'chise
en·gage'
· gaged' · gag'ing
en·gage'ment
en·gen'der
en'gine
en·gi·neer'
Eng'lish
en·gorge'
· gorged' · gorg'ing
en·grave'
· graved'
· grav'ing
en·grav'er
en·gross'
en·gulf'
en·hance'
· hanced'
· hanc'ing
e·nig'ma
e·nig·mat'ic
e·nig·mat'i·cal·ly
en·join'
en·joy'a·ble
en·joy'a·bly
en·joy'ment
en·kin'dle
· dled · dling
en·lace'
en·large'
· larged'
· larg'ing
en·large'ment
en·larg'er
en·light'en
en·light'en·ment
en·list'
en·list'ment
en·liv'en
en·mi·ty
· ties
en·no'ble
· bled · bling
en·nui'
e·nor'mi·ty
· ties
e·nor'mous
e·nough'
en·plane'
en·rage'
en·rap'ture
· tured · tur·ing
en·rich'
en·roll' or · rol'
· rolled' · roll'ing

en·roll·ee'
en·roll'ment or
en·rol'ment
en·route'
en·sconce'
· sconced'
· sconc'ing
en·sem'ble
en·shrine'
· shrined'
· shrin'ing
en'sign
en·slave'
en·snare'
en·snarl'
en·sue'
· sued' · su'ing
en·sure'
en·tail'
en·tan'gle
en·tente'
en'ter·prise'
en'ter·pris'ing
en'ter·tain'
en·thrall' or
en·thral'
· thralled'
· thrall'ing
en·throne'
en·thuse'
· thused'
· thus'ing
en·thu'si·asm
en·thu'si·as'tic
en·thu'si·as'ti·
cal·ly
en·tice'
· ticed' · tic'ing
en·tice'ment
en·tire'
en·tire'ly
en·tire'ty
· ties
en·ti'tle
· tled · tling
en'ti·ty
· ties
en·tomb'
en·to·mol'o·gy
(insect study; see
etymology)
en'tou·rage'
en·tr'acte'
en'trails
en·train'
en'trance
en·trance'
· tranced'
· tranc'ing
en'trant
en·trap'
en·treat'
en·treat'y
· ies
en'tree or · trée
en·trench'ment
en'tre·pre·neur'
en·trust'

en'try
· tries
en·twine'
e·nu'mer·ate'
· at'ed · at'ing
e·nu'mer·a'tion
e·nu'mer·a'tor
e·nun'ci·ate'
· at'ed · at'ing
(pronounce; see
annunciate)
e·nun'ci·a'tion
e·nun'ci·a'tor
en·vel'op v.
en've·lope' n.
en·ven'om
en'vi·a·ble
en'vi·a·bly
en'vi·ous
en·vi'ron·ment
en·vi'ron·men'tal
en·vi'rons
en·vis'age
· aged · ag·ing
en·vi'sion
en'voy
en'vy
· vies
· vied · vy·ing
en'zyme
e'o·lith'ic
e'on
ep'au·let' or
· lette'
e·pergne'
e·phem'er·al
ep'ic
(poem; see
epoch)
ep'i·cen'ter
ep'i·cure'
ep'i·cu·re'an
ep'i·dem'ic
ep'i·der'mis
ep'i·glot'tis
ep'i·gram'
ep'i·gram·mat'ic
ep'i·gram·mat'i·
cal·ly
ep'i·graph'
ep'i·graph'ic
ep'i·graph'i·cal·ly
ep'i·lep'sy
ep'i·lep'tic
ep'i·logue' or
· log'
E·piph'a·ny
e·pis'co·pal
E·pis'co·pa'li·an
ep'i·sode'
ep'i·sod'ic
ep'i·sod'i·cal·ly
e·pis'tle
e·pis'to·lar'y
ep'i·taph
ep'i·the'li·al
ep'i·the'li·um
· li·ums or · li·a

ep'i·thet'
e·pit'o·me
e·pit'o·mize'
· mized' · miz'ing
ep'och
(period; see epic)
ep'och·al
ep'o·nym'
ep·ox'y
ep'si·lon'
eq'ua·bil'i·ty
eq'ua·ble
eq'ua·bly
e'qual
· qualed or
· qualled
· qual·ing or
· qual·ling
e·qual'i·tar'i·an
e·qual'i·ty
· ties
e'qual·i·za'tion
e'qual·ize'
· ized' · iz'ing
e'qual·ly
e'qua·nim'i·ty
e·quate'
· quat'ed
· quat'ing
e·qua'tion
e·qua'tor
e·qua·to'ri·al
eq'uer·ry
· ries
e·ques'tri·an
e·ques'tri·enne'
e'qui·an'gu·lar
e'qui·dis'tant
e'qui·lat'er·al
e·quil'i·brant
e·quil'i·brate'
· brat'ed · brat'ing
e'qui·lib'ri·um
· ri·ums or · ri·a
e'quine
e'qui·noc'tial
e'qui·nox'
e·quip'
· quipped'
· quip'ping
e·quip'ment
e'qui·poise'
e'qui·pol'lent
eq'ui·ta·ble
eq'ui·ta·bly
eq'ui·ty
· ties
e·quiv'a·lence
e·quiv'a·lent
e·quiv'o·cal
e·quiv'o·cal·ly
e·quiv'o·cate'
· cat'ed · cat'ing
e·quiv'o·ca'tion
e·quiv'o·ca'tor
e'ra
e·rad'i·ca·ble

e·rad'i·cate'
· cat'ed · cat'ing
e·rad'i·ca'tion
e·rad'i·ca'tor
e·ras'a·ble
e·rase'
· rased' · ras'ing
e·ras'er
e·ra'sure
e·rect'
e·rec'tile
e·rec'tion
e·rec'tor
erg
er'go
er·gos'ter·ol'
er'got
er'mine
e·rode'
· rod'ed · rod'ing
e·rog'e·nous
e·ro'sion
e·ro'sive
e·rot'ic
e·rot'i·ca
e·rot'i·cal·ly
e·rot'i·cism
er'o·tism
e·ro'to·gen'ic
err
er'ran·cy
· cies
er'rand
er'rant
er·ra'ta
(sing. er·ra'tum)
er·rat'ic
er·rat'i·cal·ly
er·ro'ne·ous
er'ror
er'satz
erst'while'
e·ruct'
e·ruc'tate
· tat·ed · tat·ing
e·ruc·ta'tion
er'u·dite'
er'u·di'tion
e·rupt'
e·rupt'i·ble
e·rup'tion
e·rup'tive
e·ryth'ro·my'cin
es'ca·drille'
es'ca·lade'
· lad'ed · lad'ing
es'ca·late'
· lat'ed · lat'ing
es'ca·la'tion
es'ca·la'tor
es·cal'lop or · op
es'ca·pade'
es·cape'
· caped' · cap'ing
es·cap·ee'
es·cape'ment
es·cap'ism
es·cap'ist

es'ca·role'
es·carp'ment
es'cha·rot'ic
es'cha·tol'o·gy
es·cheat'
es·chew'
es·chew'al
es'cri·toire'
es'crow
es'cu·lent
es·cutch'eon
Es·ki·mo'
· mos' or · mo'
e·soph'a·gus
· a·gi'
es'o·ter'ic
es'o·ter'i·cal·ly
es'pa·drille'
es·pal'ier
es·pe'cial
es·pe'cial·ly
Es'pe·ran'to
es'pi·o·nage'
es'pla·nade'
es·pous'al
es·pouse'
· poused' · pous'ing
es·pres'so
· sos
es·prit' de corps'
es·py'
· pied' · py'ing
es'quire
es·say'
(try; see assay)
es'say·ist
es'sence
es·sen'tial
es·sen'ti·al'i·ty
es·sen'tial·ly
es·tab'lish
es·tab'lish·ment
es·tate'
es·teem'
es'thete
es·thet'ic
es·thet'i·cal·ly
es·thet'i·cism
es'ti·ma·ble
es'ti·mate'
· mat'ed · mat'ing
es'ti·ma'tion
es'ti·ma'tor
es'ti·val
es'ti·vate'
· vat'ed · vat'ing
es·trange'
· tranged'
· trang'ing
es·trange'ment
es'tro·gen
es'trous adj.
es'trus n.
es'tu·ar'i·al
es'tu·ar'y
· ies
et cet'er·a

et·cet'er·as
etch'ing
e·ter'nal
e·ter'nal·ly
e·ter'ni·ty
  ·ties
e'ther
e·the're·al
e·the're·al·ize'
  ·ized' ·iz'ing
e'ther·ize'
  ·ized' ·iz'ing
eth'i·cal
eth'i·cal·ly
eth'ics
eth'nic
eth'ni·cal·ly
eth'no·cen'tri·
  cal·ly
eth'no·cen'trism
eth·nog'ra·phy
eth'no·log'i·cal
eth·nol'o·gy
e'thos
eth'yl
e'ti·ol'o·gy
et'i·quette
é'tude
et'y·mo·log'i·cal
et'y·mol'o·gy
  ·gies
  (word study; see
  entomology)
et'y·mon'
eu·ca·lyp'tus
  ·tus·es or ·ti
Eu'cha·rist
eu'chre
eu·gen'i·cal·ly
eu·gen'ics
eu'lo·gize'
  ·gized' ·giz'ing
eu'lo·gy
  ·gies
eu'nuch
eu'phe·mism
eu·phe·mis'tic
eu·phe·mis'ti·
  cal·ly
eu'phe·mize'
  ·mized' ·miz'ing
eu·phon'ic
eu·pho'ni·ous
eu·pho'ni·um
eu'pho·ny
  ·nies
eu·pho'ri·a
eu·phor'ic
eu'phu·ism
eu·phu·is'tic
Eur·a'sian
Eur'a·tom'
eu·re'ka
Eu'ro·crat'
Eu'ro·dol'lars
Eu'ro·pe'an
eu·ryth'mics
eu·ryth'my

Eu·sta'chi·an
eu'tha·na'si·a
e·vac'u·ate'
  ·at'ed ·at'ing
e·vac'u·a'tion
e·vac'u·ee'
e·vade'
  ·vad'ed ·vad'ing
e·val'u·ate'
  ·at'ed ·at'ing
e·val'u·a'tion
ev'a·nesce'
  ·nesced' ·nesc'ing
ev'a·nes'cence
ev'a·nes'cent
e'van·gel'i·cal
e'van·gel'i·cal·ly
e·van'gel·ism
e·van'gel·ist
e·van'gel·is'tic
e·van'gel·ize'
  ·ized' ·iz'ing
e·vap'o·rate'
  ·rat'ed ·rat'ing
e·vap'o·ra'tion
e·va'sion
e·va'sive
e'ven·hand'ed
eve'ning
e'ven·ness
e·vent'
e'ven·tem'pered
e·vent'ful
e·ven'tu·al
e·ven'tu·al'i·ty
  ·ties
e·ven'tu·al·ly
e·ven'tu·ate'
  ·at'ed ·at'ing
ev'er·glade'
ev'er·green'
ev'er·last'ing
ev'er·more'
e·vert'
ev'er·y·bod'y
ev'er·y·day'
ev'er·y·one'
ev'er·y·thing'
ev'er·y·where'
e·vict'
e·vic'tion
ev'i·dence
  ·denced ·denc·ing
ev'i·dent
ev'i·den'tial
e'vil·do'er
e'vil·ly
e'vil·mind'ed
e·vince'
  ·vinced'
  ·vinc'ing
e·vin'ci·ble
e·vis'cer·ate'
  ·at'ed ·at'ing
e·vis'cer·a'tion
ev'o·ca'tion
e·voke'
  ·voked' ·vok'ing

ev'o·lu'tion
ev'o·lu'tion·ar'y
ev'o·lu'tion·ist
e·volve'
  ·volved' ·volv'ing
ewe
  (sheep; see yew)
ew'er
ex·ac'er·bate'
  ·bat'ed ·bat'ing
ex·ac'er·ba'tion
ex·act'
ex·act'ing
ex·ac'tion
ex·ac'ti·tude'
ex·act'ly
ex·ag'ger·ate'
  ·at'ed ·at'ing
ex·ag'ger·a'tion
ex·ag'ger·a'tor
ex·alt'
ex·al·ta'tion
ex·am'i·na'tion
ex·am'ine
  ·ined ·in·ing
ex·am'in·er
ex·am'ple
ex·as'per·ate'
  ·at'ed ·at'ing
ex·as·per·a'tion
ex'ca·the'dra
ex'ca·vate'
  ·vat'ed ·vat'ing
ex'ca·va'tion
ex'ca·va'tor
ex·ceed'
  (surpass; see
  accede)
ex·ceed'ing·ly
ex·cel'
  ·celled' ·cel'ling
ex'cel·lence
ex'cel·len·cy
  ·cies
ex'cel·lent
ex·cel'si·or'
ex·cept'
  (omit; see accept)
ex·cept'ed
  (left out; see
  accepted)
ex·cep'tion
ex·cep'tion·a·ble
ex·cep'tion·al
ex·cep'tion·al·ly
ex·cerpt'
ex·cess'
  (surplus; see
  access)
ex·ces'sive
ex·ces'sive·ly
ex·change'
  ·changed'
  ·chang'ing
ex·change'·
  a·bil'i·ty
ex·change'a·ble
ex·cheq'uer

ex·cis'a·ble
ex'cise
ex·cise'
  ·cised' ·cis'ing
ex·ci'sion
ex·cit'a·bil'i·ty
ex·cit'a·ble
ex·cit'a·bly
ex·ci'ta·tion
ex·cite'
  ·cit'ed ·cit'ing
ex·cite'ment
ex·claim'
ex'cla·ma'tion
ex·clam'a·to'ry
ex'clave
ex·clud'a·ble
ex·clude'
  ·clud'ed
  ·clud'ing
ex·clu'sion
ex·clu'sive
ex·clu·siv'i·ty
ex'com·mu'ni·
  cate'
  ·cat'ed ·cat'ing
ex·co'ri·ate'
  ·at'ed ·at'ing
ex·co'ri·a'tion
ex'cre·ment
ex·cres'cence
ex·crete'
  ·cret'ed
  ·cret'ing
ex·cre'tion
ex'cre·to'ry
ex·cru'ci·ate'
  ·at'ed ·at'ing
ex'cul·pate'
  ·pat'ed ·pat'ing
ex·cul·pa'tion
ex·cur'sion
ex·cus'a·ble
ex·cus'a·bly
ex·cuse'
  ·cused' ·cus'ing
ex'e·cra·ble
ex'e·crate'
  ·crat'ed
  ·crat'ing
ex'e·cra'tion
ex'e·cute'
  ·cut'ed ·cut'ing
ex'e·cu'tion
ex'e·cu'tion·er
ex·ec'u·tive
ex·ec'u·tor
ex'e·ge'sis
ex·em'plar
ex·em'pla·ri·ly
ex·em'pla·ri·ness
ex·em'pla·ry
ex·em'pli·fi·
  ca'tion
ex·em'pli·fy'
  ·fied' ·fy'ing
ex·empt'
ex·emp'tion

ex'er·cis'a·ble
ex'er·cise'
  ·cised' ·cis'ing
  (use; see exorcise)
ex·ert'
ex·er'tion
ex'e·unt
ex·ha·la'tion
ex·hale'
  ·haled' ·hal'ing
ex·haust'
ex·haust'i·ble
ex·haus'tion
ex·haus'tive
ex·hib'it
ex·hi·bi'tion
ex·hi·bi'tion·ism
ex·hib'i·tor
ex·hil'a·rant
ex·hil'a·rate'
  ·rat'ed ·rat'ing
ex·hil·a·ra'tion
ex·hort'
ex·hor·ta'tion
ex·hu·ma'tion
ex·hume'
  ·humed'
  ·hum'ing
ex'i·gen·cy
  ·cies
ex'i·gent
ex'ile
ex·ist'
ex·ist'ence
ex·ist'ent
ex·is·ten'tial
ex·is·ten'tial·ism
ex'it
ex'o·dus
ex' of·fi'ci·o'
ex·og'a·my
ex·on'er·ate'
  ·at'ed ·at'ing
ex·on·er·a'tion
ex·o'ra·ble
ex·or'bi·tance
ex·or'bi·tant
ex'or·cise' or
  ·cize'
  ·cised' or ·cized'
  ·cis'ing or ·ciz'ing
  (expel; see
  exercise)
ex'or·cism
ex·o·ter'ic
ex·ot'ic
ex·ot'i·ca
ex·ot'i·cal·ly
ex·pand'
ex·panse'
ex·pan'si·ble
ex·pan'sion
ex·pan'sive
ex·pa'ti·ate'
  ·at'ed ·at'ing
ex·pa'ti·a'tion
ex·pa'tri·ate'
  ·at'ed ·at'ing

ex·pa'tri·a'tion
ex·pect'
ex·pect'an·cy
ex·pect'ant
ex'pec·ta'tion
ex·pec'to·rant
ex·pec'to·rate'
  ·rat'ed ·rat'ing
ex·pec'to·ra'tion
ex·pe'di·ence
ex·pe'di·en·cy
  ·cies
ex·pe'di·ent
ex'pe·dite'
  ·dit'ed ·dit'ing
ex'pe·dit'er
ex·pe·di'tion
ex'pe·di'tion·ar'y
ex'pe·di'tious
ex·pel'
  ·pelled' ·pel'ling
ex·pel'la·ble
ex'pel·lee'
ex·pend'
ex·pend'a·bil'i·ty
ex·pend'a·ble
ex·pend'i·ture
ex·pense'
ex·pen'sive
ex·pen'sive·ly
ex·pe'ri·ence
  ·enced ·enc·ing
ex·pe'ri·en'tial
ex·per'i·ment
ex·per'i·men'tal
ex·per'i·men·
  ta'tion
ex'pert
ex'pert·ise'
ex'pi·a·ble
ex'pi·ate'
  ·at'ed ·at'ing
ex'pi·a'tion
ex'pi·a'tor
ex·pi·ra'tion
ex·pir'a·to'ry
ex·pire'
  ·pired' ·pir'ing
ex·plain'a·ble
ex'pla·na'tion
ex·plan'a·to'ry
ex'ple·tive
ex'pli·ca·ble
ex'pli·cate'
  ·cat'ed ·cat'ing
ex'pli·ca'tion
ex·plic'it
ex·plod'a·ble
ex·plode'
  ·plod'ed
  ·plod'ing
ex'ploit
ex·ploi·ta'tion
ex'plo·ra'tion
ex·plor'a·to'ry
ex·plore'
  ·plored'
  ·plor'ing

ex·plor'er
ex·plo'sion
ex·plo'sive
ex·po'nent
ex'po·nen'tial
ex·port'
ex'por·ta'tion
ex·pose'
· posed' · pos'ing
ex'po·sé'
ex'po·si'tion
ex·pos'i·tor
ex·pos'i·to'ry
ex post fac'to
ex·pos'tu·late'
· lat'ed · lat'ing
ex·pos'tu·la'tion
ex·pos'tu·la'tor
ex·po'sure
ex·pound'
ex·press'
ex·press'age
ex·press'i·ble
ex·pres'sion
ex·pres'sion·ism
ex·pres'sion·
is'tic
ex·pres'sive
ex·press'man
ex·press'way
ex·pro'pri·ate'
· at'ed · at'ing
ex·pro'pri·a'tion
ex·pul'sion
ex·punge'
· punged'
· pung'ing
ex'pur·gate'
· gat'ed · gat'ing
ex'pur·ga'tion
ex'qui·site
ex'tant
(existing; see
extent)
ex·tem'po·ra'ne·
ous
ex·tem'po·re
ex·tem'po·rize'
· rized' · riz'ing
ex·tend'
ex·ten'si·ble
ex·ten'sion
ex·ten'sive
ex·tent'
(scope; see extant)
ex·ten'u·ate'
· at'ed · at'ing
ex·ten'u·a'tion
ex·te'ri·or
ex·ter'mi·nate'
· nat'ed · nat'ing
ex·ter'mi·na'tion
ex·ter'mi·na'tor
ex·ter'nal
ex·ter'nal·ize'
· ized' · iz'ing
ex·tinct'
ex·tinc'tion

ex·tin'guish
ex'tir·pate'
· pat'ed · pat'ing
ex'tir·pa'tion
ex·tol' or ·toll'
· tolled' · toll'ling
ex·tort'
ex·tor'tion
ex·tor'tion·ate
ex·tor'tion·er
ex·tor'tion·ist
ex'tra
ex·tract'
ex·tract'a·ble
or · i · ble
ex·trac'tion
ex·trac'tor
ex'tra·cur·ric'u·
lar
ex'tra·dit'a·ble
ex'tra·dite'
· dit'ed · dit'ing
ex'tra·di'tion
ex'tra·le'gal
ex'tra·mar'i·tal
ex'tra·mu'ral
ex·tra·ne·ous
ex·traor'di·
nar'i·ly
ex·traor'di·
nar'y
ex·trap'o·late'
· lat'ed · lat'ing
ex'tra·sen'so·ry
ex'tra·ter'ri·
to'ri·al
ex·trav'a·gance
ex·trav'a·gant
ex·trav'a·gan'za
ex'tra·ve·hic'u·lar
ex·treme'
ex·treme'ly
ex·trem'ism
ex·trem'ist
ex·trem'i·ty
· ties
ex'tri·cate'
· cat'ed · cat'ing
ex'tri·ca'tion
ex·trin'sic
ex·trin'si·cal·ly
ex'tro·ver'sion
ex'tro·vert'
ex·trude'
· trud'ed
· trud'ing
ex·tru'sion
ex·u'ber·ance
ex·u'ber·ant
ex'u·da'tion
ex·ude'
· ud'ed · ud'ing
ex·ult'
ex·ult'ant
ex'ul·ta'tion
ex'urb'
ex·ur'ban·ite'
ex·ur'bi·a

eye
eyed eye'ing
or ey'ing
eye'ball'
eye'brow'
eye'-catch'er
eye'cup'
eye'ful'
eye'glass'
eye'hole'
eye'lash'
eye'let
(hole; see islet)
eye'lid'
eye liner
eye'-o'pen·er
eye'piece'
eye shadow
eye'shot'
eye'sight'
eye'sore'
eye'strain'
eye'tooth'
eye'wash'
eye'wink'
eye'wit'ness

F

fa'ble
· bled · bling
fab'ric
fab'ri·cate'
· cat'ed · cat'ing
fab'ri·ca'tion
fab'ri·ca'tor
Fab'ri·koid'
fab'u·lous
fa·çade' or · cade'
face
faced fac'ing
face'plate'
face'-sav'ing
fac'et
fa·ce'tious
fa'cial
fac'ile
fa·cil'i·tate'
· tat'ed · tat'ing
fa·cil'i·ta'tion
fa·cil'i·ty
· ties
fac·sim'i·le
· led · le·ing
fac'tion
fac'tious
fac·ti'tious
(artificial; see
fictitious)
fac'tor
fac·to'ri·al
fac'to·ry
· ries
fac·to'tum
fac'tu·al
fac'tu·al·ly

fac'ul·ty
· ties
fad'dish
fad'dism
fade
fad'ed fad'ing
fade'-in'
fade'-out'
fag
fagged
fag'ging
fag'ot·ing
Fahr'en·heit'
fail'-safe'
fail'ure
faint
(weak; see feint)
faint'heart'ed
fair'ground'
fair'-haired'
fair'ly
fair'-mind'ed
fair'-spo'ken
fair'-trade'
fair'way'
fair'-weath'er
fair'y
· ies
fair'y·land'
faith'ful
faith'ful·ly
faith'less
fake
faked fak'ing
fak'er
(fraud)
fa·kir'
(Moslem beggar)
fal'cate
fal'con
fal'con·ry
fall
fell fall'en
fall'ing
fal·la'cious
fal'la·cy
· cies
fal'li·bil'i·ty
fal'li·ble
fal'li·bly
fall'ing-out'
fall'off'
fall'out'
fal'low
false
fals'er fals'est
false'heart'ed
false'hood'
fal·set'to
fal'si·fi·ca'tion
fal'si·fi'er
fal'si·fy'
· fied' · fy'ing
fal'si·ty
· ties
fal'ter
fa·mil'ial
fa·mil'iar

fa·mil'i·ar'i·ty
· ties
fa·mil'iar·i·
za'tion
fa·mil'iar·ize'
· ized' · iz'ing
fam'i·ly
· lies
fam'ine
fam'ish
fa'mous
fan
fanned fan'ning
fa·nat'ic
fa·nat'i·cal·ly
fa·nat'i·cism
fan'ci·ful
fan'cy
· cies
· ci·er · ci·est
· cied · cy·ing
fan'cy-free'
fan'cy·work'
fan'fare'
fan'light'
fan'tail'
fan·ta'si·a
fan'ta·size'
· sized' · siz'ing
fan·tas'tic
fan·tas'ti·cal·ly
fan'ta·sy
· sies
· sied · sy·ing
far
far'ther
far'thest
far'ad
far'a·day'
far'a·way'
farce
farced farc'ing
far'ci·cal
far'ci·cal·ly
fare
fared far'ing
fare'well'
far'fetched'
far'-flung'
fa·ri'na
far'i·na'ceous
farm'hand'
farm'house'
farm'stead'
farm'yard'
far'o
far'-off'
far'-out'
far'-reach'ing
far'row
far'see'ing
far'sight'ed
far'ther
far'thing
fas'ces
fas'ci·cle
fas'ci·nate'
· nat'ed · nat'ing

fas'ci·na'tion
fas'ci·na'tor
fas'cism
fas'cist
fash'ion
fash'ion·a·ble
fash'ion·a·bly
fast'back'
fas'ten
fas'ten·er
fas'ten·ing
fas·tid'i·ous
fat
fat'ter fat'test
fat'ted fat'ting
fa'tal
fa'tal·ism
fa'tal·ist
fa'tal·is'tic
fa'tal·is'ti·cal·ly
fa·tal'i·ty
· ties
fa'tal·ly
fate'ful
fa'ther·hood'
fa'ther-in-law'
fa'thers-
in-law'
fa'ther·land'
fa'ther·less
fa'ther·li·ness
fa'ther·ly
fath'om
fath'om·a·ble
fath'om·less
fat'i·ga·ble
fa·tigue'
· tigued'
· tigu'ing
fat'-sol'u·ble
fat'ten
fat'ti·ness
fat'ty
· ti·er · ti·est
fa·tu'i·ty
· ties
fat'u·ous
fat'-wit'ted
fau'cet
fault'find'ing
fault'i·ness
fault'less
fault'y
· i·er · i·est
faun
(deity; see fawn)
fau'na
· nas or · nae
faux' pas'
faux' pas'
fa'vor·a·ble
fa'vor·a·bly
fa'vored
fa'vor·ite
fa'vor·it·ism
fawn
(deer; act ser-
vilely; see faun)

faze
  fazed faz'ing
  (*disturb;* see
  phase)
fe'al·ty
fear'ful
fear'ful·ly
fear'less
fear'some
fea·si·bil'i·ty
fea'si·ble
fea'si·bly
feast
feat
  (*deed;* see feet)
feath'er·bed'
feath'er·
  bed'ding
feath'er·
  brain'
feath'ered
feath'er·edge'
feath'er·i·ness
feath'er·stitch'
feath'er·weight'
feath'er·y
fea'ture
  ·tured ·tur·ing
fea'ture-length'
feb'ri·fuge'
fe'brile
Feb'ru·ar'y
fe'cal
fe'ces
feck'less
fe'cund
fe'cun·date'
  ·dat'ed ·dat'ing
fe·cun'di·ty
fed'er·al
fed'er·al·ism
fed'er·al·i·
  za'tion
fed'er·al·ize'
  ·ized' ·iz'ing
fed'er·ate'
  ·at'ed ·at'ing
fed'er·a'tion
fe·do'ra
fee'ble
  ·bler ·blest
fee'ble·mind'ed
feed
  fed feed'ing
feed'back'
feel
  felt feel'ing
feel'-split'ting
feet
  (*pl. of foot;*
  see feat)
feign
feint
  (*pretense;* see
  faint)
fe·lic'i·tate'
  ·tat'ed ·tat'ing
fe·lic'i·ta'tion

fe·lic'i·tous
fe·lic'i·ty
  ·ties
fe'line
fel'low·ship'
fel'on
fe·lo'ni·ous
fel'o·ny
  ·nies
fe·luc'ca
fe'male
fem'i·nine
fem'i·nin'i·ty
fem'i·nism
fem'i·nize'
  ·nized' ·niz'ing
femme fa·tale'
  femmes fa·tales'
fence
  fenced fenc'ing
fend'er
fen·es·tra'tion
fen'nel
fer'ment
fer'men·ta'tion
fern
fe·ro'cious
fe·roc'i·ty
fer'ret
fer'ri·age
Fer'ris wheel
fer'rule
  (*metal ring;*
  see ferule)
fer'ry
  ·ries
  ·ried ·ry·ing
fer'ry·boat'
fer'tile
fer·til'i·ty
fer'til·iz'a·ble
fer'til·i·za'tion
fer'til·ize'
  ·ized' ·iz'ing
fer'til·iz'er
fer'ule
  (*stick;* see
  ferrule)
fer'vent
fer'vid
fer'vor
fes'cue
fes'tal
fes'ter
fes'ti·val
fes'tive
fes·tiv'i·ty
  ·ties
fes·toon'
fe'tal
fetch'ing
fete *or* fête
  fet'ed *or* fêt'ed
  fet'ing *or* fêt'ing
fe'ti·cide'
fet'id
fet'ish
fet'ish·ism

fet'lock'
fet'ter
fet'tle
fet'tuc·ci'ne
fe'tus
  ·tus·es
feu'dal
feu'dal·ism
feu'dal·is'tic
fe'ver·ish
fez
  fez'zes
fi·an·cé' *masc.*
fi·an·cée' *fem.*
fi·as'co
  ·coes *or* ·cos
fi'at
fib
  fibbed fib'bing
fib'ber
fi'ber *or* ·bre
fi'ber-board'
Fi'ber·glas'
fi·bril·la'tion
fi'broid
fi'brous
fib'u·la
  ·lae *or* ·las
fick'le
fic'tion·al·ize'
  ·ized' ·iz'ing
fic·ti'tious
  (*imaginary;* see
  factitious)
fid'dle
  ·dled ·dling
fi·del'i·ty
  ·ties
fidg'et
fidg'et·i·ness
fidg'et·y
fi·du'ci·ar'y
  ·ies
field'er
field'-strip'
field'-test'
field'work'
fiend'ish
fierce
  fierc'er
  fierc'est
fierce'ly
fi'er·i·ness
fi'er·y
  ·i·er ·i·est
fi·es'ta
fif'teen'
fif'ti·eth
fif'ty
  ·ties
fight
fought
fight'ing
fig'ment
fig'u·ra'tion
fig'u·ra·tive
fig'ure
  ·ured ·ur·ing

fig'ure·head'
fig'u·rine'
fil'a·ment
fi'lar
fil'bert
file
  filed fil'ing
fi·let' mi·gnon'
fil'i·al
fil'i·a'tion
fil'i·bus'ter
fil'i·gree'
  ·greed'
  ·gree'ing
fill'ings
Fil'i·pi'no
  ·nos
fil'let
fill'-in'
fill'ing
fil'lip
fil'ly
  ·lies
film'strip'
film'y
  ·i·er ·i·est
fil'ter
  (*strainer;* see
  philter)
fil'ter·a·ble
filth'i·ly
filth'i·ness
filth'y
  ·i·er ·i·est
fil'trate
  ·trat·ed ·trat·ing
fin'a·ble
fi·na'gle
  ·gled ·gling
fi·na'le
fi'nal·ist
fi·nal'i·ty
fi'nal·ize'
  ·ized' ·iz'ing
fi'nal·ly
fi·nance'
  ·nanced'
  ·nanc'ing
fi·nan'cial
fi·nan'cial·ly
fin'an·cier'
find
found find'ing
find'er
fine
fin'er fin'est
fined fin'ing
firth
fine'-cut'
fine'-drawn'
fine'-grained'
fine'ly
fine'ness
fin'er·y
  ·ies
fine'spun'
fi·nesse'
  ·nessed'
  ·ness'ing

fine'-toothed'
fin'ger·board'
fin'gered
fin'ger·nail'
fin'ger·print'
finger tip
fin'i·al
fin'i·cal
fin'ick·i·ness
fin'ick·y
fi'nis
fin'ish
fin'ished
fi'nite
fin'nan had'die
fiord
fir
  (*tree;* see fur)
fire
  fired fir'ing
fire'arm'
fire'ball'
fire'boat'
fire'bomb'
fire'box'
fire'brand'
fire'break'
fire'brick'
fire'bug'
fire'clay'
fire'crack'er
fire'-cure'
fire'damp'
fire'dog'
fire'-eat'er
fire escape
fire'fly'
  ·flies'
fire'man
fire'place'
fire'plug'
fire'pow'er
fire'proof'
fire'side'
fire'trap'
fire'wa'ter
fire'wood'
fire'works'
fir'kin
fir'ma·ment
firm'ly
first'born'
first'-class'
first'hand'
first'ly
first'-rate'
firth
fis'cal
fis'cal·ly
fish'bowl'
fish'er·man
fish'er·y
  ·ies
fish'hook'
fish'i·ness
fish'mon'ger
fish'plate'
fish'pond'

fish'tail'
fish'wife'
fish'y
  ·i·er ·i·est
fis'sion
fis'sion·a·ble
fis'sure
  ·sured ·sur·ing
fis'ti·cuffs'
fis'tu·lous
fit
  fit'ted fit'ting
fit'ter fit'test
fit'ful
fit'ful·ly
fit'ness
five'fold'
fix'ate
  ·at·ed ·at·ing
fix·a'tion
fix'a·tive
fixed
fix'ed·ly
fix'ture
fiz'zle
  ·zled ·zling
fjord
flab'ber·gast'
flab'bi·ness
flab'by
  ·bi·er ·bi·est
flac'cid
flac·cid'i·ty
fla·con'
flag
flagged
flag'ging
flag'el·lant
flag'el·late'
  ·lat'ed ·lat'ing
flag'el·la'tion
fla·gel'lum
  ·la *or* ·lums
flag'eo·let'
flag'on
flag'pole'
fla'gran·cy
fla'grant
flag'ship'
flag'stone'
flag'-wav'ing
flail
flair
  (*knack;* see flare)
flake
  flaked flak'ing
flak'i·ness
flak'y
  ·i·er ·i·est
flam·bé'
flam'beau
  ·beaux *or* ·beaus
flam·boy'ance
flam·boy'ant
flame
  flamed flam'ing
fla·men'co
  ·cos

flame'out'
flame'proof'
fla·min'go
  ·gos *or* ·goes
flam'ma·bil'i·ty
flam'ma·ble
flange
  flanged
  flang'ing
flank
flan'nel
flan'nel·ette'
flan'nel-mouthed'
flap
  flapped
  flap'ping
flap'jack'
flap'per
flare
  flared flar'ing
  (*blaze;* see flair)
flare'-up'
flash'back'
flash'bulb'
flash'card'
flash'cube'
flash'i·ly
flash'i·ness
flash'light'
flash'y
  ·i·er ·i·est
flat
  flat'ter flat'test
  flat'ted flat'ting
flat'boat'
flat'car'
flat'fish'
flat'-foot'ed
flat'i'ron
flat'ten
flat'ter
flat'ter·y
flat'u·lent
flat'ware'
flat'work'
flaunt
flau'tist
fla'vor·ful
fla'vor·ing
fla'vor·less
flaw'less
flax'en
flax'seed'
flea'-bit'ten
fledg'ling
flee
  fled flee'ing
fleece
  fleeced fleec'ing
fleec'i·ness
fleec'y
  ·i·er ·i·est
fleet'ing
flesh'-col'ored
flesh'i·ness
flesh'pots'
flesh'y
  ·i·er ·i·est

fleur'-de-lis'
  fleurs'-de-lis'
flex'i·bil'i·ty
flex'i·ble
flex'i·bly
flick'er
flied
  (*only in baseball*)
fli'er *or* fly'er
flight'i·ness
flight'less
flight'y
  ·i·er ·i·est
flim'si·ly
flim'si·ness
flim'sy
  ·si·er ·si·est
flinch'ing·ly
fling
  flung fling'ing
flint'lock'
flint'y
  ·i·er ·i·est
flip
  flipped flip'ping
flip'pan·cy
  ·cies
flip'pant
flip'per
flir·ta'tion
flir·ta'tious
flit
  flit'ted flit'ting
float'er
float'ing
floc'cu·late'
  ·lat'ed ·lat'ing
floc'cu·lent
floe
  (*ice;* see flow)
flog
  flogged
  flog'ging
flood'gate'
flood'light'
  ·light'ed *or* ·lit'
  ·light'ing
floor'ing
floor'walk'er
flop
  flopped
  flop'ping
flo'ra
  ·ras *or* ·rae
flo'ral
flo·res'cence
  (*blooming;* see
  fluorescence)
flo·res'cent
flo'ret
flo'ri·cul'ture
flor'id
Flor'i·da
flo·rid'i·ty
flor'in
flo'rist
floss'y
  ·i·er ·i·est

flo·ta'tion
flo·til'la
flot'sam
flounce
  flounced
  flounc'ing
floun'der
flour'ish
flout
flow
  (*glide;* see floe)
flow'ered
flow'er·i·ness
flow'er·pot'
flow'er·y
  ·i·er ·i·est
flu
  (*influenza*)
fluc'tu·ate'
  ·at'ed ·at'ing
flue
  (*pipe*)
flu'en·cy
flu'ent
fluff'i·ness
fluff'y
  ·fi·er ·fi·est
flu'id
flu·id'i·ty
flun'ky
  ·kies
flu'o·resce'
  ·resced'
  ·resc'ing
flu'o·res'cence
  (*light;* see
  florescence)
flu'o·res'cent
fluor'i·date'
  ·dat'ed ·dat'ing
fluor'i·da'tion
fluor'i·nate'
  ·nat'ed ·nat'ing
fluor'o·scope'
flu'o·ros'co·py
flur'ry
  ·ries
  ·ried ·ry·ing
flus'ter
flute
  flut'ed flut'ing
flut'ist
flut'ter
flu'vi·al
fly
  flies
  flew flown
  fly'ing
fly'a·ble
fly'a·way'
fly'-by-night'
fly'catch'er
fly'leaf'
  ·leaves'
fly'pa'per
fly'speck'
fly'trap'
fly'weight'

fly'wheel'
foam'i·ness
foam'y
  ·i·er ·i·est
fo'cal
fo'cal·ize'
  ·ized' ·iz'ing
fo'cus
  ·cus·es *or* ·ci
  ·cused *or* ·cussed
  ·cus·ing *or*
  ·cus·sing
fod'der
fog
  fogged fog'ging
fog'bound'
fog'gi·ly
fog'gi·ness
fog'gy
  ·gi·er ·gi·est
fog'horn'
fo'gy *or* fo'gey
  ·gies *or* ·geys
foi'ble
foist
fold'a·way'
fold'er
fo'li·age
fo'li·ate'
  ·at'ed ·at'ing
fo'li·a'tion
fo'li·o'
  ·os', ·oed' ·o'ing
folk'lore'
folk'way'
fol'li·cle
fol'low·er
fol'low-through'
fol'low-up'
fol'ly
  ·lies
fo·ment'
fo'men·ta'tion
fon'dant
fon'dle
  ·dled ·dling
fond'ness
fon·due'
food'stuff'
fool'har'di·ness
fool'har'dy
fool'ish·ness
fool'proof'
fools'cap'
foot
  feet
foot'age
foot'ball'
foot'bridge'
foot'-can'dle
foot'fall'
foot'hold'
foot'ing
foot'lights'
foot'lock'er
foot'loose'
foot'note'
foot'path'

foot'-pound'
foot'print'
foot'race'
foot'rest'
foot'sore'
foot'step'
foot'stool'
foot'-ton'
foot'wear'
foot'work'
fop'pish
for'age
for'ay
for·bear'
  ·bore' ·borne'
  ·bear'ing
  (*abstain;* see
  forebear)
for·bear'ance
for·bid'
  ·bade' *or* ·bad'
  ·bid'den
  ·bid'ding
force
  forced forc'ing
force'ful
for'ceps
  ·ceps
for'ci·ble
for'ci·bly
fore'arm'
fore'bear'
  (*ancestor;* see
  forbear)
fore·bode'
  ·bod'ed ·bod'ing
fore'cast'
  ·cast' *or* ·cast'ed
  ·cast'ing
fore'cas'tle
fore·close'
fore·clo'sure
fore·doom'
fore'fa'ther
fore'fin'ger
fore'foot'
fore·go'
  ·went' ·gone'
  ·go'ing
  (*precede;* see
  forgo)
fore'go'ing
fore'ground'
fore'hand'
fore·hand'ed
fore'head
for'eign
for'eign-born'
for'eign·er
fore'knowl'edge
fore'leg'
fore'lock'
fore'man
fore'most'
fore'named'
fore'noon'
fo·ren'sic
fo·ren'si·cal·ly

fore'or·dain'
fore'paw'
fore'play'
fore'quar'ter
fore'run'ner
fore'sail'
fore·see'
  ·saw' ·seen'
  ·see'ing
fore·see'a·ble
fore·se'er
fore·shad'ow
fore·short'en
fore·show'
  ·showed',
  ·shown' *or*
  ·showed',
  ·show'ing
fore'sight'
fore'skin'
for'est
fore·stall'
for'est·a'tion
for'est·er
for'est·ry
fore'taste'
fore·tell'
  ·told' ·tell'ing
fore'thought'
for·ev'er
fore·warn'
fore'word'
  (*preface;* see
  forward)
for'feit
for'fei·ture
forge
  forged forg'ing
for'ger
for'ger·y
  ·ies
for·get'
  ·got', ·got'ten
  or ·got',
  ·get'ting
for·get'ful
for·get'-me-not'
for·get'ta·ble
for·giv'a·ble
for·give'
  ·gave' ·giv'en
  ·giv'ing
for·give'ness
for·go' *or* fore·
  ·went' ·gone'
  ·go'ing
  (*do without;*
  see forego)
forked
fork'lift'
for·lorn'
for'mal
form·al'de·hyde'
for·mal'i·ty
  ·ties
for'mal·i·za'tion
for'mal·ize'
  ·ized' ·iz'ing

for'mal·ly
for'mat
for·ma'tion
form'a·tive
for'mer
For·mi'ca
for'mi·da·ble
for'mi·da·bly
form'less
for'mu·la
· las or ·lae'
for'mu·late'
· lat'ed ·lat'ing
for'mu·la'tion
for'ni·cate'
· cat'ed ·cat'ing
for'ni·ca'tion
for'ni·ca'tor
for·sake'
· sook' ·sak'en
· sak'ing
for·swear'
· swore' ·sworn'
· swear'ing
for·syth'i·a
fort
(fortified place)
forte
(special skill)
forth'com'ing
forth'right'
forth·with'
for'ti·eth
for'ti·fi·ca'tion
for'ti·fi'er
for'ti·fy'
· fied' ·fy'ing
for'ti·tude'
for'tress
for·tu'i·tous
for·tu'i·ty
· ties
for'tu·nate
for'tune
for'tune·tell'er
for'ty
· ties
fo'rum
· rums or ·ra
for'ward
(to the front;
see foreword)
fos'sil
fos'ter
foul
(filthy; see fowl)
fou·lard'
foul'mouthed'
foun·da'tion
foun'der v.
found'er n.
found'ling
found'ry
· ries
foun'tain
foun'tain·head'
four'-flush'er
four'fold'

four'-foot'ed
Four'-H' club or
4'-H' club
four'-in-hand'
four'-post'er
four'score'
four'some
four'square'
four'teen'
fourth
fourth'-class'
four'-way'
fowl
(bird; see foul)
fox'hole'
fox'hound'
fox'i·ly
fox'i·ness
fox'y
· i·er ·i·est
foy'er
fra'cus
frac'tion
frac'tious
frac'ture
· tured ·tur·ing
frag'ile
fra·gil'i·ty
frag'ment
frag·men'tal·ly
frag'men·tar'y
fra'grance
fra'grant
frail'ty
· ties
frame
framed
fram'ing
frame'-up'
frame'work'
franc
(coin; see frank)
fran'chise
· chised ·chis·ing
fran'gi·bil'i·ty
fran'gi·ble
frank
(free; see franc)
frank'furt·er
frank'in·cense'
fran'tic
fran'ti·cal·ly
frap·pé'
fra·ter'nal
fra·ter'nal·ly
fra·ter'ni·ty
· ties
frat'er·ni·za'tion
frat'er·nize'
· nized' ·niz'ing
frat'ri·cide'
fraud'u·lence
fraud'u·lent
fraught
freak'ish
freck'le
· led ·ling

free
fre'er fre'est
freed free'ing
free'bie or ·by
· bies
free'born'
freed'man
free'dom
free'-for-all'
free'-form'
free'hand'
free'lance'
free'load'er
free'man
Free'ma'son
free'-spo'ken
free'-stand'ing
free'stone'
free'think'er
free'way'
free'wheel'ing
freez'a·ble
freeze
froze froz'en
freez'ing
(become ice; see
frieze)
freeze'-dry'
-dried' -dry'ing
freez'er
freight'age
freight'er
French cuff
French doors
French fry
French fries
French toast
fre·net'ic
fre·net'i·cal·ly
fren'zy
· zies
· zied ·zy·ing
fre'quen·cy
· cies
fre'quent
fres'co
· coes or ·cos
fresh'en
fresh'et
fresh'man
fresh'wa'ter
fret
fret'ted
fret'ting
fret'ful
fret'ful·ly
fret'work'
Freud'i·an
fri'a·bil'i·ty
fri'a·ble
fri'ar
fric'as·see'
· seed' ·see'ing
fric'tion
Fri'day
friend'li·ness
friend'ly
· li·er ·li·est

friend'ship
frieze
(in architecture;
see freeze)
frig'ate
fright'ened
fright'ful
frig'id
fri·gid'i·ty
frill'y
· i·er ·i·est
fringe
fringed
fring'ing
frip'per·y
· ies
Fris'bee
fri·sé'
frisk'i·ness
frisk'y
· i·er ·i·est
frit'ter
fri·vol'i·ty
· ties
friv'o·lous
friz'zi·ness
frog'man'
frol'ic
· icked ·ick·ing
frol'ick·er
frol'ic·some
front'age
fron'tal
fron·tier'
fron·tiers'man
fron'tis·piece'
front'let
frost'bite'
· bit' ·bit'ten
· bit'ing
frost'i·ly
frost'i·ness
frost'ing
frost'y
· i·er ·i·est
froth'i·ly
froth'i·ness
froth'y
· i·er ·i·est
fro'ward
frown
frow'zi·ness
frow'zy
· zi·er ·zi·est
fro'zen
fruc'ti·fy'
· fied' ·fy'ing
fru'gal
fru·gal'i·ty
fru'gal·ly
fruit'cake'
fruit'ful
fruit'i·ness
fru·i'tion
fruit'less
fruit'wood'
fruit'y
· i·er ·i·est

frump'ish
frus'trate
· trat·ed ·trat·ing
frus·tra'tion
frus'tum
· tums or ·ta
fry
fried fry'ing
fry'er or fri'er
f'-stop'
fuch'sia
fudge
fudged
fudg'ing
fu'el
· eled or ·elled
· el·ing or ·el·ling
fuel cell
fu'gi·tive
fugue
ful'crum
· crums or ·cra
ful·fill' or ·fil'
· filled' ·fill'ing
ful·fill'ment
or ·fil'ment
full'back'
full'-blood'ed
full'-blown'
full'-bod'ied
full'-dress'
full'-faced'
full'-fash'ioned
full'-fledged'
full'-length'
full'-scale'
full'-time'
full'y
ful'mi·nate'
· nat'ed ·nat'ing
ful'some
fum'ble
· bled ·bling
fume
fumed fum'ing
fu'mi·gant
fu'mi·gate'
· gat'ed ·gat'ing
fu'mi·ga'tion
fu'mi·ga'tor
func'tion·al
func'tion·al·ly
func'tion·ar'y
· ar'ies
fun'da·men'tal
fun'da·men'tal·
ism
fun'da·men'tal·ly
fund'-rais'er
fu'ner·al
fu·ne're·al
fun'gi·cid'al
fun'gi·cide'
fun'gous adj.
fun'gus n.
· gi or ·gus·es
fu·nic'u·lar

fun'nel
· neled or ·nelled
· nel·ing or
· nel·ling
fun'ni·ness
fun'ny
· ni·er ·ni·est
fur
furred fur'ring
(hair; see fir)
fur'be·low'
fur'bish
fu'ri·ous
fur'long
fur'lough
fur'nace
fur'nish·ings
fur'ni·ture
fu'ror
fur'ri·er
fur'ri·ness
fur'row
fur'ry
· ri·er ·ri·est
fur'ther
fur'ther·ance
fur'ther·more'
fur'ther·most'
fur'thest
fur'tive
fu'ry
· ries
fuse
fused fus'ing
fu'se·lage'
fu'si·bil'i·ty
fu'si·ble
fu'sil·lade'
· lad'ed ·lad'ing
fu'sion
fuss'i·ness
fuss'y
· i·er ·i·est
fus'tian
fust'y
· i·er ·i·est
fu'tile
fu'tile·ly
fu·til'i·ty
fu'ture
fu·tu'ri·ty
· ties
fuzz'i·ly
fuzz'i·ness
fuzz'y
· i·er ·i·est

G

gab'ar·dine'
ga'ble
gad'a·bout'
gadg'et
gag
gagged
gag'ging

gage
(*pledge;* see
gauge)
gag'gle
gag'man'
gai'e·ty
gai'ly
gain'er
gain'ful
gain'ful·ly
gain'li·ness
gain'ly
·li·er ·li·est
gain'say'
·said' ·say'ing
gait
(*way of walking;*
see gate)
gai'ter
ga'la
Gal'a·had'
gal'ax·y
·ies
gal'lant
gal'lant·ry
·ries
gal'le·on
gal'ler·y
·ies
·ied ·y·ing
gal'ley
·leys
gall'ing
gal'li·vant'
gal'lon
gal'lop
gal'lows
·lows·es *or* ·lows
gall'stone'
ga·lore'
ga·losh'
or ·loshe'
ga·lumph'
gal·van'ic
gal'va·nism
gal'va·ni·za'tion
gal'va·nize'
·nized' ·niz'ing
gal'va·nom'e·ter
gam'bit
gam'ble
·bled ·bling
(*risk;* see
gambol)
gam'bler
gam'bol
·boled *or* ·bolled
·bol·ing *or*
·bol·ling
(*frolic;* see
gamble)
gam'brel
game'cock'
game'keep'er
games'man·ship'
gam'in
gam'i·ness
gam'ma

gam'ut
gam'y
·i·er ·i·est
gan'der
Gan'dhi·ism
ga'nef *or* ·nof
gang'land'
gan'gling
gan'gli·on
·gli·a *or* ·gli·ons
gang'plank'
gan'grene
gan'gre·nous
gang'ster
gang'way'
gant'let
gan'try
·tries
gap
gapped
gap'ping
gape
gaped gap'ing
gar'bage
gar'ble
·bled ·bling
gar·çon'
·çons'
gar'den·er
gar·de'ni·a
gar'gle
·gled ·gling
gar'goyle
gar'ish
gar'land
gar'lic
gar'lick·y
gar'ment
gar'ner
gar'net
gar'nish
gar'nish·ee'
·eed' ·ee'ing
gar'nish·ment
gar'ret
gar'ri·son
gar·rote'
·rot'ed *or*
·rot'ted
·rot'ing *or*
·rot'ting
gar·ru'li·ty
gar'ru·lous
gar'ter
gas
gassed
gas'sing
gas'e·ous
gas'ket
gas'light'
gas'o·line' *or*
·lene'
gas'sy
·si·er ·si·est

gas'tric
gas'tro·nome'
gas'tro·nom'i·cal
gas·tron'o·my
gate
(*door;* see gait)
gate'way'
gath'er·ing
gauche
(*lacking grace;*
see gouache)
gau'che·rie'
gaud'i·ly
gaud'i·ness
gaud'y
·i·er ·i·est
gauge
gauged
gaug'ing
(*measure;* see
gage)
gauge'a·ble
gaunt
gaunt'let
gauze
gauz'y
·i·er ·i·est
gav'el
gawk'i·ness
gawk'y
·i·er ·i·est
gay'ly
gaze
gazed gaz'ing
ga·ze'bo
·bos *or* ·boes
ga·zelle'
ga·zette'
gaz'et·teer'
gear'box'
gear'shift'
gear'wheel'
Gei'ger
gei'sha
·sha *or* ·shas
gel
gelled gel'ling
gel'a·tin *or* ·tine
ge·lat'i·nize'
·nized' ·niz'ing
ge·lat'i·nous
geld
geld'ed *or* gelt
geld'ing
gel'id
ge·lid'i·ty
gem'i·nate'
·nat'ed ·nat'ing
Gem'i·ni'
gen'darme
gen'der
ge'ne·a·log'i·cal
ge'ne·al'o·gy
·gies
gen'er·al
gen'er·al'i·ty
·ties
gen'er·al·i·za'tion

gen'er·al·ize'
·ized' ·iz'ing
gen'er·al·ly
gen'er·ate'
·at'ed ·at'ing
gen'er·a'tion
gen'er·a'tor
ge·ner'ic
ge·ner'i·cal·ly
gen'er·os'i·ty
·ties
gen'er·ous
gen'e·sis
·ses'
ge·net'ic
ge·net'i·cal·ly
ge'nial
ge'ni·al'i·ty
ge'nial·ly
ge'nie
gen'i·tal
gen'ius
gen'o·cide'
gen'o·type'
gen're
gen·teel'
gen·teel'ly
gen'tile
gen·til'i·ty
gen'tle
·tler ·tlest
gen'tle·man
gen'tle·man·ly
gen'tle·wom'an
gent'ly
gen'try
gen'u·flect'
gen'u·ine
gen'u·ine·ly
ge'nus
gen'er·a
ge'o·cen'tric
ge·og'ra·pher
ge'o·graph'i·cal
ge·og'ra·phy
·phies
ge'o·log'ic
ge'o·log'i·cal·ly
ge·ol'o·gist
ge·ol'o·gy
·gies
ge'o·met'ric
ge'o·met'ri·cal·ly
ge·om'e·try
·tries
ge'o·phys'i·cal
ge'o·phys'i·cist
ge'o·phys'ics
ge'o·po·lit'i·cal
ge'o·pol'i·tics
Geor'gia
ge'o·stat'ics
ge·ot'ro·pism
ge·ra'ni·um
ger'bil *or* ·bille
ger'i·at'rics
ger·mane'
ger'mi·cid'al

ger'mi·cide'
ger'mi·nate'
·nat'ed ·nat'ing
ger'mi·na'tion
ger'on·tol'o·gy
ger'ry·man'der
ger'und
Ge·stalt'
ges'tate
·tat·ed ·tat·ing
ges·ta'tion
ges·tic'u·late'
·lat'ed ·lat'ing
ges·tic'u·la'tion
ges·tic'u·la'tor
ges'ture
·tured ·tur·ing
get
got, got *or*
got'ten,
get'ting
get'a·way'
get'-to·geth'er
gew'gaw
gey'ser
ghast'li·ness
ghast'ly
·li·er ·li·est
gher'kin
ghet'to
·tos *or* ·toes
ghet'to·ize'
·ized' ·iz'ing
ghil'lie
ghost'li·ness
ghost'ly
·li·er ·li·est
ghost'write'
ghost'writ'er
ghoul'ish
gi'ant
gib'ber·ish
gib'bet
gib'bon
gib·bos'i·ty
·ties
gib'bous
gibe
gibed gib'ing
(*taunt;* see jibe)
gib'let
gid'di·ly
gid'di·ness
gid'dy
·di·er ·di·est
gift'ed
gift'-wrap'
-wrapped'
-wrap'ping
gig
gigged gig'ging
gi·gan'tic
gi·gan'ti·cal·ly
gi·gan'tism
gig'gle
·gled ·gling
gig'o·lo'
·los'

gild
gild'ed *or* gilt
gild'ing
(*coat with gold;*
see guild)
gilt
(*gold;* see guilt)
gilt'-edged'
gim'bals
gim'crack'
gim'let
gim'mick
gin'ger
gin'ger·bread'
ging'ham
gi·raffe'
gird
gird'ed *or* girt
gird'ing
gird'er
gir'dle
·dled ·dling
girl'ish
gist
give
gave giv'en
giv'ing
give'a·way'
giz'zard
gla·cé'
·céed' ·cé'ing
gla'cial
gla'ci·ate'
·at'ed ·at'ing
gla'cier
glad
glad'der
glad'dest
glad'den
glad'i·a'tor
glad'i·o'lus *or* ·la
·lus·es *or* ·li, ·las
glad'some
glair
(*glaze;* see glare)
glam'or·ize
·ized' ·iz'ing
glam'or·ous
glam'our *or* ·or
glance
glanced
glanc'ing
glan'du·lar
glare
glared glar'ing
(*strong light;*
see glair)
glar'i·ness
glar'y
·i·er ·i·est
glass'ful'
·fuls'
glass·ine'
glass'i·ness
glass'ware'
glass'y
·i·er ·i·est
glau·co'ma

glaze
  glazed glaz'ing
gla'zier
glean'ings
glee'ful
glee'ful·ly
glib
  glib'ber
  glib'best
  glib'ly
glide
  glid'ed glid'ing
glid'er
glim'mer
glimpse
  glimpsed
  glimps'ing
glis·sade'
  ·sad'ed ·sad'ing
glis'ten
glit'ter
glit'ter·y
gloam'ing
gloat
glob'al
globe'-trot'ter
glob'u·lar
glob'ule
glock'en·spiel'
gloom'i·ly
gloom'i·ness
gloom'y
  ·i·er ·i·est
glo'ri·fi·ca'tion
glo'ri·fy'
  ·fied' ·fy'ing
glo'ri·ous
glo'ry
  ·ries
  ·ried ·ry·ing
glos'sa·ry
  ·ries
gloss'i·ness
gloss'y
  ·i·er ·i·est
  ·ies
glot'tal
glove
  gloved glov'ing
glow'er
glow'ing·ly
glow'worm'
glu'cose
glue
  glued glu'ing
glue'y
  glu'i·er
  glu'i·est
glum'ly
glut
  glut'ted
  glut'ting
glu'ten
glu'ten·ous
  (having gluten)
glu'ti·nous
  (gluey)
glut'ton

glut'ton·ous
  (greedy)
glut'ton·y
glyc'er·in or ·ine
gnarled
gnash
gnat
gnaw
  gnawed
  gnaw'ing
gneiss
gnoc'chi
gnome
gno'mic
gno'mon
gnos'tic
gnu
go
  went gone
  go'ing
goad
go'-a·head'
goal'keep'er
goat·ee'
gob'ble
  ·bled ·bling
gob'ble·dy·gook'
go'-be·tween'
gob'let
gob'lin
god'child'
god'daugh'ter
god'dess
god'fa'ther
God'-giv'en
god'li·ness
god'ly
  ·li·er ·li·est
god'moth'er
god'par'ent
god'send'
god'son'
God'speed'
go'-get'ter
gog'gle
  ·gled ·gling
go'-go'
goi'ter or ·tre
gold'en
gold'-filled'
gold'fish'
gold leaf
gold'smith'
golf'er
gon'do·la
gon'do·lier'
gon'or·rhe'a
  or ·rhoe'a
good
  bet'ter best
good'bye' or
  good'-bye'
  ·byes' or -byes'
good'-for-
  noth'ing
good'-heart'ed
good'-hu'mored
good'-look'ing

good'ly
  ·li·er ·li·est
good'-na'tured
good night
good'-sized'
good'-tem'pered
good'y
  ·ies
goo'ey
goo'i·er goo'i·est
goo'gol
goose
  geese
goose'neck'
goose'-step'
go'pher
gore
  gored gor'ing
gorge
  gorged gorg'ing
gor'geous
go·ril'la
  (ape; see guerrilla)
gor'i·ness
gor'mand·ize'
  ·ized' ·iz'ing
gor'y
  ·i·er ·i·est
gos'hawk'
gos'ling
gos'pel
gos'sa·mer
gos'sip
got'ten
gouache
  (painting; see
  gauche)
gouge
  gouged
  goug'ing
gou'lash
gourd
gour'mand
gour'met
gout
gov'ern·ess
gov'ern·ment
gov'ern·men'tal
gov'er·nor
grab
  grabbed
  grab'bing
grace'ful
grace'ful·ly
grace'less
gra'cious
gra'date
  ·dat·ed ·dat·ing
gra·da'tion
grade
  grad'ed grad'ing
grad'u·al
grad'u·ate'
  ·at'ed ·at'ing
grad'u·a'tion
graf·fi'ti
  (sing. graf·fi'to)
graft'er

gra'ham
grain'i·ness
grain'y
  ·i·er ·i·est
gram'mar
gram·mar'i·an
gram·mat'i·cal
gran'a·ry
  ·ries
grand'aunt'
grand'child'
grand'daugh'ter
gran'deur
grand'fa'ther
gran·dil'o·quent
gran'di·ose'
grand'moth'er
grand'neph'ew
grand'niece'
grand'par'ent
grand'son'
grand'stand'
grand'un'cle
gran'ite
gran'ite·ware'
grant·ee'
grant'in-aid'
  grants'-in-aid'
grant'or
gran'u·lar
gran'u·late'
  ·lat'ed ·lat'ing
gran'ule
grape'fruit'
grape'vine'
graph'ic
graph'i·cal·ly
graph'ite
graph·ol'o·gy
grap'nel
grap'ple
  ·pled ·pling
grap'pler
grasp'ing
grass'hop'per
grass'y
  ·i·er ·i·est
grate
  grat'ed grat'ing
grate'ful
grate'ful·ly
grat'i·fi·ca'tion
grat'i·fy'
  ·fied' ·fy'ing
gra'tis
grat'i·tude
gra·tu'i·tous
gra·tu'i·ty
  ·ties
grave
  graved, grav'en
  or graved,
  grav'ing
  (carve out)
grave
  graved grav'ing
  (clean the hull)
grave'clothes'

grav'el
  ·eled or ·elled
  ·el·ing or ·el·ling
grav'el·ly
grave'ly
grave'side'
grave'stone'
grave'yard'
grav'i·tate'
  ·tat'ed ·tat'ing
grav'i·ta'tion
grav'i·ty
  ·ties
gra'vy
  ·vies
gray
gray'-head'ed
graze
  grazed graz'ing
grease
  greased
  greas'ing
grease'paint'
greas'i·ness
greas'y
  ·i·er ·i·est
great'-aunt'
great'coat'
great'-grand'child'
great'-grand'par'·
  ent
great'ly
great'-neph'ew
great'ness
great'-niece'
great'-un'cle
greed'i·ly
greed'i·ness
greed'y
  ·i·er ·i·est
Greek'-let'ter
green'back'
green'er·y
green'-eyed'
green'gage'
green'horn'
green'house'
green'room'
green'sward'
greet'ing
gre·gar'i·ous
grem'lin
gre·nade'
gren'a·dier'
gren'a·dine'
grey'hound' or
  gray'·
grid'dle
  ·dled ·dling
grid'dle·cake'
grid'i'ron
grief'-strick'en
griev'ance
grieve
  grieved
  griev'ing
griev'ous
grif'fin

grill
  (broiler grid)
grille
  (open grating)
grill'room'
grim
  grim'mer
  grim'mest
gri·mace'
  ·maced'
  ·mac'ing
grime
  grimed grim'ing
grim'i·ly
grim'i·ness
grim'y
  ·i·er ·i·est
grin
  grinned
  grin'ning
grind
  ground
  grind'ing
grind'stone'
grip
  gripped or gript
  grip'ping
  (hold)
gripe
  griped grip'ing
  (distress)
grippe
  (influenza)
gris'li·ness
gris'ly
  ·li·er ·li·est
  (horrid)
gris'tle
gris'tly
  (of gristle)
grist'mill'
grit
  grit'ted
  grit'ting
grit'ti·ness
grit'ty
  ·ti·er ·ti·est
griz'zly bear
groan'ing
gro'cer·y
  ·ies
grog'gi·ly
grog'gi·ness
grog'gy
  ·gi·er ·gi·est
groin
grom'met
groom
groove
  grooved
  groov'ing
groov'y
  ·i·er ·i·est
grope
  groped grop'ing
gros'grain'
gross'ly
gross'ness

gro·tesque'
gro·tesque'ly
grot'to
·toes or ·tos
grouch'i·ly
grouch'i·ness
grouch'y
·i·er ·i·est
ground'less
grounds'keep'er
ground'speed'
ground'work'
group
grout
grove
grov'el
·eled or ·elled
·el·ing or ·el·ling
grow
grew grown
grow'ing
growl'er
grown'-up'
growth
grub
grubbed
grub'bing
grub'bi·ness
grub'by
·bi·er ·bi·est
grub'stake'
grudge
grudged
grudg'ing
gru'el
gru'el·ing or
gru'el·ling
grue'some
grue'some·ly
gruff'ly
grum'ble
·bled ·bling
grum'bler
grum'bly
grump'i·ness
grump'y
·i·er ·i·est
grun'ion
grunt
Gru·yère'
G'-string'
G'-suit'
guar'an·tee'
·teed' ·tee'ing
guar'an·tor'
guar'an·ty
·ties
·tied ·ty·ing
guard'ed
guard'house'
guard'i·an
guard'rail'
guard'room'
guards'man
gua'va
gu'ber·na·to'ri·al
Guern'sey
·seys

guer·ril'la or gue·
(soldier; see
gorilla)
guess'work'
guest
guid'a·ble
guid'ance
guide
guid'ed
guid'ing
guide'book'
guide'line'
guide'post'
guild
(union; see gild)
guilds'man
guile'ful
guile'less
guil'lo·tine'
·tined' ·tin'ing
guilt
(blame; see gilt)
guilt'i·ly
guilt'i·ness
guilt'y
·i·er ·i·est
guin'ea pig
guise
gui·tar'
gui·tar'ist
gulch
gul'let
gul'li·bil'i·ty
gul'li·ble
gul'li·bly
gul'ly
·lies
gum'drop'
gum'mi·ness
gum'my
·mi·er ·mi·est
gun
gunned
gun'ning
gun'cot'ton
gun'fire'
gung'-ho'
gun'lock'
gun'man
gun'ner·y
gun'ny·sack'
gun'play'
gun'point'
gun'pow'der
gun'run'ning
gun'shot'
gun'shy'
gun'smith'
gun'stock'
gup'py
·pies
gur'gle
·gled ·gling
gu'ru
gush'er
gush'i·ness
gush'y
·i·er ·i·est

gus'set
gus'ta·to'ry
gus'to
gust'y
·i·er ·i·est
gut
gut'ted
gut'ting
gut'ta-per'cha
gut'ter·snipe'
gut'tur·al
guy
guz'zle
·zled ·zling
guz'zler
gym·na'si·um
·si·ums or ·si·a
gym'nast
gym·nas'tics
gym'no·sperm'
gyn'e·col'o·gist
gyn'e·col'o·gy
gyp
gypped gyp'ping
gyp'sum
Gyp'sy
·sies
gy'rate
·rat·ed ·rat·ing
gy·ra'tion
gy'ro·com'pass
gy'ro·scope'
gy'ro·scop'ic
gy'ro·sta'bi·liz'er

H

ha'be·as cor'pus
hab'er·dash'er·y
·ies
ha·bil'i·tate'
·tat'ed ·tat'ing
hab'it
hab'it·a·ble
hab'i·tat'
hab'i·ta'tion
hab'it-form'ing
ha·bit'u·al
ha·bit'u·ate'
·at'ed ·at'ing
hab'i·tude'
ha·bit'u·é
ha'ci·en'da
hack'ney
·neys
hack'neyed
hack'saw'
had'dock
hag'gard
hag'gle
·gled ·gling
hai'ku
·ku
hail
(ice; see hale)
hail'stone'

hail'storm'
hair'breadth'
hair'cut'
hair'do'
hair'dress'er
hair'i·ness
hair'line'
hair'piece'
hair'-rais'ing
hair'split'ting
hair'spring'
hair'y
·i·er ·i·est
hal'cy·on
hale
haled hal'ing
(healthy; force;
see hail)
half
halves
half'back'
half'-baked'
half'-breed'
half'-caste'
half'-cocked'
half'heart'ed
half'-hour'
half'-mast'
half'-moon'
half'tone'
half'track'
half'-truth'
half'way'
hal'i·but
hal'i·to'sis
hal'le·lu'jah
or ·iah
hall'mark'
hal'lowed
Hal'low·een'
hal·lu'ci·nate'
·nat'ed ·nat'ing
hal·lu'ci·na'tion
hal·lu'ci·na·to'ry
hal·lu'ci·no·gen
hall'way'
hal'lo
·los or ·loes
hal'ter
halt'ing·ly
ha·lutz'
ha·lutz·im'
halve
halved halv'ing
hal'yard
ham'burg'er
ham'let
ham'mer
ham'mer·head'
ham'mock
ham'per
ham'ster
ham'string'
hand'bag'
hand'ball'
hand'bar'row
hand'bill'

hand'book'
hand'breadth'
hand'clasp'
hand'cuff'
hand'ful'
·fuls'
hand'gun'
hand'i·cap'
·capped'
·cap'ping
hand'i·craft'
hand'i·ly
hand'i·ness
hand'i·work'
hand'ker·chief
·chiefs
han'dle
·dled ·dling
han'dle·bar'
hand'ler
hand'made'
hand'-me-down'
hand'out'
hand'picked'
hand'rail'
hand'saw'
hand'sel
·seled or ·selled
·sel·ing or ·sel·ling
hand'set'
hand'shake'
hands'-off'
hand'some
hand'spring'
hand'stand'
hand'-to-hand'
hand'-to-mouth'
hand'work'
hand'writ'ing
hand'y
·i·er ·i·est
han'dy·man'
hang
hung hang'ing
(suspend)
hang
hanged hang'ing
(put to death)
hang'ar
(aircraft shed)
hang'dog'
hang'er
(garment holder)
hang'er-on'
hang'ers-on'
hang'man
hang'nail'
hang'o'ver
hang'-up'
hank'er
han'ky-pan'ky
han'som (cab)
Ha'nu·ka'
hap'haz'ard
hap'less
hap'pen
hap'pen·stance'
hap'pi·ly

hap'pi·ness
hap'py
·pi·er ·pi·est
hap'py-go-luck'y
ha'ra-ki'ri
ha·rangue'
·rangued'
·rangu'ing
ha·rangu'er
har·ass'
har'bin·ger
har'bor
hard'back'
hard'-bit'ten
hard'-boiled'
hard'-bound'
hard'-core'
hard'-cov'er
hard'en
hard'fist'ed
hard'goods'
hard'head'ed
hard'heart'ed
har'di·hood'
har'di·ly
har'di·ness
hard'ly
hard'pan'
hard'-shell'
hard'ship'
hard'tack'
hard'top'
hard'ware'
hard'wood'
har'dy
·di·er ·di·est
hare'brained'
hare'lip'
ha'rem
har'le·quin
harm'ful
harm'less
har·mon'ic
har·mon'i·ca
har·mo'ni·ous
har·mo'nize'
·nized' ·niz'ing
har'mo·ny
har'ness
harp'ist
har·poon'
harp'si·chord'
har'py
·pies
har'ri·er
har'row
har'row·ing
har'ry
·ried ·ry·ing
harsh'ness
har'te·beest'
har'um-scar'um
har'vest·er
has'-been'
ha'sen·pfef'fer
hash'ish or ·eesh
has'sle
·sled ·sling

has'sock
haste
has'ten
hast'i·ly
hast'i·ness
hast'y
· i·er ·i·est
hat'band'
hatch'er·y
· ies
hatch'et
hatch'ing
hatch'way'
hate
hat'ed hat'ing
hate'a·ble
hate'ful
hat'rack'
ha'tred
hat'ter
haugh'ti·ly
haugh'ti·ness
haugh'ty
· ti·er ·ti·est
haul'age
haunch
haunt'ed
haunt'ing
hau·teur'
have
had hav'ing
have'lock
ha'ven
have'-not'
hav'er·sack'
hav'oc
Ha·wai'i
Ha·wai'ian
hawk
hawk'-eyed'
hawk'ish
haw'ser
hay fever
hay'field'
hay'loft'
hay'ride'
haz'ard
haz'ard·ous
haze
hazed haz'ing
ha'zel·nut'
ha'zi·ly
ha'zi·ness
ha'zy
· zi·er ·zi·est
H'-bomb'
head'ache'
head'board'
head'cheese'
head'dress'
head'first'
head'gear'
head'hunt·er
head'i·ly
head'i·ness
head'land
head'less
head'light'

head'line'
head'long'
head'man
head'mas'ter
head'mis'tress
head'-on'
head'phone'
head'piece'
head'quar'ters
head'rest'
head'room'
head'set'
head'stand'
head start
head'stock'
head'strong'
head'wait'er
head'wa'ters
head'way'
head wind
head'y
· i·er ·i·est
heal
(cure; see heel)
health'ful
health'i·ly
health'i·ness
health'y
· i·er ·i·est
heap
hear
heard hear'ing
heark'en
hear'say'
hearse
heart'ache'
heart'beat'
heart'break'
heart'bro·ken
heart'burn'
heart'en
heart'felt'
hearth'stone'
heart'i·ly
heart'i·ness
heart'less
heart'-rend'ing
heart'sick'
heart'strings'
heart'-to-heart'
heart'warm·ing
heart'y
· i·er ·i·est
heat'ed·ly
heat'er
heath
hea'then
heath'er
heat'stroke'
heave
heaved or hove
heav'ing
heav'en·ly
heav'en·ward
heav'i·ly
heav'i·ness
heav'y
· i·er ·i·est

heav'y-du'ty
heav'y-hand'ed
heav'y-heart'ed
heav'y·set'
heav'y·weight'
He·bra'ic
He'brew
heck'le
· led ·ling
hec'tic
hec'ti·cal·ly
hec'to·graph'
hedge
hedged
hedg'ing
hedge'hop'
he'don·ism
he'do·nis'tic
heed'ful
heed'less
heel
(foot part;
see hcal)
heft'y
· i·er ·i·est
heif'er
height
height'en
hei'nous
heir
(inheritor; see
air)
heir'ess
heir'loom'
hel'i·cal
hel'i·cop'ter
he'li·o·graph'
he'li·o·trope'
he'i·port'
he'li·um
he'lix
· lix·es or ·li·ces'
hell'lion
hel·lo'
· los'
locd' ·lo'ing
hel'met
helms'man
help'ful
help'ful·ly
help'less
hel'ter-skel'ter
hem
hemmed
hem'ming
he'ma·tol'o·gy
hem'i·sphere'
hem'i·spher'i·cal
hem'line'
he'mo·glo'bin
he'mo·phil'i·a
hem'or·rhage
· rhaged
· rhag·ing
hem'or·rhoid'
hem'stitch'
hence'forth'
hench'man

hen'na
· naed ·na·ing
hen'ner·y
· ies
hen'pecked'
hen'ry
· rys or ·ries
he·pat'ic
hep'a·ti'tis
hep'ta·gon'
her'ald
he·ral'dic
her'ald·ry
her·ba'ceous
her'bi·cide'
her'bi·vore'
her·biv'o·rous
herds'man
here'a·bout'
here·af'ter
here'by'
he·red'i·tar'y
he·red'i·ty
· ties
here·in'
here'in·af'ter
here's
her'e·sy
· sies
her'e·tic
he·ret'i·cal
here'to·fore'
here·with'
her'it·a·ble
her'it·age
her·maph'ro·dite'
her·met'i·cal·ly
her'mit
her'ni·a
· as or ·ae'
her'ni·ate'
· at'ed ·at'ing
he'ro
· roes
he·ro'ic
he·ro'i·cal·ly
her'o·in
(narcotic)
her'o·ine
(female hero)
her'o·ism
her'pes
her'ring·bone'
her·self'
hes'i·tan·cy
· cies
hes'i·tant
hes'i·tate'
· tat'ed ·tat'ing
hes'i·ta'tion
het'er·o·dox'
het'er·o·dox'y
· ies
het'er·o·dyne'
· dyned' ·dyn'ing
het'er·o·ge·ne'i·ty
· ties
het'er·o·ge'ne·ous

het'er·o·nym'
het'er·o·sex'u·al
heu·ris'tic
heu·ris'ti·cal·ly
hew
hewed, hewed or
hewn, hew'ing
(chop; see hue)
hex'a·gon'
hex·ag'o·nal
hex'a·he'dron
· drons or ·dra
hey'day'
H'-hour'
hi·a'tus
· tus·es or ·tus
hi·ba'chi
hi'ber·nate'
· nat'ed ·nat'ing
hi'ber·na'tion
hi'ber·na'tor
hi·bis'cus
hic'cup or cough
· cuped or ·cupped
· cup·ing or
· cup·ping
hick'o·ry
· ries
hide
hid, hid'den or
hid, hid'ing
hide'a·way'
hide'bound'
hid'e·ous
hide'-out'
hie
hied, hie'ing
or hy'ing
hi'er·ar'chi·cal
hi'er·ar'chy
· chies
hi'er·o·glyph'ic
hi'-fi'
high'ball'
high'born'
high'boy'
high'bred'
high'brow'
high'chair'
high'-class'
high'er-up'
high'fa·lu'tin
high'-flown'
high'-grade'
high'hand'ed
high'-keyed'
high'land·er
high'-lev'el
high'light'
high'ly
high'-mind'ed
high'-pitched'
high'-pow'ered
high'-pres'sure
high'-priced'
high'-rise'
high'-sound'ing
high'-spir'it·ed

high'-strung'
high'-ten'sion
high'-test'
high'way'
hi'jack'
hike
hiked hik'ing
hi·lar'i·ous
hi·lar'i·ty
hill'i·ness
hill'ock
hill'side'
hill'y
· i·er ·i·est
him·self'
hind
hind'er,
hind'most' or
hind'er·most'
hin'der
hin'drance
hind'sight'
hinge
hinged hing'ing
hin'ter·land'
hip'bone'
hip'pie
hip'po·drome'
hip'po·pot'a·mus
· mus·es or ·mi
hir'a·ble or hire'-
hire
hired hir'ing
hire'ling
hiss'ing
his'ta·mine·
his·tol'o·gy
his·to'ri·an
his·tor'i·cal
· chies
his·tor'i·cal·ly
his'to·ry
· ries
his'tri·on'ic
hit
hit hit'ting
hit'-and-run'
hitch'hike'
hith'er·to'
hit'-or-miss'
hives
hoard
(reserve; see
horde)
hoar'frost'
hoar'i·ness
hoarse
hoar'y
· i·er ·i·est
hob'ble
· bled ·bling
hob'by
· bies
hob'by·horse'
hob'gob'lin
hob'nail'
hob'nob'
· nobbed' ·nob'bing

ho'bo
·bos or ·boes
hock'ey
ho'cus·po'cus
hodge'podge'
hoe
hoed hoe'ing
hoe'down'
hog'gish
hogs'head'
hog'tie'
·tied', ·ty'ing
or ·tie'ing
hog'wash'
hoi' pol·loi'
hoist
hold
held hold'ing
hold'out'
hold'o·ver
hold'up'
hole
holed hol'ing
hole'y
(with holes; see
holy, wholly)
hol'i·day'
ho'li·ly
ho'li·ness
hol'lan·daise'
hol'low
hol'lo·ware'
hol'ly
·lies
hol'ly·hock'
hol'o·caust'
ho·log'ra·phy
Hol'stein
hol'ster
ho'ly
·li·er ·li·est
·lies
(sacred; see
holey, wholly)
hom'age
hom'burg
home
homed hom'ing
home'bod'y
home'bred'
home'-brew'
home'com'ing
home'-grown'
home'land'
home'less
home'li·ness
home'ly
·li·er ·li·est
(plain; see
homey)
home'made'
home'mak'er
home'own'er
home'sick'
home'spun'
home'stead'
home'stretch'
home'ward

home'work'
home'y
hom'i·er
hom'i·est
(cozy; see
homely)
home'y·ness
hom'i·ci'dal
hom'i·cide'
hom'i·let'ics
hom'i·ly
·lies
hom'i·ny
ho'mo·ge·ne'i·ty
ho'mo·ge'ne·ous
ho·mog'e·nize'
·nized' ·niz'ing
hom'o·graph'
ho·mol'o·gous
hom'o·nym
hom'o·phone'
Ho'mo sa'pi·ens'
ho'mo·sex'u·al
ho'mo·sex'u·
al'i·ty
hone
honed hon'ing
hon'est
hon'es·ty
hon'ey
·eys, ·eyed or
·ied, ·ey·ing
hon'ey·bee'
hon'ey·comb'
hon'ey·dew'
hon'ey·moon'
hon'ey·suck'le
hon'or·a·ble
hon'o·ra'ri·um
·ri·ums or ·ri·a
hon'or·ar'y
hon'or·if'ic
hood'ed
hood'lum
hood'wink'
hoof
hoof'beat'
hook'ah or ·a
hook'up'
hook'y
hoo'li·gan
hoop'la
hoot'en·an'ny
·nies
hop
hopped hop'ping
hope
hoped hop'ing
hope'ful
hope'ful·ly
hope'less
hop'per
horde
hord'ed hord'ing
(crowd; see
hoard)
hore'hound'
ho·ri'zon

hor'i·zon'tal
hor·mo'nal
hor'mone
hor'net
horn'i·ness
horn'pipe'
horn'y
·i·er ·i·est
ho·rol'o·gy
hor'o·scope'
hor·ren'dous
hor'ri·ble
hor'ri·bly
hor'rid
hor'ri·fy'
·fied' ·fy'ing
hor'ror
hors' d'oeu'vre
·vres
horse'back'
horse'fly'
·flies'
horse'hair'
horse'hide'
horse'laugh'
horse'man
horse'play'
horse'pow'er
horse'rad'ish
horse'shoe'
·shoed' ·shoe'ing
horse'tail'
horse'whip'
horse'wom'an
hors'i·ness
hors'y
·i·er ·i·est
hor'ta·to'ry
hor'ti·cul'ture
hor'ti·cul'tur·ist
ho·san'na
hose
hosed hos'ing
ho'sier·y
hos'pice
hos'pi·ta·ble
hos'pi·ta·bly
hos'pi·tal
hos'pi·tal'i·ty
·ties
hos'pi·tal·i·za'tion
hos'pi·tal·ize'
·ized' ·iz'ing
hos'tage
hos'tel
(inn; see hostile)
hos'tel·ry
·ries
host'ess
hos'tile
(unfriendly; see
hostel)
hos'tile·ly
hos·til'i·ty
·ties
hos'tler
hot
hot'ter hot'test

hot'bed'
hot'-blood'ed
hot'box'
ho·tel'
ho·tel·ier'
hot'foot'
·foots'
hot'head'ed
hot'house'
hot'tem'pered
hound'ed
hour'glass'
hour'ly
house
housed hous'ing
house'boat'
house'break'
·broke' ·bro'ken
·break'ing
house'clean'ing
house'dress'.
house'coat'
house'fly'
·flies'
house'ful'
house'hold'
house'keep'er
house'lights'
house'maid'
house'man'
house'moth'er
house organ
house party
house'-rais'ing
house'warm'ing
house'wife'
·wives'
house'work'
hous'ing
hov'el
·eled or ·elled
·el·ing or ·el·ling
hov'er
how'dah
how·ev'er
how'itz·er
howl'ing
how'so·ev'er
how'-to'
hoy'den
hua·ra'ches
hub'bub'
hub'cap'
huck'le·ber'ry
·ries
huck'ster
hud'dle
·dled ·dling
hue
(color; see hew)
huff'i·ly
huff'i·ness
huff'y
·i·er ·i·est
hug
hugged hug'ging
huge'ness
hulk'ing

hul'la·ba·loo'
hum
hummed
hum'ming
hu'man
hu·mane'
hu'man·ism
hu'man·is'tic
hu·man·is'ti·cal·ly
hu·man'i·tar'i·an
hu·man'i·ty
·ties
hu'man·ize'
·ized' ·iz'ing
hu'man·kind'
hu'man·ly
hu'man·ness
hu'man·oid'
hum'ble
·bler ·blest
·bled ·bling
hum'bly
hum'bug'
hum'drum'
hu·mec'tant
hu'mer·us
·mer·i'
(bone; see
humorous)
hu'mid
hu·mid'i·fi·ca'tion
hu·mid'i·fi'er
hu·mid'i·fy'
·fied' ·fy'ing
hu·mid'i·ty
hu'mi·dor'
hu·mil'i·ate'
·at'ed ·at'ing
hu·mil'i·a'tion
hu·mil'i·ty
hum'ming·bird'
hum'mock
hu'mor
hu'mor·esque'
hu'mor·ist
hu'mor·ous
(funny; see
humerus)
hump'back'
hu'mus
hunch'back'
hun'dred·fold'
hun'dredth
hun'dred·weight'
hun'ger
hun'gri·ly
hun'gri·ness
hun'gry
·gri·er ·gri·est
hunt'er
hunt'ress
hunts'man
hur'dle
·dled ·dling
(barrier; see
hurtle)
hur'dy-gur'dy
hurl'er

hurl'y-burl'y
hur·rah'
hur'ri·cane'
hur'ried·ly
hur'ry
·ried ·ry·ing
hurt
hurt hurt'ing
hurt'ful
hur'tle
·tled ·tling
(rush; see hurdle)
hus'band
hus'band·ry
hush'-hush'
husk'i·ly
husk'i·ness
hus'ky
·kies
(dog)
husk'y
·i·er ·i·est, ·ies
(hoarse; robust)
hus'sy
·sies
hus'tle
·tled ·tling
hus'tler
hy'a·cinth'
hy'brid
hy'brid·ize'
·ized' ·iz'ing
hy·dran'ge·a
hy'drant
hy'drate
·drat·ed ·drat·ing
hy'dra·tor
hy·drau'lic
hy'dro·chlo'ric
hy'dro·dy·nam'ics
hy'dro·e·lec'tric
hy'dro·foil'
hy'dro·gen
hy'dro·gen·ate'
·at'ed ·at'ing
hy'dro·gen·a'tion
hy'dro·ki·net'ics
hy·drol'o·gy
hy·drol'y·sis
hy'dro·lyt'ic
hy'dro·me·
chan'ics
hy·drom'e·ter
hy'dro·naut'
hy'dro·pho'bi·a
hy'dro·plane'
hy'dro·pon'ics
hy'dro·ski'
hy'dro·stat'ics
hy'dro·ther'a·py
hy'drous
hy·e'na
hy'giene
hy'gi·en'ic
hy'gi·en'i·cal·ly
hy'gi·en·ist
hy·grom'e·ter
hy'gro·scope'

hy'men
hy'me·ne'al
hymn
hym'nal
hym·nol'o·gy
hy'per·a·cid'i·ty
hy'per·ac'tive
hy·per'bo·la
(curve)
hy·per'bo·le
(exaggeration)
hy'per·bol'ic
hy'per·crit'i·cal
(too critical; see
hypocritical)
hy'per·sen'si·tive
hy'per·son'ic
hy'per·ten'sion
hy'per·ven'ti·
la'tion
hy'phen
hy'phen·ate'
·at'ed ·at'ing
hy'phen·a'tion
hyp·no'sis
·ses
hyp·not'ic
hyp·not'i·cal·ly
hyp'no·tism
hyp'no·tiz'a·ble
hyp'no·tize'
·tized' ·tiz'ing
hy'po·chon'dri·a
hy'po·chon'dri·ac'
hy'po·chon·
dri'a·cal
hy'po·chon·
dri'a·sis
hy·poc'ri·sy
·sies
hyp'o·crite
hyp'o·crit'i·cal
(deceitful; see
hypercritical)
hy'po·der'mic
hy·pot'e·nuse'
hy·poth'e·cate'
·cat'ed ·cat'ing
hy·poth'e·sis
·ses'
hy·poth'e·size'
·sized' ·siz'ing
hy'po·thet'i·cal
hy'po·thet'i·cal·ly
hys·ter·ec'to·my
·mies
hys·te'ri·a
hys·ter'ic
hys·ter'i·cal
hys·ter'i·cal·ly

I

i·am'bic
ice
iced ic'ing

ice'berg'
ice'bound'
ice'box'
ice'break'er
ice'cap'
ice cream
ice field
ice'house'
ice'man'
ice milk
ich'thy·ol'o·gy
i'ci·cle
i'ci·ly
i'ci·ness
ic'ing
i'con
i·con'ic
i·con'o·clast'
i'cy
i'ci·er i'ci·est
I'da·ho'
i·de'a
i·de'al
i·de'al·ism
i·de'al·ist
i'de·al·is'tic
i'de·al·is'ti·cal·ly
i·de'al·i·za'tion
i·de'al·ize'
·ized' ·iz'ing
i·de'al·ly
i'de·ate'
·at'ed ·at'ing
i'de·a'tion
i·den'ti·cal
i·den'ti·cal·ly
i·den'ti·fi'a·ble
i·den'ti·fi·ca'tion
i·den'ti·fi'er
i·den'ti·fy'
·fied' ·fy'ing
i·den'ti·ty
·ties
id'e·o·gram'
id'e·o·graph'ic
i'de·o·log'i·cal
i'de·o·log'i·cal·ly
i'de·ol'o·gist
i'de·ol'o·gize'
·gized' ·giz'ing
i'de·ol'o·gy
·gies
id'i·o·cy
id'i·om
id'i·o·mat'ic
id'i·o·mat'i·cal·ly
id'i·o·syn'cra·sy
·sies
id'i·o·syn·crat'ic
id'i·ot
id'i·ot'ic
id'i·ot'i·cal·ly
i'dle
i'dler i'dlest
i'dled i'dling
(not active; see
idol, idyll))
i'dle·ness

i'dler
i'dly
i'dol
(image worshiped;
see idle, idyll)
i·dol'a·ter
i·dol'a·trous
i·dol'a·try
i'dol·ize'
·ized' ·iz'ing
i'dyll or i'dyl
(pastoral poem;
see idle, idol)
i·dyl'lic
ig'loo
·loos
ig'ne·ous
ig·nit'a·ble
or ·i·ble
ig'nite'
·nit'ed ·nit'ing
ig·ni'tion
ig·no'ble
ig'no·min'i·ous
ig'no·min'y
·ies
ig'no·ra'mus
ig'no·rance
ig'no·rant
ig·nore'
·nored' ·nor'ing
i·gua'na
il'e·um
(intestine)
il'i·um
(bone)
ill
worse worst
ill'-ad·vised'
ill'-be'ing
ill'-bod'ing
ill'-bred'
ill'-con·sid'ered
ill'-dis·posed'
il·le'gal
il'le·gal'i·ty
·ties
il·le'gal·ly
il'leg·i·bil'i·ty
il·leg'i·ble
il·leg'i·bly
il'le·git'i·ma·cy
·cies
il'le·git'i·mate
il'le·git'i·mate·ly
ill'-fat'ed
ill'-fa'vored
ill'-found'ed
ill'-got'ten
ill'-hu'mored
il·lib'er·al
il·lic'it
(unlawful; see
elicit)
il·lim'it·a·ble
il·lim'it·a·bly
Il·li·nois'
il·lit'er·a·cy

il·lit'er·ate
il·lit'er·ate·ly
ill'-man'nered
ill'-na'tured
ill'ness
il·log'i·cal
il·log'i·cal·ly
ill'-sort'ed
ill'-spent'
ill'-starred'
ill'-suit'ed
ill'-tem'pered
ill'-timed'
ill'-treat'
il·lu'mi·nate'
·nat'ed ·nat'ing
il·lu'mi·na'tion
il·lu'mi·na'tor
ill'-us'age
ill'-use'
il·lu'sion
(false idea; see
allusion, elusion)
il·lu'sive
(deceptive; see
allusive, elusive)
il·lu'so·ri·ly
il·lu'so·ri·ness
il·lu'so·ry
il'lus·trate'
·trat'ed ·trat'ing
il'lus·tra'tion
il·lus'tra·tive
il'lus·tra'tor
il·lus'tri·ous
im'age
·aged ·ag·ing
im'age·ry
·ries
i·mag'i·na·ble
i·mag'i·na·bly
i·mag'i·nar'i·ness
i·mag'i·nar'y
i·mag'i·na'tion
i·mag'i·na·tive
i·mag'ine
·ined ·in·ing
im'ag·ism
im·bal'ance
im'be·cile
im'be·cil'ic
im·be·cil'i·ty
·ties
im·bibe'
·bibed' ·bib'ing
im·bib'er
im'bri·cate'
·cat'ed ·cat'ing
im'bri·ca'tion
im·bro'glio
·glios
im·brue'
·brued' ·bru'ing
im·bue'
·bued' ·bu'ing
im'i·ta·ble
im'i·tate'
·tat'ed ·tat'ing

im'i·ta'tion
im'i·ta'tive
im'i·ta'tor
im·mac'u·late
im'ma·nent
(inherent; see
imminent)
im·ma·te'ri·al
im·ma·ture'
im·ma·tu'ri·ty
im·meas'ur·a·ble
im·me'di·a·cy
im·me'di·ate
im·me'di·ate·ly
im·me·mo'ri·al
im·mense'
im·mense'ly
im·men'si·ty
im·merge'
·merged'
·merg'ing
im·mer'gence
im·merse'
·mersed'
·mers'ing
im·mers'i·ble
im·mer'sion
im'mi·grant
im'mi·grate'
·grat'ed ·grat'ing
im'mi·gra'tion
im'mi·nence
im'mi·nent
(impending; see
eminent,
immanent)
im·mis'ci·ble
im·mit'i·ga·ble
im·mo'bile
im·mo·bil'i·ty
im·mo'bi·li·
za'tion
im·mo'bi·lize'
·lized' ·liz'ing
im·mod'er·ate
im·mod·er·a'tion
im·mod'est
im·mod'es·ty
·ties
im·mo·la'tion
im·mor'al
im·mo·ral'i·ty
·ties
im·mor'tal
im·mor·tal'i·ty
im·mor'tal·i·
za'tion
im·mor'tal·ize'
·ized' ·iz'ing
im·mov'a·bil'i·ty
im·mov'a·ble
im·mune'
im·mu'ni·ty
·ties
im'mu·ni·za'tion

im'mu·nize'
·nized' ·niz'ing
im·mu·nol'o·gy
im·mure'
·mured' ·mur'ing
im·mu'ta·bil'i·ty
im·mu'ta·ble
im·mu'ta·bly
im·pact'ed
im·pac'tion
im·pair'
im·pale'
·paled' ·pal'ing
im·pal'pa·bil'i·ty
im·pal'pa·ble
im·pan'el
·eled or ·elled
·el·ing or ·el·ling
im·part'
im·part'a·ble
im·par'tial
im'par·ti·al'i·ty
im·part'i·ble
im·pas'sa·bil'i·ty
im·pass'a·ble
(not passable;
see impassible)
im'passe
im·pas'si·bil'i·ty
im·pas'si·ble
(unfeeling; see
impassable)
im·pas'sioned
im·pas'sive
im'pas·siv'i·ty
im·pa'tience
im·pa'tient
im·peach'
im·peach'a·ble
im·pec'ca·bil'i·ty
im·pec'ca·ble
im·pec'ca·bly
im'pe·cu'ni·
os'i·ty
im'pe·cu'ni·ous
im·ped'ance
im·pede'
·ped'ed ·ped'ing
im·ped'i·ment
im·ped'i·men'ta
im·pel'
·pelled' ·pel'ling
im·pel'lent
im·pel'ler
im·pend'
im·pend'ing
im·pen'e·tra·
bil'i·ty
im·pen'e·tra·ble
im·pen'i·tence
im·pen'i·tent
im·per'a·tive
im'per·cep'ti·ble
im'per·cep'ti·bly
im·per'fect
im'per·fec'tion
im·per'fo·rate
im·pe'ri·al

im·pe'ri·al·ism
im·pe'ri·al·is'tic
im·pe'ri·al·ly
im·per'il
im·pe'ri·ous
im·per'ish·a·ble
im·per'ma·nent
im·per'me·a·ble
im'per·mis'si·ble
im·per'son·al
im·per'son·al'i·ty
im·per'son·al·ize'
im·per'son·ate'
 ·at'ed ·at'ing
im·per'son·a'tion
im·per'son·a'tor
im·per'ti·nence
im·per'ti·nent
im'per·turb'a·
 bil'i·ty
im'per·turb'a·ble
im·per'vi·ous
im·pe·ti'go
im·pet'u·os'i·ty
im·pet'u·ous
im'pe·tus
im·pi'e·ty
 ·ties
im·pinge'
 ·pinged' ·ping'ing
im·pinge'ment
im'pi·ous
imp'ish
im·pla'ca·ble
im·plant'
im'plan·ta'tion
im·plau'si·ble
im'ple·ment
im'ple·men'tal
im'ple·men·ta'tion
im'pli·cate'
 ·cat'ed ·cat'ing
im'pli·ca'tion
im'pli·ca'tive
im·plic'it
im·plode'
 ·plod'ed ·plod'ing
im·plore'
 ·plored' ·plor'ing
im·plo'sion
im·ply'
 ·plied' ·ply'ing
im'po·lite'
im·pol'i·tic
im·pon'der·a·ble
im·port'
im·port'a·ble
im·por'tance
im·por'tant
im'por·ta'tion
im·port'er
im·por'tu·nate
im'por·tune'
 ·tuned' ·tun'ing
im'por·tu'ni·ty
 ·ties
im·pose'
 ·posed' ·pos'ing

im'po·si'tion
im·pos'si·bil'i·ty
 ·ties
im·pos'si·ble
im'post
im·pos'tor
 (deceiver)
im·pos'ture
 (deception)
im'po·tence
im'po·tent
im·pound'
im·pov'er·ish
im·prac'ti·ca·
 bil'i·ty
im·prac'ti·ca·ble
im·prac'ti·cal
im'pre·cate'
 ·cat'ed ·cat'ing
im'pre·ca'tion
im'pre·cise'
im·preg'na·bil'i·ty
im·preg'na·ble
im·preg'nate
 ·nat·ed ·nat·ing
im'preg·na'tion
im'pre·sa'ri·o
 ·ri·os
im'pre·scrip'ti·ble
im·press'
im·press'i·ble
im·pres'sion
im·pres'sion·a·ble
im·pres'sion·a·bly
im·pres'sion·ism
im·pres'sive
im·pres'sive·ly
im'pri·ma'tur
im·print'
im·pris'on
im·prob'a·ble
im·promp'tu
im·prop'er
im'pro·pri'e·ty
 ·ties
im·prov'a·ble
im·prove'
 ·proved' ·prov'ing
im·prove'ment
im·prov'i·dent
im·prov'i·sa'tion
im'pro·vise'
 ·vised' ·vis'ing
im·pru'dence
im·pru'dent
im'pu·dence
im'pu·dent
im·pugn'
im·pugn'a·ble
im'pulse
im·pul'sion
im·pul'sive
im·pul'sive·ly
im·pu'ni·ty
im·pure'
im·pu'ri·ty
 ·ties
im·put'a·bil'i·ty

im·put'a·ble
im·pu·ta'tion
im·put'a·tive
im·pute'
 ·put'ed ·put'ing
in'a·bil'i·ty
in'ac·ces'si·ble
in·ac'cu·ra·cy
in·ac'cu·rate
in·ac'tion
in·ac'ti·vate'
 ·vat'ed ·vat'ing
in·ac'ti·va'tion
in·ac'tive
in·ac·tiv'i·ty
in·ad'e·qua·cy
 ·cies
in·ad'e·quate
in'ad·mis'si·ble
in'ad·vert'ence
in'ad·vert'ent
in'ad·vis'a·bil'i·ty
in'ad·vis'a·ble
in·al'ien·a·ble
in·al'ter·a·ble
in·ane'
in·an'i·mate
in·an'i·ty
 ·ties
in·ap'pli·ca·ble
in'ap·pre'ci·a·ble
in'ap·proach'a·ble
in'ap·pro'pri·ate
in·ar·tic'u·late
in'ar·tis'tic
in'as·much' as
in'at·ten'tion
in'at·ten'tive
in·au'di·ble
in·au'gu·ral
in·au'gu·rate'
 ·rat'ed ·rat'ing
in·aus·pi'cious
in'board'
in'born'
in'breed'
 ·bred' ·breed'ing
in·cal'cu·la·ble
in·cal'cu·la·bly
in·can·des'cence
in·can·des'cent
in'can·ta'tion
in'ca·pa·bil'i·ty
in·ca'pa·ble
in'ca·pac'i·tate'
 ·tat'ed ·tat'ing
in'ca·pac'i·ta'tion
in'ca·pac'i·ty
in·car'cer·ate'
 ·at'ed ·at'ing
in·car'cer·a'tion
in·car'nate
 ·nat·ed ·nat·ing
in'car·na'tion
in·cau'tious
in·cen'di·ar'y
 ·ies

in'cense
in·cense'
 ·censed' ·cens'ing
in·cen'tive
in·cep'tion
in·cep'tive
in·cer'ti·tude'
in·ces'sant
in'cest
in·ces'tu·ous
in·cho'ate
in'ci·dence
in'ci·dent
in'ci·den'tal
in'ci·den'tal·ly
in·cin'er·ate'
 ·at'ed ·at'ing
in·cin'er·a'tion
in·cin'er·a'tor
in·cip'i·ence
in·cip'i·ent
in·cise'
 ·cised' ·cis'ing
in·ci'sion
in·ci'sive
in·ci'sor
in·cite'
 ·cit'ed ·cit'ing
in·cit'er
in·ci·vil'i·ty
 ·ties
in·clem'en·cy
in·clem'ent
in·clin'a·ble
in'cli·na'tion
in·cline'
 ·clined' ·clin'ing
in·cli·nom'e·ter
in·clude'
 ·clud'ed
 ·clud'ing
in·clu'sion
in·clu'sive
in'co·er'ci·ble
in·cog'ni·to
 ·tos
in·cog'ni·zance
in·cog'ni·zant
in'co·her'ence
in'co·her'ent
in'com·bus'ti·ble
in'come
in'com'ing
in·com·men'su·
 ra·ble
in·com·men'su·
 rate
in'com·mode'
 ·mod'ed ·mod'ing
in'com·mo'di·ous
in'com·mu'ni·
 ca·ble
in'com·mu'ni·
 ca'do
in·com'pa·ra·ble
in'com·pat'i·
 bil'i·ty
 ·ties

in'com·pat'i·ble
in·com'pe·tence
in·com'pe·tent
in'com·plete'
in'com·pre·
 hen'si·ble
in'com·press'i·ble
in·com'put·a·ble
in·con·ceiv'a·ble
in·con·clu'sive
in·con'dite
in'con·form'i·ty
in·con'gru·ent
in'con·gru'i·ty
 ·ties
in·con'gru·ous
in·con'se·
 quen'tial
in'con·sid'er·a·ble
in'con·sid'er·ate
in'con·sid'er·
 ate·ly
in'con·sid'er·
 a'tion
in'con·sis'ten·cy
 ·cies
in'con·sis'tent
in'con·sol'a·ble
in'con·spic'u·ous
in·con'stan·cy
in·con'stant
in·con·sum'a·ble
in·con·test'a·ble
in·con'ti·nent
in'con·trol'la·ble
in'con·tro·vert'i·
 ble
in'con·ven'ience
in'con·ven'ient
in'con·vert'i·ble
in'co·or'di·nate
in·cor'po·rate'
 ·rat'ed ·rat'ing
in·cor'po·ra'tion
in·cor'po·ra'tor
in'cor·po're·al
in'cor·rect'
in·cor'ri·gi·bil'i·ty
in·cor'ri·gi·ble
in·cor'ri·gi·bly
in'cor·rupt'
in'cor·rupt'i·ble
in·creas'a·ble
in·crease'
 ·creased'
 ·creas'ing
in·creas'ing·ly
in·cred'i·bil'i·ty
in·cred'i·ble
in·cred'i·bly
in'cre·du'li·ty
in·cred'u·lous
in'cre·ment
in'cre·men'tal
in·crim'i·nate'
 ·nat'ed ·nat'ing
in·crim'i·na'tion
in·crim'i·na·to'ry

in·crust'
in'crus·ta'tion
in'cu·bate'
 ·bat'ed ·bat'ing
in'cu·ba'tion
in'cu·ba'tor
in·cul'cate
 ·cat·ed ·cat·ing
in·cul·ca'tion
in·culp'a·ble
in·cul·pa'tion
in·cum'ben·cy
 ·cies
in·cum'bent
in'cu·nab'u·la
in·cur'
 ·curred'
 ·cur'ring
in·cur'a·bil'i·ty
in·cur'a·ble
in·cur'a·bly
in·cu'ri·ous
in·cur'sion
in·debt'ed
in·de'cen·cy
 ·cies
in·de'cent
in·de·ci'pher·
 a·ble
in·de·ci'sion
in·de·ci'sive
in·de·clin'a·ble
in·dec'o·rous
in·de·co'rum
in·deed'
in·de·fat'i·ga·ble
in·de·fat'i·ga·bly
in·de·fea'si·ble
in·de·fect'i·ble
in·de·fen'si·ble
in·de·fin'a·ble
in·def'i·nite
in·del'i·ble
in·del'i·bly
in·del'i·ca·cy
 ·cies
in·del'i·cate
in·dem'ni·fi·
 ca'tion
in·dem'ni·fy'
 ·fied' ·fy'ing
in·dem'ni·ty
 ·ties
in·dent'
in·den·ta'tion
in·den'tion
in·den'ture
 ·tured ·tur'ing
in·de·pend'ence
in·de·pend'ent
in'-depth'
in·de·scrib'a·ble
in·de·scrib'a·bly
in·de·struct'i·ble
in·de·ter'mi·na·
 ble
in·de·ter'mi·na·cy
in·de·ter'mi·nate

in'de·ter'mi·
  na'tion
in'dex
  ·dex·es or ·di·ces'
In'di·an'a
in'di·cate'
  ·cat'ed ·cat'ing
in'di·ca'tion
in·dic'a·tive
in'di·ca'tor
in·dict'
  (accuse formally;
  see indite)
in·dict'a·ble
in·dict'ment
in·dif'fer·ence
in·dif'fer·ent
in'di·gence
in·dig'e·nous
in'di·gent
in·di·gest'i·ble
in·di·ges'tion
in·dig'nant
in·dig·na'tion
in·dig'ni·ty
  ·ties
in'di·go'
in·di·rect'
in·di·rec'tion
in'dis·cern'i·ble
in'dis·creet'
  (lacking prudence)
in'dis·crete'
  (not separated)
in'dis·cre'tion
  (indiscreet act)
in'dis·crim'i·nate
in'dis·pen'sa·ble
in'dis·pose'
in'dis·po·si'tion
in'dis·pu'ta·ble
in·dis·sol'u·ble
in·dis'tinct'
in'dis·tinc'tive
in'dis·tin'guish·
  a·ble
in·dite'
  ·dit'ed ·dit'ing
  (write; see indict)
in'di·vid'u·al
in'di·vid'u·al·ism
in'di·vid'u·al·
  is'tic
in'di·vid'u·al'i·ty
in'di·vid'u·al·ize'
  ·ized' ·iz'ing
in'di·vid'u·al·ly
in'di·vid'u·ate'
  ·at'ed ·at'ing
in'di·vis'i·bil'i·ty
in'di·vis'i·ble
in·doc'tri·nate'
  ·nat'ed ·nat'ing
in·doc'tri·na'tion
in·doc'tri·na'tor
in'do·lence
in'do·lent
in·dom'i·ta·ble

in·dom'i·ta·bly
in'door'
in'doors'
in·dorse'
  ·dorsed'
  ·dors'ing
in·du'bi·ta·ble
in·du'bi·ta·bly
in·duce'
  ·duced' ·duc'ing
in·duce'ment
in·duct'
in·duct'ance
in·duct·ee'
in·duc'tile
in·duc'tion
in·duc'tive
in·duc'tor
in·dulge'
  ·dulged'
  ·dulg'ing
in·dul'gence
in·dul'gent
in'du·rate'
  ·rat'ed ·rat'ing
in'du·ra'tion
in·dus'tri·al
in·dus'tri·al·ism
in·dus'tri·al·ist
in·dus'tri·al·i·
  za'tion
in·dus'tri·al·ize'
  ·ized' ·iz'ing
in·dus'tri·ous
in'dus·try
  ·tries
in·e'bri·ate'
  ·at'ed ·at'ing
in·e'bri·a'tion
in·e·bri'e·ty
in·ed'i·ble
in·ed'u·ca·ble
in·ef'fa·ble
in·ef'fa·bly
in'ef·face'a·ble
in'ef·fec'tive
in'ef·fec'tu·al
in'ef·fi·ca'cious
in·ef'fi·ca·cy
in'ef·fi'cien·cy
in'ef·fi'cient
in·e·las'tic
in'e·las·tic'i·ty
in·el'e·gance
in·el'e·gant
in·el'i·gi·bil'i·ty
in·el'i·gi·ble
in'e·luc'ta·ble
in'e·lud'i·ble
in·ept'
in·ept'i·tude'
in'e·qual'i·ty
  ·ties
in·eq'ui·ta·ble
in·eq'ui·ty
  ·ties
  (unfairness;
  see iniquity)

in'e·rad'i·ca·ble
in·er'ra·ble
in·er'rant
in·ert'
in·er'tia
in'es·cap'a·ble
in'es·cap'a·bly
in'es·sen'tial
in·es'ti·ma·ble
in·ev'i·ta·bil'i·ty
in·ev'i·ta·ble
in·ev'i·ta·bly
in·ex·act'
in'ex·cus'a·ble
in'ex·haust'i·ble
in·ex'o·ra·ble
in'ex·pe'di·ent
in'ex·pen'sive
in'ex·pe'ri·ence
in·ex'pert
in·ex'pi·a·ble
in·ex'pli·ca·ble
in·ex'pli·ca·bly
in'ex·press'i·ble
in'ex·press'i·bly
in'ex·pres'sive
in'ex·ten'si·ble
in'ex·tin'guish·a·
  ble
in·ex'tri·ca·ble
in·ex'tri·ca·bly
in·fal'li·bil'i·ty
in·fal'li·ble
in·fal'li·bly
in'fa·mous
in'fa·my
  ·mies
in'fan·cy
  ·cies
in'fant
in·fan'ti·cide'
in'fan·tile'
in'fan·ti·lism
in'fan·try
  ·tries
in'fan·try·man
in·fat'u·ate'
  ·at'ed ·at'ing
in·fat'u·a'tion
in·fect'
in·fec'tion
in·fec'tious
in·fec'tive
in·fec'tor
in·fe·lic'i·tous
in·fe·lic'i·ty
  ·ties
in·fer'
  ·ferred'
  ·fer'ring
in·fer'a·ble
in'fer·ence
in'fer·en'tial
in·fe'ri·or
in·fe'ri·or'i·ty
in·fer'nal
in·fer'no
  ·nos

in·fer'tile
in·fest'
in'fi·del
in'fi·del'i·ty
  ·ties
in'field'
in·fil'trate
  ·trat·ed ·trat·ing
in'fil·tra'tion
in'fil·tra'tor
in'fi·nite
in·fi'nite·ly
in·fin·i·tes'i·mal
in·fin'i·tive
in·fin'i·ty
  ·ties
in·firm'
in·fir'ma·ry
  ·ries
in·fir'mi·ty
  ·ties
in·flame'
  ·flamed'
  ·flam'ing
in·flam'ma·ble
in·flam·ma'tion
in·flam'ma·to'ry
in·flate'
  ·flat'ed
  ·flat'ing
in·fla'tion
in·fla'tion·ar'y
in·flect'
in·flec'tion
in·flex'i·ble
in·flex'i·bly
in·flict'
in·flic'tion
in'-flight'
in'flow'
in'flu·ence
  ·enced ·enc·ing
in·flu·en'tial
in·flu·en'za
in'flux'
in·form'
in·for'mal
in'for·mal'i·ty
in·form'ant
in'for·ma'tion
in·form'a·tive
in·form'er
in·frac'tion
in·fran'gi·ble
in'fra·red'
in·fre'quent
in·fringe'
in·fringe'ment
in·fu'ri·ate'
  ·at'ed ·at'ing
in·fuse'
  ·fused' ·fus'ing
in·fu'sion
in·gen'ious
  (clever; see
  ingenuous)
in·gé'nue'
in·ge·nu'i·ty

in·gen'u·ous
  (frank; see
  ingenious)
in·gest'
in·ges'tion
in·glo'ri·ous
in'got
in·grained'
in'grate
in·gra'ti·ate'
  ·at'ed ·at'ing
in·grat'i·tude'
in·gre'di·ent
in'gress
in'grown'
in'-group'
in'-house'
in·hab'it
in·hab'it·a·ble
in·hab'it·ant
in·hal'ant
in·ha·la'tion
in·hale'
  ·haled' ·hal'ing
in·hal'er
in·har·mon'ic
in·har·mo'ni·ous
in·here'
  ·hered' ·her'ing
in·her'ence
in·her'ent
in·her'it
in·her'it·a·ble
in·her'it·ance
in·her'i·tor
in·hib'it
in·hi·bi'tion
in·hib'i·tive
in·hib'i·tor
in·hos'pi·ta·ble
in·hos·pi·tal'i·ty
in'-house'
in·hu'man
in·hu·mane'
in·hu·man'i·ty
  ·ties
in·im'i·cal
in·im'i·ta·ble
in·iq'ui·tous
in·iq'ui·ty
  ·ties
  (wickedness;
  see inequity)
in·i'tial
  ·tialed or ·tialled
  ·tial·ing or ·tial·ling
in·i'tial·ly
in·i'ti·ate'
  ·at'ed ·at'ing
in·i'ti·a'tion
in·i'ti·a·tive
in·i'ti·a'tor
in·ject'
in·jec'tion
in·jec'tor
in·ju·di'cious
in·junc'tion
in'jure
  ·jured ·jur·ing

in·ju'ri·ous
in'ju·ry
  ·ries
in·jus'tice
ink'blot'
ink'ling
ink'y
  ·i·er ·i·est
in'laid'
in'land
in'-law'
in'lay'
  ·laid' ·lay'ing
  ·lays'
in'let
in'mate'
in me·mo'ri·am
in'most'
in'nards
in'nate'
in'ner·most'
in'ner·spring'
in·ner'vate
  ·vat·ed ·vat·ing
in'ning
inn'keep'er
in'no·cence
in'no·cent
in·noc'u·ous
in'no·vate'
  ·vat'ed ·vat'ing
in'no·va'tion
in'no·va'tive
in'no·va'tor
in'nu·en'do
  ·does or ·dos
in·nu'mer·a·ble
in·oc'u·late'
  ·lat'ed ·lat'ing
in·oc'u·la'tion
in·of·fen'sive
in·op'er·a·ble
in·op'er·a·tive
in·op'por·tune'
in·or'di·nate
in·or·gan'ic
in·pa'tient
in'put'
in'quest'
in·qui'e·tude'
in·quire'
  ·quired'
  ·quir'ing
in·quir'y
  ·ies
in'qui·si'tion
in·quis'i·tive
in·quis'i·tor
in'road'
in·sane'
in·san'i·tar'y
in·san'i·ty
in·sa'ti·a·ble
in·scribe'
  ·scribed'
  ·scrib'ing
in·scrip'tion
in·scru'ta·bil'i·ty

in·scru'ta·ble
in'seam'
in'sect
in·sec'ti·cide'
in·se·cure'
in·se·cu'ri·ty
in·sem'i·nate'
· nat'ed ·nat'ing
in·sem'i·na'tion
in·sen'sate
in·sen'si·bil'i·ty
in·sen'si·ble
in·sen'si·tive
in·sen'si·tiv'i·ty
in·sep'a·ra·ble
in·sert'
in·ser'tion
in'-ser'vice
in'side'
in·sid'i·ous
in'sight'
in·sig'ni·a
in'sig·nif'i·cance
in'sig·nif'i·cant
in·sin·cere'
in'sin·cere'ly
in'sin·cer'i·ty
in·sin'u·ate'
· at'ed ·at'ing
in·sin'u·a'tion
in·sip'id
in'si·pid'i·ty
in·sist'
in·sist'ence
in·sist'ent
in·so·bri'e·ty
in·so·far'
in'sole'
in'so·lence
in'so·lent
in·sol'u·ble
in·sol'vent
in·som'ni·a
in·sou'ci·ance
in·sou'ci·ant
in·spect'
in·spec'tion
in·spec'tor
in'spi·ra'tion
in·spire'
· spired' ·spir'ing
in·spir'it
in'sta·bil'i·ty
in·stall' or ·stal'
· stalled' ·stall'ing
in·stal·la'tion
in·stall'ment
or ·stal'ment
in'stance
in'stant
in'stan·ta'ne·ous
in·stan'ter
in·state'
· stat'ed ·stat'ing
in·stead'
in'step'
in'sti·gate'
· gat'ed ·gat'ing

in'sti·ga'tion
in'sti·ga'tor
in·still' or ·still'
· stilled' ·still'ing
in'stinct
in·stinc'tive
in'sti·tute'
· tut'ed ·tut'ing
in'sti·tu'tion
in'sti·tu'tion·al·
ize'
· ized' ·iz'ing
in·struct'
in·struc'tion
in·struc'tive
in·struc'tor
in'stru·ment
in'stru·men'tal
in'stru·men·
tal'i·ty
in'stru·men·
ta'tion
in·sub·or'di·nate
in·sub·or'di·
na'tion
in·sub·stan'tial
in·suf'fer·a·ble
in'suf·fi'cien·cy
· cies
in'suf·fi'cient
in'su·lar
in'su·late'
· lat'ed ·lat'ing
in'su·la'tion
in'su·la'tor
in'su·lin
in·sult'
in·su'per·a·ble
in·sup·port'a·ble
in·sup·press'i·ble
in·sur'a·bil'i·ty
in·sur'a·ble
in·sur'ance
in·sure'
· sured' ·sur'ing
in·sur'er
in·sur'gence
in·sur'gent
in'sur·mount'a·
ble
in'sur·rec'tion
in·tact'
in·tagl'io
· ios
in·take'
in·tan'gi·ble
in'te·ger
in'te·gral
in'te·grate'
· grat'ed ·grat'ing
in'te·gra'tion
in·teg'ri·ty
in·teg'u·ment
in'tel·lect'
in'tel·lec'tu·al
in'tel·lec'tu·al·ize'
· ized' ·iz'ing
in'tel·lec'tu·al·ly

in·tel'li·gence
in·tel'li·gent
in·tel'li·gent'si·a
in·tel'li·gi·bil'i·ty
in·tel'li·gi·ble
in·tel'li·gi·bly
In'tel·sat'
in·tem'per·ance
in·tem'per·ate
in·tend'
in·tend'ant
in·tense'
in·tense'ly
in·ten'si·fi·ca'tion
in·ten'si·fy'
· fied' ·fy'ing
in·ten'si·ty
in·ten'sive
in·tent'
in·ten'tion
in·ten'tion·al
in·ten'tion·al·ly
in·ter'
· terred' ·ter'ring
in'ter·act'
in'ter·ac'tion
in'ter·breed'
· bred' ·breed'ing
in'ter·cede'
· ced'ed ·ced'ing
in'ter·cept'
in'ter·cep'tion
in'ter·cep'tor
in'ter·ces'sion
in'ter·change'
in'ter·change'a·
ble
in'ter·com'
in'ter·com·mu'ni·
cate'
in'ter·con·nect'
in'ter·course'
in'ter·de·nom'i·
na'tion·al
in'ter·de·part'·
men'tal
in'ter·de·pend'·
ence
in'ter·dict'
in'ter·dis'ci·
pli·nar'y
in'ter·est
in'ter·est·ed
in'ter·faith'
in'ter·fere'
· fered' ·fer'ing
in'ter·fer'ence
in'ter·fer'on
in'ter·im
in·te'ri·or
in'ter·ject'
in'ter·jec'tion
in'ter·lace'
in'ter·leaf'
· leaves'
in'ter·leave'
· leaved'
· leav'ing

in'ter·lin'e·ar
in'ter·lin'ing
in'ter·lock'
in'ter·lo·cu'tion
in'ter·loc'u·tor
in'ter·loc'u·to'ry
in'ter·lope'
· loped' ·lop'ing
in'ter·lop'er
in'ter·lude'
in'ter·mar'riage
in'ter·mar'ry
in'ter·me'di·ar'y
· ar'ies
in'ter·me'di·ate
in·ter'ment
in'ter·mez'zo
· zos or ·zi
in·ter'mi·na·ble
in'ter·min'gle
in'ter·mis'sion
in'ter·mit'tent
in'tern
(doctor)
in·tern'
(detain)
in·ter'nal
in·ter'nal·ize'
· ized' ·iz'ing
in·ter'nal·ly
in·ter·na'tion·al
in·ter·ne'cine
in'tern·ee'
in·ter'nist
in·tern'ment
in'tern·ship'
in'ter·of'fice
in'ter·pen'e·
trate'
in'ter·per'son·al
in'ter·phone'
in'ter·plan'e·
tar'y
in'ter·play'
in·ter'po·late'
· lat'ed ·lat'ing
in·ter'po·la'tion
in'ter·pose'
in·ter'pret
in·ter'pre·ta'tion
in·ter'pret·er
in'ter·ra'cial
in'ter·re·late'
in'ter·re·la'tion
in·ter'ro·gate'
· gat'ed ·gat'ing
in·ter'ro·ga'tion
in'ter·rog'a·tive
in·ter'ro·ga'tor
in·ter'rog'a·to'ry
in·ter·rupt'
in'ter·rup'tion
in'ter·scho·las'tic
in'ter·sect'
in'ter·sec'tion
in'ter·sperse'
· spersed'
· spers'ing

in'ter·sper'sion
in'ter·state'
in'ter·stel'lar
in·ter'stice
· stic·es
in'ter·twine'
in'ter·ur'ban
in'ter·val
in'ter·vene'
· vened' ·ven'ing
in'ter·ven'tion
in'ter·view'
in'ter·view'er
in'ter·weave'
· wove' ·wov'en
· weav'ing
in·tes'tate
in·tes'tin·al
in·tes'tine
in'ti·ma·cy
· cies
in'ti·mate
in'ti·ma'tion
in·tim'i·date'
· dat'ed ·dat'ing
in·tim'i·da'tion
in·tol'er·a·ble
in·tol'er·ance
in·tol'er·ant
in'to·na'tion
in·tone'
in·tox'i·cant
in·tox'i·cate'
· cat'ed ·cat'ing
in·tox'i·ca'tion
in·trac'ta·ble
in'tra·mu'ral
in'tra·mus'cu·lar
in·tran'si·gent
in·tran'si·tive
in'tra·state'
in'tra·u'ter·ine
in'tra·ve'nous
in·trep'id
in'tre·pid'i·ty
in'tri·ca·cy
· cies
in'tri·cate
in·trigue'
· trigued'
· trigu'ing
in·trin'sic
in'tro·duce'
· duced' ·duc'ing
in'tro·duc'tion
in'tro·duc'to·ry
in'tro·spec'tion
in'tro·spec'tive
in'tro·ver'sion
in'tro·vert'
in·trude'
· trud'ed
· trud'ing
in·trud'er
in·tru'sion
in·tru'sive
in·tu·i'tion
in·tu'i·tive

in'un·date'
· dat'ed ·dat'ing
in·un·da'tion
in·ure'
· ured' ·ur'ing
in·vade'
· vad'ed ·vad'ing
in·vad'er
in'va·lid
in·val'id
in·val'i·date'
· dat'ed ·dat'ing
in·val'i·da'tion
in·val'u·a·ble
in·val'u·a·bly
in·var'i·a·ble
in·var'i·a·bly
in·va'sion
in·vec'tive
in·veigh'
in·vei'gle
· gled ·gling
in·vent'
in·ven'tion
in·ven'tive
in·ven'tor
in·ven·to'ry
· ries, ·ried ·ry·ing
in·verse'
in·ver'sion
in·vert'
in·ver'te·brate
in·vert'i·ble
in·vest'
in·ves'ti·gate'
· gat'ed ·gat'ing
in·ves'ti·ga'tion
in·ves'ti·ga'tor
in·ves'ti·ture
in·vest'ment
in·vet'er·ate
in·vi'a·ble
in·vid'i·ous
in·vig'or·ate'
· at'ed ·at'ing
in·vin·ci·bil'i·ty
in·vin'ci·ble
in·vin'ci·bly
in·vi'o·la·ble
in·vi'o·late
in·vis'i·ble
in'vi·ta'tion
in·vite'
· vit'ed ·vit'ing
in'vo·ca'tion
in'voice
· voiced ·voic·ing
in·voke'
· voked' ·vok'ing
in·vol'un·tar'i·ly
in·vol'un·tar'y
in'vo·lute'
in·volve'
· volved'
· volv'ing
in·vul'ner·a·ble
in'ward
i'o·dine'

i'on
i'on·i·za'tion
i'on·ize'
· ized' ·iz'ing
i·on'o·sphere'
i·o'ta
I'o·wa
ip'e·cac'
ip'so fac'to
i·ras'ci·bil'i·ty
i·ras'ci·ble
i·rate'
ire'ful·ly
ir'i·des'cence
ir'i·des'cent
irk'some
i'ron·bound'
i'ron·clad'
i·ron'i·cal
i·ron'i·cal·ly
i'ron·stone'
i'ron·work'
i'ro·ny
· nies
ir·ra'di·ate'
ir·ra'di·a'tion
ir·ra'tion·al
ir·ra'tion·al'i·ty
ir·ra'tion·al·ly
ir·re·claim'a·ble
ir·rec'on·cil'a·ble
ir·re·cov'er·a·ble
ir·re·deem'a·ble
ir·re·duc'i·ble
ir·ref'u·ta·ble
ir·reg'u·lar
ir·reg'u·lar'i·ty
· ties
ir·rel'e·vant
ir're·li'gious
ir·re·me'di·a·ble
ir·re·mis'si·ble
ir·re·mov'a·ble
ir·re·rep'a·ra·ble
ir·re·place'a·ble
ir·re·press'i·ble
ir·re·proach'a·ble
ir·re·sist'i·ble
ir·res'o·lute'
ir're·spec'tive
ir're·spon'si·ble
ir·re·triev'a·ble
ir·rev'er·ence
ir·rev'er·ent
ir're·vers'i·ble
ir·rev'o·ca·ble
ir'ri·ga·ble
ir'ri·gate'
· gat'ed ·gat'ing
ir'ri·ga'tion
ir'ri·ta·bil'i·ty
ir'ri·ta·ble
ir'ri·ta·bly
ir'ri·tant
ir'ri·tate'
· tat'ed ·tat'ing
ir'ri·ta'tion
ir·rupt'

ir·rup'tion
i'sin·glass'
is'land
isle
    (island; see aisle)
is'let
    (small island;
    see eyelet)
is'n't
i'so·bar'
i'so·late'
· lat'ed ·lat'ing
i'so·la'tion
i'so·la'tion·ist
i'so·mer
i'so·met'ric
i'so·met'ri·cal·ly
i·sos'ce·les'
i'so·therm'
i'so·tope'
i'so·trop'ic
Is'ra·el
Is·rae'li
is'su·ance
is'sue
· sued ·su·ing
isth'mus
· mus·es or ·mi
i·tal'ic
i·tal'i·cize'
· cized' ·ciz'ing
itch'i·ness
itch'y
· i·er ·i·est
i'tem·ize'
· ized' ·iz'ing
it'er·ate'
· at'ed ·at'ing
it'er·a'tion
i·tin'er·ant
i·tin'er·ar'y
· ies
i·tin'er·ate'
· at'ed ·at'ing
its
    (of it)
it's
    (it is)
it·self'
I've
i'vied
i'vo·ry
· ries
i'vy
i'vies

J

jab
jabbed jab'bing
jab'ber
ja·bot'
ja'cinth
jack'al
jack'a·napes'
jack'ass'

jack'boot'
jack'et
jack'ham'mer
jack'-in-the-box'
· box'es
jack'knife'
· knives'
· knifed' ·knif'ing
jack'-of-all'-
trades'
jacks'-
jack'-o'-lan'tern
· terns
jack'pot'
jack'screw'
jack'straw'
Jac·quard'
jade
jad'ed jad'ing
jag'ged
jag'uar
jai' a·lai'
jail'bird'
jail'er or ·or
jal'ou·sie'
    (door; see
    jealousy)
jam
jammed
jam'ming
jam'ba·lay'a
jam'bo·ree'
jan'gle
· gled ·gling
jan'i·tor
Jan'u·ar'y
· ar·ies
ja·pan'
· panned'
· pan'ning
jar
jarred jar'ring
jar'di·niere'
jar'gon
jas'mine
jas'per
ja'to or JA'TO
jaun'dice
· diced ·dic·ing
jaun'ti·ly
jaun'ti·ness
jaun'ty
· ti·er ·ti·est
jav'e·lin
jaw'bone'
jaw'break'er
Jay'cee'
jay'walk'er
jazz'i·ness
jazz'y
· i·er ·i·est
jeal'ous
jeal'ous·y
· ies
    (envy; see
    jalousie)
jeans
jeer'ing·ly

je·june'
jel'li·fy'
· fied' ·fy'ing
jel'ly
· lies, ·lied ·ly·ing
jel'ly·fish'
jel'ly·roll'
jen'ny
· nies
jeop'ard·ize'
· ized' ·iz'ing
jeop'ard·y
je·quir'i·ty
· ties
jer'e·mi'ad
jerk'i·ly
jer'kin
jerk'i·ness
jerk'wa'ter
jerk'y
· i·er ·i·est
    (moving fitfully)
jer'ky
    (dried beef)
Jer'sey
· seys
    (dairy cattle)
jer'sey
· seys
    (cloth; shirt)
jest'er
jet
jet'ted jet'ting
jet'-black'
jet'lin'er
jet'port'
jet'-pro·pelled'
jet'sam
jet stream
jet'ti·son
jet'ty
· ties, ·tied ·ty·ing
jew'el
· eled or ·elled
· el·ing or ·el ling
jew'el·er or
· el·ler
jew'el·ry
Jew'ish
Jew'ry
· ries
jew's'-harp' or
jews'-harp'
Jez'e·bel
jib
jibbed jib'bing
jibe
jibed jib'ing
    (nautical; agree;
    see gibe)
jig'ger
jig'gle
· gled ·gling
jig'saw'
Jim'-Crow'
jim'my
· mies
· mied ·my·ing

jin'gle
· gled ·gling
jin'go
· goes
jin'go·ism
jin'go·is'ti·cal·ly
jin·ni'
jinn
jin·rik'i·sha
jinx
jit'ney
· neys
jit'ter·y
job
jobbed job'bing
job'ber
jock'ey
· eys
· eyed ·ey·ing
jock'strap'
jo·cose'
jo·cos'i·ty
· ties
joc'u·lar
joc'u·lar'i·ty
joc'und
jo·cun'di·ty
jodh'purs
jog
jogged jog'ging
jog'ger
jog'gle
· gled ·gling
john'ny·cake'
join'er
joint'ly
join'ture
joist
joke
joked jok'ing
jol'li·ness
jol·li'ty
jol'ly
· li·er ·li·est
jon'quil
jos'tle
· tled ·tling
jot
jot'ted jot'ting
jounce
jounced
jounc'ing
jour'nal
jour'nal·ese'
jour'nal·ism
jour'nal·is'tic
jour'ney
· neys
· neyed ·ney·ing
jour'ney·man
joust
jo'vi·al
jo'vi·al'i·ty
jo'vi·al·ly
jowl
joy'ful
joy'less
joy'ous

ju'bi·lant
ju'bi·la'tion
ju'bi·lee'
Ju·da'i·ca
Ju'da·ism
judge
judged judg'ing
judg'ment or
judge'·
ju'di·ca·to'ry
· ries
ju·di'cial
ju·di'ci·ar'y
· ies
ju·di'cious
ju'do
jug
jugged jug'ging
jug'ger·naut'
jug'gle
· gled ·gling
jug'u·lar
juice
juiced juic'ing
juic'er
juic'i·ly
juic'i·ness
juic'y
· i·er ·i·est
ju·jit'su or
ju·jut'su
ju'jube
juke'box'
ju'lep
ju·li·enne'
Ju·ly'
· lies'
jum'ble
· bled ·bling
jum'bo
jump'er
jump'i·ness
jump'y
· i·er ·i·est
junc'tion
junc'ture
June
jun'gle
jun'ior
jun·ior'i·ty
ju'ni·per
junk'et
junk'man'
jun'ta
jun'to
· tos
ju·rid'i·cal
ju·rid'i·cal·ly
ju'ris·dic'tion
ju'ris·pru'dence
ju'rist
ju·ris'tic
ju'ror
ju'ry
· ries
ju'ry·man
jus'tice
jus'ti·fi'a·ble

jus'ti·fi'a·bly
jus'ti·fi·ca'tion
jus'ti·fy'
　·fied'　·fy'ing
just'ly
jut
　jut'ted jut'ting
jute
ju'ven·ile
jux'ta·pose'
　·posed'　·pos'ing
jux'ta·po·si'tion

K

Ka·bu'ki
kaf'fee·klatsch'
kai'ser
ka·lei'do·scope'
ka·lei'do·scop'ic
kal'so·mine'
ka'mi·ka'ze
kan'ga·roo'
Kan'sas
ka'o·lin
ka'puk
ka·put'
kar'a·kul
kar'at
ka·ra'te
ka'sha
ka'ty·did'
katz'en·jam'mer
kay'ak
ka·zoo'
ke·bab'
kedge
　kedged kedg'ing
keel'haul'
keel'son
keen'ness
keep
　kept keep'ing
keep'sake'
keg'ler
ke'loid
kempt
ken'nel
　·neled or ·nelled
　·nel·ing or
　·nel·ling
Ken·tuck'y
ker'a·tin
ker'chief
ker'miss or ·mess
ker'nel
　(grain; see
　colonel)
ker'o·sene' or
　·sine'
ker'sey
　·seys
ketch'up
ke'tone
ket'tle
ket'tle·drum'

key
keys
keyed key'ing
(lock; see quay)
key'board'
key club
key'hole'
key'note'
key punch
key'stone'
key'way'
kha'ki
kib'ble
kib·butz'
　kib'but·zim'
kib'itz·er
kick'off'
kid'nap'
　·napped' or
　·naped'
　·nap'ping or
　·nap'ing
kid'nap'per or
　kid'nap'er
kid'ney
　·neys
kill'er
kill'-joy'
kiln
kil'o·gram'
kil'o·hertz'
　·hertz'
kil'o·li'ter
ki·lo'me·ter
kil'o·volt'
kil'o·watt'
kil'o·watt'-hour'
kil'ter
ki·mo'no
　·nos
kin'der·gar'ten
kin'der·gart'ner
kind'heart'ed
kin'dle
　·dled ·dling
kind'li·ness
kind'ly
　·li·er ·li·est
kin'dred
kin'e·mat'ics
kin'e·scope'
ki·ne'sics
kin'es·thet'ic
ki·net'ic
kin'folk'
king'bolt'
king'dom
king'fish'
king'li·ness
king'ly
　·li·er ·li·est
king'pin'
king post
king'-size'
kink'i·ness
kink'y
　·i·er ·i·est
kin'ship'

kins'man
ki'osk
kis'met
kitch'en
kitch'en·ette'
kitch'en·ware'
kit'ten
kit'ty
　·ties
kit'ty-cor'nered
klax'on
Klee'nex
klep'to·ma'ni·ac
klieg light
knack
knack'wurst'
knap'sack'
knave
　(rogue; see nave)
knav'er·y
knav'ish
knead
　(press; see need)
knee
　kneed knee'ing
knee'cap'
knee'-deep'
knee'-high'
knee'hole'
kneel
　knelt or kneeled
　kneel'ing
knee'pad'
knell
knick'er·bock'ers
knick'knack'
knife
　knives
　knifed knif'ing
knife'-edge'
knight
　(rank; see night)
knight'hood'
knit
　knit'ted or knit
　knit'ting
knit'ter
knob'by
　·bi·er ·bi·est
knock'a·bout'
knock'down'
knock'-kneed'
knock'out'
knoll
knot
　knot'ted
　knot'ting
knot'hole'
knot'ty
　·ti·er ·ti·est
know
　knew known
know'ing
know'a·ble
know'-how'
know'-it-all'
knowl'edge
knowl'edge·a·ble

knowl'edge·a·bly
knuck'le
　·led ·ling
knurled
ko·a'la
ko'di·ak' bear
kohl'ra'bi
　·bies
Ko·ran'
ko'sher
kow'tow'
ku'chen
ku'dos
küm'mel
kum'quat
kwa'shi·or'kor

L

la'bel
　·beled or ·belled
　·bel·ing or
　·bel·ling
la'bi·al
la'bile
la'bor
lab'o·ra·to'ry
　·ries
la'bor·er
la·bo'ri·ous
la'bor-sav'ing
lab'y·rinth'
lab'y·rin'thine
lace
　laced lac'ing
lac'er·ate'
　·at'ed ·at'ing
lac'er·a'tion
lace'work'
lach'ry·mose'
lac'i·ness
lack'a·dai'si·cal
lack'ey
　·eys
lack'lus'ter
la·con'ic
la·con'i·cal·ly
lac'quer
la·crosse'
lac'tate
　·tat·ed ·tat·ing
lac·ta'tion
lac'te·al
lac'tic
lac'tose
la·cu'na
　·nas or ·nae
lac'y
　·i·er ·i·est
lad'der
lad'en
lad'ing
la'dle
　·dled ·dling
la'dy
　·dies

la'dy·bug'
la'dy·fin'ger
la'dy·like'
la'dy·ship'
lag
　lagged lag'ging
la'ger
lag'gard
la·gniappe'
la·goon'
lair
　(den; see layer)
lais'sez faire'
la'i·ty
la'ma
　(monk; see llama)
la'ma·ser'y
　·ies
lam·baste'
　·bast'ed ·bast'ing
lam'bent
lamb'kin
lam'bre·quin
lamb'skin'
lame
　(crippled)
la·mé';
　(fabric)
la·ment'
lam'en·ta·ble
lam'en·ta'tion
lam'i·nate'
　·nat'ed ·nat'ing
lam'i·na'tion
lamp'black'
lam·poon'
lamp'post'
lance
　lanced lanc'ing
lan'dau
land'fill'
land'hold'er
land'ing
land'la'dy
land'locked'
land'lord'
land'lub'ber
land'mark'
land'own'er
land'scape'
　·scaped'
　·scap'ing
land'slide'
lands'man
lan'guage
lan'guid
lan'guish
lan'guor
lan'guor·ous
lank'i·ness
lank'ness
lank'y
　·i·er ·i·est
lan'o·lin
lan'tern
lan'yard
lap
　lapped lap'ping

la·pel'
lap'i·dar'y
　·ies
lap'in
lap'is laz'u·li'
lapse
　lapsed laps'ing
lar'ce·nous
lar'ce·ny
lard'er
large
　larg'er larg'est
large'ly
large'-scale'
lar'gess or ·gesse
lar'i·at
lar'va
　·vae or ·vas
la·ryn'ge·al
lar'yn·gi'tis
lar'ynx
lar'ynx·es or
　la·ryn'ges
la·sa'gna
las·civ'i·ous
lase
　lased las'ing
　(emit laser light;
　see laze)
la'ser
lash'ing
las'si·tude'
las'so
　·sos or ·soes
last'-ditch'
Las'tex
last'ing
latch'key'
latch'string'
late
　lat'er or lat'ter
　lat'est or last
la·teen'
late'ly
la'ten·cy
la'tent
lat'er·al
la'tex
lat'i·ces' or
　la'tex·es
lath
　(wood strip)
lathe
　lathed lath'ing
　(machine)
lath'er
lath'ing
lat'i·tude'
lat'ke
　·kes
la·trine'
lat'ter-day'
lat'tice
　·ticed ·tic·ing
lat'tice·work'
laud'a·ble
laud'a·bly
laud'a·to'ry

laugh'a·ble
laugh'ing-stock'
laugh'ter
laun'der
laun'dress
laun'dro·mat'
laun'dry
·dries
laun'dry·man
lau're·ate
lau'rel
la'va
la·va'bo
·boes
lav'a·liere'
lav'a·to'ry
·ries
lav'en·der
lav'ish
law'-a·bid'ing
law'break'er
law'ful
law'ful·ly
law'giv'er
law'less
law'mak'er
lawn mower
law'suit'
law'yer
lax'a·tive
lax'i·ty
lay
laid lay'ing
(*put;* see lie)
lay'er
(*stratum;* see
lair)
lay·ette'
lay'man
lay'off'
lay'out'
lay'o·ver
laze
lazed laz'ing
(*loaf;* see lase)
la'zi·ly
la'zi·ness
la'zy
·zi·er ·zi·est
leach
(*filter;* see leech)
lead
led lead'ing
lead'en
lead'er·ship'
lead'-in'
lead'off'
leaf
leaves
leaf'let
leaf'y
·i·er ·i·est
league
leagued
leagu'ing
leagu'er
leak
(*escape;* see leek)

leak'age
leak'y
·i·er ·i·est
lean
leaned *or* leant
lean'ing
lean
(*thin;* see lien)
lean'ness
lean'-to'
-tos'
leap
leaped *or* leapt
leap'ing
leap'frog'
·frogged'
·frog'ging
learn
learned *or* learnt
learn'ing
learn'ed *adj.*
leas'a·ble
lease
leased leas'ing
lease'-back'
lease'hold'er
least
leath'er
leath'er·ette'
leath'er·i·ness
leath'er·y
leave
left leav'ing
(*let stay*)
leave
leaved leav'ing
(*bear leaves*)
leav'en·ing
leave'-tak'ing
lech'er·ous
lec'i thin
lec'tern
lec'ture
·tured ·tur·ing
ledge
ledg'er
leech
(*worm;* see
leach)
leek
(*vegetable;* see
leak)
leer'y
·i·er ·i·est
lee'ward
lee'way'
left'-hand'ed
left'ist
left'o·ver
left'-wing'er
leg
legged leg'ging
leg'a·cy
·cies
le·gal'ese'
le·gal'i·ty
·ties
le'gal·i·za'tion

le'gal·ize'
·ized' ·iz'ing
le'gal·ly
leg'a·tee'
le·ga'tion
le·ga'to
leg'end
leg'end·ar'y
leg'er·de·main'
leg'gi·ness
leg'gy
·gi·er ·gi·est
leg'i·bil'i·ty
leg'i·ble
leg'i·bly
le'gion
le'gion·naire'
leg'is·late'
·lat'ed ·lat'ing
leg'is·la'tion
leg'is·la'tive
leg'is·la'tor
leg'is·la'ture
le·git'i·ma·cy
le·git'i·mate
le·git'i·mize'
·mized' ·miz'ing
leg'man'
leg'room'
leg'ume
lei
lei'sure
lei'sure·ly
lem'on·ade'
lend
lent lend'ing
length'en
length'i·ness
length'wise'
length'y
·i·er ·i·est
le'ni·en·cy
le'ni·ent
len'i·ty
lens
len'til
leop'ard
le'o·tard'
lep'er
lep're·chaun'
lep'ro·sy
lep'rous
les'bi·an
le'sion
les·see'
less'en
(*make less*)
less'er
(*smaller*)
les'son
(*instruction*)
les'sor
(*one who leases*)
let
let let'ting
let'down'

le'thal
le·thar'gic
le·thar'gi·cal·ly
leth'ar·gize'
·gized' ·giz'ing
leth'ar·gy
let'tered
let'ter·head'
let'ter-per'fect
let'ter·press'
let'tuce
let'up'
leu·ke'mi·a
lev'ee
·eed ·ee·ing
(*embankment;*
see levy)
lev'el
·eled *or* ·elled
·el·ing *or* ·el·ling
lev'el·head'ed
lev'el·ly
lev'er·age
lev'i·a·ble
lev'i·er
le'vis
lev'i·tate'
·tat'ed ·tat'ing
lev'i·ta'tion
lev'i·ty
lev'y
·ies, ·ied ·y·ing
(*tax;* see levee)
lewd'ness
lex'i·cog'ra·pher
lex'i·con
li'a·bil'i·ty
·ties
li'a·ble
(*likely;* see libel)
li'ai·son'
li'ar
(*one who tells
lies;* see lyre)
li·ba'tion
li'bel
·beled *or* ·belled
·bel·ing *or*
·bel·ing
(*defame;* see
liable)
li'bel·ous *or*
·bel·lous
lib'er·al
lib'er·al'i·ty
lib'er·al·ize'
·ized' ·iz'ing
lib'er·ate'
·at'ed ·at'ing
lib'er·a'tion
lib'er·a'tor
lib'er·tar'i·an
lib'er·tine'
lib'er·ty
·ties
li·bid'i·nous
li·bi'do
li·brar'i·an

li'brar'y
·ies
li·bret'tist
li·bret'to
·tos *or* ·ti
Lib'ri·um
li'cense
·censed ·cens·ing
li·cen'tious
li'chen
lic'it
lic'o·rice
lie
lay lain ly'ing
(*to rest;* see lay)
lie
lied ly'ing
(*tell falsehood;*
see lye)
li'en
(*claim;* see lean)
lieu
lieu·ten'an·cy
lieu·ten'ant
life
lives
life belt
life'blood'
life'boat'
life buoy
life'-giv'ing
life'guard'
life'less
life'like'
life'line'
life'long'
life'sav'er
life'-size'
life'time'
life'work'
lift'off'
lig'a·ment
lig'a·ture
·tured ·tur·ing
light
light'ed *or* lit
light'ing
light'en
·ened ·en·ing
(*make light or less
heavy;* see lightning)
light'face'
light'-fin'gered
light'-foot'ed
light'-hand'ed
light'head'ed
light'heart'ed
light'house'
light'ly
light'-mind'ed
light'ning
(*flash of light;*
see lighten)
light'weight'
light'-year'
lig'ne·ous
lig'nite
lik'a·ble *or* like'·

like
liked lik'ing
like'li·hood'
like'ly
like'-mind'ed
lik'en
like'ness
like'wise'
li'lac
Lil'li·pu'tian
lil'y
·ies
lil'y-liv'ered
lil'y-white'
limb
(*branch;* see limn)
lim'ber
lim'bo
lime
limed lim'ing
lime'light'
lim'er·ick
lime'stone'
lim'it·a·ble
lim'i·ta'tion
lim'it·ed
limn
(*draw;* see limb)
lim'ou·sine'
lim'pid
limp'ness
lin'age *or* line'·
(*number of lines;*
see lineage)
linch'pin'
Lin'coln
lin'den
line
lined lin'ing
lin'e·age
(*ancestry;* see
lineage)
lin'e·al
lin'e·a·ment
(*feature;* see
liniment)
lin'e·ar
line'man
lin'en
lin'er
lines'man
line'up'
lin'ger
lin'ge·rie'
lin'go
·goes
lin'gual
lin'guist
lin·guis'tics
lin'i·ment
(*medication;*
see lineament)
lin'ing
link'age
links
(*golf course;*
see lynx)
li·no'le·um

lin'o·type'
lin'seed'
lin'sey-wool'sey
lin'tel
  (beam; see lentil)
li'on·ess
li'on·heart'ed
lip'-read'
  -read'-read'ing
lip'stick'
lip'-sync'
liq'ue·fac'tion
liq'ue·fi'a·ble
liq'ue·fi'er
liq'ue·fy'
  ·fied' ·fy'ing
li·ques'cent
li·queur'
liq'uid
liq'ui·date'
  ·dat'ed ·dat'ing
liq·ui·da'tion
liq'ui·da'tor
liq'uor
lisle
lisp'ing·ly
lis'some or ·som
lis'ten
list'less
lit'a·ny
  ·nies
li'tchi nut
li'ter
lit'er·a·cy
lit'er·al
  (exact; see
  littoral)
lit'er·al·ly
lit'er·ar'y
lit'er·ate
lit'er·a·ture
lithe'ly
lith'o·graph'
li·thog'ra·pher
li·thog'ra·phy
lith'o·sphere'
lit'i·ga·ble
lit'i·gant
lit'i·gate'
  ·gat'ed ·gat'ing
lit'i·ga'tion
lit'mus
li'to·tes
lit'ter
lit'ter·bug'
lit'tle
  lit'tler or less or
  less'er, lit'tlest
  or least
  lit'to·ral
  (shore; see
  literal)
li·tur'gi·cal
lit'ur·gy
  ·gies
liv'a·ble or live'·
live
  lived liv'ing

live'li·hood'
live'li·ness
live'long'
live'ly
  ·li·er ·li·est
liv'en
liv'er·wurst'
liv'er·y
  ·ies
live'stock'
liv'id
liz'ard
lla'ma
  (animal; see
  lama
load
  (burden; see lode)
load'stone'
loaf
  loaves
loaf'er
loam'y
  ·i·er ·i·est
loan
  (something lent;
  see lone)
loath
  (unwilling)
loathe
  loathed loath'ing
  (detest)
loath'some   ~
lob
  lobbed lob'bing
lob'by
  ·bies
  ·bied ·by·ing
lob'by·ist
lobe
lob'ster
lo'cal
lo·cale'
lo'cal·ism
lo·cal'i·ty
  ·ties
lo'cal·ize'
  ·ized' ·iz'ing
lo'cal·ly
lo'cate
  ·cat·ed ·cat·ing
lo·ca'tion
lock'er
lock'et
lock'out'
lock'smith'
lo'co·mo'tion
lo'co·mo'tive
lo'co·weed'
lo'cus
  ·ci
lo'cust
lo·cu'tion
lode
  (ore; see load)
lode'stone'
lodge
  lodged lodg'ing
  (house; see loge)

lodg'er
lodg'ment
loft'i·ly
loft'i·ness
loft'y
  ·i·er ·i·est
log
  logged log'ging
log'a·rithm
loge
  (theater box;
  see lodge)
log'ger·head'
log'gi·a
  ·gi·as
log'ic
log'i·cal
log'i·cal·ly
lo·gi'cian
lo·gis'tics
log'o·gram'
log'o·griph'
log'or·rhe'a
lo'gy
  ·gi·er ·gi·est
loin'cloth'
loi'ter
lol'li·pop' or ·ly·
lone
  (solitary;
  see loan)
lone'li·ness
lone'ly
  ·li·er ·li·est
lone'some
long'-dis'tance
long'-drawn'
lon·gev'i·ty
long'hand'
lon'gi·tude'
lon'gi·tu'di·nal
long'-lived'
long'-play'ing
long'-range'
long'-run'
long'shore'man
long'stand'ing
long'-suf'fer·ing
long'-term'
long'-wind'ed
look'er-on'
look'ers-on'
look'out'
loop'hole'
loose
  loosed loos'ing
  (free; see
  lose, loss)
loose'-joint'ed
loose'-leaf'
loose'ly
loos'en
loose'-tongued'
lop
  lopped lop'ping
lope
  loped lop'ing
lop'sid'ed

lo·qua'cious
lo·quac'i·ty
lor·do'sis
lor·gnette'
lor'ry
  ·ries
lose
  lost los'ing
  (mislay; see
  loose, loss)
los'er
loss
  (thing lost; see
  loose, lose)
Lo·thar'i·o'
lo'tion
lot'ter·y
  ·ies
loud'mouthed'
loud'speak'er
Lou·i'si·an'a
lounge
  lounged
  loung'ing
louse
  lice
lout'ish
lou'ver
lov'a·ble or
  love'·
love
  loved lov'ing
love'li·ness
love'lorn'
love'ly
  ·li·er ·li·est
lov'ing·kind'ness
low'boy'
low'bred'
low'brow'
low'-cost'
low'-down'
low'er
low'er·class'man
low'-grade'
low'-key'
low'-lev'el
low'li·ness
low'ly
  ·li·er ·li·est
low'-mind'ed
low'-necked'
low'-pitched'
low'-spir'it·ed
lox
loy'al
loy'al·ly
loy'al·ty
  ·ties
loz'enge
lu·au'
lu'bri·cant
lu'bri·cate'
  ·cat'ed ·cat'ing
lu'bri·ca'tion
lu'bri·ca'tor
lu'cid
lu·cid'i·ty

luck'i·ly
luck'i·ness
luck'y
  ·i·er ·i·est
lu'cra·tive
lu'cre
lu'cu·bra'tion
lu'di·crous
lug'gage
lu·gu'bri·ous
luke'warm'
lull'a·by'
  ·bies
lum'bar
  (of the loins)
lum'ber
  (timber)
lum'ber·jack'
lum'ber·yard'
lu'men
  ·mi·na or ·mens
lu'mi·nar'y
  ·ies
lu'mi·nes'cent
lu'mi·nous
lump'i·ness
lump'y
  ·i·er ·i·est
lu'na·cy
lu'nar
lu'na·tic
lunch'eon
lunge
  lunged lung'ing
lu'pine
lure
  lured lur'ing
lu'rid
lurk'ing
lus'cious
lush'ness
lus'ter
lust'i·ness
lus'trous
lust'y
  ·i·er ·i·est
lux·u'ri·ance
lux·u'ri·ant
lux·u'ri·ate'
  ·at'ed ·at'ing
lux·u'ri·ous
lux'u·ry
  ·ries
ly·ce'um
lye
  (alkaline sub-
  stance; see lie)
ly'ing-in'
lym·phat'ic
lynch'ing
lynx
  (animal; see links)
ly'on·naise'
lyre
  (harp; see liar)
lyr'ic
lyr'i·cal
lyr'i·cist

M

ma·ca'bre
mac·ad'am
mac·ad'am·ize'
  ·ized' ·iz'ing
mac·a·ro'ni
mac'a·roon'
mac'er·ate'
  ·at'ed ·at'ing
ma·che'te
Mach'i·a·vel'li·an
mach'i·nate'
  ·nat'ed ·nat'ing
mach'i·na'tion
ma·chine'
  ·chined'
  ·chin'ing
ma·chin'er·y
ma·chin'ist
mack'er·el
mack'i·naw'
mack'in·tosh'
  (coat; see
  McIntosh)
mac'ra·me'
mac'ro·bi·ot'ics
mac'ro·cosm
ma'cron
mac'u·la
  ·lae
mad
  mad'der
  mad'dest
mad'am
mad'ame
  mes·dames'
mad'cap'
mad'den·ing
Ma·deir'a
ma'de·moi·selle'
made'-to-or'der
made'-up'
mad'house'
mad'man'
ma'dras
mad'ri·gal
mad'wo·man
mael'strom
ma·es'tro
  ·tros or ·tri
Ma'fi·a or Maf'·
mag'a·zine'
ma·gen'ta
mag'got
mag'ic
mag'i·cal·ly
ma·gi'cian
mag'is·te'ri·al
mag'is·trate'
mag'na·nim'i·ty
mag·nam'i·mous
mag'nate
  (influential
  person)

mag · ne'sia
mag'net
 (*iron attracter*)
mag · net'ic
mag · net'i · cal · ly
mag'net · ism
mag'net · ize'
 · ized' · iz'ing
mag · ne'to
 · tos
mag · ni · fi · ca'tion
mag · nif'i · cence
mag · nif'i · cent
mag'ni · fi'er
mag'ni · fy'
 fied' · fy'ing
mag · nil'o · quent
mag'ni · tude'
mag · no'li · a
mag'num
mag'pie
ma · ha · ra'jah *or*
 · ra'ja
ma · ha · ra'ni *or*
 · ra'nee
ma · hat'ma
mah'-jongg'
ma · hog'a · ny
maid'en
maid'ser'vant
mail'box'
mail'man'
maim
Maine
main'land'
main'line'
main'ly
main'spring'
main'stream'
main · tain'
main'te · nance
maî'tre d'hô · tel'
maize
 (*corn;* see maze)
ma · jes'tic
ma · jes'ti · cal · ly
maj'es · ty
 · ties
ma · jol'i · ca
ma'jor
ma'jor-do'mo
 · mos
ma · jor'i · ty
 · ties
ma · jus'cule
make
 made mak'ing
make'-be · lieve'
make'shift'
make'up'
mal'a · dapt'ed
mal'ad · just'ed
mal'ad · min'is · ter
mal'a · droit'
mal'a · dy
 · dies
ma · laise'
mal'a · prop · ism

mal'ap · ro · pos'
ma · lar'i · a
mal'con · tent'
mal de mer'
mal'e · dic'tion
mal'e · fac'tion
mal'e · fac'tor
ma · lef'i · cent
male'ness
ma · lev'o · lence
ma · lev'o · lent
mal · fea'sance
mal'for · ma'tion
mal · formed'
mal · func'tion
mal'ice
ma · li'cious
ma · lign'
ma · lig'nan · cy
ma · lig'nant
ma · lig'ni · ty
 · ties
ma · lin'ger
ma · lin'ger · er
mall
 (*promenade;* see
 maul)
mal'lard
mal'le · a · bil'i · ty
mal'le · a · ble
mal'let
malm'sey
mal'nu · tri'tion
mal'oc · clu'sion
mal · o'dor · ous
mal · prac'tice
malt'ose
mam'mal
mam · ma'li · an
mam'ma · ry
mam'mon
mam'moth
man
 men, manned
man'ning
man'a · cle
 · cled · cling
man'age
 · aged · ag · ing
man'age · a · ble
man'age · ment
man'ag · er
man'a · ge'ri · al
ma · ña'na
man'-child'
men'-chil'dren
man · da'mus
man'da · rin
man'date
 · dat · ed · dat · ing
man'da · to'ry
man'di · ble
man'do · lin'
man'drel *or* · dril
 (*metal spindle*)
man'drill
 (*baboon*)

man'-eat'er
ma · nège'
 (*horsemanship;*
 see ménage)
ma · neu'ver
ma · neu'ver · a · ble
man'ful · ly
man'ga · nese'
mange
man'ger
man'gi · ness
man'gle
 · gled · gling
man'go
 · goes *or* · gos
man'grove
man'gy
 · gi · er · gi · est
man'han'dle
Man · hat'tan
man'hole'
man'hood'
man'-hour'
man'hunt'
ma'ni · a
ma'ni · ac'
ma · ni'a · cal
man'ic
man'i · cot'ti
man'i · cure'
 · cured' · cur'ing
man'i · cur'ist
man'i · fest'
man'i · fes · ta'tion
man'i · fes'to
 · toes
man'i · fold'
man'i · kin
Ma · nil'la
ma · nip'u · late'
 · lat'ed · lat'ing
ma · nip'u · la'tion
ma · nip'u · la'tive
ma · nip'u · la'tor
man'kind'
man'li · ness
man'ly
 · li · er · li · est
man'-made'
man'na
man'ne · quin
man'ner
 (*way;* see manor)
man'ner · ism
man'ner · ly
man'nish
man'-of-war'
men'-of-war'
ma · nom'e · ter
man'or
 (*residence;*
 see manner)
man'pow'er
man'sard
man'ser'vant
men'ser'vants
man'sion
man'-sized'

man'slaugh'ter
man'teau
 · teaus
man'tel
 (*fireplace fac-
 ing;* see mantle)
man'tel · et
man'tel · piece'
man · til'la
man'tis
 · tis · es *or* · tes
man'tle
 · tled · tling
 (*cloak;* see
 mantel)
man'tu · a
man'u · al
man'u · fac'to · ry
 · ries
man'u · fac'ture
 · tured · tur · ing
man'u · fac'tur · er
ma · nure'
 · nured' · nur'ing
man'u · script'
man'y
 more most
man'y-sid'ed
map
mapped
map'ping
ma'ple
mar
 marred mar'ring
mar'a · bou'
ma · ra'ca
mar'a · schi'no
ma · ras'mus
mar'a · thon'
ma · raud'
mar'ble
 · bled · bling
mar'ble · ize'
 · ized' · iz'ing
mar'ca · site'
mar · cel'
 · celled' · cel'ling
March
mar'chion · ess
Mar'di gras'
mare's'-nest'
mare's'-tail'
mar'ga · rine
mar'gin
mar'gin · al
mar'gin · al · ly
mar'i · gold'
ma'ri · jua'na *or*
 · hua'na
ma · rim'ba
ma · ri'na
mar'i · nade'
 · nad'ed · nad'ing
mar'i · nate'
 · nat'ed · nat'ing
ma · rine'
mar'i · ner
mar'i · o · nette'

mar'i · tal
 (*of marriage;*
 see martial)
mar'i · time'
mar'jo · ram.
mark'down'
marked
mark'ed · ly
mar'ket · a · bil'i · ty
mar'ket · a · ble
mar'ket · place'
marks'man
mark'up'
mar'lin
 (*fish*)
mar'line
 (*cord*)
mar'line · spike'
mar'ma · lade'
mar'mo · set'
mar'mot
ma · roon'
mar · quee'
mar'quess
mar'que · try
mar'quis
mar · quise'
mar'qui · sette'
mar'riage
mar'riage · a · ble
mar'row
mar'row · bone'
mar'ry
 · ried · ry · ing
Mar · sa'la
mar'shal
 · shaled *or*
 · shalled
 · shal · ing *or*
 · shal · ling
marsh'mal'low
mar · su'pi · al
mar · su'pi · um
 · pi · a
mar'ten
 (*animal;* see
 martin)
mar'tial
 (*military;* see
 marital)
Mar'tian
mar'tin
 (*bird;* see marten)
mar'ti · net'
mar'tin · gale'
mar · ti'ni
 · nis
mar'tyr
mar'tyr · dom
mar'tyr · ize'
 · ized' · iz'ing
mar'vel
 · veled *or* · velled
 · vel · ing *or*
 · vel · ling
mar'vel · ous
Marx'ism
Mar'y · land

mar'zi · pan'
mas · ca'ra
 · raed · ra · ing
mas'con'
mas'cot
mas'cu · line
mas · cu · lin'i · ty
ma'ser
mash'ie
mask
 (*cover;* see
 masque)
masked
mas'och · ism
mas'och · is'tic
mas'och · is'ti ·
 cal · ly
ma'son
Ma'son · ite'
ma'son · ry
masque
 (*masked ball;* see
 mask)
mas'quer · ade'
 · ad'ed · ad'ing
Mas'sa · chu'setts
mas'sa · cre
 · cred · cring
mas · sage'
 · saged' · sag'ing
mas · seur'
mas · seuse'
mas'sive
mas'ter · ful
mas'ter · ly
mas'ter · mind'
mas'ter · piece'
mas'ter · y
 · ies
mast'head'
mas'tic
mas'ti · cate'
 · cat'ed · cat'ing
mas'ti · ca'tion
mas'tiff
mas'to · don'
mas'toid
mas'tur · bate'
 · bat'ed · bat'ing
mas'tur · ba'tion
mat
mat'ted
mat'ting
mat'a · dor'
match'box'
match'less
match'lock'
match'mak'er
mate
mat'ed mat'ing
ma'te · las · sé'
ma · te'ri · al
 (*of matter;*
 see materiel)
ma · te'ri · al · ism
ma · te'ri · al · is'tic
ma · te'ri · al · ize'
 · ized' · iz'ing

ma·te'ri·al·ly
ma·te'ri·el'
 or ·té·ri·el'
 (*equipment;*
 see material)
ma·ter'nal
ma·ter'ni·ty
math'e·mat'i·cal
math'e·ma·ti'cian
math'e·mat'ics
mat'i·nee'
 or ·i·née'
ma'tri·arch'
ma'tri·ar'chal
ma'tri·ar'chy
 ·chies
ma'tri·cide'
ma·tric'u·lant
ma·tric'u·late'
 ·lat'ed ·lat'ing
ma·tric'u·la'tion
mat'ri·mo'ni·al
mat'ri·mo'ny
ma'trix
 ·tri·ces' *or* ·trix·es
ma'tron
ma'tron·li·ness
ma'tron·ly
mat'ter
mat'ter-of-fact'
mat'tock
mat'tress
mat'u·rate'
 ·rat'ed ·rat'ing
mat'u·ra'tion
ma·ture'
 ·tured' ·tur'ing
ma·ture'ly
ma·tu'ri·ty
mat'zo
 ·zot *or* ·zoth
 or ·zos
maud'lin
maul
 (*mallet; injures;*
 see mall)
maun'der
mau'so·le'um
 ·le'ums *or* ·le'a
mauve
mav'er·ick
mawk'ish
max·il'la
max'il·lar'y
max'i·mal
max'i·mize'
 ·mized' ·miz'ing
max'i·mum
 ·mums *or* ·ma
May
may'be
May'day'
may'hem
may'on·naise'
may'or
may'or·al·ty
 ·ties

May'pole'
maze
 (*labyrinth;* see
 maize)
maz'el tov'
Mc'In·tosh'
 (*apple;* see
 mackintosh)
mead'ow
mea'ger
meal'time'
meal'y
 ·i·er ·i·est
meal'y-mouthed'
mean *v.*
 meant mean'ing
mean *adj., n.*
 (*middle; low;*
 see mien)
me·an'der
mean'ing·ful
mean'ing·less
mean'ness
mean'time'
mean'while'
mea'sles
mea'sly
 ·sli·er ·sli·est
meas'ur·a·bil'i·ty
meas'ur·a·ble
meas'ur·a·bly
meas'ure
 ·ured ·ur·ing
meas'ure·less
meas'ure·ment
meas'ur·er
meat
 (*flesh;* see
 meet, mete)
meat'i·ness
me·a'tus
meat'y
 ·i·er ·i·est
me·chan'ic
me·chan'i·cal
mech'a·ni'cian
me·chan'ics
mech'a·nism
mech'a·ni·za'tion
mech'a·nize'
 ·nized' ·niz'ing
med'al
 (*award;*
 see meddle)
med'al·ist
me·dal'lion
med'dle
 ·dled ·dling
 (*interfere;*
 see medal)
med'dler
med'dle·some
me'di·a
 (*sing.* medium)
me'di·al
me'di·an
me'di·ate'
 ·at'ed ·at'ing

me'di·a'tion
me'di·a'tor
Med'i·caid'
med'i·cal
Med'i·care'
med'i·cate'
 ·cat'ed ·cat'ing
med'i·ca'tion
me·dic'i·nal
med'i·cine
me'di·e'val
 or ·ae'val
me'di·o'cre
me'di·oc'ri·ty
 ·ties
med'i·tate'
 ·tat'ed ·tat'ing
med'i·ta'tion
med'i·ta'tor
Med'i·ter·ra'ne·an
me'di·um
 ·di·ums *or* ·di·a
med'ley
 ·leys
meer'schaum
meet
 met meet'ing
 (*come upon;* see
 meat, mete)
meg'a·death'
meg'a·hertz'
meg'a·lo·ma'ni·a
meg'a·lop'o·lis
meg'a·phone'
meg'a·ton'
mel'an·cho'li·a
mel'an·chol'ic
mel'an·chol'y
me'lange'
mel'a·nin
me'lee *or* mê'lée
mel'io·rate'
 ·rat'ed ·rat'ing
mel'io·ra'tion
mel·lif'lu·ous
mel'low
me·lo'de·on
me·lod'ic
me·lo'di·ous
mel'o·dra'ma
mel'o·dra·mat'ic
mel'o·dy
 ·dies
mel'on
melt'a·ble
mel'ton
mem'ber·ship'
mem'brane
mem'bra·nous
me·men'to
 ·tos *or* ·toes
mem'oir
mem'o·ra·bil'i·a
mem'o·ra·ble
mem'o·ra·bly
mem'o·ran'dum
 ·dums *or* ·da
me·mo'ri·al

me·mo'ri·al·ize'
 ·ized' ·iz'ing
mem'o·ri·za'tion
mem'o·rize'
 ·rized' ·riz'ing
mem'o·ry
 ·ries
men'ace
 ·aced ·ac·ing
mé·nage' *or* me·
 (*household;* see
 manège)
me·nag'er·ie
men·da'cious
men·dac'i·ty
Men·de'li·an
men'di·cant
me'ni·al
men'in·gi'tis
me·nis'cus
 ·cus·es *or* ·ci
Men'non·ite'
men'o·pause'
men'ses
men'stru·al
men'stru·ate'
 ·at'ed
 ·at'ing
men'stru·a'tion
men'sur·a·ble
men'su·ra'tion
mens'wear'
men'tal
men·tal'i·ty
men'thol
men'tho·lat'ed
men'tion
men'tor
men'u
 ·us
me·phit'ic
me·pro'ba·mate'
mer'can·tile'
mer'can·til·ism
mer'ce·nar'y
 ·nar·ies
mer'cer·ize'
 ·ized' ·iz'ing
mer'chan·dise'
 ·dized' ·diz'ing
mer'chan·dis·er
mer'chant
mer'ci·ful
mer'ci·ful·ly
mer'ci·less
mer·cu'ri·al
Mer·cu'ro·
 chrome'
mer'cu·ry
mer'cy
 ·cies
mere
mer'est
mere'ly
mer·en'gue
 (*dance;* see
 meringue)
mer'e·tri'cious

merge
 merged merg'ing
merg'er
me·rid'i·an
me·ringue'
 (*pie topping;*
 see merengue)
me·ri'no
 ·nos
mer'it
mer'i·to'ri·ous
mer'maid'
mer'ri·ly
mer'ri·ment
mer'ri·ness
mer'ry
 ·ri·er ·ri·est
mer'ry-an'drew
mer'ry-go-round'
mer'ry·mak'ing
Mer·thi'o·late'
me'sa
mé·sal'li·ance
mes·cal'
mes'ca·line'
mes'dames'
mes'de·moi·selles'
me·shu'ga
mesh'work'
mes'mer·ism
mes'mer·ize'
 ·ized' ·iz'ing
mes'on
mes'sage
mes'sen·ger
mes·si'ah
mes'sieurs
mess'i·ly
mess'i·ness
mess'y
 ·i·er ·i·est
met'a·bol'ic
me·tab'o·lism
me·tab'o·lize'
 ·lized' ·liz'ing
met'al
 ·aled *or* ·alled
 ·al·ing *or* ·al·ling
 (*mineral;* see
 mettle)
me·tal'lic
met'al·lur'gi·cal
met'al·lur'gist
met'al·lur'gy
met'al·work'
met'a·mor'phic
met'a·mor'phism
met'a·mor'phose
 ·phosed ·phos·ing
met'a·mor'pho·sis
 ·ses
met'a·phor'
met'a·phor'i·cal
met'a·phor'i·
 cal·ly
met'a·phys'i·cal
met'a·phys'ics
met'a·tar'sal

me·tath'e·sis
 ·ses'
mete
 met'ed met'ing
 (*allot;* see meat,
 meet)
me'te·or
me'te·or'ic
me'te·or·ite'
me'te·or·oid'
me'te·or·o·
 log'i·cal
me'te·or·ol'o·gist
me'te·or·ol'o·gy
me'ter
meth'a·done'
meth'ane
meth'a·nol'
meth'e·drine'
meth'od
me·thod'i·cal
me·thod'i·cal·ly
Meth'od·ist
meth'od·ize'
 ·ized' ·iz'ing
meth'od·ol'o·gy
me·tic'u·lous
mé·tier'
me·ton'y·my
met'ric
met'ri·cal
met'ro·nome'
me·trop'o·lis
met'tle
 (*spirit;* see metal)
mez'za·nine'
mez'zo-so·pra'no
 ·nos *or* ·ni
mez'zo·tint'
mi·as'ma
 ·mas *or* ·ma·ta
mi'ca
Mich'i·gan
mi'cro·bar'
mi'crobe
mi·cro'bic
mi'cro·cop'y
mi'cro·cosm
mi'cro·dot'
mi'cro·fiche'
mi'cro·film'
mi'cro·groove'
mi·crom'e·ter
mi'cro·or'gan·
 ism
mi'cro·phone'
mi'cro·print'
mi'cro·read'er
mi'cro·scope'
mi'cro·scop'ic
mi'cro·scop'i·
 cal'ly
mi'cro·wave'
mid'air'
mid'cult'
mid'day'
mid'dle

mid'dle-aged'
mid'dle·brow'
mid'dle-class'
mid'dle·man'
mid'dle-of-the-
   road'
mid'dle-sized'
mid'dle·weight'
mid'dling
mid'dy
 ·dies
midg'et
mid'i'ron
mid'land
mid'night'
mid'point'
mid'riff
mid'ship'man
midst
mid'stream'
mid'sum'mer
mid'term'
mid'-Vic·to'ri·an
mid'way'
mid'week'
Mid'west'
Mid'west'ern·er
mid'wife'
 ·wives'
mid'win'ter
mid'year'
mien
 (manner; see
 mean)
miffed
might
 (power; see mite)
might'i·ly
might'i·ness
might'y
 ·i·er ·i·est
mi'gnon
mi'graine
mi'grant
mi'grate
 ·grat·ed ·grat·ing
mi·gra'tion
mi'gra·to'ry
mi·ka'do
 ·dos
mi·la'dy
mil'dew'
mild'ly
mile'age
mile'post'
mile'stone'
mi·lieu'
mil'i·tan·cy
mil'i·tant
mil'i·tar'i·ly
mil'i·ta·rism
mil'i·ta·ris'tic
mil'i·ta·ri·za'tion
mil'i·ta·rize'
 ·rized' ·riz'ing
mil'i·tar'y
mil'i·tate'
 ·tat'ed ·tat'ing

mi·li'tia
milk'i·ness
milk'maid'
milk'man'
milk'shake'
milk'shed'
milk'sop'
milk toast
 (food; see
 milquetoast)
milk'weed'
milk'y
 ·i·er ·i·est
mill'age
mill'dam'
milled
mil·len'ni·um
 ·ni·ums or ·ni·a
mill'er
mill'let
mill'liard
mil'li·bar'
mil'li·gram'
mil'li·me'ter
mill'line'
mil'li·ner
mil'li·ner'y
mill'ing
mill'lion
mil'lion·aire'
mill'lionth
mil'li·pede'
mill'pond'
mill'race'
mill'stone'
mill'stream'
mill wheel
mill'work'
mill'wright'
milque'toast'
 (timid person;
 see milk toast)
Mil·wau'kee
mime
 mimed mim'ing
mim'e·o·graph'
mim'er
mi·met'ic
mim'ic
 ·icked ·ick·ing
mim'ick·er
mim'ic·ry
mi·mo'sa
min·a'ret'
min'a·to'ry
mince
 minced minc'ing
mince'meat'
mind'ful
mind'less
mind reader
mine
 mined min'ing
mine'lay'er
min'er
 (mine worker;
 see minor)

min'er·al
min'er·al·i·za'tion
min'er·al·ize'
 ·ized' ·iz'ing
min·er·al'o·gist
min·er·al'o·gy
mi'ne·stro'ne
min'gle
 ·gled ·gling
min'i·a·ture
min'i·a·tur'i·
 za'tion
min'i·a·tur·ize'
 ·ized' ·iz'ing
min'i·bus'
min'i·fi·ca'tion
min'i·fy'
 ·fied' ·fy'ing
min'im
min'i·mal
min'i·mal·ly
min'i·mize'
 ·mized' ·miz'ing
min'i·mum
 ·mums or ·ma
min'ion
 (deputy; see
 minyan)
min'i·skirt'
min'is·ter
 (diplomat; clergy-
 man; see minster)
min·is·te'ri·al
min'is·trant
min'is·tra'tion
min'is·try
 ·tries
min'i·track'
min'i·ver
Min'ne·ap'o·lis
min'ne·sing'er
Min'ne·so'ta
min'now
mi'nor
 (lesser; see
 miner)
mi·nor'i·ty
 ·ties
min'ster
 (church; see
 minister)
min'strel
mint'age
min'u·end'
min·u·et'
mi'nus
mi·nus'cule
min'ute n.
mi·nute' adj.
mi·nute'ly
min'ute·man'
mi·nu'ti·ae'
 (sing. mi·nu'ti·a)
minx
min·yan'
min'ya·nim'
 (group; see
 minion)

mir'a·cle
mi·rac'u·lous
mi·rage'
mire
 mired mir'ing
mir'ror
mirth'ful
mirth'less
mir'y
 ·i·er ·i·est
mis'ad·ven'ture
mis'ad·vise'
mis'al·li'ance
mis'al·ly'
mis'an·thrope'
mis'an·throp'ic
mis·an'thro·py
mis'ap·pli·ca'tion
mis'ap·ply'
mis'ap·pre·hend'
mis'ap·pre·
 hen'sion
mis'ap·pro'pri·ate'
mis'be·got'ten
mis'be·have'
mis'be·hav'ior
mis'be·lief'
mis'be·lieve'
mis·cal'cu·late'
mis'cal·cu·la'tion
mis·car'riage
mis·car'ry
mis·cast'
mis'ce·ge·na'tion
mis'cel·la'ne·a
mis'cel·la'ne·ous
mis'cel·la'ny
 ·nies
mis·chance'
mis'chief
mis'chief-mak'er
mis'chie·vous
mis·ci·bil'i·ty
mis'ci·ble
mis'con·ceive'
mis'con·cep'tion
mis·con'duct
mis'con·
 struc'tion
mis'con·strue'
mis·count'
mis'cre·ant
mis·cue'
mis·date'
mis·deal'
 ·dealt' ·deal'ing
mis·deed'
mis'de·mean'or
mis'di·rect'
mi'ser
mis'er·a·ble
mis'er·a·bly
mi'ser·ly
mis'er·y
 ·ies
mis·es'ti·mate'
mis·fea'sance
mis·file'

mis·fire'
mis'fit'
mis·for'tune
mis·giv'ing
mis·gov'ern
mis·guid'ance
mis·guide'
mis·han'dle
mis'hap
mish'mash'
mis·in·form'
mis·in·for·ma'tion
mis·in·ter'pret
mis·judge'
mis·judg'ment
 or ·judge'ment
mis·lay'
 ·laid' ·lay'ing
mis·lead'
 ·led' ·lead'ing
mis·man'age
mis·man'age·
 ment
mis·match'
mis·mate'
mis·no'mer
mi·sog'a·mist
mi·sog'a·my
mi·sog'y·nist
mi·sog'y·ny
mis·place'
mis·print'
mis·pri'sion
mis'pro·nounce'
mis'pro·nun'ci·
 a'tion
mis'quo·ta'tion
mis·quote'
mis·read'
 ·read' ·read'ing
mis'rep·re·sent'
mis'rep·re·sen·
 ta'tion
mis·rule'
Miss
Miss'es
mis'sal
 (book; see
 missile, missive)
mis·shape'
mis·shap'en
mis'sile
 (weapon; see
 missal, missive)
mis'sion
mis'sion·ar'y
Mis'sis·sip'pi
mis'sive
 (letter; see
 missal, missive)
mis·speak'
 ·spoke' ·spo'ken
 ·speak'ing
mis·spell'
 ·spelled' or
 ·spelt'
 ·spell'ing

mis·spend'
 ·spent'
 ·spend'ing
mis·state'
mis·state'ment
mis·step'
mis·take'
 ·took' ·tak'en
 ·tak'ing
mist'i·ly
mist'i·ness
mis'tle·toe'
mis'tral
mis·treat'ment
mis'tress
mis·tri'al
mis·trust'
mist'y
 ·i·er ·i·est
mis·un·der·stand'
 ·stood' ·stand'ing
mis·us'age
mis·use'
mis·val'ue
mis·write'
 ·wrote' ·writ'ten
 ·writ'ing
mite
 (arachnid; tiny
 thing; see might)
mi'ter
mit'i·ga·ble
mit'i·gate'
 ·gat'ed ·gat'ing
mit'i·ga'tion
mit'i·ga'tor
mi'tral
mitt
mit'ten
mix
 mixed or mixt
mix'ing
mix'er
mix'ture
mix'-up'
miz'zen·mast
mne·mon'ic
moan'ing
moat
 (ditch; see mote)
mob
 mobbed
 mob'bing
mo'bile
mo·bil'i·ty
mo'bi·liz'a·ble
mo'bi·li·za'tion
mo'bi·lize'
 ·lized' ·liz'ing
mob·oc'ra·cy
 ·cies
moc'ca·sin
mo'cha
mock'er·y
 ·ies
mock'-he·ro'ic
mock'ing·bird'
mock'-up'

mod'a·cryl'ic
mod'al
(of a mode)
mod'el
·eled or ·elled
·el·ing or ·el·ling
(copy)
mod'er·ate'
·at'ed ·at'ing
mod'er·ate·ly
mod'er·a'tion
mod'er·a'tor
mod'ern
mod'ern·ism
mod'ern·is'tic
mo·der'ni·ty
mod'ern·i·za'tion
mod'ern·ize'
·ized' ·iz'ing
mod'ern·ness
mod'est
mod'es·ty
mod'i·cum
mod'i·fi·ca'tion
mod'i·fi'er
mod'i·fy'
·fied' ·fy'ing
mod'ish
mo·diste'
mod'u·lar
mod'u·late'
·lat'ed ·lat·ing
mod'u·la'tion
mod'u·la'tor
mod'ule
mo'gul
mo'hair
moi'e·ty
·ties
moire
moi·ré'
mois'ten
moist'ness
mois'ture
mois'tur·ize'
·ized' ·iz'ing
mo'lar
mo·las'ses
mold'board'
mold'er
mold'i·ness
mold'ing
mold'y
·i·er ·i·est
mole
mo·lec'u·lar
mol'e·cule'
mole'hill'
mole'skin'
mo·lest'
mo'les·ta'tion
mol'li·fy'
·fied' ·fy'ing
mol'lusk
mol'ly·cod'dle
·dled ·dling
molt
mol'ten

mo·lyb'de·num
mo'ment
mo'men·tar'i·ly
mo'men·tar'y
mo·men'tous
mo·men'tum
·tums or ·ta
mom'ism
mo·nan'drous
mon'arch
mo·nar'chal
mon'arch·ism
mon'arch·y
·ies
mon'as·ter'y
·ies
mo·nas'tic
mo·nas'ti·cism
mon·au'ral
Mon'day
mon'e·tar'y
mon'e·tize'
·tized' ·tiz'ing
mon'ey
·eys or ·ies
mon'ey·bag'
mon'ey-chang'er
mon'eyed
mon'ey-grub'ber
mon'ey·lend'er
mon'ey·mak'er
mon'ger
Mon'gol·ism
Mon'gol·oid'
mon'goose
·goos·es
mon'grel
mo·ni'tion
mon'i·tor
mon'i·to'ry
·ries
monk
mon'key
·keys
monk's cloth
mon'o·chro·mat'ic
mon'o·chrome'
mon'o·cle
mon'o·coque'
mo·noc'u·lar
mon'o·dra'ma
mo·nog'a·mist
mo·nog'a·mous
mo·nog'a·my
mon'o·gram'
·grammed'
·gram'ming
mon'o·graph'
mo·nog'y·ny
mon'o·lith'
mon'o·logue'
or ·log'
mon'o·logu'ist or
mo·nol'o·gist
mon'o·ma'ni·a
mon'o·met'al·lism
mon'o·nu'cle·o'sis

mon'o·plane'
mo·nop'o·list
mo·nop'o·list'tic
mo·nop'o·li·
za'tion
mo·nop'o·lize'
·lized' ·liz'ing
mo·nop'o·ly
·lies
mon'o·rail'
mon'o·syl·lab'ic
mon'o·syl'la·ble
mon'o·the'ism
mon'o·the·is'tic
mon'o·tone'
mo·not'o·nous
mo·not'o·ny
mon'o·type'
mon·ox'ide
Mon'sei·gneur'
Mes'sei·gneurs'
mon·sieur'
mes·sieurs'
Mon·si'gnor
mon·soon'
mon'ster
mon·stros'i·ty
·ties
mon'strous
mon·tage'
·taged' ·tag'ing
Mon·tan'a
month'ly
·lies
mon'u·ment
mon'u·men'tal
mood'i·ly
mood'i·ness
mood'y
·i·er ·i·est
moon'beam'
moon'-faced'
moon'light'
moon'light'ing
moon'lit'
moon'port'
moon'rise'
moon'set'
moon'shine'
moon'shot'
moon'stone'
moon'struck'
moor'age
moor'ing
moose
moose
(deer; see
mouse, mousse)
moot
(debatable;
see mute)
mop
mopped
mop'ping
mope
moped mop'ing
mop'pet
mop'-up'

mo·raine'
mor'al
mo·rale'
mor'al·ist
mor'al·is'tic
mor'al·is'ti·cal·ly
mo·ral'i·ty
mor'al·ize'
·ized' ·iz'ing
mor'al·ly
mo·rass'
mo·ra·to'ri·um
·ri·ums or ·ri·a
mor'bid
mor·bid'i·ty
mor'dant
(corrosive)
mor'dent
(musical term)
more·o'ver
mo'res
mor'ga·nat'ic
morgue
mor'i·bund'
mor'i·bun'di·ty
Mor'mon
morn'ing
(part of day;
see mourning)
mo·roc'co
mo'ron
mo·ron'ic
mo·rose'
mor'phine
mor·phol'o·gy
mor'sel
mor'tal
mor·tal'i·ty
mor'tal·ly
mor'tar
mor'tar·board'
mort'gage
·gaged ·gag·ing
mort'ga·gee'
mort'ga·gor
mor·ti'cian
mor'ti·fi·ca'tion
mor'ti·fy'
·fied' ·fy'ing
mor'tise
·tised ·tis·ing
mor'tu·ar'y
·ies
mo·sa'ic
·icked ·ick·ing
mosque
mos·qui'to
·toes or ·tos
moss'back'
moss'i·ness
moss'y
·i·er ·i·est
most'ly
mote
(speck; see moat)
mo·tel'
moth'ball'
moth'-eat'en

moth'er·hood'
moth'er-in-law'
moth'ers-in-law'
moth'er·land'
moth'er·li·ness
moth'er·ly
moth'er-of-pearl'
moth'proof'
mo·tif'
mo'tile
mo·til'i·ty
mo'tion·less
mo'ti·vate'
·vat'ed ·vat'ing
mo'ti·va'tion
mo'ti·va'tor
mo'tive
mot'ley
mo'tor·bike'
mo'tor·boat'
mo'tor·bus'
mo'tor·cade'
mo'tor·cy'cle
mo'tor·drome'
mo'tor·ist
mo'tor·ize'
·ized' ·iz'ing
mo'tor·man
mot'tle
·tled ·tling
mot'to
·toes or ·tos
mou·lage'
mound
moun'tain
moun'tain·eer'
moun'tain·ous
moun'te·bank'
mourn'ful
mourn'ing
(grieving;
see morning)
mouse
mice
moused mous'ing
(rodent; see
moose, mousse)
mous'er
mouse'trap'
mous'i·ness
mousse
(food; see
moose, mouse)
mousse·line'
de soie'
mous'y
·i·er ·i·est
mouth'ful'
·fuls'
mouth'part'
mouth'piece'
mouth'-to-mouth'
mouth'wash'
mouth'wa·ter·ing
mou'ton'
(fur; see mutton)
mov'a·ble
or move'·

mov'a·bly
move
moved mov'ing
move'ment
mov'ie
mov'ie·go·er
mov'i·o'la
mow
mowed, mowed
or mown,
mow'ing
moz'za·rel'la
Mr.
Messrs.
Mrs.
Mmes.
mu'ci·lage
mu'ci·lag'i·nous
muck'rake'
mu'cous adj.
mu'cus n.
mud'der
mud'di·ness
mud'dle
·dled ·dling
mud'dler
mud'dy
·di·er ·di·est
mud'sling'ing
Muen'ster
mu·ez'zin
muf'fin
muf'fle
·fled ·fling
muf'fler
muf'ti
mug
mugged
mug'ging
mug'gi·ness
mug'gy
·gi·er ·gi·est
mug'wump'
muk'luk'
mu·lat'to
·toes
mul'ber'ry
·ries
mulch
mulct
mul'ish
mul'li·ga·taw'ny
mul'lion
mul'ti·col'ored
mul'ti·far'i·ous
mul'ti·form'
mul'ti·lat'er·al
mul'ti·ple
mul'ti·plex'
mul'ti·pli'a·ble
mul'ti·pli·cand'
mul'ti·pli·ca'tion
mul'ti·plic'i·ty
mul'ti·pli'er
mul'ti·ply'
·plied' ·ply'ing
mul'ti·tude'
mul'ti·tu'di·nous

mul'ti·ver'si·ty
mum'ble
· bled · bling
mum'bler
mum'mer·y
mum'mi·fy'
· fied' · fy'ing
mum'my
· mies
munch
mun·dane'
mu·nic'i·pal
mu·nic'i·pal'i·ty
· ties
mu·nic'i·pal·ize'
· ized' · iz'ing
mu·nif'i·cence
mu·nif'i·cent
mu·ni'tion
mu'ral
mur'der·er
mur'der·ous
murk'i·ly
murk'i·ness
murk'y
· i·er · i·est
mur'mur
mur'mur·er
mus'ca·dine
mus'ca·tel'
mus'cle
· cled · cling
(body part;
see mussel)
mus'cle-bound'
mus'cu·lar
mus'cu·la'ture
muse
mused mus'ing
mu·sette'
mu·se'um
mush'i·ness
mush'room
mush'y
· i·er · i·est
mu'sic
mu'si·cal adj.
mu'si·cale' n.
mu·si'cian
mu'si·col'o·gist
mu'si·col'o·gy
mus'kel·lunge'
mus'ket
musk'i·ness
musk'mel'on
musk'rat'
musk'y
· i·er · i·est
mus'lin
mus'sel
(shellfish;
see muscle)
mus·tache'
or mous·
mus'tang
mus'tard
mus'ter
mus'ti·ness

mus'ty
· ti·er · ti·est
mu·ta·bil'i·ty
mu'ta·ble
mu'tant
mu'tate
· tat·ed · tat·ing
mu·ta'tion
mute
mut'ed mut'ing
(silent; see moot)
mu'ti·late'
· lat'ed · lat'ing
mu'ti·la'tion
mu'ti·neer'
mu'ti·nous
mu'ti·ny
· nies
· nied · ny·ing
mut'ter
mut'ton
(food; see
mouton)
mu'tu·al
mu'tu·al'i·ty
mu'tu·al·ly
muu'muu
Mu'zak
muz'zle
· zled · zling
my'e·li'tis
my'e·lo·gram'
my'lar
my'na or · nah
my·o'pi·a
my·op'ic
myr'i·ad
myr'i·a·pod'
myr'mi·don'
myrrh
myr'tle
my·self'
mys·te'ri·ous
mys'ter·y
· ies
mys'tic
mys'ti·cal
mys'ti·cal·ly
mys'ti·cism
mys'ti·fi·ca'tion
mys'ti·fy'
· fied' · fy'ing
mys·tique'
myth'i·cal
myth'o·log'i·cal
my·thol'o·gize'
· gized' · giz'ing
my·thol'o·gy
· gies
myth'os

N

nab
nabbed nab'bing
na·celle'

na'cre
na'cre·ous
na'dir
nag
nagged nag'ging
nail'head'
nain'sook
na·ive' or ·ïve'
na·ive·té' or ·ïve·
na'ked·ness
nam'by-pam'by
· bies
name
named nam'ing
name'a·ble
or nam'·
name'-drop'per
name'less
name'ly
name'plate'
name'sake'
nan·keen' or ·kin'
nap
napped nap'ping
na'palm
na'per·y
naph'tha
naph'tha·lene'
nap'kin
na·po'le·on
nap'per
nar·cis'sism
nar'cis·sist
nar'cis·sis'tic
nar·cis'sus
nar'co·lep'sy
nar·co'sis
nar·cot'ic
nar'co·tism
nar'rate
· rat·ed · rat·ing
nar·ra'tion
nar'ra·tive
nar'ra·tor
nar'row-mind'ed
nar'whal
na'sal
na·sal'i·ty
na'sal·ize'
· ized' · iz'ing
nas'cent
nas'ti·ly
nas'ti·ness
na·stur'tium
nas'ty
· ti·er · ti·est
na'tal
na'tant
na·ta·to'ri·um
· ri·ums or · ri·a
na·ta·to'ry
na'tion
na'tion·al
na'tion·al·ism
na'tion·al·is'ti·
cal·ly
na'tion·al'i·ty
· ties

na'tion·al·i·za'tion
na'tion·al·ize'
· ized' · iz'ing
na'tion·al·ly
na'tion·wide'
na'tive
na'tive-born'
na·tiv'i·ty
· ties
nat'ti·ly
nat'ty
· ti·er · ti·est
nat'u·ral
nat'u·ral·ism
nat'u·ral·ist
nat'u·ral·is'tic
nat'u·ral·i·za'tion
nat'u·ral·ize'
· ized' · iz'ing
nat'u·ral·ly
na'ture
naug'a·hyde'
naught
naugh'ti·ly
naugh'ti·ness
naugh'ty
· ti·er · ti·est
nau'se·a
nau'se·ate'
· at'ed · at'ing
nau'seous
nau'ti·cal
nau'ti·lus
· lus·es or · li'
na'val
(of a navy)
nave
(part of a church;
see knave)
na'vel
(umbilicus)
nav'i·cert
nav'i·ga·ble
nav'i·gate'
· gat'ed · gat'ing
nav'i·ga'tion
nav'i·ga'tor
na'vy
· vies
nay
(no; see nee,
neigh)
Ne·an'der·thal'
near'by'
near'ly
near'sight'ed
neat'ly
neat'ness
neb'bish
Ne·bras'ka
neb'u·la
· lae' or · las
neb'u·lar
neb'u·los'i·ty
neb'u·lous
nec'es·sar'i·ly
nec'es·sar'y
· ies

ne·ces'si·tate'
· tat'ed · tat'ing
ne·ces'si·tous
ne·ces'si·ty
· ties
neck'er·chief
neck'lace
neck'line'
neck'piece'
neck'tie'
neck'wear'
ne·crol'o·gy
· gies
nec'ro·man'cy
nec'tar
nec'tar·ine'
nee or née
(born; see nay,
neigh)
need
(require; see
knead)
need'ful
need'i·ness
nee'dle
· dled · dling
nee'dle·like'
nee'dle·point'
nee'dler
need'less
nee'dle·work'
need'n't
need'y
· i·er · i·est
ne'er'-do-well'
ne·far'i·ous
ne·gate'
· gat'ed · gat'ing
ne·ga'tion
neg'a·tive
neg'a·tiv·ism
neg·lect'
neg·lect'ful
neg'li·gee'
· gat'ed · gat'ing
neg'li·gence
neg'li·gent
neg'li·gi·ble
neg'li·gi·bly
ne·go'ti·a·bil'i·ty
ne·go'ti·a·ble
ne·go'ti·ate'
· at'ed · at'ing
ne·go'ti·a'tion
ne·go'ti·a'tor
Ne'gro
· groes
Ne'groid
neigh
(whinny; see
nay, nee)
neigh'bor
neigh'bor·hood'
neigh'bor·li·ness
neigh'bor·ly
nei'ther
(not either;
see nether)
nem'a·tode'

nem'e·sis
· ses'
ne'o·clas'sic
ne'o·lith'ic
ne·ol'o·gism
ne'o·my'cin
ne'on
ne'o·phyte'
ne'o·plasm
ne'o·prene'
ne·pen'the
neph'ew
ne·phri'tis
nep'o·tism
Nep'tune
nerve
nerved nerv'ing
nerve'-rack'ing
or -wrack'·
nerv'ous
nerv'y
· i·er · i·est
nes'ci·ent
nes'tle
· tled · tling
nest'ling
(young bird)
net
net'ted net'ting
neth'er
(lower; see
neither)
net'tle
· tled · tling
net'work'
Neuf·châ·tel'
neu'ral
neu·ral'gia
neu'ras·the'ni·a
neu·ri'tis
neu·ro·log'i·cal
neu·rol'o·gist
neu·rol'o·gy
neu·ro'sis
· ses
neu·rot'ic
neu'ter
neu'tral
neu·tral'i·ty
neu'tral·i·za'tion
neu'tral·ize'
· ized' · iz'ing
neu'tral·iz'er
neu·tri'no
neu'tron
Ne·vad'a
nev'er·more'
nev'er·the·less'
ne'vus
· vi
new'born'
new'com'er
new'el
new'fan'gled
new'-fash'ioned
New'found·land'
New Hamp'shire
New Jer'sey

new'ly·wed'
New Mex'i·co
news'boy'
news'cast'
news'deal·er
news'let'ter
news'man'
news'pa·per
new'speak'
news'print'
news'reel'
news'stand'
news'wor'thy
New York
next'-door'
nex'us
·us·es *or* nex'us
ni'a·cin
Ni·ag'a·ra
nib'ble
·bled ·bling
nib'lick
nice
nic'er nic'est
nice'ly
ni'ce·ty
·ties
niche
(*recess*)
nick
(*notch*)
nick'el
·eled *or* ·elled
·el·ing *or* ·el·ling
nick'el·o'de·on
nick'name'
nic'o·tine'
nic'o·tin'ism
nic'ti·tate'
·tat'ed ·tat'ing
niece
nig'gard·ly
nig'gling
night
(*darkness;* see
knight)
night'cap'
night'club'
night'dress'
night'fall'
night'gown'
night'in·gale'
night'long'
night'ly
night'mare'
night'mar·ish
night'shirt'
night'time'
ni'hil·ism
ni'hil·is'tic
nim'ble
·bler ·blest
nim'bly
nim'bus
·bi *or* ·bus·es
nin'com·poop'
nine'fold'
nine'pins'

nine'teen'
nine'ti·eth
nine'ty
·ties
nin'ny
·nies
ni'non
ninth
nip
nipped nip'ping
nip'per
nip'pi·ness
nip'ple
nip'py
·pi·er ·pi·est
nip'-up'
nir·va'na
ni'sei
·sei *or* ·seis
nit'-pick'ing
ni'tro·gen
ni'tro·glyc'er·in
or ·er·ine
nit'ty-grit'ty
no·bil'i·ty
no'ble
·bler ·blest
no'ble·man
no'bly
no'bod'y
·ies
noc·tur'nal
noc·tur'nal·ly
noc'turne
noc'u·ous
nod
nod'ded nod'ding
nod'al
node
nod'u·lar
nod'ule
no·el' *or* ·ël'
nog'gin
no'-hit'ter
noise
noised nois'ing
noise'less
noise'mak'er
nois'i·ly
nois'i·ness
noi'some
nois'y
·i·er ·i·est
no'mad
no·mad'ic
nom' de plume'
noms' de plume'
no'men·cla'ture
nom'i·nal
nom'i·nal·ly
nom'i·nate'
·nat'ed ·nat'ing
nom'i·na'tion
nom'i·na·tive
nom'i·na'tor
nom'i·nee'
non'a·ge·nar'i·an
non'-book'

nonce
non'cha·lance'
non'cha·lant'
non·com'bat·ant
non'com·mit'tal
non com'pos
men'tis
non'con·form'ist
non'co·op'er·a'·
tion
non'de·script'
non·en'ti·ty
·ties
non'es·sen'tial
none'such'
none'the·less'
non'ex·ist'ent
non·fea'sance
non'he'ro
non·nu'cle·ar
no-non'sense
non'pa·reil'
non·par'ti·san
non·plus'
·plussed' *or*
·plussed'
·plus'ing *or*
·plus'sing
non·prof'it
non·sched'uled
non'sec·tar'i·an
non'sense
non·sen'si·cal
non·sen'si·cal·ly
non' se'qui·tur
non'-sked'
non'skid'
non'stop'
non'sup·port'
non·un'ion
non·vi'o·lence
noo'dle
noon'day'
no one
noon'time'
noose
noosed noos'ing
no'-par'
nor'mal
nor'mal·cy
nor·mal'i·ty
nor'mal·ize'
·ized' ·iz'ing
nor'mal·ly
north'bound'
North Car'o·li'na
North Da·ko'ta
north'east'
north'east'er·ly
north'east'ern
north'er·ly
north'ern
north'ward
north'west'
north'west'er·ly
north'west'ern
nose
nosed nos'ing

nose'bleed'
nose cone
nose'-dive'
-dived' -div'ing
nose'gay'
nose'piece'
no'-show'
nos·tal'gia
nos·tal'gic
nos'tril
nos'trum
no'ta·ble
no'ta·bly
no'ta·ri·za'tion
no'ta·rize'
·rized' ·riz'ing
no'ta·ry public
no'ta·ries public
or no'ta·ry publics
no·ta'tion
notched
note
not'ed not'ing
note'book'
note'wor'thy
noth'ing·ness
no'tice
·ticed ·tic·ing
no'tice·a·ble
no'tice·a·bly
no'ti·fi'a·ble
no'ti·fi·ca'tion
no'ti·fy'
·fied' ·fy'ing
no'tion
no'to·ri'e·ty
no·to'ri·ous
no'-trump'
not'with·stand'ing
nou'gat
nought
nour'ish·ment
nou'veau riche'
nou'veaux riches'
no'va
·vas *or* ·vae
nov'el
nov'el·ette'
nov'el·ist
no·vel'la
nov'el·ty
·ties
No·vem'ber
nov'ice
no·vi'ti·ate
now'a·days'
no'where'
no'wise'
nox'ious
noz'zle
nu'ance
nub'bi·ness
nub'by
·bi·er ·bi·est
nu'bile
nu'cle·ar
nu'cle·ate'
·at'ed ·at'ing

nu'cle·on'ics
nu'cle·us
·cle·i' *or*
·cle·us·es
nude
nudge
nudged nudg'ing
nud'ist
nu'di·ty
nu'ga·to'ry
nug'get
nui'sance
nul'li·fi·ca'tion
nul'li·fy'
·fied' ·fy'ing
num'ber
num'ber·less
numb'ly
numb'ness
nu'mer·a·ble
nu'mer·al
nu'mer·ate'
·at'ed ·at'ing
nu'mer·a'tion
nu'mer·a'tor
nu·mer'i·cal
nu'mer·ol'o·gy
nu'mer·ous
nu·mis·mat'ic
nu·mis'ma·tist
num'skull'
nun'ner·y
·ies
nup'tial
nurse
nursed nurs'ing
nurse'maid'
nurs'er·y
·ies
nur'ture
·tured ·tur·ing
nut'crack'er
nut'gall'
nut'meat'
nut'meg'
nut'pick'
nu'tri·a
nu'tri·ent
nu'tri·ment
nu·tri'tion
nu·tri'tious
nu'tri·tive
nut'shell'
nuz'zle
·zled ·zling
ny'lon
nymph
nym'pho·
ma'ni·ac'

O

oaf'ish
oa'kum
oar
(*pole;* see ore)

oar'lock'
oars'man
o·a'sis
·ses
oath
oat'meal'
ob'bli·ga'to
·tos *or* ·ti
ob'du·ra·cy
ob'du·rate
o·be'di·ence
o·be'di·ent
o·bei'sance
o·bei'sant
ob'e·lisk'
o·bese'
o·be'si·ty
o·bey'
ob'fus·cate'
·cat'ed ·cat'ing
ob'i·ter dic'tum
ob'i·ter dic'ta
o·bit'u·ar'y
·ies
ob'ject
ob·jec'tion
ob·jec'tion·a·ble
ob·jec'tion·a·bly
ob·jec'tive
ob·jec'tive·ly
ob'jec·tiv'i·ty
ob·jec'tor
ob'jet d'art'
ob'jets d'art'
ob'jur·gate'
·gat'ed ·gat'ing
ob'jur·ga'tion
ob·la'tion
ob'li·gate'
·gat'ed ·gat'ing
ob'li·ga'tion
ob·lig'a·to'ry
o·blige'
o·bliged'
o·blig'ing
ob·lique'
ob·lique'ly
ob·liq'ui·ty
ob·lit'er·ate'
·at'ed ·at'ing
ob·lit'er·a'tion
ob·lit'er·a'tor
ob·liv'i·on
ob·liv'i·ous
ob'long
ob'lo·quy
·quies
ob·nox'ious
o'boe
o'bo·ist
ob·scene'
ob·scen'i·ty
·ties
ob·scure'
·scured' ·scur'ing
ob·scure'ly
ob·scu'ri·ty
·ties

ob'se·quies	oc·cur'	off'shoot'	om·niv'o·rous	o·pin'ion	or'ches·tra
ob·se'qui·ous	·curred'	off'shore'	once'-o'ver	o·pin'ion·at'ed	or·ches'tral
ob·serv'a·ble	·cur'ring	off'side'	on'com'ing	o·pin'ion·a'tive	or'ches·trate'
ob·serv'ance	oc·cur'rence	off'spring'	one'ness	o'pi·um	·trat'ed ·trat'ing
ob·serv'ant	o'cean	·spring' or	on'er·ous	o·pos'sum	or'ches·tra'tion
ob'ser·va'tion	o'cean·go'ing	·springs'	one'self'	op·po'nent	or'chid
ob·serv'a·to'ry	o'ce·an'ic	off'-white'	one'-sid'ed	op'por·tune'	or·dain'
·ries	o'ce·a·nog'ra·phy	of'ten	one'-time'	op'por·tun'ism	or·deal'
ob·serve'	o'ce·an·ol'o·gy	of'ten·times'	one'-track'	op'por·tun'ist	or'der
served' ·serv'ing	o'ce·lot'	o'gle	one'-up'	op'por·tu'ni·ty	or'der·li·ness
ob·serv'er	o'cher or o'chre	o'gled o'gling	-upped'	·ties	or'der·ly
ob·sess'	o'·clock'	o'gre	-up'ping	op·pos'a·ble	·lies
ob·ses'sion	oc'ta·gon'	o'gre·ish or	one'-up'man·ship'	op·pose'	or'di·nal
ob·ses'sive	oc·tag'o·nal	o'grish	one'-way'	·posed' ·pos'ing	or'di·nance
ob·sid'i·an	oc'ta·he'dron	O·hi'o	on'go'ing	op·pos'er	(law; see
ob'so·lesce'	oc'tane	ohm'me'ter	on'ion·skin'	op'po·site	ordnance)
lesced' ·lesc'ing	oc·tan'gu·lar	oil'cloth'	on'-line'	op'po·si'tion	or'di·nar'i·ly
ob'so·les'cence	oc'tave	oil'i·ness	on'look'er	op·press'	or'di·nar'y
ob'so·les'cent	oc·ta'vo	oil'pa'per	on'ly	op·pres'sion	·ies
ob'so·lete'	·vos	oil'skin'	on'o·mat'o·poe'ia	op·pres'sive·ly	or'di·nate
ob'sta·cle	oc·tet' or ·tette'	oil'stone'	on'rush'	op·pres'sor	or'di·na'tion
ob·stet'ric	Oc·to'ber	oil'y	on'set'	op·pro'bri·ous	ord'nance
ob·stet'ri·cal	oc'to·ge·nar'i·an	·i·er ·i·est	on'shore'	op·pro'bri·um	(artillery; see
ob'ste·tri'cian	oc'to·pus	oint'ment	on'side'	op'tic	ordinance)
ob'sti·na·cy	·pus·es or ·pi'	OK or O.K.	on'slaught'	op'ti·cal	or'dure
·cies	or oc·top'o·des'	OK's or O.K.'s	o'nus	op·ti'cian	ore
ob'sti·nate	oc'tu·ple	OK'd or O.K.'d	on'ward	op'ti·mal	(mineral; see oar)
ob'sti·nate·ly	oc'tu·lar	OK'ing or O.K.'ing	on'yx	op'ti·mism	o·reg'a·no
ob·strep'er·ous	oc'u·list	O'kla·ho'ma	oo'long	op'ti·mist	Or'e·gon
ob·struct'	odd'i·ty	old'-fash'ioned	ooze	op'ti·mis'tic	or'gan
ob·struc'tion	·ties	old'ish	oozed ooz'ing	op'ti·mis'ti·cal·ly	or'gan·dy or ·die
ob·struc'tion·ist	odd'ly	old'-line'	oo'zi·ness	op'ti·mize'	or·gan'ic
ob·struc'tive	odds'-on'	old'ster	oo'zy	·mized' ·miz'ing	or·gan'i·cal·ly
ob·tain'	o'di·ous	old'-tim'er	·zi·er ·zi·est	op'ti·mum	or'gan·ism
ob·trude'	o'di·um	old'-world'	o·pac'i·ty	·mums or ·ma	or'gan·ist
·trud'ed	o·dom'e·ter	o'le·o'	o'pal	op'tion	or'gan·iz'a·ble
·trud'ing	o'dor	o'le·o·mar'ga·	o'pal·es'cent	op'tion·al	or'gan·i·za'tion
ob·tru'sion	o'dor·if'er·ous	rine or ·rin	o·paque'	op'tion·al·ly	or'gan·ize'
ob·tru'sive	o'dor·ous	ol·fac'tion	o'pen-and-shut'	op·tom'e·trist	·ized' ·iz'ing
ob·tru'sive·ly	Od'ys·sey	ol·fac'to·ry	o'pen-end'	op·tom'e·try	or'gan·iz'er
ob·tuse'	of'fal	·ries	o'pen-end'ed	op'u·lence	or·gan'za
ob·verse'	off'beat'	ol'i·garch'	o'pen·er	op'u·lent	or'gasm
ob·vert'	off'-col'or	ol'i·garch'y	o'pen-eyed'	o'pus	or·gas'mic
ob'vi·ate'	of·fend'	·ies	o'pen·hand'ed	op'er·a or	or'gy
·at'ed ·at'ing	of·fense'	ol'i·gop'o·ly	o'pen·heart'ed	o'pus·es	·gies
ob'vi·ous	of·fen'sive	·lies	o'pen-hearth'	or'a·cle	O'ri·ent n.
ob'vi·ous·ly	of'fer	ol'ive	o'pen·ly	(wise person;	o'ri·ent' v.
oc'a·ri'na	of'fer·ing	O·lym'pic	o'pen-mind'ed	see auricle)	O'ri·en'tal
oc·ca'sion	of'fer·to'ry	o·me'ga	o'pen-mouthed'	o·rac'u·lar	o'ri·en·tate'
oc·ca'sion·al	·ries	om'e·let or	o'pen·ness	o'ral	·tat'ed ·tat'ing
oc·ca'sion·al·ly	off'hand'	·lette	o'pen·work'	(of the mouth;	o'ri·en·ta'tion
Oc'ci·dent	off'hand'ed·ly	o'men	op'er·a or	see aural)	or'i·fice
Oc'ci·den'tal	of'fice	om'i·nous	op'er·a·ble	o'ral·ly	or'i·ga'mi
oc·cip'i·tal	of'fi·cer	o·mis'si·ble	op'er·ate'	or'ange	or'i·gin
oc·clude'	of·fi'cial·ese'	o·mis'sion	·at'ed ·at'ing	or'ange·ade'	o·rig'i·nal
·clud'ed	of·fi'cial	o·mit'	op'er·at'ic	or'ange·wood'	o·rig'i·nal'i·ty
·clud'ing	of·fi'ci·ate'	o·mit'ted	op'er·a'tion	o·rang'u·tan'	o·rig'i·nal·ly
oc·clu'sion	·at'ed ·at'ing	o·mit'ting	op'er·a'tion·al	o·ra'tion	o·rig'i·nate'
oc·cult'	of·fi'ci·a'tion	om'ni·bus'	op'er·a'tion·al·ly	or'a·tor	·nat'ed ·nat'ing
oc'cul·ta'tion	of·fi'ci·a'tor	om'ni·far'i·ous	op'er·a'tive	or'a·tor'i·cal	o·rig'i·na'tion
oc·cult'ism	of·fi'cious	om·nip'o·tence	op'er·a'tor	or'a·tor'i·o'	o·rig'i·na'tor
oc'cu·pan·cy	off'ing	om·nip'o·tent	op'er·et'ta	·os'	o'ri·ole'
·cies	off'-key'	om'ni·pres'ence	oph'thal·mol'o·	or'a·to'ry	or'lon
oc'cu·pant	off'-lim'its	om'ni·pres'ent	gist	·ries	or'na·ment
oc'cu·pa'tion	off'-line'	om'ni·range'	oph'thal·mol'o·gy	or·bic'u·lar	or'na·men'tal
oc'cu·pa'tion·al·ly	off'print'	om·nis'cience	oph·thal'mo·	or'bit	or'na·men·ta'tion
oc'cu·py'	off'set'	om·nis'cient	scope'	or'chard	or·nate'
·pied' ·py'ing			o'pi·ate		

or·nate'ly
or'ni·thol'o·gy
o'ro·tund'
or'phan·age
or'thi·con'
or'tho·don'tics
or'tho·don'tist
or'tho·dox'
or'tho·dox'y
·ies
or·thog'ra·phy
or'tho·pe'dics
or'tho·pe'dist
os'cil·late'
·lat'ed ·lat'ing
(fluctuate; see
osculate)
os'cil·la'tion
os'cil·la'tor
os·cil'lo·scope'
os'cu·late'
·lat'ed ·lat'ing
(kiss; see
oscillate)
os·mo'sis
os'prey
·preys
os'si·fy'
·fied' ·fy'ing
os·ten'si·ble
os·ten'si·bly
os·ten'sive
os·ten'sive·ly
os'ten·ta'tion
os'ten·ta'tious
os'te·o·path'
os'te·op'a·thy
os'tra·cism
os'tra·cize'
·cized' ·ciz'ing
os'trich
oth'er-di·rect'ed
oth'er·wise'
o'ti·ose'
ot'ter
ot'to·man
·mans
ought
(be obliged; see
aught)
our·self'
our·selves'
oust'er
out'-and-out'
out'bid'
·bid' ·bid'ding
out'board'
out'bound'
out'break'
out'build'ing
out'burst'
out'cast'
out'class'
out'come'
out'crop'
out'cry'
·cries
out'dat'ed

out'dis'tance
·tanced ·tanc·ing
out'do'
·did' ·done'
·do'ing
out'door'
out'doors'
out'er·most'
out'er space
out'er·wear'
out'face'
out'field'er
out'fit'
out'fit'ter
out'flank'
out'flow'
out'go'
·went' ·gone'
·go'ing
out'go'
·goes'
out'go'ing
out'-group'
out'grow'
·grew' ·grown'
·grow'ing
out'growth'
out'guess'
out'house'
out'ing
out'land'er
out·land'ish
out·last'
out'law'
out'law·ry
·ries
out'lay'
·laid' ·lay'ing
out'let'
out'li'er
out'line'
out'live'
out'look'
out'ly'ing
out'man'
out'ma·neu'ver
out'mod'ed
out'most'
out'num'ber
out'-of-date'
out'-of-doors'
out'-of-pock'et
out'-of-the-way'
out'-of-town'er
out'pa'tient
out'post'
out'pour'ing
out'put'
out'rage'
out·ra'geous
out'rank'
out'reach'
out'ride'
·rode' ·rid'den
·rid'ing
out'rid'er
out'rig'ger
out'right'

out'run'
·ran' ·run'
·run'ning
out'sell'
·sold' ·sell'ing
out'set'
out'shine'
·shone' ·shin'ing
out'side'
out'sid'er
out'sit'
·sat' ·sit'ting
out'size'
out'skirts'
out'smart'
out'speak'
·spoke' ·spo'ken
·speak'ing
out'spo'ken·ness
out'spread'
·spread'
·spread'ing
out'stand'ing
out'stare'
out'sta'tion
out'stay'
out'stretch'
out'strip'
out'talk'
out'think'
·thought'
·think'ing
out'vote'
out'ward
out'wear'
·wore' ·worn'
·wear'ing
out'weigh'
out'wit'
·wit'ted
·wit'ting
out'work'
o'val
o'val·ly
o·var'i·an
o'va·ry
·ries
o·va'tion
ov'en
o'ver·age
o'ver·all'
o'ver·alls'
o'ver·awe'
·awed' ·aw'ing
o'ver·bal'ance
o'ver·bear'
·bore' ·borne'
·bear'ing
o'ver·bid'
·bid' ·bid'ding
o'ver·bite'
o'ver·blouse'
o'ver·board'
o'ver·cap'i·tal·
ize'
o'ver·cast'
o'ver·charge'
o'ver·coat'

o'ver·come'
·came' ·come'
·com'ing
o'ver·com'pen·
sate'
o'ver·con'fi·dent
o'ver·crowd'ed
o'ver·do'
·did' ·done'
·do'ing
o'ver·dose'
o'ver·draft'
o'ver·draw'
·drew' ·drawn'
·draw'ing
o'ver·dress'
o'ver·drive'
o'ver·due'
o'ver·flight'
o'ver·flow'
o'ver·fly'
·flew' ·flown'
·fly'ing
o'ver·gar'ment
o'ver·glaze'
o'ver·grow'
·grew' ·grown'
·grow'ing
o'ver·hand'
o'ver·hang'
·hung'
·hang'ing
o'ver·haul'
o'ver·head'
o'ver·hear'
·heard'
·hear'ing
o'ver·heat'
o'ver·in·dul'·
gence
o'ver·is'sue
o'ver·joy'
o'ver·lad'en
o'ver·lap'
o'ver·lay'
·laid' ·lay'ing
o'ver·leap'
o'ver·lie'
·lay' ·lain'
·ly'ing
o'ver·load'
o'ver·look'
o'ver·ly
o'ver·nice'
o'ver·night'
o'ver·pass'
o'ver·pay'
·paid' ·pay'ing
o'ver·pop'u·late'
o'ver·pow'er
o'ver·pro·duce'
o'ver·pro·tect'
o'ver·rate'
o'ver·reach'
o'ver·ride'
·rode' ·rid'den
·rid'ing
o'ver·rule'

o'ver·run'
·ran' ·run'
·run'ning
o'ver·seas'
o'ver·see'
·saw' ·seen'
·see'ing
o'ver·se'er
o'ver·sell'
·sold' ·sell'ing
o'ver·sexed'
o'ver·shad'ow
o'ver·shoe'
o'ver·shoot'
·shot' ·shoot'ing
o'ver·sight'
o'ver·sim'pli·fy'
o'ver·size'
o'ver·skirt'
o'ver·slaugh'
o'ver·sleep'
·slept' ·sleep'ing
o'ver·spend'
·spent' ·spend'ing
o'ver·spread'
o'ver·state'
o'ver·stay'
o'ver·step'
o'ver·stock'
o'ver·strung'
o'ver·stuff'
o'ver·sub·scribe'
o'ver·sup·ply'
o·vert'
o'ver·take'
·took' ·tak'en
·tak'ing
o'ver·tax'
o'ver-the-count'er
o'ver·throw'
·threw' ·thrown'
·throw'ing
o'ver·time'
o'ver·tone'
o'ver·ture
o'ver·use'
o'ver·view'
o'ver·ween'ing
o'ver·weight'
o'ver·whelm'
o'ver·wind'
·wound' ·wind'ing
o'ver·work'
o'ver·write'
·wrote' ·writ'ten
·writ'ing
o'ver·wrought'
o·vip'a·rous
o'void
o'vu·late'
·lat'ed ·lat'ing
o'vu·la'tion
o'vule
o'vum
o'va
owe
owed ow'ing
owl'ish

own'er·ship'
ox
ox'en
ox'blood'
ox'bow'
ox'ford
ox'i·da'tion
ox'i·dize'
·dized' ·diz'ing
ox'tail'
ox'y·gen
ox'y·gen·ate'
·at'ed ·at'ing
ox'y·gen·a'tion
ox'y·mo'ron
·mo'ra
ox'y·tet'ra·cy'·
cline
oys'ter
o'zone

P

pab'lum
pace
paced pac'ing
pace'mak'er
pach'y·derm'
pach'y·san'dra
pac'i·fi'a·ble
pa·cif'ic
pac'i·fi·ca'tion
pac'i·fi'er
pac'i·fism
pac'i·fy'
·fied' ·fy'ing
pack'age
·aged ·ag·ing
pack'et
pack'ing
pack'sad'dle
pack'thread'
pact
pad
pad'ded
pad'ding
pad'dle
·dled ·dling
pad'dock
pad'dy
·dies
(rice; see patty)
pad'lock'
pa'dre
·dres
pae'an
(song; see peon)
pa'gan
page
paged pag'ing
pag'eant
pag'eant·ry
·ries
page'boy'
pag'i·nate'
·nat'ed ·nat'ing

pag'i·na'tion
pa·go'da
pail
  (bucket; see
  pale)
pail'ful'
  ·fuls'
pain
  (hurt; see pane)
pain'ful
pain'less
pains'tak'ing
paint'brush'
paint'er
pair
  (two; see pare,
  pear)
pais'ley
pa·ja'mas
pal'ace
pal'an·quin'
pal'at·a·ble
pal'at·a·bly
pal'a·tal
pal'ate
  (roof of mouth;
  see palette, pallet)
pa·la'tial
pal'a·tine'
pa·lav'er
pale
  paled pal'ing
  (white; see pail)
pale'face'
pale'ly
pa'le·o·lith'ic
pa'le·on·tol'o·gy
pal'ette
  (paint board; see
  palate, pallet)
pal'in·drome'
pal'ing
pal·i·sade'
pall
  palled pall'ing
pal·la'di·um
pall'bear'er
pal'let
  (tool; bed; see
  palate, palette)
pal'li·ate'
  ·at'ed ·at'ing
pal'li·a'tive
pal'lid
pall'-mall'
  (game; see
  pell-mell)
pal'lor
palm
pal·met'to
  ·tos or ·toes
palm'is·try
pal'o·mi'no
  ·nos
pal'pa·ble
pal'pa·bly
pal'pate
  ·pat·ed ·pat·ing

pal'pi·tate'
  ·tat'ed ·tat'ing
pal'pi·ta'tion
pal'sy
  ·sied ·sy·ing
pal'tri·ness
pal'try
  ·tri·er ·tri·est
  (trifling;
  see poultry)
pam'pas
pam'per
pam'phlet
pam'phlet·eer'
pan
  panned pan'ning
pan'a·ce'a
pa·nache'
Pan'-A·mer'i·can
pan'a·tel'a
pan'cake'
pan'chro·mat'ic
pan'cre·as
pan'cre·at'ic
pan·dem'ic
pan'de·mo'ni·um
pan'der
pan·dow'dy
  ·dies
pane
  (window; see
  pain)
pan'e·gyr'ic
pan'e·gyr'i·cal
pan'el
  ·eled or ·elled
  ·el·ing or ·el·ling
pan'el·ist
pan'-fry'
  -fried' -fry'ing
pan'han'dle
pan'ic
  ·icked ·ick·ing
pan'ic·al·ly
pan'ick·y
pan'ic-strick'en
panne
pan'nier
pan'o·ply
  ·plies
pan'o·ra'ma
pan'o·ram'ic
pan'o·ram'i·cal·ly
pan'ta·loons'
pant'dress'
pan'the·ism
pan'the·is'tic
pan'the·on'
pan'ther
pant'ies
pan'to·graph
pan'to·mime'
  ·mimed'
  ·mim'ing
pan'to·mim'ic
pan'to·mim'ist
pan'try
  ·tries

pant'suit' or
  pants suit
pan'ty hose
pa'pa·cy
  ·cies
pa'pal
pa'paw
pa·pa'ya
pa'per·back'
pa'per·bound'
pa'per·hang'er
pa'per·weight'
pa'per·y
pa'pier-mâ·ché'
pa·pri'ka
pap'ule
pa·py'rus
  ·ri or ·rus·es
par
  parred par'ring
par'a·ble
pa·rab'o·la
par'a·bol'ic
par'a·bol'i·cal·ly
par'a·chute'
  ·chut'ed
  ·chut'ing
par'a·chut'ist
pa·rade'
  ·rad'ed ·rad'ing
par'a·digm
par'a·dise'
par'a·dox'
par'a·dox'i·cal
par'a·dox'i·cal·ly
par'af·fin
par'a·gon'
par'a·graph'
par'a·keet'
par'al·lax'
par'al·lel'
  ·leled' or ·lelled'
  ·lel'ing or
  ·lel'ling
par'al·lel·ism
par'al·lel'o·gram'
pa·ral'y·sis
par'a·lyt'ic
par'a·lyze'
  ·lyzed' ·lyz'ing
par'a·me'ci·um
  ·ci·a
par'a·med'ic
par'a·med'i·cal
pa·ram'e·ter
  (math. term; see
  perimeter)
par'a·mount'
par'a·mour'
par'a·noi'a
par'a·noi'ac
par'a·noid'
par'a·pet
par'a·pher·na'li·a
par'a·phrase'
  ·phrased'
  ·phras'ing

par'a·ple'gi·a
par'a·ple'gic
par'a·prax'is
  ·es
par'a·psy·chol'o·
  gy
par'a·res'cue
par'a-sail'
par'a·site'
par'a·sit'ic
par'a·sol'
par'a·troops'
par'boil'
par'buck'le
par'cel
  ·celed or ·celled
  ·cel·ing or
  ·cel·ling
parch'ment
par'don·a·ble
par'don·a·bly
pare
  pared par'ing
  (trim; see pair,
  pear)
par'e·gor'ic
par'ent
par'ent·age
pa·ren'tal
pa·ren'the·sis
  ·ses'
pa·ren'the·size'
  ·sized' ·siz'ing
par'en·thet'i·cal
par'ent·hood'
pa·re'sis
par'e·ve
par ex·cel·lence'
par·fait'
par·he'li·on
  ·li·a
pa·ri'ah
pa·ri'e·tal
par'i·mu'tu·el
par'ish
pa·rish'ion·er
par'i·ty
  ·ties
par'ka
park'way'
parl'ance
par'lay
  (bet)
par'ley
  (confer)
par'lia·ment
par'lia·men·
  tar'i·an
par'lia·men'ta·ry
par'lor
pa·ro'chi·al
par'o·dist
par'o·dy
  ·died ·dy·ing
pa·role'
  ·roled' ·rol'ing
pa·rol·ee'

pa·rot'id
par'ox·ysm
par'ox·ys'mal
par·quet'
  ·queted'
  ·quet'ing
par'quet·ry
par·ra·keet'
par'ri·cid'al
par'ri·cide'
par'rot
par'ry
  ·ries
  ·ried ·ry·ing
par'sec'
par'si·mo'ni·ous
par'si·mo'ny
pars'ley
pars'nip
par'son
par'son·age
par·take'
  ·took' ·tak'en
  ·tak'ing
par·terre'
par'the·no·gen'e·
  sis
par'tial
par'ti·al'i·ty
par'tial·ly
par'ti·ble
par·tic'i·pant
par·tic'i·pate'
  ·pat'ed ·pat'ing
par·tic'i·pa'tion
par·tic'i·pa'tor
par·tic'i·ple
par'ti·cle
par·ti·col'ored
par·tic'u·lar
par·tic'u·lar'i·ty
  ·ties
par·tic'u·lar·ize'
  ·ized' ·iz'ing
par·tic'u·lar·ly
par'ti·san
par·ti'tion
part'ner
part'ner·ship'
par'tridge
part'-time'
par·tu'ri·ent
par·tu·ri'tion
par'ty
  ·ties
par've·nu'
  ·nus'
pas'chal
pass'a·ble
pass'a·bly
pas'sage
pas'sage·way'
pass'book'
pas·sé'
passed
  (pp. of pass;
  see past)

pas'sen·ger
passe'-par·tout'
pass'er-by'
  pass'ers-by'
pas'sion
pas'sion·ate
pas'sion·ate·ly
pas'sive
pas'sive·ly
pas·siv'i·ty
pass'key'
Pass'o'ver
pass'port'
pass'-through'
pass'word'
past
  (gone by; over;
  see passed)
paste
  past'ed past'ing
paste'board'
pas·tel'
pas'teur·i·za'tion
pas'teur·ize'
  ·ized' ·iz'ing
pas·tille'
pas'time'
past'i·ness
pas'tor
pas'to·ral
pas'tor·ate
pas·tra'mi
pas'try
  ·tries
pas'ture
  ·tured ·tur·ing
past'y
  ·i·er ·i·est
pat
  pat'ted pat'ting
patch'work'
patch'y
  ·i·er ·i·est
pâ·té' de foie'
  gras'
pa·tel'la
  ·las or ·lae
pat'ent
pat'ent·ee'
pa·ter'nal
pa·ter'nal·is'tic
pa·ter'ni·ty
pa·thet'ic
pa·thet'i·cal·ly
path'find'er
path'o·gen'ic
path'o·log'i·cal
pa·thol'o·gy
  ·gies
pa'thos
pa'tience
pa'tient
pat'i·na
pa'ti·o'
  ·os'
pa·tis'se·rie
pat'ois
  ·ois

pa'tri·arch'
pa'tri·ar'chal
pa'tri·ar'chy
 ·chies
pa·tri'cian
pat'ri·cide'
pat'ri·mo'ny
 ·nies
pa'tri·ot
pa'tri·ot'ic
pa'tri·ot'i·cal·ly
pa'tri·ot·ism
pa·trol'
 ·trolled'
 ·trol'ling
pa·trol'man
pa'tron
pa'tron·age
pa'tron·ize'
 ized' iz'ing
pat'ro·nym'ic
pat'ter
pat'tern·mak'er
pat'ty
 ·ties
 (*cake;* see paddy)
pau'ci·ty
paunch'i·ness
paunch'y
pau'per
pause
 paused paus'ing
pave
 paved pav'ing
pave'ment
pa·vil'ion
pawn'bro'ker
pawn'shop'
pay
 paid pay'ing
pay'a·ble
pay'check'
pay'day'
pay·ee'
pay'load'
pay'mas·ter
pay'ment
pay'off'
pay'roll'
peace
 (*harmony;*
 see piece)
peace'a·ble
peace'a·bly
peace'ful
peace'ful·ly
peace'mak'er
peace pipe
peace'time'
peach
pea'cock'
peak
 (*highest point;*
 see peek, pique)
peaked
 (*pointed*)
peak'ed
 (*thin and drawn*)

peal
 (*sound;* see peel)
pea'nut
pear
 (*fruit;* see pair, pare)
pearl
 (*gem;* see purl)
pearl'y
 ·i·er ·i·est
pear'-shaped'
peas'ant
peas'ant·ry
peat moss
peau' de soie'
peb'ble
 ·bled ·bling
peb'bly
 ·bli·er ·bli·est
pe·can'
pec'ca·dil'lo
 ·loes *or* ·los
pec'cant
peck
pec'tin
pec'to·ral
pec'u·late'
 ·lat'ed ·lat'ing
pec'u·la'tion
pec'u·la'tor
pe·cul'iar
pe·cu'li·ar'i·ty
 ·ties
pe·cu'ni·ar'i·ly
pe·cu'ni·ar'y
ped'a·gog'ic
ped'a·gogue'
 or ·gog'
ped'a·go'gy
ped'al
 aled *or* ·alled
 ·al·ing *or*
 ·al·ling
 (*foot lever;* see peddle)
ped'ant
pe·dan'tic
pe·dan'ti·cal·ly
ped'ant·ry
 ·ries
ped'dle
 ·dled ·dling
 (*sell;* see pedal)
ped'dler
ped'es·tal
pe·des'tri·an
pe'di·a·tri'cian
pe'di·at'rics
ped'i·cure'
ped'i·gree'
ped'i·greed'
ped'i·ment
pe·dom'e·ter
peek
 (*look;* see peak, pique)
peel
 (*skin;* see peal)

peep'hole'
peer
 (*equal; look;* see pier)
peer group
peer'less
peeve
 peeved peev'ing
pee'vish
peg
 pegged peg'ging
peg'board'
peign·oir'
pe'jo·ra'tion
pe·jo'ra·tive
Pe'king·ese'
pe'koe
pel'i·can
pel·la'gra
pel'let
pell'-mell'
 (*without order;* see pall-mall)
pel·lu'cid
pel'vic
pel'vis
pem'mi·can
pen
 penned *or* pent
 pen'ning
 (*enclose*)
pen
 penned pen'ning
 (*write with pen*)
pe'nal
pe'nal·i·za'tion
pe'nal·ize'
 ized' iz'ing
pen'al·ty
 ·ties
pen'ance
pen'chant
pen'cil
 ·ciled *or* ·cilled
 ·cil·ing *or*
 ·cil·ling
pend'ant *or*
 ·ent n.
pend'ent *or*
 ·ant adj.
pend'ing
pen'du·lous
pen'du·lum
pen'e·tra·bil'i·ty
pen'e·tra·ble
pen'e·tra·bly
pen'e·trate'
 ·trat'ed ·trat'ing
pen'e·tra'tion
pen'e·trom'e·ter
pen'guin
pen'hold'er
pen'i·cil'lin
pen·in'su·la
pen·in'su·lar
pe'nis
 ·nis·es *or* ·nes
pen'i·tence

pen'i·tent
pen'i·ten'tial
pen'i·ten'tia·ry
 ·ries
pen'knife'
 ·knives'
pen'light' *or* ·lite'
pen'man·ship'
pen name
pen'nant
pen'non
Penn'syl·va'ni·a
pen'ny
 ·nies
pen'ny ante
pen'ny·weight'
pen'ny-wise'
pen'ny·worth'
pe'no·log'i·cal
pe·nol'o·gist
pe·nol'o·gy
pen'sion
pen'sion·ar'y
 ·ies
pen'sive
pen'sive·ly
pen'stock'
pen'ta·gon'
pen·tag'o·nal
pen'ta·he'dral
pen'ta·he'dron
 ·drons *or* ·dra
pen·tam'e·ter
Pen'ta·teuch'
pen·tath'lon
Pen'te·cost'
pent'house'
pen·tom'ic
pent'-up'
pe·nu'che *or* ·chi
pe'nult
pe·nul'ti·mate
pe·num'bra
 ·brae *or* ·bras
pe·nu'ri·ous
pen'u·ry
pe'on
 (*laborer;* see paean)
pe'on·age
pe'o·ny
 ·nies
peo'ple
 ·pled ·pling
pep'lum
 ·lums *or* ·la
pep'per-and-salt'
pep'per·corn'
pep'per·i·ness
pep'per·mint'
pep'per·o'ni
 ·nis *or* ·ni
pep'per·y
 ·i·er ·i·est
pep'pi·ly
pep'pi·ness
pep'py
 ·pi·er ·pi·est

pep'sin
pep'tic
per·am'bu·late'
 ·lat'ed ·lat'ing
per·am'bu·la'tion
per·am'bu·la'tor
per an'num
per·cale'
per cap'i·ta
per·ceiv'a·ble
per·ceiv'a·bly
per·ceive'
 ·ceived' ·ceiv'ing
per·cent' *or*
 per cent
per·cent'age
per·cen'tile
per'cept
per·cep'ti·ble
per·cep'ti·bly
per·cep'tion
per·cep'tive
per·cep'tive·ly
per·cep'tu·al
per·chance'
Per'che·ron'
per·cip'i·ent
per'co·late'
 ·lat'ed ·lat'ing
per'co·la'tion
per'co·la'tor
per·cus'sion
per·cus'sive
per di'em
per·di'tion
per·du' *or* ·due'
per·dur'a·ble
per'e·gri·nate'
 ·nat'ed ·nat'ing
per'e·gri·na'tion
per·emp'to·ri·ly
per·emp'to·ri·ness
per·emp'to·ry
per·en'ni·al
per'fect
per·fect'i·bil'i·ty
per·fect'i·ble
per·fec'tion
per·fec'tion·ism
per·fec'to
 ·tos
per·fid'i·ous
per'fi·dy
 ·dies
per'fo·rate'
 ·rat'ed ·rat'ing
per'fo·ra'tion
per'fo·ra'tor
per·force'
per·form'
per·form'ance
per·fume'
 ·fumed' ·fum'ing
per'fume n.
per·fum'er
per·func'to·ri·ly
per·func'to·ry
per'go·la

per·haps'
per'i·gee'
per'i·he'li·on
 ·li·ons *or* ·li·a
per'il
 ·iled *or* ·illed
 ·il·ing *or* ·il·ling
per'il·ous
per'i·lune'
pe·rim'e·ter
 (*boundary;* see parameter)
pe'ri·od
pe'ri·od'ic
pe'ri·od'i·cal
pe'ri·od'i·cal·ly
pe'ri·o·dic'i·ty
per'i·pa·tet'ic
pe·riph'er·al
pe·riph'er·y
 ·ies
pe·riph'ra·sis
per'i·phras'tic
pe·rique'
per'i·scope'
per'i·scop'ic
per'ish
per'ish·a·bil'i·ty
per'ish·a·ble
per'i·stal'sis
per'i·style'
per'i·to·ni'tis
per'jure
 ·jured ·jur·ing
per'jur·er
per'ju·ry
 ·ries
perk'i·ness
perk'y
 ·i·er ·i·est
per'ma·frost'
perm'al·loy
per'ma·nence
per'ma·nent
per'me·a·bil'i·ty
per'me·a·ble
per'me·ate'
 ·at'ed ·at'ing
per'me·a'tion
per·mis'si·bil'i·ty
per·mis'si·ble
per·mis'si·bly
per·mis'sion
per·mis'sive
per·mis'sive·ly
per·mit'
 ·mit'ted
 ·mit'ting
per·mut'a·ble
per'mu·ta'tion
per·ni'cious
per·nod'
per'o·rate'
 ·rat'ed ·rat'ing
per'o·ra'tion
per·ox'ide
 ·id·ed ·id·ing
per'pen·dic'u·lar

per'pe·trate'
  ·trat'ed ·trat'ing
per'pe·tra'tion
per'pe·tra'tor
per·pet'u·al
per·pet'u·al·ly
per·pet'u·ate'
  ·at'ed ·at'ing
per·pet'u·a'tion
per·pet'u·a'tor
per'pe·tu'i·ty
  ·ties
per·plex'
per·plexed'
per·plex'ed·ly
per·plex'i·ty
  ·ties
per'qui·site
  (privilege; see
  prerequisite)
per se
per'se·cute'
  ·cut'ed ·cut'ing
  (harass; see
  prosecute)
per'se·cu'tion
per'se·cu'tor
per'se·ver'ance
per'se·vere'
  ·vered' ·ver'ing
per'si·flage'
per·sim'mon
per·sist'
per·sist'ence
per·sist'ent
per'son
per'son·a·ble
per'son·age
per'son·al
  (private; see
  personnel)
per'son·al'i·ty
  ·ties
per'son·al·ize'
  ·ized' ·iz'ing
per'son·al·ly
per'son·ate'
  ·at'ed ·at'ing
per'son·a'tion
per'son·a'tor
per·son'i·fi·
  ca'tion
per·son'i·fy'
  ·fied' ·fy'ing
per'son·nel'
  (employees; see
  personal)
per·spec'tive
  (view; see
  prospective)
per·spi·ca'cious
per'spi·cac'i·ty
per'spi·cu'i·ty
per·spic'u·ous
per'spi·ra'tion
per·spir'a·to'ry
per·spire'
  ·spired' ·spir'ing

per·suad'a·ble
per·suade'
  ·suad'ed
  ·suad'ing
per·sua'si·bil'i·ty
per·sua'sion
per·sua'sive
per·tain'
per'ti·na'cious
per'ti·nac'i·ty
per'ti·nence
per'ti·nent
pert'ly
per·turb'
per·tur·ba'tion
pe·rus'al
pe·ruse'
  ·rused' ·rus'ing
per·vade'
  ·vad'ed ·vad'ing
per·va'sion
per·va'sive
per·verse'
per·verse'ly
per·ver'sion
per·ver'si·ty
per·vert'
per'vi·ous
Pe'sach
pe'so
  ·sos
pes'si·mism
pes'si·mist
pes'si·mis'tic
pes'si·mis'ti·
  cal·ly
pes'ter
pest'hole'
pes'ti·cide'
pes'ti·lence
pes'ti·lent
pes'ti·len'tial
pes'tle
  ·tled ·tling
pet
  pet'ted pet'ting
pet'al
pet'al·like'
pet'cock'
pe·tite'
pe'tit four'
  pe'tits fours'
  or pe'tit fours'
pe·ti'tion
pet'it jury
pe·tit' mal'
pet'it point
pe'tri dish
pet'ri·fac'tion
pet'ri·fy'
  ·fied' ·fy'ing
pet'ro·la'tum
pe·tro'le·um
pet'ti·coat'
pet'ti·fog'
  ·fogged'
  ·fog'ging
pet'ti·fog'ger

pet'ti·ly
pet'ti·ness
pet'ti·pants'
pet'tish
pet'ty
  ·ti·er ·ti·est
pet'u·lance
pet'u·lant
pew'ter
pha'e·ton
pha'lanx
  ·lanx·es or
  pha·lan'ges
phal'lic
phal'lus
  ·li or ·lus·es
phan'tasm
phan'tom
phar'i·sa'ic
phar'i·see'
phar'ma·ceu'ti·cal
phar'ma·cist
phar'ma·col'o·gy
phar'ma·co·pe'ia
phar'ma·cy
  ·cies
phar'ynx
  ·ynx·es or
  pha·ryn'ges
phase
  phased phas'ing
  (stage; see faze)
phase'-out'
pheas'ant
phe'no·bar'bi·tal'
phe·nom'e·nal
phe·nom'e·nal·ly
phe·nom'e·non'
  ·na or ·nons'
phi'al
Phil'a·del'phi·a
phi·lan'der·er
phil'an·throp'ic
phi·lan'thro·pist
phi·lan'thro·py
  ·pies
phil'a·tel'ic
phi·lat'e·list
phi·lat'e·ly
phil'har·mon'ic
Phil'ip·pine'
Phil'is·tine'
phil'o·den'dron
phil'o·log'i·cal
phi·lol'o·gist
phi·lol'o·gy
phi·los'o·pher
phil'o·soph'ic
phil'o·soph'i·
  cal·ly
phi·los'o·phize'
  ·phized' ·phiz'ing
phi·los'o·phy
  ·phies
phil'ter
  (potion; see
  filter)
phle·bi'tis

phlegm
phleg·mat'ic
phlox
pho'bi·a
pho'bic
phoe'be
Phoe'nix
phone
  phoned phon'ing
pho'neme
pho·net'ic
pho·net'i·cal·ly
pho'ne·ti'cian
phon'ics
pho'ni·ness
pho'no·graph'
pho·nol'o·gy
pho'ny
  ·ni·er ·ni·est
  ·nies
phos'phate
phos'pho·
  res'cence
phos'pho·res'cent
pho'to·chron'o·
  graph
pho'to·cop'i·er
pho'to·cop'y
  ·ied ·y·ing
pho'to·e·lec'tric
pho'to·en·grave'
  ·graved'
  ·grav'ing
pho'to·flash'
pho'to·flood'
pho'to·gen'ic
pho'to·graph'
pho·tog'ra·pher
pho'to·graph'ic
pho·tog'ra·phy
pho'to·gra·vure'
pho'to·lith'o·
  graph
pho'to·li·thog'ra·
  phy
pho'to·map'
pho·tom'e·ter
pho'to·met'ric
pho·tom'e·try
pho'to·mon·tage'
pho'to·mu'ral
pho'to-off'set'
pho'to·sen'si·tive
pho'to·stat'
  ·stat'ed or
  ·stat'ted
  ·stat'ing or
  ·stat'ting
pho'to·stat'ic
pho'to·syn'the·sis
phras'al
phras'al·ly
phrase
phrased
phras'ing

phra'se·ol'o·gy
  ·gies
phre·net'ic
phre·nol'o·gy
phy·lac'ter·y
  ·ies
phy'lum
  ·la
phys'ic
  ·icked ·ick·ing
phys'i·cal
phys'i·cal·ly
phy·si'cian
phys'i·cist
phys'ics
phys'i·og'no·my
phys'i·og'ra·phy
phys'i·o·log'i·cal
phys'i·ol'o·gy
phys'i·o·ther'a·
  pist
phys'i·o·ther'a·py
phy·sique'
pi
  pied
  pie'ing or pi'ing
  (jumble; see pie)
pi
  (Greek letter;
  see pie)
pi'a·nis'si·mo'
pi·an'ist
pi·an'o
  ·os
pi·a·no'la
pi·az'za
pi'ca
pic'a·dor'
pic'a·resque'
pic'a·yune'
Pic'ca·dil'ly
pic'ca·lil'li
pic'co·lo'
  ·los'
pick'ax' or ·axe'
pick'er·el
pick'et
pick'le
  ·led ·ling
pick'pock'et
pick'up'
pic'nic
  ·nicked
  ·nick·ing
pic'nick·er
pi'cot
  ·coted ·cot·ing
pic'to·graph'
pic·to'ri·al
pic·to'ri·al·ly
pic'ture
  ·tured ·tur·ing
pic'tur·esque'
pid'dle
  ·dled ·dling
pidg'in English
pie
  (food; see pi)

pie'bald'
piece
  pieced piec'ing
  (part; see peace)
pièce de ré·sis·
  tance'
piece'-dyed'
piece'meal'
piece'work'
pied'mont
pier
  (structure; see
  peer)
pierce
pierced
pierc'ing
pier glass
pi'e·tism
pi'e·ty
  ·ties
pi'geon
pi'geon-hole'
  ·holed' ·hol'ing
pi'geon-toed'
pig'gish
pig'gy·back'
pig'head·ed
pig iron
pig'let
pig'ment
pig'men·ta'tion
pig·no'li·a
pig'pen'
pig'skin'
pig'sty'
  ·sties
pig'tail'
pi·laf' or ·laff'
pi·las'ter
pile
  piled pil'ing
pi'le·ous
pile'up'
pil'fer
pil'fer·age
pil'grim
pil'grim·age
pil'lage
  ·laged ·lag·ing
pil'lar
pill'box'
pil'lion
pil'lo·ry
  ·ries
  ·ried ·ry·ing
pil'low
pil'low·case'
pi'lose
pi'lot
pi'lot·house'
Pil'sener or
  Pil'sner
pi·men'to or
  ·mien'·
  ·tos
pim'ple
pim'ply
pin'a·fore'

pi·ña'ta
pin'ball'
pince'-nez'
pin'cers
pinch'beck'
pinch'-hit'
　-hit'　·hit'ting
pin'cush·ion
pine
　pined pin'ing
pine'ap'ple
pin'feath'er
ping'-pong'
pin'head'
pin'hole'
pin'ion
pink'eye'
pin'na·cle
　·cled　·cling
　(acme)
pi'noch'le or
　·noc'·
　(game)
pin'point'
pin stripe
pin'to
　·tos
pint'-size'
pin'up'
pin'wale'
pin'wheel'
pin'worm'
pi'o·neer'
pi'ous
pipe
　piped pip'ing
pipe'ful'
　·fuls'
pipe'line'
pip'er
pipe'stem'
pi·pette' or ·pet'
　·pet'ted　·pet'ting
pip'pin
pi'quan·cy
pi'quant
pique
　piqued piqu'ing
　(offend; see
　peak, peek)
pi·qué' or ·que'
　(fabric)
pi'ra·cy
pi·ra'nha
pi'rate
　·rat·ed　·rat·ing
pir'ou·ette'
　·et'ted　·et'ting
pis'ca·to'ri·al
pis'ci·cul'ture
pis·ta'chi·o'
　·os'
pis'til
　(part of plant)
pis'tol
　·toled or ·tolled
　·tol·ing or ·tol·ling
　(firearm)

pis'tol-whip'
pis'ton
pit
　pit'ted pit'ting
pitch'-black'
pitch'blende'
pitch'-dark'
pitch'er·ful'
　·fuls'
pitch'fork'
pitch pipe
pit'e·ous
pit'fall'
pith'i·ness
pith'y
　·i·er　·i·est
pit'i·a·ble
pit'i·ful
pit'i·less
pit'tance
Pitts'burgh
pi·tu'i·tar'y
pit'y
　·ies, ·ied　·y·ing
piv'ot
piv'ot·al
pix'ie or ·y
　·ies
piz'za
piz'ze·ri'a
piz'zi·ca'to
plac'a·bil'i·ty
plac'a·ble
plac'a·bly
plac'ard
pla'cate
　·cat·ed　·cat·ing
place
　placed plac'ing
pla·ce'bo
　·bos or ·boes
place'ment
pla·cen'ta
　·tas or ·tae
plac'er
plac'id
pla·cid'i·ty
plack'et
pla'gia·rism
pla'gia·rize'
　·rized'　·riz'ing
pla'gia·ry
　·ries
plague
　plagued
　plagu'ing
plagu'er
plaid
plain
　(clear; simple;
　see plane)
plain'ness
plains'man
plain'song'
plain'-spo·ken
plain'tiff
plain'tive
plain'tive·ly

plait
　(pleat; braid;
　see plate)
plan
　planned
　plan'ning
plane
　planed plan'ing
　(level; see plain)
plan'et
plan'e·tar'i·um
　·i·ums or ·i·a
plan'e·tar'y
plan'e·tes'i·mal
plan'et·oid'
plank'ing
plank'ton
plan'ner
plan'tain
plan'tar
　(of the sole)
plan·ta'tion
plant'er
　(one that plants)
plan'ti·grade'
plaque
plas'ma
plas'ter
plas'ter·board'
plas'ter·er
plas'tic
plas'ti·cal·ly
plas'ti·cine
plas·tic'i·ty
plas'ti·cize'
　·cized'　·ciz'ing
plat
　plat'ted
　plat'ting
　(map)
plate
　plat'ed plat'ing
　(dish; see plait)
pla·teau'
　·teaus' or
　·teaux'
plate'ful'
　·fuls'
plat'en
plat'form'
plat'i·num
plat'i·tude
plat'i·tu'di·nous
pla·ton'ic
pla·ton'i·cal·ly
pla·toon'
plat'ter
plau'dit
plau'si·bil'i·ty
plau'si·ble
plau'si·bly
play'back'
play'bill'
play'boy'
play'-by-play'
play'ful·ly
play'go'er
play'ground'

play'house'
play'mate'
play'-off'
play'pen'
play'room'
play'thing'
play'wright'
pla'za
plea
plead
　plead'ed or plead
　plead'ing
pleas'ant
pleas'ant·ry
　·ries
please
　pleased
　pleas'ing
pleas'ur·a·ble
pleas'ur·a·bly
pleas'ure
pleat
ple·be'ian
pleb'i·scite'
plec'trum
　·trums or ·tra
pledge
　pledged
　pledg'ing
pledg·ee'
ple'na·ry
plen'i·po·ten'ti·
　ar'y
　·ies
plen'i·tude'
plen'te·ous
plen'ti·ful
plen'ti·ful·ly
plen'ty
ple'num
　·nums or ·na
ple'o·nasm
pleth'o·ra
pleu'ral
　(of the pleura;
　see plural)
pleu'ri·sy
Plex'i·glas'
pli'a·bil'i·ty
pli'a·ble
pli'an·cy
pli'ant
pli'ers
plight
plis·sé' or ·se'
plod
　plod'ded
　plod'ding
plop
　plopped
　plop'ping
plot
　plot'ted
　plot'ting
plow'share'
pluck'i·ness
pluck'y
　·i·er　·i·est

plug
　plugged
　plug'ging
plum
　(fruit)
plum'age
plumb
　(lead weight)
plumb'er
plumb'ing
plume
　plumed
plum'ing
plum'met
plu'mose
plump'ness
plun'der
plunge
　plunged
　plung'ing
plung'er
plu·per'fect
plu'ral
　(more than one;
　see pleural)
plu'ral·ism
plu'ral·is'tic
plu·ral'i·ty
　·ties
plu'ral·ize'
　·ized'　·iz'ing
plush'i·ness
plush'y
　·i·er　·i·est
plu·toc'ra·cy
　·cies
plu'to·crat'
plu'to·crat'ic
plu·to'ni·um
plu'vi·al
ply
　plies
　plied ply'ing
ply'wood'
pneu·mat'ic
pneu·mo'ni·a
poached
poach'er
pock'et·book'
　(purse)
pocket book
　(small book)
pock'et·ful'
　·fuls'
pock'et·knife'
　·knives'
pock'et-size'
pock'mark'
po·di'a·trist
po·di'a·try
po'di·um
　·di·a or ·di·ums
po'em
po·et'ic
po·et'i·cal·ly
po'et·ry
po·go'ni·a
po'go stick

po·grom'
poign'an·cy
poign'ant
poin·set'ti·a
point'-blank'
point'ed·ly
point'er
point'less
poise
　poised pois'ing
poi'son·ous
poke
　poked pok'ing
pok'er
pok'i·ness
pok'y
　·i·er　·i·est
po'lar
po·lar'i·ty
po'lar·i·za'tion
po'lar·ize'
　·ized'　·iz'ing
pole
　poled pol'ing
　(rod; see poll)
pole'ax' or ·axe'
po·lem'ic
po·lem'i·cist
pole'star'
pole'-vault' v.
po·lice'
　·liced'　·lic'ing
po·lice'man
po·lice'wom·an
pol'i·clin'ic
　(outpatient clinic;
　see polyclinic)
pol'i·cy
　·cies
pol'i·cy·hold'er
po·li·o·my'e·li'tis
pol'ish
po·lite'ly
po·lite'ness
pol'i·tic
　·ticked　·tick·ing
po·lit'i·cal
po·lit'i·cal·ly
　(in a political
　manner)
pol'i·ti'cian
pol'i·tic·ly
　(shrewdly)
po·lit'i·co'
　·cos'
pol'i·tics
pol'i·ty
　·ties
pol'ka
pol'ka dot
poll
　(vote; see pole)
poll·ee'
pol'len
pol'li·nate'
　·nat'ed　·nat'ing
pol'li·na'tion
pol'li·wog'

poll'ster
poll tax
pol·lu'tant
pol·lute'
 · lut'ed · lut'ing
pol·lu'tion
poll'ter·geist'
pol·troon'
pol'y·an'drous
pol'y·an'dry
pol'y·clin'ic
 (hospital; see
 policlinic)
pol'y·es'ter
pol'y·eth'yl·ene'
po·lyg'a·mous
po·lyg'a·my
pol'y·glot'
pol'y·gon'
pol'y·graph'
po·lyg'y·ny
pol'y·mer
pol'y·sty'rene
pol'y·syl·lab'ic
pol'y·syl'la·ble
pol'y·tech'nic
pol'y·the·ism
pol'y·un·sat'u·
 rat'ed
pom'ace
 (pulp; see
 pumice)
po·ma'ceous
po·made'
pome'gran'ate
pom'mel
 ·meled or
 ·melled
 ·mel·ing or
 ·mel·ling
pom'pa·dour'
pom'pa·no'
Pom·pei'i
pom'pon'
pom·pos'i·ty
pom'pous
pon'cho
 ·chos
pon'der
pon'der·a·ble
pon'der·ous
pon·gee'
pon'iard
pon'tiff
pon·tif'i·cal
pon·tif'i·cate'
 ·cat'ed ·cat'ing
pon·toon'
po'ny
 ·nies
po'ny·tail'
poo'dle
pooh'-pooh'
pool'room'
poor'house'
pop
 popped pop'ping
pop'corn'

pop'eyed'
pop'lar
 (tree; see
 popular)
pop'lin
pop'o'ver
pop'per
pop'pet
pop'py
 ·pies
pop'u·lace
 (the masses;
 see populous)
pop'u·lar
 (liked by many;
 see poplar)
pop'u·lar'i·ty
pop'u·lar·i·
 za'tion
pop'u·lar·ize'
 ·ized' ·iz'ing
pop'u·late'
 ·lat'ed ·lat'ing
pop'u·la'tion
pop'u·lous
 (full of people;
 see populace)
por'ce·lain
por'cu·pine'
pore
 pored por'ing
 (ponder; tiny
 opening; see
 pour)
pork'er
por'no·graph'ic
por·nog'ra·phy
po·ros'i·ty
po'rous
por'phy·ry
 ·ries
por'poise
por'ridge
por'rin·ger
port'a·bil'i·ty
port'a·ble
por'tage
 ·taged ·tag·ing
por'tal
port·cul'lis
por·tend'
por'tent
por·ten'tous
por'ter
por'ter·house'
port·fo'li·o'
 ·os'
port'hole'
por'ti·co'
 ·coes' or ·cos'
por·tiere'
por'tion
port'li·ness
port'ly
 ·li·er ·li·est
port·man'teau
 ·teaus or ·teaux
por'trait

por'trai·ture
por·tray'
por·tray'al
Por'tu·guese'
por'tu·lac'a
pose
 posed pos'ing
posh
po·si'tion
pos'i·tive
pos'i·tive·ly
pos'i·tiv·ism
pos'se
pos·sess'
pos·sessed'
pos·ses'sion
pos·ses'sive
pos·ses'sor
pos'si·bil'i·ty
 ·ties
pos'si·ble
pos'si·bly
post'age
post'al
post'box'
post card
post'date'
post'er
pos·te'ri·or
pos·ter'i·ty
post'grad'u·ate
post'haste'
post'hu·mous
post'hyp·not'ic
pos·til'lion
post'man
post'mark'
post'mas'ter
post'mis'tress
post'-mor'tem
post'na'tal
post'paid'
post·pon'a·ble
post·pone'
 ·poned' ·pon'ing
post·pone'ment
post'script'
pos'tu·late'
 ·lat'ed ·lat'ing
pos'tu·la'tion
pos'tu·la'tor
pos'tur·al
pos'ture
 ·tured ·tur·ing
post'war'
pot
 pot'ted pot'ting
po'ta·ble
po·ta'tion
po·ta'to
 ·toes
pot'bel'lied
pot'bel'ly
 ·lies
pot'boil'er
po'ten·cy
po'tent
po'ten·tate'

po·ten'tial
po·ten'ti·al'i·ty
 ·ties
po·ten'tial·ly
po'tent·ly
poth'er
pot'hold'er
pot'hole'
pot'hook'
po'tion
pot'latch'
pot'luck'
pot'pour·ri'
pot'sherd'
pot'shot'
pot'tage
pot'ter·y
 ·ies
pouch'i·ness
poul'tice
poul'try
 (fowls; see
 paltry)
pounce
 pounced
 pounc'ing
pound'-fool'ish
pour
 (flow; see pore)
pout
pov'er·ty
pow'der·y
 ·i·er ·i·est
pow'er·ful
pow'er·ful·ly
pow'er·house'
pow'er·less
pow'wow'
pox
prac'ti·ca·bil'i·ty
prac'ti·ca·ble
prac'ti·ca·bly
prac'ti·cal
prac'ti·cal'i·ty
 ·ties
prac'ti·cal·ly
prac'tice
 ·ticed ·tic·ing
prac'tic·er
prac'ti·cum
prac·ti'tion·er
prag·mat'ic
prag·mat'i·cal·ly
prag'ma·tism
prag'ma·tist
prai'rie
praise
 praised
 prais'ing
praise'wor'thy
pra'line
prance
 pranced
 pranc'ing
prank'ish
prate
 prat'ed
 prat'ing

prat'tle
 ·tled ·tling
pray
 (implore; see
 prey)
pray'er
 (one who prays)
prayer
 (an entreaty)
preach'er
pre'am'ble
pre'ar·range'
 ·ranged'
 ·rang'ing
pre'ar·range'ment
preb'end
pre·can'cel
pre·car'i·ous
pre·cau'tion
pre·cau'tion·ar'y
pre·cede'
 ·ced'ed ·ced'ing
 (come before;
 see proceed)
prec'e·dence
 (priority)
prec'e·dent
 (example)
pre'-cen'sor
pre'cept
pre·cep'tor
pre·ces'sion
 (a going before;
 see procession)
pre·ces'sion·al
pre'cinct
pre·ci·os'i·ty
pre'cious
prec'i·pice
pre·cip'i·tate'
 ·tat'ed ·tat'ing
pre·cip'i·ta'tion
pre·cip'i·tous
pré·cis'
 ·cis'
 (abstract)
pre·cise'
 (definite)
pre·cise'ly
pre·ci'sion
pre·clude'
 ·clud'ed
 ·clud'ing
pre·clu'sion
pre·co'cious
pre'cog·ni'tion
pre'con·ceive'
pre'con·cep'tion
pre'con·scious
pre·cur'sor
pre·cur'so·ry
pre·da'cious
pre·date'
pred'a·tor
pred'a·to'ry
pre'de·cease'
pred'e·ces'sor
pre·des'ti·na'tion

pre·des'tine
 ·tined ·tin·ing
pre'de·ter'mine
pred'i·ca·bil'i·ty
pred'i·ca·ble
pre·dic'a·ment
pred'i·cate'
 ·cat'ed ·cat'ing
pred'i·ca'tion
pre·dict'
pre·dict'a·ble
pre·dic'tion
pre·dic'tive
pre·dic'tor
pre·di·gest'
pre'di·lec'tion
pre·dis·pose'
pre'dis·po·si'tion
pre·dom'i·nant
pre·dom'i·nate'
pre·em'i·nence
pre·em'i·nent
pre·empt'
pre·emp'tion
pre·emp'tive
pre·emp'tor
pre·es·tab'lish
pre·ex·ist'
pre·ex·ist'ence
pre'fab'
pre·fab'ri·cate'
pref'ace
 ·aced ·ac·ing
pref'a·to'ry
pre'fect
pre'fec·ture
pre·fer'
 ·ferred' ·fer'ring
pref'er·a·ble
pref'er·a·bly
pref'er·ence
pref'er·en'tial
pre·fer'ment
pre·fig'u·ra'tion
pre·fig'ur·a·tive
pre·fig'ure
pre'fix
pre'flight'
preg'na·ble
preg'nan·cy
 ·cies
preg'nant
pre·hen'sile
pre'his·tor'ic
pre·judge'
pre·judg'ment or
 ·judge'·
prej'u·dice
 ·diced ·dic·ing
prej'u·di'cial
prel'a·cy
prel'ate
pre·lim'i·nar'y
 ·ies
prel'ude
pre·mar'i·tal
pre'ma·ture'
pre'ma·ture'ly

pre·med'i·cal	pre·serv'a·tive	pre'view	pri'or·ess	proc'u·ra'tor	prog·nos'ti·ca'tor
pre·med'i·tate'	pre·serve'	pre'vi·ous	pri·or'i·ty	pro·cure'	pro'gram
pre·mier'	·served'	pre·vi'sion	·ties	·cured' ·cur'ing	·grammed
(chief)	·serv'ing	pre'war'	pri'o·ry	pro·cure'ment	or ·gramed
pre·mière'	pre·set'	prey	·ries	prod	·gram·ming
·mièred'	pre'-shrunk'	(victim; see	prism	prod'ded	or ·gram·ing
·mièr'ing	pre·side'	pray)	pris·mat'ic	prod'ding	pro'gram·mat'ic
(first showing)	·sid'ed ·sid'ing	pri'a·pism	pris'on	prod'i·gal	pro'gram·mer
prem'ise	pres'i·den·cy	price	pris'on·er	prod'i·gal'i·ty	or ·gram·er
·ised ·is·ing	·cies	priced pric'ing	pris'tine	pro·di'gious	prog'ress
pre'mi·um	pres'i·dent	price'less	pri'va·cy	prod'i·gy	pro·gres'sion
pre'mo·ni'tion	pres'i·dent-e·lect'	prick'le	pri'vate	·gies	pro·gres'sive
pre·mon'i·to'ry	pres·i·den'tial	·led ·ling	pri'va·teer'	(genius; see	pro·gres'siv·ism
pre·na'tal	pre·sid'i·um	prick'li·ness	pri·va'tion	protégé)	pro·hib'it
pre·oc'cu·pan·cy	·i·a or ·i·ums	prick'ly	priv'et	pro·duce'	pro·hi·bi'tion
pre·oc'cu·pa'tion	pre·sig'ni·fy'	·li·er ·li·est	priv'i·lege	·duced'	pro·hib'i·tive
pre·oc'cu·py'	press box	pride	·leged ·leg·ing	·duc'ing	pro·hib'i·to'ry
·pied' ·py'ing	press'ing	prid'ed prid'ing	priv'y	pro·duc'er	proj'ect
pre'or·dain'	press'man	pri'er	·ies	pro·duc'i·ble	pro·jec'tile
pre·pack'age	pres'sure	(one who pries;	prize	prod'uct	pro·jec'tion
pre·paid'	·sured ·sur·ing	see prior)	prized priz'ing	pro·duc'tion	pro·jec'tive
prep'a·ra'tion	pres'sur·ize'	priest'ess	prize'fight'	pro·duc'tive	pro·jec'tor
pre·par'a·tive	·ized' ·iz'ing	priest'hood	prob'a·bil'i·ty	pro·duc'tive·ly	pro·lep'sis
pre·par'a·to'ry	press'work'	priest'ly	prob'a·ble	pro'duc·tiv'i·ty	·ses
pre·pare'	pres'ti·dig'i·ta'tor	·li·er ·li·est	prob'a·bly	prof'a·na'tion	pro'le·tar'i·an
·pared' ·par'ing	pres·tige'	prig'gish	pro'bate	pro·fane'	pro'le·tar'i·at
pre·par'ed·ness	pres·ti'gious	prim	·bat·ed ·bat·ing	·faned' ·fan'ing	pro·lif'er·ate'
pre·pay'	pre'stressed'	prim'mer	pro·ba'tion·ar'y	pro·fane'ly	·at'ed ·at'ing
·paid' ·pay'ing	pre·sum'a·ble	prim'mest	pro·ba'tion·er	pro·fan'i·ty	pro·lif'ic
pre·pay'ment	pre·sume'	pri'ma·cy	pro'ba·tive	·ties	pro·lix'
pre·pon'der·ance	·sumed'	pri'ma don'na	probe	pro·fess'	pro·lix'i·ty
pre·pon'der·ant	·sum'ing	pri'ma fa'ci·e'	probed prob'ing	pro·fessed'	pro·loc'u·tor
pre·pon'der·ate'	pre·sump'tion	pri'mal	prob'i·ty	pro·fess'ed·ly	pro'logue
·at'ed ·at'ing	pre·sump'tive	pri·ma'ri·ly	prob'lem	pro·fes'sion	pro·long'
prep'o·si'tion	pre·sump'tu·ous	pri'ma·ry	prob'lem·at'ic	pro·fes'sion·al·ly	pro·lon'gate
pre·pos·sess'	pre'sup·pose'	·ries	pro·bos'cis	pro·fes'sor	·gat·ed ·gat·ing
pre'pos·sess'ing	pre'sup·po·si'tion	pri'mate	·cis·es or ·ci·des'	pro·fes'so·ri·al	pro'lon·ga'tion
pre·pos'ter·ous	pre·tend'	prime	pro·ce'dur·al	pro·fes'so·ri·ate	prom'e·nade'
pre're·cord'	pre·tend'er	primed prim'ing	pro·ce'dure	prof'fer	·nad'ed
pre·req'ui·site	pre·tense'	prim'er	pro·ceed'	pro·fi'cien·cy	·nad'ing
(requirement; see	pre·ten'sion	pri·me'val	(go on; see	pro·fi'cient	prom'i·nence
perquisite)	pre·ten'tious	prim'i·tive	precede)	pro'file	prom'i·nent
pre·rog'a·tive	pre'ter·nat'u·ral	prim'i·tive·ly	pro'ceeds	·filed ·fil·ing	prom'is·cu'i·ty
pre·sage'	pre'text	prim'i·tiv·ism	proc'ess	prof'it	·ties
·saged' ·sag'ing	pre'tri'al	pri'mo·gen'i·tor	pro·ces'sion	(gain; see	pro·mis'cu·ous
pres'by·ter	pret'ti·fy'	pri'mo·gen'i·ture	(parade; see	prophet)	prom'ise
Pres'by·te'ri·an	·fied' ·fy'ing	pri·mor'di·al	precession)	prof'it·a·ble	·ised ·is·ing
pre'school'	pret'ti·ly	primp	pro·ces'sion·al	prof'it·a·bly	prom'is·so'ry
pre'sci·ence	pret'ti·ness	prim'rose'	proc'es·sor or	prof'i·teer'	prom'on·to'ry
pre'sci·ent	pret'ty	prince'ling	proc'ess·er	prof'li·ga·cy	·ries
pre·scribe'	·ti·er ·ti·est	prince'ly	pro·claim'	prof'li·gate	pro·mot'a·ble
·scribed'	·tied ·ty·ing	·li·er ·li·est	proc'la·ma'tion	pro·found'	pro·mote'
·scrib'ing	pret'zel	prin'cess	pro·cliv'i·ty	pro·fun'di·ty	·mot'ed ·mot'ing
(order; see	pre·vail'	prin'ci·pal	·ties	·ties	pro·mot'er
proscribe)	pre·vail'ing	(chief; see	pro·cras'ti·nate'	pro·fuse'	pro·mo'tion
pre·scrip'tion	prev'a·lence	principle)	·nat'ed ·nat'ing	pro·fuse'ly	prompt'er
pre·scrip'tive	prev'a·lent	prin'ci·pal'i·ty	pro·cras'ti·na'tion	pro·fu'sion	promp'ti·tude'
pres'ence	pre·var'i·cate'	·ties	pro·cras'ti·na'tor	pro·gen'i·tor	prompt'ly
pres'ent	·cat'ed ·cat'ing	prin'ci·pal·ly	pro'cre·ant	prog'e·ny	prom'ul·gate'
pre·sent'a·ble	pre·var'i·ca'tion	prin'ci·ple	pro'cre·ate'	·nies	·gat'ed ·gat'ing
pre'sen·ta'tion	pre·var'i·ca'tor	(basic rule; see	·at'ed ·at'ing	prog'na·thous	prom'ul·ga'tion
pres'ent-day'	pre·ven'ient	principal)	pro'cre·a'tor	prog·no'sis	prom'ul·ga'tor
pre·sent'i·ment	pre·vent'	prin'ci·pled	proc·tol'o·gy	·ses	prone
(premonition)	pre·vent'a·ble or	print'a·ble	proc'tor	prog·nos'tic	pronged
pre·sent'ment	·i·ble	print'out'	proc'to·scope'	prog·nos'ti·cate'	pro'noun
(presentation)	pre·ven'tion	pri'or	pro·cum'bent	·cat'ed ·cat'ing	pro·nounce'
pre·serv'a·ble	pre·ven'tive or	(previous; see	pro·cur'a·ble	prog·nos'ti·	·nounced'
pres'er·va'tion	·vent'a·tive	prier)		ca'tion	·nounc'ing

pro·nounce'a·ble	pro·sa'ic	pro·thon'o·tar'y	pru'dent·ly	pub'lic	punc'tu·al·ly
pro·nounce'ment	pro·sa'i·cal·ly	·ies	prud'er·y	pub'li·ca'tion	punc'tu·ate'
pro·nun'ci·a'tion	pro·sce'ni·um	pro'to·col'	prud'ish	pub'li·cist	·at'ed ·at'ing
proof'read'	·ni·ums or ·ni·a	pro'ton	prune	pub·lic'i·ty	punc'tu·a'tion
·read' ·read'ing	pro·sciut'to	pro'to·plasm	pruned prun'ing	pub'li·cize'	punc'tu·a'tor
prop'a·gan'da	pro·scribe'	pro'to·typ'al	pru'ri·ence	·cized' ·ciz'ing	punc'tur·a·ble
prop'a·gan'dize	·scribed'	pro'to·type'	pru'ri·ent	pub'lic·ly	punc'ture
·dized ·diz·ing	·scrib'ing	pro'to·zo'an	pry	pub'lish	·tured ·tur·ing
prop'a·gate'	(forbid; see	pro·tract'	pries, pried pry'ing	puck'er	pun'dit
·gat'ed ·gat'ing	prescribe)	pro·tract'ed·ly	psalm'book'	pud'ding	pun'gen·cy
prop'a·ga'tion	pro·scrip'tion	pro·tract'i·ble	psal'mo·dy	pud'dle	pun'gent
prop'a·ga'tor	prose	pro·trac'tile	psal'ter·y	·dled ·dling	pu'ni·ness
pro'pane	pros'e·cut'a·ble	pro·trac'tion	·ies	pudg'i·ness	pun'ish
pro·pel'	pros'e·cute'	pro·trac'tor	pse·phol'o·gy	pudg'y	pun'ish·a·ble
·pelled' ·pel'ling	·cut'ed ·cut'ing	pro·trude'	pseu'do	·i·er ·i·est	pun'ish·ment
pro·pel'lant or	(legal term;	·trud'ed	pseu'do·nym'	pueb'lo	pu'ni·tive
·lent	see persecute)	·trud'ing	pseu'do·nym'i·ty	·los	pun'ster
pro·pel'ler	pros'e·cu'tion	pro·tru'sile	pseu·don'y·mous	pu'er·ile	pu'ny
pro·pen'si·ty	pros'e·cu'tor	pro·tru'sion	psit'ta·co'sis	Puer'to Ri'co	·ni·er ·ni·est
·ties	pros'e·lyte'	pro·tru'sive	pso·ri'a·sis	puff'i·ness	pu'pil
prop'er·ly	·lyt'ed ·lyt'ing	pro·tu'ber·ance	psy'che	puff'y	pup'pet
prop'er·tied	pros'e·lyt·ism	pro·tu'ber·ant	psy'che·de'li·a	·i·er ·i·est	pup'pet·eer'
prop'er·ty	pros'e·lyt·ize'	proud'ly	psy'che·del'ic	pu'gil·ism	pup'py
·ties	·ized' ·iz'ing	prov'a·bil'i·ty	psy'che·del'i·cal·	pug·na'cious	·pies
proph'e·cy n.	pros'o·dy	prov'a·ble	ly	pug·nac'i·ty	pur'chas·a·ble
·cies	·dies	prov'a·bly	psy·chi'a·trist	pul'chri·tude'	pur'chase
proph'e·sy' v.	pros'pect	prove	psy·chi'a·try	pul'chri·tu'di·	·chased
·sied' ·sy'ing	pro·spec'tive	proved, proved	psy'chic	nous	·chas·ing
proph'et	(expected; see	or prov'en,	psy'chi·cal·ly	pull	pure'bred'
(predictor; see	perspective)	prov'ing	psy'cho·a·	pul'let	pu·rée'
profit)	pros'pec·tor	prov'en·der	nal'y·sis	pul'ley	·réed' ·rē'ing
pro·phet'ic	pro·spec'tus	prov'erb	psy'cho·an'a·lyst	·leys	pure'ly
pro·phet'i·cal·ly	pros'per	pro·ver'bi·al	psy·cho·an'a·	pull'out'	pur·ga'tion
pro'phy·lac'tic	pros·per'i·ty	pro·ver'bi·al·ly	lyt'ic	pull'o·ver	pur'ga·tive
pro'phy·lax'is	pros'per·ous	pro·vide'	psy'cho·an'a·	pul'mo·nar'y	pur'ga·to'ry
·lax'es	pros'tate	·vid'ed ·vid'ing	lyt'i·cal·ly	pul'mo'tor	purge
pro·pin'qui·ty	(gland; see	prov'i·dence	psy'cho·an'a·lyze'	pul'pit	purged purg'ing
pro·pi'ti·ate'	prostrate)	prov'i·dent	·lyzed' ·lyz'ing	pulp'wood'	pu'ri·fi·ca'tion
·at'ed ·at'ing	pros'the·sis	prov'i·den'tial	psy'cho·dra'ma	pulp'y	pu'ri·fi'er
pro·pi'ti·a'tion	·the·ses	pro·vid'er	psy'cho·dy·nam'·	·i·er ·i·est	pu'ri·fy'
pro·pi'ti·a'tor	pros·thet'ic	prov'ince	ics	pul'sate	·fied' ·fy'ing
pro·pi'ti·a·to'ry	pros'ti·tute'	pro·vin'cial	psy'cho·gen'ic	·sat·ed ·sat·ing	pur'ism
pro·pi'tious	·tut'ed ·tut'ing	pro·vin'cial·ism	psy'cho·log'i·cal	pul·sa'tion	pu'ri·tan
pro·po'nent	pros'ti·tu'tion	pro·vin'cial·ly	psy·chol'o·gist	pulse	pu'ri·tan'i·cal
pro·por'tion	pros'trate	pro·vi'sion	psy·chol'o·gize'	pulsed puls'ing	pu'ri·ty
pro·por'tion·al	·trat·ed ·trat·ing	pro·vi'sion·al	·gized' ·giz'ing	pul'ver·iz'a·ble	purl
pro·por'tion·al·ly	(prone; see	pro·vi'sion·al·ly	psy·chol'o·gy	pul'ver·i·za'tion	(stitch; see pearl)
pro·por'tion·ate	prostate)	pro·vi'so	psy·chom'e·try	pul'ver·ize'	pur·loin'
pro·por'tion·ate·	pros·tra'tion	·sos or ·soes	psy'cho·neu·ro'sis	·ized' ·iz'ing	pu'ro·my'cin
ly	pros'y	pro·vi'so·ry	·ses	pum'ice	pur'ple
pro·pos'al	·i·er ·i·est	prov'o·ca'tion	psy'cho·neu·rot'ic	(rock; see pomace)	pur'plish
pro·pose'	pro·tag'o·nist	pro·voc'a·tive	psy'cho·path'ic	pum'mel	pur'port'
·posed' ·pos'ing	pro·tect'	pro·voc'a·tive·ly	psy'cho·path·ol'·	·meled or	pur'pose
prop'o·si'tion	pro·tec'tion	pro·voke'	o·gy	·melled	·posed ·pos·ing
pro·pound'	pro·tec'tive	·voked' ·vok'ing	psy'cho·sex'u·al	·mel·ing or	pur'pose·ful
pro·pri'e·tar'y	pro·tec'tor	pro'vo·lo'ne	psy·cho'sis	·mel·ling	pur'pose·ful·ly
·ies	pro·tec'tor·ate	pro'vost	·ses	pump'er·nick'el	pur'pose·less
pro·pri'e·tor	pro·té·gé'	prow'ess	psy'cho·so·mat'ic	pump'kin	pur'pose·ly
pro·pri'e·tress	(one helped by	prowl'er	psy'cho·ther'a·py	pun	purr
pro·pri'e·ty	another; see	prox'i·mal	psy·chot'ic	punned	purs'er
·ties	prodigy)	prox'i·mate	pter'o·dac'tyl	pun'ning	pur·su'ance
pro·pul'sion	pro'tein	prox·im'i·ty	pto'maine	punch card	pur·sue'
pro·pul'sive	pro·tem'po·re'	prox'i·mo'	pu'ber·ty	pun'cheon	·sued' ·su'ing
pro·ra'ta	pro·test'	prox'y	pu·bes'cence	punc·til'i·o'	pur·suit'
pro·rate'	Prot'es·tant	·ies	pu'bic	·os'	pu'ru·lence
·rat'ed ·rat'ing	prot'es·ta'tion	pru'dence		punc·til'i·ous	pu'ru·lent
pro·ro·ga'tion	pro·test'er or	pru'dent		punc'tu·al	pur·vey'
	·tes'tor	pru·den'tial		punc'tu·al'i·ty	pur·vey'ance

pur·vey'or
pur'view
push'cart'
push'o·ver
push'-up'
pu·sil·lan'i·mous
pus'sy
· si·er ·si·est
(with pus)
puss'y
· ies
(cat)
pus'tu·lant
pus'tule
put
put put'ting
(place; see putt)
pu'ta·tive
pu'tre·fac'tion
pu'tre·fy'
· fied' ·fy'ing
pu·tres'cence
pu·tres'cent
pu'trid
putt
(golf term; see
put)
put·tee'
putt'er
(golf club)
put'ter
(busy oneself)
put'ty
· tied ·ty·ing
puz'zle
· zled ·zling
puz'zler
pyg'my
· mies
py'lon
py'or·rhe'a
pyr'a·mid
py·ram'i·dal
pyre
py·ret'ic
Py'rex
py·rog'ra·phy
py'ro·ma'ni·a
py'ro·ma'ni·ac'
py'ro·tech'nics
py·rox'y·lin
Py·thag'o·ras
py'thon

Q

quack'er·y
· ies
quad'ran·gle
quad·ran'gu·lar
quad'rant
quad'rate
· rat·ed ·rat·ing
quad·rat'ic
quad·ren'ni·al
quad'ri·lat'er·al

qua·drille'
quad·ril'lion
quad'ri·ple'gi·a
quad'ru·ped'
quad·ru'ple
· pled ·pling
quad·ru'plet
quad·ru'pli·cate'
· cat'ed ·cat'ing
quaff
quag'mire'
quail
quaint'ly
quake
quaked
quak'ing
qual'i·fi·ca'tion
qual'i·fi'er
qual'i·fy'
· fied' ·fy'ing
qual'i·ta'tive
qual'i·ty
· ties
qualm
quan'da·ry
· ries
quan'ti·ta'tive
quan'ti·ty
· ties
quan'tum
· ta
quar·an·tin'a·ble
quar'an·tine'
· tined' ·tin'ing
quar'rel
· reled or ·relled
· rel·ing or
· rel·ling
quar'rel·some
quar'ry
· ries
· ried ·ry·ing
quart
quar'ter
quar'ter·back'
quar'ter-deck'
quar'ter·ly
· lies
quar'ter·mas·ter
quar'ter·saw'
· sawed', ·sawed'
or ·sawn',
· saw'ing
quar·tet' or ·tette'
quar'tile
quar'to
· tos
quartz
qua'sar
quash
qua'si
qua'ter·na'ry
· ries
quat'rain
qua'ver
quay
(wharf; see key)
quea'si·ness

quea'sy
· si·er ·si·est
queen'li·ness
queen'ly
· li·er ·li·est
queen'-size'
queer
quell
quench'a·ble
quer'u·lous
que'ry
· ries
· ried ·ry·ing
quest
ques'tion
ques'tion·a·ble
ques·tion·naire'
queue
queued
queu'ing
(line; see cue)
quib'ble
· bled ·bling
quick'en
quick'-freeze'
-froze' -froz'en
-freez'ing
quick'sand'
quick'sil'ver
quick'-tem'pered
quick'-wit'ted
quid'nunc'
qui·es'cence
qui·es'cent
qui'et
(still; see quite)
qui'e·tude'
qui·e'tus
quill
quilt'ing
quince
qui·nel'la
quin·quen'ni·al
quin·tes'sence
quin·tet'
or ·tette'
quin·til'lion
quin·tu'ple
· pled ·pling
quin·tu'plet
quin·tu'pli·cate'
· cat'ed ·cat'ing
quip
quipped
quip'ping
quire
(of paper; see
choir)
quirk
quis'ling
quit
quit or quit'ted
quit'ting
quit'claim'
quite
(fully; see quiet)
quit'tance
quit'ter

quiv'er
quix·ot'ic
quiz
quiz'zes
quizzed
quiz'zing
quiz'zi·cal
quoin
(wedge; corner;
see coign, coin)
quoit
quon'dam
Quon'set hut
quo'rum
quo'ta
quot'a·ble
quo·ta'tion
quote
quot'ed quot'ing
quo'tient

R

rab'bet
(cut; see rabbit)
rab'bi
· bis or ·bies
rab·bin'i·cal
rab'bit
(hare; see rabbet)
rab'ble
· bled ·bling
rab'id
ra'bies
rac·coon'
race
raced rac'ing
race'horse'
rac'er
race track
race'way'
ra'cial
ra'cial·ly
rac'i·ly
rac'i·ness
rac'ism
rack'et
rack'et·eer'
rack'-rent'
rac'on·teur'
rac'y
· i·er ·i·est
ra'dar
ra'di·al
ra'di·ance
ra'di·ant
ra'di·ate'
· at'ed ·at'ing
ra'di·a'tion
ra'di·a'tor
rad'i·cal
rad'i·cal·ism
rad'i·cal·ly
ra'di·o'
· os', ·oed' ·o'ing
ra'di·o·ac'tive

ra'di·o·gram'
ra'di·o·graph'
ra·di·og'ra·phy
ra'di·o·i'so·tope'
ra'di·ol'o·gist
ra'di·ol'o·gy
ra'di·o·phone'
ra'di·o·pho'no·
graph'
ra'di·o·pho'to
· tos
ra'di·os'co·py
ra'di·o·sonde'
ra'di·o·tel'e·
phone'
ra'di·o·ther'a·py
ra'di·o·ther'my
rad'ish
ra'di·um
ra'di·us
· di·i' or ·di·us·es
ra'dix
ra'di·ces' or
ra'dix·es
ra'don
raf'fi·a
raf'fle
· fled ·fling
raft'er
rag'a·muf'fin
rage
raged rag'ing
rag'ged
rag'lan
ra·gout'
rag'pick'er
rag'time'
rag'weed'
raid'er
rail'ing
rail'ler·y
· ies
rail'road'
rail'-split'ter
rail'way'
rai'ment
rain
(water; see
reign, rein)
rain'bow'
rain check
rain'coat'
rain'drop'
rain'fall'
rain'i·ness
rain'proof'
rain'storm'
rain'y
· i·er ·i·est
raise
raised rais'ing
(lift; see raze)
rai'sin
rai'son d'être'
ra'jah or ·ja
rake
raked rak'ing
rak'ish

ral'li·er
ral'ly
· lies
· lied ·ly·ing
ram
rammed
ram'ming
ram'ble
· bled ·bling
ram'bler
ram·bunc'tious
ram'e·kin or ·quin
ram'i·fi·ca'tion
ram'i·fy'
· fied' ·fy'ing
ram'jet'
ramp
ram·page'
· paged' ·pag'ing
ram·pa'geous
ramp'ant
ram'part
ram'rod'
ram'shack'le
ranch'er
ran'cid
ran'cor
ran'cor·ous
ran'dom
ran'dom·ize'
· ized' ·iz'ing
range
ranged
rang'ing
rang'i·ness
rang'y
· i·er ·i·est
ran'kle
· kled ·kling
ran'sack
ran'som
rap
rapped rap'ping
(strike; see wrap)
ra·pa'cious
ra·pac'i·ty
rape
raped rap'ing
rap'id-fire'
ra·pid'i·ty
rap'id·ly
ra'pi·er
rap'ine
rap'ist
rap·port'
rap·proche'ment
rap·scal'lion
rap·to'ri·al
rap'ture
rap'tur·ous
rare
rar'er rar'est
rare'bit
rar'e·fy'
· fied' ·fy'ing
rare'ly
rar'i·ty
· ties

ras'cal
ras·cal'i·ty
ras'cal·ly
rash'er
rash'ness
rasp'ber'ry
·ries
rasp'i·ness
rasp'ing
rasp'y
·i·er ·i·est
rat
rat'ted rat'ting
rat'a·ble or rate'·
ratch'et
rate
rat'ed rat'ing
rath'er
raths'kel·ler
rat'i·fi·ca'tion
rat'i·fi'er
rat'i·fy'
·fied' ·fy'ing
ra'tio
·tios
ra·ti·o'ci·nate'
·nat'ed ·nat'ing
ra'tion·al
ra'tion·ale'
ra'tion·al·ism
ra'tion·al'i·ty
ra'tion·al·i·za'tion
ra'tion·al·ize'
·ized' ·iz'ing
ra'tion·al·ly
rat'line or ·lin
rat'tail'
rat·tan' or ra·tan'
rat'tle
·tled ·tling
rat'tle·brained'
rat'tler
rat'tle·snake'
rat'tle·trap'
rat'tly
rau'cous
rav'age
·aged ·ag·ing
rave
raved rav'ing
rav'el
·eled or ·elled
·el·ing or ·el·ling
ra'ven
rav'e·nous
ra·vine'
ra'vi·o'li
rav'ish
raw'boned'
raw'hide'
ray'on
raze
razed raz'ing
(demolish; see raise)
ra'zor
ra'zor·back'
reach

re·act'
(respond)
re'-act'
(act again)
re·ac'tion
re·ac'tion·ar'y
·ies
re·ac'ti·vate'
·vat'ed ·vat'ing
re·ac'tive·ly
re·ac'tor
read
read read'ing
read·a·bil'i·ty
read'a·ble
read'i·ly
read'i·ness
re'ad·just'
read'out'
read'y
·i·er ·i·est
·ied ·y·ing
read'y-made'
re·a'gent
re'al
(actual; see reel)
re'al·ism
re'al·ist
re'al·is'tic
re'al·is'ti·cal·ly
re·al'i·ty
·ties
(real thing; see realty)
re'al·iz'a·ble
re'al·i·za'tion
re'al·ize'
·ized' ·iz'ing
re'al-life'
re'al·ly
realm
Re'al·tor
re'al·ty
(real estate; see reality)
ream'er
re·an'i·mate'
·mat'ed ·mat'ing
reap'er
re'ap·por'tion
rear guard
re·ar'ma·ment
re·ar·range'
re·ar·range'ment
rear'ward
rea'son·a·ble
rea'son·a·bly
re·as·sur'ance
re·as·sure'
·sured' ·sur'ing
re'bate
·bat·ed ·bat·ing
reb'el n.
re·bel' v.
·belled' ·bel'ling
re·bel'lion
re·bel'lious
re·birth'

re·bound'
re·buff'
(blunt refusal)
re'-buff'
(buff again)
re·buke'
·buked'
·buk'ing
re'bus
re·but'
·but'ted
·but'ting
re·but'tal
re·cal'ci·trant
re·call'
re·cant'
re·cap'
·capped'
·cap'ping
re·ca·pit'u·late'
·lat'ed ·lat'ing
re·ca·pit'u·la'tion
re·cap'pa·ble
re·cap'ture
re·cede'
·ced'ed ·ced'ing
re·ceipt'
re·ceiv'a·ble
re·ceive'
·ceived'
·ceiv'ing
re·ceiv'er·ship'
re·cen'sion
re'cent
re·cep'ta·cle
re·cep'tion
re·cep'tive
re·cep'tor
re'cess
re·ces'sion
re·ces'sive
re·charge'a·ble
re·cher'ché
re·cid'i·vism
rec'i·pe
re·cip'i·ent
re·cip'ro·cal
re·cip'ro·cal·ly
re·cip'ro·cate'
·cat'ed ·cat'ing
re·cip'ro·ca'tion
re·cip'ro·ca'tor
rec'i·proc'i·ty
re·ci'sion
re·cit'al
rec'i·ta'tion
rec'i·ta·tive'
re·cite'
·cit'ed ·cit'ing
reck'less
reck'on·ing
re·claim'
(restore for use)
re'-claim'
(claim back)
rec'la·ma'tion
re·cline'
·clined' ·clin'ing

rec'luse
re·clu'sion
rec'og·ni'tion
rec'og·niz'a·ble
re·cog'ni·zance
rec'og·nize'
·nized' ·niz'ing
re·coil'
(draw back)
re'-coil'
(coil again)
re·coil'less
rec'ol·lect'
(remember)
re'-col·lect'
(collect again)
rec'ol·lec'tion
rec'om·mend'
rec'om·men·da'tion
re'com·mit'
rec'om·pense'
·pensed'
·pens'ing
rec'on·cil'a·ble
rec'on·cile'
·ciled' ·cil'ing
rec'on·cil'i·a'tion
rec'on·dite'
re·con·di'tion
re·con'nais·sance
re·con·struct'
rec'on·noi'ter
re·con·sid'er
re·con·ver'sion
re·con·vert'
re·cord' v.
rec'ord n.
re·cord'er
re·count'
(narrate)
re'-count'
(count again)
re·coup'
re'course
re·cov'er
(get back)
re'-cov'er
(cover again)
re·cov'er·y
·ies
rec're·ant
rec're·ate'
·at'ed ·at'ing
(refresh)
re'-cre·ate'
·at'ed ·at'ing
(create anew)
rec're·a'tion
re'-cre·a'tion
re·crim'i·nate'
·nat'ed ·nat'ing
re·crim'i·na'tion
re·cruit'
rec'tal
rec'tan'gle
rec·tan'gu·lar
rec'ti·fi'a·ble

rec'ti·fi·ca'tion
rec'ti·fi'er
·fied' ·fy'ing
rec'ti·lin'e·ar
rec'ti·tude'
rec'tor
rec'to·ry
·ries
rec'tum
·tums or ·ta
re·cum'ben·cy
re·cum'bent
re·cu'per·ate'
·at'ed ·at'ing
re·cu'per·a'tion
re·cur'
·curred'
·cur'ring
re·cur'rence
re·cur'rent
rec'u·sant
re·cy'cle
re·dact'
re·dac'tion
re·dac'tor
red'bait'
red'-blood'ed
red'den
re·deem'a·ble
re·demp'tion
re·de·ploy'
re·de·vel'op·ment
red'-hand'ed
red'head'
red'-hot'
re·di·rect'
red'-let'ter
re·do'
·did' ·done'
·do'ing
red'o·lence
red'o·lent
re·dou'ble
re·doubt'
re·doubt'a·ble
re·dound'
red'out'
re'dress'
(remedy)
re'-dress'
(dress again)
re·duce'
·duced' ·duc'ing
re·duc'i·ble
re·duc'tion
re·dun'dan·cy
·cies
re·dun'dant
re·du'pli·cate'
re·du'pli·ca'tion
re·ech'o
reed'i·ness
re·ed'it
re·ed'u·cate'
reed'y
·i·er ·i·est

reek
(emit a smell; see wreak)
reel
(whirl; dance; spool; see real)
re·e·lect'
re'e·lec'tion
re·em·bark'
re·em·bod'y
re·em·brace'
re·e·merge'
re·em'pha·sis
re·em'pha·size'
re·em·ploy'
re·en·act'
re·en·dow'
re·en·gage'
re·en·list'
re·en'ter
re·en'try
re·e·quip'
re·es·tab'lish
re·e·val'u·ate'
re·ex·am'ine
re·ex·change'
re·ex·hib'it
re·ex·pe'ri·ence
re·ex·plain'
re·ex·port'
re·fec'tion
re·fer'
·ferred'
·fer'ring
ref'er·a·ble or ·i·ble
ref'er·ee'
·eed' ·ee'ing
ref'er·ence
ref'er·en'dum
·dums or ·da
ref'er·ent
re·fer'ral
re·fill'a·ble
re·fine'
·fined' ·fin'ing
re·fine'ment
re·fin'er·y
·ies
re·fit'
re·fla'tion
re·flect'
re·flec'tion
re·flec'tive
re·flec'tor
re'flex
re·flex'ive
re·for·est·a'tion
re·form'
(make better)
re'-form'
(form again)
ref'or·ma'tion
re·form'a·to'ry
·ries
re·fract'
re·frac'tion
re·frac'to·ry

re·frain'
re·fran'gi·ble
re·fresh'
re·fresh'ment
re·frig'er·ant
re·frig'er·ate'
· at'ed · at'ing
re·frig'er·a'tion
re·frig'er·a'tor
ref'uge
ref'u·gee'
re·ful'gent
re·fund'
re·fur'bish
re·fus'al
re·fuse' v.
· fused' · fus'ing
ref'use n.
re·fut'a·ble
ref'u·ta'tion
re·fute'
· fut'ed · fut'ing
re·gain'
re'gal adj.
re·gale' v.
· galed' · gal'ing
re·ga'li·a
re·gal'i·ty
· ties
re·gard'ing
re·gard'less
re·gat'ta
re'gen·cy
· cies
re·gen'er·ate'
· at'ed · at'ing
re·gen'er·a'tion
re·gen'er·a'tive
re·gen'er·a'tor
re'gent
reg'i·cide'
re·gime' or ré·
reg'i·men
reg'i·ment
reg'i·men'tal
reg'i·men·ta'tion
re'gion·al
reg'is·ter
reg'is·trant
reg'is·trar'
reg'is·tra'tion
reg'is·try
· tries
re'gress
re·gres'sion
re·gres'sive
re·gret'
· gret'ted
· gret'ting
re·gret'ful
re·gret'ful·ly
re·gret'ta·ble
re·gret'ta·bly
reg'u·lar
reg'u·lar'i·ty
· ties
reg'u·late'
· lat'ed · lat'ing

reg'u·la'tion
reg'u·la'tor
re·gur'gi·tate'
· tat'ed · tat'ing
re·gur'gi·ta'tion
re'ha·bil'i·tate'
· tat'ed · tat'ing
re'ha·bil'i·ta'tion
re·hears'al
re·hearse'
· hearsed'
· hears'ing
reign
(rule; see rain, rein)
re'im·burs'a·ble
re'im·burse'
· bursed'
· burs'ing
rein
(control; see rain, reign)
re'in·car'nate
· nat·ed · nat·ing
re'in·car·na'tion
re'in·cur'
rein'deer
re'in·force'
· forced'
· forc'ing
re'in·force'ment
re'in·state'
· stat'ed
· stat'ing
re·it'er·ate'
· at'ed · at'ing
re·ject'
re·jec'tion
re·joice'
· joiced' · joic'ing
re·join'der
re·ju've·nate'
· nat'ed · nat'ing
re·lapse'
· lapsed'
· laps'ing
re·lat'a·ble
re·late'
· lat'ed · lat'ing
re·la'tion·ship'
rel'a·tive
rel'a·tive·ly
rel'a·tiv'i·ty
re·lax'
re·lax'ant
re'lax·a'tion
re'lay
· layed · lay·ing
(send by relay)
re'-lay'
-laid' -lay'ing
(lay again)
re·lease'
· leased'
· leas'ing
(set free)
re'-lease'
(lease again)

rel'e·gate'
· gat'ed · gat'ing
rel'e·ga'tion
re·lent'less
rel'e·vance
rel'e·vant
re·li'a·bil'i·ty
re·li'a·ble
re·li'a·bly
re·li'ance
re·li'ant
rel'ic
re·lief'
re·liev'a·ble
re·lieve'
· lieved' · liev'ing
re·liev'er
re·li'gion
re·li'gious
re·lin'quish
rel'i·quar'y
· ies
rel'ish
re·luc'tance
re·luc'tant
re·ly'
· lied' · ly'ing
re·main'der
re·make'
· made' · mak'ing
re·mand'
re·mark'a·ble
re·mark'a·bly
re·me'di·a·ble
re·me'di·al
rem'e·dy
· dies
· died · dy·ing
re·mem'ber
re·mem'brance
re·mind'er
rem'i·nisce'
· nisced'
· nisc'ing
rem'i·nis'cence
rem'i·nis'cent
rem'i·nis'cer
re·miss'
re·mis'si·ble
re·mis'sion
re·mit'
· mit'ted
· mit'ting
re·mit'ta·ble
re·mit'tance
re·mit'tent
rem'nant
re·mod'el
re·mon'strance
re·mon'strate
· strat·ed
· strat·ing
re'mon·stra'tion
re·mon'stra·tor
re·morse'ful
re·morse'less
re·mote'
re·mote'ly

re·mov'a·ble
re·mov'al
re·move'
· moved'
· mov'ing
re·mu'ner·ate'
· at'ed · at'ing
re·mu'ner·a'tion
re·mu'ner·a'tive
re·mu'ner·a'tor
ren'ais·sance'
re·nas'cent
rend
rent rend'ing
ren'der
ren'dez·vous'
· vous'
· voused'
· vous'ing
ren·di'tion
ren'e·gade'
re·nege'
· neged' · neg'ing
re·new'al
ren'net
re·nounce'
· nounced'
· nounc'ing
ren'o·vate'
· vat'ed · vat'ing
ren'o·va'tion
re·nown'
re·nowned'
rent'al
rent'-free'
re·nun'ci·a'tion
re·or'der
re'or·gan·i·za'tion
re·or'gan·ize'
· ized' · iz'ing
re·pair'man
rep'a·ra·ble
rep'a·ra'tion
rep'ar·tee'
re·past'
re·pa'tri·ate'
· at'ed · at'ing
re·pa'tri·a'tion
re·pay'
· paid' · pay'ing
(pay back)
re'-pay'
-paid' -pay'ing
(pay again)
re·peal'
re·peat'
re·pel'
· pelled' · pel'ling
re·pel'lent
re·pent'
re·pent'ance
re·pent'ant
re'per·cus'sion
rep'er·toire'
rep'er·to'ry
· ries
rep'e·ti'tion
(a repeating)

re'-pe·ti'tion
(petition again)
rep'e·ti'tious
re·pet'i·tive
re·phrase'
re·place'
re·place'a·ble
re·place'ment
re·plen'ish
re·plete'
re·ple'tion
re·plev'in
rep'li·ca
re·ply'
· plies'
· plied' · ply'ing
re·port'ed·ly
re·port'er
re·pose'
· posed' · pos'ing
(rest)
re'-pose'
(pose again)
re·pos'i·to'ry
· ries
re·pos·sess'
re'pos·ses'sion
rep're·hend'
rep're·hen'si·ble
rep're·hen'sion
rep're·sent'
(stand for)
re'-pre·sent'
(present again)
rep're·sen·ta'tion
rep're·sent'a·tive
re·press'
(restrain)
re'-press'
(press again)
re·pressed'
re·press'i·ble
re·pres'sion
re·prieve'
· prieved'
· priev'ing
rep'ri·mand'
re·print'
re·pris'al
re·proach'
re·proach'ful
rep'ro·bate'
· bat'ed · bat'ing
re·proc'essed
re'pro·duce'
re'pro·duc'i·ble
re'pro·duc'tion
re'pro·duc'tive
re·proof'
re·prove'
· proved'
· prov'ing
(rebuke)
re'-prove'
(prove again)
rep'tile
rep·til'i·an
re·pub'lic

re·pub'li·can
re·pu'di·ate'
· at'ed · at'ing
re·pu'di·a'tion
re·pug'nance
re·pug'nant
re·pulse'
· pulsed'
· puls'ing
re·pul'sion
re·pul'sive
rep'u·ta·bil'i·ty
rep'u·ta·ble
rep'u·ta·bly
rep'u·ta'tion
re·pute'
· put'ed · put'ing
re·quest'
Re'qui·em
re·quire'
· quired'
· quir'ing
re·quire'ment
req'ui·site
req'ui·si'tion
re·quite'
· quit'ed
· quit'ing
rere'dos
re·route'
re·run'
· ran' · run'
· run'ning
re·sal'a·ble
re'sale'
re·scind'
re·scind'a·ble
re·scis'sion
res'cu·a·ble
res'cue
· cued · cu·ing
res'cu·er
re·search'
re·sem'blance
re·sem'ble
· bled · bling
re·sent'
(feel a hurt)
re'-sent'
(sent again)
re·sent'ful
re·sent'ment
res'er·va'tion
re·serve'
· served'
· serv'ing
(set aside)
re'-serve'
(serve again)
re·serv'ed·ly
re·serv'ist
res'er·voir'
re·set'
· set' · set'ting
re·ship'ment
re·side'
· sid'ed · sid'ing

res'i·dence
res'i·den·cy
·cies
res'i·dent
res'i·den'tial
re·sid'u·al
re·sid'u·ar'y
res'i·due'
re·sign'
  (give up)
re'-sign'
  (sign again)
res'ig·na'tion
re·sil'i·ence
re·sil'i·ent
res'in
res'in·ous
re·sist'
re·sist'ance
re·sist'ant
re·sist'er
  (one who resists)
re·sist'i·ble
re·sist'or
  (electrical device)
re'sole'
  ·soled' ·sol'ing
res'o·lute'
res'o·lu'tion
re·solv'a·ble
re·solve'
  ·solved'
  ·solv'ing
  (break into parts)
re'-solve'
  (solve again)
re·sol'vent
res'o·nance
res'o·nant
res'o·na'tor
re·sort'
  (go for help)
re'-sort'
  (sort again)
re·sound'
  (echo)
re'-sound'
  (sound again)
re'source
re·source'ful
re·spect'a·bil'i·ty
re·spect'a·ble
re·spect'ful
re·spect'ful·ly
re·spec'tive
re·spec'tive·ly
res'pi·ra'tion
res'pi·ra'tor
res'pi·ra·to'ry
re·spire'
  ·spired'
  ·spir'ing
res'pite
  ·pit·ed ·pit·ing
re·splend'ence
re·splend'ent
re·spond'
re·spond'ent

re·sponse'
re·spon'si·bil'i·ty
  ·ties
re·spon'si·ble
re·spon'si·bly
re·spon'sive
re·state'
  ·stat'ed ·stat'ing
res'tau·rant
res'tau·ra·teur'
rest'ful
res'ti·tu'tion
res'tive
rest'less
res'to·ra'tion
re·stor'a·tive
re·store'
  ·stored' ·stor'ing
re·strain'
  (hold back)
re'-strain'
  (strain again)
re·straint'
re·strict'
re·stric'tion
re·stric'tive
rest'room'
re·struc'ture
re·sult'
re·sult'ant
re·sum'a·ble
re·sume' v.
  ·sumed'
  ·sum'ing
ré'su·mé' n.
re·sump'tion
re·sur'face
re·sur'gence
re·sur'gent
res'ur·rect'
res'ur·rec'tion
re·sus'ci·tate'
  ·tat'ed ·tat'ing
re·sus'ci·ta'tion
re·sus'ci·ta'tor
re'tail
re·tain'
re·tain'er
re·take'
  ·took' ·tak'en
  ·tak'ing
re·tal'i·ate'
  ·at'ed ·at'ing
re·tal'i·a'tion
re·tal'i·a·to'ry
re·tard'
re·tard'ant
re·tar'date
re'tar·da'tion
retch
  (strain to vomit;
  see wretch)
re·ten'tion
re·ten'tive
re'ten·tiv'i·ty
re·think'
ret'i·cence
ret'i·cent

re·tic'u·lar
re·tic'u·late'
  ·lat'ed ·lat'ing
ret'i·cule'
ret'i·na
  ·nas or ·nae'
ret'i·nue'
re·tire'
  ·tired' ·tir'ing
re·tir'ee'
re·tire'ment
re·tool'
re·tort'
re·touch'
re·trace'
  (go back over)
re'-trace'
  (trace again)
re·trace'a·ble
re·tract'
re·tract'a·ble
re·trac'tile
re·trac'tion
re·trac'tor
re'tread' v.
  ·tread'ed
  ·tread'ing
re'tread' n.
re·treat'
  (go back)
re'-treat'
  (treat again)
re·trench'
ret'ri·bu'tion
re·triev'a·ble
re·triev'al
re·trieve'
  ·trieved'
  ·triev'ing
re·triev'er
ret'ro·ac'tive
ret'ro·ces'sion
ret'ro·fire'
ret'ro·fit'
ret'ro·grade'
  ·grad'ed
  ·grad'ing
ret'ro·gress'
ret'ro·gres'sion
ret'ro-rock'et or
  ret'ro-rock'et
ret'ro·spect'
ret'ro·spec'tion
re·turn'
re·turn'ee'
re·un'ion
re'u·nite'
re·us'a·ble
re·use'
rev
  revved rev'ving
re·vamp'
re·veal'
re·veil'·le
rev'el
  ·eled or ·elled
  ·el·ing or ·el·ling
rev'e·la'tion

rev'el·ry
re·venge'
  ·venged'
  ·veng'ing
re·venge'ful
re·veng'er
rev'e·nue'
re·ver'ber·ant
re·ver'ber·ate'
  ·at'ed ·at'ing
re·ver'ber·a'tion
re·ver'ber·a'tor
re·ver'ber·a·to'ry
re·vere'
  ·vered' ·ver'ing
rev'er·ence
rev'er·end
rev'er·ent
rev'er·en'tial
rev'er·ie
re·ver'sal
re·vers'
  ·vers'
  (part of garment)
re·verse'
  ·versed'
  ·vers'ing
  (turned backward)
re·vers'i·ble
re·vers'i·bly
re·ver'sion
re·ver'sion·ar'y
re·vert'
re·view'
re·view'al
re·view'er
re·vile'
  ·viled' ·vil'ing
re·vise'
  ·vised' ·vis'ing
re·vi'sion
re·vi'so·ry
re·vi'tal·ize'
re·viv'a·ble
re·viv'al
re·vive'
  ·vived' ·viv'ing
re·viv'i·fy'
rev'o·ca·ble
rev'o·ca·bly
rev'o·ca'tion
re·voke'
  ·voked' ·vok'ing
re·volt'
re·volt'ing
rev'o·lu'tion
rev'o·lu'tion·ar'y
  ·ies
rev'o·lu'tion·ize'
  ·ized' ·iz'ing
re·volv'a·ble
re·volve'
  ·volved'
  ·volv'ing
re·volv'er
re·vue' or ·view'
re·vul'sion
re·ward'

re·wind'
  ·wound'
  ·wind'ing
re·write'
  ·wrote' ·writ'ten
  ·writ'ing
rhap·sod'ic
rhap·sod'i·cal·ly
rhap'so·dize'
  ·dized' ·diz'ing
rhap'so·dy
  ·dies
rhe'o·stat'
rhe'sus
rhet'o·ric
rhe·tor'i·cal
rhe·tor'i·cal·ly
rhet'o·ri'cian
rheu·mat'ic
rheu'ma·tism
rheu'ma·toid'
rheum'y
  ·i·er ·i·est
Rh factor
rhine'stone'
rhi·ni'tis
rhi·noc'er·os
rhi'zome
Rhode Island
rho'do·den'dron
rhom'boid
rhom'bus
  ·bus·es or ·bi
rhu'barb
rhyme
  rhymed
  rhym'ing
  (verse; see rime)
rhythm
rhyth'mic
rhyth'mi·cal·ly
rib
  ribbed
  rib'bing
rib'ald
rib'ald·ry
rib'bon
ri'bo·fla'vin
rice
  riced ric'ing
rich'ness
rick'et·i·ness
rick'ets
rick·ett'si·a
  ·si·ae' or ·si·as
rick'et·y
rick'ey
rick'rack'
rick'shaw or ·sha
ric'o·chet'
  ·cheted' or
  ·chet'ted
  ·chet'ing or
  ·chet'ting
ri·cot'ta
rid
  rid or rid'ded
  rid'ding

rid'a·ble or ride'·
rid'dance
rid'dle
  ·dled ·dling
ride
  rode rid'den
  rid'ing
rid'er·less
ridge
  ridged ridg'ing
ridge'pole'
rid'i·cule'
  ·culed' ·cul'ing
ri·dic'u·lous
rife
rif'fle
  ·fled ·fling
  (shoal; shuffle)
riff'raff'
ri'fle
  ·fled ·fling
  (gun; plunder)
ri'fle·man
rig
  rigged rig'ging
ri'ga·to'ni
rig'ger
  (one who rigs;
  see rigor)
right
  (correct; see rite)
right'-an'gled
right'eous
right'ful·ly
right'-hand'ed
right'ist
rig'id
ri·gid'i·ty
rig'ma·role'
rig'or
  (stiffness; see
  rigger)
rig'or mor'tis
rig'or·ous
rile
  riled ril'ing
rim
  rimmed
  rim'ming
rime
  rimed rim'ing
  (hoarfrost; rhyme;
  see rhyme)
ring
  rang rung
  ring'ing
  (sound; see
  wring)
ring
  ringed ring'ing
  (circle; see
  wring)
ring'er
ring'lead·er
ring'let
ring'mas'ter
ring'side'
rink

rinse
  rinsed rins'ing
ri'ot·ous
rip
  ripped rip'ping
ri·par'i·an
rip'en
ripe'ness
ri·poste' or
  ·post'
rip'per
rip'ple
  ·pled ·pling
rip'saw'
rip'tide'
rise
  rose ris'en
  ris'ing
ris'er
ris'i·bil'i·ty
  ·ties
ris'i·ble
risk'i·ly
risk'i·ness
risk'y
  ·i·er ·i·est
ris·qué'
ris'sole
rite
  (ceremonial act;
  see right, write)
rit'u·al
rit'u·al·is'tic
rit'u·al·ly
ri'val
  ·valed or ·valled
  ·val·ing or
  ·val·ling
ri'val·ry
  ·ries
rive
  rived, rived or
  riv'en, riv'ing
riv'er·side'
riv'et
riv'et·er
riv'u·let
roach
road'a·bil'i·ty
road'bed'
road'block'
road'show'
road'side'
road'ster
road'way'
road'work'
roam'er
roan
roar'ing
roast'er
rob
  robbed rob'bing
rob'ber
rob'ber·y
  ·ies
robe
  robed rob'ing
rob'in

ro'bot
ro·bust'
rock'-and-roll'
rock'-bound'
rock'er
rock'et
rock'e·teer'
rock'et·ry
rock'i·ness
rock·oon'
rock'y
  ·i·er ·i·est
ro·co'co
ro'dent
ro'de·o'
  ·os'
roe
  (fish eggs; see
  row)
roent'gen
rogue
  rogued rogu'ing
ro'guer·y
  ·ies
ro'guish
roil
  (stir up; see royal)
roist'er·er
roist'er·ous
role or rôle
  (actor's part)
roll
  (revolve)
roll'a·way'
roll'back'
roll call
roll'er
rol'lick·ing
roll'-top'
ro·maine'
ro·mance'
  ·manced'
  ·manc'ing
ro·man'tic
ro·man'ti·cal·ly
ro·man'ti·cism
ro·man'ti·cize'
  ·cized' ·ciz'ing
ron'deau
  ·deaux
  (poem)
ron'do
  ·dos
  (music)
rood
  (cross; see rude)
roof'er
rook
rook'er·y
  ·ies
rook'ie
room'er
  (lodger; see
  rumor)
room·ette'
room'ful'
  ·fuls'
room'i·ness

room'mate'
room'y
  ·i·er ·i·est
roos'ter
root beer
root'er
root'less
root'let
rope
  roped rop'ing
rope'walk'
Roque'fort
ro'sa·ry
  ·ries
ro·sé'
ro'se·ate
rose'bud'
rose'bush'
rose'-col'ored
ro·se'o·la
ro·sette'
rose'wood'
Rosh' Ha·sha'na
ros'i·ly
ros'in
ros'i·ness
ros'ter
ros·trum
  ·trums or ·tra
ros'y
  ·i·er ·i·est
rot
  rot'ted
  rot'ting
ro'ta·ry
  ·ries
ro'tat·a·ble
ro'tate
  ·tat·ed ·tat·ing
ro·ta'tion
ro'ta·tor
rote
  (routine; see
  wrote)
ro·tis'ser·ie
ro'to·gra·vure'
ro'tor
rot'ten
ro·tund'
ro·tun'da
ro·tun'di·ty
rou·é'
rouge
  rouged roug'ing
rough
  (not smooth;
  see ruff)
rough'age
rough'cast'
  ·cast' ·cast'ing
rough'-dry'
  -dried' -dry'ing
rough'en
rough'-hew'
  -hewed', -hewed'
  or -hewn',
  -hew'ing
rough'ly

rough'shod'
rou·lade'
rou·leau'
  ·leaux' or ·leaus'
rou·lette'
round'a·bout'
roun'de·lay'
round'house'
round'up'
round'worm'
rouse
  roused rous'ing
roust'a·bout'
rout
  (noisy mob; dig
  up; defeat)
route
  rout'ed rout'ing
  (course)
rou·tine'
rove
  roved rov'ing
row n., v.
  (line; use oars;
  brawl; see roe)
row'boat'
row'di·ness
row'dy
  ·dies
  ·di·er ·di·est
row'dy·ism
row'el
  ·eled or ·elled
  ·el·ing or ·el·ling
roy'al
  (regal; see roil)
roy'al·ist
roy'al·ly
roy'al·ty
  ·ties
rub
  rubbed
  rub'bing
rub'ber·ize'
  ·ized' ·iz'ing
rub'ber·y
rub'bish
rub'ble
  (stone; see ruble)
rub'down'
ru·bel'la
ru'bi·cund'
ru'ble
  (money; see
  rubble)
ru'bric
ru'by
  ·bies
ruche
ruch'ing
ruck'sack'
rud'der
rud'di·ness
rud'dy
  ·di·er ·di·est
rude
  (crude; see rood)
rude'ly

ru'di·ment
ru'di·men'ta·ry
rue
  rued ru'ing
rue'ful
ruff
  (collar; see rough)
ruf'fi·an
ruf'fle
  ·fled ·fling
rug'ged
ru'in·a'tion
ru'in·ous
rule
  ruled rul'ing
rul'er
rum'ble
  ·bled ·bling
ru'mi·nant
ru'mi·nate'
  ·nat'ed ·nat'ing
ru'mi·na'tor
rum'mage
  ·maged
  ·mag·ing
ru'mor
  (hearsay; see
  roomer)
rum'ple
  ·pled ·pling
run
  ran run
  run'ning
run'a·bout'
run'a·way'
run'-down'
rung
  (crossbar; pp. of
  ring; see wrung)
run'-in'
run'ner-up'
run'ners-up'
run'ni·ness
run'ny
  ·ni·er ·ni·est
run'off'
run'-on'
run'way'
rup'ture
  ·tured ·tur·ing
ru'ral
ru'ral·ly
ruse
rush
rus'set
rus'tic
rus'ti·cal·ly
rus'ti·cate'
  ·cat'ed ·cat'ing
rust'i·ness
rus'tle
  ·tled ·tling
rus'tler
rust'proof'
rust'y
  ·i·er ·i·est
rut
  rut'ted rut'ting

ru'ta·ba'ga
ruth'less
rye
  (grain; see wry)

S

Sab'bath
sab·bat'i·cal
sa'ber or ·bre
sa'ble
sa'bot
sab'o·tage'
  ·taged' ·tag'ing
sab'o·teur'
sac
  (pouch; see sack)
sac'cha·rin n.
sac'cha·rine adj.
sac'er·do'tal
sa·chet'
sack
  (bag; see sac)
sack'cloth'
sack'ful'
  ·fuls'
sack'ing
sac'ra·ment
sac'ra·men'tal
sa'cred
sac'ri·fice'
  ·ficed' ·fic'ing
sac'ri·fi'cial
sac'ri·lege
sac'ri·le'gious
sac'ris·tan
sac'ris·ty
  ·ties
sac'ro·il'i·ac'
sac'ro·sanct'
sa'crum
  ·cra or ·crums
sad
  sad'der sad'dest
sad'den
sad'dle
  ·dled ·dling
sad'dle·bag'
sad'dle·cloth'
sad'dler
sad'i'ron
sad'ism
sad'ist
sa·dis'tic
sa·dis'ti·cal·ly
sa·fa'ri
  ·ris
safe
saf'er saf'est
safe'-con'duct
safe'-de·pos'it
safe'guard'
safe'keep'ing
safe'ty
  ·ties
saf'fron

sag
sagged sag'ging
sa'ga
sa·ga'cious
sa·gac'i·ty
sage
sag'er sag'est
sage'brush'
sag'gy
·gi·er ·gi·est
sa'go
·gos
sail'boat'
sail'cloth'
sail'er
(boat)
sail'fish'
sail'or
(person; hat)
saint'li·ness
saint'ly
·li·er ·li·est
sa'ke
(rice wine)
sake
(purpose)
sa·laam'
sal'a·ble or
sale'·
sa·la'cious
sal'ad
sal'a·man'der
sa·la'mi
sal'a·ried
sal'a·ry
·ries
sal'e·ra'tus
sales'clerk'
sales'man
sales'man·ship'
sales'peo'ple
sales'per'son
sales'wom'an
sa'lient
sa'line
sa·lin'i·ty
sa·li'va
sal'i·var'y
sal'i·vate'
·vat'ed ·vat'ing
sal'low
sal'ly
·lies, ·lied ·ly·ing
sal'ma·gun'di
salm'on
sal'mo·nel'la
·lae or ·la or ·las
sa·lon'
sa·loon'
sa·loon'keep'er
sal'si·fy'
salt'box'
salt'cel'lar
salt'i·ly
salt·ine'
salt'i·ness
salt'pe'ter
salt'shak'er

salt'wa'ter
salt'works'
·works'
salt'y
·i·er ·i·est
sa·lu'bri·ous
sal'u·tar'y
sal'u·ta'tion
sa·lu'ta·to'ri·an
sa·lu'ta·to'ry
·ries
sa·lute'
·lut'ed ·lut'ing
sal'vage
·vaged ·vag·ing
sal'vage·a·ble
sal·va'tion
salve
salved salv'ing
sal'ver
sal'vo
·vos or ·voes
Sa·mar'i·tan
same'ness
sam'i·sen'
sam'o·var'
sam'pan
sam'ple
·pled ·pling
sam'pler
sam'u·rai'
·rai'
san'a·tive
sanc'ti·fi·ca'tion
sanc'ti·fy'
·fied' ·fy'ing
sanc'ti·mo'ni·ous
sanc'ti·mo'ny
sanc'tion
sanc'ti·ty
sanc'tu·ar'y
·ies
sanc'tum
·tums or ·ta
san'dal
san'daled or
·dalled
san'dal·wood'
sand'bag'
sand bar
sand'blast'
sand'box'
san'dhi
sand'hog'
sand'i·ness
sand'lot'
sand'man'
sand'pa'per
sand'stone'
sand'storm'
sand'wich
sand'y
·i·er ·i·est
sane'ly
San'for·ize'
·ized' ·iz'ing
sang'-froid'
san'gui·nar'y

san'guine
san'i·tar'i·um
·i·ums or ·i·a
san'i·tar'y
san'i·ta'tion
san'i·tize'
·tized' ·tiz'ing
san'i·ty
San'skrit
sap
sapped sap'ping
sap'ling
sa·pon'i·fy'
·fied' ·fy'ing
sap'phire
sap'py
·pi·er ·pi·est
sap'suck'er
sa·ran'
sar'casm
sar·cas'tic
sar·cas'ti·cal·ly
sar·co'ma
·mas or ·ma·ta
sar·coph'a·gus
·a·gi
sar·dine'
sar·don'ic
sar·don'i·cal·ly
sar'do·nyx
sa'ri
·ris
sa·rong'
sar'sa·pa·ril'la
sar·to'ri·al
sas'sa·fras'
sa·tan'ic
sa·tan'i·cal·ly
satch'el
sate
sat'ed sat'ing
sa·teen'
sat'el·lite'
sa'tia·ble
sa'ti·ate'
·at'ed ·at'ing
sa'ti·a'tion
sa·ti'e·ty
sat'in
sat'in·wood'
sat'in·y
sat'ire
sa·tir'i·cal
sat'i·rist
sat'i·rize'
·rized' ·riz'ing
sat'is·fac'tion
sat'is·fac'to·ri·ly
sat'is·fac'to·ry
sat'is·fy'
·fied' ·fy'ing
sa·to'ri
sa'trap
sat'su·ma
sat'u·ra·ble
sat'u·rate'
·rat'ed ·rat'ing

sat'u·ra'tion
Sat'ur·day
sat'ur·nine'
sat'yr
sat'y·ri'a·sis
sauce'pan'
sau'cer
sau'ci·ness
sau'cy
·ci·er ·ci·est
sau'er·bra'ten
sau'er·kraut'
sau'na
saun'ter
sau'sage
sau·té'
·téed' ·té'ing
sau·terne'
sav'a·ble or
save'·
sav'age
sav'age·ly
sav'age·ry
sa·van'na
sa·vant'
save
saved sav'ing
sav'ior
sa'voir-faire'
sa'vor
sa'vor·i·ness
sa'vor·y
·i·er ·i·est
sa·voy'
saw
sawed saw'ing
saw'dust'
saw'horse'
saw'mill'
saw'-toothed'
saw'yer
sax'o·phone'
sax'o·phon'ist
say
said say'ing
says
say'-so'
scab
scabbed scab'bing
scab'bard
scab'bi·ness
scab'by
·bi·er ·bi·est
scab'rous
scaf'fold
scagl·io'la
scal'a·ble
scal'a·wag'
scald
scale
scaled scal'ing
scale'less
sca·lene'
scal'i·ness
scal'lion
scal'lop
scal'op·pi'ne
scal'pel

scalp'er
scal'y
·i·er ·i·est
scam'per
scan
scanned
scan'ning
scan'dal
scan'dal·ize'
·ized' ·iz'ing
scan'dal·mon'ger
scan'dal·ous
scan'na·ble
scan'ner
scan'sion
scant'i·ly
scant'i·ness
scant'ling
scant'ness
scant'y
·i·er ·i·est
scape'goat'
scape'grace'
scap'u·la
·lae' or ·las
scap'u·lar
scar
scarred
scar'ring
scar'ab
scar'a·mouch'
scarce'ly
scar'ci·ty
·ties
scare
scared scar'ing
scare'crow'
scarf
scarfs or scarves
(long cloth)
scarf
scarfs
(joint; cut)
scar'i·fi·ca'tion
scar'i·fy'
·fied' ·fy'ing
scar'i·ness
scar'let
scarp
scar'y
·i·er ·i·est
scat
scat'ted
scat'ting
scathe
scathed
scath'ing
scat'ter
scat'ter·brain'
scav'enge
·enged ·eng·ing
scav'eng·er
sce·nar'i·o'
·os'
sce·nar'ist
scene
sce'ner·y
·ies

sce'nic
scent
(odor; see sent)
scep'ter
sched'ule
·uled ·ul·ing
sche'ma
·ma·ta
sche·mat'ic
sche·mat'i·cal·ly
scheme
schemed
schem'ing
scher'zo
·zos or ·zi
schism
schis·mat'ic
schiz'oid
schiz'o·phre'ni·a
schiz'o·phren'ic
schnau'zer
schol'ar·ly
schol'ar·ship'
scho·las'tic
scho·las'ti·cal·ly
scho·las'ti·cism
school'boy'
school'girl'
school'house'
school'mate'
school'room'
school'teach'er
school'work'
schoon'er
schwa
sci·at'i·ca
sci'ence
sci'en·tif'ic
sci'en·tif'i·cal·ly
sci'en·tist
scim'i·tar
scin·til'la
scin'til·late'
·lat'ed ·lat'ing
scin'til·la'tor
sci'on
scis'sors
scle·ro'sis
scoff
scold'ing
sconce
scone
scoop'ful'
·fuls'
scoot'er
scope
scorch'ing
score
scored scor'ing
score'less
scorn'ful
scor'pi·on
scot'-free'
scoun'drel
scour
scourge
scourged
scourg'ing

scout'mas'ter
scowl
scrab'ble
·bled ·bling
scrag'gly
·gli·er ·gli·est
scrag'gy
·gi·er ·gi·est
scram'ble
·bled ·bling
scrap
scrapped
scrap'ping
scrap'book'
scrape
scraped
scrap'ing
scrap'er
scrap'heap'
scrap'ple
scrap'py
·pi·er ·pi·est
scratch'i·ness
scratch'y
·i·er ·i·est
scrawl
scraw'ny
·ni·er ·ni·est
scream'ing
screech'y
screen'play'
screw'driv'er
scrib'ble
·bled ·bling
scrib'bler
scribe
scribed scrib'ing
scrim'mage
·maged ·mag·ing
scrimp'i·ness
scrimp'y
·i·er ·i·est
scrip
(certificate)
script
(manuscript)
scrip'tur·al
scrof'u·la
scroll'work'
scro'tum
·ta or ·tums
scrounge
scrounged
scroung'ing
scrub
scrubbed
scrub'bing
scrub'by
·bi·er ·bi·est
scruff
scrunch
scru'ple
·pled ·pling
scru'pu·lous
scru'ta·ble
scru'ti·nize'
·nized' ·niz'ing
scru'ti·ny

scu'ba
scuff
scuf'fle
·fled ·fling
scull
(oar; boat; see
skull)
scul'ler·y
·ies
sculpt
sculp'tor
sculp'tur·al
sculp'ture
·tured ·tur·ing
scum'my
·mi·er ·mi·est
scup'per·nong'
scur·ril'i·ty
·ties
scur'ril·ous
scur'ry
·ried ·ry·ing
scur'vy
·vi·er ·vi·est
scut'tle
·tled ·tling
scythe
scythed
scyth'ing
sea'board'
sea'borne'
sea'coast'
sea'far'er
sea'far'ing
sea'food'
sea'go'ing
seal'ant
sea level
seal'skin'
seam
sea'man
seam'less
seam'stress
seam'y
·i·er ·i·est
sé'ance
sea'plane'
sea'port'
sear
(burn; see seer)
search'light'
sea'scape'
sea'shell'
sea'shore'
sea'sick'ness
sea'side'
sea'son
sea'son·a·ble
sea'son·al
seat belt
sea'ward
sea'way'
sea'weed'
sea'wor'thy
se·ba'ceous
se'cant
se·cede'
·ced'ed ·ced'ing

se·ces'sion
se·clude'
·clud'ed
·clud'ing
se·clu'sion
se·clu'sive
sec'ond
sec'ond·ar'i·ly
sec'ond·ar'y
sec'ond-class'
sec'ond-guess'
sec'ond·hand'
sec'ond-rate'
se'cre·cy
se'cret
sec're·tar'i·al
sec're·tar'i·at
sec're·tar'y
·ies
se·crete'
·cret'ed ·cret'ing
se·cre'tion
se'cre·tive
se·cre'to·ry
sect
sec·tar'i·an
sec'tion·al
sec'tion·al·ize'
·ized' ·iz'ing
sec'tor
sec'u·lar
sec'u·lar·ize'
·ized' ·iz'ing
se·cur'a·ble
se·cure'
·cured' ·cur'ing
se·cure'ly
se·cu'ri·ty
·ties
se·dan'
se·date'
·dat'ed ·dat'ing
se·date'ly
se·da'tion
sed'a·tive
sed'en·tar'y
sed'i·ment
sed'i·men'ta·ry
sed'i·men·ta'tion
se·di'tion
se·di'tious
se·duce'
·duced' ·duc'ing
se·duc'i·ble
se·duc'tion
se·duc'tive
se·du'li·ty
sed'u·lous
see
saw seen see'ing
seed'bed'
seed'i·ness
seed'ling
seed'y
·i·er ·i·est
seek
sought seek'ing
seem'ing·ly

seem'li·ness
seem'ly
·li·er ·li·est
seep'age
seer
(prophet; see
sear)
seer'suck'er
see'saw'
seethe
seethed
seeth'ing
seg'ment
seg·men'tal
seg'men·ta'tion
seg're·gate'
·gat'ed ·gat'ing
seg're·ga'tion
seg're·ga'tion·ist
sei'del
seis'mic
seis'mi·cal·ly
seis'mo·graph'
seis·mog'ra·pher
seis·mol'o·gist
seis·mol'o·gy
seize
seized seiz'ing
sei'zure
sel'dom
se·lect'
se·lect'ee'
se·lec'tion
se·lec'tive
se·lec·tiv'i·ty
se·lec'tor
self
selves
self'-act'ing
self'-ad·dressed'
self'-ap·point'ed
self'-as·sur'ance
self'-as·sured'
self'-cen'tered
self'-con'fi·dence
self'-con'scious
self'-con·tained'
self'-con·trol'
self'-de·fense'
self'-dis'ci·pline
self'-driv'en
self'-ed'u·cat'ed
self'-em·ployed'
self'-es·teem'
self'-ev'i·dent
self'-ex·plan'a·
to'ry
self'-ex·pres'sion
self'-gov'ern·ing
self'-im'age
self'-im·por'tant
self'-im·posed'
self'-im·prove'·
ment
self'-in·duced'
self'-in·dul'gence
self'-in·flict'ed
self'-in'ter·est

self'ish
self'less
self'-load'ing
self'-love'
self'-made'
self'-pit'y
self'-por'trait
self'-pos·sessed'
self'-pres·er·va'·
tion
self'-reg'u·lat'ing
self'-re·li'ance
self'-re·proach'
self'-re·spect'
self'-re·straint'
self'-right'eous
self'-ris'ing
self'-sac'ri·fice'
self'same'
self'-sat'is·fied'
self'-seal'ing
self'-serv'ice
self'-start'er
self'-styled'
self'-suf·fi'cient
self'-sup·port'
self'-taught'
self'-tor'ture
self'-willed'
self'-wind'ing
sell
sold sell'ing
sell'-off'
sell'out'
sel'vage or
·vedge
se·man'tic
sem'a·phore'
·phored'
·phor'ing
sem'blance
se'men
sem'i·na
se·mes'ter
sem'i·an'nu·al
sem'i·au'to·
mat'ic
sem'i·cir'cle
sem'i·co'lon
sem'i·con·duc'tor
sem'i·con'scious
sem'i·de·tached'
sem'i·fi'nal
sem'i·for'mal
sem'i·month'ly
sem'i·nal
sem'i·nar'
sem'i·nar'y
·ies
sem'i·of·fi'cial
sem'i·pre'cious
sem'i·pri'vate
sem'i·pro·fes'·
sion·al
sem'i·rig'id
sem'i·skilled'
sem'i·sol'id
Sem'ite

Se·mit'ic
sem'i·trail'er
sem'i·trop'i·cal
sem'i·week'ly
sem'i·year'ly
sem'o·li'na
sen'ate
sen'a·tor
sen·a·to'ri·al
send
sent send'ing
send'-off'
se·nes'cent
se'nile
se·nil'i·ty
sen'ior
sen·ior'i·ty
sen·sa'tion
sen·sa'tion·al·ly
sense
sensed sens'ing
sense'less
sen·si·bil'i·ty
·ties
sen'si·ble
sen'si·bly
sen'si·tive
sen·si·tiv'i·ty
sen'si·ti·za'tion
sen'si·tize'
·tized' ·tiz'ing
sen'so·ry
sen'su·al
sen·su·al'i·ty
sen'su·ous
sent
(transmitted;
see scent)
sen'tence
·tenced ·tenc·ing
sen·ten'tious
sen'tient
sen'ti·ment
sen'ti·men'tal
sen'ti·men·
tal'i·ty
sen'ti·men'tal·
ize'
·ized' ·iz'ing
sen'ti·nel
·neled or ·nelled
·nel·ing or
·nel·ling
sen'try
·tries
sep'a·ra·ble
sep'a·rate'
·rat'ed ·rat'ing
sep'a·ra'tion
sep'a·ra·tism
sep'a·ra'tor
se'pi·a
Sep·tem'ber
sep·tet' or
·tette'
sep'tic
sep·tu·a·ge·
nar'i·an

sep·tu'ple
·pled ·pling
sep'ul·cher
se·pul'chral
se'quel
se'quence
se·quen'tial
se'quin
se·quoi'a
se·ra'pe
ser'e·nade'
·nad'ed ·nad'ing
ser'en·dip'i·ty
se·rene'
se·ren'i·ty
serf
(slave; see surf)
serge
(fabric; see surge)
ser'geant
se'ri·al
(in a series;
see cereal)
se'ri·al·ize'
·ized' ·iz'ing
se'ries
·ries
ser'if
se·ri·o·com'ic
se'ri·ous
se'ri·ous-mind'ed
ser'mon
se'rous
ser'pent
ser'pen·tine'
ser·rate'
·rat'ed ·rat'ing
se'rum
·rums or ·ra
ser'vant
serve
served serv'ing
serv'ice
·iced ·ic·ing
serv'ice·a·bil'i·ty
serv'ice·a·ble
serv'ice·a·bly
serv'ice·man'
ser'vi·ette'
ser'vile
ser·vil'i·ty
ser'vi·tor
ser'vi·tude'
ses'a·me'
ses'qui·cen·ten'·
ni·al
ses'sion
(meeting; see
cession)
set
set set'ting
set'back'
set'-in'
set'off'
set'screw'
set·tee'
set'ter

set'tle
·tled ·tling
set'tle·ment
set'tler
set'-to'
·tos'
sev'en·teen'
sev'enth
sev'en·ti·eth
sev'en·ty
·ties
sev'er
sev'er·al
sev'er·al·ly
sev'er·ance
se·vere'
se·vere'ly
se·ver'i·ty
·ties
sew
sewed, sewn or
sewed, sew'ing
(stitch; see sow)
sew'age
sew'er
sew'er·age
sex'a·ge·nar'i·an
sex'i·ly
sex'i·ness
sex'less
sex'tant
sex·tet' or
·tette'
sex'ton
sex·tu'ple
·pled ·pling
sex·tu'plet
sex'u·al
sex'u·al'i·ty
sex'u·al·ly
sex'y
·i·er ·i·est
shab'bi·ly
shab'bi·ness
shab'by
·bi·er ·bi·est
shack'le
·led ·ling
shade
shad'ed
shad'ing
shad'i·ness
shad'ow
shad'ow·y
shad'y
·i·er ·i·est
shaft
shag
shagged
shag'ging
shag'gi·ness
shag'gy
·gi·er ·gi·est
shak'a·ble or
shake'a·ble
shake
shook shak'en
shak'ing

Shake'speare'
Shake·spear'e·an
or ·i·an
shake'-up'
shak'i·ly
shak'i·ness
shak'y
·i·er ·i·est
shal'low
sha·lom'
sham
shammed
sham'ming
sham'ble
·bled ·bling
shame
shamed
sham'ing
shame'faced'
shame'ful
shame'ful·ly
shame'less
sham·poo'
·pooed' ·poo'ing
shang'hai
·haied ·hai·ing
shank
shan'tung'
shan'ty
·ties
shape
shaped shap'ing
shape'less
shape'li·ness
shape'ly
·li·er ·li·est
share
shared shar'ing
share'crop'per
shar·c'hold'er
shark'skin'
sharp'en·er
sharp'-eyed'
sharp'shoot'er
sharp'-sight'ed
sharp'-tongued'
sharp'-wit'ted
shat'ter
shat'ter·proof'
shave
shaved, shaved
or shav'en,
shav'ing
shawl
sheaf
sheaves
shear
sheared, sheared
or shorn,
shear'ing
(cut; see sheer)
shears
sheath
(a case; dress)
sheathe
sheathed
sheath'ing
(put into a sheath)

sheave
sheaved
sheav'ing
shed
shed shed'ding
sheen
sheep'ish·ly
sheep'skin'
sheep'walk'
sheer
(thin; steep;
see shear)
sheet'ing
sheik or sheikh
shelf
shelves
shell
shel·lac' or ·lack'
·lacked'
·lack'ing
shell'fish'
shell'-like'
shell'proof'
shel'ter
shelve
shelved
shelv'ing
she·nan'i·gan
shep'herd
sher'bet
sher'iff
sher'ry
·ries
shib'bo·leth
shield
shift'i·ly
shift'i·ness
shift'less
shift'y
·i·er ·i·est
shil·le'lagh or
shil·la'lah
shil'ly-shal'ly
·lied ·ly·ing
shim
shimmed
shim'ming
shim'mer·y
shim'my
·mies
·mied ·my·ing
shin
shinned
shin'ning
shine
shone or shined
shin'ing
shin'gle
·gled ·gling
shin'i·ness
shin'y
·i·er ·i·est
ship
shipped
ship'ping
ship'board'
ship'mate'
ship'ment

ship'own'er
ship'pa·ble
ship'per
ship'shape'
ship'wreck'
ship'wright'
ship'yard'
shirk'er
shirr'ing
shirt'waist'
shiv'a·ree'
·reed' ·ree'ing
shiv'er
shoal
shock'ing
shock'proof'
shod'di·ly
shod'di·ness
shod'dy
·di·er ·di·est
shoe
shod or shoed,
shod or shoed
or shod'den,
shoe'ing
shoe'horn'
shoe'lace'
shoe'mak'er
sho'er
shoe'shine'
shoe'string'
shoe tree
shoo
shooed shoo'ing
shoot
shot shoot'ing
shop
shopped
shop'ping
shop'keep'er
shop'lift'er
shop'per
shop'talk'
shop'worn'
Shor'an or
shor'-
shore'line'
shore'ward
shor'ing
short'age
short'bread'
short'cake'
short'change'
short'-cir'cuit
short'com'ing
short'cut'
short'en
short'en·ing
short'hand'
short'-hand'ed
short'horn'
short'-lived'
short'-range'
short'sight'ed
short'stop'
short'-tem'pered
short'-term'
short'-waist'ed

short'wave'
short'-wind'ed
shot'gun'
should
shoul'der
should'n't
shov'el
·eled or ·elled
·el·ing or ·el·ling
shov'el·ful'
·fuls'
show
showed, shown
or showed,
show'ing
show'boat'
show'case'
show'down'
show'er
show'i·ly
show'i·ness
show'man
show'off'
show'piece'
show'place'
show'room'
show'y
·i·er ·i·est
shrap'nel
shred
shred'ded or
shred
shred'ding
shrewd
shriek
shrill'ness
shril'ly
shrine
shrink
shrank or shrunk,
shrunk or
shrunk'en,
shrink'ing
shrink'age
shriv'el
·eled or ·elled
·el·ing or ·el·ling
shroud
shrub'ber·y
shrug
shrugged
shrug'ging
shuck
shud'der
shuf'fle
·fled ·fling
shuf'fle·board'
shun
shunned
shun'ning
shunt
shut
shut shut'ting
shut'down'
shut'-in'
shut'-off'
shut'out'
shut'ter

shut'tle
·tled ·tling
shut'tle·cock'
shy
shy'er or shi'er
shy'est or shi'est
shies
shied shy'ing
Si'a·mese'
sib'i·lance
sib'i·lant
sib'ling
sick'bed'
sick'en
sick'le
sick'li·ness
sick'ly
·li·er ·li·est
sick'room'
side
sid'ed sid'ing
side'arm'
side arms
side'board'
side'burns'
side'car'
side'light'
side'line'
side'long'
si·de're·al
side'sad'dle
side'show'
side'slip'
side'split'ting
side'step' v.
side'stroke'
side'swipe'
side'track'
side'walk'
side'ways'
side'wise'
sid'ing
si'dle
·dled ·dling
siege
si·en'na
si·er'ra
si·es'ta
sieve
sieved siev'ing
sift'er
sigh
sight
(view; see
cite, site)
sight'less
sight'ly
·li·er ·li·est
sight'see'ing
sight'se'er
sign
(signal; see sine)
sig'nal
·naled or ·nalled
·nal·ing or
·nal·ling
sig'nal·ize'
·ized' ·iz'ing

sig'nal·ly
sig'na·to'ry
·ries
sig'na·ture
sign'board'
sig'net
sig·nif'i·cance
sig·nif'i·cant
sig'ni·fi·ca'tion
sig'ni·fy'
·fied' ·fy'ing
sign'post'
si'lage
si'lence
·lenced ·lenc·ing
si'lenc·er
si'lent
si'lex
sil'hou·ette'
·et'ted ·et'ting
sil'i·ca
sil'i·cate
si·li'ceous
sil'i·cone'
sil'i·co'sis
silk'en
silk'i·ness
silk'-screen'
silk'worm'
silk'y
·i·er ·i·est
sil'li·ness
sil'ly
·lies, ·li·er ·li·est
si'lo
·los, ·loed ·lo·ing
sil'ver
sil'ver·fish'
silver plate
sil'ver·smith'
sil'ver-tongued'
sil'ver·ware'
sil'ver·y
sim'i·an
sim'i·lar
sim'i·lar'i·ty
·ties
sim'i·le'
si·mil'i·tude'
sim'mer
si'mon-pure'
sim'per
sim'ple
·pler ·plest
sim'ple-mind'ed
sim'ple·ton
sim·plic'i·ty
·ties
sim'pli·fi·ca'tion
sim'pli·fi'er
sim'pli·fy'
·fied' ·fy'ing
sim'ply
sim'u·lant
sim'u·late'
·lat'ed ·lat'ing
sim'u·la'tion
sim'u·la'tor

si'mul·cast'
·cast' or ·cast'ed
·cast'ing
si'mul·ta'ne·ous
sin
sinned sin'ning
sin·cere'
·cer'er ·cer'est
sin·cere'ly
sin·cer'i·ty
sine
(ratio; see sign)
si'ne·cure'
sin'ew·y
sin'ful
sing
sang sung
sing'ing
singe
singed
singe'ing
sin'gle
·gled ·gling
sin'gle-breast'ed
sin'gle-hand'ed
sin'gle-space'
sin'gle·ton
sin'gly
sing'song'
sin'gu·lar
sin'gu·lar'i·ty
sin'gu·lar·ize'
·ized' ·iz'ing
sin'is·ter
sink
sank or sunk,
sunk sink'ing
sin'ner
sin'u·ous
si'nus
si'nus·i'tis
sip
sipped sip'ping
si'phon
sire
sired sir'ing
si'ren
sir'loin
si·roc'co
·cos
si'sal
sis'ter·hood'
sis'ter-in-law'
sis'ters-in-law'
sis'ter·li·ness
sis'ter·ly
sit
sat sit'ting
si·tar'
sit'-down'
site
(place; see sight)
sit'-in'
sit'ter
sit'u·ate'
·at'ed ·at'ing
sit'u·a'tion
sit'-up' or sit'up'

sitz bath
six'fold'
six'pen'ny
six'teenth'
sixth
six'ti·eth
six'ty
·ties
siz'a·ble or
size'·
size
sized siz'ing
siz'zle
·zled ·zling
skate
skat'ed skat'ing
skein
skel'e·ton
skep'tic
skep'ti·cal
skep'ti·cal·ly
skep'ti·cism
sketch'book'
sketch'i·ly
sketch'i·ness
sketch'y
·i·er ·i·est
skew'er
ski
skis or ski
skied ski'ing
skid
skid'ded
skid'ding
ski'er
skill'let
skill'ful
skim
skimmed
skim'ming
skimp'i·ly
skimp'i·ness
skimp'y
·i·er ·i·est
skin
skinned
skin'ning
skin'-deep'
skin'flint'
skin'ni·ness
skin'ny
·ni·er ·ni·est
skip
skipped
skip'ping
ski'plane'
skip'per
skir'mish
skit'tish
skul·dug'ger·y
or skull·
skulk
skull
(head; see scull)
skull'cap'
sky
skies
sky'cap'

sky'-dive'
·dived' -div'ing
sky'-high'
sky'lark'
sky'light'
sky'line'
sky'rock'et
sky'scrap'er
sky'ward
sky'ways'
sky'writ'ing
slack'en
slack'er
slake
slaked slak'ing
sla'lom
slam
slammed
slam'ming
slan'der
slan'der·ous
slang'y
·i·er ·i·est
slant'wise'
slap
slapped
slap'ping
slap'dash'
slap'stick'
slash
slate
slat'ed slat'ing
slat'tern
slaugh'ter
slave
slaved slav'ing
slav'er
slav'er·y
slav'ish·ly
slay
slew slain
slay'ing
(kill; see sleigh)
slea'zi·ness
slea'zy
·zi·er ·zi·est
sled
sled'ded
sled'ding
sledge
sledged
sledg'ing
sleek'ly
sleep
slept sleep'ing
sleep'i·ly
sleep'i·ness
sleep'less
sleep'walk'ing
sleep'y
·i·er ·i·est
sleet
sleeve'less
sleigh
(snow vehicle;
see slay)
sleight
(skill; see slight)

slen'der
slen'der·ize'
·ized' ·iz'ing
sleuth
slew or slue
(a lot; see slue)
slice
sliced slic'ing
slick'er
slide
slid slid'ing
slide rule
slight
(frail; see
sleight)
slim
slim'mer
slim'mest
slimmed
slim'ming
slim'i·ness
slim'ness
slim'y
·i·er ·i·est
sling
slung sling'ing
sling'shot'
slink
slunk slink'ing
slip
slipped slip'ping
slip'cov'er
slip'knot'
slip'-on'
slip'page
slip'per·i·ness
slip'per·y
·i·er ·i·est
slip'shod'
slip'stream'
slip'-up'
slit
slit slit'ting
slith'er
sliv'er
sli'vo·vitz'
slob'ber
sloe
(fruit; see slow)
sloe'-eyed'
slog
slogged
slog'ging
slo'gan
sloop
slop
slopped
slop'ping
slope
sloped slop'ing
slop'pi·ly
slop'pi·ness
slop'py
·pi·er ·pi·est
slosh
slot
slot'ted slot'ting
sloth'ful

slouch'y	smog'gy	snif'ter	so'cial·ize'	so·lid'i·fi·ca'tion	so·phis'ti·cate'
·i·er ·i·est	·gi·er ·gi·est	snip	·ized' ·iz'ing	so·lid'i·fy'	·cat'ed ·cat'ing
slough	smok'a·ble or	snipped	so·ci'e·tal	·fied' ·fy'ing	so·phis'ti·ca'tion
slov'en·li·ness	smoke'a·ble	snip'ping	so·ci'e·tal·ly	sol'id-state'	soph'is·try
slov'en·ly	smoke	snipe	so·ci'e·ty	so·lil'o·quize'	·tries
·li·er ·li·est	smoked	sniped snip'ing	·ties	·quized'	soph'o·more'
slow	smok'ing	sniv'el	so'ci·o·cul'tu·ral	·quiz'ing	soph'o·mor'ic
(not fast; see	smok'er	·eled or ·elled	so'ci·o·e'co·	so·lil'o·quy	sop'o·rif'ic
sloe)	smoke screen	·el·ing or	nom'ic	·quies	so·pra'no
slow'-wit'ted	smoke'stack'	·el·ling	so'ci·o·gram'	sol'i·taire'	·nos or ·ni
sludge	smok'i·ness	snob'ber·y	so'ci·o·log'i·cal	sol'i·tar'y	sor'cer·er
sludg'y	smok'y	snob'bish	so'ci·ol'o·gist	sol'i·tude'	sor'cer·y
·i·er ·i·est	·i·er ·i·est	snoop'er·scope'	so'ci·ol'o·gy	so'lo	·ies
slue or slew	smol'der	snore	so'ci·o·path'	·los	sor'did
slued or slewed	smooth	snored snor'ing	so'ci·o·po·lit'i·cal	so'lo·ist	sore
slu'ing or	smooth'bore'	snor'kel	sock'et	sol'stice	(painful; see
slew'ing	smooth'-faced'	snout	sock'eye'	sol'u·bil'i·ty	soar)
(turn; see slew)	smooth'-shav'en	snow'ball'	sod	sol'u·ble	sore'ly
slug	smooth'-spo'ken	snow'-blind'	sod'ded sod'ding	sol'ute	sor'ghum
slugged	smor'gas·bord'	snow'bound'	so·dal'i·ty	so·lu'tion	so·ror'i·ty
slug'ging	smoth'er	snow'drift'	·ties	solv'a·bil'i·ty	·ties
slug'gard	smudge	snow'fall'	sod'den·ness	solv'a·ble	sor'rel
slug'gish	smudged	snow'flake'	sod'om·y	solve	sor'ri·ly
sluice	smudg'ing	snow line	soft'ball'	solved	sor'ri·ness
sluiced sluic'ing	smudg'i·ness	snow'mo·bile'	soft'-boiled'	solv'ing	sor'row
slum	smudg'y	·biled· ·bil'ing	soft'-cov'er	sol'ven·cy	sor'row·ful
slummed	·i·er ·i·est	snow'plow'	soft'en·er	sol'vent	sor'ry
slum'ming	smug	snow'shoe'	soft'heart'ed	som'ber	·ri·er ·ri·est
slum'ber	smug'ger	·shoed'	soft'-shell'	som·bre'ro	sor'tie
slum'ber·ous	smug'gest	·shoe'ing	soft'-spo'ken	·ros	so'-so'
slump	smug'gle	snow'storm'	soft'ware'	some'bod'y	sou·brette'
slur	·gled ·gling	snow'-white'	sog'gi·ness	some'day'	souf·flé'
slurred	smut'ty	snow'y	sog'gy	some'how'	soul
slur'ring	·ti·er ·ti·est	·i·er ·i·est	·gi·er ·gi·est	some'one'	(spirit; see sole)
slush'y	snack bar	snub	soil	som'er·sault'	soul'ful
·i·er ·i·est	snaf'fle	snubbed	soi·ree' or ·rée'	some'thing'	soul'-search'ing
slut'tish	·fled ·fling	snub'bing	so'journ	some'time'	sound'proof'
sly	sna·fu'	snub'-nosed'	sol'ace	some'times'	soup·çon'
sli'er or sly'er	snag	snuff'ers	·aced ·ac·ing	some'what'	source'book'
sli'est or sly'est	snagged	snuf'fle	so'lar	some'where'	sour'dough'
sly'ly or sli'ly	snag'ging	·fled ·fling	so·lar'i·um	som·nam'bu·late'	sour'ness
smack	snail'-paced'	snug	·lar'i·a	·lat'ed ·lat'ing	sou'sa·phone'
small'-mind'ed	snake	snug'ger	sol'der	som'no·lent	souse
small'pox'	snaked snak'ing	snug'gest	(metal alloy)	so'nar	soused sous'ing
small'-scale'	snak'y	snug'gle	sol'dier	so·na'ta	South Car'o·li'na
smart	·i·er ·i·est	·gled ·gling	(man in an army)	sonde	South Da·ko'ta
smash'up'	snap	soak'ers	sole	song'ster	south·east'
smat'ter·ing	snapped	soap'box'	soled sol'ing	son'ic	south·east'er·ly
smear'i·ness	snap'ping	soap'suds'	(bottom surface;	son'-in-law'	south·east'ern
smear'y	snap'drag·on	soap'y	only; see soul)	sons'-in-law'	south·east'ward
·i·er ·i·est	snap'pish	·i·er ·i·est	sol'e·cism	son'net	south'er·ly
smell	snap'shot'	soar	sole'ly	son'net·eer'	south'ern
smelled or smelt	snare	(fly; see sore)	sol'emn	so·nor'i·ty	south'ern·er
smell'ing	snared snar'ing	sob	so·lem'ni·fy'	so·no'rous	south'ern·most'
smell'i·ness	snarl'y	sobbed	·fied' ·fy'ing	soon'er	south'ward
smell'y	·i·er ·i·est	sob'bing	so·lem'ni·ty	soothe	south·west'
·i·er ·i·est	snatch	so'ber-mind'ed	·ties	soothed	south·west'er·ly
smidg'en	sneak'i·ly	so·bri'e·ty	sol'em·nize'	sooth'ing	south·west'ern
smile	sneak'i·ness	so'bri·quet'	·nized' ·niz'ing	sooth'say'er	south·west'ward
smiled smil'ing	sneak'y	so'-called'	so'le·noid'	soot'i·ness	sou've·nir'
smirch	·i·er ·i·est	soc'cer	sole'plate'	soot'y	sov'er·eign
smirk	sneer'ing·ly	so'cia·bil'i·ty	so·lic'it	·i·er ·i·est	sov'er·eign·ty
smite	sneeze	so'cia·ble	so·lic'i·ta'tion	sop	·ties
smote, smit'ten	sneezed	so'cia·bly	so·lic'i·tor	sopped	so'vi·et
or smote,	sneez'ing	so'cial	so·lic'i·tous	sop'ping	sow
smit'ing	snick'er	so'cial·ism	so·lic'i·tude'	soph'ism	sowed, sown or
smock'ing	snif'fle	so'cial·ite'	sol'id	soph'ist	sowed, sow'ing
smog	·fled ·fling	so'cial·i·za'tion	sol'i·dar'i·ty	so·phis'ti·cal	(plant; see sew)

soy'bean'
space
 spaced spac'ing
space'craft'
 ·craft'
space'flight'
space'man
space'port'
space'ship'
space'suit'
space'walk'
spa'cious
spack'le
 ·led ·ling
spade
 spad'ed
 spad'ing
spade'work'
spa·ghet'ti
span
 spanned
 span'ning
span'dex
span'drel
span'gle
 ·gled ·gling
span'iel
span'sule
spar
 sparred
 spar'ring
spare
 spared spar'ing
spare'ribs'
spar'kle
 ·kled ·kling
spar'kler
spar'row
sparse'ly
spasm
spas·mod'ic
spas·mod'i·cal·ly
spas'tic
spa'tial
spat'ter
spat'u·la
spawn
spay
speak
 spoke spo'ken
 speak'ing
speak'er
spear'head'
spear'mint'
spe'cial
spe'cial·ist
spe'cial·ize'
 ·ized' ·iz'ing
spe'cial·ly
spe'cial·ty
 ·ties
spe'cie
 (coin money)
spe'cies
 ·cies
 (kind)
spec'i·fi'a·ble
spe·cif'ic

spe·cif'i·cal·ly
spec'i·fi·ca'tion
spec'i·fy'
 ·fied' ·fy'ing
spec'i·men
spe'cious
speck'le
 ·led ·ling
spec'ta·cle
spec'ta·cled
spec·tac'u·lar
spec'ta·tor
spec'ter
spec'tral
spec'tro·scope'
spec·tros'co·py
spec'trum
 ·tra or ·trums
spec'u·late'
 ·lat'ed ·lat'ing
spec'u·la'tion
spec'u·la'tive
spec'u·la'tor
speech'less
speed
 sped or speed'ed
 speed'ing
speed'boat'
speed'i·ly
speed'i·ness
speed·om'e·ter
speed'up'
speed'y
 ·i·er ·i·est
spe'le·ol'o·gy
spell
 spelled or spelt
 spell'ing
 (name the letters)
spell
 spelled spell'ing
 (work in place of)
spell'bind'
 ·bound' ·bind'ing
spell'down'
spe·lunk'er
spend
 spent spend'ing
spend'thrift'
sper'ma·ce'ti
spew
sphere
spher'i·cal
sphe'roid
sphinx
 sphinx'es or
 sphin'ges
spice
 spiced spic'ing
spic'i·ness
spick'-and-span'
spic'y
 ·i·er ·i·est
spi'der
spi'er
spig'ot
spike
 spiked spik'ing

spill
 spilled or spilt
 spill'ing
spin
 spun spin'ning
spin'ach
spi'nal
spin'dle
 ·dled ·dling
spin'dly
 ·dli·er dli·est
spin'drift'
spine'less
spin'et
spin'ner
spin'off'
spin'ster
spin'y
 ·i·er ·i·est
spi'ral
 ·raled or ·ralled
 ·ral·ing or
 ·ral·ling
spir'it
spir'it·u·al
spir'it·u·ous
spit
 spit'ted
 spit'ting
 (impale)
spit
 spit or spat
 spit'ting
 (eject saliva)
spite
 spit'ed
 spit'ing
spite'ful
spit'fire'
spit'tle
spit·toon'
spitz
splash'down'
splat'ter
splay'foot'
 ·feet'
spleen'ful
splen'did
splen'dor
sple·net'ic
splice
 spliced
 splic'ing
splin'ter
split
 split split'ting
split'-lev'el
split'-up'
splotch
splurge
 splurged
 splurg'ing
splut'ter
spoil
 spoiled or spoilt
 spoil'ing
spoil'age
spoil'sport'

spoke
 spoked spok'ing
spoke'shave'
spokes'man
spo'li·a'tion
sponge
 sponged
 spong'ing
sponge'cake'
spon'gi·ness
spon'gy
 ·gi·er ·gi·est
spon'sor
spon'ta·ne'i·ty
 ·ties
spon·ta'ne·ous
spoon'er·ism
spoon'-feed'
 -fed' -feed'ing
spoon'ful'
 ·fuls'
spo·rad'ic
sport'ing
spor'tive
sports'man
sports'wear'
spot
 spot'ted
 spot'ting
spot'-check'
spot'light'
spot'ti·ness
spot'ty
 ·ti·er ·ti·est
spout'less
sprain
sprawl
spray
spread
 spread
 spread'ing
sprig
 sprigged
 sprig'ging
spright'li·ness
spright'ly
 ·li·er ·li·est
spring
 sprang or
 sprung, sprung,
 spring'ing
spring'board'
spring'i·ness
spring'time'
spring'y
 ·i·er ·i·est
sprin'kle
 ·kled ·kling
sprin'kler
sprint'er
spritz
sprock'et
sprout
spruce
 spruc'er
 spruc'est
 spruced
 spruc'ing

spry
 spri'er or spry'er
 spri'est or
 spry'est
spry'ly
spry'ness
spume
 spumed
 spum'ing
spu·mo'ni or ·ne
spur
 spurred
 spur'ring
spu'ri·ous
spurn
spurt
sput'nik
sput'ter
spu'tum
spy
 spies
 spied spy'ing
spy'glass'
squab'ble
 ·bled ·bling
squab'bler
squad'ron
squal'id
squall
squal'or
squan'der
square
 squared
 squar'ing
square'-rigged'
squar'ish
squash'i·ness
squash'y
 ·i·er ·i·est
squat
 squat'ted
 squat'ting
squawk
squeak'i·ly
squeak'y
 ·i·er ·i·est
squeal'er
squeam'ish
squee'gee
 ·geed ·gee·ing
squeez'a·ble
squeeze
 squeezed
 squeez'ing
squelch
squig'gle
 ·gled ·gling
squint'-eyed'
squire
 squired
 squir'ing
squirm'y
 ·i·er ·i·est
squir'rel
squirt
stab
 stabbed
 stab'bing

sta·bil'i·ty
sta'bi·li·za'tion
sta'bi·lize'
 ·lized' ·liz'ing
sta'bi·liz'er
sta'ble
 ·bled ·bling
sta'bly
stac·ca'to
 ·tos
stack'up'
sta'di·um
 ·di·a or di·ums
staff
 staffs or staves
 (stick; music)
 staffs
 (people)
stage
 staged
 stag'ing
stage'craft'
stage'hand'
stage'-struck'
stag'ger
stag'nan·cy
stag'nant
stag'nate
 ·nat·ed ·nat·ing
stag·na'tion
stag'y
 ·i·er ·i·est
staid
 (sober; see stay)
stain'less
stair'case'
stake
 staked
 stak'ing
 (post; share;
 see steak)
stake'hold'er
stake'out'
sta·lac'tite
sta·lag'mite
stale
 stal'er stal'est
 staled stal'ing
stale'mate'
 ·mat'ed ·mat'ing
stalk'ing-horse'
stall
stal'lion
stal'wart
stam'i·na
stam'mer
stam·pede'
 ·ped'ed ·ped'ing
stance
stan'chion
stand
 stood stand'ing
stand'ard
stand'ard-bear'er
stand'ard·i·
 za'tion
stand'ard·ize'
 ·ized' ·iz'ing

stand'by'
·bys'
stand·ee'
stand'-in'
stand'off'
stand'pat'
stand'point'
stand'still'
stand'-up'
stan'za
staph'y·lo·coc'cus
·coc'ci
sta'ple
·pled ·pling
sta'pler
star
starred
star'ring
star'board
starch'i·ness
starch'y
·i·er ·i·est
star'dom
stare
stared
star'ing
star'gaze'
·gazed' ·gaz'ing
stark'-nak'ed
star'let
star'light'
star'lit'
star'ry
·ri·er ·ri·est
star'-span'gled
start'er
star'tle
·tled ·tling
star·va'tion
starve
starved
starv'ing
starve'ling
stat'a·ble
state
stat'ed stat'ing
State'hood'
state'li·ness
state'ly
·li·er ·li·est
state'ment
state'room'
states'man
state'-wide'
stat'ic
stat'i·cal·ly
sta'tion
sta'tion·ar'y
(not moving)
sta'tion·er
sta'tion·er'y
(writing paper)
sta·tis'tic
sta·tis'ti·cal
sta·tis'ti·cal·ly
stat'is·ti'cian
stat'u·ar'y
·ies

stat'ue
stat'u·esque'
stat'u·ette'
stat'ure
sta'tus
sta'tus quo'
stat'ute
stat'u·to'ry
staunch
stave
staved or stove
stav'ing
stay
stayed stay'ing
(stop; see staid)
stead'fast'
stead'i·ly
stead'i·ness
stead'y
·i·er ·i·est
·ied ·y·ing
steak
(meat; see stake)
steal
stole stol'en
steal'ing
stealth'i·ly
stealth'y
·i·er ·i·est
steam'boat'
steam'er
steam'roll'er
steam'ship'
steam shovel
steam'y
·i·er ·i·est
steel mill
steel wool
steel'work'er
steel'yard'
stee'ple
stee'ple·chase'
stee'ple·jack'
steer'age·way'
steers'man
stein
stel'lar
stem
stemmed
stem'ming
stem'-wind'ing
sten'cil
·ciled or ·cilled
·cil·ing or
·cil·ling
ste·nog'ra·pher
sten'o·graph'ic
ste·nog'ra·phy
sten'o·type'
sten'o·typ'ist
sten'o·typ'y
sten·to'ri·an
step
stepped
step'ping
step'broth'er
step'child'
·chil'dren

step'daugh·ter
step'-down'
step'fa'ther
step'lad'der
step'moth'er
step'par'ent
steppe
(treeless plain)
stepped'-up'
step'ping·stone'
step'sis'ter
step'son'
step'-up'
ster'e·o'
ster'e·o·phon'ic
ster'e·op'ti·con
ster'e·o·scope'
ster'e·o·scop'ic
ster'e·o·type'
·typed ·typ'ing
ster'e·o·typ'ic
ster'ile
ste·ril'i·ty
ster'i·li·za'tion
ster'i·lize'
·lized' ·liz'ing
ster'ling
stern'ness
stern'-wheel'er
stet
stet'ted
stet'ting
steth'o·scope'
ste've·dore'
stew'ard
stew'ard·ess
stick
stuck stick'ing
stick'i·ness
stick'le
·led ·ling
stick'ler
stick'pin'
stick-to'-it·ive·
ness
stick'y
·i·er ·i·est
stiff'en
stiff'-necked'
sti'fle
·fled ·fling
stig'ma
·mas or ·ma·ta
stig'ma·tize'
·tized' ·tiz'ing
stile
(steps; see style)
sti·let'to
·tos or ·toes
still'born'
still life
still'y
stilt'ed
stim'u·lant
stim'u·late'
·lat'ed ·lat'ing
stim'u·la'tion
stim'u·la'tive

stim'u·lus
·li'
sting
stung sting'ing
stin'gi·ly
stin'gi·ness
stin'gy
·gi·er ·gi·est
stink
stank or stunk,
stunk stink'ing
stint'ing·ly
sti'pend
sti·pen'di·ar'y
·ar'ies
stip'ple
·pled ·pling
stip'u·late'
·lat'ed ·lat'ing
stip'u·la'tion
stip'u·la'tor
stir
stirred stir'ring
stir'rup
stitch
stock·ade'
·ad'ed ·ad'ing
stock'bro'ker
stock'hold'er
stock'i·ness
stock'i·nette' or
·net'
stock'ing
stock'pile'
stock'room'
stock'-still'
stock'y
·i·er ·i·est
stock'yard'
stodg'i·ness
stodg'y
·i·er ·i·est
sto'gie or ·gy
·gies
sto'ic
sto'i·cal
sto'i·cism
stoke
stoked stok'ing
stoke'hole'
stok'er
stole
stol'en
(pp. of steal)
stol'id
stol'len
(sweet bread)
stom'ach
stom'ach·ache'
stone
stoned ston'ing
stone'-blind'
stone'cut'ter
stone'-deaf'
stone'ma'son
stone'ware'
stone'work'
ston'i·ly

ston'y
·i·er ·i·est
stoop
(porch; bend;
see stoup)
stop
stopped
stop'ping
stop'cock'
stop'gap'
stop'light'
stop'o'ver
stop'page
stop'per
stop'ple
·pled ·pling
stop'watch'
stor'a·ble
stor'age
store
stored stor'ing
store'house'
store'keep'er
store'room'
storm'bound'
storm door
storm'i·ly
storm'i·ness
storm'y
·i·er ·i·est
sto'ry
·ries
·ried ·ry·ing
sto'ry·tell'er
stoup
(basin; see
stoop)
stout'heart'ed
stove'pipe'
stow'a·way'
stra·bis'mus
strad'dle
·dled ·dling
Strad'i·var'i·us
strafe
strafed straf'ing
strag'gle
·gled ·gling
strag'gler
straight
(not bent;
see strait)
straight'a·way'
straight'edge'
straight'ened
(made straight;
see straitened)
straight'-faced'
straight'for'ward
strain'er
strait
(waterway; see
straight)
strait'ened
(limited; see
straightened)
strait'jack'et
strait'-laced'

strange
strang'er
strang'est
strange'ly
stran'ger
stran'gle
·gled ·gling
stran'gle·hold'
stran'gu·late'
·lat'ed ·lat'ing
stran'gu·la'tion
strap
strapped
strap'ping
strat'a·gem
stra·te'gic
stra·te'gi·cal·ly
strat'e·gist
strat'e·gy
·gies
strat'i·fi·ca'tion
strat'i·fy'
·fied' ·fy'ing
strat'o·sphere'
stra'tum
·ta or ·tums
stra'tus
·ti
straw'ber'ry
·ries
stray
streak'i·ness
streak'y
·i·er ·i·est
stream'line'
·lined' ·lin'ing
street'car'
strength'en
stren'u·ous
strep'to·coc'cal
strep'to·coc'cus
·coc'ci
strep'to·my'cin
stretch'er
stretch'i·ness
stretch'y
·i·er ·i·est
streu'sel
strew
strewed, strewed
or strewn,
strew'ing
stri'ate
·at·ed ·at·ing
stri·a'tion
strict'ly
stric'ture
stride
strode strid'den
strid'ing
stri'dent
strid'u·late'
·lat'ed ·lat'ing
strife
strike
struck, struck or
strick'en,
strik'ing

strike'break·er
string
 strung
 string'ing
strin'gen·cy
 ·cies
strin'gent
string'halt'
string'i·ness
string'y
 ·i·er ·i·est
strip
 stripped
 strip'ping
stripe
 striped
 strip'ing
strip'ling
strip'tease'
strive
 strove or strived,
 striv'en or
 strived, striv'ing
strobe
stroke
 stroked
 strok'ing
stroll'er
strong'-arm'
strong'box'
strong'hold'
strong'-mind'ed
strong'-willed'
stron'ti·um
strop
 stropped
 strop'ping
struc'tur·al
struc'ture
 ·tured ·tur·ing
stru'del
strug'gle
 ·gled ·gling
strum
 strummed
 strum'ming
strut
 strut'ted
 strut'ting
strych'nine
stub
 stubbed
 stub'bing
stub'ble
stub'bly
 ·bli·er ·bli·est
stub'born
stub'by
 ·bi·er ·bi·est
stuc'co
 coes or ·cos
 ·coed ·co·ing
stud
 stud'ded
 stud'ding
stud'book'
stu'dent
stud'horse'

stu'di·o'
 ·os'
stu'di·ous
stud'y
 ·ies, ·ied ·y·ing
stuff'i·ness
stuff'y
 ·i·er ·i·est
stul'ti·fy'
 ·fied' ·fy'ing
stum'ble
 ·bled ·bling
stun
 stunned
 stun'ning
stu'pe·fac'tion
stu'pe·fy'
 ·fied' ·fy'ing
stu·pen'dous
stu'pid
stu·pid'i·ty
 ·ties
stu'por
stur'di·ly
stur'di·ness
stur'dy
 ·di·er ·di·est
stur'geon
stut'ter
stut'ter·er
sty
 sties
 stied sty'ing
 (pig pen)
sty or stye
 sties
 (eyelid swelling)
style
 styled styl'ing
 (mode; see stile)
style'book'
styl'ish
styl'ist
sty·lis'tic
styl'i·za'tion
styl'ize
 ·ized ·iz·ing
sty'lus
 ·lus·es or ·li
sty'mie
 ·mied ·mie·ing
styp'tic
sty'rene
Sty'ro·foam'
su'a·ble
sua'sion
suave
suave'ly
suav'i·ty
sub'as·sem'bly
sub'base'ment
sub'com·mit'tee
sub·con'scious
sub·con'tract
sub'cul'ture
sub'cu·ta'ne·ous
sub'di·vide'
sub'di·vi'sion

sub·due'
 ·dued' ·du'ing
sub'gum'
sub'ject
sub·jec'tive
sub·jec·tiv'i·ty
sub·join'der
sub'ju·gate'
 ·gat'ed ·gat'ing
sub'ju·ga'tion
sub'ju·ga'tor
sub·junc'tive
sub'lease'
sub·let'
 ·let' ·let'ting
sub'li·mate'
 ·mat'ed ·mat'ing
sub'li·ma'tion
sub·lime'
 ·limed' ·lim'ing
sub·lim'i·nal
sub·lim'i·ty
 ·ties
sub·mar'gin·al
sub'ma·rine'
sub·merge'
 ·merged'
sub·mer'gence
sub·mer'gi·ble
sub·merse'
 ·mersed'
 ·mers'ing
sub·mers'i·ble
sub·mer'sion
sub·mis'sion
sub·mis'sive
sub·mit'
 ·mit'ted
 ·mit'ting
sub·nor'mal
sub'nor·mal'i·ty
sub·or'di·nate'
 ·nat'ed ·nat'ing
sub·or'di·na'tion
sub'or·na'tion
sub'plot'
sub·poe'na
 ·naed ·na·ing
sub ro'sa
sub·scribe'
 ·scribed'
 ·scrib'ing
sub'script
sub·scrip'tion
sub'se·quent
sub·ser'vi·ent
sub·side'
 ·sid'ed ·sid'ing
sub·sid'i·ar'y
 ·ies
sub'si·di·za'tion
sub'si·dize'
 ·dized' ·diz'ing
sub'si·dy
 ·dies
sub·sist'ence
sub'soil'
sub'stance
sub·stand'ard
sub·stan'tial

sub·stan'tial·ly
sub·stan'ti·ate'
 ·at'ed ·at'ing
sub·stan'ti·a'tion
sub'stan·ti'val
sub'stan·tive
sub·sta'tion
sub'sti·tut'a·ble
sub'sti·tute'
 ·tut'ed ·tut'ing
sub'sti·tu'tion
sub·stra'tum
 ·ta or ·tums
sub·struc'tur·al
sub'struc'ture
sub'ter·fuge'
sub'ter·ra'ne·an
sub'ti'tle
sub'tle
 ·tler ·tlest
sub'tle·ty
sub'tly
sub·tract'
sub·trac'tion
sub'tra·hend'
sub·trop'i·cal
sub'urb
sub·ur'ban
sub·ur'ban·ite'
sub·ur'bi·a
sub·ver'sion
sub·ver'sive
sub·vert'
sub'way'
suc·ceed'
suc·cess'
suc·cess'ful
suc·cess'ful·ly
suc·ces'sion
suc·ces'sive
suc·ces'sor
suc·cinct'
suc'cor
 (help; see sucker)
suc'co·tash'
suc'cu·lence
suc'cu·lent
suc·cumb'
suck'er
 (one that sucks;
 see succor)
suck'le
 ·led ·ling
su'crose
suc'tion
sud'den·ly
sud'den·ness
su'dor·if'ic
suds'y
 ·i·er ·i·est
sue
 sued su'ing
suede or suède
su'et
suf'fer
suf'fer·ance
suf'fer·ing

suf·fice'
 ·ficed' ·fic'ing
suf·fi'cien·cy
suf·fi'cient
suf'fix
suf'fo·cate'
 ·cat'ed ·cat'ing
suf'fo·ca'tion
suf'frage
suf'fra·gette'
suf'fra·gist
suf·fuse'
 ·fused' ·fus'ing
suf·fu'sion
sug'ar
sug'ar·coat'
sug'ar-cured'
sug'ar·plum'
sug'ar·y
sug·gest'
sug·gest'i·ble
sug·ges'tion
sug·ges'tive
su'i·ci'dal
su'i·cide'
suit
 (set; see suite)
suit'a·bil'i·ty
suit'a·ble
suit'a·bly
suit'case'
suite
 (rooms; furniture;
 see suit, sweet)
suit'or
su'ki·ya'ki
sul'fa
sul'fur
sulk'y
 ·i·er ·i·est
sul'len
sul'ly
 ·lied ·ly·ing
sul'tan
sul·tan'a
sul'tri·ness
sul'try
 ·tri·er ·tri·est
sum
 summed
 sum'ming
su'mac
sum·mar'i·ly
sum'ma·rize'
 ·rized' ·riz'ing
sum'ma·ry
 ·ries
 (brief account)
sum·ma'tion
sum'mer·time'
sum'mer·y
 (like summer)
sum'mit
sum'mon
sum'mons
 ·mons·es
sump'tu·ar'y
sump'tu·ous

sun
 sunned sun'ning
sun bath
sun'bathe'
 ·bathed' ·bath'ing
sun'bath'er
sun'beam'
sun'burn'
sun'burst'
sun'-cured'
sun'dae
Sun'day
sun'di·al
sun'down'
sun'-dried'
sun'dries
sun'dry
sun'glass·es
sunk'en
sun'lamp'
sun'light'
sun'lit'
sun'ni·ness
sun'ny
 ·ni·er ·ni·est
sun'proof'
sun'rise'
sun'set'
sun'shade'
sun'shine'
sun'spot'
sun'stroke'
sun'tan'
sun'-tanned'
sup
 supped sup'ping
su·perb'
su'per·car'go
 ·goes or ·gos
su'per·charge'
su'per·cil'i·ous
su'per·e'go
su'per·fi'cial
su'per·fi'ci·al'i·ty
 ·ties
su·per·fi'cial·ly
su'per·fine'
su'per·flu'i·ty
 ·ties
su·per'flu·ous
su'per·het'er·
 o·dyne'
su'per·hu'man
su'per·im·pose'
su'per·in·duce'
su'per·in·tend'ent
su·pe'ri·or
su·pe'ri·or'i·ty
su·per'la·tive
su'per·man'
su'per·mar'ket
su'per·nat'u·ral
su'per·nu'mer·
 ar'y
 ·ar'ies
su'per·scribe'
su'per·script'
su'per·scrip'tion

su'per·sede'	surf'boat'	swad'dle	swim	syn'a·gogue'	ta'ble d'hôte'
·sed'ed ·sed'ing	surf'-cast'	·dled ·dling	swam swum	syn'chro·mesh'	ta'ble-hop'
su·per·se'dure	sur'feit	swag'ger	swim'ming	syn'chro·nism	ta'ble·land'
su'per·sen'si·tive	surf'er	swal'low	swim'ming·ly	syn'chro·ni·	ta'ble·spoon'ful
su·per·ses'sion	surge	swal'low-tailed'	swim'suit'	za'tion	·fuls
su'per·son'ic	surged surg'ing	swa'mi	swin'dle	syn'chro·nize'	tab'let
su·per·sti'tion	(sudden rush;	·mis	·dled ·dling	·nized' ·niz'ing	ta'ble·ware'
su'per·sti'tious	see serge)	swamp'y	swing	syn'chro·nous	tab'loid
su'per·struc'ture	sur'geon	·i·er ·i·est	swung	syn'chro·tron'	ta·boo' or ·bu'
su'per·vene'	sur'ger·y	swan's'-down'	swing'ing	syn'co·pate'	·boos' or ·bus'
·vened'	·ies	swap	swing'by'	·pat'ed ·pat'ing	·booed' or ·bued'
·ven'ing	sur'gi·cal	swapped	swin'ish	syn·co·pa'tion	·boo'ing or
su'per·ven'tion	sur'gi·cal·ly	swap'ping	swipe	syn'co·pe	·bu'ing
su'per·vise'	sur'li·ness	sward	swiped	syn'cre·tize'	ta'bor or ·bour
·vised' ·vis'ing	sur'ly	(turf; see sword)	swip'ing	·tized' ·tiz'ing	tab'o·ret
su'per·vi'sion	·li·er ·li·est	swarm	swirl	syn'di·cal·ism	tab'u·lar
su'per·vi'sor	sur·mise'	swarth'y	switch'board'	syn'di·cate'	tab'u·late'
su'per·vi'so·ry	·mised' ·mis'ing	·i·er ·i·est	switch'man	·cat'ed ·cat'ing	·lat'ed ·lat'ing
su·pine'	sur·mount'	swash'buck'ler	swiv'el	syn'drome	tab'u·la'tion
sup'per	sur'name'	swas'ti·ka	·eled or ·elled	syn·ec'do·che	tab'u·la'tor
sup·plant'	·named'	swat	·el·ing or ·el·ling	syn'e·col'o·gy	ta·chis'to·scope'
sup'ple	·nam'ing	swat'ted	swol'len	syn'er·gism	ta·chom'e·ter
sup'ple·ly	sur·pass'	swat'ting	sword	syn'od	tac'it
sup'ple·ment	sur'plice	swath n.	(weapon; see	syn·od'i·cal	tac'i·turn'
sup'ple·men'tal	(cloak)	(strip)	sward)	syn'o·nym	tac'i·tur'ni·ty
sup'ple·men'ta·ry	sur'plus	swathe v., n.	sword'fish'	syn·on'y·mous	tack'i·ness
sup'ple·men·	(excess)	swathed	sword'play'	syn·on'y·my	tack'le
ta'tion	sur·prise'	swath'ing	swords'man	·mies	·led ·ling
sup'pli·ant	·prised' ·pris'ing	(bandage)	syb'a·rite'	syn·op'sis	tack'y
sup'pli·cant	sur·pris'ing·ly	sway'backed'	syc'a·more'	·ses	·i·er ·i·est
sup'pli·cate'	sur·re'al	swear	syc'o·phant	syn·op'size	tact'ful
·cat'ed ·cat'ing	sur·re'al·ism	swore	syc'o·phan'tic	·sized ·siz·ing	tact'ful·ly
sup'pli·ca'tion	sur·ren'der	sworn	syl·lab'ic	syn·op'tic	tac'ti·cal
sup·pli'er	sur'rep·ti'tious	swear'ing	syl·lab'i·fi·ca'tion	syn·tac'tic	tac·ti'cian
sup·ply'	sur'rey	swear'word'	syl·lab'i·fy'	syn·tac'ti·cal·ly	tac'tics
·plied' ·ply'ing	·reys	sweat	·fied' ·fy'ing	syn'tax	tac'tile
·plies'	sur'ro·gate'	sweat or	syl'la·ble	syn'the·sis	tact'less
sup·port'	·gat'ed ·gat'ing	sweat'ed,	syl'la·bus	·ses'	tac'tu·al
sup·port'ive	sur·round'	sweat'ing	·bus·es or ·bi'	syn'the·size'	tad'pole'
sup·pose'	sur'tax'	sweat'band'	syl'lo·gism	·sized' ·siz'ing	taf'fe·ta
·posed' ·pos'ing	sur·veil'lance	sweat'er	sylph	syn·thet'ic	taf'fy
sup·pos'ed·ly	sur'vey	sweat shirt	syl'van	syn·thet'i·cal·ly	tag
sup'po·si'tion	·veys	sweat'shop'	sym'bi·ot'ic	syph'i·lis	tagged tag'ging
sup·pos'i·to'ry	sur·vey'or	sweat'y	sym'bol	syph'i·lit'ic	tail'gate'
·ries	sur·viv'a·ble	·i·er ·i·est	(mark; see	sy·ringe'	·gat'ed ·gat'ing
sup·press'	sur·viv'al	sweep	cymbal)	·ringed' ·ring'ing	tail'less
sup·pres'si·ble	sur·vive'	swept sweep'ing	sym·bol'ic	syr'up	tail'light'
sup·pres'sion	·vived' ·viv'ing	sweep'stakes'	sym'bol·ism	sys'tem	tai'lor
sup·pres'sor	sur·vi'vor	·stakes'	sym'bol·is'tic	sys'tem·at'ic	tai'lor-made'
sup'pu·rate'	sus·cep'ti·bil'i·ty	sweet	sym'bol·ize'	sys'tem·at'i·	tail'piece'
·rat'ed ·rat'ing	sus·cep'ti·ble	(like sugar;	·ized' ·iz'ing	cal·ly	tail'race'
sup'pu·ra'tion	sus·pect'	see suite)	sym·met'ri·cal	sys'tem·a·tize'	tail'spin'
su·prem'a·cist	sus·pend'	sweet'bread'	sym'me·try	·tized' ·tiz'ing	tail wind
su·prem'a·cy	sus·pense'	sweet corn	·tries	sys·tem'ic	taint'ed
su·preme'ly	sus·pen'sion	sweet'en·er	sym·pa·thet'ic		tak'a·ble or take'·
sur'charge	sus·pen'so·ry	sweet'heart'	sym'pa·thet'i·		take
sur'cin·gle	sus·pi'cion	sweet'meat'	cal·ly		took tak'en
sure	sus·pi'cious	swell	sym'pa·thize'	**T**	tak'ing
sur'er sur'est	sus·tain'	swelled, swelled	·thized' ·thiz'ing		take'off'
sure'-foot'ed	sus·tain'a·ble	or swol'len,	sym'pa·thy		take'out'
sure'ly	sus'te·nance	swell'ing	·thies	tab'ard	take'o'ver
sur'e·ty	sut·tee'	swel'ter	sym·phon'ic	tab'by	talc
·ties	su'ture	swept'back'	sym'pho·ny	·bies	tal'cum
surf	·tured ·tur·ing	swerve	·nies	tab'er·nac'le	tale'bear'er
(waves; see serf)	svelte	swerved	sym·po'si·um	ta'ble	tal'ent·ed
sur'face	swab	swerv'ing	·ums or ·a	·bled ·bling	ta'les·man
·faced ·fac·ing	swabbed	swift'ness	symp'tom	tab'leau	(juryman)
surf'board'	swab'bing	swill	symp'to·mat'ic	·leaux or ·leaus	tale'tell'er
				ta'ble·cloth'	

tal'is·man
·mans
(*good luck charm*)
talk'a·tive
talk'y
tal'low
tal'ly
·lies, ·lied ·ly·ing
Tal'mud
tal'on
tam'a·ble *or*
tame'·
ta·ma'le
tam'bour
tam'bou·rine'
tame
tamed tam'ing
tam'-o'-shan'ter
tamp'er *n.*
tam'per *v.*
tam'per·er
tam'pi·on
tam'pon
tan
tan'ner tan'nest
tanned tan'ning
tan'dem
tan'ge·lo'
·los'
tan'gent
tan·gen'tial
tan'ge·rine'
tan'gi·ble
tan'gi·bly
tan'gle
gled ·gling
tan'go
·gos
tang'y
·i·er ·i·est
tank'age
tank'ard
tank'er
tank'ful
·fuls
tan'ner·y
·ies
tan'nic
tan'nin
tan'ta·lize'
·lized' ·liz'ing
tan'ta·mount'
tan'trum
tap
tapped
tap'ping
tape
taped tap'ing
tape deck
ta'per
(*candle; decrease;*
see tapir)
tape'-re·cord'
tape recorder
tap'es·try
·tries
tape'worm'
tap'i·o'ca

ta'pir
(*animal; see*
taper)
tap'pet
tap'room'
tap'root'
tar
tarred tar'ring
tar'an·tel'la
ta·ran'tu·la
tar·boosh'
tar'di·ness
tar'dy
·di·er ·di·est
tare
tared tar'ing
(*weight deduction;*
see tear)
tar'get
tar'iff
tar'nish
ta'ro
·ros
(*plant*)
tar'ot
(*playing cards*)
tar·pau'lin
tar'pon
tar'ra·gon'
tar'ry
·ried ·ry·ing
tar'tan
tar'tar
tar'tar sauce
tart'ly
task force
task'mas'ter
tas'sel
·seled *or* ·selled
·sel·ing *or*
·sel·ling
taste
tast'ed tast'ing
taste'ful
taste'ful·ly
taste'less
tast'er
tast'i·ness
tast'y
·i·er ·i·est
tat'ter·de·mal'ion
tat'tered
tat'ter·sall'
tat'tle
·tled ·tling
tat'tle·tale'
tat·too'
·toos'
·tooed' ·too'ing
taught
(*trained; see* taut)
taunt
taupe
taut
(*tight; see* taught)
tau·tol'o·gy
·gies
tav'ern

taw'dry
·dri·er ·dri·est
taw'ny
·ni·er ·ni·est
tax'a·bil'i·ty
tax'a·ble
tax·a'tion
tax'-de·duct'i·ble
tax'-ex·empt'
tax'i
·is, ·ied
·i·ing *or* ·y·ing
tax'i·cab'
tax'i·der'mist
tax'i·der'my
tax'i·me'ter
tax'i·way'
tax·on'o·my
tax'pay'er
tea bag
teach
taught teach'ing
teach'a·ble
teach'er
teach'-in'
tea'cup'
tea'cup·ful'
·fuls'
teak
tea'ket'tle
team
(*group; see* teem)
team'mate'
team'ster
team'work'
tea'pot'
tear
tore torn
tear'ing
(*rip; see* tare)
tear
teared tear'ing
(*eye fluid;*
see tier)
tear'drop'
tear'ful
tear gas
tear'i·ness
tea'room'
tear'y
·i·er ·i·est
tease
teased teas'ing
tea'sel
·seled *or* ·selled
·sel·ing *or*
·sel·ling
tea'spoon·ful'
·fuls'
teat
tea'-ta'ble
tea'tast'er
tea'time'
tech'nic
tech'ni·cal
tech'ni·cal'i·ty
·ties
tech'ni·cal·ly

tech·ni'cian
tech'ni·col'or
tech·nique'
tech·noc'ra·cy
tech·nog'ra·phy
tech'no·log'i·cal
tech·nol'o·gy
te'di·ous
te'di·um
tee
teed tee'ing
teem
(*abound; see*
team)
teen'-age'
teen'-ag'er
tee'ter-tot'ter
teethe
teethed teeth'ing
tee·to'tal·er
tee·to'tal·ism
Tef'lon
teg'u·ment
tel·au'to·graph'
tel'e·cast'
·cast' *or* ·cast'ed
·cast'ing
tel'e·com·mu'·
ni·ca'tion
tel'e·course'
tel'e·gen'ic
tel'e·gram'
tel'e·graph'
te·leg'ra·pher
tel'e·graph'ic
te·leg'ra·phy
tel'e·ki·ne'sis
tel'e·me'ter
te'le·o·log'i·cal
te·le·ol'o·gy
tel'e·path'ic
te·lep'a·thy
tel'e·phone'
·phoned'
·phon'ing
tel'e·phon'ic
te·leph'o·ny
tel'e·pho'to
tel'e·pho'to·graph'
tel'e·pho·tog'ra·
phy
tel'e·play'
tel'e·prompt'er
tel'e·ran'
tel'e·scope'
·scoped' ·scop'ing
tel'e·scop'ic
tel'e·thon'
Tel'e·type'
·typed' ·typ'ing
tel'e·type'writ'er
tel'e·view'er
tel'e·vise'
·vised' ·vis'ing
tel'e·vi'sion
tell
told tell'ing
tell'a·ble

tell'er
tell'tale'
tel'pher *or* ·fer
Tel'star'
te·mer'i·ty
tem'per
tem'per·a
tem'per·a·ment
tem'per·a·
men'tal
tem'per·ance
tem'per·ate
tem'per·a·ture
tem'pered
tem'pest
tem·pes'tu·ous
tem'plate *or* ·plet
tem'ple
tem'po
·pos *or* ·pi
tem'po·ral
tem'po·rar'i·ly
tem'po·rar'i·ness
tem'po·rar'y
tem'po·rize'
·rized' ·riz'ing
temp·ta'tion
tempt'er
tempt'ing
tempt'ress
tem'pus fu'git
ten'a·ble
te·na'cious
te·nac'i·ty
ten'an·cy
·cies
ten'ant
ten'ant·a·ble
ten'ant·ry
·ries
tend'en·cy
·cies
ten'der
(*soft; offer*)
tend'er
(*one who tends*)
ten'der·foot'
·foots' *or* ·feet'
ten'der·heart'ed
ten'der·ize'
·ized' ·iz'ing
ten'der·iz'er
ten'der·loin'
ten'don
ten'dril
ten'e·ment
ten'et
ten'fold'
Ten'nes·see'
ten'nis
ten'on
ten'or
(*tendency; singer;*
see tenure)
ten'pins'
tense
tens'er tens'est
tensed tens'ing

tense'ly
tense'ness
ten'sile
ten·sil'i·ty
ten'sion
ten'ta·cle
ten'ta·tive
ten'ta·tive·ly
ten'ter
ten'ter·hook'
tenth
ten·u'i·ty
ten'u·ous
ten'ure
(*time held;*
see tenor)
ten·u'ri·al
te'pee *or* tee'·
tep'id
te·pid'i·ty
te·qui'la
ter'cen·te'nar·y
·ies
ter'gi·ver·sate'
·sat'ed ·sat'ing
ter'gi·ver·sa'tor
ter'ma·gant
ter'mi·na·ble
ter'mi·na·bly
ter'mi·nal
ter'mi·nate'
·nat'ed ·nat'ing
ter'mi·na'tion
ter'mi·nol'o·gy
·ni' *or* ·nus·es
ter'mite
ter'na·ry
terp'si·cho·re'an
ter'race
·raced ·rac·ing
ter'ra cot'ta
ter'ra fir'ma
ter·rain'
Ter'ra·my'cin
ter'ra·pin
ter·rar'i·um
·i·ums *or* ·i·a
ter·raz'zo
ter·res'tri·al
ter'ri·ble
ter'ri·bly
ter'ri·er
ter·rif'ic
ter·rif'i·cal·ly
ter'ri·fy'
·fied ·fy'ing
ter'ri·to'ri·al
ter'ri·to'ri·al'i·ty
ter'ri·to'ry
·ries
ter'ror
ter'ror·ism
ter'ror·ist
ter'ror·is'tic
ter'ror·i·za'tion
ter'ror·ize'
·ized' ·iz'ing

ter'ry
terse
ters'er ters'est
terse'ness
ter'ti·ar'y
tes'sel·late'
 ·lat'ed ·lat'ing
tes'sel·la'tion
test'a·ble
tes'ta·ment
tes'ta·men'ta·ry
tes'tate
tes'ta·tor
tes'ti·cle
tes'ti·fi'er
tes'ti·fy'
 ·fied' ·fy'ing
tes'ti·ly
tes'ti·mo'ni·al
tes'ti·mo'ny
 ·nies
tes'ti·ness
tes'ty
 ·ti·er ·ti·est
tet'a·nus
tête'-à-tête'
teth'er
tet'ra·cy'cline
tet'ra·he'dron
 ·drons or ·dra
te·tral'o·gy
 ·gies
Tex'as
text'book'
tex'tile
tex'tu·al
tex'tur·al
tex'ture
than conj., prep.
thank'ful
thank'less
thanks'giv'ing
that
 those
thatch
thaw
the·a'ter or ·tre
the·at'ri·cal
theft
their
 (poss. form of
 they; see there,
 they're)
theirs
 (belonging to
 them; see there's)
the'ism
the·is'tic
the·mat'ic
theme
them·selves'
then
 (at that time)
thence'forth'
the·oc'ra·cy
 ·cies
the·od'o·lite'
the·o·lo'gian

the'o·log'i·cal
the·ol'o·gy
 ·gies
the'o·rem
the'o·ret'i·cal
the'o·ret'i·cal·ly
the'o·re·ti'cian
the'o·rize'
 ·rized' ·riz'ing
the'o·ry
 ·ries
the·os'o·phy
 ·phies
ther'a·peu'tic
ther'a·pist
ther'a·py
 ·pies
there
 (at that place;
 see their, they're)
there'a·bouts'
there·af'ter
there·at'
there·by'
there·for'
 (for it)
there'fore'
 (for that reason)
there·in'
there·in·af'ter
there·in'to
there's
 (there is; see
 theirs)
there'to·fore'
there·up·on'
there·with'
ther'mal
therm'i·on'ics
ther'mo·dy·
 nam'ics
ther'mo·e·lec'·
 tric'i·ty
ther·mom'e·ter
ther'mo·nu'cle·ar
ther'mo·pile'
ther'mo·plas'tic
ther'mos
ther'mo·stat'
ther'mo·stat'i·
 cal·ly
the·sau'rus
 ·ri or ·rus·es
the'sis
 ·ses
they'd
they'll
they're
 (they are; see
 their, there)
they've
thi'a·mine'
thick'en·ing
thick'et
thick'ness
thick'set'
thick'-skinned'
thick'-wit'ted

thief n.
thieves
thieve v.
 thieved thiev'ing
thiev'er·y
 ·ies
thiev'ish·ly
thigh'bone'
thim'ble·ful'
 ·fuls'
thin
thin'ner
thin'nest
thinned
thin'ning
thing
think
 thought
think'ing
thin'-skinned'
third'-class'
third'-rate'
thirst'i·ly
thirst'i·ness
thirst'y
 ·i·er ·i·est
thir'teenth'
thir'ti·eth
thir'ty
 ·ties
this
 these
this'tle·down'
thith'er·to'
thole
thong
tho·rac'ic
tho'rax
 ·rax·es or ·ra·ces
tho'ri·um
thorn'y
 ·i·er ·i·est
thor'ough
thor'ough·bred'
thor'ough·fare'
thor'ough·go'ing
though
thought
thought'ful·ly
thought'ful·ness
thought'less
thou'sand·fold'
thrall'dom
thrash
thread'bare'
thread'i·ness
thread'y
 ·i·er ·i·est
threat'en
3'-D'
three'-deck'er
three'-di·men'·
 sion·al
three'fold'
three'-ply'
three'-quar'ter
three'score'
three'some

three'-way'
three'-wheel'er
thren'o·dy
 ·dies
thresh'er
thresh'old
threw
 (pt. of throw;
 see through)
thrice
thrift'i·ly
thrift'i·ness
thrift'y
 ·i·er ·i·est
thrill'er
thrive
 thrived or throve,
 thrived or
 thriv'en,
 thriv'ing
throat'y
 ·i·er ·i·est
throb
throbbed
throb'bing
throe
 (pang; see throw)
throm·bo'sis
throne
throned
thron'ing
throng
throt'tle
 ·tled ·tling
through
 (from end to end
 of; see threw)
through·out'
throw
 threw thrown
 throw'ing
 (hurl; see throe)
throw'a·way'
throw'back'
thrum
thrummed
thrum'ming
thrust
thrust thrust'ing
thud
thud'ded
thud'ding
thumb'nail'
thumb'screw'
thumb'stall'
thumb'tack'
thump
thun'der·bolt'
thun'der·cloud'
thun'der·head'
thun'der·ous
thun'der·show'er
thun'der·squall'
thun'der·storm'
thun'der·struck'
Thurs'day
thus
thwack

thwart
thyme
 (herb; see time)
thy'mus
thy'roid
ti·ar'a
tib'i·a
tic
 (muscle spasm)
tick
 (click; insect)
tick'er tape
tick'et
tick'ing
tick'le
 ·led ·ling
tick'ler
tick'lish
tick'-tack-toe'
tick'y tack'y
tid'al
tid'bit'
tide'land'
tide'mark'
tide'wa·ter
ti'di·ly
ti'di·ness
ti'dings
ti'dy
 ·di·er ·di·est
 ·died ·dy·ing
tie
 tied ty'ing
tie'back'
tie'-dye'
 -dyed' -dye'ing
tie'-in'
tie'pin'
tier
 (row; see tear)
ti'er
 (one that ties;
 see tire)
tie tack
tie'-up'
ti'ger
ti'ger's eye
tight'en
tight'fist'ed
tight'fit'ting
tight'knit'
tight'-lipped'
tight'rope'
ti'gress
tile
 tiled til'ing
till'a·ble
tilt'-top'
tim'bale
tim'ber
 (wood)
tim'ber·line'
tim'bre
 (quality of sound)
time
 timed tim'ing
 (duration;
 see thyme)

time'card'
time clock
time'-con·sum'ing
time'-hon'ored
time'keep'er
time'less
time'li·ness
time'ly
 ·li·er ·li·est
time'out'
time'piece'
tim'er
time'sav'ing
time'ta'ble
time'-test'ed
time'worn'
time zone
ti·mid'i·ty
tim'id·ly
tim'or·ous
tim'o·thy
tim'pa·ni
tim'pa·nist
tin
 tinned tin'ning
tinc'ture
 ·tured ·tur·ing
tin'der·box'
tin'foil'
tinge
 tinged, tinge'ing
 or ting'ing
tin'gle
 ·gled ·gling
tin'gly
 ·gli·er ·gli·est
ti'ni·ness
tin'ker
tin'ker·er
tin'kle
 ·kled ·kling
tin'ni·ness
tin·ni'tus
tin'ny
 ·ni·er ·ni·est
tin'-plate'
 -plat'ed -plat'ing
tin'sel
 ·seled or ·selled
 ·sel·ing or
 ·sel·ling
tin'smith'
tin·tin·nab'u·
 la'tion
tin'type'
tin'ware'
ti'ny
 ·ni·er ·ni·est
tip
 tipped tip'ping
tip'-off'
tip'pet
tip'ple
 ·pled ·pling
tip'sy
 ·si·er ·si·est
tip'toe'
 ·toed' ·toe'ing

tip'top'
ti'rade
tire
　tired tir'ing
　(weary; rubber
　hoop; see tier)
tired'ly
tire'less
tire'some
tis'sue
ti'tan
tithe
　tithed tith'ing
ti'tian
tit'il·late'
　·lat'ed ·lat'ing
tit'il·la'tion
ti'tle
　·tled ·tling
ti'tle·hold'er
tit'mouse'
　·mice'
tit'ter
tit'u·lar
toad'stool'
toad'y
　·ies, ·ied ·y·ing
toad'y·ism
to'-and-fro'
toast'mas'ter
to·bac'co
　·cos
to·bac'co·nist
to·bog'gan
toc·ca'ta
toc'sin
　(alarm; see toxin)
to·day'
tod'dle
　·dled ·dling
tod'dler
tod'dy
　·dies
to-do'
toe
　toed toe'ing
toe'-dance'
　·danced'
　·danc'ing
toe'hold'
toe'-in'
toe'less
toe'nail'
tof'fee or ·fy
to'ga
　·gas or ·gae
to·geth'er
tog'gle
　·gled ·gling
toi'let
toi'let·ry
　·ries
toil'some
toil'worn'
to'ken
tole
tol'er·a·ble
tol'er·a·bly

tol'er·ance
tol'er·ant
tol'er·ate'
　·at'ed ·at'ing
tol'er·a'tion
tol'er·a'tor
toll'booth'
toll bridge
toll call
toll'gate'
toll'keep'er
toll road
tom'a·hawk'
to·ma'to
　·toes
tom'boy'
tomb'stone'
tom'cat'
tom'fool'er·y
to·mor'row
tom'-tom'
ton
　(weight; see tun)
ton'al
to·nal'i·ty
　·ties
tone
　toned ton'ing
tone'-deaf'
tongs
tongue
tongued
tongu'ing
tongue'-lash'ing
tongue'-tie'
　-tied' -ty'ing
ton'ic
to·night'
ton'nage
ton·neau'
　·neaus' or
　·neaux'
ton'sil
ton'sil·lec'to·my
　·mies
ton'sil·li'tis
ton·so'ri·al
ton'sure
　·sured ·sur·ing
ton'tine
tool'mak'er
tooth
　teeth
tooth'ache'
tooth'brush'
tooth'paste'
tooth'pick'
tooth'some
top
　topped top'ping
to'paz
top'coat'
top'-drawer'
top'-dress'ing
top'-flight'
top'-heav'y
to'pi·ar'y
top'ic

top'i·cal
top'knot'
top'less
top'-lev'el
top'most'
top'-notch'
to·pog'ra·pher
top'o·graph'i·cal
to·pog'ra·phy
　(surface features;
　see typography)
top'ple
　·pled ·pling
top'sail
top'-se'cret
top'soil'
top'sy-tur'vy
toque
to'rah or ·ra
torch'bear'er
torch·ier' or
　·iere'
torch'light'
tor'e·a·dor'
tor'ment
tor·men'tor
tor·na'do
　·does or ·dos
tor·pe'do
　·does
tor'pid
tor·pid'i·ty
tor'por
torque
tor'rent
tor·ren'tial
tor'rid
tor·rid'i·ty
tor'sion
tor'so
　·sos or ·si
tort
　(wrongful act)
torte
　(cake)
tor·til'la
tor'toise
tor·to'ni
tor'tu·ous
　(winding)
tor'ture
　·tured ·tur·ing
tor'tur·ous
　(agonizing)
toss'up'
to'tal
　·taled or ·talled
　·tal·ing or
　·tal·ling
to·tal'i·tar'i·an
to·tal'i·ty
to'tal·i·za'tor
to'tal·ly
tote
　tot'ed tot'ing
to'tem
tot'ter
touch'back'

touch'down'
tou·ché'
touch'hole'
touch'i·ly
touch'i·ness
touch'stone'
touch'-type'
touch'-typ'ist
touch'y
　·i·er ·i·est
tough'en
tough'-mind'ed
tou·pee'
tour' de force'
　tours' de force'
tour'ism
tour'ist
tour'ma·line
tour'na·ment
tour'ney
　·neys
tour'ni·quet
tou'sle
　·sled ·sling
tow'age
to·ward'
tow'boat'
tow'el
　·eled or ·elled
　·el·ing or ·el·ling
tow'er·ing
tow'head'
tow'line'
town'ship
towns'peo'ple
tow'path'
tow'rope'
tox·e'mi·a
tox'ic
tox'i·cant
tox'i·col'o·gy
tox'in
　(poison; see
　tocsin)
trace
　traced trac'ing
trace'a·ble
trac'er
trac'er·y
　·ies
tra'che·a
　·ae' or ·as
tra·cho'ma
track
　(trace)
tract
　(land; leaflet)
trac'ta·ble
trac'tile
trac'tion
trac'tor
trad'a·ble or
　trade'a·ble
trade
　trad'ed trad'ing
trade'-in'
trade'-last'
trade'mark'

trade name
trades'man
trades'peo'ple
trade wind
tra·di'tion
tra·di'tion·al
tra·duce'
　·duced' ·duc'ing
traf'fic
　·ficked ·fick·ing
traf'fick·er
tra·ge'di·an
tra·ge'di·enne'
trag'e·dy
　·dies
trag'ic
trag'i·cal·ly
trag'i·com'e·dy
　·dies
trag'i·com'ic
trail'blaz'er
trail'er
train·ee'
train'man
trait
trai'tor
trai'tor·ous
trai'tress
tra·jec'to·ry
　·ries
tram'mel
　·meled or ·melled
　·mel·ing or
　·mel·ling
tram'ple
　·pled ·pling
tram'po·line'
trance
tranced
tranc'ing
tran'quil
　·quil·er or ·quil·ler
　·quil·est or
　·quil·lest
tran'quil·ize'
　or ·quil·lize'
　·ized' or ·lized'
　·iz'ing or ·liz'ing
tran'quil·iz'er or
　·quil·liz'er
tran·quil'li·ty or
　·quil'i·ty
tran'quil·ly
trans·act'
trans·ac'tion
trans·ac'tor
trans·at·lan'tic
trans·ceiv'er
tran·scend'
tran·scend'ent
tran·scen·den'tal
trans·con·ti·
　nen'tal
tran·scribe'
　·scribed' ·scrib'in,
tran'script'
tran·scrip'tion
tran'sept

trans·fer'
　·ferred
　·fer'ring
trans·fer'a·ble
　or ·fer'ra·ble
trans·fer'al
　or ·fer'ral
trans·fer·ee'
trans·fer'ence
trans·fer'rer
trans·fig'u·ra'tion
trans·fig'ure
trans·fix'
trans·form'
trans·for·ma'tion
trans·form'er
trans·fuse'
trans·fus'i·ble
trans·fu'sion
trans·gress'
trans·gres'sion
trans·gres'sor
tran'sient
tran·sis'tor
tran·sis'tor·ize'
　·ized' ·iz'ing
trans'it
tran·si'tion
tran·si'tion·al·ly
tran'si·tive
tran'si·to'ry
trans·lat'a·ble
trans·late'
　·lat'ed ·lat'ing
trans·la'tion
trans·la'tor
trans·lit'er·ate'
　·at'ed ·at'ing
trans·lit'er·a'tion
trans·lu'cence
trans·lu'cent
trans·mi'grate
　·grat·ed ·grat·ing
trans'mi·gra'tion
trans·mis'si·ble
trans·mis'sion
trans·mit'
　·mit'ted
　·mit'ting
trans·mit'tal
trans·mit'tance
trans·mit'ter
trans·mut'a·ble
trans'mu·ta'tion
trans·mute'
　·mut'ed
　·mut'ing
trans·o·ce·an'ic
tran'som
tran·son'ic
trans·pa·cif'ic
trans·par'en·cy
　·cies
trans·par'ent
tran·spire'
　·spired' ·spir'ing
trans·plant'
tran·spon'der

trans·port'
trans'por·ta'tion
trans·pos'a·ble
trans·pose'
·posed' ·pos'ing
trans'po·si'tion
trans·sex'u·al
trans·ship'
·shipped'
·ship'ping
tran'stage'
tran'sub·stan'ti·
ate'
trans·val'ue
trans·ver'sal
trans·verse'
trans·verse'ly
trans·ves'tite
trap
trapped trap'ping
trap'door'
tra·peze'
tra·pe'zi·um
trap'e·zoid'
trap'per
trap'pings
trap'shoot'ing
trash'i·ness
trash'y
·i·er ·i·est
trau'ma
·mas or ·ma·ta
trau·mat'ic
trau·mat'i·cal·ly
trav'ail
(hard work)
trav'el
·eled or ·elled
·el·ing or ·el·ling
(journey)
trav'el·er or
·el·ler
trav'e·logue' or
·log'
trav·ers'a·ble
trav·ers'al
trav·erse'
·ersed' ·ers'ing
trav'er·tine'
trav'es·ty
·ties
·tied ·ty·ing
trawl'er
tray
(holder; see
trey)
treach'er·ous
treach'er·y
·ies
trea'cle
tread
trod, trod'den or
trod, tread'ing
trea'dle
·dled ·dling
tread'mill'
trea'son
trea'son·ous

treas'ure
·ured ·ur·ing
treas'ur·er
treas'ure-trove'
treas'ur·y
·ies
treat'a·ble
trea'tise
treat'ment
trea'ty
·ties
tre'ble
·bled ·bling
tree
treed
tree'ing
tree'nail'
tree'top'
tre'foil
treill'age
trek
trekked
trek'king
trel'lis
trem'ble
·bled ·bling
tre·men'dous
trem'o·lo'
·los'
trem'or
trem'u·lous
trench'ant
trench mouth
trend
trep'i·da'tion
tres'pass
tress'es
tres'tle
tres'tle·work'
trey
(a three; see
tray)
tri'a·ble
tri'ad
tri'al
tri'an'gle
tri·an'gu·lar
tri·an'gu·late'
·lat'ed ·lat'ing
tri·an'gu·la'tion
trib'al
trib'al·ism
tribes'man
trib'u·la'tion
tri·bu'nal
trib'une
trib'u·tar'y
·ies
trib'ute
tri'cen·ten'ni·al
tri'ceps
·cep·ses or ·ceps
tri·chi'na
·nae
trich'i·no'sis
tri·chot'o·my
tri'chro·mat'ic
trick'er·y

trick'i·ly
trick'i·ness
trick'le
·led ·ling
trick'ster
trick'y
·i·er ·i·est
tri'col'or
tri'cot
tri'cy·cle
tri'di·men'sion·al
tri·en'ni·al
tri·en'ni·um
·ums or ·a
tri'er
tri'fle
·fled ·fling
tri·fo'cal
trig'ger
trig'o·no·met'ric
trig'o·nom'e·try
tri·lat'er·al
tri·lin'gual
tril'lion
tril'li·um
tril'o·gy
·gies
trim
trimmed
trim'ming
trim'mer
trim'mest
tri·mes'ter
tri·month'ly
trin'i·ty
·ties
trin'ket
tri·no'mi·al
tri'o
·os
trip
tripped trip'ping
tri·par'tite
trip'ham'mer
tri'ple
·pled ·pling
tri'ple-space'
tri'plet
trip'li·cate'
·cat'ed ·cat'ing
tri'ply
tri'pod
trip'per
trip'tych
tri·sect'
triste
tris·tesse'
trite
trit'er trit'est
trite'ly
trit'u·rate'
·rat'ed ·rat'ing
tri'umph
tri·um'phal
tri·um'phant
tri·um'vi·rate
triv'et
triv'i·a

triv'i·al
triv'i·al'i·ty
·ties
triv'i·al·ly
tri·week'ly
·lies
tro'che
(lozenge)
tro'chee
(poetic meter)
trod'den
trof'fer
trog'lo·dyte'
troll
trol'ley
·leys
·leyed ·ley·ing
trol'lop
trom·bone'
trom·bon'ist
troop
(of soldiers;
see troupe)
troop'ship'
tro'phy
·phies
trop'ic
trop'i·cal
tro'pism
trop'o·sphere'
trot
trot'ted trot'ting
trot'ter
trou'ba·dour'
trou'ble
·bled ·bling
trou'ble·mak'er
trou'ble-shoot'er
trou'ble·some
trough
trounce
trounced
trounc'ing
troupe
trouped
troup'ing
(of actors;
see troop)
troup'er
trou'sers
trous'seau
·seaux or ·seaus
trout
trow'el
·eled or ·elled
·el·ing or ·el·ling
tru'an·cy
·cies
tru'ant
truce
truck farm
truck'le
·led ·ling
truc'u·lence
truc'u·lent
trudge
trudged
trudg'ing

true
tru'er tru'est
trued tru'ing
or true'ing
true'-blue'
·lies
true'-life'
true'love'
truf'fle
tru'ism
tru'ly
trump
trumped'-up'
trump'er·y
·ies
trum'pet
trum'pet·er
trun'cate
·cat·ed ·cat·ing
trun·ca'tion
trun'cheon
trun'dle
·dled ·dling
trunk line
trun'nion
truss
trus·tee'
·teed' ·tee'ing
(manager; see
trusty)
trus·tee'ship'
trust'ful
trust'ful·ly
trust'i·ness
trust'wor'thy
trust'y
·ies, ·i·er ·i·est
(relied upon;
see trustee)
truth'ful
truth'ful·ly
truth'ful·ness
try
tries
tried try'ing
try'out'
tryst
tset'se fly
T'-shirt'
tsim'mes
tsor'is
T square
tsu·na'mi
tub
tubbed tub'bing
tu'ba
·bas or ·bae
tub'ba·ble
tub'bi·ness
tub'by
·bi·er ·bi·est
tube
tubed tub'ing
tu'ber
tu'ber·cle
tu·ber'cu·lar
tu·ber'cu·lin
tu·ber'cu·lo'sis
tu·ber'cu·lous

tube'rose'
(plant)
tu'ber·ous
(having tubers)
tu'bu·lar
tuck'er
Tu'dor
Tues'day
tuft'ed
tug
tugged tug'ging
tug'boat'
tu·i'tion
tu·la·re'mi·a
tu'lip
tulle
tum'ble
·bled ·bling
tum'ble·down'
tum'bler
tum'ble·weed'
tum'brel
tu'me·fy'
·fied' ·fy'ing
tu·mes'cence
tu·mes'cent
tu'mid
tu'mor
tu'mor·ous
tu'mult
tu·mul'tu·ous
tun
tunned tun'ning
(cask; see ton)
tun'a·ble
or tune'·
tun'dra
tune
tuned tun'ing
tune'ful
tune'less
tun'er
tune'up' or
tune'-up'
tung'sten
tu'nic
tun'nel
·neled or ·nelled
·nel·ing or
·nel·ling
tu'pe·lo'
·los'
tur'ban
(headdress)
tur'bid
tur'bine
(engine)
tur'bo·jet'
tur'bo·prop'
tur'bu·lence
tur'bu·lent
tu·reen'
turf
tur'gid
tur'key
tur'mer·ic
tur'moil
turn'a·bout'

turn'a·round'
turn'buck'le
turn'coat'
turn'down'
tur'nip
turn'key'
·keys'
turn'off'
turn'out'
turn'o·ver
turn'pike'
turn'stile'
turn'ta·ble
tur'pen·tine'
tur'pi·tude'
tur'quoise
tur'ret
tur'tle
tur'tle·dove'
tur'tle·neck'
tus'sle
·sled ·sling
tu'te·lage
tu'te·lar'y
tu'tor
tu·to'ri·al
tut'ti-frut'ti
tu'tu
tux·e'do
·dos
TV
TVs or TV's
twang
tweak
tweed
tweed'y
·i·er ·i·est
tweeze
tweezed
tweez'ing
tweez'ers
twelfth
twelve'fold'
twen'ti·eth
twen'ty
·ties
twen'ty·fold'
twice'-told'
twid'dle
·dled ·dling
twi'light'
twi'lit
twill
twine
twined twin'ing
twin'-en'gined
twinge
twinged
twing'ing
twi'-night'
twin'kle
·kled ·kling
twirl'er
twist'er
twitch
twit'ter
two'-by-four'
two'-edged'

two'-faced'
two'-fist'ed
two'fold'
two'-hand'ed
two'-leg'ged
two'-piece'
two'-ply'
two'-sid'ed
·at'ed ·at'ing
two'some
two'-way'
ty·coon'
tym·pan'ic
typ'a·ble or type'·
typ'al
type
typed typ'ing
type'bar'
type'cast'
·cast' ·cast'ing
(in acting)
type'-cast'
-cast' -cast'ing
(in printing)
type'script'
type'set'
·set' ·set'ting
type'set'ter
type'write'
·wrote' ·writ'ten
·writ'ing
type'writ'er
ty'phoid
ty·phoon'
ty'phus
typ'i·cal
typ'i·cal·ly
typ'i·fy'
·fied' ·fy'ing
typ'ist
ty·pog'ra·pher
ty'po·graph'i·cal
ty·pog'ra·phy
(setting of type;
see topography)
ty·pol'o·gy
ty·ran'ni·cal
tyr'an·nize'
·nized' ·niz'ing
tyr'an·nous
tyr'an·ny
·nies
ty'rant
ty'ro
·ros
ty'ro·thri'cin

U

u·biq'ui·tous
u·biq'ui·ty
ud'der
(milk gland;
see utter)
u·fol'o·gist
ug'li
(fruit)

ug'li·ness
ug'ly
·li·er ·li·est
u'kase
u'ku·le'le
ul'cer
ul'cer·ate'
·at'ed ·at'ing
ul'cer·ous
ul'ster
ul·te'ri·or
ul'ti·mate
ul'ti·mate·ly
ul'ti·ma'tum
·tums or ·ta
ul'tra
ul'tra·con·serv'·
a·tive
ul'tra·ism
ul'tra·ma·rine'
ul'tra·mi'cro·
scope'
ul'tra·mod'ern
ul'tra·na'tion·al·
ism
ul'tra·son'ic
ul'tra·sound'
ul'tra·vi'o·let
ul'u·late'
·lat'ed ·lat'ing
um'ber
um·bil'i·cal
um·bil'i·cus
·ci'
um'bra
·brae or ·bras
um'brage
um·bra'geous
um·brel'la
u'mi·ak' or ·ack'
um'laut
um'pire
·pired ·pir·ing
un·a'ble
un·a'bridged'
un·ac·count'a·ble
un·ac·count'ed-
for'
un·ac·cus'tomed
un·af·fect'ed
un'-A·mer'i·can
u'na·nim'i·ty
u·nan'i·mous
un·apt'
un·armed'
un·as·sum'ing
un'at·tached'
un·a·void'a·ble
un·a·ware'
un·a·wares'
un·bal'anced
un·bear'a·ble
un·beat'a·ble
un'be·com'ing
un'be·known'
un·be·lief'
un'be·liev'a·ble
un'be·liev'er

un·bend'
·bent' or ·bend'ed,
·bend'ing
un·bi'ased or
·assed
un·bid'den
un·bolt'ed
un·bos'om
un·bound'ed
un·bri'dled
un·bro'ken
un·buck'le
un·but'ton
un·called'-for'
un·can'ni·ly
un·can'ni·ness
un·can'ny
un·cared'-for'
un'cer·e·mo'ni·
ous
un·cer'tain
un·cer'tain·ty
·ties
un·char'i·ta·ble
un·chris'tian
un'ci·al
un·civ'il
un·civ'i·lized'
un·clad'
un·class'i·fied
un'cle
un·clothe'
·clothed' or
·clad', ·cloth'ing
un·com'fort·a·ble
un·com'pro·
mis'ing
un'con·cerned'
un'con·di'tion·al
un·con'scion·a·
ble
un·con'scious
un'con·sti·
tu'tion·al
un·cou'ple
un·couth'
unc'tion
unc'tu·ous
un·daunt'ed
un·de·cid'ed
un·de·ni'a·ble
un'der·age'
un'der·age
un'der·brush'
un'der·buy'
·bought' ·buy'ing
un'der·car'riage
un'der·class'man
un'der·clothes'
un'der·coat'
un'der·cov'er
un'der·cur'rent
un'der·cut'
un'der·de·vel'·
oped
un'der·do'
·did' ·done'
·do'ing

un'der·dog'
un'der·em·ployed'
un'der·es'ti·mate'
un'der·fired'
un'der·foot'
un'der·gar'ment
un'der·glaze'
un'der·go'
·went' ·gone'
·go'ing
un'der·grad'u·ate
un'der·ground'
un'der·growth'
un'der·hand'
un'der·hand'ed
un'der·hung'
un'der·lay'
·laid' ·lay'ing
un'der·lie'
·lay' ·lain'
·ly'ing
un'der·line'
un'der·ling
un'der·lin'ing
un'der·mine'
un'der·neath'
un'der·nour'ish
un'der·pants'
un'der·part'
un'der·pass'
un'der·pay'
·paid' ·pay'ing
un'der·pin'ning
un'der·play'
un'der·priv'i·
leged
un'der·proof'
un'der·rate'
un'der·score'
un'der·sea'
un'der·sec're·
tar'y
·ies
un'der·sell'
·sold' ·sell'ing
un'der·sexed'
un'der·shirt'
un'der·shot'
un'der·side'
un'der·signed'
un'der·sized'
un'der·staffed'
un'der·stand'
·stood' ·stand'ing
un'der·stand'a·
ble
un'der·stand'a·bly
un'der·state'ment
un'der·stud'y
·ies, ·ied ·y·ing
un'der·take'
·took' ·tak'en
·tak'ing
un'der·tak'ing
un'der·tone'
un'der·tow'
un'der·val'ue
un'der·wa'ter

un'der·wear'
un'der·weight'
un'der·world'
un'der·write'
·wrote' ·writ'ten
·writ'ing
un·do'
·did' ·done'
·do'ing
un·doubt'ed·ly
un·dress'
un·due'
un'du·lant
un'du·late'
·lat'ed ·lat'ing
un·du'ly
un·dy'ing
un·earned'
un·earth'
un·eas'y
un·em·ploy'a·ble
un·e'qualed
or ·qualled
un'e·quiv'o·cal·ly
un·err'ing
un·es·sen'tial
un·e'ven·ness
un'e·vent'ful·ly
un'ex·cep'tion·
a·ble
un'ex·cep'tion·al
un'ex·pect'ed
un·faith'ful
un·fa·mil'iar
un·feel'ing
un·feigned'
un'for·get'ta·ble
un·for'tu·nate
un·found'ed
un·freeze'
·froze' ·froz'en
·freez'ing
un·frock'
un·furl'
un·gain'ly
un·god'ly
un'guent
un'gu·late
un·hand'
un·heard'-of'
un·hoped'-for'
un·horse'
·horsed'
·hors'ing
u'ni·cam'er·al
u'ni·cel'lu·lar
u'ni·corn'
u'ni·cy'cle
u'ni·fi'a·ble
u'ni·fi·ca'tion
u'ni·fi'er
u'ni·form'
u'ni·form'i·ty
u'ni·fy'
·fied' ·fy'ing
u'ni·lat'er·al
un·im·peach'a·ble
un·in·hib'it·ed

un·in·tel'li·gi·ble
un'ion
un'ion·ize'
·ized· iz'ing
u·nique'
u'ni·son
u'nit
U'ni·tar'i·an
u·nite'
·nit'ed ·nit'ing
u'nit·ize'
·ized' ·iz'ing
u'ni·ty
·ties
u'ni·ver'sal
u'ni·ver·sal'i·ty
u'ni·ver'sal·ly
u'ni·verse'
u'ni·ver'si·ty
·ties
un·kempt'
un·known'
un·lade'
·lad'ed, ·lad'ed
or ·lad'en,
·lad'ing
un·law'ful
un·less'
un·let'tered
un·like'li·hood'
un·like'ly
un·lim'it·ed
un·list'ed
un·looked'-for'
un·loose'
·loosed' ·loos'ing
un·loos'en
un·luck'y
un·make'
·made' ·mak'ing
un·man'
·manned'
·man'ning
un·men'tion·a·ble
un·mer'ci·ful
un'mis·tak'a·ble
un·mit'i·gat'ed
un·nat'u·ral
un·nec'es·sar'y
un·nerve'
·nerved'
·nerv'ing
un·num'bered
un·oc'cu·pied'
un·or'gan·ized'
un·paid'-for'
un·par'al·leled'
un·pleas'ant
un·prec'e·dent'ed
un·prej'u·diced
un·prin'ci·pled
un·qual'i·fied
un·ques'tion·a·
bly
un'quote'
un·rav'el
·eled or ·elled
·el·ing or ·el·ling

un're·al·is'tic
un·rea'son·a·ble
un're·gen'er·ate
un·rest'
un·rul'i·ness
un·rul'y
·i·er ·i·est
un·said'
un·sa'vor·i·ness
un·sa'vor·y
un·scathed'
un·scru'pu·lous
un·seat'
un·seem'ly
un·shod'
un·sight'li·ness
un·sight'ly
un·speak'a·ble
un·stead'y
un·strung'
un·sung'
un·tan'gle
·gled ·gling
un·ten'a·ble
un·think'a·ble
un·thought'-of'
un·ti'dy
un·tie'
·tied' ·ty'ing or
·tie'ing
un·til'
un·time'ly
un·told'
un·touch'a·ble
un·to'ward
un·truth'ful
un·tu'tored
un·u'su·al
un·veil'ing
un·want'ed
(not wanted;
see unwonted)
un·war'y
un·whole'some
un·wield'i·ness
un·wield'y
un·wit'ting·ly
un·wont'ed
(not usual;
see unwanted)
un·wor'thy
un·writ'ten
un·zip'
up'-and-com'ing
up'-and-down'
up'beat'
up·braid'
up'bring'ing
up'coun'try
up·date'
up·end'
up'grade'
up·heav'al
up'hill'
up·hold'
·held' ·hold'ing
up·hol'ster
up·hol'ster·er

up·hol'ster·y
·ies
up'keep'
up'land
up·lift'
up·on'
up'per-case'
·cased' ·cas'ing
up'per·class'man
up'per·most'
up'right'
up·ris'ing
up'roar'
up·roar'i·ous
up·root'
up·set'
·set' ·set'ting
up'shot'
up'stage'
·staged'
·stag'ing
up'stairs'
up·stand'ing
up'start'
up'state'
up'stream'
up'swept'
up'swing'
up'take'
up'thrust'
up'-tight' or
up'tight'
up'most'
up'-to-date'
up'town'
up·turn'
up'ward
u·ra'ni·um
ur'ban
(of the city)
ur·bane'
(socially poised)
ur'ban·ism
ur·ban'i·ty
·ties
ur'ban·i·za'tion
ur'ban·ize'
·ized' ·iz'ing
ur'chin
u·re'mi·a
u·re'ter
u·re'thra
·thrae or ·thras
urge
urged urg'ing
ur'gen·cy
·cies
ur'gent
u'ri·nal
u'ri·nal'y·sis
·ses'
u'ri·nar'y
u'ri·nate'
·nat'ed ·nat'ing
u'rine
urn
u'ro·log'i·cal
u·rol'o·gy
u·ros'co·py

us'a·ble or use'·
us'age
use
used us'ing
use'ful
use'less
us'er
ush'er
ush'er·ette'
u'su·al
u'su·al·ly
u'su·fruct'
u'su·rer
u·su'ri·ous
u·surp'
u'sur·pa'tion
u'su·ry
·ries
U'tah
u·ten'sil
u'ter·ine
u'ter·us
·ter·i'
u·til'i·tar'i·an
u·til'i·ty
·ties
u'ti·liz'a·ble
u'ti·li·za'tion
u'ti·lize'
·lized' ·liz'ing
ut'most'
u·to'pi·a
ut'ter
(speak; see udder)
ut'ter·ance
U'-turn'
ux·o'ri·ous

V

va'can·cy
·cies
va'cant
va'cate
·cat·ed ·cat·ing
va·ca'tion
vac'ci·nate'
·nat'ed ·nat'ing
vac'ci·na'tion
vac·cine'
vac'il·late'
·lat'ed ·lat'ing
vac'il·la'tion
vac'il·la'tor
va·cu'i·ty
·ties
vac'u·ous
vac'u·um
·ums or ·a
vag'a·bond'
va·gar'y
·ies
va·gi'na
·nas or ·nae
va'gran·cy
·cies

va'grant
vague
vague'ly
vain
(futile; conceited;
see vane, vein)
vain'glo'ri·ous
vain'glo'ry
val'ance
(drapery; see
valence)
vale
(valley; see veil)
val'e·dic'tion
val'e·dic·to'ri·an
val'e·dic'to·ry
·ries
va'lence
(term in chemis-
try; see valance)
val'en·tine'
val'et
val'iant
val'id
val'i·date'
·dat'ed ·dat'ing
val'i·da'tion
va·lid'i·ty
va·lise'
val'ley
·leys
val'or
val'or·i·za'tion
val'u·a·ble
val'u·a'tion
val'ue
·ued ·u·ing
val'ue·less
valve
val'vu·lar
vam'pire
van'dal
van'dal·ism
van'dal·ize'
·ized' ·iz'ing
Van·dyke'
vane
(blade; see
vain, vein)
van'guard'
va·nil'la
van'ish
van'i·ty
·ties
van'quish
van'tage
vap'id
va'por
va'por·i·za'tion
va'por·ize'
·ized' ·iz'ing
va'por·iz'er
va'por·ous
va·que'ro
·ros
var'i·a·ble
var'i·a·bly
var'i·ance

var'i·ant
var'i·a'tion
var'i·col'ored
var'i·cose'
var'ied
var'i·e·gate'
·gat'ed ·gat'ing
var'i·e·ga'tion
va·ri'e·tal
va·ri'e·ty
·ties
var'i·o'rum
var'i·ous
var'nish
var'si·ty
·ties
var'y
·ied ·y·ing
(change; see very)
vas'cu·lar
vas de'fe·rens'
vas'e·line'
vas'sal
(a subordinate;
see vessel)
vast'ness
vat
vat'ted vat'ting
vat'-dyed'
vaude'ville
vault'ing
vaunt
vec'tor
vec·to'ri·al
V'-E' Day
veer
veg'e·ta·ble
veg'e·tar'i·an
veg'e·tate'
·tat'ed ·tat'ing
veg'e·ta'tion
veg'e·ta'tive
ve'he·mence
ve'he·ment
ve'hi·cle
ve·hic'u·lar
veil
(screen; see vale)
vein
(blood vessel;
streak; see
vain, vane)
Vel'cro
vel'lum
ve·loc'i·pede'
ve·loc'i·ty
·ties
ve·lour' or ·lours'
·lours'
ve·lure'
vel'vet
vel'vet·een'
vel'vet·y
ve'nal
(corrupt; see
venial)
ve·nal'i·ty
·ties

vend·ee'
ven·det'ta
ven'dor *or*
  vend'er
ve·neer'
ven'er·a·ble
ven'er·ate'
  ·at'ed ·at'ing
ven'er·a'tion
ve·ne're·al
Ve·ne'tian
venge'ance
venge'ful
ve'ni·al
  (*pardonable;* see
  venal)
ven'i·son
ven'om·ous
ve'nous
ven'ti·late'
  ·lat'ed ·lat'ing
ven'ti·la'tion
ven'ti·la'tor
ven'tri·cle
ven·tril'o·quist
ven'ture
  ·tured ·tur·ing
ven'ture·some
ven'tur·ous
ven'ue
ve·ra'cious
  (*truthful;* see
  voracious)
ve·rac'i·ty
ve·ran'da *or* ·dah
ver'bal
ver'bal·i·za'tion
ver'bal·ize'
  ·ized' ·iz'ing
ver'bal·ly
ver·ba'tim
ver·be'na
ver'bi·age
ver·bose'
ver·bos'i·ty
ver'dant
ver'dict
ver'di·gris'
ver'dure
verge
  verged verg'ing
ver'i·fi'a·ble
ver'i·fi·ca'tion
ver'i·fy'
  ·fied' ·fy'ing
ver'i·ly
ver'i·si·mil'i·tude'
ver'i·ta·ble
ver'i·ta·bly
ver'i·ty
  ·ties
ver'mi·cel'li
ver'mi·cide'
ver·mic'u·lar
ver·mic'u·lite'
ver'mi·form'
ver'mi·fuge'
ver·mil'ion

ver'min
Ver·mont'
ver·mouth'
ver·nac'u·lar
ver'nal
ver'ni·er
ver'sa·tile
ver'sa·tile·ly
ver'sa·til'i·ty
versed
ver'si·fi·ca'tion
ver'si·fy'
  ·fied' ·fy'ing
ver'sion
ver'sus
ver'te·bra
  ·brae' *or* ·bras
ver'te·bral
ver'te·brate
ver'tex
  ·tex·es *or* ·ti·ces'
ver'ti·cal
ver·tig'i·nous
ver'ti·go'
verve
ver'y
  ·i·er ·i·est
  (*complete; exceed-
  ingly;* see vary)
ves'i·cant
ves'i·cate'
  ·cat'ed ·cat'ing
ves'i·cle
ves'per
ves'sel
  (*container; ship;*
  see vassal)
ves'tal
ves'ti·bule
ves'tige
ves·tig'i·al
vest'ment
vest'-pock'et
ves'try
  ·tries
vet'er·an
vet'er·i·nar'i·an
vet'er·i·nar'y
  ·ies
ve'to
  ·toes
  ·toed ·to·ing
vex·a'tion
vex·a'tious
vi'a·bil'i·ty
vi'a·ble
vi'a·duct'
vi'al
  (*bottle;* see
  vile, viol)
vi'and
vi'brant
vi'bra·phone'
vi'brate
  ·brat·ed ·brat·ing
vi·bra'tion
vi·bra'to
  ·tos

vi'bra'tor
vi'bra·to'ry
vic'ar
vic'ar·age
vi·car'i·al
vi·car'i·ous
vice
  (*evil conduct;
  flaw;* see vise)
vice'-chair'man
vice'-chan'cel·lor
vice'-con'sul
vice'-pres'i·dent
vice'roy
vi'ce ver'sa
vi'chy·ssoise'
vi·cin'i·ty
  ·ties
vi'cious
vi·cis'si·tude'
vic'tim
vic'tim·ize'
  ·ized' ·iz'ing
vic'tor
vic·to'ri·a
vic·to'ri·ous
vic'to·ry
  ·ries
vi·cu'ña
vid'e·o'
vid'i·con
vie
  vied vy'ing
view'point'
vig'il
vig'i·lance
vig'i·lant
vig'i·lan'te
vi·gnette'
vig'or
vig'or·ous
vile
  (*evil; offensive;*
  see vial, viol)
vile'ly
vil'i·fi·ca'tion
vil'i·fy'
  ·fied' ·fy'ing
vil'la
vil'lage
vil'lag·er
vil'lain
  (*scoundrel;*
  see villein)
vil'lain·ous
vil'lain·y
  ·ies
vil'lein
  (*serf;* see
  villain)
vin'ai·grette'
vin'ci·ble
vin'di·cate'
  ·cat'ed ·cat'ing
vin'di·ca'tion
vin'di·ca'tive
vin'di·ca'tor
vin·dic'tive

vin'e·gar
vin'er·y
  ·ies
vine'yard
vin'i·cul'ture
vi'nous
vin'tage
vint'ner
vi'nyl
vi'ol
  (*instrument;*
  see vial, vile)
vi·o'la
vi'o·la·ble
vi'o·late'
  ·lat'ed ·lat'ing
vi'o·la'tion
vi'o·la'tor
vi'o·lence
vi'o·lent
vi'o·let
vi'o·lin'
vi'o·lin'ist
vi'o·lon·cel'lo
  ·los
VIP *or* V.I.P.
vi'per
vi·ra'go
  ·goes *or* ·gos
vi'ral
vir'gin
vir'gin·al
Vir·gin'ia
vir·gin'i·ty
vir'gule
vir'ile
vi·ril'i·ty
vi·rol'o·gy
vir·tu'al
vir'tu·al·ly
vir'tue
vir·tu·os'i·ty
vir·tu·o'so
  ·sos *or* ·si
vir'tu·ous
vir'u·lence
vir'u·lent
vi'rus
vi'sa
vis'age
vis-à-vis'
vis'cer·a
vis'cid
vis·cos'i·ty
vis'count
vis'count·ess
vis'cous
vise
  vised vis'ing
  (*clamp;* see vice)
vis'i·bil'i·ty
vis'i·ble
vis'i·bly
vi'sion
vi'sion·ar'y
  ·ies
vis'it

vis'it·ant
vis'it·a'tion
vis'i·tor
vis'or
vis'ta
vis'u·al
vis'u·al·ize'
  ·ized' ·iz'ing
vi'ta
  ·tae
vi'tal
vi·tal'i·ty
  ·ties
vi'tal·ize'
  ·ized' ·iz'ing
vi'ta·min
vi'ti·a·ble
vi'ti·ate'
  ·at'ed ·at'ing
vi'ti·a'tion
vi'ti·a'tor
vit're·ous
vit'ri·fy'
  ·fied' ·fy'ing
vit'ri·ol
vit'ri·ol'ic
vi·tu'per·ate'
  ·at'ed ·at'ing
vi·tu'per·a'tion
vi·va'cious
vi·vac'i·ty
viv'id
viv'i·fy'
  ·fied' ·fy'ing
vi·vip'a·rous
viv'i·sect'
viv'i·sec'tion
vix'en
V'-J' Day
V'-neck'
vo·cab'u·lar'y
  ·ies
vo'cal cord
vo'cal·ist
vo'cal·ize'
  ·ized' ·iz'ing
vo·ca'tion
vo·cif'er·ate'
  ·at'ed ·at'ing
vo·cif'er·ous
vo'cod'er
vod'ka
vogue
voice'less
voice'print'
void'a·ble
voi·là'
voile
vol'a·tile
vol'a·til'i·ty
vol·can'ic
vol·ca'no
  ·noes *or* ·nos
vol'i·tant
vo·li'tion
vol'ley
  ·leys
  ·leyed ·ley·ing

vol'ley·ball'
volt'age
vol·ta'ic
vol·tam'e·ter
volt'me'ter
vol'u·bil'i·ty
vol'u·ble
vol'u·bly
vol'ume
vo·lu'mi·nous
vol'un·tar'i·ly
vol'un·tar'y
vol'un·teer'
vo·lup'tu·ar'y
  ·ies
vo·lup'tu·ous
vo·lute'
vo·lu'tion
vom'it
voo'doo
  ·doos
vo·ra'cious
  (*greedy;* see
  veracious)
vo·rac'i·ty
vor'tex
  ·tex·es *or* ·ti·ces'
vo'ta·ble *or* vote'-
vo'ta·ry
  ·ries
vote
  vot'ed vot'ing
vo'tive
vouch'er
vouch·safe'
  ·safed' ·saf'ing
vow
vow'el
voy'age
  ·aged ·ag·ing
voy'ag·er
vo·yeur'
vroom
vul'can·i·za'tion
vul'can·ize'
  ·ized' ·iz'ing
vul'gar
vul·gar'i·an
vul'gar·ism
vul·gar'i·ty
  ·ties
vul'gar·ize'
  ·ized' ·iz'ing
vul'ner·a·bil'i·ty
vul'ner·a·ble
vul'ner·a·bly
vul'ture
vul'tur·ous
vul'va
vy'ing

W

wad
wad'ded
wad'ding

wad'dle
· dled ·dling
wade
wad'ed
wad'ing
wa'fer
waf'fle
waft
wag
wagged
wag'ging
wage
waged wag'ing
wa'ger
wag'ger·y
· ies
wag'gish
wag'gle
·gled ·gling
Wag·ne'ri·an
wag'on·load'
wa·hi'ne
waif
wail
(cry; see wale,
whale)
wain'scot
·scot·ed or
·scot·ted
·scot·ing or
·scot·ting
wain'wright'
waist'band'
waist'coat
waist'-high'
waist'line'
wait'er
wait'ress
waive
waived waiv'ing
(give up; see
wave)
waiv'er
(a relinquishing;
see waver)
wake
woke or waked,
waked or wok'·
en, wak'ing
wake'ful
wak'en
wale
waled wal'ing
(ridge; see
wail, whale)
walk
walk'a·way'
walk'ie-talk'ie
walk'-in'
walk'-on'
walk'out'
walk'-through'
walk'-up'
walk'way'
wall'board'
wal'let
wall'eyed'
wall'flow'er

wal'lop·ing
wal'low
wall'pa'per
wall'-to-wall'
wal'nut
wal'rus
waltz
wam'pum
wan
wan'ner
wan'nest
wan'der
(stray; see
wonder)
wan'der·lust'
wane
waned wan'ing
wan'gle
·gled ·gling
want'ing
wan'ton
(unjustifiable;
see won ton)
war
warred war'ring
war'ble
·bled ·bling
ward
war'den
ward'robe'
ward'room'
ware'house'
·housed'
·hous'ing
war'fare'
war'head'
war'i·ly
war'i·ness
war'like'
war'lock'
warm'blood'ed
warmed'-o'ver
warm'heart'ed
war'mon'ger
warmth
warm'-up'
warn'ing
warp
war'path'
warped
war'plane'
war'rant
war'ran·ty
·ties
war'ren
war'ri·or
war'ship'
wart
war'time'
war'y
·i·er ·i·est
wash'a·ble
wash'-and-wear'
wash'board'
wash'bowl'
wash'cloth'
washed'-out'
washed'-up'

wash'er
wash'er·wom'an
Wash'ing·ton
wash'out'
wash'room'
wash'stand'
wash'tub'
was'n't
wasp'ish
was'sail
wast'age
waste
wast'ed
wast'ing
waste'bas'ket
waste'ful
waste'land'
waste'pa'per
waste pipe
wast'rel
watch'band'
watch'case'
watch'dog'
watch fire
watch'ful
watch'mak'er
watch'man
watch'tow'er
watch'word'
wa'ter·borne'
wa'ter·col'or
wa'ter-cooled'
water cooler
wa'ter·course'
wa'ter·craft'
wa'ter·cress'
wa'ter·cy'cle
wa'tered
wa'ter·fall'
wa'ter·front'
water glass
water hole
wa'ter·less
wa'ter·line'
wa'ter·logged'
wa'ter·mark'
wa'ter·mel'on
water pipe
water power
wa'ter·proof'
wa'ter-re·pel'lent
wa'ter-re·sist'ant
wa'ter·scape'
wa'ter·shed'
wa'ter·side'
wa'ter-ski'
-skied' -ski'ing
wa'ter-ski'er
water skis
wa'ter-soak'
wa'ter-sol'u·ble
wa'ter·spout'
wa'ter·tight'
water tower
wa'ter·way'
water wheel
water wings

wa'ter·works'
wa'ter·worn'
wa'ter·y
watt'age
watt'-hour'
wat'tle
·tled ·tling
watt'me'ter
wave
waved wav'ing
(curving motion;
see waive)
wave'length'
wav'er
(one that waves;
see waiver)
wa'ver
(falter; see
waiver)
wav'i·ness
wav'y
·i·er ·i·est
wax
wax'en
wax'i·ness
wax'work'
wax'y
·i·er ·i·est
way
(route; manner;
see weigh, whey)
way'bill'
way'far'er
way'far'ing
way'lay'
·laid' ·lay'ing
way'side'
way'ward
weak'en
weak'-kneed'
weak'ling
weak'ly
·li·er ·li est
weak'-mind'ed
weak'ness
weal
(ridge; welfare;
see wheal, wheel)
wealth'i·ness
wealth'y
·i·er ·i·est
wean
weap'on
wear
wore worn
wear'ing
wear'a·ble
wea'ri·ly
wea'ri·ness
wea'ri·some
wea'ry
·ri·er ·ri·est
·ried ·ry·ing
wea'sel
weath'er
(atmospheric con-
ditions; see
whether)

weath'er-beat'en
weath'er-bound'
weath'er·cock'
weath'er·man'
weath'er·proof'
weath'er·strip'
·stripped'
·strip'ping
weather vane
weave
wove, wov'en or
wove, weav'ing
(interlace)
weave
weaved
weav'ing
(move in and out
as in traffic)
weav'er
web
webbed
web'bing
web'foot'
·feet'
web'-foot'ed
wed
wed'ded,
wed'ded or
wed, wed'ding
we'd
wedge
wedged
wedg'ing
Wedg'wood'
wed'lock
Wednes'day
wee
we'er we'est
weed'i·ness
week'day'
week'end' or
week'-end'
week'ly
·lies
weep
wept weep'ing
weep'i·ness
weep'y
·i·er ·i·est
wee'vil
weigh
weighed
weigh'ing
(measure weight
of; see way, whey)
weight'i·ness
weight'less
weight'y
·i·er ·i·est
weir
(dam; see we're)
weird
wel'come
·comed ·com·ing
weld'er
wel'fare'
well'-ad·vised'
well'-ap·point'ed

well'-bal'anced
well'-be·haved'
well'-be'ing
well'-be·loved'
well'born'
well'-bred'
well'-chos'en
well'-con·tent'
well'-dis·posed'
well'do'ing
well'-done'
well'-fa'vored
well'-fed'
well'-found'ed
well'-groomed'
well'-ground'ed
well'-han'dled
well'head'
well'-in·formed'
well'-in·ten'·
tioned
well'-knit'
well'-known'
well'-made'
well'-man'nered
well'-mean'ing
well'-meant'
well'-nigh'
well'-off'
well'-or'dered
well'-pre·served'
well'-read'
well'-round'ed
well'-spo'ken
well'spring'
well'-thought'-of'
well'-timed'
well'-to-do'
well'-turned'
well'-wish'er
well'-worn'
we'll
Welsh rabbit
or rarebit
welt'er
welt'er·weight'
we're
(we are; see
weir)
weren't
were'wolf'
·wolves'
wes'kit
west'er·ly
·lies
west'ern·er
west'ern·ize'
·ized' ·iz'ing
west'-north'west'
west'-south'west'
West Vir·gin'ia
west'ward
wet
wet'ter wet'test
wet or wet'ted
wet'ting
(moistened;
see whet)

wet'back'
wet'ta·ble
whale
  whaled whal'ing
  (fishlike mammal;
  see wail, wale)
whale'boat'
whale'bone'
whal'er
wharf
  wharves or
  wharfs
wharf'age
wharf'in·ger
what·ev'er
what'not'
what'so·ev'er
wheal
  (pimple; see
  weal, wheel)
wheat
whee'dle
  ·dled ·dling
wheel
  (disk for turning;
  see weal, wheel)
wheel'bar'row
wheel'base'
wheel'chair'
wheel'house'
wheel'wright'
wheeze
  wheezed
  wheez'ing
wheez'y
  ·i·er ·i·est
whelp
when
whence
when·ev'er
where
where'a·bouts'
where·as'
where·by'
where'fore'
where·in'
where·of'
where'up·on'
wher·ev'er
where·with'
where'with·al'
wher'ry
  ·ries, ·ried ·ry·ing
whet
  whet'ted
  whet'ting
  (sharpen; see wet)
wheth'er
  (if; see weather)
whet'stone'
whey
  (thin part of milk;
  see way, weigh)
which·ev'er
whiff
while
  whiled whil'ing
  (time; see wile)

whim
whim'per
whim'si·cal
whim'sy
  ·sies
whine
  whined whin'ing
  (cry; see wine)
whin'i·ness
whin'ny
  ·nies
  ·nied ·ny·ing
  (neigh)
whin'y
  ·i·er ·i·est
  (complaining)
whip
  whipped
  whip'ping
whip'cord'
whip'lash'
whip'pet
whip'poor·will'
whip'saw'
whip'stitch'
whip'stock'
whir or whirr
  whirred
  whir'ring
whirl
whirl'pool'
whirl'wind'
whisk broom
whisk'er
whis'key
  ·keys or ·kies
whis'per
whis'tle
  ·tled ·tling
whis'tler
whit
  (bit; see wit)
white
  whit'ed whit'ing
white'cap'
white'-col'lar
white'-haired'
white'-hot'
white'-liv'ered
whit'en·er
white'ness
whit'en·ing
white room
white'wall'
white'wash'
whith'er
  (where; see
  wither)
whit'ing
whit'tle
  ·tled ·tling
whiz or whizz
  whizzed
  whiz'zing
who·ev'er
whole'heart'ed
whole'sale'
  ·saled ·sal'ing

whole'sal'er
whole'some
whole'-wheat'
whol'ly
  (completely; see
  holey, holy)
whom·ev'er
whom'so·ev'er
whoop'ee
whop'per
whore
whorl
who's
  (who is; who has)
whose
  (poss. of who)
who'so·ev'er
why
wick'ed
wick'er·work'
wick'et
wide'-an'gle
wide'-a·wake'
wide'-eyed'
wid'en
wide'-o'pen
wide'spread'
wid'get
wid'ow
wid'ow·er
width
wield
wield'y
  ·i·er ·i·est
wie'ner
wife
  wives
wife'ly
wig'gle
  ·gled ·gling
wig'gly
wig'let
wig'wam
wild'cat'
  ·cat'ted ·cat'ting
wil'de·beest'
wil'der·ness
wild'-eyed'
wild'fire'
wild'life'
wile
  wiled wil'ing
  (trick; see while)
wil'i·ness
will'ful or wil'·
  will'ing·ness
will'-o'-the-wisp'
wil'low·y
will'pow'er
will'y-nil'ly
wi'ly
  ·li·er ·li·est
wim'ple
  ·pled ·pling
win
  won win'ning
wince
  winced winc'ing

wind
  wound wind'ing
wind'blown'
wind'-borne'
wind'break'er
wind'burn'
wind'fall'
wind'i·ness
wind'lass
  (winch)
wind'less
  (without wind)
wind'mill'
win'dow
win'dow·pane'
win'dow·shop'
wind'row'
wind'shield'
wind'storm'
wind'-swept'
wind'up'
wind'ward
wind'y
  ·i·er ·i·est
wine
  wined win'ing
  (drink; see whine)
wine cellar
wine'-col'ored
wine'glass'
wine'grow'er
wine press
win'er·y
  ·ies
Wine'sap'
wine'skin'
wing chair
wing'span'
wing'spread'
win'ner
win'now
win'some
win'ter
win'ter·green'
win'ter·ize'
  ·ized' ·iz'ing
win'ter·time'
win'try
  ·tri·er ·tri·est
wipe
  wiped wip'ing
wire
  wired wir'ing
wire'draw'
  ·drew' ·drawn'
  ·draw'ing
wire'hair'
wire'-haired'
wire'less
Wire'pho'to
wire'pull'er
wire'tap'
wire'work'
wir'i·ness
wir'y
  ·i·er ·i·est
Wis·con'sin
wis'dom

wise
  wis'er wis'est
wise'ly
wish'bone'
wish'ful
wisp
wist'ful
wit
  (sense; see whit)
witch'craft'
witch'er·y
  ·ies
with·draw'
  ·drew' ·drawn'
  ·draw'ing
with·draw'al
with'er
  (wilt; see whither)
with·hold'
  ·held' ·hold'ing
with·in'
with·out'
with·stand'
  ·stood'
  ·stand'ing
wit'less
wit'ness
wit'ti·cism
wit'ti·ness
wit'ty
  ·ti·er ·ti·est
wiz'ard
wiz'ard·ry
wiz'ened
wob'ble
  ·bled ·bling
woe'be·gone'
woe'ful
wolf
  wolves
wolf'hound'
wom'an
  wom'en
wom'an·hood'
wom'an·kind'
wom'an·li·ness
wom'an·ly
womb
wom'en·folk'
won'der
  (marvel; see
  wander)
won'der·ful
won'der·land'
won'der·work'
won'der·work'er
won'drous
wont
  (accustomed)
won't
  (will not)
won' ton'
  (food; see wanton)
wood'carv'ing
wood'chuck'
wood'craft'
wood'cut'
wood'ed

wood'land'
wood'peck'er
wood'pile'
wood pulp
wood'shed'
woods'man
wood'sy
  ·si·er ·si·est
wood'wind'
wood'work'
wood'y
  ·i·er ·i·est
woof'er
wool'en
wool'gath'er·ing
wool'grow'er
wool'lies or
  wool'ies
wool'li·ness or
  wool'i·ness
wool'ly or
  wool'y
  ·li·er or ·i·er
  ·li·est or ·i·est
Worces'ter·shire'
word'age
word'book'
word'i·ly
word'i·ness
word'less
word'-of-mouth'
word'play'
wood'y
  ·i·er ·i·est
work
  worked or
  wrought
  work'ing
work'a·ble
work'a·day'
work'bench'
work'book'
work'day'
work'house'
work'ing·man'
work'load'
work'man·like'
work'man·ship'
work'out'
work'room'
work'shop'
work'ta·ble
work'week'
world'li·ness
world'ly
  ·li·er ·li·est
world'ly-wise'
world'-shak'ing
world'-wea'ry
world'wide'
worm'-eat'en
worm gear
worm'hole'
worm'i·ness
worm wheel
worm'wood'
worm'y
  ·i·er ·i·est

worn'-out'
wor'ri·er
wor'ri·ment
wor'ri·some
wor'ry
·ries
·ried ·ry·ing
wor'ry·wart'
worse
wors'en
wor'ship
·shiped or
·shipped
·ship·ing or
·ship·ping
wor'ship·er or
wor'ship·per
wor'ship·ful
worst
wor'sted
wor'thi·ly
wor'thi·ness
worth'less
worth'while'
wor'thy
·thi·er ·thi·est
would
would'-be'
wound
wrack
wraith
wran'gle
·gled ·gling
wran'gler
wrap
wrapped or
wrapt
wrap'ping
(cover; see rap)
wrap'a·round'
wrap'per
wrath'ful
wreak
(inflict; see reek)

wreath n.
wreathe v.
wreathed
wreath'ing
wreck'age
wreck'er
wrench
wres'tle
·tled ·tling
wres'tler
wretch
(miserable
person; see
retch)
wretch'ed
wrig'gle
·gled ·gling
wring
wrung wring'ing
(twist; see ring)
wrin'kle
·kled ·kling
wrin'kly
·kli·er ·kli·est
wrist'band'
wrist'let
wrist pin
wrist'watch'
writ
write
wrote writ'ten
writ'ing
(inscribe; see
right, rite)
write'-in'
write'-off'
writ'er
write'-up'
writhe
writhed
writh'ing
wrong'do'er
wrong'do'ing
wrong'ful

wrote
(pt. of write;
see rote)
wrought
wrought'-up'
wrung
(pt. and pp. of
wring; see rung)
wry
wried wry'ing
wri'er wri'est
(twisted; see rye)
wry'ly
Wy·o'ming

X

x
x-ed or x'd
x-ing or x'ing
xan'thous
xe'bec
xen·o·pho'bi·a
xe·rog'ra·phy
xe·roph'i·lous
Xe'rox
Xmas
X'-ray' or
X ray
xy'lo·phone'
xy'lo·phon'ist

Y

yacht
yachts'man
Yan'kee

yard'age
yard'arm'
yard'mas'ter
yard'stick'
yarn'-dyed'
yawl
yawn
yea
year'book'
year'ling
year'long'
year'ly
yearn
year'-round'
yeast
yel'low
yelp
yen
yenned yen'ning
yeo'man
yes
yessed yes'sing
ye·shi'va
yes'ter·day
yes'ter·year'
yet
yew
(tree; see ewe)
Yid'dish
yield
yip'pie
yo'del
·deled or ·delled
·del·ing or
·del·ling
yo'del·er or
yo'del·ler
yo'ga
yo'gi
·gis
yo'gurt
yoke
yoked yok'ing
(harness)

yolk
(of an egg)
Yom Kip'pur
yon'der
you'd
you'll
young'ster
your
(poss. of you)
you're
(you are)
yours
your·self'
·selves'
youth'ful
you've
yowl
yo'-yo'
yule log
yule'tide'

Z

zai'ba·tsu'
·tsu'
za'ni·ness
za'ny
·nies, ·ni·er
·ni·est
zeal
zeal'ot
zeal'ous
ze'bra
ze'brass'
ze'bu
Zeit'geist'
Zen
ze'nith
ze'o·lite'

ze'o·lit'ic
zeph'yr
zep'pe·lin
ze'ro
·ros or ·roes
·roed ·ro·ing
zest'ful·ly
zest'ful·ness
zig'zag'
·zagged'
·zag'ging
zinc
zincked or zinced
zinck'ing or
zinc'ing
zin'ni·a
Zi'on·ism
zip
zipped zip'ping
ZIP Code
zip'per
zir'con
zith'er
zo'di·ac'
zo·di'a·cal
zom'bie
zon'al
zone
zoned zon'ing
zoo
zo'o·ge·og'ra·phy
zo'o·log'i·cal
zo·ol'o·gist
zo·ol'o·gy
zoom lens
zoy'si·a
zuc·chet'to
·tos
zuc·chi'ni
·ni or ·nis
zwie'back
zy'gote
zy·mol'o·gy
zy'mur·gy

Index